THE CULTURE OF SECRECY
BRITAIN, 1832–1998

David Vincent

OXFORD UNIVERSITY PRESS
1998

Oxford University Press, Great Clarendon Street, Oxford OX2 6DP

Oxford   New York
Athens Auckland Bangkok Bogotá Buenos Aires Calcutta
Cape Town Chennai Dar es Salaam Delhi Florence Hong Kong Istanbul
Karachi Kuala Lumpur Madrid Melbourne Mexico City Mumbai
Nairobi Paris São Paulo Singapore Taipei Tokyo Toronto Warsaw
and associated companies in Berlin Ibadan

Oxford is a registered trade mark of Oxford University Press

Published in the United States
by Oxford University Press Inc., New York

British Library Cataloguing in Publication Data
Data available

Library of Congress Cataloging in Publication Data
Vincent, David, 1949–
      The culture of secrecy in Britain, 1832–1998 / David Vincent.
         p.   cm.
      Includes bibliographical references and index.
      1. Official secrets—Great Britain—History—20th century.
   2. Official secrets—Great Britain—History—19th century.
   3. Government information—Great Britain—History—20th century.
   4. Government information—Great Britain—History—19th century.
   5. Great Britain—Politics and government—20th century.   6. Great
   Britain—Politics and government—1837–1901.   7. Great Britain—
   Politics and government—1830–1837.   I. Title.
JN329.S4V56   1998
302.2—dc21   98-17247

ISBN 0-19-820307-1

1 3 5 7 9 10 8 6 4 2

Typeset by Best-set Typesetter Ltd., Hong Kong
Printed in Great Britain
on acid-free paper by
Bookcraft Ltd, Midsomer Norton,
Nr. Bath, Somerset

For

Anna, Rebecca, and Michael

PREFACE

Secrecy first came to my attention when I was working on the history of reading and writing. The most direct application of the skills of penmanship which the early nineteenth-century elementary schools were trying to teach was correspondence, and thus I turned to the introduction of the Penny Post in 1840. As I pursued its implications, I came across the first great controversy over official secrecy which erupted four years later when the government was forced to defend its clandestine practice of letter-opening. The implications of the debate which took place both inside and outside Parliament form the subject matter of the study that follows.

The Culture of Secrecy is, in this sense, the other side of the coin of the growth of literacy and of later technologies of communication, the obverse of the process by which the minds of the mass of the population were opened to unprecedented resources of knowledge and imagination. This is not, however, a study merely of the darker aspects of this long revolution. Secrecy is as integral to a liberal democracy as openness; the latter indeed could not exist either as a concept or as a practice without the former. The word itself has acquired such negative connotations that it is necessary to resist the instinct to condemn past practices and mock more recent behaviour. At times this is not easy. When we remind ourselves that in the 1980s it was still the case that every scrap of official information was potentially a legally enforceable secret, that sane, respected statesmen could still refuse to name the directors of the secret services whom all our enemies knew as intimates, there is little need to deploy the past to make strange the present. A central concern of this book is to recapture the logic and function of arrangements whose survival merits at least the respect if not the approbation of those who study them. The task is to understand the forces which created the particular configurations of blocked communication which characterized the making of modern Britain.

The title is as much a question as a description. The notion of a culture of secrecy is seen here not as an object to be delineated, like a war or an election, but rather as an explanation to be interrogated. It is evident from the outset that an account which confines itself to laws and their making will illuminate very little. But equally it is clear that the notion of culture has frequently been used to evade or obscure the historical identity of systems of controlling the flow of information. At each stage the relation between institutional structures and the associated bundles of attitudes, values, and conventions needs to be carefully articulated. If it is the case that informal controls were, wherever possible, preferred to statutory regulations, then we need to know why, and we need to examine the means by which the particular balance between them was generated, maintained, and undermined. The book commences at the moment when the problem of secrecy took on its modern form. The main text concludes in 1989, the year in which the major legislative instruments were reconfigured to meet the next millennium. The research and writing took place during the course of the fourth consecutive Conservative Administration, and the complex if inconclusive developments of that period have not been addressed in what is essentially an historical study. However the book went to press in the month of the Labour election victory, and it has been possible to include an Afterword on the implications of the new government's epochal White Paper, *Your Right to Know. The Government's proposals for a Freedom of Information Act*. The scale of this document's engagement with what the Prime Minister describes as the 'traditional culture of secrecy' permits a review of the process and prospects of change in the 1990s. The place is Great Britain and not the United Kingdom or the Empire. Both Ireland and the colonies play their part in the development of domestic systems, but each in the matter of structures of secrecy has a history too complex to be encompassed within these pages. It is Britain and not England, although here the boundary is more fluid. Most of the practices and institutions examined here applied with occasional variations to the three countries of the mainland, but the cultural constructs were at times less consistently applied. There was a discernible tendency to attribute key virtues in the national identity, in this context particularly that of the gentleman, to England, and characteristic vices, including in the end the culture of secrecy, to Britain at large. The liberties which required defending were British, but the qualities which sustained them were frequently conceived in narrower terms. A final disclaimer concerns the forbidden fruit itself. This is not an account of secrets, but rather of why they were kept.

This book begins and concludes in the House of Commons. The chapters rarely stray far from the behaviour of the state, either in its own development, or in its interaction with the professions, commerce, and private neighbourhoods and households. It may thus be termed a political history, but it is one which pays little heed to the traditional boundaries of the genre. In his useful recent survey, *The Transformation of British Politics*, Brian Harrison has complained that historians have been paying too little attention to the development of those constitutional arrangements which are now under widespread attack. If this is true, the fault lies in part with those who once turned away from the traditional narratives of the past and sought instead to write accounts in which prime ministers and permanent secretaries were present, if at all, as distant bystanders. This enterprise is yielding diminishing returns. In Britain, as in any modernizing democracy, the social and the political, and the concepts, institutions, and practices in which they were embodied, have developed in a particular relation to each other. Neither is comprehensible in isolation, and any history which excludes civil servants from an understanding of civil society, or divorces the study of public from private archives, will tell much less than half the story.

These points have particular force in relation to the study of blocked communication. If we take forward, for instance, the implications of the growing use of correspondence inside and outside government, we are immediately engaged with both the developing infrastructure of the state and the increasing complexity of domestic relations. As soon as questions are asked about the justifications for covertly opening letters, we are faced with the deployment of concepts which have served as the navigation lights for the voyage of modern liberalism. Privacy and confidentiality, honour and integrity, openness and freedom of expression, secrecy itself in all its positive and negative connotations, are terms which have been fundamental to the delineation of the legitimate boundaries of the state and society. By concentrating on the single issue of the blocking of communication it is possible to examine the historically contingent meanings of these central concepts, and to deepen our knowledge of how these were constructed, embodied, and challenged. Because of the nature of secrecy as a process, and because of the particular British tradition of clothing secrecy in secrecy, this book represents a first approach to the social history of trust. Every chapter in one way or another constitutes an examination of the ethical basis of power in the public, professional, commercial, and private domains. At a time when the probity of all sources of authority is under attack, it may be appropriate to begin to consider how structures of mutual confidence have been created and eroded in our recent history.

Such an enterprise is almost limitless in the topics which could be considered. The coming pages pay even attention to ballots and birth control, to gossip and gay rights, to doctors and dole investigators, and much else besides. In order, however, to provide some focus to the discussion, a limited number of issues have been pursued right through the book because they highlight key tensions within the overall process. These include the civil service and its control of public information, the interception of letters and later forms of communication, and the home visit, whether by volunteers, professionals, or official inspectors. Between the introduction and conclusion the chapters are arranged in broad blocks of time which take the arguments at a consistent pace from the construction of the liberal state after the Reform Act to the various attempts at reform and reconstruction in the 1970s and 1980s. Each chapter contains its own preface and coda, and three or four discrete discussions of key developments within its period.

The pursuit of secrecy and its meanings has taken me far from my point of departure, and I am grateful to a range of experts for guiding my steps across many unfamiliar fields. These include Olive Anderson, Harry Cocks, Anne Crowther, Bobby Farsides, Maurice Frankel, Gordon Fyfe, Peter Hennock, Kevin Hetherington, Martin Hewitt, Kathryn Hughes, Steve Jefferies, David Laven, Rolland Munro, Margaret Pelling, Mike Rose, Mark Roseman, Mike Savage, and

Anne Worrall. My particular thanks for reading the entire text go to my colleagues at Keele, Chris Harrison, Ray Cocks, and Charles Townshend, and to my friends in the Manchester school of new political history, James Vernon and Pat Joyce. Charlolte Vincent has made possible the dedication and all that follows.

DAVID VINCENT
KEELE AND SHRAWARDINE,
May 1997

Contents

| # THE PROBLEM OF SECRECY

Secrecy Becomes Modern

In the beginning were poppy seeds and grains of sand. During the spring of 1844, a well-connected Italian exile in London, Joseph Mazzini, started to send himself letters containing minuscule ingredients in order to discover whether the British Government was opening his correspondence at the behest of the Austrian ambassador.[1] When the envelopes arrived empty, he arranged for the radical MP Thomas Duncombe to present a petition to the House of Commons protesting at the introduction of 'the spy system of foreign states', which was 'repugnant to every principle of the British constitution, and subversive of the public confidence, which was so essential to a commercial country'.[2] The subsequent refusal of the Home Secretary, Sir James Graham, to confirm or deny the practice drove Duncombe to make the first modern attack on official secrecy:

the answer of the right hon. Baronet was, that he must firmly but respectfully decline to answer any question on that subject. If a Secretary of State, or the Government, were justified in screening and sheltering themselves behind this official secrecy, he wanted to know what became of that responsibility of which we heard so much when any measure was submitted giving more extensive powers to the Secretary of State or the Government?[3]

The revelations about postal espionage provoked what Graham's biographer called a 'paroxysm of national anger'.[4] It was the major political scandal of the year, stimulating widespread comment in the daily and periodical press, and much gleeful satire in the recently launched *Punch*. The cause of Young Italy and its persecuted leader received enormous publicity, although Mazzini him-

---

[1] J. Mazzini, *Life and Writings of Joseph Mazzini* (new edn., London, 1891), iii. 188; [J. Mazzini], 'Mazzini and the Ethics of Politicians', *Westminster Review*, 82 (Sept.–Dec. 1844), 242. Mazzini's most recent English biographer confirms the substance of his fears. D. Mack Smith, *Mazzini* (New Haven, 1994), 41–4.

[2] *Hansard*, 3rd Series, LXXV, 14 June 1844, col. 892. For an example of what he was talking about, see the account of contemporary practice in Russia: R. Hingley, *The Russian Secret Service* (London, 1970), 33–5.

[3] *Hansard*, 3rd Series, LXXV, 24 June 1844, col. 1264.

[4] T. M. Torrens, *The Life and Times of the Right Honourable Sir James R. G. Graham* (London, 1863), ii. 348.

self was never again to trust his correspondence, and continued to use code in his letters up to his death in 1872.[5] In the domestic arena Duncombe won powerful support in both the Commons and the Lords, eventually forcing Sir Robert Peel to set up a secret select committee to consider his allegations,[6] which by this time extended to the charge that the letters of MPs were being opened. In a series of set-piece debates which lasted until February 1845, an increasingly embattled government was subjected to a more extensive interrogation of official secrecy than was to be permitted again for well over a century.[7]

In one sense the controversy appears to mark an intermission in the history of the subject. Two months after Mazzini's initial petition, the Secret Department of the Post Office was abolished, the official decipherer of foreign correspondence, Francis Willes, whose family had held the position since 1703, was pensioned off with secret service money,[8] and Britain became the only major power bereft of the most effective weapon for spying on external enemies. In the absence of a public refusal to change its policy, its internal enemies could never be confident that their letters were secure; Marx and Engels certainly continued to believe that their correspondence was vulnerable.[9] Nonetheless, once the crisis of 1848 had passed,[10] the state began a quarter of a century when for what may have been the first time in its history, and certainly was the last, it largely refrained from the surveillance of the thoughts and actions of its citizens.[11]

Yet it may be argued that the Mazzini affair, and the debate which surrounded it, represented not the end but the beginning of a tradition of public secrecy whose effects were more profound and pervasive than the specific matter of opening letters. At the centre of a complex set of arguments was the fundamental relationship between the post-Reform Act state and popular communication. It was barely a decade since the enlargement of the franchise in 1832, and Peel was hard at work building upon the extensive foundations laid

---

[5] Mack Smith, *Mazzini*, 42, 224.

[6] Under pressure, he conceded the appointment of a select committee, but its proceedings were kept secret. See, *Report from the Select Committee on the Post Office* (1844), PP 1844, XIV.

[7] The fullest account of the event is to be found in, F. B. Smith, 'British Post Office Espionage 1844', *Historical Studies*, 4 (1970). See also, A. P. Donajgrodzki, 'Sir James Graham at the Home Office', *Historical Journal*, 20: 1 (1977); B. Porter, *Plots and Paranoia* (London, 1989), 76–8; H. Robinson, *Britain's Post Office* (Cambridge, 1953), 47, 55, 91–2; E. Troup, *The Home Office* (2nd edn., London, 1926), 109–10; D. Vincent, 'Communications, Community and the State', in C. Emsley and J. Walvin (eds.), *Artisans, Peasants and Proletarians, 1760–1860* (London, 1985), 166–86.

[8] C. Andrew, *Secret Service: The Making of the British Intelligence Community* (London, 1985), 3; Porter, *Plots and Paranoia*, 78.

[9] See, for instance, comments in correspondence between them 2 Mar. 1852; 5 Mar. 1852; 24 Sept. 1852; 28 Sept. 1852; 25 Oct. 1852; 27 Oct. 1852; 2 Nov. 1852. K. Marx and F. Engels, *Collected Works*, vol. 39 (London, 1983), 56, 58, 196, 200, 215–16, 219, 235.

[10] On the extent of surveillance during the final Chartist challenge, see J. Saville, *1848* (Cambridge, 1987), 125, 161–3, 185.

[11] B. Porter, *The Origins of the Vigilant State* (London, 1987), 1–18.

by Grey and Melbourne. The deep concern about ministerial responsibility was generated by the visible expansion of the scope of Government activity. Duncombe chose the New Poor Law to illustrate why it was now so important that public accountability was not undermined by official secrecy. At just the moment when Parliament needed to exert its authority over an ever-more ambitious Executive, it appeared that ministers were overturning established safeguards. In the Commons, Macaulay pressed home the charge against Graham:

the line of conduct he adopted was utterly inconsistent with all notions of Ministerial responsibility. I now say, that in my opinion, there is a wide distinction between the conduct of the right hon. Gentleman (Sir J. Graham) and that of any persons who have preceded him in his present office; for who, when called upon in the face of this House to state on what principle he had exercised the power we are now discussing, ever declined to do so before the right hon. Baronet?[12]

The Tory Government stood accused of imperilling progress by abandoning tradition. The enterprise of increasing liberty by increasing the activity of government was critically dependent on the free flow of information between the rulers and the ruled. A year before the Mazzini affair, Bentham's seminal essay 'Of Publicity', which he never managed to publish in his lifetime, finally appeared in the first complete edition of his *Works*. 'Publicity', he insisted, 'is the fittest law for securing the public confidence, and causing it constantly to advance towards the end of its institution.'[13] It was more than just a mechanical device for checking abuse of power. Open communication lay at the very heart of the Utilitarian enterprise: 'Without publicity, no good is permanent: under the auspices of publicity, no evil can continue.'[14] There might be a case for restricting publicity when a nation was at war, but such controls had no place in peacetime: 'Secrecy is an instrument of conspiracy; it ought not, therefore, to be the system of a regular government.'[15] Secrecy was at once an obstacle to progress and a measure of its absence. As John Stuart Mill wrote in *Thoughts on Parliamentary Reform*: 'The moral sentiment of mankind, in all periods of tolerably enlightened morality, has condemned concealment.'[16]

Fired by this conviction, the previous Whig Administration had made substantial efforts to accompany the extension of its powers with an expansion in the structures of communication. Immediately following the Reform Act it had laid the basis of the modern government information service with the creation of the Statistical Department of the Board of Trade under

[12] *Hansard*, 3rd Series, LXXVI, 2 July 1844, col. 249.
[13] J. Bentham, 'Of Publicity', in J. Bowring (ed.), *The Works of Jeremy Bentham* (London, 1843), ii. 310.
[14] Ibid. 314.
[15] Ibid. 315.
[16] J. S. Mill, 'Thoughts on Parliamentary Reform', in *Collected Works of John Stuart Mill* (Toronto, 1977), xix. 337. (The essay was first published in 1859.)

G. R. Porter;[17] a year later it had committed itself to the creation of a literate population through the grant of a subsidy to elementary education; in 1836 it had legalized the political reading of the people through the reduction of the newspaper stamp from fourpence-halfpenny to a penny; in 1838 it had promoted access to the Parliamentary process by installing a gallery for shorthand writers and putting *Hansard* on public sale for the first time;[18] and in 1840 it had made a bold attempt to liberalize the principal application of writing by the costly introduction of the Penny Post.[19] Ironically, Mazzini's suspicions were first aroused when, to save money, the Post Office put a penny stamp on an intercepted overseas letter it was forwarding to him.

The conviction that popular elected government depended on an uncontaminated flow of information to the electorate and its representatives was not confined to the English Utilitarians. As was noted by Georg Simmel, the greatest theorist of modern secrecy: 'Every democracy holds publicity to be an intrinsically desirable situation, on the fundamental premise that everybody should know the events and circumstances that concern him, since this is the condition without which he cannot contribute to decisions about them.'[20] However in 1844 there were grounds for setting the behaviour of Peel's Administration in a quite specific historical context. As the Secret Select Committee was later able to show in numbing detail,[21] governments of every complexion had been opening the letters of suspected criminals and political opponents since at least the time of the Commonwealth, but following the reforms of the Whigs the resonance of this mode of espionage had radically altered. The Penny Post of 1840, described by Richard Cobden as 'a terrible engine for upsetting monopoly and corruption',[22] had doubled the flow of letters and cost the Government in lost profits a sum equivalent to nearly a third of the yield of the new Income Tax which Peel introduced in 1841.[23] It now appeared that the Home Secretary was appropriating this terrible engine to mount a double attack on the fledgling democratic process, by both interfering with the free flow of written communication and obstructing Parliamentary scrutiny of its actions.

For the keepers of the pure flame of modern liberalism, the matter was straightforward. The freedom from public interference of personal possession,

---

[17] See below, Ch. 2, p. 46.

[18] Prior to this date, it had been printed for members only.

[19] D. Vincent, *Literacy and Popular Culture* (Cambridge, 1989), 32–49, 69–72, 233–6.

[20] K. H. Wolff (ed. and trans.), *The Sociology of Georg Simmel* (Toronto, 1950), 337. Also, P. Birkinshaw, *Freedom of Information: The Law, the Practice and the Ideal* (London, 1988), 63; S. Bok, *Secrets: On the Ethics of Concealment and Revelation* (Oxford, 1984), 179; G. Drewry, 'The Official Secrets Acts', *Political Quarterly*, 44: 1 (1973) 92; A. F. Westin, *Privacy and Freedom* (New York, 1967), 24.

[21] *Report from the Select Committee on the Post Office* (1844), PP 1844, XIV.

[22] R. and G. B. Hill, *The Life of Sir Rowland Hill and the History of the Penny Postage* (London, 1880), 478.

[23] Vincent, *Literacy and Popular Culture*, 38–9.

action, and thought encompassed the materials through which individuals communicated with each other. A letter was a letter, argued Macaulay, whether on a desk or in transit: 'they are both alike my property; and the exposure of my secrets is the same, and attended with the same consequences, whether from the reading of a letter which is yet to be delivered or from the reading of a letter which has been delivered.'[24] The free flow of information constituted a seamless web of democratic and moral principle. The authoritative figure of Lord Denman, Lord Chief Justice since the first Reform Act, summarized the issue with stark simplicity:

He did not consider this a question of expediency or inexpediency—he thought it a question of right and wrong. He could no more believe it necessary to show that such a power ought not to be vested in the discretion of any individual, than he felt it necessary to argue that it was wrong to pick a pocket.[25]

Britain recognized itself as a free country precisely by the absence of the multiple forms of public secrecy which characterized repressive regimes abroad.[26] It was central to the liberal narrative of history that concealment be replaced by transparency as democracy succeeded despotism.

History itself, however, proved more complex. At the very end of the nineteenth century one of the chief protagonists in the Mazzini affair, the Prime Minister Sir Robert Peel, was the subject of a biographical study by a later Liberal Premier Lord Rosebery. As a historian he was faced with the intractable difficulty of discovering what took place during the crucial debates inside Peel's Cabinet. No record was available either to contemporaries or to subsequent scholars. If instead of complacently looking down on our backward neighbours, wrote Rosebery, one tried to observe Britain as a critical outsider, there appeared to be a large element of inconsistency in the way in which power was exercised at the very heart of modern government:

To the inquiring foreigner . . . nothing can seem more extraordinary, in a country with so much of democracy about it, than the spectacle of a secret council, on the Vatican model, and sworn to absolute silence, conducting the business of a nation which insists on publicity for everything less important . . . Whether the system of Cabinet government be an efficient one or not is not now the question . . . but what may confidently be asserted is that of all anomalous arrangements for executive government in an Anglo-Saxon community, during the present epoch and under present conditions, the strangest is the government of the British Empire by a secret committee.[27]

---

[24] *Hansard*, 3rd Series, LXXVII, 20 Feb. 1845, col. 841.

[25] Ibid., LXXV, 25 June 1845, col. 1341.

[26] As, for instance, in Russia, where the 'Black Office' engaged in widespread postal espionage from the time of Catherine the Great. Z. A. Medvedev, *Secrecy of Correspondence Guaranteed by Law* (Nottingham, 1975), 75–80.

[27] Lord Rosebery, *Sir Robert Peel* (London, 1899), 35–6.

Cabinet secrecy was guaranteed by the Privy Councillor's Oath, which supplied the only constitutional definition of a Government Minister.[28] The Councillor was sworn to 'keep secret all matters committed and revealed unto you, or that be treated of secretly in Council'.[29] This was the basis of Graham's refusal to answer questions on postal espionage, and he himself bitterly attacked Macaulay and other Whig Privy Councillors for breaking ranks and criticizing him for upholding their common obligation.[30]

In practice, anomalous arrangements were the rule rather than the exception in this particular political community as it emerged in its modern form in the aftermath of the Reform Act. Bentham was unduly sanguine in his assumption that publicity was an unmixed blessing which everywhere was successfully doing battle with the evil of secrecy.[31] Communication was a double-edged tool, its growth in the nineteenth century as much a condition of increased secrecy as of greater openness. There was no intrinsic reason why the enlarged production of information should lead to its untrammelled diffusion. As Alexander Welsh argues, 'Valuable information is usually valuable as someone either reveals or conceals it'.[32] In ways which will be explored throughout this study, the central issue was one of power.[33] If not the meaning of words, then at least their dissemination depended on who was master, and, of equal importance, who was seen as a potential rival of that mastery. The anomalies of the period reflected the fact that the liberal state was suspended between hope and fear as it sought to develop a strategy for managing the unprecedented flow of information.

The pre-Reform tradition of dealing with criticism by attempting to silence it, which found its final form in the Six Acts of 1819, had finally been abandoned. It was now accepted that it was more dangerous to prevent than to permit political communication.[34] Yet in the uncertain years of the 1830s and 1840s, it was by no means self-evident to successive governments that it was either inevitable or desirable that all controls over official information should be abandoned. The critics of the Home Secretary might argue that in the summer of 1844, with trade recovering and Chartism receding, there were no domestic threats to the security of the state, but Graham could reply that it was barely two years since the country had been convulsed by the Plug Plot riots and attendant disorders following the rejection of the Second Chartist Petition, which, as it happened, had been presented to the Commons by none other than Thomas Duncombe. Peel went so far as to claim that Britain was menaced

---

[28] S. Low, *The Governance of England* (London, 1904), 29–40.

[29] *Hansard*, 3rd Series, LXXVII, 18 Feb. 1845, cols. 728–9.

[30] Bok, *Secrets*, 173–4.

[31] D. Leigh, *The Frontiers of Secrecy* (London, 1980), 1.

[32] A. Welsh, *George Eliot and Blackmail* (Cambridge, 1985), 44.

[33] P. Hennessy, *Whitehall* (London, 1989), 572; D. Goren, *Secrecy and the Right to Know* (Ramat Gan, 1979), 27.

[34] Vincent, *Literacy and Popular Culture*, 233–4.

by the prospect of civil war in August 1842, and was quite unapologetic about the widespread use of letter-opening at that time, which he regarded as an acceptable alternative to more overt and provocative forms of repression.[35] The question was not one of complete transparency or total restriction, but rather of where and more particularly how the line was drawn.

To some observers at the time, the Government was in trouble not because it had kept secrets, but because it had failed to do so. The leader of the 'Young England' group, Lord John Manners, remarked to Graham that 'The right hon. Gentleman says that official secrecy restrains him. Why the whole grievance in my eyes is, that secrecy has somehow or other been abandoned.'[36] In fact there was not a single speaker in the long series of often bitter debates who argued for the abolition of every form of official secrecy. Parliament's collective memory was not so short. In the discussions which followed the publication of the secret Select Committee report, the argument was focused on not so much the legitimacy of espionage, but on the codification of the Government's powers and the publicizing of their use. In terms which were to be repeated time and again during the subsequent century and a half, it was argued that the legal basis for secret activity was vague and insubstantial. The relevant Acts of 1711 and 1837 merely permitted letter carriers to withhold mail on the instruction of the Secretary of State; the actual powers of the Minister were not otherwise specified. Furthermore it was claimed that the most recent legislation had been passed by subterfuge. In the words of one MP: 'The House believed that it was a consolidation only, and not an alteration; but words had been introduced insidiously, and without the knowledge of Members.'[37]

The critics of the Government, who included many of their own MPs, wanted a new Act which would compel the Post Office to notify the recipient of a letter that it had been opened. Surveillance might be necessary in times of national crisis, but its existence should not itself be secret. Disraeli, who caused much grief to Peel on this issue, cheerfully offered up his own correspondence to the Home Office: 'they may open all my letters, provided they answer them.'[38] Of course such openness would diminish the effectiveness of the action, but that was a price worth paying. A modern liberal state had to learn how to sacrifice some of its reserve powers in order to promote the greater good of public confidence. The Adminstration looked at the same equation and came up with the opposite answer. In an uncertain world, such a procedure would inflame public opinion and hamstring those responsible for maintaining public order. A speaker in the debate accurately summarized the strategy of Peel's Government, which in one form or another was to be followed by all its successors, regardless of party: 'It was evident that they had arrived at the conclusion that it

---

[35] *Hansard*, 3rd Series, LXXVII, 18 Feb. 1845 cols. 728–30.
[36] Ibid., 20 Feb. 1845, col. 860.
[37] Ibid., LXXV, 14 June 1844, col. 900.
[38] Ibid., LXXVII, 20 Feb. 1845, col. 909.

would not be safe nor prudent to deprive Government of a power which it would be fit for it to exercise in case of emergency.'[39] The maintenance of the existing arrangements would permit the maximum flexibility of response with the minimum danger of publicity. Further legislation would invite debate and restrict action.

The tension between the increasing capacity to interfere with communication and the growing demand for freedom of expression was to be resolved by silence. Such a policy fitted both the unpredictable condition of domestic tranquillity and the established practice of the British state, which had escaped revolution in 1830. The situation was otherwise in Louis Phillipe's France, which had reacted against the era of royal tyranny by formally outlawing letter-opening by the post office, although it may have been continued in a muted form by other government agencies.[40] At home, the sheer density of the inherited structure of hidden instruments was cogently surveyed by Lord John Russell, the former Whig Home Secretary and next Prime Minister, who had been shamed by Graham into giving somewhat oblique support to a fellow Privy Councillor:

I believe, Sir, that the employment of spies does not at present exist; but you have no sanction in law to secure you against that policy; no declaration on the part of this House; no enactment to secure you against the employment of spies. The secret service money is placed entirely at the disposal of the Secretary of State, to be disposed of in a way which he believes to be most fitting for the service of the State; and if you enact that there shall be no opening of letters, are you secure—are you certain—that no future Secretary, anxious to preserve the public peace, feeling himself charged with the responsibility of its preservation, will not have recourse to means still more objectionable than the opening of letters?[41]

It was a paradoxical but compelling argument. Nothing had come of earlier attempts to place the use of secret service money on the official record, and although mounting public disquiet had curtailed the use of domestic spies, there had been no change in the law. The breadth of concealed powers, which mirrored and was sustained by the unwritten constitution, was a powerful disincentive to piecemeal reform and was to remain so as the exercise of government discretion evolved in subsequent decades.

In 1844 the Government's rigid refusal to give details of its actions caused it much unnecessary embarrassment. Unable to confirm what he had done, the Home Secretary was thus incapable of denying what he had not done, and by the end of the debate he was being accused of an ever-widening range of malpractice, including the wholesale opening of MPs' letters.[42] But then as later,

[39] *Hansard*, 3rd Series, LXXVII, 21 Feb. 1845, col. 946.
[40] E. Vaillé, *Le Cabinet noir* (Paris, 1950), 384–403.
[41] *Hansard*, 3rd Series, LXXVII, 21 Feb. 1845, cols. 987–8.
[42] Records of warrants had been kept since 1822, and do not support Duncombe's claim that his own mail was subject to surveillance, although at one stage a warrant was issued for the mail of Cobden. F. C. Mather, *Public Order in the Age of the Chartists* (London, 1959), 221.

the short-term difficulty was worth the long-term preservation of independence from Parliamentary scrutiny. Peel's successful insistence that the Select Committee which was forced upon him should meet behind closed doors ensured that there would be no break in continuity. Eventually it dawned upon the Government's chief critic Thomas Duncombe that the double secrecy with which he was faced was a summation rather than a betrayal of the national tradition: 'It was said before that it was an un-English custom, but it now appeared to be peculiarly English, particularly in the way we carried it out.'[43] Secrecy about secrecy was the British way.

The Culture of Secrecy

Both sides in the Mazzini affair made every effort to broaden their arguments from the particular to the general. The origins of both the offence and its justification were located well outside the immediate circumstances of the case. The Government's strategy during the controversy was to overwhelm the issue with precedents, which served the dual purpose of incriminating their opponents and diffusing their criticism. The report of the Commons Secret Select Committee said almost nothing about what had or had not been done in the spring of 1844, but instead supplied a hundred-page treatise on postal espionage down the ages.[44] Lord John Russell mordantly observed that the Committee members

described so many warrants that had been issued in former days, and showed so much antiquarian research, that I may wonder they did not go still further back: that they did not instance the case of Hamlet, Prince of Denmark, who opened the letters which had been committed to his charge, and got Rosencrantz and Guildenstern put to death instead of himself.[45]

In spite of their protests, Mazzini's supporters were capable of reaching even further back, one speaker claiming that, 'it had been the glory of England now for six centuries, that England should be the refuge of the foreigner'.[46] At every point the particular grievance was set in the context of what Macaulay termed the 'genius of the English people',[47] a concept at once charged with meaning and empty of precision.

The re-emergence of official secrecy as a public issue in the last twenty-five years has generated a similar breadth of argument. No serious approach to the subject, whether by academics, politicians, or bureaucrats, has confined itself

[43] *Hansard*, 3rd Series, LXXVI, 2 July 1844, col. 216.

[44] *Report from the Select Committee on the Post Office* (1844), PP 1844, XIV.

[45] *Hansard*, 3rd Series, LXXVII, 21 Feb. 1845, col. 991.

[46] Ibid., 20 Feb. 1845, col. 870.

[47] Ibid., LXXV, 24 June 1844, col. 1274. See also the remarks by Duncombe, ibid. 18 June 1844, col. 1014.

merely to the substance and operation of the more than one hundred separate pieces of legislation which currently restrict the flow of government information.[48] Richard Crossman, whose *Diaries of a Cabinet Minister* recorded the Wilson Governments' obsession with leaks of information and were themselves the subject of a landmark court action over the freedom to publish Cabinet secrets,[49] described secrecy as the 'British disease',[50] and every subsequent attempt at diagnosis has extended through and beyond the body politic. Peter Hennessy, the first journalist ever accredited to Whitehall and the best-informed observer of its activities, has written in terms which echo but invert Macaulay: 'Secrecy is as much a part of the English landscape as the Cotswolds. It goes with the grain of our society. Its curtailment, not its continuity, would be aberrational. Whitehall . . . is only its greatest, not its sole monument.'[51] 'National character' is invoked in his work not as the bulwark against secrecy but the chief obstacle to its removal. Where once, in the blissful dawn of the liberal state, to be English (or British—the terms tend to blur in this rhetoric)[52] was to boast of our leadership of the struggle against the despotic regimes of Europe, now it was a way of apologizing for the backwardness of our civil liberties amongst the western democracies.

The various explanatory frameworks are most often held together by the notion of culture. Thus, for instance, Clive Ponting, who has featured in the most dramatic official secrets trial of recent times and also written the only historical introduction to the subject, summarizes the path of change over the last two centuries:

A powerful and persistent culture of secrecy—reflecting the basic assumption that good government is closed government and the public should only be allowed to know what the government decides they should know—was carried over from the nineteenth century and refined in the twentieth century when it was given statutory backing through Britain's formidable secrecy laws.[53]

The fourth chapter of his *Secrecy in Britain* is entitled 'The Culture of Secrecy', and sets out to show how 'Britain has fostered a culture of secrecy, which ex-

---

[48] C. Ponting, *Secrecy in Britain* (London, 1990), 1.

[49] R. Crossman, *The Diaries of a Cabinet Minister*, 3 vols. (London, 1975); H. Young, *The Crossman Affair* (London, 1976).

[50] For Crossman's use of the phrase, see J. Michael, *The Politics of Secrecy* (Harmondsworth, 1982), 12. The phrase is employed as the title for the 'Charter 88' pamphlet, G. Robertson, *Freedom of Information: The Cure for the British Disease* (London, 1993). Also M. Frankel, 'Addicted to Secrecy, Lies and Distortion', *Observer* (10 Apr. 1994), 18.

[51] Hennessy, *Whitehall*, 347. Also 'A Malign Legacy', *Index on Censorship*, 15: 6 (1986), 9. Switching metaphors, he describes it elsewhere as 'built into the calcium of a British policy-maker's bones': C. Bennett and P. Hennessy, 'Introduction' to: Outer Circle Policy Unit, *A Consumer's Guide to Open Government* (London, 1980), 1.

[52] See below, Ch. 7 for a more extended discussion of the British tradition.

[53] Ponting, *Secrecy*, p. 1.

tends far beyond central government in many different and often unsuspected ways'.[54] What Hennessy has recently described as 'that famous British culture of secrecy'[55] is widely invoked to give depth and substance to descriptions of the structures of official secrecy which appear to resist more limited explanations of their form and survival.

Two different dimensions are embodied in this approach. In the first instance there is a direct appeal to history. Most commentators on modern practices seek to found their account outside the contemporary world, with bolder spirits such as Hennessy ranging widely across the centuries. At one point he manages to link the Whitehall mandarins to 'a 700 year-old culture of administrative secrecy'.[56] Whether or not the Privy Councillor's Oath was the foundation of our present discontents, there is a general sense that any convincing analysis must possess a broad temporal perspective. Those fearing change invoke the value of tradition and the lessons of earlier crises; those depressed by its absence perceive the dead hand of the past frustrating their endeavours.

Secondly, there is a lateral dimension, an assumption that the legal framework, most notably Section 2 of the 1911 Official Secrets Act, which remained in force until 1989, can be understood only by reference to related categories of structure and ideology. It is a view partly that the law itself is only one element of a broader constellation of forces which together impede the free flow of information, and partly that the survival of the legislation is dependent on a range of extra-legal agencies. In addition, the appeal to culture is a way of trying to measure the significance of the law. For most of its existence, Section 2 of the Official Secrets Act was used very sparingly, with an average of no more than one prosecution every two years up to 1979.[57] The handful of highly publicized dramas featuring well-connected MPs or journalists have obscured the fact that the great majority of the cases involved relatively trivial offences committed by otherwise unknown citizens. Compared, for instance, with any one of the multitude of social security enactments which stemmed from the introduction of National Insurance in that same year of 1911,[58] the direct impact of this most notorious piece of secrecy legislation on the daily lives of the mass of the population was negligible. Even though the rate of prosecutions increased sharply under Mrs Thatcher, it was still only being employed

---

[54] Ibid. 42.

[55] P. Hennessy, 'On Secrecy', Radio 4 broadcast, 25 June 1992. Also D. Goldberg, 'Executive Secrecy, National Security, and Freedom of Information in the United Kingdom', *Government Information Quarterly*, 4: 1 (1987), 43; P. Kellner, 'The Lobby, Official Secrets and Good Government', *Parliamentary Affairs*, 36: 3 (1983), 280.

[56] P. Hennessy, 'Not by Teabags Alone', *Index on Censorship*, 17: 8 (1988), 50.

[57] Lord Franks, *Departmental Committee on Section 2 of the Official Secrets Act, 1911* (London, 1972), Cmnd. 5104, i. 116–18; C. M. Regan, 'Anonymity in the British Civil Service: Facelessness Diminished', *Parliamentary Affairs*, 39: 4 (1986), 424.

[58] Forty National Insurance Acts were passed between 1920 and 1934 alone, modifying and extending the initial legislation. D. Vincent, *Poor Citizens* (London, 1991), 69.

four or five times a year.[59] If the Act mattered at all, it was in relation to the patterns of behaviour which it sustained amongst those in authority, and the more general habits of deference and ignorance which it engendered amongst society at large.

The most obvious context of analysis is the machinery of government. Official secrecy relates directly to public servants, particularly those required to 'sign the Official Secrets Act', a formal device which in fact has no force in law. It is commonly claimed that this ritual exercises a pervasive influence over the outlook of those who are thereby initiated into the ruling order. Peter Kellner and Lord Crowther-Hunt argue in their study of the civil service that

The real impact of the Act lies in the environment of secrecy that it creates inside Whitehall. The fact that tens of thousands of people each year 'sign' the Act has almost nothing to do with national security; it has a great deal to do with indoctrinating civil servants into the culture of closed government.[60]

Beyond the machinery lies the political system in general.[61] Thus, for instance, Drewry and Butcher, in a more recent study of Whitehall, appeal to a wider set of attitudes in seeking to understand the role of the Act: 'It is important to remember that legislation tells only part of the story of government secrecy in Britain. The rest is embedded in British political culture, constitutional conventions and the understandings and habits of civil service behaviour.'[62] And beyond the political culture lies almost everything. When the British secrecy record is compared with that of other western democracies, concluded Lord Franks in his 1972 report on Section 2, it becomes evident that the law is only one of a number of relevant factors: 'constitutional arrangements, political tradition, and national character, habits and ways of thought, all have their influence.'[63] There was no aspect of mentality or action, no period of time, incapable of yielding insights into the current system, which in the event was to prove highly resistant to Franks's attempt at reform.

There are good reasons for welcoming this breadth of approach. As it has operated for most of the twentieth century, the law on official secrecy has been frequently absurd and almost always opaque. Logic and clarity can only be brought to the subject if it is viewed through a wide lens. Any agenda for research must contain fields of study well outside both the topic and the period.

---

[59] K. D. Ewing and C. A. Gearty, *Freedom Under Thatcher: Civil Liberties in Modern Britain* (Oxford, 1990), 139.

[60] P. Kellner and Lord Crowther-Hunt, *The Civil Servants: An Inquiry into Britain's Ruling Class* (London, 1980), 265; also Kellner, 'The Lobby, Official Secrets and Good Government', 280.

[61] The concluding point in D. G. T. Williams's wide-ranging 1968 survey: 'Official Secrecy in England', *Federal Law Review*, 3: 1 (June 1968), 50.

[62] G. Drewry and T. Butcher, *The Civil Service Today* (Oxford, 1988), 175; A. Rogers, *Secrecy and Power in the British State: A History of the Official Secrets Act* (London, 1997), 120; J. B. Christoph, 'A Comparative View: Administrative Secrecy in Britain', *Public Administration Review*, 35 (Jan.–Feb. 1975), 28.

[63] Franks, *Departmental Committee on Section 2 of the Official Secrets Act, 1911*, i. 34.

However, it may be argued that what appears to offer an explanation of a set of practices often constitutes an evasion of a systematic understanding. The idea of a 'culture of secrecy' seems inherently historical but can represent almost a negation of an effective historical analysis. The most obvious difficulty is the ever-receding boundary of the programme of study. It sounds fine for the Civil Service Department report on open government in 1979 to conclude that, 'A comprehensive examination of all its various aspects would require a study in depth of the history and culture of most western democracies',[64] but in reality this looks more like a withdrawal from the field than a call to arms. To require to know everything before you can understand anything is to guarantee ignorance. There is no agreement on when to begin or where, and, more importantly, no clear sense of how any alterations have come to pass. Indeed the term is frequently deployed as a warning against the prospect of effective reform taking place at all. Either the intangible cultural forces will entrap the legislators, or their laws will be powerless against hidden sources of convention and authority. Whereas history is the study of change, culture, in this discourse, can be the denial of its existence or possibility.

Observers of official secrecy are not the first to have difficulty with the notion of culture, and it is perhaps not surprising that the term has obscured as much as it has illuminated. Here, as elsewhere, the central difficulty is that of articulating the parts within the whole. Unless this is done, the state, whose historical identity has been shrouded by the exercise of secrecy, is further concealed by the category of analysis. The bundle of tradition, sentiment, language, and interest has to be disentangled in a way which displays the relationships between them. In their frustration with the frequent failure of reform, critics of successive governments have been prone to attribute to them a coherence of vision and a consistency of purpose which are wholly misleading. As with the unwritten constitution, so with the traditions of secrecy which were embedded within it, the very absence of formal definition was a source of instability and argument.[65] From the agonies suffered by Sir James Graham sitting mutely on the Treasury Bench whilst his opponents used his silence to accuse him of every political crime short of treason,[66] through to the governments of the most recent past clutching on to the tiger of open government for fear of being eaten by it, conflict and contradiction have been at the heart of official secrecy. It has been in the interest of those in power to pretend otherwise, and they have often been assisted in this enterprise by the blurred pessimism of their opponents.[67]

[64] Cited in Michael, *Politics of Secrecy*, 19.

[65] J. Vernon, 'Notes Towards an Introduction', in id. (ed.), *Re-reading the Constitution* (Cambridge, 1996), 2.

[66] On the personal suffering of Graham during the crisis, see Torrens, *Life and Times of Graham*, ii. 302. Also A. B. Erikson, *The Public Career of Sir James Graham* (Oxford, 1952), 268–75; J. T. Ward, *Sir James Graham* (London, 1967), 209–11, 306.

[67] For instance, R. Holme, 'The Democratic Deficit', in B. Pimlott, A. Wright, and T. Flower (eds.), *The Alternative* (London, 1990), 104.

Despite the actual and constructed elements of continuity, the present is not interchangeable with the past in this field; an effective deployment of the concept of culture has to supply an explanation of the major developments in attitude and behaviour which have taken place and will continue to do so during the remainder of this century.

Secrecy is a profoundly volatile compound. As Georg Simmel pointed out, it is precisely because the rules are so easily breached that any system of regulation has to be embedded in a dense set of values: 'The preservation of secrecy is something so unstable; the temptations of betrayal are so manifold; the road from discretion to indiscretion is in many cases so continuous, that the unconditional trust in discretion involves an incomparable preponderance of the subjective factor.'[68] For this reason, legal and procedural histories of the subject, although valuable in themselves,[69] cannot fully comprehend the sequence of change. A full account needs to be focused not on the detail of the legislation and its implementation but rather on the means by which the inherent tensions and contradictions are resolved over time. At the intersection of intention and consequence stands the issue of trust, which, as Simmel argues, is doubly inherent in any secret body: 'as soon as the society becomes secret, it adds to the trust determined by its particular purpose, the formal trust in secrecy.'[70] The 'regime of publicity' by contrast, was, as Bentham insisted, 'a system of *distrust*'. 'Whom ought we to distrust', he asked, 'if not those to whom is committed great authority, with great temptation to abuse it?'[71] It was those who would block communication who demanded the greatest confidence. The question is therefore why a particular organization saw secrecy as a device for enhancing the trust it required, and whether and in what fashion it was successful in sustaining trust in the secrecy it attempted to establish.

The answer can be located in the particular conjunction of forces which were first displayed in their modern form in the Mazzini affair. New social groups were competing for power, with a nascent democratic system as their arena and the emerging forms of mass communication amongst their principal weapons. The exponential growth of formal means of generating, storing,

[68] Wolff, *Sociology of Georg Simmel*, 348. On the axis between secrecy and suspicion, see D. H. Johnson, 'Criminal Secrecy: The Case of the Zande "Secret Societies" ', *Past and Present*, 130 (1991), 192–3.

[69] The most recent full surveys are: J. D. Baxter, *State, Security, Privacy and Information* (London, 1990); R. M. Thomas, *Espionage and Secrecy: The Official Secrets Acts 1911–1989 of the United Kingdom* (London, 1991); R. Thurlow, *The Secret State* (Oxford, 1994); Rogers, *Secrecy and Power*. For earlier surveys, see J. Aitken, *Officially Secret* (London, 1971); Birkinshaw, *Freedom of Information*; D. Hooper, *Official Secrets* (London, 1987); Leigh, *Frontiers of Secrecy*; K. Robertson, *Public Secrets*, (London, 1982); D. Williams, *Not in the Public Interest* (London, 1965).

[70] Wolff, *Sociology of Georg Simmel*, 348.

[71] Bentham, 'Of Publicity', ii. 314. See also the very useful discussion of this point in I. Burney, 'Making Room at the Public Bar: Coroners' Inquests, Medical Knowledge and the Politics of the Constitution in Early-Nineteenth-Century England', in J. Vernon (ed.), *Re-reading the Constitution* (Oxford, 1996), 137.

and reproducing information was placing a new status on secular knowledge as a key to authority, but at the same time presenting fresh difficulties in respect of its validation. As the largely (though never wholly) oral communities were invaded by ever-more elaborate versions of the printed word, and the influence of those who had heard and remembered the most was displaced by those who had read and learned the most,[72] it became less easy to confirm information by appeal to tradition or immediate experience. The growth of a self-regulating capitalist economy meant that an increasing number of transactions were taking place at a distance, placing an ever-greater premium on mutual confidence.[73] As the knowledge became more important yet less complete, so the integrity of the individual or organization which controlled it became more critical.[74] But as it became more abstract so the established means of guaranteeing its provenance became less visible. Trust was every-where sought and constantly contested. Placing some form of embargo on in-formation enhanced both its value and the power of those who held it, but doubled the requirement to demonstrate moral worth. Concealment was so naturally allied to vice that it needed an especial display of virtue if it was to gain consent. Secrecy and trust constituted twin magnetic poles, forever re-pelling and attracting each other as written communication grew in volume and significance.

Withholding information became at once a claim to probity and a demand for deference. It implied a sense of responsibility which arose from and defined a position of moral authority. As groups within and beyond the state struggled to establish and defend their position, controlling the dissemi-nation of formal knowledge became a means of asserting not just their strength but their right to exercise it. Conversely, their opponents challenged both the substance of their learning and their fitness to determine its acces-sibility. The ethical basis of power was inextricably bound up with the infor-mation revolution, the more so in Britain where overt legal regulation was avoided wherever possible. The tradition of the unwritten constitution made restrictions on the written word more often a matter of engineered consensus than direct compulsion. Where organizations did codify their powers and impose formal controls over the knowledge in their possession, individual and collective rectitude remained the justification of their action.[75] Trust was the bridge between private and public good in this matter. The notion of the 'public interest' was constantly deployed in the Mazzini

---

[72] Vincent, *Literacy and Popular Culture*, 180.

[73] M. Savage and A. Miles, *The Remaking of the British Working Class, 1840–1940* (London, 1994), 70–1; Welsh, *George Eliot and Blackmail*, 72.

[74] S. Shapin, *A Social History of Truth: Civility and Science in Seventeenth-Century England* (Chicago, 1994), 7–17.

[75] T. Osborne, 'On Liberalism, Neo-Liberalism and the "Liberal Profession" of Medicine' *Economy and Society*, 22: 3 (Aug. 1993), 348.

debate,[76] as it was whenever a group was suspected of manipulating the flow of information for its own purpose. The term was never defined, nor, in a particular sense, could it ever be. Just as the issue of secrecy was in essence not about the substance of concealed knowledge but the right to determine its release, so the concept of public interest was not about a legal entity but the capacity of those in power to judge what was good for the nation at large.[77]

The pivotal relationship between secrecy and trust defines the boundaries of this study. It supplies first of all the point of departure. As has been suggested, the related transitions to mass communication and mass democracy associated with the first Reform Act gave the problem its modern form. It is of course the case that public secrecy was not invented in 1832, and both sides in the first controversy of the new era could find lengthy precedents for their arguments and actions. Equally, the machinery of government whose extension generated significant new difficulties in the flow of information had been developing over many decades before the reforming Whig Administration took office.[78] But it may be argued that this was the time when the practices and the debate over their scope and legitimacy took on a character which separated them from the pre-Reform period and launched them towards the procedures and controversies of the late twentieth century. As will be shown in Chapter 2, it is of particular importance that the analysis begins half a century before the first Official Secrets Act of 1889 and the associated creation of the Special Branch in 1887.[79] After the drama of 1844, successive governments were careful to avoid any possibility of renewed public concern, but it will be demonstrated that beneath the tranquil surface of mid-Victorian Britain, key innovations were being made, and powerful long-term positions taken up. The main text will conclude with the belated major revision of the Official Secrets Act in 1989, although whether and in what form that represented a watershed in the history of the subject will be a matter of discussion in the final two chapters and the Afterword.

The book begins and ends with official secrecy, but the focus is on the process rather than the substance of restriction. This is not a study of secret policemen or spies. The definitive volumes on the history of the domestic secret services combine erudition with humour in a way which must deter competition from all but the most dedicated espionage hunters.[80] The events are generally

---

[76] For examples of the use of this phrase or some variant, see *Hansard*, 3rd Series, LXXV, 14 June 1844, col. 894; 24 June 1844, cols. 1272, 1285; LXXVI, 4 July 1844, col. 310; LXXVII, 18 Feb. 1845, col. 698.

[77] See the valuable discussion of the use and misuse of the sister concept of 'national security', in L. Lustgarten and I. Leigh, *In From the Cold: National Security and Parliamentary Democracy* (Oxford, 1994), 3–35.

[78] J. M. Bourne, *Patronage and Society in Nineteenth-Century England* (London, 1986), 162–5.

[79] 'Special Branch' evolved from the 'Special Irish Branch' formed in 1883 to combat Fenian terrorism. Porter, *The Origins of the Vigilant State*, 35–67.

[80] Especially Porter, ibid., and Andrew, *Secret State*.

obscure, the sources are often themselves secret, the characters frequently bizarre. On some occasions the spies and spymasters held the fate of nations in their hands, on others they represented little more than a pioneering form of care in the community for distressed former public-schoolboys. It is not clear at times whether their obscurity was a defence against ridicule, or their eccentricity a constructed distraction from their more deliberate purpose. The dominant figure in the first phase of the implementation of the 1911 Official Secrets Act ended up in the dock on a charge of committing an act in violation of public decency in Hyde Park,[81] and there should be no surprise that the only victim of the Act to have turned his experiences into a novel should have written a farce rather than a tragedy, and that during the next world war, the fiction supplied guidance to Kim Philby,[82] and was reproduced for use as a training manual by the OSS.[83] From at least the Mazzini affair onwards, governments have frequently blurred the distinction between political, bureaucratic, and national interest, and between internal and external espionage, and for this reason it will be necessary to explore the creation and substance of these connections, which were notoriously enshrined in the two parts of the 1911 Act. But the concern throughout is with the control of public information, which, as a former Conservative Prime Minister has lately argued, 'lies at the heart of the relationship between the individual and the executive'.[84]

As this category of secrecy at every point raised the contentious issue of public trust, so the analysis must spread into the disputed body of corporate and private values and the struggles for ascendancy which they represented. This in turn demands that full consideration is given to other institutional restrictions on the flow of information which were growing or in some cases being outlawed in this period. Official secrecy as defined by the Privy Councillor's Oath, civil service regulation, or legal statute, is best seen as a special case of a phenomenon which became ever-more complex and diverse as the volume and status of formal communication expanded. The ethical basis of authority was an issue throughout the modernizing society, and doubly so wherever knowledge was concealed from view. Neither the development

---

[81] i.e. Basil Thomson, Head of Special Branch, 1913–21 and head of the Directorate of Intelligence, 1919–21. He was fined £5 for 'fondling' a prostitute, one Thelma de Lava, in Hyde Park in December 1925. He claimed he had in been in the Park on secret service business. Andrew, *Secret Service*, 283–4; Porter, *Plots and Paranoia*, 157–8.

[82] K. Philby, *My Secret War* (London, 1968), 40–1.

[83] See Compton Mackenzie's *Water on the Brain* (London, 1933; 2nd edn., London, 1954). On the book's later use, see A. Linklater, *Compton Mackenzie: A Life* (London, 1987), 254. Also below, Ch. 4, pp. 182–5.

[84] E. Heath, 'A State of Secrecy', *New Statesman and Society* (10 Mar. 1989), 10; A. May and K. Rowan (eds.), *Inside Information* (London, 1982), 36. See also the similar observation by Lord Franks, that issues surrounding the control of official information 'touch the heart of government in a Parliamentary democracy'. Franks, *Departmental Committee on Section 2 of the Official Secrets Act, 1911*, i. 13.

nor the significance of government controls can be properly understood without a parallel examination of professional, commercial, welfare, and domestic secrecy, and what Harriet Martineau in a famous attack called the 'Secret Organisation of Trades'.[85] If the concept of a culture of secrecy is to be usefully deployed, it requires a full-scale study, which has not yet been undertaken for this country,[86] of the ways in which both the practices and their associated meanings evolved in relationship to each other over the last century and a half.

Secrecy and Privacy

At first sight, the problem of defining secrecy resolves itself into a series of oppositions. The period begins with Jeremy Bentham setting it against 'publicity' and all that was progressive in the modern state, and ends with Tony Benn, who became a leading proponent of open government on the Parliamentary left in the 1970s and 1980s, denouncing it in equally sweeping terms: 'Secrecy is the great enemy of democracy and science.'[87] With the possible exception of warfare, there was not a single aspect of the state's behaviour which could be undertaken in camera without provoking a hostile challenge from some quarter. Even diplomacy became the subject of a vigorous campaign for more open conduct during the years before and after the first World War.[88] As C. J. Friedrich observes: 'Secrecy belongs to the group of phenomena which while ubiquitous in politics are considered morally objectionable or at least dubious, such as corruption, violence, betrayal.'[89] Whatever liberal democracy was for, secrecy seemed to be against.

Every vice requires for its existence a corresponding virtue. In the case of secrecy perhaps the most obvious was openness, but presented without qualification such a term could seem little more than a negative of a negative. During the period under review, much the most fertile and complex polarity was between secrecy and privacy. Here the opposing concept expressed not merely the absence of sin, but a positive condition which embodied a range of key aspirations of nineteenth and twentieth-century society. Letter-opening, in common with later forms of intercepting communication such as

---

[85] The title of an article published in the *Edinburgh Review*, 110 (1859).

[86] The one serious (and very successful) attempt to do this is by a literary critic writing on George Eliot. See Welsh, *George Eliot and Blackmail*, esp. 31–81.

[87] T. Benn, *The Right to Know* (Nottingham, 1978), 1.

[88] See below, Ch. 4, pp. 177–80.

[89] C. J. Friedrich, 'Secrecy versus Privacy: The Democratic Dilemma', *Nomos* (New York, 1971), 105. Also S. T. Gabis, 'Political Secrecy and Cultural Conflict: A Plea for Formalism', *Administration and Society*, 10 (1978), 145–50; I. Harden and N. Lewis, *The Noble Lie: The British Constitution and the Rule of Law* (London, 1986), 8, 41.

phone-tapping, aroused such fierce passions because it exposed with particular clarity the conflict between the power of government and the vulnerability of the individual. The almost feminine frailty of the envelope rendered its violation especially ignoble.[90] Mr Punch protested in 1844 that 'my letters—and the thousands I receive!—had all of them been defiled by the eyes of a spy; that all my most domestic secrets had been rumpled and touzled, and pinched here and pinched there—searched by an English Minister as shuddering modesty is searched by a French custom-house!'[91] A letter was in most cases written and meant to be read in private.[92] In their search for seditious material, the interceptors would be privy to the most personal information meant only for the eyes of the recipient. As one speaker in the Mazzini debate asserted, 'it is a grave thing that the correspondence of the country should be tampered with; that the private family secrets should be known'.[93] When the focus of the controversy shifted from the correspondence of foreigners and Chartists to that of the MPs themselves, their indignation at the prospect of lowly Post Office clerks feasting their eyes on the domestic communications of honourable gentlemen could scarcely be contained: 'He could place no confidence', declaimed another speaker, 'in a Minister of Police in Great Britain who could be guilty of the violation of privacy by the secret opening of letters of a Member of Parliament.'[94] A free country was founded upon a respect for the integrity of the private realm; a hallmark of the despotic regime was its capacity to appropriate at will the knowledge which defined the domestic sphere. As Josephine Butler wrote in the late 1880s, when the state was laying the foundations of the modern surveillance systems, 'the records of private and family life, gathered by espionage and treasured up in the secret cabinets of the police, constitute the instruments of an occult and immoral tyranny'.[95]

However, if we step back from the polemics and consider each term separately, their identities start to blur. There are two broad approaches to the notion of privacy. The first stresses the condition, 'the right', as Mervyn Jones has it, 'to be left alone'.[96] It is held that there is a fundamental value in the capacity to withdraw from the gaze or company of other persons or groups.[97]

---

[90] Wolff, *Sociology of Georg Simmel*, 352.

[91] *Punch*, VII (1844), 2. For further cartoons and satirical attacks, see ibid. 3, 14, 34, 41, 44, 73, 106, 117–8, 148.

[92] In communities where the skills of literacy were not widely distributed, it was still common at this time for the less educated to seek the assistance of other members of the family or neighbourhood for composing or reading letters. Vincent, *Literacy and Popular Culture*, 50–1.

[93] *Hansard*, 3rd Series, LXXVII, 20 Feb. 1845, col. 891.

[94] Ibid., 21 Feb. 1845, col. 948.

[95] J. E. Butler, *Government by Police* (London, 1888), 18.

[96] M. Jones (ed.), *Privacy* (Newton Abbot, 1974), 1. The phrase is usually attributed to Judge Cooley in 1888: see D. Madgwick and T. Smythe, *The Invasion of Privacy* (London, 1974), 2–6.

[97] L. C. Velecky, 'The Concept of Privacy', in J. B. Young (ed.), *Privacy* (London, 1978), 18.

Although the concept is nowhere defined in English law,[98] Britain is now covered by Article 8 of the European Convention for the Protection of Human Rights which declares that: 'Everyone has the right to respect for his private and family life, his home and his correspondence.'[99] The second approach lays particular emphasis on the restriction of access to a person. Privacy does not mean isolation, but rather the capacity to decide who knows how much about your life. In the words of Alan Westin's influential definition, 'Privacy is the claim of individuals, groups or institutions to determine for themselves when, how and to what extent information about them is communicated to a third party.'[100] Whether this conception is properly regarded as the means or the end of privacy,[101] every treatment of the term at some stage lays emphasis on what Professor Arthur Miller calls 'the individual's ability to control the circulation of information relating to him'.[102]

Another way of putting this would be the right to keep secrets. Secrecy has been described in the leading theoretical treatment of the subject as simply 'blocked communication'.[103] The more elaborate the definition, the closer it comes to privacy. Thus, S. K. Tefft establishes it as 'the mandatory or voluntary, but calculated, concealment of information, activities or relationships'.[104] Little effort is required to merge the terms altogether. Their Latin forms, *privatus* and *secretus*, are derived from verbs meaning 'to free from' and 'to separate from'.[105] Samuel Johnson saw the two words as virtually interchangeable, defining privacy as 'state of being secret; secrecy', and secrecy as, 'privacy; state of being hidden'.[106] In practice, the identity of each term in relation to the other belongs to the historical context in which they are employed. The key to understanding how, in the period following the compilation of Johnson's *Dictionary*, secrecy could come to be seen as both the greatest defence and principal enemy of privacy, lies in the emergence of a new sense of the public.

During the nineteenth century the notion of the public came to represent

---

[98] The most thorough discussion of the problem of reaching a legally satisfactory definition of privacy is to be found in *Report of the Committee on Privacy* [Younger] Cmnd. 5012 (London, 1972), 17–34. Also M. Hurwitt and P. Thornton, *Civil Liberty* (4th edn., London, 1989), 84.

[99] See also Article 12 of the Universal Declaration of the Rights of Man: 'No person shall be subject to arbitrary interference with his private life, family, domicile, or correspondence or to attacks on his house or reputation.'

[100] Westin, *Privacy and Freedom*, 7. Also J. Michael, 'Privacy', in P. Wallington (ed.), *Civil Liberties 1984* (Oxford, 1984), 134–5.

[101] Verlecky, 'Concept of Privacy', 21.

[102] A. R. Miller, *The Assault on Privacy* (Ann Arbor, 1971), 25. Also C. Hakim, 'Census Confidentiality in Britain', in M. Bulmer (ed.), *Census, Surveys and Privacy* (London, 1979), 133.

[103] Bok, *Secrets*, 6.

[104] S. K. Tefft (ed.), *Secrecy: A Cross-Cultural Perspective* (New York, 1980), 320.

[105] Respectively *privere* and *secernere*. For a discussion of the derivation of the word 'secrecy', see G. Vincent, 'A History of Secrets?', in A. Prost and G. Vincent (eds.), *A History of Private Life*, vol. V, *Riddles of Identity in Modern Times* (Cambridge, Mass., 1991), 163.

[106] 2nd edn., 1760, vol. II.

first of all the clamour and the stress of modern living which increasingly threatened the stability and integrity of the inner personality. This polarity, as Ralph Waldo Emerson put it, between 'society and solitude'[107] was incorporated into the legal discourse in a classic article by Warren and Brandeis in the 1890 *Harvard Law Review*:

The intensity and complexity of life, attendant upon advancing civilisation, have rendered necessary some retreat from the world, and man, under the refining influence of culture, has become more sensitive to publicity, so that solitude and privacy have become more essential to the individual; but modern enterprise and invention have, through invasions upon his privacy, subjected him to mental pain and distress, far greater than could be inflicted by mere bodily injury.[108]

It was assumed that in more backward civilizations the collective exposure to the forces of nature and the pervasive presence of magic and ritual left no place for the concept of privacy.[109] Progress, argued Simmel, took the form of a 'general scheme of cultural differentiation': 'what is public becomes ever more public, and what is private becomes ever more private.'[110] The division of labour, the growth of towns, the separation of the home from the work-place, and the spread of literacy and literature created the material base for the emergence of a new sense of the fragile self. Secrecy guaranteed the space within which the individual could flourish, making possible what Simmel called 'an immense enlargement of life'.[111]

The second and more instrumental notion of the public was the state. The emancipation of politics from the mutually reinforcing vices of mystery and corruption was the necessary counterpart to the growth of individual liberty. Publicity ensured that the public sphere was independent of private influence, and allowed the private sphere to flourish independently of the state.[112] Furthermore, in the event of the invasion of privacy by 'modern enterprise and invention', it might be possible, as Warren and Brandeis were claiming, to summon the legal resources of the state to its defence. In the realm of politics, the Janus face of secrecy became fully evident. Its value was contingent on agency and context. Should the state succumb to the more powerful forms of concealment and surveillance that were now within its reach, it would threaten the individual's crucial capacity to control what was known about his or her own life. Secret police destroyed the ability to police your own secrets. As the issue of postal espionage so graphically illustrated, the same forces that were creating

[107] R. W. Emerson, *Society and Solitude* (London, 1895 edn.), esp. 19–20.

[108] S. D. Warren and L. D. Brandeis, 'The Right to Privacy', *Harvard Law Review*, 4: 5 (15 Dec. 1890), 196. On the making of this article, see M. L. Ernst and A. U. Schwartz, *Privacy: The Right To Be Let Alone* (London, 1968), 45–8.

[109] Westin, *Privacy and Freedom*, 18–21.

[110] Wolff, *Sociology of Georg Simmel*, 337.

[111] Ibid. 330. See also D. Vincent, 'Secrecy and the City, 1870–1939', *Urban History*, 22: 3 (Dec. 1995), 341–2.

[112] Harden and Lewis *The Noble Lie: The British Constitution and the Rule of Law*, 57.

the possibilities of genuine privacy were also creating the weapons of its extinction. Private secrecy guaranteed the growth of liberal democracy, public secrecy paved the way to totalitarian dictatorship.[113]

This particular duality was a product of the nineteenth century, and buried within it were a number of unresolved difficulties characteristic of the age. A central problem was the place in the model of those groupings which lay between the private and the public. On the one side was the state, emancipated from personal interest and committed to publicity, on the other was the individual, fully protected from unwelcome intrusion. As was evident in the Mazzini debate and throughout the rest of the Victorian period, the realm of the private was held to extend no further than the family. No man was an island, but as far as possible his household was. There remained, however, the social structures which were larger than the domestic unit, and the organized bodies which were independent of government. It was not immediately apparent whether these had an obligation of openness to strengthen the public sphere, or a privilege of seclusion to reinforce the private. The failure to resolve or in many cases even to recognize these latent tensions were to provoke major inconsistencies in the treatment of secrecy during the period under review.

The most pressing issue was the impenetrable working-class community.[114] In the middle decades of the nineteenth century this seemed as much a threat to progress as the secret state, and indeed its existence was one of the few possible justifications for continuing surveillance. Once the urgent political danger had passed, this conflict between the acceptable and unacceptable forms of social seclusion was most clearly exposed in the dual response to the growth of towns and cities.[115] Here were found the detached villas surrounded by their fenced and carefully tended gardens which provided hitherto undreamt-of possibilities of withdrawal, but here also were located the teeming communities of the poor who could not afford to turn their homes into retreats from the pressures of modern life, where they could be exposed to the 'refining influence of culture'.[116] The consequence was the development of a strategy of urban development which sought maximum privacy for the civilized, and complete publicity for the unwashed.[117] This ambition and the associated growth of the home-visitors movement which will be discussed in Chapter 3,

[113] B. Moore, *Privacy* (New York, 1984), 271.

[114] The general danger to the state posed by secrecy amongst the public is discussed in Johnson, 'Criminal Secrecy', 170.

[115] For a general survey of the increasing preoccupation with these communities, see A. Lees, 'The Metropolis and the Intellectual', in A. Sutcliffe (ed.), *Metropolis 1890–1940* (London, 1984), 67–9.

[116] J. Bensman and R. Lilienfeld, *Between Public and Private: The Lost Boundaries of the Self* (New York, 1979), 31.

[117] D. J. Olsen, 'Victorian London: Specialization, Segregation and Privacy', *Victorian Studies* (March 1974), 12–13.

exposed the deep vein of class discrimination which informed the conception of legitimate secrecy. It was assumed that, in the absence of material comfort and the refining influence of education, privacy was neither a right nor an aspiration.

Outside the home, there was an increasing tendency to organize. John Stuart Mill wrote his classic defence of individual liberty against what he saw as a characteristic phenomenon of the age: 'The greatness of England is now all collective: individually small, we only appear capable of anything great by our habit of combining.'[118] The form of combination which came to depend most completely on the control of information in this period was the chartered profession. The members of an increasingly broad range of learned associations delineated their authority in terms of the exclusive possession of a codified, formally examinable body of knowledge. Doctors, lawyers, accountants, ever-more specialized groups of engineers, exercised their power in the market by means of their legally safeguarded intellectual monopoly and an associated set of ethical standards designed to insure against its misuse.[119] Much attention will be devoted to development of professions in this study because they straddled the boundary between the private and the public, the secret and the open. They were independent of the state but dependent upon its statutory protection. Their identity was defined collectively but their trade was practised individually. Their knowledge was established through open inquiry but its application was closed to the uncertificated. Whilst denying every connection with the occult secret societies of the past, they derived solidarity and status from their ownership of information denied to the population at large.

As in the case of informal social groups, the question of which side of the boundary professions properly belonged was bound up with the issue of class. The new or redefined learned associations were a vehicle for the upwardly mobile middle ranks of society, extensively and expensively educated at public schools and universities. In trade after trade they sought to place a barrier between themselves and those who had acquired their knowledge by means of traditional apprenticeships. This exercise was founded on an historically contingent distinction between malign and beneficial controls on the flow of information. Guilds, and their modern counterparts the trade societies, were stigmatized because their knowledge was uncodified, untestable, and protected for sectional gain rather than public benefit. By contrast, the closures characteristic of the professions were held to be necessary for the maintenance of progressive standards of service from which everybody would ultimately gain. The possibility that the opposing forms of restricting

[118] J. S. Mill, *On Liberty* (London, New Universal Library edn., n.d.), 102.
[119] For a good recent survey of this process, see P. J. Corfield, *Power and the Professions in Britain 1700–1850* (London, 1995), 20–1 and *passim*.

communication had more to connect than divide them was rarely admitted. However much the professions sought to associate unacceptable secrecy with backward occupations, they could not divorce themselves from charges of private self-interest in the far more powerful constraints they developed. As Simmel observed, 'secrecy is an interim arrangement for rising as well as sinking forces'.[120] It was not just the losers in the modernizing economy who saw advantage in controlling access to their knowledge.

The final unresolved tension lay at the heart of government itself. Just how far and in what way the civil service was becoming a profession as it was enlarged and reformed in the nineteenth century was a matter of continuing argument. There was certainly more than mere respectability linking public servants to the expanding ranks of doctors and lawyers. At one level, the civil service was another manifestation of the information revolution of the period. Weber claimed that, 'among essentially technical factors, the specifically modern means of communication enter the picture as pacemakers of bureaucratisation'.[121] Like the professions, authority was founded on formal expertise: 'Bureaucratic administration means fundamentally the exercise of control on the basis of knowledge. This is the feature which makes it specifically rational.'[122] Furthermore, in Weber's view it was axiomatic that in order to generate control, knowledge itself had to be controlled: 'While not peculiar to bureaucratic organisations, the concept of "official secrets" is certainly typical of them. It stands in relation to technical knowledge in somewhat the same position as commercial secrets do to technological training. It is a product of the striving for power.'[123]

The question was, whose power? Weber was doing no more than constructing an ideal type of what he described as 'the most crucial phenomenon of the modern Western state'.[124] The actual historical process required a separate study.[125] According to the model, 'the development of bureaucracy greatly favours the levelling of social classes [and] inevitably foreshadows the development of mass democracy'.[126] In practice, the weapon of official secrecy could be employed to frustrate both processes. In their struggle to defend their position, old and new elites could come together to resist the challenge from below by exercising control over the proliferating body of official information. Again, it was a matter of where the boundary between public and private secrecy was drawn. There was undoubtedly a case for a disinterested state bureaucracy imposing limited closures in the interests of efficiency and administrative

---

[120] Wolff, *Sociology of Georg Simmel*, 347.
[121] M. Weber, *From Max Weber*, ed. H. H. Gerth and C. Wright Mills (London, 1948), 213.
[122] M. Weber, *The Theory of Social and Economic Organisation*, ed. T. Parsons (New York, 1947), 339.
[123] Ibid. 339.
[124] Ibid. 337.
[125] G. Morgan, *Organisations in Society* (London, 1990), 66.
[126] Weber, *Theory of Social and Economic Organisation*, 340.

justice.[127] Equally, there was a clear possibility that such powers would come to be exercised largely on behalf of the social elites which populated the corridors of power before and after patronage was eroded by examination. In these terms, the history of official secrecy in Britain can be viewed as a long struggle between the private and public control of government.

---

[127] Bok, *Secrecy*, 174–5; Friedrich, 'Secrecy versus Privacy', 19.

| # HONOURABLE SECRECY, 1832–1870

The Vice-President's Eyesight

Twenty years after the Mazzini affair, a second Parliamentary controversy erupted over the issue of official secrecy. On this occasion the Minister in the dock was a Liberal, Robert Lowe, who was Vice-President of the Board of Education. In hostile debates in both Houses of Parliament, followed by a Select Committee of Inquiry, he stood accused of suppressing critical reports by a number of Her Majesty's Inspectors of Education, including their leading spokesman Matthew Arnold. As with Sir James Graham, the earlier target of public outrage, Lowe behaved with a combination of brute intransigence and what an admiring colleague described as 'sensitive delicacy'[1] in defending both his own honour and that of his department. Unlike the first occasion, however, the dispute over an apparent extension of Government restrictions on the flow of information was to cost the principal protagonist his job.

At the centre of the altercation was the management of the final drive towards universal literacy. Alarmed by the spiralling cost of the state subsidy and the continuing reluctance of a substantial minority of working-class families to patronize the denominational elementary schools, Lowe had introduced the Revised Code in 1862.[2] This sought to meet requirements of taxpayers anxious to save money and parents concerned to equip their children with the basic tools of reading, writing, and arithmetic, by making grants to schools and their teachers dependent on attendance levels and the results of annual tests of the literacy and numeracy of their pupils. Although the narrowing of the curriculum had some effect—expenditure was held down and the system at last began to reach the poorest sections of the community[3]—the introduction of the Code put a double strain on relations between the Inspectors and their department.

---

[1] *Hansard*, 3rd Series, CLXXIV, 18 Apr. 1864, col. 1188.

[2] For the growing crisis and the attempts to resolve it, see M. Sturt, *The Education of the People* (London, 1967), 238–58; A. J. Marcham, 'The Revised Code of Education 1862: Reinterpretation and Misinterpretations', *History of Education*, 10: 2 (1981), 87–90; A. Ellis, *Educating Our Masters* (Aldershot, 1985), 93.

[3] Vincent, *Literacy and Popular Culture*, 86–90.

On the one hand they were bitterly critical of a reform upon which they had never been consulted;[4] on the other, their annual reports were now moved to the very centre of the distribution of Government money. The attempt to achieve mass communication threw into sharp relief their own freedom to communicate to a wider audience.

From within the department, it was now essential that the Inspectors be brought into line. Public dissent could no longer be tolerated from a group of well-paid employees responsible for disbursing an eighth of total civil expenditure.[5] 'It seems to me', explained Ralph Lingen, the department's secretary, 'that with 60 gentlemen all over the country upon whose reports money depends, unless some sort of control is exercised over those reports which form part of the Committee of Council's own communications, you will be dispensing money on the various terms.'[6] More generally, it was a matter of establishing a single structure of command in an area which was becoming an increasing locus of public and Parliamentary concern.[7] Lowe protested that he could not be answerable to both his civil servants and his political masters:

I can understand no gentleman who values his character undertaking the working of an office under such circumstances. It would really be a divided responsibility, one part of it to the House of Commons, and the other part to a special bureaucracy, constituted out of the subordinates of the office itself.[8]

In terms which were to be repeated down the decades, he argued that the essential point was not the substance of the criticism, in which he affected little interest, but the right to make it: 'My object was not to suppress any opinion of these Inspectors, but to preserve the discipline and subordination of the office.'[9] The position which had to be defended at all costs was one of authority over the disclosure of any opinion contrary to official policy.

To his critics, Lowe was arguing the wrong case at precisely the wrong time. The Education Department was in the process of implementing the biggest change to the system since the original subsidy of 1833, argued one speaker,

and just at this moment, when we are most anxious to get all the information possible as to facts, the right hon. Gentleman comes forward and pleads for the

---

[4] N. J. Smelser, *Social Paralysis and Social Change: British Working Class Education in the Nineteenth Century* (Berkeley, 1991), 344. On the growth of the Inspectors, see G. Rhodes, *Inspectors in British Government* (London, 1981).

[5] B. R. Mitchell and P. Deane, *Abstract of British Historical Statistics* (Cambridge, 1971), 397.

[6] *Report from the Select Committee on Education* (Inspectors' Reports) (1864), PP 1864, IX, p. 13.

[7] J. E. Dunford, 'Robert Lowe and Inspectors' Reports', *British Journal of Educational Studies*, 25: 2, (June 1977), 164–8.

[8] *1864 SC on Education*, 59. The argument is amplified in A. Patchett Martin, *Life and Letters of the Right Honourable Robert Lowe, Viscount Sherbrooke* (London, 1893), ii. 221–35.

[9] *1864 SC on Education*, 61.

discipline of his Office—what none of his predecessors found it necessary to do—by saying that it was not the original understanding that all the Inspectors' Reports should be published.[10]

The more senior inspectors, led by Matthew Arnold, vigorously denied that the Department's right of censorship, which had been set out in Minutes drafted by Lingen in 1861 and 1863, 'was consistent with the instructions under which we were appointed'.[11] Behind the operational issues lay two points of principle. The first concerned the relationship between Parliament and its executive branches. Lowe's claim to ownership of the information generated by his officials was challenged by Lord Robert Cecil, who introduced the censure motion:

I do not believe that in the service of the Crown any loyalty is due to heads of department as against the House of Commons. The heads of departments and those departments themselves are alike subject to our jurisdiction; and if persons employed there see what they deem to be abuses they do no wrong in laying them before the representatives of the people.[12]

In as many as eight departments of state, inspectors were now acting as the eyes and ears of Government.[13] If they and other experienced civil servants were prevented from communicating directly with MPs, the capacity of Parliament to exercise informed and independent judgement on matters of national interest would be fatally diminished.

The second point concerned the status of the officials themselves. They were all gentlemen, and in the case of the Inspectors, particularly well-educated and paid. As such their own ethical standards were a sufficient guarantee of their conduct. To require their subordination to a body of departmental rules was both insulting and unnecessary. Their upbringing and training rendered them fully competent to form their own opinion on what they saw and to whom they should transmit their findings. As he struggled to silence the Inspectors' public opposition to the Revised Code, Lowe attempted to turn their claimed virtues to his own advantage. Except in a handful of particularly provocative cases, he abandoned direct censorship, but instead returned unacceptable drafts without comment: 'it was presumed that those Inspectors, being gentleman of great intelligence, would know very well what it was that was objected to, and would, if they were so disposed, be able to alter it, and if not that, the reports should be laid aside and not published.'[14] He was seeking to create a culture of instinctive self-censorship

---

[10] *Hansard*, 3rd Series, CLXXIV, 18 Apr. 1864, col. 910.

[11] *1864 SC on Education*, 43.

[12] *Hansard* 3rd Series, CLXXIV, 18 Apr. 1864, col. 1213.

[13] R. M. Mcleod (ed.), *Government Expertise: Specialists, Administrators and Professionals, 1860–1919* (Cambridge, 1988), 14.

[14] *1864 SC on Education*, 51.

which, once the immediate crisis had passed, would render unnecessary the overt use of formal regulations. At the heart of the enterprise was an appeal to what Lord Granville, his superior in the House of Lords, termed 'that honourable discretion which I believe to be the characteristic of the civil service of this country'.[15]

In the short term, the matter was decided by the state of Lowe's eyesight.[16] When his opponents produced the marked texts of draft reports to refute his denial of direct censorship, he was forced to admit that he could see so little without glasses that his papers were read to him by his private secretary.[17] He had no means of knowing that what he heard was adorned with critical comments by his civil servants. The spectacle of the man in charge of enlarging the nation's capacity to read and write being himself unable to read the writings of those responsible for examining the progress of literacy was too absurd not to be believed. Nonetheless, Lowe insisted that his veracity had been impugned and resigned from office.[18] The issues raised by the controversy outlasted his departure, and were still in the process of resolution when he and Lingen were reunited fourteen years later as Chancellor of the Exchequer and Permanent Secretary at the Treasury. The point of departure for this chapter is the contested notion of gentlemanly honour, which was variously deployed in 1864 to justify and condemn official secrecy, and was finally invoked by Lowe to explain what seemed at the time to be the termination of his ministerial career. As the Reform-Act state rose from its foundations, this became the key concept in establishing the scope, function, and legitimacy of secrecy in relations between Parliament, the executive, and the electorate, and between the conflicting social groups as they struggled for power in a country in which, partly as a consequence of the Revised Code, an increasing proportion of the population had access to the tools of mass communication.

Bureaucrats and Gentlemen

Amidst the flurry of articles in the daily and quarterly press called forth by the initial crisis of official secrecy in 1844, was a lengthy diatribe in the *Westminster Review* written by the leading victim of the affair. In accordance with prevailing conventions,[19] the authorship of 'Mazzini and the Ethics of Politicians' was nominally secret, but the detailed and forceful argument provided plenty of

---

[15] *Hansard*, 3rd Series, CLXXIV, 18 Apr. 1864, col. 1187.

[16] Lowe was an albino, and extremely short-sighted. On Lowe's problems in reading books, see A. Briggs, 'Robert Lowe and the Fear of Democracy', in *Victorian People* (Harmondsworth, 1965), 242, 263–5.

[17] *Hansard*, 3rd Series, CLXXIV, 18 Apr. 1864, col. 1209.

[18] P. Horn, 'Robert Lowe and HM Inspectorate, 1859–1864', *Oxford Review of Education*, 7: 2 (1981), 138–41.

[19] See below, pp. 65–8, on anonymity in periodical writing.

clues as to its identity.[20] Mazzini rehearsed the widespread complaints about the betrayal of 'official trust' and 'British honour', and about the widening gulf between public and private morality, and concluded by setting the matter in a broader context:

This anxiety for secrecy on the part of public officers is a growing evil. In the Customs, in the Stamp office, in various Government departments, we hear now of common clerks sworn to secrecy, or told by their superiors that if they communicate to the public any information connected with the business of the office, they will be instantly dismissed . . . Why, who are these men who treat as enemies their fellow subjects of the realm? Is it their business to prey upon the public or to serve it? Let diplomacy have its secrets, for diplomacy is but a refined mode of modern warfare, effecting its objects by tricks; but there needs no diplomacy between a servant and his employer. For public servants, we want responsibility; and responsibility cannot be obtained without publicity. Secrecy is but another word for fear.[21]

This was the earliest recognition of the emergence of a new ambition to control the flow of information within and beyond government. The linking factor was correspondence. At the centre of Weber's model of modern bureaucracy was the clerk with a pen in his hand:

Administrative acts, decisions and rules are formulated and recorded in writing, even in cases where oral discussion is the rule or is even mandatory . . . The combination of written documents and a continuous organisation of civil functions constitutes the 'office' which is the central focus of all types of modern corporate action.[22]

In the structures taking their form in the second quarter of the nineteenth century, the clerk spent most of his time writing letters and reading those sent to him. John Stuart Mill, occasional theorist of the liberal state and full-time Examiner of Indian Correspondence, described the practices of his organization, which in many respects provided the template for the domestic innovations: 'the whole Government of India is carried on in writing. All the orders given, and all the acts of the executive officers, are reported in writing, and the whole of the original correspondence is sent to the Home Government.'[23]

At home, the particular needs of communicating with the colonies were replicated by the expanding domestic bureaucracies, such as the Boards responsible for the Poor Law, Trade, and Education, which developed ever-more intricate contacts with other parts of the government machine, with their

---

[20] On the authorship of the article, see J. W. Mario, *The Birth of Modern Italy* (London, 1909), 81; H. Rudman, *Italian Nationalism and English Letters* (London, 1940), 65.

[21] 'Mazzini and the Ethics of Politicians', 251.

[22] Weber, *Theory of Social and Economic Organisations*, 332.

[23] *Report from the Select Committee of the House of Lords on the East India Company's Charter* (1852), PP 1852–3, XXX, 305.

own distant offices, and with the public in general. The labour of opening, reading, docketing, drafting, writing, copying, filing, and posting letters occupied the relatively short working days of clerks throughout their frequently lengthy careers. The ebb and flow of business during the year was measured by the size of the postbag. Problems were initiated by incoming correspondence, considered by consulting past letters, and resolved by composing new despatches.[24] The opportunity might be found for discussion with other officials and politicians, audiences were sometimes granted to visitors, but the main channel of administration was through handwritten communication.[25] In one sense the terminology of clerks and secretaries gives a misleading impression of the status, income, and power of the bureaucrats who created and were created by the liberal state; in another it accurately reflects the bulk of their work.[26]

For this reason, the route taken by correspondence within a government office was virtually coextensive with its entire organization.[27] At no point in the period was one state bureaucracy typical of another, but all were exposed to two conflicting pressures. First, there was the insistence by those who ran them that they should maintain an almost literally 'hands-on' control of their department's business. If he was embarrassed about opening Mazzini's mail, Sir James Graham was proud to admit to seeing all the correspondence which was actually addressed to the Home Office.[28] As Foreign Secretary, Palmerston not only dealt with every letter, but minutely corrected the handwriting and punctuation of his officials.[29] Secondly, there was a remorseless growth in the volume of correspondence which had to be processed. Ministries came and went, but year by year the postbags became heavier. The form and timing of the stages of organizational reform through which every department passed in the nineteenth century depended on the evolving balance between oversight and efficiency as the correspondence continued to multiply.

---

[24] See, for instance, the accounts given of the basic routine of the Colonial Office in 'Regulation for Numbering and Docketing Despatches and Papers Sent to the Colonial Office', Jan. 1818, reprinted as App. 9 of D. M. Young, *The Colonial Office in the Early Nineteenth Century* (London, 1961); *Report from the Select Committee on Official Salaries* (1850), PP 1850, XV, 359; *Reports of Committees of Inquiry into Public Offices* (1854), PP 1854, XXVII, 79.

[25] The later arrival of the telegraph and then the telephone diminished the absolute centrality of correspondence, but drafting letters remained a basic task of civil servants. For an account of its presence in the lives of senior officials more than a century later, see R. A. Chapman, *The Higher Civil Service in Britain* (London, 1970), 60.

[26] H. Parris, *Constitutional Bureaucracy* (London, 1969), 106–11; J. Pellew, *The Home Office, 1848–1914* (London, 1982), 7; N. Chester, *The English Administrative System, 1780–1870* (Oxford, 1981), 282–3.

[27] Chester, *The English Administrative System*, 300. One of the few attempts to identify the technology of communication as an agent of administrative reform is to be found in J. W. Cell, *British Colonial Administration in the Mid-Nineteenth Century* (New Haven, 1970), 43–6. Cell also draws attention to the later impact of the telegraph, which forced the involvement of junior clerks in dealing with incoming messages.

[28] *1850 SC on Official Salaries*, 474.

[29] E. Herstlet, *Recollections of the Old Foreign Office* (London, 1901), 77–81.

The key characteristic of what the Northcote–Trevelyan Report termed the 'great and continuing accumulation of public business'[30] was that it was both inescapable and inconsistent. The flow of paperwork was everywhere growing, yet nowhere at the same rate. During the second quarter of the century, the correspondence dealt with in the Home Office multiplied four-fold, in the Foreign Office and Board of Trade threefold, in the Admiralty it nearly doubled, and in the Treasury and Colonial Office it increased by less than half.[31] Fittingly, the largest increase of official letters was recorded in the department in charge of private letters.[32] In each case the number of officials employed to read and reply to the correspondence grew more slowly. The permanent establishment of the Foreign Office, for instance, only expanded from thirty-five to forty between 1830 and 1849.[33] There was a shared perception that the pressure of work was intensifying and would continue to do so, but no atmosphere of general crisis. Instead, separate departments were able to choose their own moment to embark on a common series of administrative changes.

There were two broad areas of reform which could be applied to the handling of correspondence. At the lower end of the bureaucracy, most departments, beginning with the Foreign Office in 1810,[34] established registries so that incoming mail at least could be listed and sorted before it was sent up to the senior officials, and a retrievable record made of their replies.[35] In the higher reaches of the service, it was gradually becoming physically impossible for the Secretary of State personally to reply to every letter. Whilst the Minister could be assisted by his Parliamentary Under-Secretary, the increasing complexity of business demanded a more long-term engagement with the work of the department than could be provided by the more transient, political, appoint-

---

[30] *Northcote–Trevelyan Report* (1854), republished in *Public Administration*, 32 (Spring 1954), 1. The Report, which was submitted to the Houses of Parliament in February 1854, was the culmination of a series of economy reviews into government departments during the preceding four years, in the course of which Charles Trevelyan, the head of the Treasury, developed his ideas of defining merit by examination and dividing the administrative labour into intellectual and routine categories. On the background to the report, see Hennessy, *Whitehall*, 31–43.

[31] *1850 SC on Official Salaries*, 88, 204, 458; J. Barrow, *An Auto-Biographical Memoir* (London, 1847), 418; A. P. Donajgrodzki, 'New Roles for Old: The Northcote–Trevelyan Report and the Clerks of the Home Office, 1822–48', in G. Sutherland (ed.), *Studies in the Growth of Nineteenth-Century Government* (London, 1972), 93; Chester, *The English Administrative System*, 283; R. Jones, *The Nineteenth-Century Foreign Office* (London, 1971), 13, 32; J. A. C. Tilley and S. Gaselee, *The Foreign Office* (London, 1933), 66.

[32] *1850 SC on Official Salaries*, 505–6.

[33] Tilley and Gaselee, *Foreign Office*, 53, 65–7.

[34] Herstlet, *Recollections*, 29.

[35] By the 1840s some departments were experimenting with separate grades of copying clerks. R. C. Snelling and T. J. Brown, 'The Colonial Office and its Permanent Officials, 1801–1914', in Sutherland (ed.), *Studies in . . . Nineteenth-Century Government*, 150; B. L. Blakeley, *The Colonial Office, 1868–1892* (Durham, NC, 1972), 4–15. On the early reform of the Board of Trade, see R. Prouty, *The Transformation of the Board of Trade, 1830–1855* (London, 1957), 100.

ments.[36] Thus the Permanent Under-Secretary began to become the focal point for processing the correspondence of the office.

Epistolary momentum provided a common basis for the emergence of a routine based on a nascent division of labour. However, by mid-century, even in the most progressive ministries this fell far short of a full hierarchical specialization of function. A Secretary of State would still see most of the department's mail, even if his Permanent Under-Secretary first put it in order and then supervised the writing, copying, and despatching of the replies. Amongst the established staff there was no effective device for filtering the flow of correspondence. At the Treasury, Charles Trevelyan, the apostle of rational reform, personally wrote the immense body of correspondence generated by the Irish Famine.[37] His vision of a state bureaucracy consistently divided into intellectual and mechanical classes, each recruited by examination, was behind and ahead of its time.[38] Both the necessity and the terminology of reform had been clearly set forth nearly two decades earlier in Henry Taylor's *The Statesman*: 'As to their functions', he wrote of clerks, 'they are of two kinds, intellectual and mechanical; and it were reasonable, therefore, that they should be divided into two classes, those who are fit for the one sort of employment, and those who are competent to the other only.'[39] Most civil servants could see the course which change must take, and many had embarked on it; few, on the other hand, could see the justification for so crude and so precipitate a resolution to problems with which they had been living since the Reform Act state came into being.

If the Northcote–Trevelyan Report of 1854 had only a limited and inconsistent impact on the machinery of the civil service, it did at least clarify the issues surrounding reform. At the heart of the recommendations was the reciprocal relationship between selection and performance. The endless labour of processing correspondence was repelling potential entrants and destroying the minds of those who were recruited.[40] It was absurd to suppose, argued Henry Taylor from his experience at the Colonial Office, that the drudgery of transcribing despatches constituted a necessary training for a career as a statesman.[41] As one of the *Committees of Inquiry into Public Offices* put it,

---

[36] S. Finer, 'Jeffersonian Bureaucracy and the British Tradition', *Public Administration*, 30 (1952), 347–8.

[37] J. Hart, 'The Genesis of the Northcote–Trevelyan Report', in Sutherland (ed.), *Studies in . . . Nineteenth-Century Government*, 102. See also the similar behaviour of the reforming James Stephen in Cell, *British Colonial Administration*, 7–11.

[38] *Northcote–Trevelyan Report*, 11; O. MacDonagh, *Early Victorian Government, 1830–1870* (London, 1977), 202–8.

[39] H. Taylor, *The Statesman* (1836; New York, 1958), 109.

[40] For a fierce attack on the lack of intellectual stimulus in the traditional civil service, see Byerley Thomson's survey of the profession, published before the Northcote–Trevelyan reforms had begun to have a visible effect. H. B. Thomson, *Choice of a Profession* (London, 1857), 239–66.

[41] Taylor, *The Statesman*, 109–10. Also Blakeley, *Colonial Office*, 6–10.

If, after ten or fifteen years spent in incessant copying and other routine work, the spirit, the mental activity, and the wide extent of acquired knowledge necessary for vigorous intellectual exertion in the transaction of business like that of the Colonial Office, are wanting, it is the fault of the system, and not of the individuals who have been placed in circumstances so unfavourable to them.[42]

A clear separation of function would enable the department to establish formal criteria for selection and identify and reward good performance.

The prospect of appointing two separate grades of clerks by examination, and the associated intention finally to replace seniority by merit as the basis of promotion, brought into sharp focus the issue of the character of the British civil servant. As with every other aspect of its affairs, the ethos of the state bureaucracy had been evolving in an unspoken and unsystematic fashion during the previous decades. Now both advocates and opponents of reform had to articulate what was required, and, perhaps more urgently, what was to be avoided in the personality and behaviour of the public official. During the debate it fell to Sir George Cornewall Lewis, then editing *The Edinburgh Review* prior to returning to Parliament in 1855 as political head of Trevelyan's Treasury, to identify the major danger:

One of the first qualities required in the clerks of a public office is trustworthiness. In many public offices, papers containing information respecting pending questions of great importance, and of deep interest to private individuals, to companies and associations, to the public at large, and to the whole civilised world, necessarily pass through the hands of clerks in their successive stages of preparation. The honourable secrecy which has distinguished the clerks of our superior offices, and their abstinence from communicating information to interested parties or public journals, cannot be too highly commended. But this discreet reserve depends on qualities which cannot be made the subject of examination by a central board, or be expressed by marks upon a paper of written answers.[43]

The notion of 'honourable secrecy' was central both to Lewis's response to civil service reform, and to the whole modern history of restricting official communication. At first sight it was a paradoxical phrase. To the Home Office's critics a decade earlier, personal honour and public secrecy were mutually exclusive. In his article on political ethics, Mazzini claimed that if 'private gentlemen' had behaved like the government, they would have been punished 'with a horsepond or the treadmill'.[44] There could be no morality in this form of concealment. By engaging in postal espionage and then refusing to discuss it, Ministers were betraying not only the sanctity of the home but the structure of values upon which all civilized society was based. An understanding of how

---

[42] *1854 Reports of Committees of Inquiry into Public Offices*, 82.
[43] *Papers on the Re-Organisation of the Civil Service* (1855), PP 1854–5, XX, 116.
[44] 'Mazzini and the Ethics of Politicians', 228.

this apparent oxymoron came to occupy so central place in the emerging culture of the civil service requires a closer examination of the choice of honour, amongst all the possible garments, as the appropriate dress for secrecy. The conjunction was founded on the press of business. The increasing volume and formality of exchanges between the state and its citizens inevitably heightened awareness of the quality of public ethics. Here, as elsewhere in society, the less transactions were conducted between familiar faces, the more critical became the issue of trust.[45] Yet the more public funds were expended by these means, the more important became the question of competence. In 1860 Lord Robert Cecil entered the debate over the implementation of Northcote–Trevelyan. Citing with approval Lewis's concern about the threat to the 'discreet reserve' of the civil servant, he identified the priorities in any system of recruitment and promotion: 'Every man who lives by his labour offers to his employer two distinct qualities—capacity and trustworthiness. In the open market of the world trustworthiness bears the highest price, and capacity the second.'[46] The attempt to replace nomination by examination raised in an acute form the relation between qualities which in an earlier age might have been seen as interchangeable. To most of those taking part in the debate, there could be little doubt about the proper order. As Earl Grey put it in 1855: 'Brilliant talents and great acquirements are far less useful than moral qualities, in the holders of permanent offices.'[47]

The question was whether, in Cecil's terms, substituting the 'regime of cram' for the 'regime of patronage' would lead to the appointment of 'clever men of dissipated habits and of mixed character'.[48] The most eloquent presentation of the counter-argument was furnished by the short-lived Administrative Reform Association. This was founded in 1855 as a reaction to alleged aristocratic mismanagement of the Crimean War, which had begun just as the Northcote–Trevelyan Report was published and appeared to be a timely confirmation of its central message.[49] The Association demanded a new era of transparency in the organization and conduct of the civil service: 'There must be an end put to every mystery of office—how the Administration of the country is carried on must be made plain to the most ordinary capacity.'[50] Open competition would serve the double purpose of clarifying the process of selection and introducing to the bureaucracy a cohort of officials capable of exposing what Dickens, in an address to the Association, described as 'the ghastly absurdity of that vast labyrinth of misplaced men and misdirected

---

[45] Welsh, *George Eliot and Blackmail*, 54.

[46] [Lord R. Cecil], 'Competitive Examinations', *Quarterly Review*, 18 (Oct. 1860), 599.

[47] Earl Grey, *Parliamentary Government* (London, 1858), 170.

[48] Cecil, 'Competitive Examinations', 596, 599.

[49] O. Anderson, 'The Administrative Reform Association, 1855–1857', in P. Hollis (ed.), *Pressure from Without* (London, 1974), 262–88.

[50] Administrative Reform Association, *Address of the Committee to the People of England* (10 May 1855), 7. Also W. R. Greg, *The Way Out* (London, 1855), 3–17.

things'.[51] The widely canvassed fear that examination would favour amoral intelligence over well-bred integrity was countered by an appeal to the inherent value of mental toil, a case much favoured by John Stuart Mill. A paper on 'Appointments for Merit Discussed in Official Answers to Official Objections to the Abolition of Patronage' argued that a successful candidate

must have exercised self-denial and have been industrious and attentive; he will seldom have been enabled to give his mind to horse-racing or gambling, or to absorbing and expensive pleasures. Negatively, by excluding vices, the qualifications which ensure success in competition, are security, at all events, for humble virtue and honour.[52]

At one level the Administrative Reform Association represented a vigorous attack by the metropolitan professional and business interests on the still-pervasive role of the aristocracy in government.[53] The controversy has been seen as the beginning of the admittedly distant end of the power of inherited privilege in the democratic state.[54] Amidst the polemics, however, it is possible to identify a striking commonality of language. 'Humble virtue and honour' was the objective of every contribution to the debate. It was around these terms that a search was begun for a compromise which would pacify the reformers and satisfy their opponents. The solution was found in the figure of the gentleman, the endlessly malleable bedrock of the social hierarchy. Senior members of the civil service had never doubted the status which was both a condition and a consequence of their appointment. Contemplating promotion within the Colonial Office, Henry Taylor looked forward to the deference he would receive: 'The official rank would go for a good deal with the middle classes, the country gentlemen, and the humdrum aristocracy.'[55] Whatever its shortcomings, the ramshackle structure of private and political patronage had at least preserved the personal standing if not the corporate efficiency of the civil servant. As the author of *Our Government Offices* wrote in 1855:

The manner of their appointment, however much it may be objected to, has secured also a general quality of gentleman-like feeling. Parliamentary patronage has some evils,—but it at all events contributes towards placing in the Service men who can only be described by that vague word 'gentleman'—that is, if one would attempt a definition, persons having some social station, and thus giving collateral guarantee for good conduct.[56]

---

[51] Administrative Reform Association, *Speech of Charles Dickens, Esq., Delivered at the Meeting of the Administrative Reform Association at the Theatre Royal, Drury Lane* (27 June 1855). See also Dickens's satire on 'The Circumlocution Office' in *Dombey and Son* (1847–8).

[52] Administrative Reform Association, *Appointments for Merit Discussed in Official Answers to Official Objections to the Abolition of Patronage* (London, 1855), 32.

[53] O. Anderson, 'The Janus Face of Mid-Nineteenth-Century English Radicalism: The Administrative Reform Association of 1855', *Victorian Studies*, 8 (Mar. 1965), 234–5.

[54] J. V. Beckett, *The Aristocracy in England, 1660–1914* (Oxford, 1986), 456–60.

[55] H. Taylor, *The Autobiography of Henry Taylor* (London, 1885), i. 266.

[56] J. H. Stack, *Our Government Offices* (London, 1855), 4.

The challenge now was to find a way of modernizing the gentleman without sacrificing the assurance of ethical behaviour which was more than ever required of the public official.

Throughout the nineteenth century, it was both essential and impossible to map the features of a gentleman. Everyone needed to know his identity. As Taine observed, 'the vital question in the case of a man is always put thus: "Is he a gentleman?" '[57] But no one could supply an objective set of rules which could determine the answer in advance.[58] The concept was so central to the distribution of social status that every commentator became part of his own explanation. 'Not only is the definition of the word "gentleman" difficult because the exact meaning of the term is illusive,' noted Arthur Ponsonby, 'but because each one who attempts to define it is slightly biased according to his own social status.'[59] Everything depended on perspective. The category was rigid to those on the outside, elastic to those on the inside.[60] It was both divisive and encompassing. A line was drawn in order to exclude the majority of the population and to integrate the privileged minority into a single cultural entity. There were no formal regulations to establish membership. Defoe was not the first writer on the subject to insist that the station was open to those who had either inherited or achieved their status.[61] To many apologists the absence of fixed criteria made the figure of the gentleman particularly appropriate for the era of democratic reform, unlike that of the aristocrat, trammelled round with the outmoded conventions of his caste. 'The character of the gentleman', wrote the American commentator Frederick Lieber in 1846, 'produces an equality of social claims and supersedes rank, office, or title.'[62] It was moving the centre of its existence from the field of leisure to that of work,[63] and, as Lieber stressed, it had emancipated itself from the arcane rituals of the medieval period: 'The character of the cavalier was essentially aristocratic; that of the gentleman is rather of a popular cast, or of a civic nature, and shows in this, likewise, that it belongs to modern times.'[64]

The modernization was achieved by a reworking rather than a rejection of the basic characteristics of the landed elite. One property in particular was seen as the parent of every other: 'The character of the gentleman', continued

[57] H. Taine, *Notes on England* (3rd. edn., London, 1872), 173. Also 'Gentlemen', *Cornhill Magazine*, 5 (Jan.-June 1852), 330.

[58] The absence of a clear definition is discussed in [W. J. Browne], 'The English Gentleman', *The National Review*, 7: 38 (Apr. 1886), 261.

[59] A. Ponsonby, *The Decline of the Aristocracy* (London, 1912), 24.

[60] W. L. Burn, *The Age of Equipoise* (London, 1964), 259.

[61] D. Defoe, *The Compleat English Gentleman*, ed. K. D. Buelbring (London, 1900), 22. [This was left unpublished at Defoe's death in 1731, and first published in 1890]. Also, M. Curtin, *Propriety and Position: A Study of Victorian Manners* (New York, 1987), 101–4.

[62] F. Lieber, *The Character of the Gentleman* (Cincinnati, 1846), 7.

[63] This shift in the locus of character is examined in S. Collini, 'The Idea of "Character" in Victorian Political Thought', *Transactions of the Royal Historical Society*, 35 (1985), 39.

[64] Lieber, *Character of the Gentleman*, 12.

Lieber, 'includes whatever was valuable in the cavalier and the earlier knight, but he stands above him even with reference to that very element which constituted a chief attribute of the earlier—to honour.'[65] A constellation of qualities surrounded this core virtue. The honourable gentleman was expected to display courage, truthfulness, honesty, unselfishness, generosity, modesty, composure, thoughtfulness, and a self-denying lack of ambition for external recognition. A man of honour needed no honours to know his own standing.[66]

A major obstacle to the renovation of these values was the custom of defending honour by mortal combat. This most lethal means of silencing an adversary was still sufficiently accepted to permit Wellington as Prime Minister in 1828 to demand of Lord Winchelsea, who had criticized him in a newspaper article, 'to give me that satisfaction for your conduct which a gentleman has a right to require, and which a gentleman never refuses to give',[67] and for his successor as Conservative leader to call out his opponent in the 1837 General Election after he had been accused of the violation of 'honour, principle and truth' by acting 'under the mask of secrecy' to influence the result.[68] The practice at this time occupied a grey area of legality, neither specifically prohibited nor immune to charges ranging from breach of the peace to murder.[69] Attempts were made in the 1820s to subject the practice to a modern code, which might permit honour to be defended with both discipline and impunity, especially in the armed forces.[70] Unlike Germany, however, the military played too small a part in public life for its traditions of personal violence to determine the development of the gentlemanly ideal.[71] On the eve of the Mazzini affair an anti-duelling association was formed which succeeded in amending the Articles of War in 1844 to allow army officers to apologize without compromising their honour, and in outlawing the practice altogether in 1852.[72] There were two reasons for haste. First, as the divisions in society were renegotiated in the aftermath of the Reform Act, it no longer seemed appropriate for one section to demand the privilege of taking life with legal sanction.[73] 'It was', wrote Ponsonby, 'a class distinction which was doomed to die out in a more democratic age.'[74] Secondly, and more seriously, the increasing tendency to permit gentlemanly honour to

[65] Lieber, *Character of the Gentleman*, 12.

[66] A. Welsh, *The Hero of the Waverley Novels* (New Haven, 1963), 219–20.

[67] They met at Battersea Fields, climbing over a fence to avoid the gaze of some workmen, and both aimed wide. E. Longford, *Wellington: Pillar of State* (London, 1972), 186–8.

[68] The affair was eventually settled by seconds, although not before Peel had arranged to arm himself. N. Gash, *Sir Robert Peel* (London, 1972), 189–91; Rosebery, *Sir Robert Peel*, 25.

[69] J. P. Gilchrist, *A Brief Display of the Origin and History of Ordeals* (London, 1821), pp. xiv–xxxv.

[70] See *The British Code of Duel* (London, 1824).

[71] U. Frevert, 'Honour and Middle-Class Culture: The History of the Duel in England and Germany', in J. Kocka and A. Mitchell (eds.), *Bourgeois Society in Nineteenth-Century Europe* (Oxford, 1993), 224.

[72] V. Kiernan, *The Duel in European History* (Oxford, 1988), 204–22.

[73] D. T. Andrew, 'The Code of Honour and its Critics: The Opposition to Duelling in England, 1700–1850', *Social History*, 5: 3 (Oct. 1980), 429.

[74] Ponsonby, *Decline of the Aristocracy*, 60.

float free of its landed base invited the participation in the ritual of every wronged greengrocer and outraged clerk.[75] As *The Gentleman's Pocket Book of Etiquette* of 1838 put it,

> The SPIRIT OF HONOR is confined to no class, its abode is not subject to the regulations of Etiquette—it is a godlike spirit, is uncontrollable in its will, and will not confine its wanderings or its waitings to the breasts of the ARISTOCRACY; therefore if Duel be allowable to any, it is allowable to all who are influenced by this spirit.[76]

The abolition of duelling, which took place just as the Northcote–Trevelyan Report was being written, left unresolved the basic dilemma of the modern code of the gentleman—how to preserve its identity when both its forms and its personnel were in such dangerous proximity to the behaviour of those so firmly denied its status. One solution was to retreat to a reinvented world of chivalry and there make a stand against the further spread of democracy.[77] But events such as the Eglington Tournament of 1839 did more to bury than revive the medieval code. It reminded the emerging ruling order of the unwisdom not only of organizing large, open-air events in a rainy climate, but also of prolonging the association with weapons and violence. At the heart of the shift in emphasis was the transition from physical to moral courage. As the new model gentleman lived out his life in a century of increasing comfort and almost unbroken peace, the issue was no longer the readiness to sacrifice life for a greater cause, but rather the willingness to withstand mental pain for the sake of truth and honour. The element of renunciation was transferred from the realm of action to that of communication. The gentleman's character, stated Charles Kingsley, 'endureth all things, keeps its temper, and keeps its tongue'.[78] Self-restraint founded on a combination of self-respect and self-denial became its most visible quality.[79] 'It is the characteristic of the gentleman', insisted *The Art of Conversation*, 'that he never speaks of himself at all.'[80] Volubility, especially about one's own self, was the mark of a foreigner.[81] In the words of the *Gentleman's Handbook of Etiquette*,

> A Gentleman is distinguished as much by his composure as by any other quality. His exertions are always subdued, and his efforts easy. He is never surprised into an exclamation or startled by anything. Throughout his life he avoids what the French call *scenes*—occasions of exhibition, in which the vulgar delight. He of course has feelings, but he never exhibits any to the world. He hears of the death of his

---

[75] Frevert, 'Honour and Middle-Class Culture', 221–2.

[76] A. Freeling, *The Gentleman's Pocket-Book of Etiquette* (8th edn., Liverpool, 1838), 68.

[77] M. Girouard, *The Return to Camelot* (New Haven, 1981), 260–70.

[78] Cited in A. Smythe-Palmer, *The Ideal of a Gentleman* (London, [1908]), 117. Kingsley borrowed the phrase from St Paul. Also Andrew, 'The Code of Honour and its Critics', 426–7.

[79] S. R. Letwin, *The Gentleman in Trollope* (London, 1982), 26.

[80] J. Mitchell, ['Captain Orlando Sabertash'], *The Art of Conversation* (London, 1842), 63. Also, *How to Behave, or, Etiquette of Society* (London [1879]), 17.

[81] 'Au Fait', *Social Observances: A Series of Essays on Practical Etiquette* (London, 1896), 203.

favourite pointer or the loss of an estate with entire calmness when others are present.[82]

Gentlemanly self-restraint was not an invention of the democratic age. Chaucer, in the *Wife of Bath*, had urged that virtue rather than birth, self-restraint rather than self-indulgence, were the making of a the true gentleman: 'he is gentil that dooth gentil deedes.'[83] By the seventeenth century it was widely argued that moral self-control lay at the heart of both the identity of the gentleman and his claim to authority and respect.[84] Richard Brathwait's *The English Gentleman* of 1630 noted how 'a true and generous Moderation of his affections, hath begot in him an absolute command and conquest of himself'.[85] Surveying the tradition towards the end of the nineteenth century, Emerson claimed to be able to trace back the 'reputation of taciturnity' for 'six or seven hundred years'.[86] However, there was a particular reason why the quality of reticence came to occupy such prominence in contemporary attempts to define a gentleman. Bulwer Lytton, writing the year after the Reform Act, drew attention to the 'immense varieties of gradation' prevailing in the upper reaches of English society.[87] Unlike in other countries, such as Germany, there were few clear indicators of rank, and the consequence of 'nobody being really fixed in society' was a general reluctance to risk drawing undue attention to feelings and opinions for fear of exposure to unexpected condescension. Thus, he concluded, 'proceeds the most noticeable trait in our national character: our reserve . . .'.[88] The best defence of self-conceit against self-doubt was a form of silence which could be presented as evidence of hidden depths of character. The public display of reticence flowed equally from pride and insecurity. The necessity of maintaining visible authority in a world of increasingly obscure distinctions generated a pervasive lack of openness.[89] As T. H. S. Escott, explained,

In England, where the antecedents of many of those who are admitted to the 'best society' are obscure, and where the connections between the families of the peerage and the commonalty are infinite and invisible, it is natural and it is right, that considerable caution should be exercised. Hence, in a great measure, the proverbial reserve for which Englishmen and women are celebrated.[90]

---

[82] J. Millar, *The Gentleman's Handbook of Etiquette* (Edinburgh, 18–), republished as *How to be a Perfect Gentleman* (London, 1989), 16. Also, Duncan (Lecturer on Elocution), *The Gentleman's Book of Manners or Etiquette; Showing How to Become a Perfect Gentleman* (London, 1875), 75; [Browne], 'The English Gentleman', 264.

[83] E. T. Donaldson, (selected and ed.), *Chaucer's Poetry* (New York, 1958), *The Wife of Bath's Tale*, l. 314. See also Chaucer's poem, 'Gentilesse', 546–7.

[84] See the excellent discussion of this issue in Shapin, *Social History of Truth*, 65–70, 103–7.

[85] R. Brathwait, *The English Gentleman* (London, 1860; 1st pub. 1630), 460.

[86] R. W. Emerson, *English Traits* (London, 1883), 104.

[87] E. Bulwer Lytton, *England and the English* (Paris, 1833 edn.), 17.

[88] Ibid. 17–18.

[89] Curtin, *Propriety and Position*, 129.

[90] T. H. S. Escott, *England: Its People, Polity, and Pursuits* (London, 1890), 319. Also, Taylor, *The Autobiography of Henry Taylor*, i. 72.

It is of course possible that what Price Collier called 'the almost universal reticence of manner and speech among the better classes'[91] had a simpler explanation. A recent examination of the 'English Gentleman' concluded that 'he does not use long words largely because he does not know any'.[92] But in practice the strength of this trait arose precisely from its easy association with what was becoming the only consistent external mark of a gentleman, the possession of an extensive formal education. The public schools and the universities which were beginning to provide the institutional means of integrating the better sort of the middling ranks with the least unintelligent of the upper, transmitted not just knowledge but an attitude towards its use. An early guide was supplied by Defoe's celebration of the meritocratic gentleman:

He is frugal without avarice, managing without rigour, humble without meanness, and great without haughtiness; he is pleasant without levity, grave without affectacion; if he has learning, his knowledge is without pedantry and his parts without pride; modesty and humility govern him, and he applyes his learning purely to do good to others and to instruct himself further in the good government of himself.[93]

An educated man knew what to say and when not to say it. 'The power of preserving silence' stated *The Art of Conversation*, 'is in fact the very first requisite to all who wish to shine, or even please in discourse.'[94] The primary function of his programme of study was the development of his inward character rather than his outward presence. His enhanced powers of communication were far removed from the facile verbosity of the self-taught. The value of his learning was revealed in the discretion with which it was deployed. It is not for nothing that the most influential definition of a gentleman in this period is to be found in a treatise on higher education. Newman's *The Idea of a University*, a series of lectures given in 1852 and published the following year, presented the ideal figure in a long sequence of negatives. 'Hence it is', he began, 'that it is almost a definition of a gentleman to say he is one who never inflicts pain'; as to his conversation: 'He never speaks of himself except when compelled, never defends himself by mere retort, he has no ears for slander or gossip, is scrupulous in imputing motives to those who interfere with him, and interprets everything for the best.'[95]

In its most developed version, the gentleman's schooled self-possession extended even to his bodily presence. 'He should have the complete command', wrote Hazlitt, 'not only over his countenance, but over his limbs and

---

[91] Collier, *England and the English from an American Point of View* (London, 1910), 400.

[92] D. Sutherland, *The English Gentleman* (London 1978), 69.

[93] Defoe, *Compleat English Gentleman*, 240.

[94] *The Art of Conversation*, 39. Also 'Gentlemen', 336.

[95] J. H. Newman, *The Idea of a University*, ed. I. T. Ker (Oxford, 1976), 179. On Newman's contribution to the concept of the gentleman, see P. Mason, *The English Gentleman: The Rise and Fall of an Ideal* (London, 1993), 185–7.

motions.'[96] However, the central emphasis was always on the quality of social discourse. 'The extreme of candour', observed *The Manners of the Aristocracy, by One of Themselves*, was one of the 'most fatal' social blunders.[97] Careless talk cost status. 'Never repeat conversations,' insisted *The Gentleman's Pocket Book of Etiquette*, '—never gossip—abjure tattling.'[98] The main object of concern was knowledge gained in confidence. Whereas the gentleman's real estate, should he have any, was largely secure against attack, his reputation was a fragile possession, protected only by the habitual self-discipline of his peers. The shared sense of discretion, stated another contemporary guide, 'teaches us to be careful in everything we say and do; to pay the greatest attention to affairs of importance; to be cautious in our conversations, that we reveal not our own secrets, nor those of others'.[99] Honour, which could no longer be championed by combat, was the proud parent and defenceless child of this particular form of cultivated secrecy. Unthinking disclosure, or, still worse, deliberate revelation, struck not just at the individual victim but at the entire structure of values which sustained the identity of the gentleman. 'Talking of yourself is an impertinence to the company,' insisted *The Gentleman's Book of Manners*, 'your affairs are nothing to them, besides they cannot be kept too secret. As to the affairs of others, what are they to you?'[100]

Hence the acute sensitivity, in 1844 and thereafter, to the interception of private communication. 'What is a Gentleman?' asked Frederick Wills:

The essence, then, of a gentleman is unselfishness, and the laws by which a gentleman is governed are the laws of honour. Honour implies perfect courage, honesty, truth and good faith. It forbids anything underhanded or mean, such as listening at doors, or opening other people's letters, reading their correspondence, or breaking confidence.[101]

The letter, however, both reinforced the private sphere and connected it to the world beyond. The contents might be family news, but if the recipient were the husband rather than the wife, they might equally be official business. It was at the point of contact between the domestic and the public realm that the notion of the gentleman became specifically masculine. If ladies enjoyed the same status and were expected to embrace the same code, they were not faced with the same level of temptation to abuse their authority. Their dramas were confined

[96] W. Hazlitt, 'On the Look of a Gentleman', *The Plain Speaker* (1826), reprinted in P. P. Howe (ed.), *The Complete Works of William Hazlitt*, Vol. 12 (London, 1931), 210. Also E. Cheadle, *Manners of Modern Society* (London, 1872), 45.

[97] *The Manners of the Aristocracy: By One of Themselves* (London, 1881), 61.

[98] Freeling, *The Gentleman's Pocket-Book of Etiquette*, 54. Also *The Habits of Good Society: A Handful of Etiquette for Ladies and Gentlemen* (London, 1855), 69.

[99] W. Pinnock, *The Golden Treasury* (London, 1848), 156. Also Lady Colin Campbell, *Etiquette of Good Society* (London, 1895), 46; *How to Behave*, 55; Curtin, *Propriety and Position*, 127.

[100] Duncan, *The Gentleman's Book of Manners or Etiquette*, 61.

[101] F. Wills, 'What is a Gentleman?', in F. Wills (ed.), *Lay Sermons for Practical People* (London, 1890), 44. Also Lieber, *Character of the Gentleman*, 20.

to the small stage of the domestic realm.[102] Only the heads of their households could gain entry to the proper theatre of assertion and restraint which was at the heart of their identity. Self-control gained real meaning where there was a capacity for significant intervention in the affairs of the world at large. The gentleman asserted his manhood as he controlled his power, and by this means demonstrated his moral authority over both the lower orders and the weaker sex.

The remaining issue was how well the coat that was being woven for the re-fashioned gentleman could be made to fit the figure of the reformed civil servant. There was an evident danger that the attack on patronage and the introduction of modern forms of bureaucratic management would render the occupation unfit for those of gentle birth and thus detach the old ruling class from the machinery of government. As one of the critics of the Northcote–Trevelyan Report put it: 'The more the civil service is recruited from the lower classes, the less will it be sought after by the higher, until at last the aristocracy will be altogether dissociated from the permanent civil service of the country.'[103] However, in the eyes of Gladstone, who as Chancellor of the Ex-chequer from 1852 had a central role to play in the Report's implementation, its abiding virtue was that it would achieve precisely the reverse effect:

One of the great recommendations of the change in my eyes would be its tendency to strengthen and multiply the ties between the higher classes and the possession of administrative power . . . I have a strong impression that the aristocracy of this country are even superior in natural gifts, on the average, to the mass: but it is plain that with their acquired advantages, their insensible education, irrespective of book learning, they have an immense superiority. This applies in its degree to all those who may be called gentlemen by birth and training; and it must be remem-bered that an essential part of any such plan as is now under discussion is the sepa-ration of *work*, wherever it can be made, into mechanical and intellectual, a separation which will open to the higher educated class a career and give them a command over all the higher parts of the civil service, which up to this time they have never enjoyed.[104]

Gladstone's confidence was founded on the clear affinity between the pre-cepts of 'those who may be called gentlemen by birth and training', and the requisites of the redefined upper echelons of the administrative sector. The dual stress on authority and abnegation exactly suited the emerging bureau-cratic ethos. Public service was a burden which the gentleman was expected to shoulder for the sake of his country, without thought of gain and irrespective of hardship.[105] As *The Christian Gentleman's Daily Walk* of 1850 put it, 'he is careful

---

[102] See below, Ch. 2, pp. 71–5.

[103] Cited in J. Morley, *The Life of Gladstone* (London, 1908), i. 380. The critic was Lord Romilly.

[104] Ibid. 607. Letter to Lord John Russell, 20 June 1854.

[105] D. Duman, 'The Creation and Diffusion of a Professional Ideology in Nineteenth Century England', *Sociological Review*, 27 (1979), 117–23.

to be guided by regard to merit and the public service, rather than by motives of private interest or partizanship'.[106] He brought to the task the virtues of a balanced, composed judgement and an instinctive reluctance to engage in open controversy: 'though he may feel strongly, he never loses sight of moderation, and as studiously avoids any indication of party violence as he does a tendency towards wavering laxity.'[107] Above all, there was a visceral dislike of the needless exchange of information. Sir James Stephen, the archetype of the new mandarin, and without question a gentleman, caught something of the attitude in a letter to his wife in 1841:

There is a Christian virtue to which I never heard an allusion from the pulpit, and of which I have scarcely witnessed the practice in any circle in which I have mixed, though all Roman Catholic books are full of it. I mean the duty of silence. Unless I am much mistaken, frivolity of discourse, mere talk for talk's sake, is one of the most besetting sins of our generation.[108]

There was some distance to travel before the conduct of Stephen's peers matched his own, but the destination had been identified. A lack of self-possession was the enemy. In its more superficial aspect, such a shortcoming consistently undermined the reticence demanded of the new public servant. As Henry Taylor, one of Stephen's subordinates, observed in 1836: 'In nine cases out of ten of betrayed confidence in affairs of state, vanity is the traitor.'[109] At a more profound level the problem was the inability to withstand criticism without recourse to active and voluble protest. It was necessary to inculcate a virtue which pre-dated Christianity, although it was compatible with it. In the words of the *Gentleman's Handbook of Etiquette*: 'The precept of stoicism, is the precept for conduct among gentlemen.'[110] The public schools, themselves undergoing reformation at this time, were inculcating an ideal of public service based on the subordination of personal to group interest.[111] They taught that character rather than written law was the key to honourable conduct, and that it was expressed not through self-aggrandisement but rather through physical and above all mental resilience.[112] Turning a silent face to a foe was the sign of a higher calling. 'Truly men's judgment is to him a little matter', wrote Edmonstone of the Christian gentleman:—'his rule of conduct is within; and as he hears the voice of God which speaks to his conscience, he pursues his way unswervingly, firm and steadfast to the end.'[113] In the political arena the

---

[106] Sir A. Edmonstone, *The Christian Gentleman's Daily Walk* (London 1850), 93.

[107] Ibid. 85. Also Duncan, *The Gentleman's Book of Manners or Etiquette*, 63; *The Habits of Good Society*, 71.

[108] C. E. Stephen, *The Rt. Hon. Sir James Stephen: Letters with Biographical Notes* (Gloucester, 1906), letter to wife, 27 Oct. 1841.

[109] Taylor, *The Statesman*, 89.

[110] Millar, *Gentleman's Handbook*, 74.

[111] Frevert, 'Honour and Middle-Class Culture', 226; Duman, 'The Creation and Diffusion of a Professional Ideology', 121.

[112] R. Wilkinson, *Gentlemanly Power* (London, 1964), 10–13, 29–37.

[113] Edmonstone, *Christian Gentleman's Daily Walk*, 86.

stiffening of resolve was exemplified in the contrast between Peel's attempted recourse to arms in 1837 and the behaviour of his Home Secretary seven years later when subjected to a far more comprehensive attack on his integrity. Graham could not respond in kind to his critics, neither would his own code of honour permit him to reveal his inner feelings. His nineteenth-century biographer pictured him sitting in mute anguish in the Commons: 'Silently and secretly he suffered infinitely more than many of his accusers were capable of comprehending.'[114]

Whilst Graham was resisting assaults on his discreet reserve, attempts were being made to instil the same quality in his civil servants. The gradual separation of the duties of the permanent and political heads of departments of state was accompanied by a division of rights of communication. Over time, and with considerable friction, a deal was struck. The politicians accepted that within a given department all lines of correspondence should flow through the permanent head; an incoming Minister would have to respect the hierarchical structure of clerks and secretaries and refrain from intervening directly in its operation. In return they demanded that civil servants should abandon the privilege of writing public letters and articles on issues relating to their work. Bureaucrats would forfeit the right to criticize their political masters, but in exchange could expect full protection from attacks levelled at them by an increasingly inquisitive Parliament and a decreasingly deferential press.[115]

The voluntary acceptance of anonymity by men of strong personality was integral to the reworking of their corporate ethos. The convention of the Privy Councillor's Oath, that the advice of ministers became the possession of the monarch, was translated to the relationship between civil servants and their political masters. As at the higher constitutional level, the cloak of confidentiality both protected and obscured the distribution of power. Frustrated and rebellious as senior civil servants often were in this period of transition, they could now employ their secrecy as both a shield and a banner. 'Silence has been my only defence,' wrote Sir James Stephen in 1844, 'because any other vindication would have involved a breach of confidence.'[116] The refusal to respond to praise or criticism was turned into a celebration of the civil servant's calling. It became a matter of pride to endure the intense discomfort imposed by this Trappist stance. Stephen's stoic outlook was described by his biographer:

The understanding upon which the permanent offices of the Civil Service are held is that those who accept them shall give up all claim to personal reputation on the one hand, and shall be shielded from personal responsibility on the other. Though

[114] Torrens, *Life of Graham*, ii. 302. Also Erikson, *The Public Career of Sir James Graham*, 268–75; Ward, *Sir James Graham*, 209–11, 306.

[115] G. Kitson Clark, ' "Statesmen in Disguise": Reflexions on the History of the Neutrality of the Civil Service', *Historical Journal*, 3 (1959), 21–38.

[116] E. Hughes, 'Sir James Stephen and the Anonymity of the Civil Servant', *Public Administration*, 36 (Spring 1958), 30.

Sir James Stephen was at one time the object of the most bitter personal attacks (often for measures to which he had opposed all the resistance in his power) he never complained of this compact.[117]

Only men secure in their status and their authority could pretend to such indifference about their standing with the populace. The growth of anonymity both reinforced and depended on the emergence of a more sharply defined collective identity. Bereft of credit for what they did, officials demanded the respect of society for who they were.

It is important to recognize the element of individual and corporate sacrifice embodied in this notion of secrecy. Because the refusal to disclose official information was presented as a form of administrative purgatory rather than bureaucratic arrogance, the logical conflict with the liberal state's commitment to publicity was not apparent. Thus it was that the development of the culture of discreet reserve exactly coincided with the creation of the modern system of collecting and disseminating government information. The same individuals who were learning not to disclose the basis upon which decisions were taken were at the same time heavily engaged in the establishment of machinery to collate and publish the data which both informed the legislative process and measured its consequences.[118] In 1833 the newly reformed state appointed eleven new Royal Commissions to gather information for its legislative programme.[119] At the same time the first step towards the creation of the Statistical Department of the Board of Trade was taken, and its work was subject to a further reorganization and extension by Edward Cardwell just as Cornewall Lewis was expounding the doctrine of honourable secrecy.[120] By now almost every department of state was making a conscious effort to present to the public authoritative facts and figures about its work, the labour of clerks reinforced in half-a-dozen cases by the reports of specially appointed Inspectors. As Olive Anderson observes: 'British government in the mid-nineteenth century surely led the world in its faith in information and its zeal for social statistics.'[121]

In the early 1830s it was strongly argued that our main competitors, especially France, were well ahead of us in the centralized collection of national information.[122] In Britain, by contrast, there was a growing mound of Blue Books

[117] Stephen, *The Rt. Hon. Sir James Stephen*, 50–1.

[118] H. M. Clokie and J. W. Robinson, *Royal Commissions of Inquiry* (Stanford, 1937), 54–148.

[119] T. J. Cartwright, *Royal Commissions and Departmental Committees in Britain* (London, 1975), 38.

[120] H. Llewellyn Smith, *The Board of Trade* (London, 1928), 209–13; L. Brown, *The Board of Trade and the Free Trade Movement, 1830–42* (Oxford, 1958), 76–93; Prouty, *Transformation of the Board of Trade*, 8–9; M. J. Cullen, *The Statistical Movement in Early Victorian Britain* (Hassocks, 1975), 19–27.

[121] Anderson, 'The Administrative Reform Association', 283. Also Welsh, *George Eliot and Blackmail*, 66. For an excellent discussion of the breadth of the statistical movement in the early 1830s, see A. Desmond, *The Politics of Evolution: Morphology, Medicine and Reform in Radical London* (Chicago, 1989), 28–9.

[122] *Second Report from the Select Committee on Public Documents* (1833), PP 1833, XII, p. 24; [J. R. McCulloch], 'State and Defects of British Statistics', *Edinburgh Review*, 61, (Apr. 1835), 154–9.

and other official publications whose value was severely compromised by the absence of a means of sifting and reconciling their contents. As a witness to the 1833 Select Committee on Public Documents put it: 'The great difficulty arises in bringing them into focus, so as to show all the different interests of the country in a concise and perspicuous point of view.'[123] The case was presented in the context of central liberal preoccupations. On the one hand, it would save money by preventing the unnecessary duplication of material; on the other, it would be a means of measuring in detail what G. R. Porter, the Department's first head, termed 'the social progress of this vast and growing empire'.[124] The state had no means of quantifying the impact of change, nor the potential for intervention by the reformed Parliament. J. R. McCulloch observed that, 'neither the Government, the legislature, nor the public, can at present form any just estimate of the influence of any measure, or any truth of any statement, that may be made as to the conduct of any class of people'.[125] More urgently, the generation of accurate information would help to deal with the threats to that progress which had been so apparent during the Reform Bill crisis. As one of the advocates of reform wrote:

A more general diffusion of accurate knowledge regarding the state of public affairs would tend to check that excitement and party spirit which has often been created by misrepresentation or exaggeration, and has produced an annoyance to the government, and at least a temporary disaffection in the public mind.[126]

The possibility that such knowledge might be employed to inflame still further popular discontent was countered partly by the liberal faith in the rationality of their case and the ultimate capacity of the mass of the population to understand it, and partly by the state's retention of the final decision as to the substance and form of publication. It was suggested in evidence to the 1833 Committee that the Board of Trade establish a 'Public Opinion Branch' to ascertain, through the study of newspapers and other sources, the 'state of the public mind' and how it was changing.[127] In the event, the flow of information was to be in the opposite direction. The exercise was expected to instil in the minds of present and prospective voters a more detailed grasp of the achievements of the post-Reform Act state and a sounder understanding of the principles upon which they were based.[128]

---

[123] *First Report from the Select Committee on Public Documents* (1833), PP 1833, XII, p. 7.

[124] Ibid. 25.

[125] [J. R. McCulloch], 'State and Defects of British Statistics', 179.

[126] W. Jacob, 'Observations and Suggestions Respecting the Collation, Concentration, and Diffusion of Statistical Knowledge Regarding the State of the United Kingdom', *Transactions of the Statistical Society of London*, 1: 1 (1837), 1.

[127] The proposal was contained in a letter from the statistician John Bowring to Lord John Russell, 25 Feb. 1833, which was submitted to the Committee. *1833 Second Report from the SC on Public Documents*, 59.

[128] Cullen, *Statistical Movement*, 140.

A similar set of priorities was apparent in the concurrent attempts to modernize the procedures for storing and retrieving official records. Complaints about the mismanagement of the mounting body of government documents provoked a Select Committee in 1836 and the passage two years later of the first Public Record Office Act.[129] This authorized the Master of the Rolls to provide appropriate accommodation for the material, which led to the construction of a building in Chancery Lane between 1851 and 1855. On the face of it, the Act was an ambitious and expensive concession to the needs of the public, who were guaranteed free access to the new Record Office, and in particular to historians, whose problems were extensively rehearsed before the Select Committee.[130] In practice, the reforms of the period transferred authority to rather than away from the state. At the beginning of the nineteenth century the phrase 'public record' referred merely to legal documents which embodied the rights of individuals and were preserved for open consultation. The 1838 Act specifically referred only to this field, but a series of administrative amendments, particularly agreements with the Treasury in 1845 and 1846, widened the *de facto* scope of the legislation to cover all categories of paperwork generated by government departments. However, as the notion of record expanded, that of public contracted. The term ceased to relate to material which was about and belonged to the population at large, and instead came to describe documents created and owned by the state.[131]

The change in emphasis was made more apparent as the issue of the systematic destruction of papers had to be faced. By the middle of the century it was becoming evident that the rapidly expanding state bureaucracy was creating potential records on a scale which would overwhelm any affordable building programme. Pressure from the Treasury led to the formation of a committee to consider the question of weeding out what were held to be the 40 per cent of documents of no conceivable value to historians, and its recommendations were eventually consolidated into a second Act of 1877, which, with some modification in 1898, governed procedures until after the Second World War. The Master of the Rolls was charged with overseeing the formulation of rules covering the methods by which departments selected documents for preservation. But he had neither the staff nor the power to intervene directly in the treatment of papers before they reached the Public Record Office, and as a consequence individual departments retained effective autonomy over what they destroyed, and thereafter what they decided to deposit at Chancery Lane and under what conditions. Whilst the absolute flow of material increased

---

[129] The fullest account of the creation of the Public Record Office is to be found in *Report of the Committee on Departmental Records* [Grigg] (1954), PP 1953–4, XI, pp. 8–28.

[130] *Report from the Select Committee appointed to Inquire into the Management and Affairs of the Record Commission, and Present State of the Records of the United Kingdom* (1836), PP 1836, XVI, xxviii, 302, 335, 505–6, 534, 549, 558, 567, 630, 640.

[131] *1954 Report on Departmental Records*, 8–9.

dramatically, the practical control of its dissemination was held by the officials who had produced it. The result was extensive variation in the processes for establishing what was either destroyed altogether or removed from circulation for an unspecified period of time.[132] The only consistency was in the maintenance of the capacity of departmental civil servants and their political superiors to determine what was to be hidden from the gaze of the public and subsequent generations of historians.

In some senses, the phrase 'discreet reserve' most accurately described the emerging civil service attitude to the dissemination of information. It conveyed the gentlemanly distaste for unnecessary noise of any sort, and the more general concern for self-restraint in all dealings with the wider world. Moreover, it placed the emphasis not on a Whitehall version of *omertà*, a total refusal to reveal anything to anybody, but rather on the issue of authority in the release of official material. Communication was to be at the discretion of the bureaucrat rather than at the demand of the elector, the journalist, or the historian. Nonetheless, the larger concept of 'honourable secrecy' more eloquently captured the range of attitudes and associations embedded in the new administrative culture. In two important respects it served to deflect attention away from the more ambiguous connotations of restricting the flow of information. First, it implied that the controls were a function not of the power of the state but of the values of a private community, some of whose members had chosen to sacrifice their comforts for the good of the country. In the middle decades of the nineteenth century, the machinery in charge of the world's most successful economy and most rapidly expanding empire was defining itself by the absence of its own public interest. Britain was inventing the non-bureaucratic bureaucracy. In accordance with contemporary liberalism, the behaviour of individual officials was conditioned not by external regulation but internal moral imperatives policed by a section of society which was independent of the political sphere. Only at points of inadvertent crisis, such as occurred over Mazzini's letters or Lowe's attempts to censor in the interests of official secrecy those charged with reporting official practice, was it possible to glimpse a government acting merely in its own interest, or a bureaucracy committed only to its own preservation.

Secondly, the term proposed that the necessary restrictions be placed in the context of the broader security that honour would bring to public service. The associated values of truth, integrity, and honesty were promised and to a large extent delivered. Despite the long rearguard action fought by family interest and political patronage, there was negligible personal corruption in an organization with ever-increasing opportunities to line its pockets at the expense of the taxpayer. For as long as the public perceived that this was so, and that

---

[132] N. Cox, 'The Thirty-Year Rule and Freedom of Information: Access to Government Records', in G. H. Martin and Spufford (eds.), *The Records of the Nation* (Woodbridge, 1990), 75–6.

honourable behaviour was compatible with efficiency, it was disinclined to subject the potentially negative traits of gentlemanly conduct to a more searching interrogation. British secrecy was not to be confused with continental despotism, because in the end it was in the hands of men of honour.

Professional Boundaries

Amongst the critics of the attempt to turn the civil service into a meritocracy was a novelist who had failed his initial interview for a place in the Post Office because his handwriting was too poor. He had been given a night to improve his fair copy, and was thus able to begin a career which he pursued for thirty-three years until the dividends on his invested royalties finally exceeded his generous official salary.[133] In 1861 Trollope entered the lists against Northcote–Teveleyan in an article in the *Cornhill Magazine* entitled 'The Civil Service as a Profession'. He readily confessed to the material attractions of the 'life of moderate safety' which was open to those with little other than their education and a few distant connections to keep them, but nonetheless insisted on the higher qualities of his work: 'there is no profession by which a man can earn his bread in these realms, admitting of a brighter honesty, of a nobler purpose, or of an action more manly and independent.'[134] His criticism of examinations and of the substitution of merit for seniority in promotions (to which he himself was to fall victim three years later), was provoked, he explained, by an overriding concern to enhance the relative status of his chosen occupation: 'My chief object in these remarks—indeed, I may say my only object—has been to assist in raising that profession to the level of other professions.'[135]

Trollope's ambition was at once misplaced and inescapable. In a formal sense, the civil service was not a profession in the middle of the nineteenth century, and had no intention of becoming one. It was committed to a generalist tradition of administration, which denied the existence of a body of technical skills and hence the necessity for a specialized training.[136] The new Civil Service Commission based its examinations on the liberal curriculum of the universities rather than the vocational qualifying tests of the doctors and solicitors which were favoured by the Administrative Reform Association.[137] At the same time medical men, lawyers, and bureaucrats were bound together in a common struggle for gentlemanly status. Each calling was recruited from the same pool of families and schools, each sought to cloak its activities in the mantle of honourable conduct. The differences between them were a function less of

---

[133] R. Mullen, *Anthony Trollope* (London, 1990), 67, 82.
[134] [A. Trollope], 'The Civil Service as a Profession', *Cornhill Magazine*, 3 (Jan.–June 1861), 215.
[135] Ibid. 227.
[136] R. A. Chapman and J. R. Greenaway, *The Dynamics of Administrative Reform* (London, 1980), 220.
[137] Anderson, 'Administrative Reform Association', 278–9.

their formal structures, and more of their tactical resources in the contemporary struggle for success.[138] Civil servants derived authority from the political heads of their departments to whom they proffered their wide-ranging skills. Those who would cure ills or right wrongs, by contrast, had to establish their ascendancy in what initially was an open market-place, where they offered services to clients who might go elsewhere.[139] In this more anarchic context, the definition of professional expertise assumed much greater significance. The identification of an exclusive body of paper-based learning underpinned the structure of education and examinations, which in turn determined membership of the occupational group and permitted the disqualification of competing practitioners.[140] Equally, the deference of the client was engineered by an acceptance of the practitioner's possession of authoritative information. Historic identity, security, and income were guaranteed by the control of knowledge.[141] It is not surprising, therefore, that the restrictions on its communication were more specific and more complex than the unwritten conventions which governed the early forms of official secrecy.[142]

The doctors were first into the field of regulation, asserting precedence in part through their possession of the Hippocratic Oath. This was nothing if not forthright on the improper transmission of information: 'All that may come to my knowledge in the exercise of my profession or outside my profession or in daily commerce with men, which ought not to be spread abroad, I will keep secret and will never reveal.'[143] In reality, its role was neither as antique nor as straightforward as it appeared. Although the Victorian doctors laid claim to an authority which pre-dated the New Testament, the continuity was largely an artifice. One amongst a number of possible codes was resurrected in the eighteenth century as much as a consequence, as a cause of, the profession's growing self-confidence.[144] When applied to the increasingly diverse institutional and personal relationships in which medical men were beginning to operate,

[138] C. Davies, 'Professionals in Bureaucracies: The Conflict Thesis Revisited', in R. Dingwall and P. Lewis (eds.), *The Sociology of the Professions* (London, 1983), 177–92.

[139] E. Friedson, *Professional Powers* (Chicago, 1986), 73.

[140] J. M. Jacob, *Doctors and Rules* (London, 1988), 42. For a survey of the role of education in defining group closure, and promoting the 'demonopolization' of less powerful rival groups, see R. Collins, 'Market Closure and the Conflict Theory of the Professions', in M. Burrage and H. Tortendahl (eds.), *Professions in Theory and History* (London, 1990), 34–8.

[141] Wilkinson, *Gentlemanly Power*, 20.

[142] *Pace* R. Lewis and A. Maude, *Professional People* (London, 1952), 63, who argue that the civil service is distinguished from the private professions by its greater reliance on regulation.

[143] Jacob, *Doctors and Rules*, 192. There are various translations in circulation. For alternative modern renderings, see L. Edelstein, 'The Hippocratic Oath: Text, Translation and Interpretation', *Bulletin of the History of Medicine*, Supp. 1 (1943), 3; A. V. Campbell, *Moral Dilemmas in Medicine* (Edinburgh, 1972), 194–5; P. Hewitt, *Privacy* (London, 1977), 39. For a detailed examination of various renditions in the ancient world, see W. H. S. Jones, *The Doctor's Oath: An Essay in the History of Medicine* (Cambridge, 1924), 2–38.

[144] I. E. Thompson, 'The Nature of Confidentiality', *Journal of Medical Ethics*, 5 (1979), 57–8. Edelstein attributes the severity of the injunction on secrecy to the influence of the small Pythagorean school rather than Greek medicine in general. 'The Hippocratic Oath', 37–8, 57–8, 63–4.

the simple appeal to secrecy dissolved into a series of conflicting priorities and stubborn contradictions.

Many of the difficulties were anticipated in the founding text of modern medical ethics, written in 1803 by the Manchester surgeon Thomas Percival. He dedicated the book to his son, who had followed him into the profession, in terms which emphasized ultimate goal of their endeavours:

The study of professional Ethics, therefore, cannot fail to invigorate and enlarge your understanding; whilst the observance of the duties which they enjoin, will soften your manners, expand your affections, and form you to that propriety and dignity of conduct, which are essential to the character of a GENTLEMAN.[145]

The driving force in the early stage of professionalization was hospital medicine, and it was here that Percival began. Some of his precepts were peculiar to the era, especially his advice on whether doctors conducting an operation should converse with the all-too conscious patient. He concluded that,

A decorous silence ought to be observed. It may be humane and salutary however, for one of the attending physicians or surgeons to speak occasionally to the patient; to comfort him under his sufferings; and to give him assurance, if consistent with the truth, that the operation goes on well, and promises a speedy and successful termination.[146]

Percival's general concerns, however, were of much broader relevance. He was acutely aware of the problems caused by the lack of privacy in a hospital: 'In the wards of an Infirmary the patients should be interrogated concerning their complaints in a *tone of voice* which cannot be *overheard*. *Secrecy*, also, when required by peculiar circumstances, should be strictly observed.'[147] The patient did not want his symptoms to be overheard, and it was equally important that conversations between surgeons did not reach the ears of the sufferer in question, because 'misapprehension may magnify real evils, or create imaginary ones'.[148] The basis of the doctor's reticence should be a respect for the state of mind of those under his care:

The *feelings* and *emotions* of the patients, under critical circumstances, require to be known and to be attended to, no less than the symptoms of their diseases . . . Even the *prejudices* of the sick are not to be contemned or opposed with harshness. For although silenced by authority, they will operate secretly and forcibly on the mind, creating fear, anxiety, and watchfulness.[149]

---

[145] T. Percival, *Medical Ethics; or, A Code of Institutes and Precepts Adapted to the Professional Conduct of Physicians and Surgeons* (Manchester, 1803), pp. viii-ix. See also W. O. Porter, *Medical Science and Ethicks* (Bristol, 1837), 7.

[146] Percival, *Medical Ethics*, 21.

[147] Ibid. 11.

[148] Ibid. 10.

[149] Ibid. 11.

The importance of the patient's psychological condition had long been recognized, but its assertion in the context of the developing medical structures raised new problems. Through his own long experience in a hospital, Percival had come to realize that the deferential relationship the profession was seeking to create with patients could impede the communication that was necessary for effective treatment.

Outside the hospital, the doctor was enjoined to total confidentiality. The opening paragraph of Percival's chapter on general practice laid out the basic principle: 'Secrecy, and delicacy when required by peculiar circumstances, should be strictly observed. And the familiar and confidential intercourse, to which the faculty are admitted in the professional visits, should be used with discretion, and with the most scrupulous regard to fidelity and honour.'[150] The sense of trust which distinguished the professional from the mere entrepreneur was nowhere more vulnerable than in the release of private information to third parties. 'If he divulges those personal weaknesses,' warned Gisborne's *Duties of Physicians*,

or betrays those domestic secrets, which come to his knowledge in the course of his employment; if he bears tales of slander from house to house; if he foments quarrels and aggravates misunderstandings; he is deserving of severer censure that words can say. Whatever he witnesses humiliating or disgraceful in the habitation of one patient, he should wish to forget before he enters that of another.[151]

A case in 1780 had established that a doctor's confidentiality had no absolute legal protection;[152] everything depended on his judgement and self-control. A successful relationship with a patient, observed another guide, was founded 'on the discipline of our own feelings'.[153]

The question here, as elsewhere, was whether such injunctions reflected or sought to correct contemporary practice. According to Glenn's *Manual of the Laws Affecting Medical Men* of 1871, prevailing expectations were that doctors would readily yield to the illicit pleasure of revealing privileged information:

Medical practitioners of all kinds often make mistakes by talking of the diseases of their patients to third persons. The nature of the disease is the patient's secret, and ought never to be talked about. It is usual for everyone to apply to the doctor to know what is the matter with C.D., and some men like to be officious in stating the case. But the doctor has no real right to divulge its nature, any more than the lawyer has

---

[150] Ibid. 30.

[151] T. Gisborne, *On the Duties of Physicians Resulting from their Profession* (Oxford, 1847), 42. This was taken from a work published in 1811.

[152] A. Carpenter, 'Medical Etiquette', in R. C. Glenn, *A Manual of the Laws Affecting Medical Men* (London, 1871), 282.

[153] Porter, *Medical Science and Ethicks*, 28.

to mention the contents of a will on which he has been engaged. It is necessary for this rule to be strictly observed, and for medical men to refuse to answer such inquiries on all occasions.[154]

The doctor was caught between competing aspirations. He was committed to the truth, but it was difficult to answer such enquiries without some form of evasion. He profited from the status of possessing secrets, but could only demonstrate their existence by exposing them. He sought membership of a common culture of gentlemanly professionals, but was then expected to share his knowledge with fellow members of the local elite in the interests of their collective authority and responsibility. As late as 1907, the author of a new textbook on medical ethics found it necessary to warn his readers of the pressures they would face: 'In a country parish the vicar deems he has a right to know all about the ailments of, at any rate, the labouring classes of his parishioners, while the vicar's wife is even more catholic in her sympathy or curiosity.'[155] If the poor were to have the same rights to privacy as the respectable sections of society, it would be necessary to set up barriers between the professions, not only in the old rural communities, but, as we shall see in later chapters, in the expanding towns where employers, the police, and the developing welfare system posed new challenges to the doctor's ability to hold his tongue.

Despite the solicitude for the well-being of patients, the central focus of Percival's text, as of most subsequent nineteenth-century manuals, was on dealings within the profession.[156] Although the terminology was not employed with any great consistency in this period, 'ethics' tended to refer to the general moral conduct of doctors, and 'etiquette' to relations between practitioners.[157] The essential question, as Banks's *Medical Etiquette* of 1839 put it, was how 'persons possessing the highest notion of honour' should observe each other's rights and deal with each other's shortcomings.[158] The long debate which led up to the Medical Registration Act of 1858 was principally concerned with fixing the relative status, powers, and obligations of the different sections of medicine. The controversies frequently spilled over into the public domain, but once the legislative framework had been established, every effort was made to resolve further disputes behind the closed doors of the professional bodies.[159] As the rules of conduct were codified, confidential committees were set up to judge individual shortcomings. The justification for excluding the patients or their representatives from hearing breaches of etiquette or

---

[154] Glenn, *A Manual of the Laws Affecting Medical Men*, 369.
[155] R. Saundby, *Medical Ethics: A Guide to Professional Conduct* (London, 1907), 117.
[156] I. Waddington, 'The Development of Medical Ethics: A Sociological Analysis', *Medical History*, 19 (1975), 39–49.
[157] See the definition given by Carpenter in 'Medical Etiquette'.
[158] A. Banks, *Medical Etiquette* (London, 1839), p. ix.
[159] W. Dale, *The State of the Medical Profession in Great Britain* (London, 1875), 70.

ethics was that any publicity would harm the standing of the profession as a whole, which would in turn damage the interests of the public who needed to repose trust in those who treated them. Percival laid out the basic principle: 'The medical gentlemen of every charitable institution are, in some degree, responsible for, and the guardians of, the honour of each other. No physician or surgeon, therefore, should *reveal* occurrences in the hospital, which may injure the reputation of any one of his colleagues.'[160] Whereas honour preserved the secrets of patients, secrecy protected the honour of doctors.

On the face of it, this desire to prevent the flow of information from the profession to the public was in direct conflict with its conception of the nature of its core expertise. An article on 'Medical Ethics' in 1848 celebrated the past achievements of medical science and the 'brilliant results' which lay in the future. It posed the question, 'how far the communication of this knowledge should be oral and private, and how far oral and public, or even published?',[161] and gave a firmly positive answer: 'such a diffusion is really one of the necessities of the age.'[162] The growth of the modern scientific community was founded on the assertion that its findings, in the words of E. W. Holm, constituted 'what we may call public knowledge, that is not the partially incommunicable knowledge of one individual'.[163] Despite a growing tendency to use Latin rather than English in communicating with patients,[164] the contrast was drawn between the shared, accessible discoveries of professional doctors, and the private, secret remedies of commercial salesmen.[165] In this context, secrecy was the parent of dishonesty. As Percival put it:

No physician or surgeon should dispense a secret *nostrum*, whether it be his invention, or exclusive property. For if it be of real efficacy, the concealment of it is inconsistent with beneficence and professional liberality. And if mystery alone gives it value and importance, such craft implies either disgraceful ignorance or fraudulent avarice.[166]

The conflict between the commitment to liberality and the desire to keep patients in the dark about the inner workings of the profession was resolved by refining the role of honour. The problem with what were termed quack medicines was not so much their therapeutic contents, which were not subjected to

---

[160] Percival, *Medical Ethics*, 14.

[161] 'Medical Ethics', *British and Foreign Medico-Chirurgical Review* (July, 1848), 16.

[162] Ibid. 17.

[163] Cited in D. K. Himrod, 'Secrecy in Modern Science', in K. W. Bolle (ed.), *Secrecy in Religions* (Leiden, 1987), 104. See also E. McMullin, 'Openness and Secrecy in Science: Some Notes on Early History', *Science, Technology and Human Values*, 51 (1985), 14–15; D. Hull, 'Openness and Secrecy in Science: Their Origins and Limitations', *Science, Technology and Human Values*, 51 (1985), 8.

[164] M. E. Fissell, *Patients, Power and the Poor in Eighteenth-Century Bristol* (1991), 11.

[165] M. J. Peterson, *The Medical Profession in Mid-Victorian London* (Berkeley, 1978), 256–8.

[166] Percival, *Medical Ethics*, 45. See also *Report from the Select Committee on Medical Education* (1834), PP 1834, XIII, p. 151.

systematic chemical analysis until late in the century,[167] but their mode of validation. The purveyors of secret remedies relied upon the judgement of their customers to establish a demand for their products. Any hope that improvements in educational standards might emancipate the public from a belief in these heavily advertised pills and treatments was frustrated by the continuing inability of institutional medicine actually to cure virtually all the serious illnesses of the time.[168] As Macaulay and Graham were told by a witness to the 1847 Select Committee on Medical Registration: 'There will always be a tendency to employ quacks, because all must die in their turn. The medical profession can never do all that is required of them to do, and those who cannot be relieved by the regular craft will of course naturally look to others.'[169] In the resulting market-place, not only was the customer king, but the monarch, or at least the most distinguished members of society, were customers. For the professionals this was irrefutable proof of the unfitness of any patient ever to be trusted with medical knowledge: 'it is a commodity of which the public cannot judge', explained one doctor; 'we see that every hour of our lives: for instance, the most eminent subject in the State is the president of a homeopathic hospital. A Cabinet Minister . . . is president of a Mesmeric Institute.'[170] As the mere possession of honour was no defence against credulity, it must be left to the honourable discretion of the profession to determine what information was communicated to the public, and in what form.

Secrecy in medicine was by turns legitimate and illegitimate according to the varying requirements of the nascent profession. The search for ascendancy over patients and non-qualified practitioners dictated a complex and unstable body of prescriptions and behaviour which would need to be constantly reviewed in future decades. In a range of circumstances, the honour of professional gentlemen could justify the withholding of information and guarantee that such a privilege would not be misused. The one absolute principle was that those motivated by personal gain rather than the public good should not be trusted with the power to conceal knowledge. The authority of the doctor, as of every other emergent professional, was founded on a public acceptance of their emancipation from what William Rivington called 'trade propensities and trade practices'.[171] At an individual level, the natural tendency of those seeking

---

[167] The need for such an analysis had been recognized much earlier—the first editions of *The Lancet* regularly carried analyses of about five medicines in each number (*Lancet*, 1: 1 (5 Oct. 1823), 30; (12 Oct. 1823), 62–3; (19 Oct. 1823), 89; (26 Oct. 1823), 138; (7 Dec. 1823), 345) but it was not until the full weight of the BMA was brought to bear on the subject in 1909 that a full public debate began. See British Medical Association, *Secret Remedies* (London, 1909).

[168] F. B. Smith, 'Health', in J. Benson (ed.), *The Working Class in England, 1875–1914* (London, 1985), 36–7; A. J. Youngson, *The Scientific Revolution in Victorian Medicine* (London, 1979), 9–41; Vincent, *Literacy and Popular Culture*, 165–6.

[169] *Report from the Select Committee on Medical Registration* (1847), PP 1847, IX, p. 174.

[170] Ibid. 107.

[171] W. Rivington, *Medical Education and Medical Organisation* (London, 1879), 9.

private profit to keep secrets from each other merely confirmed their inferior status. But what was a characteristic weakness became a national menace when those in trade operated their own corporate forms of secrecy.

The most obvious manifestation of this danger were the multiplying combinations of artisans. In the early 1830s respectable opinion was still coming to terms with the partial legalization of trade unions which had taken place in 1824 and 1825. A leading objective of the repeal of the Combination Acts had been the destruction of the culture of conspiracy into which the unions had been forced by the emergency legislation of the Revolutionary Wars. The outburst of general unions in the aftermath of the Reform Act raised fears that the labourers were using their new freedoms to entrench their old vices. The prosecution of the Tolpuddle Martyrs in 1834 for administering illegal oaths reflected the acute official sensitivity on the issue. As E. C. Tufnell explained, the problem was not so much the swearing as the associated forms of concealment: 'the objection to voluntary oaths acquires much greater weight, when they are not only voluntary but secret, and used as a bond of union by large bodies of men, deriving perhaps an additional force, as we have seen they do in the cases before us, from the cunningly devised terms of a superstitious ritual.'[172] During the following three decades, the central concern was whether covert behaviour would flourish more in the absence than the presence of overt repression.

The matter was brought to a head by the bitter London master-builders' lockout of 1859, and the revelation eight years later of the 'Sheffield Outrages'. The two crises exposed the growing union movement to unprecedented scrutiny, and brought into sharp focus the apparent disjuncture between the increasingly transparent public sphere and the persistently clandestine world of labour. For Harriet Martineau, writing on the very visible dispute in London, 'the distinguishing characteristic of society and government in Great Britain is perfect openness and publicity in its arrangements, its legislation, and its executive action'.[173] The nation knew itself precisely by the absence of collective conspiracy: 'when we hear of continental nations, from the Mediterranean to the Volga, and from the Black Sea to the Channel, being honeycombed with secret societies, we are wont to rejoice that with us everything is open and aboveboard, and that the soil is sound under our feet.'[174] There was, for this reason 'something frightful' in the exercise of 'a secret and irresponsible authority' by the carpenters and bricklayers.[175] When the sequence of intimidation and murder in Sheffield became known, a similar contrast was drawn between the seemingly incompatible traditions of the nation and the unions. The *Edinburgh Review* returned to the subject:

---

[172] E. C. Tufnell, *Character, Object and Effects of Trade Unions* (London, 1834), 122.
[173] [H. Martineau], 'Secret Organisation of Trades', *Edinburgh Review*, 110 (1859), 527.
[174] Ibid. 527.
[175] Ibid. 558.

It is difficult to realise the fact that in a country in which the external face of things wears the semblance of tranquillity and order, where respect for the law is supposed to be a feature of the national character, and where the value attached to human life is manifested sometimes almost in a morbid degree, there exists, and has existed for many years a power above the law, secret, arbitrary, irresponsible—exercising a despotic control on the wills and consciences, and wreaking its vengeance with absolute impunity upon the lives and limbs of those who, through fear or infatuation, have submitted themselves to its dominion. We had supposed that tyranny in all its forms, but particularly when it works through the agency of secret tribunals, was particularly odious to the English character.[176]

In practice, the unions were as English as the other forms of collective authority of the period. Not only were the state and its genteel supporters less consistent in their regard for publicity than contemporary commentators supposed, but the skilled working men were more sophisticated in their attitude towards secrecy than the more alarming incidents in Sheffield suggested. As with the professions which now sought to place such distance between themselves and those who worked with their hands, it was a matter of striking a provisional balance between strategic objectives and tactical resources. From at least the late eighteenth century onwards it had been obvious to the groups of artisans who came together to assert their position in the market-place that the success of their endeavours depended upon a flexible approach to the release of information about their activities.

On the one hand, the survival of combinations in the face of fluctuations in the economy and attacks by employers required the development of increasingly formal means of communication. Disputes were resolved by finance. If the union was unable to pay benefits to its members, or failed to prevent the employer from recruiting new labour to keep his business going, then the strike was lost, and at least until the early 1850s the very existence of the union was imperilled. The maintenance of funds, at first in the primitive 'box clubs' and then in larger organizations, required systematic administration. Rules had to be devised for collecting, storing, and above all disbursing the weekly dues. For the sake of consistency over time and distance, the regulations needed to be written down and made accessible to subsequent members. From the 1830s onwards, handwriting was supplemented by print as the rule-books became more permanent, and the benefits they guaranteed became more extensive. As unions began to spread their geographical coverage, they introduced the device of the 'fortnightly return' as a means of formalizing the flow of information between the centre and the periphery. The Operative Masons, for instance, started their publication in the same year that the Dorsetshire labourers were transported.[177] For the elected officials

---

[176] [G. K. Rickards], 'Trades' Unions', *Edinburgh Review*, 126 (1867), 438.

[177] The return was handwritten until 1836, printed thereafter. Operative Society of Masons, *Fortnightly Returns*, 26 May–9 June 1836. For similar developments amongst the brushmakers, see W. Kiddier, *The Old Trade Unions from the Unprinted Records of the Brushmakers* (London, 1930), 54–65.

the printed columns were a means of extending their authority beyond face-to-face relationships; for the local societies they supplied a crucial source of intelligence about the state of the market beyond their immediate horizons. Trade societies no less than the Board of Trade were becoming bureaucracies with a similar need to establish clear and consistent lines of communication between their constituent parts.[178]

As with the expanding departments of state, however, there were reasons for exercising discretion over the flow of information beyond the confines of the organization. They were faced with a series of constraints. At the outset there was the state itself. The repeal of the Combination Acts left the unions in a kind of limbo, neither without nor within the law. Until the Friendly Societies Act of 1846 it remained technically illegal for any working-class organization to engage in written communication.[179] The subsequent Act of 1855 gave legal protection to those bodies which confined their activities to the payment of insurance benefits, provided they deposited their rules with the Registrar of Friendly Societies and opened their books for inspection. Combinations seeking to engage in collective bargaining were offered no such incentive to openness. They had no standing in law in the event of the fraudulent misuse of their funds, and were forced to subsist in a private, twilight world which maximized the fears of both their members and the general public.

Bereft of the support of the courts, the unions had to engage in elaborate devices to extend the scope of their own laws. The ceremony of oath-taking persisted well beyond the period of outright repression. What Clive Behagg terms the 'Theatre of secrecy' dramatized both the traditions of trade societies, which were under mounting attack from employers, and their boundaries, which were persistently undermined by non-members.[180] If the parodies of Christian ritual outraged polite churchgoers, they gave comfort to the initiates by emphasizing brotherhood in a world of increasing individualism, and by celebrating the distinctiveness of their calling in an economy which was seeking to erode all divisions within the labouring population. The only concession to the repeal of the legalization which had forced all their activities underground was a new willingness to embody such rites in their printed rules. Unlike the state, which was developing a custom of denying the possession of secrets, the artisans sought to make a virtue of the opacity of their practices. It was impossible to codify the combination of manual and cognitive skills which defined their skills, despite attempts by enterprising publishers from the 1840s

---

[178] On the increasing use of paper by trade unions during the first half of the nineteenth century, see Vincent, *Literacy and Popular Culture*, 135–40.

[179] E. Yeo, 'Some Practices and Problems of Chartist Democracy', in J. Epstein and D. Thompson (eds.), *The Chartist Experience* (London, 1982), 360–2. Also Vincent, 'Community, Communication and the State', 166–8.

[180] C. Behagg, 'Secrecy, Ritual and Folk Violence: The Opacity of the Workplace in the First Half of the Nineteenth Century', in R. D. Storch (ed.), *Popular Culture and Custom in Nineteenth-Century England* (London, 1982), 160.

onwards to produce learn-it-yourself manuals.[181] As the doctors defended their privileges by an appeal to the public's need for their expertise, so also the trades justified their controls over entry and practice in terms of the customer's interest in the quality of the goods and services which were purchased. Trust in the integrity of the practitioner was as relevant to the manufacture of a surgeon's knives as it was to his use of them. It was therefore necessary to preserve the institution of apprenticeship in which the knowledge, the manipulative capabilities, and above all the values of good workmanship were learned by guided imitation rather than formal instruction. The enclosed transmission of trade secrets was at the root of the skilled worker's sense of his worth, and constituted the basis of his bargaining power in the market-place.

Controlling the number of those permitted to take up an apprenticeship was a means of asserting the artisan's position against both masters and unskilled workers. This double perspective dictated a deliberately ambiguous policy towards the publicity given to the activities of the trade as a collective entity. In even the best-organized sectors, no mid-century union could establish an effective closed shop. The mysteries of initiation were partly a means of projecting a larger shadow than the actual size of a given body justified. The same function was performed by the line which was drawn between published and unpublished rules. Those regulations which defined the strength of a union in areas which were acceptable to employers and to the public at large, especially in relation to the good management of their funds, were printed and made available. But those by-laws which dealt with a range of working practices which could not be openly enforced over either masters or non-society men were left in the realm of unwritten custom, to be defended or advanced as the conditions of the local labour market permitted. The premature recording of issues such as maximum speeds of work or lengths of meal-breaks would only invite open attack from employers or breaches of discipline from those disinclined to pay their dues. The transition from implicit to explicit regulation had to be handled with great care if the union's limitations were not to be exposed. Where an advantage had been gained through a long dispute, particularly in relation to wages, the resulting agreement would stay pinned to workshop walls for years on end. But the mass of privileges and obligations which had never been subject to formal negotiation were rarely visible from a distance. In these areas, the unions demanded quiet conformity rather than vocal obedience. Amongst the masons, the Operative Society required only that non-members 'tacitly' accepted customs governing such matters as the permitted daily work-rate.[182] Such reticence applied particularly to devices which flagrantly breached the precepts of orthodox liberal economics.

---

[181] See, for instance, the list of manuals in J. Weale, *Catalogue of Books on Architecture and Engineering, Civil, Mechanical, Military, and Naval, New and Old* (London, 1854).

[182] *Eleventh and Final Report of the Royal Commissioners Appointed to Inquire into the Organisation and Rules of Trade Unions and other Associations*, PP 1868–9, XXXI, p. 53.

Thus, for instance, the saw-grinders of Sheffield, perpetrators of some of the worst 'outrages', had well-defined laws about contributions and benefits, but there were 'no formal rules and no formal resolutions' governing their enforcement through the device of rattening—disabling a worker's machinery or hiding his tools.[183]

The variable patterns of open and hidden regulation were a reflection of both the worldliness and the vulnerability of organized labour. Every member of a trade was expected to display a weathered judgement as he navigated his way across a sea of projecting and submerged rules. But the discretionary role of published regulation was born of weakness and was itself vulnerable to breakdown. In the mid-1860s the extremist behaviour of both the judiciary and the judicial bodies of some trade societies threatened to bring the delicate structure of compromise and adjustment crashing to the ground. On the one hand, a series of court decisions, particularly *Hornby* v. *Close* and *R.* v. *Drewitt*, demolished any illusion that over the decades since the repeal of the Combination Acts the trade unions had gained *de facto* legal protection. It was confirmed that organized labour had no right to apply to the courts to prevent embezzlement of their funds, whereas employers were free to use them to prosecute strikers for conspiracy. On the other hand, the recourse to violence by sections of the Sheffield metal trade undermined the movement's claim that the hidden aspects of their activities were governed by the same regard for honourable conduct as those which were made public. The legal system appeared to be condemning the unions to a world of secrecy, which in turn was threatening a widespread breakdown of law and order.

There were two ways forward. The first was to face squarely the evil of secret combinations and return to the strategy of open repression. The second was to bring the unions firmly within the law in the hope that they would respond by exposing more of their procedures to public scrutiny. The partial implementation of the latter strategy through the Trade Union Acts of 1871 and 1875 reflected a grudging acceptance that skilled working-men now possessed sufficient maturity to be trusted with their own secrets. This conclusion, which was forged through a series of debates culminating in the 1869 Royal Commission, was partly a concession to the capacity of the working class to withstand unwelcome scrutiny. In the case of the 'Sheffield Outrages', most of the city's trades had not been involved in bombing and murder; the community nonetheless united in the face of outside inquiry, and the facts only came to light after an unprecedented grant of immunity from prosecution. It was painful to name those responsible for the crimes and then let them walk free, but there was no other way of breaking down the wall of silence. The

---

[183] *Report Presented to the Trades Unions Commissioners by the Examiners Appointed to Inquire into Acts of Intimidation, Outrage, or Wrong Alleged to have been Promoted, Encouraged, or Connived at by Trades Unions in the Town of Sheffield* (1867), repr. in S. Pollard, (ed.), *The Sheffield Outrages* (London, 1867), 4, 102.

experience confirmed a lesson first learned a generation earlier, that it was beyond the power of the liberal state to flatten the barriers erected by an embattled working class. An article on 'Work and Murder' in the less than
sympathetic *Blackwood's Magazine* drew the only possible conclusion:

If the law were to try to prohibit Trades-unions, they would, in spite of the law, continue to exist, as long as the working man considered them necessary for the protection of their real or supposed interests—with this difference, that they would be
organised as secret societies with secret oaths and passwords, and that, being secret
and illegal, they would be more bloodthirsty in their vengeance against employers
and against their own class, than they are ever likely to be under a system of comparative legality and publicity.[184]

No strategy was without its risks. But the scale of the conflict which would
ensue if the government drove underground a movement which had now
established its own permanent bureaucracies and was about to set up a national presence in the form of the Trades Union Congress was too large to be
contemplated. Faith in the alternative road was sustained by the confidence
which was still invested in the agencies of mass communication. Back in 1834,
a year after the first grant to the elementary school societies, Tufnell had
observed that 'it is curious to mark, how every evil that afflicts the country
is resolvable into ignorance, and how directly education offers a remedy'.[185]
Although further legislation was still required to achieve a universal system
of basic schooling, virtually all skilled working-men were already literate.[186]
The more they engaged in collective activity, the more they learned how to employ the tools with which they had been equipped, and the more, so it was
hoped, would they read of the truths of laissez-faire economics. Furthermore,
in the same year that the judges turned on the unions, Parliament enfranchised the bulk of their members through the Second Reform Act of 1867. With
the working class partially admitted to the state, it was now necessary to
permit at least an element of the freedom enjoyed by the professional men
who had possessed the vote since 1832. In the case of the unions, reforms took
the form not of positive rights, but rather of a set of legal immunities.[187] At
the beginning of the crisis over union secrecy, Harriet Martineau wrote that:
'Men are not more fit to be trusted with secret and irresponsible power when
they meet round an ale-house table in fustian jackets than when they assemble
in the courts of kings or the council chambers of the great.'[188] The outcome
of the controversy turned this observation inside out. The men in fustian
jackets were to be allowed something of the same licence as the men in the

---

[184] 'Work and Murder', *Blackwood's Magazine*, 102 (1867), 504.
[185] Tufnell, *Character of Trade Unions*, 105.
[186] Vincent, *Literacy and Popular Culture*, 96–104.
[187] C. Crouch, 'Sharing Public Space: States and Organized Interests in Western Europe', in J. Hall
(ed.), *States in History* (Oxford, 1986), 193.
[188] [Martineau], 'Secret Organisation of Trades', 562.

council chambers now enjoyed to set their own limits to what was known about their corporate affairs.

In 1870 the Prime Minister-in-waiting took up his pen once more. *Lothair*, Disraeli's first novel for more than twenty years, was an immense popular success. Its eponymous hero is a rich young landowner, who at the time of the Second Reform Act sets out in search of a new source of spiritual authority in a world in which the old certainties have been undermined by the twin forces of German biblical scholarship and Darwinian science. As Disraeli's Preface to a contemporary edition of his *Collected Works* observed, liberalism has sapped 'the institutions which were the bulwarks of the multitude', and 'nothing had been substituted for them'.[189] Throughout the novel, a vigorous campaign for Lothair's soul and money is mounted by the Catholic Church, which presents itself as the last bulwark against atheism and communism in Europe. His joint guardian, the Newman-like Cardinal Grandison, denies that Catholicism is reactionary, 'but if you mean by political freedom the schemes of the illuminati and the freemasons which perpetually torture the Continent, all the dark conspiracies of the secret societies, there I admit, the Church is in antagonism with such aspirations after liberty'.[190] Disraeli shared with Harriet Martineau the widespread belief that Europe was indeed honeycombed with secret societies.[191] His hero becomes involved with the shadowy Standing Committee of the Holy Alliance of Peoples, which stands behind all the continental conspiratorial movements, such as the 'Mary-Anne' in France and the 'Madre Nature' in Italy. Lothair nearly loses his life fighting on behalf of Mazzini, who is introduced once more to the British public in the thin disguise of the republican leader 'Mirandola'.

The threat of the secret societies was, however, conceived as largely external. The organizations represented the dark forces of European politics which imperilled native freedoms from across the Channel. Their leaders used Britain as a safe haven and repaid her hospitality by fomenting sedition, most notably in the novel in the form of the Fenians, whose first bombing campaign on the mainland took place in the period which it covers. In particular, a line was drawn between the continental freemasons, who were held to have been implicated in every revolutionary outbreak since 1789, and the flourishing British lodges, which excited no serious concern. The freemasons had been specifically exempted from the 1799 Secret Societies Act, not least because of their close connections with the throne.[192] The Grand Lodge had been led by members of the royal family since 1782, and the Grand Master for the last three decades of

[189] B. Disraeli, *Collected Edition of the Novels and Tales by the Right Honourable B. Disraeli*, Vol. 1, *Lothair* (London, 1970), p. x.

[190] Ibid. 260.

[191] Disraeli's belief in the sinister role of secret societies is discussed in J. M. Roberts, *The Mythology of the Secret Societies* (London, 1972), 3–7.

[192] D. Wright (rev. and ed.), *Guild's History of Freemasonry* (London, 1931), iii. 96; M. Short, *Inside the Brotherhood* (London, 1990), 66.

the nineteenth century was the future Edward VII.[193] The domestication of the British branch reflected the growing identity and self-assurance of the public sphere. Freemasonry had flourished across Europe in the eighteenth century as a protected arena in which new ideas of intellectual progress could be pursued beyond the all-pervasive gaze of the monarchy and the church.[194] But where the political, professional, and scientific radicals developed their own institutional forms, they became less and less dependent on private structures of bonding and support. Open arrangements were made with the state to protect their confidential knowledge and enhance their corporate standing. In Britain the lodges scaled down their ambitions as they increased their numbers, becoming a grown-up version of the public schools, where local bourgeois elites could integrate themselves with the old ruling order in an atmosphere of male ritual and conviviality.[195] Eventually the genuine stonemasons and their artisan brothers were admitted to the public arena, a process completed by Disraeli himself in the legislation of 1875. Their version of freemasonry, the Oddfellows and the other friendly societies, were accepted as benevolent recreational and mutual aid bodies, whose rituals presented no threat to a free society.

The fear of external secret societies in the pages of *Lothair* was deep-rooted and was to renew itself in various guises in the succeeding decades, with Irish terrorists joined later by anarchists and then from 1917 by the international conspiracy of Bolshevism. But in the novel the plot turns not on the defeat of the Standing Committee of the Holy Alliance of Peoples, but rather on the failure of the Catholics to answer the hero's search for authority. He eventually rejects their appeal precisely because of their disregard for the distinctive identity of the public and private spheres which were now central to British liberties. On the one hand the church is presented as hostile the secular political process. 'The world is wearied of statesmen', argues the Cardinal, 'whom democracy has degraded into politicians, and of orators who have become what they call debaters.'[196] On the other, the familiar charge that Popery was inimical to the sanctity of the home is given a full airing. Lothair's second joint guardian, the non-Catholic Lord Culloden, gives him some necessary fatherly advice:

---

[193] Roberts, *Mythology of the Secret Societies*, 25–6. The Prince of Wales was succeeded by his brother, the Duke of Connaught, and later by the future Edward VIII and George VI. J. J. Robinson, *Born in Blood: The Lost Secrets of Freemasonry* (London, 1989), 176.

[194] M. C. Jacob, *Living the Enlightenment: Freemasonry and Politics in Eighteenth-Century Europe* (Oxford, 1991), 23–72; K. Hetherington, *The Badlands of Modernity* (London, 1997), 77–102. I am grateful to my colleague for allowing me access to a pre-publication copy of his important book.

[195] The affinities between the public schools and the freemasons, and thence with the imperial civil service, are energetically explored in P. J. Rich's *Elixir of Empire* (London, 1989) and *Chains of Empire* (London, 1991).

[196] Disraeli, *Lothair*, 70.

A man should be master in his own house. You will be taking a wife some day; at least it is to be hoped so; and how will you like one of these Monsignores to be walking into her bedroom, eh; and talking to her alone when he pleases, and where he pleases; and when you want to consult your wife, which a wise man should often do, to find there is another mind between hers and yours?[197]

In the concluding pages, Lothair finally sees the light, proposes to Lady Corisande, and accepts his duties as a responsible Anglican landowner.

The Naming of Names

A major source for the history of honourable secrecy is the writing of men whose honour demanded that their names be kept secret. The leading periodicals and the national daily press of the second quarter of the nineteenth century operated a policy of anonymity in the publication of their reviews and articles. Personal signatures were omitted in the interests of collective authority. As one (anonymous) proponent of the convention put it: 'The individual is merged in the court which he represents, and he speaks out not in his own name, but *ex cathedra*.'[198] The proliferation of the written word made the concealment of names both easier and more important. Print had greater power than speech, and was more readily separated from its begetter. As more and more divisive opinion clamoured for yet wider attention, it appeared that, as the author and journalist H. D. Traill wrote, the 'unnamed contributor' constituted 'the area of calm in the heart of the cyclone'.[199] Higher journalism assumed the task defined by Coleridge in his proposal for a clerisy. With traditional forms of spiritual authority in decline there was required a new body which, through its common social standing and its shared commitment to honourable thought and behaviour, could promote truth and order in a fractured age. If the serious periodicals and newspapers were to stand in for the proposed entity, it was necessary to curtail the identity of the individual contributor. Every opinion was that of the publication as a whole, and in the absence of a named editor, every publication could be seen as a variation of a larger moral and intellectual presence. The suppression of signatures permitted debate but prevented it from unleashing the forces of anarchy which would render all civilized discussion impossible.[200]

The first serious breaches in the wall of authorial secrecy were made by the launch of *Macmillan's Magazine* in 1859, followed by the *Fortnightly* and

[197] Ibid. 246–7.

[198] 'On the Anonymous in Periodicals', *New Monthly Magazine* (1853), 5.

[199] H. D. Traill, 'The Anonymous Critic', *Saturday Review*, 10 (1860), 11.

[200] C. Kent, 'Higher Journalism and the Mid-Victorian Clerisy', *Victorian Studies*, 13 (1969), 182–4.

Contemporary Reviews in 1865 and 1866.[201] Their decision to make a regular practice of signing articles was the culmination of a debate which had been growing for more than two decades. The argument revolved around the consequence of concealing individual dissent within the ranks of the opinion-makers. It was claimed in defence of the practice that naming critics would exacerbate personal rivalries, and thus, 'the bitterness of malice between contending rivals, which now flows in an under-current, and which is scarcely known to exist but to the parties themselves, would then rise up to the surface, and become the object of universal disgust'.[202] However, in the first influential assault on this form of secrecy published in the year of the Reform Act, Bulwer Lytton alleged that it was serving to undermine precisely those sections of society it was designed to protect: 'the anonymous system which favours all personal slander, and which, to feed the public taste, must slander distinguished, and not obscure, station, has forwarded the progress of opinion against the aristocratic body by the most distorted exaggeration of the individual vices or foibles of its members.'[203]

The central problem was the activity of what Traill called 'the small fry of authordom'.[204] Anonymity had in part been a device to elevate the struggling profession above the Grub Street hacks. Just as the doctors and lawyers were defining their calling against mere trade by imposing restrictions on personal advertisement, so too the gentlemanly journalists distinguished themselves from those writing just for money by their distaste for self-publicity. Their individual aspirations were subordinated to the larger ethical goals of their publications. The disinterested pursuit of truth mattered more than the accumulation of wealth and fame. There were also more instrumental considerations. Anonymity concealed the widespread practice of journalists working for several newspapers at once—only *The Times* attempted the curb the activities of its staff—and also the fact that many of the contributors to the press were otherwise building their careers in law, medicine, or the civil service, and thought it prudent not to reveal their literary moonlighting. Thomas Hughes observed in 1861 that, 'it is still true that a young man is damaged in a strictly professional sense if it is known that he has any serious pursuit outside his profession, especially if it is known that he writes for newspapers'.[205]

In one sense, the need to keep such activities secret was becoming more urgent, as the learned occupations and the state bureaucracy tightened their formal and informal restrictions on extramural communication. But in another it was becoming more difficult to sustain, as the walls which had been

---

[201] O. Maurer, Jr., 'Anonymity vs. Signature in Victorian Reviewing', *Studies in English*, 27 (June 1948), 4–5.

[202] 'On the Anonymous in Periodicals', 3.

[203] Bulwer Lytton, *England and the English*, 269.

[204] Traill, 'The Anonymous Critic', 9.

[205] T. Hughes, 'Anonymous Journalism', *Macmillan's Magazine*, 5 (Dec. 1861), 166.

erected around high journalism were undermined by the insatiable public demand for print and the endless supply of hungry writers willing to meet it. Whilst the professions and the civil service were developing new means of controlling the number and calibre their recruits, there was a diminishing prospect of doing so in the newspaper and periodical offices. Individual publications might hope to maintain their standards, and the long-established reviews continued to plough their unsigned furrows throughout the century. However, the proliferation of the smaller fry of authordom and their papers rendered the principle of anonymity increasingly dangerous. What had been a badge of the honourable was becoming the cloak of the unprincipled. Instead of enhancing impartiality and truth it fostered bias and slander. By the 1860s there was a growing case for demanding of the gentlemanly writers that they offer up their names for the larger cause of responsible journalism. As Hughes argued in the *Saturday Review*, 'it is much better for the country that the few should have to put some force on themselves, and sacrifice their desire for privacy, than that the many should go on familiarising themselves and their readers with the sort of licence and recklessness which is now the rule'.[206]

Anonymous communication by the non-respectable sections of society had always been a cause of anxiety. The sending of threatening letters signed with nothing more specific than a generic *nom de guerre* had been a standard device of collective protest since the early eighteenth century.[207] It was a capital offence until 1823, and then punishable by transportation for life. The practice declined after the Captain Swing rising of 1830, as a consequence not of repression but of the growing confidence of radical movements, at least in the towns. It seemed less necessary to conceal individual participation in political or trade-union activity, and more profitable to engage in public discourse with opponents.[208] By putting their names to documents and petitions, and publishing the oaths of union secrecy, the organizations challenged the holders of power to adopt similar standards of openness. Professing individual identity was a sign of a mature liberal democracy. Only despots and those subject to them had the need to deny who they were. The expansion of the machinery of correspondence multiplied the opportunities for oblique communication, and it was in the interests of the state and its supporters not to give implicit endorsement to a such practices. Whilst they had ceased to be a threat to national security, unsigned letters remained a major public nuisance, as *The Times* pointed out in 1861: 'Few people would guess before hand the numbers and grotesqueness of anonymous letters that strew the breakfast tables of public men.'[209] As in other respects, the reform of 1840 was proving a mixed blessing:

---

[206] Hughes, 'Anonymous Journalism', 167.

[207] E. P. Thompson, 'The Crime of Anonymity', in D. Hay *et al.* (eds.), *Albion's Fatal Tree* (Harmondsworth, 1977), 283.

[208] Vincent, 'Communication, Community and the State', 170–5.

[209] *The Times* (27 Apr. 1861), 8.

The penny post, which would have penetrated the outworks of DANAN's chamber itself, sometimes enables the most insignificant of men to converse for a moment in black and white with the most illustrious. Hence all the threatening, whining, hortatory, and objurgatory epistles which are meant to disturb the peace of Royal personages, Prime Ministers, Bishops and Chancellors . . .[210]

Only those without self-respect and undeserving of the respect of others had need to omit their signatures.

Although the capacity of anonymity to enhance authority remained a powerful attraction, it was increasingly at odds with the spirit of the age. Immediately after the First Reform Act, the state had set about naming its citizens. The Registration of Births, Deaths, and Marriages Act of 1836 ensured that every inhabitant would appear in a public record on at least two occasions, and more if they formed a family. At birth and marriage their names would be given in full together with those of their parents; at death they were listed alone. Unlike the information entered in the Census Enumerators' Handbooks every decade since 1801, these personal details were available for inspection. The registration forms had spaces for addresses, but in the early years of the new system these were rarely completed with any precision. In most cases it was assumed by the vicar or the registrar that those with an interest in the event would know where everyone lived, or if not then whom to ask. Except in parts of London, there was as yet no requirement to number houses. The parish, or at most the street, was a sufficient guide to location.

The pressure to tie individual names to particular residences came not from registrars but postmasters. Before 1840 the delivery of mail demanded extensive personal contact. The letter-carrier had to call on the house to extract payment, which might require prolonged negotiation if the recipient was unable to read or unwilling to pay for the infrequent and unexpected missive.[211] As often as not the letters were left at the post office to await collection while a reader or some money was found. With the arrival of the Penny Post, the era of the leisurely, discursive service had to come to an end. Prepayment made it unnecessary to speak to the addressee, and the increasing volume of business meant that it was no longer practical for the safe passage of an envelope to depend on the letter-carrier's detailed knowledge of his area. Although the sharp reduction of the price of a letter from an average of sixpence to a flat rate of a penny did not have quite as dramatic an impact as was anticipated, the per-capita flow of mail doubled immediately from four to eight, and increased a further fourfold by 1870.[212] Mass communication required mass organization. The Post Office rapidly became the largest civilian organization in the country; by 1851 the growing army of postmasters, sorters, and carriers were dealing

---

[210] *The Times* (27 Apr. 1861), 8. The reference is to the princess confined to an inaccessible tower who was seduced by Zeus under the form of a shower of golden rain, and became the mother of Perseus.

[211] Robinson, *The British Post Office*, 198, 204.

[212] *Twenty-Seventh Annual Report of the Postmaster General on the Post Office* (1881), App. A.

with a million items a day.[213] The central intention of the reform had been to eradicate distance as an obstacle to personal contact, and to a large extent this was achieved.[214] Even in London, less than half the deliveries came from within the postal districts.[215] More and more letters were sent to strangers, as commercial firms and pressure groups began to despatch circulars by the hundred thousand.[216] And more and more letters were handled by strangers as they were moved with unprecedented speed to destinations in every corner of Britain.

The more impersonal the machinery, the more standardized had to be the material which it processed. A systematic attack was launched on the way in which individuals described themselves and each other. To avoid expense and delay it was essential that the correspondent was able to discriminate much more accurately between the recipient and the household, between the home and the street, and the street and the village or town. Physical changes were required. Along with the gummed stamp and the ready-made envelope came street signs, house numbers, and letter-boxes in doors. Less visibly came a new mentality, as the association between name and place was remade. It took at least a generation to complete the transition. On a sample day in 1843, three-and-a-half thousand letters were sorted bearing only a name and 'London', and two decades later the same sorting office was returning one-and-a-half million letters a year on the grounds of inadequate or absent addresses.[217] Gradually, however, the Penny Post taught the population to distinguish the name from the community in a way which those who knew neither could understand.

The letter folded into its exactly addressed envelope enhanced and protected individual identity. Attaching the name to the house and the street was part of a larger process of specifying personal difference. The act of written communication deepened the sense of the unique self. It encouraged reflection on intimate affairs, and consideration of an alternative perspective upon them. Singularity was established through personal contact. By putting pen to paper the correspondent was at once connected with and separated from another discrete personality. There was no point to the reading and writing unless something new was told to someone who already knew enough to understand it. So much was true of speech, but now there was more space for contemplation,

[213] B. R. Mitchell, *Abstract of European Historical Statistics* (2nd edn., London, 1981), 680.
[214] Vincent, 'Communication, Community and the State', 168.
[215] *Tenth Annual Report of the Postmaster General on the Post Office* (1864), 34–6.
[216] Pickford and Company dispatched 240,000 letters to potential customers as early as 1843, and in 1844 the Anti-Corn Law League, then at the height of its operations, sent out 300,000 letters and over 2 million other items. The 'junk mail' side of the Post Office expanded rapidly after the book post service was extended to cover circulars in 1856, and the pattern post was introduced in 1863. *Report from the Select Committee on Postage*, PP 1843, VIII, p. 15; H. Ashworth, *Recollections of Richard Cobden, MP, and the Anti-Corn Law League* (2nd edn., London, 1878), 185; *Eleventh Annual Report of the Postmaster General on the Post Office* (1865), 8.
[217] *Report from the Select Committee on Postage*, PP 1843, VIII, 283; *Seventh Report of the Postmaster General on the Post Office* (1862), 12.

and no regard for the distance over which the discourse took place. Whilst, as we have seen, the letter was all too vulnerable to interception, it was intrinsically enclosed whereas conversation was inherently accessible. In every respect it enlarged the private realm.

Once the factor of cost had been removed for all but the poorest sections of society, the principal obstacle to the exploitation of the reform was the lack of functional literacy. Although two-thirds of grooms and nearly half of brides could now sign their names, the capacity to engage in sustained, fluent composition, a skill not taught to even the senior levels of the elementary schools until 1871, was much less widely distributed.[218] This was the major factor behind the sharply differentiated use of the Penny Post throughout the nineteenth century. The expected transformation in the pattern of communication amongst the working class failed to materialize. Instead, the new flat-rate benefit was, as one critic put it, 'a boon to the rich instead of the poor'.[219] It was eagerly seized upon by those who worked with a pen in their hand, and their wives and children in suburban retreats or on their annual holidays beside the sea. Brighton's flow of mail in 1863 was five times heavier than Wigan's, despite similar populations.[220] Those whose education extended no further than elementary school suffered a double denial of privacy. They rarely engaged in confidential discourse, and if some family crisis forced them to make use of the post, they often had to expose their domestic secrets to their neighbours as they sought assistance with composing or reading the letter. When they did finally begin to make extensive use of the postal service at the very end of the nineteenth century, it was in the form of the picture postcard, which could be read by everyone who handled it.[221]

A further obstacle to writing was the lack of adequate peace and quiet in the overcrowded terraces of the labouring poor. For those now enjoying the fruits of commercial prosperity, the ability to peruse and reply to correspondence in a quiet, comfortable, secluded room defined the central object of the emerging tradition in domestic architecture. As the author of *The Gentleman's House* put it, 'it is a first principle with the better classes of English people that the Family Rooms shall be essentially private'.[222] The Englishman's castle became a home, and the commuter's villa became a castle.[223] Both were designed to exclude the outside world and, as far as resources permitted, to separate worlds of those

---

[218] Vincent, *Literacy and Popular Culture*, 43. Even then, less than one pupil in fifty received instruction in how to set out a letter.

[219] *The Administration of the Post Office from the Introduction of Mr. Rowland Hill's Plan of Penny Postage up to the Present Time* (London, 1844), 196.

[220] *Tenth Annual Report on the Post Office*, 34–6.

[221] The use of this form of communication was made possible by successive relaxations of the regulations on the use of cards between 1894 and 1902. F. Staff, *The Picture Postcard and its Origins* (London, 1966), 7–91.

[222] R. Kerr, *The Gentleman's House* (2nd edn., London, 1865), 67.

[223] S. Muthesius, *The English Terraced House* (New Haven, 1982), 39–48, 99; M. Girouard, *Life in the English Country House* (New Haven, 1978), 285.

who resided within. *How To Behave, A Pocket Manual of Etiquette* advised that: 'each person in a dwelling should, if possible, have a room as sacred from intrusion as the house is to the family'.[224] In the country houses, rooms ceased to be thoroughfares and instead opened off a connecting corridor with a single door which could be shut against the rest of the household. In the suburban developments every ingenuity was exercised to create as much sequestered space as possible. The principle of specialization of function was observed. Where income was limited, priority was given to a separate bedroom for the parents and then for each adolescent child; where the consumption of time was more of a problem than the expenditure of money, there would be an ever-proliferating range of recreational arenas. The overriding concern was to preserve modesty by ensuring that none of the bodily functions reached any of the sensory organs. This meant separate lavatories and bathrooms, and beds with quiet springs. Sex was immoral if it could be heard.

The architect's blueprint offered the prospect of a virtuous circle of privacy. Secluded space permitted the controlled communication which developed the personal qualities which justified the material privileges which paid for the new construction. The only problem was the servants. In theory, there was a straightforward solution. 'The idea which underlies all', explained *The Gentleman's House*, 'is simply this. The family constitutes one community: the servants another. Whatever may be their mutual regard and confidence as dwellers under the same roof, each class is entitled to shut its door on the other and be alone.'[225] In practice it had long been difficult to maintain so complete a divorce between the separate spheres.[226] Even in its ideal form, privacy was a one-way street. Servants had no right to know their employer's secrets, but both prudence and compassion dictated that a mistress should learn as much as possible of the 'hopes and fears' of her subordinates, and should be able to open at will the closed doors of their rooms to inspect their condition.[227] The larger difficulty, however, was that of preventing the maids and valets from abusing their necessary access to the household's affairs. The more intense the commitment to domestic seclusion, the more vulnerable it appeared. By the middle of the nineteenth century, no pretence of gentility was conceivable without the use of one or more servants to relieve the wife of any physical labour, but by the same measure, no guarantee of confidentiality was possible where the family's life was played out in front of one or more alien witnesses.[228] Growing comfort was everywhere accompanied by increasing paranoia. Servants, wrote one guide, 'are domestic spies, who continually embarrass the intercourse of the

---

[224] *How To Behave, A Pocket Manual of Etiquette* (Glasgow and London, 1865), 49.

[225] Kerr, *Gentleman's House*, 68.

[226] For a valuable discussion of this dilemma in former centuries, see L. A. Pollock, 'Living on the Stage of the World: The Concept of Privacy Among the Elite of Early Modern England,' in A. Wilson (ed.), *Rethinking Social History* (Manchester, 1993), 86–9.

[227] J. E. Panton, *From Kitchen to Garrett: Hints to Young Householders* (London, 1890), 151–7.

[228] B. Harrison, *The Transformation of British Politics 1860–1995* (Oxford, 1996), 135.

members of a family, or possess themselves of private information that renders their presence hateful and their absence dangerous'.[229] The increasing emphasis on the quality of reserve in the character of the gentleman could only be strengthened by the vulnerability of his honour in his domestic domain.[230]

The crude threat of dismissal without a character offered only limited security. A better device was to educate servants into to the habit of keeping secrets, particularly where they waited on the personal needs of the employer. As Mrs Beeton advised: 'A lady's maid having so much more intercourse with her mistress than any other servant should not only possess, but learn, discretion from day to day.'[231] Such lessons, however, were frequently undermined by the behaviour of the mistress herself. Self-discipline was the precondition of any exercise of authority. The frequently inexperienced and lonely new housewife was constantly tempted into the kind of indiscretion which could ruin all that she was trying to achieve. The reticence which the well-bred woman displayed in public was even more critical in private, as she whiled away the time between her husband's departure and return. It was essential that she school herself not to talk openly to the only adults with whom she was in regular contact during the long hours of the day.

The fear of complicity in the exposure of family affairs was all the more acute where the employee was from the same social background. An instinctive class superiority might inhibit indiscreet conversation with a manual servant, but there was no such obstacle in the case of the governess, whose ambiguous status reflected all the tensions in the ideology of domestic seclusion. By the middle of the century there were about 25,000 women of impoverished respectability working mostly as resident teachers of the sons and especially daughters of the upper classes and those of the middle class best able to imitate their way of life.[232] Although governesses formed only a small proportion of the total body of servants, they attracted immense attention in the fiction and commentaries of the period.[233] They occupied a liminal position in the household. It was a mark of distinction to give employment to a well-born woman, and essential that the delicate task of forming the personality of a growing child be entrusted to someone brought up to the same standards of conduct. Yet if the governess mingled too freely with her master and mistress, the critical barriers between kin and non-kin, between employer and employee, and between leisured lady and working woman, were overthrown. Spurned by the other servants for her air of superiority, she was distanced from the family by her claim to equality.

---

[229] Millar, *Gentleman's Handbook of Etiquette*, 116–17.

[230] Pollock, 'Living on the Stage of the World', 89.

[231] I. Beeton, *The Book of Household Management* (London, 1895), 1471. The *Book* was first published in 1859.

[232] The 1851 Census figure includes also the small number of non-resident governesses.

[233] K. Hughes, *The Victorian Governess* (London, 1993), 1–25.

In every direction, the boundary between inclusion and exclusion was uncertain. A much-debated issue was whether the governess should remain in company after dinner. She was served by the domestic staff during the meal and might be tempted to linger in conversation once they had withdrawn. This would not be welcomed by the master of the house, who, explained Elizabeth Sewell,

comes home from his day's employment weary, and perhaps irritable, and he wishes to be with his wife and children alone. The presence of a third person is irksome: and, therefore, when the governess undertakes her duties, she is made to understand that she will only be expected to spend the evening in the drawing room when she is invited.[234]

When the husband entered through the front door, he left the public sphere for the private. The essence of his domestic existence was the freedom to exchange confidences with his wife. Unless the governess spent her spare time alone, it would be impossible for him to enjoy the protected communication which his home was designed to permit.

Yet if the head of the household might hope to restrict his contact with the governess to the formal evening meal, his wife was far more exposed to her company. She had no job to go to, except perhaps a little charity work, and would expect to be regularly consulted by the woman who was deputizing for her position as a mother. It was an asymmetrical relationship. The mistress had the power to instruct, but had received no formal education in her duties. The schooled governess was subordinated to a woman who was still learning through uncertain experience how to comport herself as joint head of her miniature universe. Reclining on the most solidly built furniture in the history of domestic interiors, the wife wielded the most fragile authority. A slip of the tongue, a blurted confidence between two isolated women, and all was undone. The path to self-destruction was paved with the intentions of friendship. As the former governess Mary Maurice observed:

Many a young girl who, from mere ignorance of the forms of society, commits to such a governess tales of the family, or foolish secrets of her own, may thus be exposed to ridicule and disgrace, where a wise and judicious person would have pointed out to her the imprudence she was committing, and would have given her for life a lesson of practical wisdom. How many circumstances are now well known, which could never have been blazed abroad but for such agency.[235]

The situation was still more dangerous when the union between master and mistress fell short of the ideal. Either or both parties might seek to break out of their restricting family circle to seek advice or comfort from the nearest intelligent person of similar social background. It was imperative, wrote another

---

[234] E. M. Sewell, *Principles of Education* (1856), ii. 250.
[235] M. Maurice, *Governess Life* (1849), 101.

former governess, Anna Jameson, that the governess resist this flattering appeal to her judgement:

The lady may be troubled with the *besoin de faire les confidences*—the gentleman may choose to make you the umpire in a conjugal dispute; be warned,—in no case is prudence more requisite: there is just a possibility that a sensible and experienced woman might do secret good, but the case is a rare one, and remains for ever a secret.[236]

Jameson regarded reticence as a habit which could be readily learned: 'If you are obliged to see, hear and understand much, let it be with reluctant sense and sealed lips. Secrecy will not be a great burthen; for in such extraneous matters it is surprising how soon we forget that of which we do not allow ourselves to speak.'[237] Other observers were not so sanguine. The problem was that the substance of the undisciplined communication was not confined to the merely confidential, the trivia of domestic existence which gave flesh to private life. Rather, it extended to matters which were secret in the fullest and most vital sense of the term. These ranged from sexual or other misconduct to entirely innocent situations whose exposure would nonetheless be deeply damaging. 'Are there not,' argued Mary Maurice, 'for instance, in families, painful inherited maladies, perhaps the saddest of all, mental aberration, which all desire to conceal from public observation, and the exposure of which may be ruinous to the peace of whole families?'[238] Every closet had its skeleton, and, so it was feared, every governess sooner or later acquired its key.

In this context, as in any other, secrets were inherently fascinating, and always powerful. It was expecting too much to rely on the self-restraint of the governess, however well trained and well disposed she might be. The only possible solution was to recognize that in the hierarchy of domestic employment the governesses constituted the professional class, set apart by their background and education from other servants, and acting as specialist advisers to the heads of the domestic kingdoms. Just as doctors and lawyers had developed a code of ethics in relation to the disclosure of information, policed by various forms of regulation, so might those women who likewise combined gentle birth with a need to earn their living. Mary Maurice set out the requirement:

A physician once told the writer that it was once customary, before receiving the degree of MD to take what was called the hypocratic oath, which bound him never in any way to make use of information which he might obtain of family secrets, through the delirium of patients, or the necessary confessions which they made to him, in order to enable him to understand their cases or in any other way which his

---

[236] A. Jameson, 'On the Relative Position of Mothers and Governesses', in *Memoirs and Essays* (1846), 285.
[237] Ibid. 286.
[238] Maurice, *Governess Life*, 101.

profession should reveal to him. Now, should not a similar determination, though not enforced by the sanctity of an oath, be that of every governess when she enters a family? She must learn many things by living in the house, which she would never have known, but for that temporary connexion. She witnesses the tempers, and she discovers sometimes the estrangements amongst relations, and learns portions of their history, but she takes up the story in the midst of it—she knows nothing of the causes which have led to these conditions, nor is she in any way qualified to judge of the circumstances themselves. She has a very imperfect acquaintance with the things going on about her, and if she cannot shut her eyes or her ears to them, at all events she can be silent. Let her shrink from the base gossiping which would carry the tale beyond the doors of the house in which she resides.[239]

There was little prospect of fulfilling such an ambition. Governesses were and continued to be notorious gossips.[240] Neither the Governesses' Benevolent Institution nor the later and more exclusive Union of Private Governesses could provide the necessary corporate discipline. The emergence of a fully fledged profession was inhibited by the prevailing notion of female gentility which regarded a respectable upbringing as incompatible with a serious career. It was necessary to maintain the fiction that governesses were essentially well-trained amateurs. As a consequence, the privacy of those who could afford to employ them remained dependent upon secrets and endlessly vulnerable to their exposure.

The Black Satin Waistcoat

Just as the Northcote–Trevelyan Report was launching the civil service on its long journey towards professional competence, Dickens published his ferocious satire on the growing power of the professions, especially the law.[241] The malevolent heart of *Bleak House* is Mr Tulkinghorn, the 'severely and strictly self-repressed' solicitor to the Dedlock family.[242] Almost every character in the novel possesses or is possessed by a secret of some sort, but the main repository of confidential information is the man who, in the view of Sir Leicester Dedlock, is 'always welcome' and 'deservedly respected' because he is 'always discreet wheresoever he is'.[243] Although he is 'of course handsomely paid', it is made abundantly clear that his primary motivation is not wealth but power, especially over those from the upper reaches of society with whom 'he associates almost on a footing of equality'.[244] His whole life is immersed in other people's

---

[239] Ibid. 100–1. Maurice was in fact overstating the role of the Hippocratic Oath in the training of most doctors, but she reflected a wide belief in its significance.

[240] Hughes, *Victorian Governess*, 103.

[241] The novel was first published in parts between 1852 and 1853, and appeared in volume form at the end of 1853.

[242] C. Dickens, *Bleak House* (Everyman edn., London, 1907), Ch. 40, p. 547.

[243] Ibid. 543.   [244] Ibid.

secrets. He is pictured enjoying a bottle of vintage wine in his bachelor chambers:

As if it whispered to him of its fifty years of silence and seclusion, it shuts him up the closer. More impenetrable than ever, he sits, and drinks, and mellows as it were, in secrecy; pondering, at that twilight hour, on all the mysteries he knows, associated with darkening woods in the country, and vast blank shut-up houses in town . . .[245]

His access to the hidden affairs of the propertied is provided by the property itself. Their need for his services to purchase, maintain, and bequeath the houses in which their private lives can flourish allows him entry into every nook and cranny of their lives. Within the novel, Tulkinghorn represented the future more than the past. The baroque malpractices of Chancery had already been checked by the time *Bleak House* appeared, whilst conveyancing, and the other property-related forms of non-contentious litigation, were steadily increasing their significance in the work of the profession.[246] Dickens describes Tulkinghorn taking what turns out to be his last walk before he is murdered by the Dedlock's former maid:

He passes out into the streets, and walks on, with his hands behind him, under the shadow of the lofty houses, many of whose mysteries, difficulties, mortgages, delicate affairs of all kinds, are treasured up within his old black satin waistcoat. He is in the confidence of the very bricks and mortar. The high chimney-stacks telegraph family secrets to him.[247]

The melodramatic climax of the novel is set in motion by Tulkinghorn's discovery and threatened disclosure of Lady Dedlock's long-concealed secret, that before her marriage she had conceived a daughter by a Captain Hawdon, who is not drowned, as she had thought, but eking out a literally nameless existence as a legal copyist known as Nemo. Lady Dedlock herself is driven to flight and death by her anguish at the dishonour she will bring upon her husband. The name of her family will be ruined by the naming of her former lover. The plot centres on the deep ambivalence felt towards the expanding ranks of the professional orders. In a world of increasingly complex political, economic, and social transactions, the services of men in black satin waistcoats were becoming indispensable to the maintenance of forms of privilege which were under constant threat from below. Their discreet reserve patrolled the boundaries between the propertied and the propertyless. Where the self-discipline of the experts and advisers was maintained, it merged easily with the self-possession of their masters, creating an immensely resilient structure of oblique power.

---

[245] Dickens, *Bleak House*, Ch. 22, p. 291.
[246] M. Birks, *Gentlemen of the Law* (London, 1960), 208–38. There is a similar, although much more benevolent figure (Mr Putney Giles) in Disraeli's *Lothair* (see above).
[247] Dickens, *Bleak House*, Ch. 47, pp. 630–1.

Where it failed, it was as if the guns of the guards had been turned inwards rather than outwards. Everything depended on the trustworthiness of public and private servants who were exposed to a wide range of pressures and temptations.

The union of honour and secrecy was founded on necessity. It was a creative, modern, response to the growing requirement of publicity in the exercise of authority. Overt censorship was no longer feasible, complete transparency was out of the question. Instead, there emerged an understated doctrine of restraint, which drew attention only to the absence of direct controls on the flow of information. Amongst the ranks of the state officials, the reworked gentlemanly values served both to define and to conceal the emerging bureaucratic ethos. The absence of a formally embodied code accorded with the want of a written constitution and the imprecision of the fundamental divisions in society. However, it left unresolved the problem of how the schooled habits of abnegation were to be instilled into the second-class civil servants whose recruitment had been foreshadowed by Northcote–Trevelyan. The members of the learned professions turned more readily to controls over the transmission of their knowledge, but discovered more rapidly the complexities of administering them. Those outside the protecting walls of the state or the officially licensed professional bodies were least able to mount a public justification of their attempts to keep private what mattered to them, and found it most difficult to sustain acceptable codes of practice. Everywhere the expansion in formal communication created new possibilities of secrecy and threatened new possibilities of its abuse or betrayal. For the possessors of the greatest privilege, the worst nightmare was captured in Tulkinghorn's patient explanation of the altered condition of his employer's secret:

Now, Lady Dedlock, this is a matter of business, and in a matter of business the ground cannot be kept too clear. It is no longer your secret. Excuse me. That is just the mistake. It is my secret, in trust for Sir Leicester and the family. If it were your secret, Lady Dedlock, we should not be here holding this conversation.[248]

---

[248] Ibid. 628.

CHAPTER THREE

THE ROAD TO REGULATION, 1870–1911

The Master of Mastery

One day in 1875, a throng of down-at-heel men, representing 'every degree of broken fortunes',[1] gathered at the Civil Service Commission to take the examination for civil service writers, the lowest grade of government clerical employment. Amongst their number was a talented linguist called Charles Marvin, whose estimation of his own worth comfortably exceeded the tenpence an hour which the unestablished position offered. But he had failed at his chosen profession of journalism, and underpaid gentility was preferable to starvation. He listed his prior career on an application form, which, he later discovered, was passed around for the amusement of 'a number of fourpennies' in the records department, and sat the demanding four-hour paper.[2] A week later he was informed that he had passed, and was asked to supply birth and medical certificates, whilst further forms were sent to his referees and previous employers.

The outcome of this elaborate bureaucratic procedure was a posting, first to the Custom House, and then to the dog-licensing department of the Inland Revenue at Somerset House. There he was set to work dealing with a characteristic product of the growth of official regulation, the anonymous letter denouncing the behaviour, not of the state but of the correspondent's neighbours: 'As regards the amateur tell-tales', he observed,

they were chiefly persons ashamed of their treachery, and wrote to us on the strangest scraps of paper in the most illiterate of handwriting, signing their communications with some uncommon name or title, such as 'A Friend to the Revenue,' 'An Indignant Neighbour,' 'Where's the Police?', or as often as not, refrained from signing at all.[3]

He was then, appropriately, transferred to the Post Office itself at St Martin's le Grand, where he passed the examination to become a permanent writer, and in

---

[1] C. Marvin, *Our Public Offices* (2nd edn., London, 1880), p. 2.
[2] Ibid. 4.
[3] Ibid. 61–2.

his spare time tried to eke out his meagre salary by starting a language school under the immodest title of 'Marvin, Master of Mastery'.[4] This failed to prosper, and he was relieved to accept a new posting to the Foreign Office, where he arrived in July 1877, equipped with a burning conviction that the world in general and the civil service in particular owed him a better standard of living.

The Foreign Office was still holding out against a full implementation of the Northcote–Trevelyan reforms, not least because its closer involvement with state secrets justified more emphasis on the traditional structures of honourable behaviour and less on the mechanical skills measured by open examination.[5] Nonetheless, its internal procedures displayed the basic dichotomy which characterized every contemporary government department. The progress of paper was the subject of an elaborate and rigid system organized around the library, where all correspondence was registered and bound into volumes for future consultation.[6] However, the conduct of the clerks was controlled not by a rule-book but a code of honour, which in the socially exclusive diplomatic service seemed more than adequate security. Marvin, who as the only full-time writer on the staff was employed to copy every important document entering or leaving the building, found it all too easy to exploit the contradiction. His moral scruples were quickly extinguished by his sense of personal wrong; as he recorded in his best-selling and self-serving memoirs: 'I was so disgusted with the Foreign Office for 'sucking' the best years of my life for the miserable sum of £90, that I resolved from that moment to place upon the market every piece of information that chance threw in my way.'[7] The library, largely unoccupied before and after the six-hour working day, provided a perfect base for his renewed career as a journalist, and he was able to sell a series of revelations culminating in the draft of a secret treaty with the Russian government concerning the Congress of Berlin, which was published in the *Globe* on 31 May 1878, just two-and-a-half hours after it was signed.[8]

The Government was seriously embarrassed by the disclosure. It stood exposed to the double charge of dissimulation and incompetence. In terms which foreshadowed later controversies over the conduct of diplomacy before and after the First World War, *The Pall Mall Gazette* attacked the secrecy surrounding the negotiations with the Tsarist autocracy:

---

[4] His new method, appropriated from a Mr Prendergast, made use of a whole sentence approach to teaching which had recently been popularized in the literacy lessons of the inspected elementary schools. See Vincent, *Literacy and Popular Culture*, 84–5.

[5] Tilley and Gaselee, *The Foreign Office*, 153.

[6] On the standard pattern of organizing the progress of correspondence, which had altered little since the 1840s, see Escott, *England: Its People, Polity and Pursuits*, 365–8. The Foreign Office differed only in that more correspondence was deemed confidential, and fewer junior officials were allowed to open letters.

[7] Marvin, *Our Public Offices*, 248.

[8] Herstlet, *Recollections*, 191–2; Tilley and Gaselee, *The Foreign Office*, 139–40; Hooper, *Official Secrets*, 19–21; Aitken, *Officially Secret*, 7–15.

before long the country must know why it was thought necessary that England—strong in her own strength, strong in the respect and support of every free people in Europe, secure in the glaring weakness of the military despotisms which can no longer lean upon each other or make their subjects' blood a matter of family traffic—should leave the straight path she was pledged to follow and take to secret and tortuous ways.[9]

Since the closing years of the unreformed Parliament, there had indeed been a visible reduction in the transparency with which foreign policy was conducted. Whilst official despatches between the Foreign Office and its ambassadors were carefully prepared with a view to possible publication, these were increasingly accompanied by private letters of exegesis which need never be acknowledged, let alone revealed.[10] In the words of Harold Temperley's authoritative survey, 'our diplomacy became more secret as our constitution became more democratic'.[11] The paradox stemmed partly from the growth of the two-party system, which permitted Foreign Secretaries to maintain greater discipline over inquisitive back-benchers, and allowed their civil servants to exercise more control over the timing and volume of material that was put before Parliament. Tenterden, the current Permanent Secretary at the Foreign Office (and like his political master a hereditary peer) had been particularly keen to exploit the opportunities which had been growing since the passage of the Second Reform Act. More generally, the attraction of secret diplomacy reflected the unconfessed decline in national self-confidence since the time of Canning and Palmerston. The gap between the rhetoric of diplomatic autonomy and the requirement of international collaboration was bridged in silence. Salisbury had no wish to draw any more attention than was necessary to the need to engage in more structured relations with other great powers.[12] The days of straight paths were in the past.

The immediate problem was to find the source of the leak. Salisbury and Tenterden organized a search for the culprit, and Marvin was arrested and charged under the 1861 Larceny Act. His defence at the trial was founded on the contrast between the absence of official regulation and the presence of widespread interest in Government policy, mediated through a politically conscious press. According to his counsel, 'there was no law which made the defendant liable to punishment for the alleged offence, even if such an indiscretion had been really committed in the eagerness to satisfy the public craving for information upon matters of the deepest interest to the community at large'.[13] Marvin claimed that the Foreign Office was now regularly leaking to

---

[9] *Pall Mall Gazette* (19 June 1878).

[10] Cf. the 'secret pages' attached to unemployment benefit inspectors (below, Ch. 4, p. 156).

[11] H. Temperley, 'British Secret Diplomacy from Canning to Grey', *Cambridge Historical Journal*, 6: 1 (1938), 1.

[12] Ibid. 31.

[13] *The Times* (28 June 1878).

the newspapers for its own ends, and that he had merely anticipated the likely appearance of the information in some later edition of *The Times*. More specifically, he denied the charge of theft on the grounds that he had memorized the text of the treaty, and had not physically removed it from the building.

The trial ended in an acquittal. Marvin enjoyed fifteen minutes of notoriety, and his masters were left with a long-term dilemma. The indiscretion confirmed Salisbury's determination to restrict the flow of diplomatic information to the public, but left him less certain of the means of doing so.[14] The more honour had been identified with secrecy, the more secrecy had become vulnerable to the socially inferior. The personality which would observe and respect the conventions of discreet reserve could not be manufactured. Neither ambition nor application were any substitute for a good background and the right sort of education. The 'master of mastery' represented exactly the able but unprincipled product of competitive examinations against whom Cornewall Lewis had warned a quarter of a century earlier. 'I hope after this', wrote Tenterden to Salisbury, 'we may have properly appointed Clerks for such work and not have to depend on this cheap and untrustworthy class of people.'[15] However, the mode of selection was now established, at least for this level of government employee. The issue now was one of discipline. The 'cheap and untrustworthy class' not only had no past which would guarantee conduct; they had no future which could be the subject of sanctions. They were paid so little in relation to their abilities and responsibilities, and had such poor career prospects, that dismissal was scarcely a threat. As Tenterden gloomily observed, 'the worst of these people is that there is no hold of them'.[16]

One solution was to keep highly sensitive papers out of the hands of junior staff altogether. Arthur Conan Doyle re-created the circumstances of the Marvin affair a few years later in his story 'The Naval Treaty'. The document in question, as the Foreign Secretary explains, is the 'secret treaty between England and Italy of which, I regret to say, some rumours have already got into the public press. It is of enormous importance that nothing further should leak out. The French or the Russian embassy would pay an immense sum to learn the contents of these papers.'[17] 'Lord Holdhurst'—like Salisbury, 'that not too common type, a nobleman who is in truth noble'[18]—entrusts the task of transcribing the treaty not to a lowly copyist this time but to a senior official, who, in the unreconstructed ways of the Foreign Office, happens also to be his nephew. The official, conscious of his position of 'trust and honour',[19]

[14] Temperley, 'British Secret Diplomacy from Canning to Grey', 14.
[15] PRO, FO/363/3, Tenterden Papers. Tenterden to Salisbury, 15 June 1878.
[16] Ibid. 21 June 1878.
[17] A. Conan Doyle, 'The Naval Treaty', in *The Penguin Complete Sherlock Holmes* (Harmondsworth, 1981), 450. The story first appeared in *Memoirs of Sherlock Holmes* in 1894.
[18] Ibid. 459.
[19] Ibid. 447.

waits until all the lesser clerks have left for the night before starting work on the text. But when he leaves his desk to fetch some coffee the copy is stolen, as Sherlock Holmes later discovers, by his fiancée's brother, who calls to accompany him home and seizes the opportunity to restitute his heavy losses on the stock exchange.

There were, however, too many confidential papers, and too few detectives of the calibre of Holmes, for the fiction to offer much comfort to those charged with maintaining honourable secrecy. The various manifestations of this dilemma, and the attempts to resolve it, form the central topic of this chapter. There were a series of emerging conflicts which required new kinds of solution. As it became increasingly difficult to exclude those who could never be gentlemen from either working for the government or influencing its activities, it became less easy to evade the question of formal regulation. During the middle third of the nineteenth century, the uncertain social boundaries had been patrolled by a culture of reserve which camouflaged the latent tension between free and restricted communication. Where the state had been forced to choose between overt repression and reluctant tolerance, as in the case of the trade unions, it had, after much hesitation, adopted the latter course. However, the balance between legitimate and illegitimate secrets, and between acceptable and unacceptable means of protecting them, had never been stable, and as the century grew old, and the threats from inside and outside the nation intensified, the role of the law and the agencies of enforcement came closer to the surface. The hope remained that informal means of intervention and control could be refashioned to meet the new challenge. The fear was that an enforced descent into the statute books and the courts would destroy the liberties which distinguished Britain from her illiberal neighbours.

Writers and Rules

In 1869 Ralph Lingen was transferred from the Education Department to the Treasury to work once more with the hyperopic Robert Lowe. Released from the burden of managing the insubordinate School Inspectors, he took to his new post with enthusiasm. Within a year he had drafted the crucial Order in Council which not only codified the principle of competitive examinations, but formally extended the authority of the Treasury and its Permanent Secretary from the domain of finance to that of departmental organization.[20] Armed with his enlarged powers, he then set about tackling expenditure and discipline right across the service. At the head of his agenda were two related problems which stemmed from the initial attempt at reform.

[20] For a detailed summary of the 1870 Order in Council, see *Fourth Report of the Royal Commission on the Civil Service* [MacDonnell] (1914), PP 1914, XVI, p. 10.

The first of these was the group of employees variously known as 'temporary clerks, extra clerks, writing clerks, copyists, writers, law stationers' clerks, and Treasury extra clerks'.[21] In 1854 it had been hoped to avoid the dangers posed by the lower status of the 'mechanical' clerks by adapting established patterns of remuneration and recruitment. The Treasury calculated that a salary of £200 to £300, which was roughly the bottom of the existing scale, would be 'sufficient to secure the services of persons of respectable character who are perfectly equal to the performance of all ordinary clerical duties'.[22] No such guarantee could be offered in respect of the staff who were recruited on an *ad hoc* basis to cope with sharp fluctuations in correspondence which had to be written and copied. Many had been supplied originally by law stationers, but had stayed on and gained quasi-permanent status with implicit rights to promotion and even pensions.[23] They had no place in the new scheme, where such routine labour was to be the responsibility of the lower level of the established service. There were two solutions: either absorption into the ranks of the Regulation II clerks or exile to the outer circle of the truly temporary. In 1871 Lingen decided to adopt the latter course on the grounds of both economy and morale. The background of this motley crew of ink-stained scribes did not justify the kind of salary associated with the standards of honourable conduct which were required of the remodelled civil servant. By means of a further Order in Council he ruthlessly repealed all existing agreements and imposed a uniform rate of tenpence an hour with no possibility of increments or tenure.[24] There were by now some two thousand of these writers scattered across government departments, whose latent unity was made a militant reality by what was widely perceived to be a harsh and unjust decree. Although they lacked the connections and the platform which the School Inspectors had exploited, their protests rapidly reached the ears of MPs who were uneasy about the growing pretensions of the Treasury.

In the meantime, concern was increasing about the capacity of the civil service as a whole to keep its distance from the press. On the one hand, it was becoming established that no civil servant of principle would maintain a second career in journalism as had been the common practice during the pioneering days of the post-1832 bureaucracy. On the other, the newspapers were becoming increasingly unprincipled in their pursuit of official information. The question was whether the ethos of gentlemanly reserve would be sufficiently powerful and pervasive to withstand the new temptations. In 1858 the first recognizably modern trial for leaking public documents took place, when William Guernsey, 'described in the calendar as "a gentleman"',[25] was

---

[21] *Reports of Committees of Inquiry into Public Offices*, 11.
[22] PP 1854, XXVII, p. 44.
[23] PP 1914, XVI, pp. 124–6.
[24] *Report from the Select Committee on Civil Service Writers* (1873), PP 1873, XI.
[25] *The Times* (16 Dec. 1858).

prosecuted at the Old Bailey in connection with the premature publication in the *Daily News* of despatches from Gladstone's mission to the Ionian Islands.[26] The Attorney-General was wheeled out to promulgate the doctrine of the Government's right of property in all documents prepared for its use, and to outline the existence of a 'public interest' in the maintenance of their secrecy. He encountered a judge not easily panicked by talk of the danger of war, and a jury not convinced that the defendant's actions came within the prevailing definition of theft. Nevertheless, in agreeing with the acquittal, the judge joined with the prosecution's condemnation of the violation of the code of a gentleman: 'he could not refrain from expressing his surprise that a man who had filled the position in society of Mr. Guernsey should have been guilty of such an act.'[27] Although Guernsey was not in fact a civil servant but an unsuccessful applicant who had stolen the documents from the Colonial Office library as an act of revenge, his unpunished crime posted a warning about the efficacy of both the emerging administrative ethos and the existing legal structure.[28] Despite the Larceny Act of 1861, which specifically extended the law of theft to cover official documents, the flow of material to the newspapers continued, giving rise to growing concern that the honour of government employees was not proving an adequate defence against the blandishments of ever-more aggressive editors.

Matters came to a head in June 1873. On the third of the month, following a leak concerning, as it happened, the salaries of letter-carriers, Lingen took the unprecedented step of issuing a general Treasury Minute to all departments on the subject of disclosing information. This document laid out the four basic assumptions which were to inform the Government's concept of official secrecy throughout all the subsequent legislation. In the first place, the problem was seen as one of process rather than substance. 'I am directed by the Lords Commissioners of Her Majesty's Treasury', Lingen began, 'to state that their attention has been called to certain cases which have recently occurred, in which information derived from an official source has been communicated without authority to the public press apparently by members of the Civil Service.'[29] The issue was not the content of the information, nor any identifiable damage that had been caused, but the fact that it had been transmitted without the explicit or implicit sanction of the appropriate official. With permission, there was no clear limit to what could be said; in its absence, there were no legal, constitutional, or ethical requirements to say anything at all.

Secondly, the major threat was seen to be internal rather than external. From the Guernsey case through to the 1911 Act and beyond, the issue of national se-

---

[26] Robertson, *Public Secrets*.

[27] *The Times* (16 Dec. 1858).

[28] On the development of the civil service corporate ethos, see Donajgrodzki, 'New Roles for Old: The Northcote–Trevelyan Report and the Clerks of the Home Office 1822–48', 100–6.

[29] *Premature Publication of Official Documents. Treasury Minute* (13 Mar. 1884), PP 1884, LXII, App. No. 1, *Minute of 1873*, 335. Also Robertson, *Public Secrets*, 52–4.

curity was frequently invoked to justify the enforcement or extension of restrictions, but the consistent, central apprehension was of the domestic press and its readership. Lingen was concerned less with the integrity of national frontiers and more with the strength of the boundaries between the government and the governed. The Minute was designed to ensure that ministers and their senior advisors ceded as little control as possible over the flow of information to journalists and the public for whom they wrote.

Thirdly, unlicensed communication was held to be a mortal rather than a venial sin. The loss of grace incurred by any such infraction of the bureaucratic code was total and irreversible. 'My Lords are of opinion', wrote Lingen with characteristic delicacy, 'that such breaches of official confidence are offences of the very gravest character which a public officer can commit, and they will not hesitate in any case where they themselves possess the power of dismissal, to visit such an offence with this extreme penalty.'[30] Having spent several decades establishing the main features of a modern career structure,[31] including job security, incremental progression, formal promotion procedures, and retirement pensions, the Government was now about to beat its ploughshare into a sword. The benefits of official employment were to become the principal means of imposing discipline within the civil service. If it still seemed improper to threaten professional gentlemen with prison, it was entirely feasible to present them with the prospect of unemployment and the loss of a reliable income in old age.

Finally, the honour of the civil service was seen as both the means and the end of the maintenance of secrecy. Lingen's phrase 'official confidence' had a double charge. It referred at once to the confidentiality of the information, and to the faith the public vested in the discretion of officials. The reputation of the bureaucracy stood as the bulwark against unauthorized disclosure and the major victim of any lapse. The argument was essentially self-referential. The rights of the population at large were presented solely in terms of their need to trust in the machinery of state. Their role was to demand standards of conduct, not bodies of information. The Minute concluded:

My Lords, in communicating their views upon this subject to the Heads of Departments, do so in full confidence that they are representing the public opinion of the Service itself which may be trusted to check practices injurious to its character for fidelity and honour, as soon as attention has been called to their existence.[32]

A fortnight after the circulation of the Treasury Minute, Lingen and Lowe were finally forced to give way to the mounting Parliamentary concern about

---

[30] PP 1884, LXII, p. 356.

[31] For a full discussion of the contemporary developments in career structures, see H. Jayaweera, A. Miles, M. Savage, and D. Vincent, *Pathways and Prospects: The Development of the Modern Bureaucratic Career, 1850–1950* (Cambridge, forthcoming).

[32] PP 1884, LXII, p. 356.

their treatment of the writers, and for the second time in their careers a Select Committee was called to investigate their actions.[33] This took evidence from the aggrieved parties, and reported after six weeks that the loss of employment rights had so undermined their morale that it was seriously affecting the performance of their duties. 'Men will not work without hope', warned the Committee,[34] and their 'sense of injustice' was acting as a powerful disincentive to loyal service.[35] Neither the public airing of the complaints, nor a subsequent concession to let recent recruits to sit an examination for the permanent grades, did anything to resolve the difficulty.[36] It was proving impossible to re-allocate the ever-increasing body of routine copying work amongst the relatively well-educated and well-paid Second Division Clerks, and there seemed no way of reconciling the conflicting requirements of economy and discipline. The less the government paid its employees, the less it could rely on their loyalty.

Two years later there was another double-handed approach to the problems. In February Lingen issued a further Minute on premature publication, drawing attention to

the fact that several members of the Civil Service have openly connected themselves with the public press, either as editors or members of the staffs of newspapers, or as Directors of a Company which has undertaken the publication of a periodical much engaged in the discussion of matters relating to the Civil Service.[37]

Those 'gentlemen' who 'communicated to the public journals without the sanction of the responsible heads of Departments', were once more threatened with 'instant dismissal'.[38] In 1875 the first report of the Playfair Commission on the Civil Service was published, which addressed once more the fact that 'the amount of simple routine work in the bulk of public Offices is very great in proportion to the amount of work of a higher class'.[39] Its solution was to restrict the number of those now termed 'Regulation One Clerks', who performed tasks 'which need high social and educational attainments',[40] to make the 'Regulation Two Clerks' a larger and more distinct entity, and to outline a possible solution to the lowest grade of work by creating a new class of 'boy clerks' and welcoming the Post Office's experiment of employing women for such tasks.

In the meantime, both the leaks and the unestablished writers persisted. In every respect, Marvin was a disaster waiting to happen. His inferior social

---

[33] The Select Committee on Civil Service Writers reported on 30 July 1893.
[34] *Report from the Select Committee on Civil Service Writers*, 24.
[35] PP 1873, XI, p. 21.
[36] *First Report of the Civil Service Inquiry Commission* [Playfair] (1875), PP 1875, XXIII, pp. 6–12.
[37] PP 1884, LXII, App. 2, p. 356.
[38] Ibid.
[39] PP 1875, XXIII, p. 14.
[40] Ibid. 6.

status and highly active journalism represented all Lingen's fears made flesh. He united in one unapologetic and seemingly immune form the twin threat of mass communication and the low-born. The two existing Minutes might as well have been written on water for all the notice that had been taken of them. Nonetheless in 1884, following the appearance in the newspapers of General Gordon's appointment to the Sudan before it had been circulated to MPs, Lingen made one last effort to deal with the issue by internal regulation. A third Treasury Minute was drafted and laid before Parliament, together with its two predecessors. This sought to clarify any lingering confusion by emphasizing that the prohibition applied not just to matters under discussion but to agreed decisions, and that the misdemeanour was embodied in the fact of improper communication rather than the communication of improper facts. In a sure sign of weakness, Lingen resorted to italics to make his point:

The First Lord and the Chancellor of the Exchequer state to the Board that in their opinion, in all these cases, *the publication without authority, of official information* constitutes the offence; and that the danger, to which all Governments are equally exposed by it, cannot be adequately guarded against if distinctions are allowed to be drawn between one kind of unauthorised publication and another.[41]

Although the wording changed, this blanket definition of official secrecy was at the heart of all the Acts which followed. In a manner which was to be rehearsed by governments of every persuasion in the coming century, Lingen was forbidding not only the unsanctioned release of information, but all debate about its consequences. Any attempt to measure the damage of a given disclosure would undermine the entire edifice of honourable secrecy. It would shift the burden of proof from the interests of the civil service to the rights of those they were supposed to serve, and invite every last copyist to make a stand on behalf of the people. Unless discretion was itself discreet, indiscipline would be doubled.

Alongside the renewed attempt to cut off the unauthorized supply of material to the newspapers, the Government sought to extend its influence over the demand for official information. With a further extension of the franchise about to be implemented, there was no longer any prospect of returning to the uncomplicated ways of the first half of the nineteenth century, when the Treasury could attempt to purchase the loyalty of sections of the political press. The era of mass politics had now arrived, and it was necessary to develop less overt means of suborning newspaper editors, who were increasingly prone to see themselves not so much as clients of parties and their leaders, and more as representatives of a vague but powerful entity called the people.[42] The more far-sighted faction leaders, led by Joseph Chamberlain, began to create permanent

---

[41] PP 1884, LXII, p. 355.

[42] S. Koss, *The Rise and Fall of the Political Press in Britain*, Vol. 1, *The Nineteenth Century* (London, 1981), 215–87, 418.

political machines, which sought to establish a regular means of communication with the expanding electorate. It was now too expensive and undemocratic to own or bribe individual newspapers, so instead politicians increasingly bought their loyalty with the cheap and intangible currency of inside knowledge.[43] Leaking to the press became, and was to remain, the most plastic of practices, a natural extension of democratic communication or a vicious corruption of the governing process depending on the pronoun employed by the commentator. Stimulated by the competitive ventures of the separate parties, the state itself took a decisive step to institutionalize the process in 1884 by establishing the lobby system. Preferred journalists were licensed by the Speaker to operate behind the barriers which excluded the remainder of their profession, thus exchanging the prospect of genuine independence for the possibility of privileged access to the parts of the corridors of power those in authority were prepared to illuminate.[44]

The moment of the Third Reform Act in 1884 represented the high tide of the attempt to control the dissemination of sensitive information by non-statutory devices alone. Already Britain was beginning to retreat from the elevated moral ground it had occupied for a half a century, when it had measured its superiority over continental Europe by the absence of the paraphernalia of state secrecy. Eighteen eighty-four was the first full year of operation of the Irish Branch of the Metropolitan Police, which marked the rebirth of political surveillance on the mainland.[45] The requirement for a department to undertake espionage against internal enemies of public order was a product of the Fenian bombing campaign which had been gathering momentum since 1881, and of the creation of a secret intelligence organization in Dublin in 1882 which rapidly exposed the lack of a comparable service in London.[46] But the manner in which it was created and managed owed everything to the established domestic convention of shrouding secrecy in secrecy.

Neither the temporary Irish Branch, nor the permanent Special Branch which emerged alongside it in 1887 and took over its work three years later, possessed any specific authorization from Parliament, or any line of reporting to the government as a whole. Indeed, the control of the handful of secret policemen who were hastily recruited from the perimeters of the Empire, confirmed the emergence of the practice of erecting barriers to communication within the inner workings of the state itself. By this time the doctrine of Cabinet secrecy was fully established. It was given a standard defence by *The Times* in 1878:

The Cabinet is a Committee of Council, and the propriety of keeping its deliberation secret is obvious. This select body of statesmen, who constitute the Government of

---

[43] J. F. Naylor, *A Man and an Institution: Sir Maurice Hankey, the Cabinet Secretariat and the Custody of Cabinet Secrecy* (Cambridge, 1984), 41.

[44] Hennessy, *Whitehall*, 364.

[45] Porter, *Origins of the Vigilant State*, 35–49.

[46] C. Townshend, *Political Violence in Ireland* (Oxford, 1983), 170–2.

the nation, must discuss many questions of policy on which their opinions are frequently divided; and it would be impossible that their confidential intercourse could be maintained and the administrations of public affairs conducted as the interest of the country requires if it were not a point of honour as well as a principle of law among the members of the Cabinet that their deliberations be kept secret.[47]

However, there were beginning to be secrets not just between the inner and outer circles of government, but within the select body itself. Salisbury, who first became Foreign Secretary in the same year as *The Times*'s pronouncement, consolidated the tradition of marking the covers of official telegrams with the names of ministers permitted to see them.[48] It was becoming accepted that in the name of national security, not all members of the Cabinet would know the substance of the secrets they were charged with keeping.

Below the ministerial level, doubts were growing whether honour reinforced by departmental regulation could hold the line much longer. Exactly three years after the final Treasury Minute, the long struggle to avoid legislation was finally abandoned. In March 1887 the government's resolve was broken by the publication in the newspapers of secret instructions to the Naval Intelligence Department, followed just a week later by the dismissal of a draughtsman in Chatham Dockyard 'for betraying the trust reposed in him by selling information acquired by him in his official capacity'.[49] The twin breaches of security, especially the second, which involved the possible loss of warship designs to a foreign power, exposed the First Lord of the Admiralty to an embarrassing interrogation in Parliament. The key questions were put by the Conservative MP Robert Hanbury:

What classes of officials or workmen engaged at Chatham or other public Dockyards are employed in positions of confidence and secrecy; who are permitted to possess information of a confidential nature which has a money value; what precautions are taken as to character, or by means of an oath or some other binding engagement, to guard against a breach of trust; and, what are the lowest salaries or wages paid to any of such persons.[50]

It was impossible to supply a reassuring response. The dockyards presented an extreme form of concern about secrecy, not only because their business was so vital to national defence, but also because they employed so large a proportion of the lower white-collar and manual workers in the civil service. The great majority of these clerks and artisans were a potential security risk. 'All officials,' admitted the First Lord, 'and many of the workmen, are necessarily in

[47] *The Times* (13 Apr. 1878).

[48] P. Gordon Walker, 'Secrecy and Openness in Foreign Policy Decision-Making: A British Cabinet Perspective', in T. M. Franck and E. Weisbrand (eds.), *Secrecy and Foreign Policy* (New York, 1974), 44.

[49] *Hansard*, 3rd Ser., CCCXI, 10 Mar. 1887, col. 1745.

[50] Ibid., CCCXII, 11 Mar. 1887, col. 20. Hanbury was the Member for Preston, and eventually became President of the Board of Agriculture in 1900.

possession of information relating to the work upon which they are employed that is more or less confidential.'[51] Whilst 'only men of the best character are promoted or placed in positions of trust',[52] it was impossible to offer cast-iron guarantees about their behaviour, especially in so large an establishment as an Admiralty dockyard. The repeated incidence of improper communication was clear evidence that 'means ... recently adopted which it was hoped would have stopped the supply of information to the public except through authorized channels'[53] were not proving effective, particularly where there was so large a gap between responsibility and pay. The reluctant answer to Hanbury's final question was five shillings a day.

The government was now caught between irreconcilable objectives. It wished to avoid further Parliamentary inquisitions on so sensitive a matter, but could only placate the mounting anxiety of Members by undergoing the public process of legislation. There were, therefore, two announcements at the end of the debate. First ministers would henceforth abandon Lingen's recent innovation of tabling departmental regulations. Any further additions to the Treasury Minutes would be not be brought to the House, 'because any publicity thus occasioned might defeat their object'.[54] Secondly, there would be a Bill to provide penal sanctions for breaches of official trust.[55] This was a momentous step. For the first time since the Mazzini affair, the state's conception and enforcement of secrecy would have to be openly defined and discussed. Since 1844 it had done its best to keep the issue beneath the political horizon, and only its failure to stem the haemorrhage of its privy information had forced it into the legal arena. All that could now be done was to restrict to a minimum the debate over the passage of the Bill.

As was to be the case in 1911, great care was taken with the drafting of the Bill. Work started on the text in July 1887,[56] but it was nearly two years before the Government felt confident enough to engineer its passage through Parliament. As was also to be the case in 1911, there were separate clauses dealing with overseas espionage and domestic leaking, and every effort was made to distract attention from the latter by dramatizing the former. Early drafts had been variously entitled 'Breach of Official Trust Bill' and 'The Public Documents Act',[57] but by the time the legislation was brought to the House of Commons, the emphasis had shifted from the general issue of confidentiality to the particular problem of spying and the associated military dangers. What was now termed the 'Official Secrets Bill' was presented as the exclusive prod-

[51] *Hansard*, 3rd Ser., CCCXII, 11 Mar. 1887, col. 20.
[52] Ibid., col. 21.
[53] Ibid., CCCXI, 3 Mar. 1887, col. 1083.
[54] Ibid., CCCXIII, 5 Apr. 1887, col. 488.
[55] Ibid., col. 488.
[56] PRO, T[/8308B/16646.
[57] *Departmental Committee on Section 2 of the Official Secrets Act 1911* [Franks] (London, 1972), Cmnd. 5104, i. 121 PRO, T[/8308B/16646.

uct of those in charge of the nation's defences. The Second Reading was commended by the Attorney-General in the following terms:

Sir, I wish to say just a word or two with regard to this Bill. It has been prepared under the direction of the Secretary of State for War and the First Lord of the Admiralty, in order to punish the offence of obtaining information, and communicating it, against the interests of the State. The Bill is an exceedingly simple one, and I beg to move its second Reading.'[58]

In reality, Clause 2 represented a complex and carefully worded extension of the criminal law into the activities of not only current but also retired civil servants. They were exposed to prosecution if they transmitted any document to any person who 'ought not' to receive it.[59] An attempt to define the boundary of permissible communication in terms of the 'interests of any department of the Government' was withdrawn after protests from the persistent Hanbury that this would frustrate the necessary exposure of administrative shortcomings, and instead the line was drawn by reference to the vaguer and less contentious concept of 'the interest of the State or otherwise in the public interest'. The debate was short in the Commons, and shorter still in the Lords, where the threat posed by the 'Queen's enemies' dominated the Government's presentation.[60] Speed was all. Public secrecy became a legal entity with barely a ripple of public discussion.

Poor Visiting

The issue of official secrecy legislation stemmed in large part from the growing requirement to recruit to government offices those whose breeding, education, and pay excluded them from the rank of gentleman. The reverse of this problem was how far the expansion of the democratic state affected the freedom of the mass of the population to conceal their thoughts and actions, and whether it was prudent to employ the law either to defend or prohibit their secrets. In its modern form, this debate had been gathering momentum since 1832, and nowhere more obviously than in the exercise of the franchise itself. By the beginning of the period covered by this chapter, the secret ballot had been on the Parliamentary agenda for more than three decades.[61] The eventual passage of the Ballot Act in 1872 is generally viewed as an inevitable milestone along the road to a full democracy, but in fact the reform was regarded with the utmost misgiving not just by those hostile to any extension of the political

---

[58] *Hansard*, 3rd Ser., CCCXXXV, 28 Mar. 1889, col. 1110.
[59] For the text of the Bill, see PP 1889, VI.
[60] *Hansard*, 3rd Ser., CCCXXXVIII, 11 July 1889, col. 85.
[61] The fullest survey of the debate is found in B. L. Kinzer, *The Ballot Question in Nineteenth-Century English Politics* (New York, 1982).

nation, but by many of the leading liberal politicians and thinkers of the day. It was by no means self-evident that protecting the individual voter from the scrutiny of his peers and betters was either safe or necessary. Here, as elsewhere, the intervention of the law was seen to be, in Gladstone's words, 'a choice of evils'.[62]

From the outset, critics of the secret ballot were at pains to stress how it conflicted with the progressive tendencies of the new era. Contributors to the first major Parliamentary debate in 1838 placed the reform in opposition to the historical process. 'It is a system', claimed one speaker, 'totally at variance with all the institutions, usages, and feelings of the people of this country, with all the maxims which have taught them to believe that free discussion, that publicity, that the light of day, that public opinion, are the great checks upon abuse.'[63] The consequence of such abuse would be the erosion of public morality. Instead of enhancing the power of the newly enfranchised, making the ballot secret would destroy their integrity and with it the justification for entrusting them with the privilege of taking part in elections. 'If you accustom the voter to the violation of a solemn promise,' warned another speaker, 'if you make him believe that a lie told to a landlord is of little comparative consequence, you will dearly purchase the advantage of a secret vote, at the price of promises disregarded—truth habitually violated—the sense of honour destroyed, and self-esteem extinguished.'[64] Conservatives whose perspective began and ended with the threatened landlord were joined by liberals who fervently believed that the expansion of open communication lay at the root of social and political advance. 'The moral sentiment of mankind,' wrote John Stuart Mill,

in all periods of tolerably enlightened morality, has condemned concealment, unless when required by some overpowering motive; and if it be one of the paramount objects of national education to foster courage and public spirit, it is high time now that people should be taught the duty of asserting and acting openly on their opinions. Disguise in all its forms is a badge of slavery.[65]

At the centre of the argument was the concept of trust. Proponents of the secret ballot asserted that the vote was a species of private property which the possessor had a right to dispose of as he pleased, guided only by his inner reason and conscience. Just as he was free to enjoy without interference from his neighbours the house or land which qualified him for the franchise, so he should be able to choose his Member of Parliament without surveillance or intimidation. The defenders of open voting deplored this atomistic view of the political culture. Their position, which was most closely identified with Lord Palmerston, a major obstacle to reform until his death in 1865, was that the

---

[62] Cited by Assheton Cross in *Hansard*, 3rd Ser., CCVII, 22 June 1871, col. 413.
[63] Ibid., XL, 15 Feb. 1838, col. 1203.
[64] Ibid., col. 1212.
[65] Mill, 'Thoughts on Parliamentary Reform', 337.

franchise was held in trust for the community at large.[66] The minority who were granted the privilege had a duty to exercise it on behalf of the majority who were not. If they failed to do so, the unequal distribution of power would become untenable. They were under a positive obligation to discuss their decision with those amongst whom they lived, and to demonstrate beyond doubt that they had cast their vote in accordance with their professed intention. Hiding the action in an enclosed booth sowed suspicion amongst fellow voters and alienated the unenfranchised from the entire electoral process. 'You are changing what is a public duty', warned the former Home Secretary Gathorne-Hardy on the eve of reform, '—for which the elector is responsible—first to his conscience and then to his neighbours and everybody about him, into a system of distrust, and in its place you are making hypocrisy an absolute duty.'[67]

Although there was much discussion of the moral peril to which the existing elite would be exposed, the real concern was with the labouring population whose enfranchisement was set in motion by the Second Reform Act. They had most need of the protection offered by secrecy, and it was the nature of their reaction to legally sanctioned privacy which most exercised commentators. As Beresford Hope put it in 1871, 'for a voter in the higher classes the Ballot is of no value whatever. It is a poor man's question. It is a social question.'[68] Above all, it was a question of whether the lower sections of society would now be placed beyond the supervision and influence of their better-born and educated superiors. Mill was converted from an early enthusiasm for the secret ballot to a forthright opposition by his growing apprehension that new voters, when left to their own, unobserved devices, would consult neither their best selves nor the best available advice. In his 'Thoughts on Parliamentary Reform' he warned that: 'People will give dishonest or mean votes from lucre, from malice, from pique, from personal rivalry, from the interests or prejudices of class or sect, far more readily in secret than in public.'[69] Such an innovation would inhibit the active discussion of contemporary issues which was crucial to the education of the politically illiterate, and substitute for the fading role of the old ruling order malignant class loyalties which dared not speak their name in public. Instead of accelerating the integration of society into a single political nation, shrouding the ballot in secrecy would erect still-higher barriers to communication between the propertied and the propertyless. The widespread apprehension, shared by many who were now about to support the reform, was summarized by the Conservative MP Stephen Cave in the penultimate debate on the issue: 'it was said that the different classes in this country never knew the real feelings, the inner life of each other; that there was a reserve they never

[66] See Gladstone's full and sympathetic summary of Palmerston's position in *Hansard*, 3rd Ser., CCIII, 27 July, 1870, cols. 1029–30.

[67] Ibid., CCVII, 26 June, 1871, col. 572.

[68] Ibid., col. 597. See also the arguments that George Cornewall Lewis puts into the mouth of 'Democraticus' in his *A Dialogue on the Best Form of Government* (London, 1863), 84.

[69] Mill, 'Thoughts on Parliamentary Reform', 336.

penetrated. That was a misfortune which this new element could not fail to intensify.'[70]

Eventually, the Liberal Government which took office after the Second Reform Act was forced to accept that this was a risk which had to be taken. Despite earlier optimism, traditional forms of rural intimidation had not faded into insignificance, especially in Ireland, whose problems were now rising up the political agenda at Westminster.[71] In the towns, newly enfranchised voters faced fresh species of pressure from employers and customers, and lacked, for the most part, the protection against harassment afforded by the possession of property. So far from declining in the face of free communication, electoral corruption appeared to be flourishing in the conditions of modern democracy. At the same time, technical obstacles to reform, such as the possible illiteracy of new voters, were receding. Versions of secret voting were now successfully employed elsewhere in the world, particularly in Australia, and in some domestic contexts, such as elections to the London School Board. Gladstone's attitude turned on the issue of trust. Long an upholder of Palmerston's position, he came to realize that the prospect of universal suffrage, at least for men, had decisively altered the landscape of the debate: 'there is', he conceded 'no longer, properly so called, a limited constituency acting and exercising a trust on behalf of the whole people.'[72] All that remained for the voter was 'a trust which he holds on behalf of his wife and children'.[73] Where virtual representation was now inappropriate across the community at large, it was fully acceptable within the domestic arena. As participation in elections was driven off the streets, the private role of the voter became the key to his political being.[74] Women stayed at home in elections, while their husbands went out to vote in silence. The working-class male head of household, who had gained the vote in the boroughs in 1867, became the fellow citizen of the upper- and middle-class *paterfamilias*. Patriarchy replaced property as the guarantor of responsible and rational conduct in the public sphere.[75]

In *A New Defence of the Ballot*, written for the Reform League in the aftermath of their 1867 triumph, George Holyoake made off with the language of his enemies: 'I am told that the vote is "a trust" then let me be *trusted* with it! I am not trusted so long as my use of it is watched.'[76] The independence of the respectable artisan, a key figure in the Liberal Party's response to mass democracy, required both the physical protection and the moral confidence of the state. The change of policy on the part of the Liberal leadership represented an

---

[70] *Hansard*, 3rd Ser., CCVII, 22 June 1871, col. 467.
[71] Kinzer, *The Ballot Question*, 78–9, 123–36.
[72] *Hansard*, 3rd Ser., CCIII, 27 July 1870, col. 1031.
[73] Ibid.
[74] J. Vernon, *Politics and the People* (Cambridge, 1993), 157–8.
[75] A. Clark, 'Gender, Class and the Constitution: Franchise Reform in England, 1832–1928', in J. Vernon (ed.), *Re-reading the Constitution* (Cambridge, 1996), 239–51.
[76] G. J. Holyoake, *A New Defence of the Ballot* (London, 1868), 5.

unpalatable concession to the forces of darkness. Forty years of open debate and broadening education had failed to eradicate the abuses inherited from the pre-Reform era. The shameful solitude of the voting booth proved that corruption was mightier than pure reason. All that could be argued was that there were contrasting categories of secrecy, and that viewed in its proper light, the ballot was a justifiable protection of the individual's 'personal interests in the state'.[77] Yet if the association of honour and privacy with the secret ballot restored a moral dimension to the reform, it left unresolved the impenetrable reserve of the enlarged electorate. Holyoake was celebrating precisely the state of affairs which most alarmed Mill and many other educated commentators, the capacity of any householder to resist contact with outside influence. On the particular issue of the electoral process, the position was now lost, but the ending of the long controversy over the ballot coincided with a new and far more ambitious phase of the practice of calling upon the residences of the poor in order to expose their inner life to the guidance of well-meaning superiors.

In the midst of the passage of the Second Reform Act, Mill made the first serious attempt to extend the franchise to women. The failure of his amendment ensured their continuing exclusion from the political sphere, and instead their energies and social concern were channelled into the home-visiting movement which reached its peak in the final quarter of the nineteenth century. During this period, almost every urban parish spawned one or more visiting societies, almost every middle-class woman felt compelled to make at least an occasional call on her less fortunate sisters, and virtually every poor household was invaded by outsiders who, in Holyoake's terms, frequently appeared both intrusive and impertinent.[78] It was a well-established proceeding. Women, and occasionally men, had been leaving the comfort of their firesides to distribute small material benefits and large moral lessons since the beginning of the Evangelical revival.[79] There was a widespread sense that the new urban communities presented uncharted dangers, but also unprecedented opportunities for what Robert Vaughan described as 'spontaneous benevolence'.[80] Mrs Pardiggle with her tracts in hand had cast a shadow over many a working-class threshold before the 1870s.[81] What gave the movement its late-nineteenth-century form was partly the sheer scale of the endeavour, which

[77] Holyoake, A New Defence of the Ballot, 4.

[78] F. K. Prochaska, Women and Philanthropy in Nineteenth-Century England (Oxford, 1980), 97–137; J. Lewis, Women and Social Action in Victorian and Edwardian England (Aldershot, 1991), 32–46, 303–8; M. Brasnett, Voluntary Social Action (London, 1969), 4–15.

[79] A. F. Young and E. T. Ashton, British Social Work in the Nineteenth Century (London, 1956), 88–90; A. Summers, 'A Home from Home—Women's Philanthropic Work in the Nineteenth Century', in S. Burman (ed.), Fit Work for Women (London, 1979), 35–41. For an early guide to this work, see The Ladies' Companion for Visiting the Poor (London, 1813), which contained a perceptive estimation of the value of the charity the poor gave to the poor (p. xii).

[80] R. Vaughan, The Age of Great Cities (London, 1843), 298.

[81] See Dickens's angry satire on the insensitive and intrusive visitor of the poor in Bleak House, esp. Ch. 8, pp. 95–106.

represented the last great effort to penetrate by direct personal contact what Dickens described as the 'iron barrier' between the classes,[82] and partly the sophistication of its organization. Poor visiting was founded in reaction to a collectivist approach to social deprivation, but was driven to adopt collective means of managing the work by the immense ambition of the enterprise. Over time, this transition raised acute and eventually insoluble difficulties about the rights to secrecy of the subjects of the visitations.

The essence of the visitor's mission was that the poor, as Octavia Hill wrote, 'must be dealt with as individuals, by individuals'.[83] They should not be treated simply as categories by public officials or by socialist agitators. They were neither paupers nor revolutionary cadres, but unique personalities living in separate families, each one of which possessed its particular history, its complex present, and its unpredictable hopes for the future.[84] Personal communication was all. Charles Bosanquet, the first secretary of the Charity Organisation Society (COS), argued that 'the marked separation between the classes in England makes it especially desirable to promote intercourse amongst them',[85] and this was best achieved if the generalities of religious and social teaching were embodied and transmitted by a representative individual in the actual home of the troubled family. Undifferentiated alms-giving demoralized those in distress, incarceration in the workhouse deprived them of the dignity which was the basis of self-respect. The only effective mechanism was, in the words of Mary Steer of the Female Mission to the Fallen, a 'merging of our lives with theirs'.[86] This opening of hearts was to be conducted within clear limits. The visitors were not expected to reveal their deepest secrets, neither was it anticipated that their inmost beings would be reconstructed by the encounter. On the other hand, it was essential that every last facet of the private lives of their hosts be exposed to detailed commentary. It was an uneven relationship with only one end in view. 'I feel most deeply', urged Octavia Hill, 'that the disciplining of our immense poor population must be effected by individual influence.'[87]

The visit was designed to substitute one process of learning for another. Much of the compassion of the volunteers, and not a little of their fear was provoked by the vision of the vulnerable child receiving the worst sort of education in the overcrowded slums. In his 1883 study of *How the Poor Live*, G. R. Sims dwelt at length on 'the familiarity of the children of the poor with all manners of

---

[82] Dickens, *Bleak House*, Ch. 8, p. 103.

[83] O. Hill, *Homes of the London Poor* (2nd edn., 1883, repr. London, 1970), 56. Also C. S. Loch, *How to Help Cases of Distress* (London, 1883), 9.

[84] M. Roof, *A Hundred Years of Family Welfare* (London, 1972), 258; R. Humphreys, *Sin, Organized Charity and the Poor Law in Victorian England* (London, 1995), 53–5; Lewis, *Women and Social Action*, 38–9.

[85] C. Bosanquet, *A Handy Book for Visitors of the Poor in London* (London, 1874), 3. Also G. Stedman Jones, *Outcast London* (Harmondsworth, 1976), 241–61.

[86] M. H. Steer, 'Rescue Work by Women among Women', in Baroness Burdett-Coutts, *Women's Mission to Women* (London, 1893), 153.

[87] Hill, *Homes of the London Poor*, 25.

wickedness and crime. Of all the evils arising from this one-room system there is perhaps none greater than the utter destruction of innocence in the young.'[88] Incest was the unspoken sin at the heart of a mass of contemporary eyewitness accounts of the late-Victorian inner cities.[89] It was the ultimate degradation, the most secret of crimes which flourished in the most enclosed of environments. For as long as the poor had only the poor as instructors, for as long as the child had no other model but its already corrupted parents and elder siblings, there was no possibility of moral growth and development. There had long been a hope that the subsidized church schools would be able to counter the malign lessons of the domestic curriculum, but the Revised Code of 1862 marked the beginning of a scaling down of so large an ambition.[90] Although the elementary school system was made comprehensive in 1870 and fully compulsory ten years later, there was no longer an expectation that the schoolmaster alone could rectify the indoctrination which went on day and night in the homes of the fallen classes.

Instead, the educated outsider had to intervene to provide an alternative framework for the pattern of learning, particularly for those family members whose characters were at their most formative stage. However, to operate effectively as teachers, the visitors had first to become dedicated students of their subject-matter. If they were serious about their mission—and despite the mocking commentary of *Punch* most were—they were faced with a task which would challenge all their qualities of energy, intellect, and empathy. It was necessary to absorb every detail of the history of every member of the family, to piece together the intricate material and emotional relationships which bound the domestic unit together, and to establish the trajectory of its likely and possible development. This would require close and sensitive enquiry within the household, and further investigation amongst neighbours, past landlords, employers, tradesmen, and local clergy and relieving officers to check impressions and establish the economic and cultural context of the stories they were hearing.[91] In the experience of the former COS worker Beatrice Webb, the rigour of their search for often-concealed knowledge rendered them counterparts of the emerging body of criminal investigators: 'well-to-do men and women of goodwill who had gone out to offer personal service and friendship to the dwellers in the slums, found themselves transformed into a body of amateur detectives.'[92] The thoroughness of this approach was fundamental to the self-image

[88] G. R. Sims, *How the Poor Live* (London, 1883), 10. Also A. Mearns, *The Bitter Cry of Outcast London* (London, repr. London, 1870), 9; E. Bowmaker, *The Housing of the Working Class* (London, 1895), 13; T. Wright, *The Great Unwashed* (London, 1868), 149.

[89] See A. S. Wohl, 'Sex and the Single Room: Incest Among the Victorian Working Class', in id. (ed.), *The Victorian Family* (London, 1978), 197–218.

[90] Vincent, *Literacy and Popular Culture*, 86–8.

[91] Bosanquet, *A Handy Book for Visitors*, 11–14. On the scale of the neighbourhood enquiries, see J. Fido, 'The Charity Organisation Society and Social Casework in London 1869–1900', in A. P. Donajgrodzki, (ed.), *Social Control in Nineteenth-Century Britain* (London, 1977), 218.

[92] B. Webb, *My Apprenticeship* (Harmondsworth, 1938), i. 230.

of the movement. The depth and range of the programme of study formed the basis of its subsequent critique of the large-scale, and consequently superficial social surveys conducted by Booth, Rowntree, and their successors.[93]

The scale of the task and the size of the army of volunteers engaged in it, imposed a double requirement for organization. In the first case, the students had to be taught how to learn. Whilst a lengthy schooling, reinforced by the imperceptible instruction of the middle-class home, provided the basis of the volunteers' skills, it was necessary to give them a practical focus if the visiting was to be efficient and effective. Casual instruction by vicars or experienced fieldworkers in the parish gradually developed into a more formal pedagogy, particularly after the establishment of the Charity Organisation Society in 1869.[94] The guidance in what to ask about, how to conduct the questioning, and what to do with the resulting knowledge was embodied in training courses and in a series of instruction manuals which could be carried in the pockets of the visitors as they made their rounds.

Secondly, a system of record-keeping had to be established if the long-term process of surveillance and reconstruction was to be successfully undertaken and monitored. 'Scientific charity' required both human sympathy and good paperwork.[95] The visit only had value if it could be revisited by others. It was unrealistic to expect every individual caller to remain in permanent contact with a particular case, or to be personally possible for transmitting information to other professionals. They were, after all, volunteers, whose enthusiasm waxed and waned and who were vulnerable to illness and to other demands on their time, not least taking family holidays away from the district.[96] However, there were no intermissions in the lives of the poor, and it was important that there were no gaps in their treatment. There was an increasing recognition of the necessity of building up what Young and Ashton describe as 'a body of transmissible knowledge'[97] about the work of the visiting societies. Making a systematic and accessible note of what had been learned about a given family and about the progress of its treatment, was the only means of preventing waste of effort and unnecessary confusion as one visitor took over a case from another. *A Manual of Hints to Visiting Friends of the Poor* of 1871 instructed the volunteer in the need to inscribe their findings: 'Keep accurate your record of visits, and enter legibly in it any facts you may learn as to the condition of each family, so that if you have to relinquish the work your successor many know at once how to be

[93] C. Booth, *Life and Labour of the People in London* (London, 1889–1902); B. S. Rowntree, *Poverty: A Study of Town Life* (London, 1901). For a summary of the Charity Organisation Society's critique of quantitative social surveys, see C. S. Loch, *Charity and Social Life* (London, 1910), 386–7. Also Vincent, *Poor Citizens*, 31–4.

[94] Loch, *Charity and Social Work*, 402; Roof, *A Hundred Years of Family Welfare*, 275–7.

[95] On the centrality of record-keeping in the endeavours of the COS, see Humphreys, *Sin, Organised Charity and the Poor Law*, 136–7.

[96] In the somewhat jaundiced words of the report to the COS's First Committee on Training, the volunteers were 'away all summer and ill all winter'. Cited in Roof, *Hundred Years of Family Welfare*, 275.

[97] Young and Ashton, *British Social Work*, 104.

most useful in your place.'[98] To ensure consistency in the note-taking, *pro-forma* case-books were published, and offices and filing systems were set up for their storage and consultation.[99]

The consequence of giving, in the words of Angela Burdett-Coutts, 'collective form to efforts which were formerly left to individuals',[100] was that increasing attention began to be paid to the attitudes of the subjects of the investigations to their own privacy. The reflection on accumulated experience by often highly intelligent administrators and writers led for the first time to a serious consideration of the consequences of ignoring the interests that the poor might have in controlling the release of information about their circumstances. The earliest indication of a growing sensitivity was the frequent exhortation to inexperienced visitors to employ 'tact' in their inquiries. This developed into the beginnings of a proper technique of interviewing, which recognized that an oblique approach was always the most productive. 'One of the voluntary worker's most common duties', observed the health visitor Margaret Loane, 'must be the collection of full and trustworthy information, and in dealing with uneducated people it should constantly be remembered that it is useless to ask direct questions.'[101] It was not only that the poor were seen to lack the intellectual competence to structure their own life histories, but also that they were likely to resist too crude an assault on their most sensitive knowledge. There was a natural reserve in the face of outsiders, however well-meaning, which needed to be understood and respected. The more thoughtful observers began to grapple with the basic paradox which lay at the heart of their enterprise. They were engaged in the moral reconstruction of the fallen family by means so intrusive as to accelerate still further the collapse of its pride and dignity. 'There is already far too little independence amongst the London poor', warned Charles Bosanquet, and thus a constant danger that the 'inexperienced or undiscriminating Visitor' would 'destroy the little he may meet with.'[102] Nothing was more likely to frustrate the good intentions and hard labour of the volunteer than the clumsy or careless treatment of the confidences that the visit was designed to elicit. As the author of *Friendly Visiting Among the Poor* observed, unnecessary publicity about the household's affairs led to the 'destruction of the natural conditions of

[98] H. A. D. Surridge, *A Manual of Hints to Visiting Friends of the Poor* (London, 1871), 6. Also The Society for Organising Charitable Relief and Repressing Mendicity, *House-to-House Visitation* (London, 1871), 7.

[99] Young and Ashton, *British Social Work*, 89, 103–5; Fido, 'The Charity Organisation Society and Social Casework in London 1869–1900', 218. As an example of the new *pro-forma* aids, see *The District Visitor's Note Book* (London, 1866), which contained 150 pages of report forms followed by index pages. Space was given to record name, age, occupation, family, residence, schooling, place of worship, date of visit, relief given, and further remarks.

[100] Burdett Coutts, *Women's Mission to Women*, p. xvii. For a protest at the speed at which 'machinery and organisation are advancing', see the anonymous *District Visitors, Deaconesses* (London, 1890), 11.

[101] M. Loane, *Neighbours and Friends* (London, 1910), 12.

[102] Bosanquet, *A Handy Book for Visitors*, 6.

family life, and leaves behind a train of demoralisation that lasts long after the relief has been exhausted'.[103]

The caution applied not just to the conduct of the interviews, but to the subsequent use of the information which had been gleaned. 'Be scrupulously polite to all', enjoined the Reverend Surridge's *Manual of Hints*; 'deferential to the aged; very gentle with the sick; and keep faithfully all secrets that may be intrusted to you, either by the clergyman for the benefit of the people, or by the people for the counsel of the clergyman.'[104] It was not merely a matter of courtesy. Charles Bosanquet tempered his advice to the apprentice visitor with an urgent warning:

Listen to, and if possible, interest yourself in, what people are willing to say of their own concerns; but avoid repeating to others anything that you may have thus learnt, unless it be for the purpose of benefitting your informant. Disregard of this recommendation to reticence is often attended with the most disastrous consequences.[105]

The concern about keeping the secrets of the poor from the poor was a feature of the COS from its inception.[106] It was central to the attempt to inform the voluntary impulse with a degree of professional rigour. Good works required self-censorship. Drawing the line between responsible communication and careless gossip encapsulated the transition from the old style of casual inquiry to the new mode of systematic investigation. In the same period the contemporary code of conduct for the police forces stressed that the new recruit had to forswear the civilian's natural pleasure in gossip: 'The first duty of a police officer is to maintain absolutely secret (except to his superiors), all information he becomes possessed of, in his official capacity. Gossiping, even without any such intention, may wholly defeat the ends of justice, and be the cause of the greatest mischief.'[107] At the outset it was a matter of talking out of turn, but as bureaucracy invaded social work, so the issue of maintaining the secrecy of written records was raised. Octavia Hill was aware of the problem by the early 1880s, although with typical bravura she tried to dismiss it out of hand:

The privacy of the poor is not infringed by the use of these records, since the books remain exclusively in the hands of the visitors and referee, and it rests with the visitor to report of the committee only that which she deems essential to the right decision of the case. And, moreover, nothing of a private nature—nothing which could imply a breach of confidence—ought ever to be entered in the books at all.[108]

---

[103] M. E. Richmond, *Friendly Visiting Among the Poor* (London, 1899), 147.

[104] Surridge, *Manual of Hints*, 5.

[105] Bosanquet, *A Handy Book for Visitors*, 6. Also C. Neil, *The Christian Visitor's Handbook* (London, 1882), 31–2.

[106] Roof, *A Hundred Years of Family Welfare*, 238.

[107] C. E. Howard Vincent, *A Police Code and Manual of the Criminal Law* (London, 1881), 333.

[108] Hill, *Homes of the London Poor*, 64.

However, as time went by it became less easy to recognize the distinction between personal details which were and were not confidential, and more likely that the records would be stored in a central location away from the immediate control of those by whom and for whom originally they had been written.

In general, the growing concern about confidentiality was confined to the release of information to other members of the respondent's family and neighbourhood, and to the unresolved issue of whether it was acceptable to approach employers and tradesmen without first asking permission of the individual concerned.[109] Much less consideration was given to communication between the volunteers and other professionals. Indeed, in so far as the parish visitors were initially viewed as the eyes and ears of the vicar, they had a positive duty to share their discoveries with him.[110] Furthermore, bodies such as the COS were called into being precisely in order to co-ordinate the work of the church, the police, the doctors, the school-board visitors, and the Poor Law authorities, which implied open access to all the case histories. The committees of the COS branches brought together in a common enterprise representatives of all the senior professions in the area.[111] The whole point of inscribing, indexing, and storing the records was to facilitate co-operation over individual families and prevent waste of effort. The visitors were actively encouraged to exchange notes with those whose work brought them into contact with the families for which they were responsible. 'If you should meet any of the medical men who attend the poor in your district,' advised the Reverend Surridge, 'endeavour to establish friendly relations with them. You will find none who have more insight than they into the character and condition of the poor, and, as a rule, none who will aid your work more heartily by valuable hints and information.'[112] As was noted in the previous chapter,[113] the Hippocratic Oath was applied last and least to intercourse within the local elite. The possibilities of improper communication between doctor and vicar in a rural parish were multiplied by the attempt to orchestrate the work of the welfare and surveillance agencies in the urban communities. In the short term there was little reaction to the complex problems that were being created. The established professionals had too little respect for the volunteer workers to take seriously the status of their case records; the visiting societies had too urgent a task on their hands to place additional obstacles in the way of greater collaboration.

In the longer term, the continuing dialectic of experiment and reflection forced a sharper awareness of the significance of privacy within the communities of the urban poor. By the first decade of the twentieth century the

---

[109] Fido, 'The Charity Organisation Society and Social Casework in London 1869–1900', 221.
[110] 'H. F.', *Hints to District Visitors* (London, 1858), 4.
[111] Humphreys, *Sin, Organized Charity and the Poor Law*, 64.
[112] Surridge, *Manual of Hints*, 10–11.
[113] See above, pp. 51–6.

more perceptive theorists of the nascent social work movement were beginning to stress that the classes were united rather than divided by an overriding concern to control the dissemination of domestic secrets. Seclusion was in its way as relevant to the seething slums as it was to the detached villas on the leafy outskirts of the towns and cities.[114] Intricate, invisible communication frontiers criss-crossed the overcrowded houses and packed terraces. Husbands said little to their wives about what they earned, wives kept to themselves their devices to make the little they had go further.[115] What brought the family together was its joint resistance to the prying tongues of their endlessly inquisitive neighbours. Margaret Loane, one of the new breed of professional health visitors, observed in 1908 that: 'Secrecy is strongly developed among the poor, and although often sustained by deceitfulness and even fraud, is closely connected with self-respect and independence. Wages and the expenditure of money are always shrouded in thick darkness.'[116] The descent from respectable to rough, from indigence to real poverty, could be measured by the decline in the family's capacity to conceal its problems from outsiders.[117] Physical signs of deprivation began to show in faces and clothes, overstretched budgets were exposed by furtive visits to the pawnbroker. The workhouse was the final defeat, and was intended to be so, precisely because it was the most public form of relief.[118]

The interdependence of privacy and respectability presented the manager of a troubled domestic economy with an insoluble problem. The more she strove to maintain the status of the family, the more isolated she became from the sources of support in the neighbourhood which alone could prevent its total collapse.[119] It also presented a major difficulty to the outsiders who sought to render assistance. The strategy of the Charity Organisation Society and its sister bodies was founded on strengthening the division between rough and respectable families.[120] The task of the visitor was to distinguish one from the other in order that resources might be concentrated where there was a real prospect of success. Loane's perception implied either that the sought-after family would be the most effective in resisting inquiry, or that it would suffer the most damage from intrusion into its affairs. The dilemma could be resolved

[114] The strength of domestic privacy amongst the lower orders often struck foreign observers. See e.g. C. Peters, *England and the English* (London, 1904), 279–80, which contrasted English with German society.

[115] Vincent, *Poor Citizens*, 14.

[116] M. Loane, *From their Point of View* (London, 1908), 74–5.

[117] Webb, *My Apprenticeship*, ii. 325.

[118] For a detailed account of an eventually unsuccessful attempt to avoid the humiliation of exposure by a family whose poverty was forcing it towards the workhouse, see F. Steel, *Ditcher's Row* (London, 1939), 57, 72–8.

[119] E. Ross, '"Not the Sort that Would Sit on the Doorstep"; Respectability in Pre-World War London Neighbourhoods', *International Labor and Working Class History*, 27 (Spring 1985), 52.

[120] Stedman Jones, *Outcast London*, 303.

by either collapsing or increasing the gulf between the poor and their benefactors. The former path led to the settlement movement, a yet more labour-intensive and self-sacrificial attempt to penetrate the iron barrier, whereby volunteers sought to make contact with distressed families not as visitors but as neighbours.[121] They would learn, not by asking questions but by living alongside the victims of progress, and teach as much by example as by explicit instruction.

The latter path led in one of two directions, both of which propelled the response to poverty away from the voluntarist attack on the enclosed working-class community. The first was to intensify the professionalization of poor visiting which had been under way since the 1870s. Margaret Loane drew confidence from the possibility that the properly trained visitor, alert to the sensitivities of her subjects, might be exempted from the restrictions imposed on those who lived in permanent proximity to the distressed household. As she wrote in a later study:

Reticence is developed to an extraordinary degree among the heroic members of the poorest classes: 'Not to let any one know your business,' is at once a duty, a joy, a burden, an absorbing occupation, and a consolation. It is often practised more strictly with regard to near neighbours than with regard to educated visitors.[122]

There was no more talk of merging lives. Rather, it was the disciplined otherness of the welfare worker that was expected to open the jealously guarded door to the family's secrets. There was still a place for volunteers, but their autonomy was in sharp decline. As the early waves of amateur visitors had broken against the steep ramparts of the poor man's castle, their enthusiasm had wilted.[123] 'Impulsive Lady Bountiful may be, and often is, indiscreet', Loane observed,[124] and it was partly because of her reputation for verbal incontinence that Lady Bountiful had become frustrated and dispirited. Spontaneity had to be encased in organization if it was to survive. The bureaucratic structures were now needed not just for co-ordination, but for animation, education, regulation, and control.

Furthermore, there was a growing sense that the caller would receive a better welcome if she knocked at the door armed not just with the goodwill of a fellow housewife and Christian but with the specific skills of an institutionally trained professional. The boundless enterprise of moral regeneration was starting to be separated into more specialized and more manageable tasks,

---

[121] D. B. McIlhiney, *A Gentleman in Every Slum: Church of England Missions in East London, 1837–1914* (Allison Park, Penn., 1988), 26, 48, 71; Humphreys, *Sin, Organized Charity and the Poor Law in Victorian England*, 155–61.

[122] Loane, *Neighbours and Friends*, 2.

[123] On the height of the 'ramparts', see Lady Bell, *At the Works* (London, 1907), 288.

[124] Loane, *Neighbours and Friends*, 2.

such as the care of small children or the healthy mental and physical develop-ment of their older siblings. Qualified midwives and health visitors were an increasing presence after 1902.[125] More generally there was a move to redefine the relationship between home and school. The provision of school meals and medical inspection in 1906 and 1907 were a recognition that exhortation alone was not sufficient to turn out alert and healthy pupils, and there was a corresponding shift in pedagogic methods. Where once teachers had been charged with the total reconstruction of the domestic curriculum, now the manuals of the training colleges began to urge that they form an alliance with parents against the culture of the streets.[126] Instead of mounting a head-long attack on every value in the home, teachers were now encouraged to exploit the respectable family's instinctive misgivings about the rougher com-pany into which their children might fall when they were in neither the house nor the classroom.[127] The desire for privacy was coming to be seen not as an obstacle but an essential building block in the process of social improvement.

The second solution was both an extension and negation of the first. In spite of their bureaucratization of the voluntary impulse, bodies such as the COS re-mained opposed to state welfare. However, they were interacting ever more closely with the officially qualified or employed and with a growing body of legislation. The Children's Act of 1908 assisted their endeavour by providing legal penalties for parents who persistently refused access to mistreated chil-dren, but also represented an unwelcome removal of responsibility for defining and policing proper child-rearing. Much less ambiguous were the two most dramatic extensions of the welfare role of the state, the Pensions Act of the same year followed by the National Insurance Acts of 1911. These repre-sented a denial of all that the home-visitor movement had stood for, in that they not only supplied material rather than moral support, but they did so without close scrutiny of the circumstances of the individual recipients. There were some behavioral clauses attached to the Pensions Act, but they were gen-eralized and unworkable.[128] In the case of insurance benefits, the only require-ment was a proven contribution record together with written evidence of sickness or unemployment.

The evasion of domestic inspection was quite deliberate. The growth and evo-lution of the home-visiting movement had convinced a broad spectrum of liberal and socialist opinion that invading the privacy of distressed households

[125] W. A. Brend, *Health and the State* (London, 1917), 106.

[126] See e.g. G. Collar and C. W. Crook, *School Management and Methods of Instruction* (London, 1900), 3–4, 100–1.

[127] Vincent, *Literacy and Popular Culture*, 93; A. Digby and P. Searby, *Children, School and Society in Nineteenth-Century England* (London, 1981), 90–1.

[128] Pensions were to be denied to those who had been in receipt of Poor Law Relief during the pre-vious ten years, or who had a recent criminal record. The provisions were dropped in 1919.

was inefficient or offensive or both.[129] To the new Labour Party, the paternalist, or maternalist, intrusion transgressed the dignity of individual working-class families and conflicted with their growing political status. For the Liberal Government which took office in 1905, the decades of voluntary endeavour had patently failed to remove either poverty or its supposed moral foundations. The more professional the visitors became in response to domestic insensitivies, the more cumbersome and costly was their casework. They had organized and regulated themselves out of the field of mass relief. Instead, the state went back to the original ambition of the New Poor Law, and sought to establish a system of relieving distress that would make a virtue out of ignorance about the detailed circumstances of recipients.

The sense of urgency which informed the process of inquiry and legislation in 1834 had been provoked in part by a crisis of knowledge. Rapid urban growth was destroying all possiblity of maintaining a personal familiarity with the histories of individual claimants. The *Poor Law Report* drew attention to 'the difficulty often amounting to impossibility on the part of those who administer and award relief of ascertaining whether any and what necessity for it exists . . . the difficulty of ascertaining the wants of the applicant, operates most strongly in the large towns'.[130] A strength of the 'self-acting system' of the workhouse test was that it required the supplicant rather than the relieving officer to conduct an inquiry into the trajectory of the domestic economy. If a family concluded that it was necessary to undergo the humiliation of pauperization, any further investigation of its moral or physical circumstances was superfluous. Thus it was feasible to group the crowded parishes into larger unions which forbade any return to the knowable community of the rural idyll. In the event, the unforseen persistence of outdoor relief made it impossible to dispense altogether with the process of interrogation and verification, but this remained a relatively superficial exercise.

The Poor Law shifted the emphasis from embarrassing inquiry prior to relief to demeaning treatment on its receipt. During the remainder of the century this balance was increasingly challenged. Inside the Poor Law system, the increasing tendency to distinguish between 'deserving' and 'undeserving' paupers focused attention on relative rights to privacy. As separate institutional provision was made for categories of the non-able-bodied poor, consideration began to be given to the way in which those who received help were publicly labelled. The greatest progress was made with children. The regime of head-shaving and uniforms which destroyed their individual identity was modified, and they were allowed to attend conventional schools in or-

---

[129] For a deeply pessimistic verdict of the attempts to reach the enclosed urban working-class communities, see C. F. G. Masterman, 'Realities at Home', in *The Heart of Empire* (London, 1902), 28–35. Also P. Keating, *Into Unknown England* (London, 1976), 20.

[130] *Administration and Operation of the Laws for the Relief of the Poor* (1834), PP 1834, XXVII (Harmondsworth, 1974 edn.), 116.

dinary clothes.[131] In a move of both real and symbolic importance, the Registrar-General issued instructions in 1904 that birth certificates should obscure any association with the workhouse, thus enabling the blameless children to keep secret the circumstances of their entry into the *world*. Fifteen years later a similar privilege was granted to paupers leaving their vale of tears.[132] Outside the system the whole principle of attempting to rebuild the moral lives of families without first discovering their inmost secrets was challenged by the home-visiting movement which sought to revive the parish as an effective community of personal knowledge.

By the first decade of the new century, only the Friendly Societies were succeeding in responding to need without compromising either their familiarity with claimants, or respect for their privacy. However, it was believed that the actuarial basis of their insurance provision was coming under increasing demographic pressure. They were experiencing difficulty meeting the claims of their existing members and were in no position to extend their service to the labouring population as a whole without substantial external assistance. In the face of the diminishing acceptability of pauperism and the declining potential of domestic missionaries, the Liberal Government was forced to seek an alternative relationship with the more deserving cases of want.

Limited in scope and value as they were, non-contributory pensions and subsidized sickness and unemployment insurance represented a critical recognition of the right of poor families to retain at least some control of information about their private affairs both before and after claiming assistance.[133] An attenuated Poor Law and an increasingly professional home-visiting system still remained, and the ambition of combining relief with the moral improvement of its recipients had not been abandoned—the insurance system was itself conceived as a self-acting means of fiscal education. There was no final resolution to the question of how much those who dispensed assistance required to know of those who asked for it; this was a battleground which would be fought across by different armies in every succeeding decade of the new century. But the Acts of 1908 and especially 1911 marked the burial of the assumption that deprivation could justify the wholesale exposure of domestic secrecy. In the midst of his satire of Mrs Pardiggle, Dickens caused his heroine Esther Summerson to observe that 'What the poor are to the poor is little known, excepting to themselves and GOD'.[134] There was now less desire to seek the vision of the Almighty.

---

[131] For accounts of the ritual public humiliation of workhouse children, see S. A. Reilly, *I Walk with the King* (London, 1931), 22; H. M. Stanley, *The Autobiography of Sir Henry Morton Stanley* (London, 1909), 10–11; Steel, *Ditcher's Row*, 78–90.

[132] M. A. Crowther, *The Workhouse System, 1834–1929* (London, 1983), 88.

[133] Churchill resisted pressure from his civil servants to conduct investigations into the conduct of those who had become unemployed. B. B. Gilbert, *The Evolution of National Insurance* (London, 1966), 271–2.

[134] Dickens, *Bleak House*, 161.

Commercial Confidence

By and large, secrecy is not susceptible to counting. The suppression of communication, particularly in the British context, was more often a continuous process than a series of discrete acts, and more often unrecorded than set down in a tabulated form. However, there is one long-run statistical measure of restricting the dissemination of knowledge, which displays a dramatic upward movement. In 1832 147 patents were sealed in England, which was roughly double the number at the end of the eighteenth century.[135] In 1732 just three had been sealed. The number tripled over the next two decades, and then leapt to more than 2,000 in the aftermath of the 1852 Patent Amendment Act, which was the first major reform to the system since 1624.[136] Following a further period of slow growth there was a second sharp rise after the Patent Designs and Trade Marks Act of 1883, which laid the basis of the modern structure of registration and protection. The figure first exceeded 10,000 in the year of the first Official Secrets Act, and reached its pre-war peak of 17,164 in the year of the second.

The Acts of 1852 and 1883 introduced no major new principles, but their success in modernizing the antiquated and cumbersome system of registration which had developed since the seventeenth century did much to consolidate the concept of intellectual property. The growing agitation for a system which gave genuine protection in return for manageable costs indicated a number of significant changes in the way in which the formation of knowledge was viewed. A sharper distinction was being drawn between expertise and originality. The weight of emphasis in the traditional processes of occupational learning was on gaining a mastery of established techniques. Their application to fresh tasks might generate incremental improvements, but radical departures from inherited wisdom were neither expected nor valued.[137] At the same time, innovation was coming to be seen as a literary practice, or at least as a form of mental activity which could be recorded and reproduced in a printed form. It was held to be a human rather than a God-given undertaking, and the achievements were those of individuals rather than groups. The period between the two nineteenth-century Patent Acts saw a climax in the celebration of the

---

[135] The figures in this paragraph are taken from Mitchell and Deane, *Abstract of British Historical Statistics*, 268–9; R. J. Solliran, 'England's "Age of Invention": The Acceleration of Patents and Patentable Invention during the Industrial Revolution', *Explorations in Economic History*, 26: 4 (1989), Table A1. Until 1852 they relate to England only, thereafter to the United Kingdom.

[136] For historical surveys of patent reforms, see A. A. Gomme, *Patents of Invention: Origin and Growth of the Patent System in Britain* (London, 1946), 13–60; K. Boehm, *The British Patent System*, Vol. 1 (Cambridge, 1967), 14–37; H. I. Dutton, *The Patent System and Inventive Activity During the Industrial Revolution, 1750–1852* (Manchester, 1984); C. Macleod, 'Strategies for Innovation: The Diffusion of New Technology in Nineteenth-Century British Industry', *Economic History Review*, 45: 2 (1992), 288–9.

[137] E. McMullin, 'Openness and Secrecy in Science: Some Notes on Early History', *Science, Technology and Human Values*, 51 (1985), 15–21.

inventor as a lone genius.[138] Smiles's *Lives of the Engineers* of 1861–2 was the most famous single text, but the list of letters patent represented a more complete conspectus of heroic achievement since the onset of the industrial revolution. In the words of the leading patent barister Thomas Welster, 'a very large proportion of the progressive improvement which has gone on from the time of Arkwright and Roberts has been the subject of patents'.[139] Furthermore, as the market for Smiles's book indicated, creative thinking was seen to be critical to economic growth. Although the eighteenth-century optimism about the productive potential of pure science had yet to be fulfilled, it seemed evident that Britain's industrial success was a consequence of an accumulating body of separate inventions. Finally, knowledge had a nationality, at least when it applied to manufacture. From the 1829 Select Committee on Patents onwards,[140] it was argued that continental rivals were gaining advantage from their more efficient and effective patent laws, and that Britain's commercial lead was threatened by the prospect of espionage against her poorly protected discoveries.

The strengthening conviction that recorded creative knowledge could be a valuable species of private property was reflected in the parallel consolidation of the copyright laws. Here also an unsatisfactory legal inheritance was clarified and extended by two key Acts of Parliament. The first, in 1842, prolonged the author's possession from twenty-eight years or life, to forty-two years or life plus seven, and the second, in the epochal year of 1911, established the convention of life plus fifty years.[141] As in the case of inventions, reform was both a consequence and a cause of an exponential rise in the volume of protected material. However, the patent system, which retained the unit of fourteen years it had once shared with copyright,[142] raised far more acute and complex issues of information control. The assumptions which underpinned the notion of individual ownership generated a set of conflicts over the question of whether, where, and in what form legal protection should be applied.

The most obvious difficulty was the inherent contradiction between an open economy and a controlled market in precisely those ideas upon which economic growth was seen to depend. At the beginning of the period covered by this chapter, a determined effort was being made to halt the apparently inexorable rise in the annual returns. A vigorous patent-abolition movement had

---

[138] For the emergence of this view of the technological innovator, see C. Macleod, *Inventing the Industrial Revolution* (Cambridge, 1988), 220.

[139] Report and Minutes of Evidence taken before the Select Committee of the House of Lords (in) Letter Patent for Inventions (1851), PP 1851, XVIII, p. 250.

[140] *Report from the Select Committee on the Law Relative to Patents for Invention* (1829), PP 1829, III, p. 450.

[141] F. Mackinnon, 'Notes on the History of English Copyright', in M. Drabble (ed.), *The Oxford Companion to English Literature* (Oxford, 1985), App. III.

[142] At the first attempt to give statutory protection to copyright in 1709 the period was set as two terms of fourteen years.

emerged after the 1852 Act, which argued that granting a legal monopoly over inventions was inconsistent with the ruling principles of free trade. John Coryton's *Treatise on the Laws of Letters-Patent* pointed out that: 'In every department of productive industry which has as yet had a fair trial, direct interference by the Legislature had proved detrimental to its interests.'[143] Whereas the state had been engaged in the systematic abolition of taxes on knowledge, it had granted to patentees what Robert Macfie described as the 'right to tax without rule, limit or control, all who use their inventions'.[144] The privilege was a glaring anomaly in the era of laissez faire, the more so as it lay at the very heart of the industrial revolution. Patents promoted concealment rather than open discourse and encouraged inventors to pursue their private interests at the expense of the public at large. 'They substitute', argued Macfie, 'a desire for money in the place of the more legitimate desire for doing good and earning a laudable distinction; they make every discovery a matter of money-value.'[145] If inventors required recognition as either an incentive or as a reward from a grateful nation, it should be in the form of a single payment or a public honour, not as a right to limit access to their discovery so long a period.

The failure of the abolition movement, which was confirmed by the 1883 Act, may have owed something to the onset of the Great Depression and the emergence of a more protectionist climate,[146] but it also revealed the strength of the pressure to exempt categories of commercially sensitive knowledge from the tendency towards the unfettered exchange of ideas. As in the contemporary controversy over the secret ballot, the issue seemed to many liberal reformers to require the acceptance of a lesser evil to avoid the encouragement of a greater. Unless the inventor were given the protection of the law, he would use every private means to keep his discovery hidden from all his competitors for as long as he could.[147] There would be no licensed exploitation of what might be a device of immense value to some productive process, and no prospect of its eventual release into the open market. A witness to the 1851 Select Committee on Letters Patent explained the implied contract: 'The State says, in consideration of your disclosing the secret, and not practising it in secret, but permitting the public to have the enjoyment of it, when you like to give up the patent, or when your patent expires, you shall have the exclusive enjoyment of it for a reasonable time.'[148] This bargain was formally embodied in the 1883 Act which established the 'exchange for secret principle', the legal requirement to make a

---

[143] J. Coryton, *A Treatise on the Law of Letters-Patent* (London, 1855), 21.

[144] R. A. Macfie, *The Patent Question* (London, 1863), 19.

[145] *Report and Minutes of Evidence taken before the Select Committee of the House of Lords (in) Letters Patent for Inventions*, 391.

[146] Dutton, *The Patent System*, 29.

[147] F. Machlup and E. Penrose, 'The Patent Controversy in the Nineteenth Century', *Journal of Economic History*, 10 (1950), 10–11, 25–8. On the extent of secrecy, particularly before the reform of 1852, see Macleod, 'Strategies for Innovation', 293, 304.

[148] PP 1851, XVIII, *1851 SC on Letters Patent*, 251.

full disclosure of the inventor's secret as a prior condition of the patent.[149] The continuing absence of such a device would only encourage a culture of deception, plagiarism, and theft. It was another version of honourable secrecy. A qualified control of the flow of information would enhance the ethical conduct of trade. Commercial espionage would be discouraged and mutual confidence between entrepreneurs enhanced.

A less apparent but equally important difficulty was provoked by the figure of the ingenious artisan. The notion of intellectual property represented a direct attack on the concept of knowledge embodied in a skilled trade. The learning of apprenticed workers was oral, collective, and conservative. It was, in their own language, a mystery, resistant to codification and publication, owned by no individual but held in trust on behalf of past and future members of the society. Artisans sought legal protection not for the knowledge itself, which was no business of the state or any other external agency, but for their institutional forms which sustained the process of transmission and renewal. When only a few dozen patents were issued a year, as was the case in the first phase of the industrial revolution, there was only rarely a need to force the distinction between the time-served mechanic tinkering with his machinery and the Promethean innovator making a radical departure from inherited wisdom. Arkwright had a better claim to originality in the means he adopted to defend his spinning frame than in the device itself. But as the factory system spread and the ideology of invention began to take shape, the role of the artisan required a clearer definition.

The long debate which culminated in the Act of 1852 revealed a continuing division of opinion between the collectivist and individualist approach to innovation. On the one hand it was still argued that invention was largely a matter of low-level modifications implemented by figuratively if not literally anonymous men. As one observer put it in 1851, 'in all established businesses and trades, I have no doubt the mass of the improvements are made by workmen, that is, persons engaged in the actual working of them'.[150] Even where an innovation could be attributed to a single individual, he would be in some way dependent on skilled assistants, or working in such close proximity with them as to make it impossible to keep the new process hidden. Against this it was asserted that not only was the self-sufficient inventor a key figure, but also that mechanization was increasing his separation from the bulk of the work-force.

---

[149] Boehm, *British Patent System*, 30. Previously, an inadequate disclosure could only be the subject of invalidity proceedings.

[150] PP 1851 XVIII, *1851 SC on Letters Patent*, 253. On the failure of the unreformed patent system to release the inventive power of the artisan, see W. Hindmarsh, *Observations on the Defects of the Patent Laws of this Country with Suggestions for the Reform of Them* (London, 1851), 13. The value of invention though cumulative improvement is endorsed by more recent scholarship. See Macleod, 'Strategies for Innovation', 290–1; N. F. R. Crafts, 'Exogenous or Endogenous Growth? The Industrial Revolution Reconsidered', *Journal of Economic History*, 55: 4 (Dec. 1995), 761.

'In olden times,' observed a witness to the 1851 *Select Committee on Letters Patent*,

an inventor used to be one of that handy class of men who could turn their attention to anything; in modern times, such has been the division of labour, that a workman in a factory at the present day has only to pursue one beaten track, neither turning to the right hand or the left . . . By reason of that he does not use any inventive faculties or ingenuity.[151]

This argument about the degree of creativity which would be expected or required of the industrial worker spread out into wide areas of education and management during the second half of the century.[152] In the case of patents, Parliament decided in 1852 to back the heroic model, and deliberately set fees at a level which was affordable by educated inventors and the growing number of professional patent agents, but too expensive for a toiling artisan to contemplate. The clinching argument for a government not anxious to incur excessive administrative costs, was the danger identified by Brunel at the beginning of the reform campaign, that if the legal protection of technical secrets was available to all, the patent machinery would be overwhelmed by poor men seeking an instant fortune.[153] In the event, the new Patent Commissioners not only curtailed expenditure but actually made a profit on protecting secrets of £2 million between 1852 and 1880, despite the notorious mismanagement of their office.[154] The 1883 Act applied a correction to the charges to render the service financially neutral, but it was to remain a form of security largely confined to those with time on their hands or money in their pockets.

Lack of resources was also an obstacle to non-statutory remedies for the improper communication of technical information. A pressing argument for expanding the patent system was that manual workers were generally too poor to be sued for betrayal of faith. There remained, however, a need to enlarge the role of equity alongside that of patents. The expansion of the economy generated an ever-increasing range of commercially sensitive knowledge which could not be translated into formal specifications. As transactions became more complex and more distant, a greater premium was placed on trust in the market, and greater recourse was had to the courts when it was held to be broken. The modern action of breach of confidence emerged during the nineteenth century, beginning with cases such as *Green* v. *Felgham re Dr. Johnson's Ointment for the Eyes* in 1823, which ruled that the law could recognize secrets even if they were embodied orally. By the 1890s it was clearly established that those able to risk the legal expense could use the common law to protect

---

[151] Ibid. 161.
[152] Vincent, *Literacy and Popular Culture*, 104–19.
[153] PP 1829, III, *SC on Patents for Invention*, 452.
[154] Boehm, *British Patent System*, 30–1.

secrets which a rival had obtained by underhand means.[155] It was no accident that many of the key decisions of the period, including that of Morrison's Universal Medicines of 1851, involved the trade in proprietary medicines. Here the relationship between substantive discovery and market exploitation was at its weakest. In most cases, the value of a trade secret was confined to the mere fact that it was secret. Manufacturers rushed to the courts to protect assets which might not exist at all if their composition was publicly known.

The growing exploitation by the proprietary medicine industry of both patents and breach of confidence highlighted the third and in many respects most intractable difficulty in the relationship between commerce and the legal regulation of secrets. To many observers, particularly within the increasingly self-confident medical profession, the series of statutes and judgements had tipped the balance of power in the market-place against the interests of the general public. If it was necessary to bring this form of intellectual property within the law, there might also be a case for developing a new category of legislation forcing its publication. A start had been made with the 1875 and 1899 Sale of Food and Drugs Acts and the 1897 Merchandise Marks Act,[156] but the owners of patented medicines had gained exemption from the clauses on inadequate or false labelling. Neither the original Medical Registration Act of 1858 nor its extension in 1911 had succeeded in outlawing the prescribing, making, and selling of supposedly therapeutic drugs by unqualified practitioners.[157] The 1912 Select Committee on Patent Medicines lamented that,

For all practical purposes British law is powerless to prevent any person from processing any drug or making any mixture, whether patent (or not), advertising it in any decent terms as a cure for any disease or ailment, recommending it by bogus testimonials and the invented opinion and facsimile signatures of fictitious physicians, and selling it under any name he chooses, on the payment of a small stamp duty, for any price he can persuade the credulous public to pay.[158]

The capacity of the trade to evade the mounting calls for control reflected both the strength of its market position and the weakness and complicity of its principal opponents. The rapid growth of the large-scale manufacture and sale of untested medicines was a child of the age of mass communication. As the demand for print was transformed, wordsmiths and pill-makers consummated a relationship which had been developing since the very beginning of journalism. The proliferating national and provincial newspapers of the second half of the nineteenth century, and the ever-more numerous and varied periodicals, promoted and were in turn sustained by cures for every kind of ailment, real or

---

[155] B. C. Reid, *Confidentiality and the Law* (London, 1986), 7–16; D. D. Fatterley, 'Historical Perspectives on Criminal Laws Relating to the Theft of Trade Secrets', *Business Law*, 25 (1970), 1543–4.

[156] *Report from the Select Committee on Patent Medicines* (1913), PP 1913, X, p. vi.

[157] I. Waddington, *The Medical Profession in the Industrial Revolution* (Dublin, 1974), 96–132, 147–8.

[158] PP 1913, X, *SC on Patent Medicines*, p. ix.

imagined.[159] Advertisements created a national demand for branded products, making a millionaire out of 'Professor' Holloway, who as early as the 1850s was spending £30,000 a year selling his wares.[160] The purchase of space in periodical publications enlarged their revenues and quelled their doubts about the content of the cures and the claims which were made for them. Moral judgements were only made in the case of the more indecorous conditions and their remedies, but there were always plenty of editors eager for the money to be earned from syphilis, impotence, and unwanted pregnancies. Just how unprincipled the search for advertising revenue had become was revealed by the fate of *Secret Remedies*, the British Medical Association's chemical analysis of the actual ingredients of the most common products on the market. With the single exception of the *Spectator*, the press, which was now in receipt of £2 million a year from this source, not only continued to publicize the unmasked preparations but in some cases actually refused to carry notices for the BMA's exposé.[161]

Instead of making more transparent the workings of nature, the spread of education and the improvements in means of disseminating the written word were encouraging mystery and concealment.[162] Print was employed to give authority to what could not be revealed, and the Penny Post was from the outset exploited for hidden communication.[163] Where once those who had engaged too little or too unwisely in sexual relations would have to visit a wise-woman at night to avoid the gaze of neighbours, now they could respond in private to advertisements, and receive well-wrapped and overpriced remedies through their letter-box. After the first reply, the vendor was able to persist with the correspondence, encouraging further self-diagnosis and warning of the dire effects of failing to purchase yet more medicines. Pro-forma circulars were devised, and mailing lists were bought and sold. At the bottom end of the market, the supply of venereal cures and abortifacients was followed up by attempts at blackmail. It was a world of secret fears, secret letters, and secret profits.

By the early 1900s the medical establishment was in full cry against those it termed quacks, and against the proprietary preparations which it regarded as frauds on the public. The publication of *Secret Remedies* in 1909 was followed by a Select Committee on unqualified practice in 1910,[164] a further campaign in the *British Medical Journal* 1911, and in 1913 a second lengthy Select Committee inquiry, this time on patent medicines. Apart from a marginal tightening of

---

[159] A. J. Lees, *The Origins of the Popular Press in England, 1855–1914* (London, 1976), 85; L. Brown, *Victorian News and Newspapers* (Oxford, 1985), 15–24.

[160] 'Advertisements', *Quarterly Review*, 97 (1855), 212; E. S. Turner, *The Shocking History of Advertising* (London, 1952), 63–6; F. B. Smith, *The People's Health* (London, 1979), 344.

[161] PP 1913, X, *SC on Patent Medicines*, 96.

[162] Vincent, *Literacy and Popular Culture*, 159–71.

[163] 'Unqualified Practice through the Post', *British Medical Journal* (27 May 1911), 1281.

[164] *Report on the Practice of Medicine and Surgery by Unqualified Persons in the United Kingdom* (1910), PP 1910, XLII.

the law on medical registration in 1911, nothing happened. The only comfort that could be taken from the legislation of the period was that the beginning of national health insurance promised to reduce the recourse to self-medication to avoid doctors' fees. In the end, the BMA's campaign did more to educate itself than its intended audience of patients and politicians. The sequence of enquiry and debate forced upon its attention two unpalatable truths. The first was that, for all their power and impropriety, the advertisers were not solely responsible for creating the demand for their products. Rather, the scale of the market revealed an alarming level of mistrust in the capacity of the qualified practitioners.

After half-a-century of statutory professional development, the doctors were still a long way short of establishing the kind of hegemony which they sought, even amongst those of their own class. Although the least educated were held to be the most credulous, and women were seen as generally more susceptible to the 'nostrums of quacks' than men,[165] it was impossible to find any sector of society which was invulnerable to the wiles of the hucksters. *Secret Remedies* discovered that,

the well-to-do and the highly placed will often, when not very ill, take a curious pleasure in experimenting with mysterious compounds. In them it is perhaps to be traced to a hankering to break safely with orthodoxy; they scrupulously obey the law and the Church and Mrs. Grundy, but will have their fling against medicine.[166]

As other branches of commerce were later to discover, concealment was itself a drug: 'One of the reasons for the popularity of secret remedies is their secrecy', began the Preface to the BMA exposé.[167] At a higher moral level, there remained the principle of freedom of choice. The more critical the category of consumption, the greater the resistance to controls in the market-place. 'The average Englishman', observed the *British Medical Journal*, 'will not tolerate the infringement of his right to use his liberty, as the citizen of a free country, to seek counsel of any oracle of healing he chooses, or to take any pill he "finds good of" as Bacon says, or anoint himself with any salve in whose virtues he believes.'[168]

The second lesson to be derived from the inability of registered practitioners to drive other oracles from the field concerned the limitations of their professional claims. Those in pain or in fear of death turned to other sources of wisdom and medication because the formally qualified could offer such limited guarantees of success. Advances in diagnosis during the nineteenth century

---

[165] Sir J. Byers, 'Quackery—With Special Reference to Female Complaints', *British Medical Journal* (27 May 1911), 1241.

[166] BMA *Secret Remedies*, p. vii.

[167] Ibid. p. v.

[168] 'The Causes of Quackery', *British Medical Journal* (27 May 1911), 1292.

had far outstripped improvements in therapeutic intervention. Doctors could explain and predict with growing conviction, but their capacity to cure remained extremely limited. In opposition to the profession's demand for a monopoly, sufferers adopted a pluralist approach to recovery. Where there was choice there was hope. If the official medicine men could not prove that their treatment would work, they could never convince their impatient patients that some unofficial treatment would not. The preparations both sold and were sold by their appeal to mystery. The vendor claimed access to sources of knowledge which lay outside the limited resources of orthodox medicine. He proclaimed 'that his product possesses virtues beyond the ken of the mere doctor; his herbs have been culled in some remote prairie in America or among the mountains of Central Africa, the secret of their virtues having been confided to him by some venerable chief'.[169] Furthermore, the medical profession's attempt to derive authority from the superiority of service ethics over entrepreneurial greed was seriously undermined by the post-mortem on the failure of *Secret Remedies* to make a greater impact on law and public opinion. It transpired that by no means all the signatures on endorsements for proprietary medicines were bogus. Doctors were selling their names for products about which they knew little or nothing. And on a much wider scale, they were continuing to prescribe drugs merely on the basis of the unsubstantiated claims made for them in advertisements.[170] Under cover of their own professional secrecy, they were still in bed with the exploiters of commercial secrecy.

The effective immunity of proprietary medicine from both professional and legal supervision reflected the condition of commerce in general in the second half of the nineteenth century. The world's most dynamic economy generated an ever-increasing volume of paper-based information, whose control was vested almost entirely in the hands of those who stood to gain most from its manipulation. The requirement in the first modern company legislation of 1844 that annual accounts be audited was abandoned in 1856 and not reimposed for all registered companies until 1900.[171] Established businesses were free to withhold from shareholders, the public, and the state virtually any detail of their practices beyond a basic, unsupervised balance sheet, and the promoters of new enterprises were at liberty to present any prospectus of their activities which suited their purposes. As the economy matured, so the legal regulation of commercially sensitive communication increasingly fell behind our international competitors. Not until the Companies Act of 1948 did Britain begin to acquire a disciplinary framework which approximated to good practice in other advanced states.

---

[169] BMA, *Secret Remedies*, p. v.

[170] PP 1913, X, *SC on Patent Medicines*, 674.

[171] See the Joint Stock Companies Acts of 1844 and 1856 and the Companies Act of 1900. T. A. Lee, 'A Brief History of Company Audits: 1840–1900', in T. A. Lee and R. H. Parker, *The Evolution of Corporate Financial Accounting* (New York and London, 1984), 153–4.

The consequence was deception, fraud, and commercial scandal. Old crimes such as embezzlement were practised on an unprecedented scale as more and more wealth was handled by those who did not own it, and new crimes, such as manipulating share prices and issuing false prospectuses, were invented and allowed to flourish for decades before the law recognized their existence.[172] Proliferating paper transactions encouraged money to be made from money, out of sight of those who had invested it, and beyond the confines of the simple profit-and-loss accounts of the small partnerships which had financed early industrialization. Unlike the machinery of government, where national growth was causing an equally rapid expansion of sensitive documents, there was no necessary association between secrecy and honour. Information was withheld, or was published in a misleading form with only market confidence to guarantee its authenticity. The Institute of Chartered Accountants was established in England in 1880, but its impact on either the practices or the standing of business before 1914 was limited.[173] The only area of significant advance was banking. This was partly because it was so central to the whole economy that after a series of insolvencies culminating in the failure of the City of Glasgow Bank in 1878 it attracted specific legislation on auditing practice.[174] And it was partly because a sequence of amalgamations generated early forms of large-scale commercial bureaucracies, which gradually developed effective in-house accounting systems. Elsewhere, the weakness of formal and informal standards of disclosure continually threatened both the prosperity and the good name of the honest and the competent. In an era of rapid economic growth and innovation, there was a tendency for inexperienced investors to trust in what they were not told, until it was too late to demand more accurate knowledge. What was lost, besides the savings of the unlucky, was public confidence in the culture of commerce.

1911

One result of the traumatic controversy over letter-opening in 1844 was that the Home Office prudently ceased to keep a record of what employment, if any, it was making of the authority to intercept mail which it still held under the Post Office Act of 1837. However, in the early 1870s it began once more to make copies of warrants,[175] and subsequently commissioned a confidential internal

---

[172] G. Robb, *White-Collar Crime in Modern England* (Cambridge, 1992), 2–75, 80–107, 125–42.
[173] H. Howitt, *The History of the Institute of Chartered Accountants in England and Wales, 1870–1965* (New York, 1984), 2–25.
[174] The Companies Act, 1879, which imposed compulsory auditing for limited liability banks registered after that date.
[175] See PRO, HO151/1–9.

study of the recent history of the practice.[176] This took the Mazzini affair as its starting-point, and examined developments in both the mechanism of espionage and the policy controlling its use. The report was particularly excited about the opportunities presented by recent innovations in the technology of communication. Letters had never been a very satisfactory subject for surveillance. Detection was too easy, the public was too sensitive to the sanctity of the mail, particularly since Macaulay and his friends had taken up the issue, and the common malefactor too rarely put pen to paper. 'But', noted the report,

a great difference has been made in modern times by the introduction of telegrams. Telegrams not merely multiply communications, but remain for some time as a record in the Post Office, which, if necessary, can be consulted during that time without any risk of the person whose telegrams are examined, finding it out and taking alarm, as is the case where letters are detained or appear to have been opened.[177]

The rapidly expanding telegraph industry had been nationalized in 1868, by which time it was carrying over $5\frac{1}{2}$ million inland messages a year,[178] and the first authorized interception was made just seven years later.[179]

There was much less difference, on the other hand, in the Home Office's attitude towards Parliamentary scrutiny of its exploitation of these new opportunities. After a thirty-five year gap, questions about postal espionage were once more raised in the Commons as the Government began to turn its attention to the Fenians. They were met with a timeless response. The Home Secretary did possess the power to open letters, explained Sir William Harcourt, 'but the very nature of the dangers which might demand its employment is such as requires the Minister intrusted by Parliament with the right and duty of putting it in force to ask the support of this House in declining to make any statement which might baffle and defeat the object for which it was conferred.'[180] No detail would be given of present or past warrants; those whose letters or telegrams had been opened would not be informed after the event. The Minister had been given the duty of maintaining public order, and until his powers were removed, he must be trusted to exercise them according to his judgement. MPs were allowed to see no further than the blind Postmaster-General of the time. On the face of it, this instinctive refusal to discuss any aspect of domestic security was at best unnecessary, and at worst counter-

---

[176] PRO, HO45/9752/A59329, 'Production of Telegrams and Post Letters on the Warrant of the Secretary of State'. The paper is dated 19 Feb. 1886, but contains material up to 1890. Comparison with the contemporary Home Office Minute Books confirms the accuracy of the report.

[177] Ibid. 6.

[178] J. Kieve, *The Electric Telegraph* (Newton Abbot, 1973), 73, 138–53.

[179] The first warrant for the interception of a telegram was issued in 1875. PRO, HO151/1.

[180] *Hansard*, 3rd ser., CCLVIII, 14 Feb. 1881, col. 766.

productive. As in 1844, the refusal to confirm or deny anything merely inflamed suspicions. Had Parliament been allowed to read the secret history of interceptions drawn up at the end of the decade, it would have discovered little to criticize and much to praise. Apart from the Irish surveillance, of which the victims, as ever, were well aware, there was little in the record to arouse controversy. The public would scarcely have complained about opening telegrams in order to identify the accomplices of a 'noted procuress', or to establish the guilt of a master suspected of scuttling his ship. The Home Office had much to gain from revealing the action it had taken against the sender of threats to the Queen and Princess Beatrice, and much to lose from the mistrust which its silence engendered.

Nevertheless, the desire to preserve freedom of action in an uncertain world always appeared a more persuasive consideration. The attraction of the wall of confidentiality which Sir James Graham had fought to preserve was that it permitted maximum adaptability with minimum formality. Dicey's contemporary celebration of the British political tradition applied exactly to the system which had been created to protect it: 'Every part of it can be expanded, curtailed, amended, or abolished, with equal ease. It is the most flexible polity in existence, and is therefore utterly different in character from the "rigid" constitutions ... the whole or some part of which can be changed only by some extraordinary method of legislation.'[181] If dangers could appear without warning, so also could counter-measures be taken without notice. Although there was always a risk of exposure, the process of espionage was becoming safer as more attention was paid to telegrams, copies of which were kept by the Post Office for three months after transmission. Postal espionage could be quietly combined with the first Official Secrets Act, as first happened in 1899.[182] A few months later, the Intelligence Office of the War Office was able to employ the GPO to open all letters addressed to the officers of the South African Republic and the Orange Free State.[183] When war threatened in Europe in 1911, Captain Kell of the newly created Secret Service Bureau was allowed to add the weapon of postal interception to his armoury.[184] Powers which had been most recently used in the hunt for Crippen and Le Neve were unobtrusively turned over to the pursuit of German spies, helped by Churchill's unannounced decision to issue general as well as individual warrants.[185] The following March, Special Branch, which had been set up with a similar absence of formal regulation,[186] began opening the letters of suffragettes.[187]

---

[181] A. V. Dicey, *Introduction to the Study of the Law of the Constitution* (1885; 10th edn., London, 1959), 91.

[182] PRO, HO151/8. Warrant of 29 Sept. 1899.

[183] Ibid. Warrants of 13 Jan. and 19 Jan. 1900.

[184] Ibid. Warrant of 15 Sept. 1911. See also N. Hiley, 'The Failure of British Counter-Espionage against Germany, 1907–1914', *Historical Journal*, 28: 4 (1985), 857.

[185] W. S. Churchill, *The World Crisis, 1911–1914* (2nd edn., London, 1923), i. 52; Andrew, *Secret Service*, 50; Thurlow, *Secret State*, 42.

[186] Porter, *Origins of the Vigilant State*, 67–78.   [187] PRO, HO151/9. Warrant of 23 Mar. 1912.

Rapidity of response was valued for its own sake. The first Official Secrets Act of 1889 was almost immediately found wanting because, as the Committee of Imperial Defence later noted, 'the restrictive conditions regarding the arrest and search of offenders largely paralysed the effectiveness of the statute for emergency purposes'.[188] It was necessary to apply first to the Attorney-General and then to the courts before the police could move against a suspect.[189] But the commitment to tactical mobility was itself part of a broader strategy. The freedom to capture enemies of the state depended on a licence to escape the state's principle democratic structures.[190] The drama of 1844 had taught governments a lesson which they never forgot, that official secrecy was an explosive substance when exposed to the oxygen of public debate. The ingrained apprehension of Parliamentary scrutiny was laid bare by the confidential discussions surrounding the proposed Post Office (Obscene Matter) Acts of 1897 and 1898.

The bulk of the Home Office-sponsored espionage during the last decade of the nineteenth century and the early years of the twentieth was directed against not foreign spies but overseas pornographers. As so often, the objective was to defend the moral integrity of the ruling class or rather, in this case, its sons. There was particular concern about the public schools, whose crucial responsibility for inculcating in the next generation of Christian gentlemen a healthy sense of manliness was continually threatened by the consequences of confining large numbers of adolescent boys in closed communities. Following complaints from the headmasters of Eton and Winchester about the volume of obscene literature being obtained from abroad by their pupils, the Home Secretary began issuing warrants to intercept suspected packages.[191] The Post Office complained that its surveillance system was being severely stretched and requested a clarification of the law, arguing, 'that unless this is done at some time or other there is great danger of strong popular feeling against the exercise of the present undefined power by the Secretary of State, and that it would be much better that the power should be defined and rest on distinct statutory authority'.[192]

The Home Office was sympathetic to its problems but anxious to confine legislation to obscenity. Whereas public opinion might be quiescent on this narrow topic, wrote the Permanent Under-Secretary, 'it is much more likely that at some time or another there may be a row about the exercise of the power as

[188] PRO, CAB16/8, *Proceedings of a Sub-Committee of the Committee of Imperial Defence Appointed by the Prime Minister to Consider the Question of Foreign Espionage in the United Kingdom* (1909), App. IV, p. 21; PRO, HO45/10629/199699, p. 41.

[189] In addition, it was very difficult for a court to issue a search warrant under the terms of the Act. PRO, CAB16/8, pp. 8–9.

[190] *Pace* K. G. Robertson, who in *Public Secrets*, 42, argues that official secrecy 'was one of the mechanisms used to enhance control of elected representatives over unelected administrators'.

[191] PRO, HO45/9752/A59329, p. 2. The complaint from Eton College was received in 1890, and from Winchester College 'and other places' in 1894. The first warrants were issued in 1891.

[192] Ibid. Memorandum from Ridley to Walpole, 28 Jan. 1898.

regards crimes or suspected crimes of other kinds—especially at times of political excitement'.[193] The pervasive fear of 'strong popular feeling' produced an impasse. As it was to do again prior to the First World War, the Post Office fiercely rejected any attempt to transfer to its officials the authority to initiate espionage, on the grounds that, 'public sentiment is very strong in the support of the supposed inviolability of letters passing through the post'.[194] Unable to divest itself of even part of its responsibilities, the Home Office permitted the drafting of two successive Bills on obscene publications, but then withdrew its support altogether when advised by the law officers that it would not be able to limit discussion to the specific issue: 'questions might arise as to the existing powers of the Secretary of State, which it is undesirable to discuss.'[195] It was impossible to unravel the blanket of secrecy row by row.

The case of the public schools and the pornographers was a microcosm of the dilemma facing the state apparatus as a whole after 1889. Once it had broken with precedent and committed itself to legislation, there was no going back. To the contrary, it was immediately apparent that further intervention would be required. Rather than putting an end to the lengthy process of drafting and re-drafting, the hurried passage of the first Official Secrets Act denoted merely a brief intermission. The search for a replacement began after the judge at the initial prosecution under the new law in 1892 protested that the defendant, a former army draughtsman found guilty of trying to sell details of the fortifications at Malta and Gibraltar to the French, had been charged with a misdemeanour not a felony.[196] Larger doubts were soon raised about the difficulty of proving that any unauthorized communication was contrary to the well-being of the state and intended to be so, and about the wisdom of confining the scope of the Act to those actually employed by the government or its contractors. More generally, the pressures which had forced the state to come to Parliament in 1889 were intensifying rather than diminishing. The press was no less eager to publish leaks, and the source showed little sign of drying up. The numbers of manual and routine clerical workers continued to expand, and, more disturbingly still, there was growing evidence of a 'trade union spirit' amongst public employees, initially within the massed ranks of the Post Office, and then more generally across the civil service.[197] By the end of the Edwardian period, formal or informal recognition had been given to Associations of Second Division Clerks, Assistant Clerks, Boy Clerks, and Female

[193] PRO, HO45/9752/A59329, p. 2. Digby to Sir Spencer Walpole, Secretary of the Post Office, 29 Oct. 1897. Also R. M. Kamm, 'The Home Office, Public Order and Civil Liberties, 1870–1914', unpublished Ph.D thesis (Cambridge University, 1987), 274–5.

[194] PRO, HO45/9752/A59329, p. 2. See also the observations of Sydney Buxton, the then Postmaster General, to the 1909 Imperial Defence Sub-Committee. PRO, CAB16/8, p. 9.

[195] PRO, HO45/9752/A59329, p. 2. Report of Law Officers, dated 5 Apr. 1898.

[196] *The Times* (6 Apr. 1892), 6. Also Hooper, *Official Secrets*, 23–4.

[197] *Second Report of the Royal Commission appointed to inquire into the Civil Establishments of the different Offices of State at Home and Abroad* [Ridley] (1898), PP 1888, XXVII, p. 276; *Fourth Report of the Royal Commission on the Civil Service* [MacDonnell] (1914), PP 1914, XVI, p. 98.

Typists, as well as the various groups of postal workers.[198] Furthermore, the expansion of the mines inspectorate began to draw ex-trade unionists into relatively senior and well-paid levels of the official machine, a process accelerated by Liberal social legislation, such as the creation of labour exchanges in 1909 and the national insurance system in 1911.[199] Men whose cultural identity had been formed in a world of minutes and meetings rather than public schools and Oxbridge colleges were now integral elements of the modern state.

A second Act was only a matter of time; the problem was one of maintaining operational silence. Means had to be found of forestalling an outcry over removing the defence of public interest and *mens rea* (criminal intent) and extending the scope of the law to cover all possessors of official information whether government employees or not, and all publishers of unauthorized communication, including the press. The total success of the Liberal Government's manoeuvre in the late summer of 1911, when it rushed through these modifications in half-an-hour on a somnolent Friday afternoon, has attracted much criticism from historians, but little explanation.[200] It is necessary to stand back from the undoubted manipulation and deception which took place before and during the brief debate on 18 August,[201] and consider the related group of factors which eased the passage of legislation which has dominated the twentieth-century treatment of public secrecy in Britain.

The most obvious of these was the abiding caution of successive governments. Once the decision to legislate was taken in 1887, scarcely a year passed when one or more Bills were not at some stage of preparation in the Home Office or elsewhere. Two attempts were made at the first Official Secrecy Bill before it was tabled in 1889, and the Parliamentary draughtsmen were soon back at work. Into the wastepaper basket containing the abandoned Obscenity Acts were thrown Secrecy Bills of 1896, 1908, and 1912; a series of Bills from 1905 onwards to enforce press censorship in an emergency, and two aliens Acts in 1911 which were due to be attached to the Secrets Act of that year.[202] It was not the absence of Parliamentary time or a potential majority which determined the fate of these Bills, but the danger of their provoking any discussion at all. In most cases, prudence dictated inaction, although occasionally misjudgements were made. A Bill to make all breaches a felony rather than a misdemeanour reached its first reading in 1896 but was withdrawn after opposition from the Treasury, which wanted to maintain the freedom to mount prosecutions

[198] The Fawcett Association, the Postmen's Federation, and the Postal Telegraph Clerks' Association were recognized in 1906, and eventually combined into the Union of Post Office Workers in 1920. Robinson, *Britain's Post Office*, 232.

[199] Harrison, *The Transformation of British Politics*, 305.

[200] Birkinshaw, *Freedom of Information*, 75–8; Robertson, *Public Secrets*, 63; Hooper, *Official Secrets*, 29–31; Thurlow, *Secret State*, 37–42; *Franks Report*, iv. 123.

[201] See the shameless account by the principal Government manager of the passage of the Bill, the Secretary of State for War, Colonel Seely: J. E. B. Seely, *Adventure* (London, 1930), 144–6.

[202] PRO, CAB/17/91; HO45/10629/199699, pp. 3, 9.

against the most trivial of offences. In 1908 a premature attempt to bring the press within the law of official secrecy was hurriedly withdrawn following an orchestrated campaign of protest.[203]

Despite the combination of scrupulous preparation and quite unscrupulous tactics inside Parliament once the plunge had been taken, the muffled passage of the 1911 Bill still came as a relief. As Colonel Seely recalled,

> It was open to anyone of all the members of the House of Commons to get up and say that no bill had ever yet passed through all its stages in one day without a word of explanation from the ministry in charge . . . But to the eternal honour of those members, to whom I now offer, on behalf of that and all succeeding governments, my most grateful thanks, not one man seriously opposed.[204]

The appeal to honour was addressed to each of the players in the modern state. The code of the British gentleman had been reformulated to engineer the discretion of the bureaucrat, the deference of the legislator, and the indifference of the elector. By 1911 it represented a powerful and complex set of definitions about both a specific social ethos and a particular political nation.

In a perceptive essay on the machinery of government published the year before the second Official Secrets Act, Ramsay Muir, then Professor of Modern History at Liverpool, observed that, 'both the word bureaucracy and the thing have an evil savour in the nostrils of most Englishmen'.[205] Yet it seemed to be the case that the civil service was generally free of such obloquy. The last of the generation recruited by patronage alone had now retired, and their departure coincided with a growing tendency to celebrate the peculiar excellence of the British administrative system. 'Our Civil Service is our glory and our pride', wrote the former Liberal Prime Minister Lord Rosebery in 1898; 'It is the admiration of all foreigners who see it.'[206]

The difference, argued Francis Montague, stemmed from national tradition. The continental official had begun as the servant of despots, and had become modern through the accumulation of laws: 'In all the great monarchies of the Continent the administrative corporation rules; but it rules without responsibility and without glory.'[207] The British civil servant, by contrast, was answerable not to a separate legal code such as the *Droit administratif*, but rather to diffuse agencies of public opinion, and, ultimately, to the common law and an independent judiciary. 'All these circumstances are peculiar to our own

---

[203] For the campaign organized by the Newspaper Proprietors' Association, see *The Times* (27 Apr. 1908), 11; (4 May 1908), 3; (7 May 1908), 11. Also *Hansard*, 4th Ser. CLXXXVIII, 11 May 1908, cols. 673–4; CXC, 23 June 1908, cols. 1476–8.

[204] Seely, *Adventure*, 145.

[205] R. Muir, *Peers and Bureaucrats: Two Problems of English Government* (London, 1910), 3. He later moved to Manchester University, and served as a Liberal MP from 1923 to 1924.

[206] Lord Rosebery, *The Duty of Public Service* (Edinburgh, 1898), 32.

[207] F. C. Montague, *The Limits of Individual Liberty* (London, 1885), 222. Montague was also a historian, Professor at University College London.

country,' he concluded, 'and all afford guarantees against bureaucratic tyranny.'[208]

Muir developed further the virtue of culture against formal regulation. The key to the non-bureaucratic bureaucracy lay in the peculiar combination of integrity and invisibility which was the true legacy of the Northcote-Trevelyan reforms. On the one hand, the honour of the gentlemanly professional administrators was a real and bankable asset. It was so manifest a condition as to excite little comment: 'Nor is there ever a whispered suspicion of corrupt interest . . . So much do we take their incorruptibility for granted that we do not even think of praising them for it.'[209] They were above money, outside politics, and—which was still of real significance—independent of sectarian religious loyalties. On the other hand, they had succeeded in removing themselves so completely from the public gaze that their very absence was rarely noticed. The more power they acquired, the less they were seen to exercise it. 'There has been the most astonishing conspiracy of silence to maintain this illusion', wrote Muir. 'Neither in debates nor in the press have the actions of the bureaucrats, who are in so many ways our real masters, been openly and independently discussed.'[210]

The Treasury was an active party to this conspiracy. After 1884 it avoided a public discussion of its regulatory activities, but instead proceeded in private to strengthen the bonds of administrative secrecy. Through a series of minutes and memoranda it tightened the rules on the disclosure of inspectors' reports, limited the right of civil servants to take part in politics, restricted the information they could give to select committees, and imposed more systematic rules on the release of documents to the Public Record Office.[211] A deliberate attempt was made to insulate administrators from the democratic pressures of the period. They were increasingly protected from direct inquisition by Members of Parliament, and until 1912, expressly prohibited from standing for election for any body larger than a parish council. Thereafter, their Heads of Department might permit participation in Borough or County Councils, but the MacDonnell Royal Commission of 1914 issued firm guidance on the use of this discretion. In a chapter entitled, 'The Civil Service in Relation to the Duties of Citizenship', it reviewed the implications of the coming era of universal suffrage, and reached a clear conclusion:

we think that with regard to political questions a proper reserve and reticence both in speech and writing should be observed by the members of the General and Professional Civil Service, and that a similar obligation should be imposed on officers

---

[208] Montague, *The Limits of Individual Liberty*, 223. See also Dicey's lengthy attack on the *Droit administratif* of France, and, by extension, of other European states: Dicey, *Introduction to the Study of the Law of the Constitution*, Ch. 12, pp. 328–415.

[209] Muir, *Peers and Bureaucrats*, 30.

[210] Ibid. 22.

[211] Birkinshaw, *Freedom of Information*, 75; Robertson, *Public Secrets*, 75.

belonging to other branches which are directly connected with departmental administration.[212]

It was the moment of maturity for honourable secrecy. Although the Treasury had yet to achieve total hegemony over the other departments, its growing body of regulations both sustained and reflected a recognizable bureaucratic culture in which the 'proper reserve and reticence' was becoming second nature for the highly educated professionals who occupied the upper ranks.[213] Not only inside, but, perhaps more importantly, outside the civil service, it was becoming accepted that efficiency and anonymity, honesty and silence, were mutually reinforcing qualities. Occasionally a critical voice could be heard. In 1902 J. A. Hobson drew attention to the narrow social base of the university-trained elite: 'The chief danger arises where this official class is drawn from a small section of the people and is thus identified with the interests of a few.'[214] Ramsay Muir concluded his study with the caution that secrecy 'may provide a cloak for the man who wants to magnify his power or conceal his inefficiency by a parade of mystery and a multiplication of complicated regulations or unintelligible verbiage'.[215] But these were isolated if prophetic warnings which failed to develop into a systematic critique of Whitehall. The revolutionary left saw little profit in engaging with the constitutional niceties of freedom of speech within a bourgeois state.[216] For those engaged in the more conventional struggle to establish the legal and political presence of organized labour, the machinery of government appeared a haven of benevolent neutrality. The former civil servant Sidney Webb was at the time doing all that he could to persuade the young trade-union bureaucracies to become more rather than less like his first employer.[217] Until it tasted power in the 1920s, the new Labour Party maintained a critical stance towards the misuse of secrecy and its leaders were amongst the few MPs to vote against the 1911 Bill.[218] However, they lacked both the ideological and political resources to withstand the manipulation of the agenda by the Government's parliamentary managers, and were unable to influence the course of the legislation through the Commons.

The celebration of the non-bureaucratic bureaucracy was merely another chapter in the long and oft-told tale of the peculiar excellence of the national

---

[212] PP 1914, XVI, *RC on Civil Service*, 97.

[213] Muir, *Peers and Bureaucrats*, 40.

[214] J. A. Hobson, 'The Restatement of Democracy', *Contemporary Review*, 81 (1902), 272. The narrow educational background of the leadership of the civil service at this time is examined in K. Theakston and G. K. Fry, 'Britain's Administrative Élite: Permanent Secretaries 1900–1986', *Public Administration*, 67: 2 (Summer 1989), 134–6.

[215] Muir, *Peers and Bureaucrats*, 50.

[216] E. Hobsbawm, 'Labour and Human Rights', in *Workers* (London, 1984), 304–10.

[217] S. and B. Webb, *Industrial Democracy* (London, 1897), 807–52.

[218] The ten notes cast against the Bill include those of Keir Hardie, Arthur Henderson, George Lansbury, Ramsay MacDonald, and Philip Snowden.

constitutional tradition. However, it is possible to detect a significant shift of emphasis in the narrative. The search for formal controls over official information was both provoked and sustained by an emerging sense of a common trajectory in the political institutions of Europe. Back in 1844 the critics of domestic secrecy had charged the government with manipulating its unwritten powers to support a foreign tyrant. The outcome of the controversy was a defeat for Mazzini's case, but a victory for his cause. Young Italy became a focus of Liberal enthusiasm and a model for other liberation campaigns.[219] All were based on an unshakeable assumption that freedom of communication was both a measure of the superiority of the British system and a vital weapon in the fight against repressive regimes abroad. As *The Times* observed in 1858: 'Any defence of so important a department of the liberty of the press as the right to criticise foreign Governments is happily a work of supererogation.'[220] During the succeeding decades, the frame of reference became more ambiguous. The tradition of defining national liberties against foreign tyranny survived—in the argument over the abortive 1908 Secrecy Act *The Times* could protest that 'We are asked to graft upon British laws some of the worst features of Continental bureaucracy'[221]—and was to burst forth in all its glory when Germany invaded Belgium in 1914. However, as the need to impose restrictions on the flow of information increased, so there developed a greater respect for the constitutional arrangements of neighbouring countries.

By the final quarter of the nineteenth century there was a growing sense that, rather than representing a beacon of hope in a dark world, Britain was merely one amongst a number of modernizing states facing common problems requiring similar solutions. Where once it could claim the most liberal constitution, now it was struggling to keep pace with progress towards a fully democratic franchise. As part of the careful preparation for the first Official Secrets Act, the Foreign Office was asked to supply detailed summaries of the machinery which had been established to prevent the disclosure of information in France, Germany, Italy, and Austria-Hungary.[222] Ironically, the one continental statute which was cited specifically as a model for sections of the 1889 Act had been passed in 1875 by the country to whose creation Mazzini had devoted his life.[223] By the second Act, ministers had become well versed in the twin appeal to the strength of foreign secrecy regulations and the superiority of domestic constitutional safeguards. Virtually the only argument set forth by Seely in the brief debate on the 1911 Bill was that: 'Every other country has legislation of this kind I understand, and in no case would the powers be used to infringe any

---

[219] On the impact of the 1844 controversy on the cause of Italian Nationalism in Britain, see Smith, 'British Post Office Espionage', 202.

[220] *The Times* (7 May 1908), 11.

[221] Ibid. (6 Dec. 1858).

[222] PRO, T1/8308B/16646.

[223] PRO, WO32/6347. MS note on drafting secrecy legislation, 24 Dec. 1887.

of the liberties of His Majesty's subjects.'[224] In most other countries the powers were much more sharply defined, but it was the glory of the British constitution to leave as much as possible unwritten.

The state's capacity to generate both complacency and anxiety by reference to overseas rivals was apparent in its campaign to quieten the newspapers' opposition to further secrecy legislation. On the one hand, fears about the possible misuse of extra power were met with the assurance that if editors behaved as gentlemen should, then the British tradition of liberty would be security enough. As the Lord Chancellor put it in 1908, 'it should be clear that anyone in the Press conducting his duties honourably would be quite safe'.[225] On the other, it was urged with ever-increasing stridency that the failure to observe the discretion expected of gentlemen was imperilling the safety of the nation.

The vulnerability of the press to this double appeal stemmed from the equivocal nature of its own position. This was nowhere better illustrated than in the affair of 'Defenceless Dover'. In March 1908 the *Morning Post* published an article which began with the provocative claim that 'Dover is a fortress as strong as Nature can make it and as weak as the present Government can leave it'.[226] The War Office, which had been exercised by unauthorized disclosures about the nation's defences for a decade,[227] was outraged by the detailed discussion of the disposition of the batteries around the port, and successfully pressed the Government to introduce its long-prepared Bill to expose newspapers to prosecution for publishing official information.[228] This in turn provoked a spirited and temporarily effective defence by the newly formed Newspaper Proprietors' Association. However, the *Post* article was itself merely the latest instalment in the 'invasion scare' campaign in which most of Fleet Street was vigorously participating.[229] In 1909 the indefatigable fabulist William Le Queux asserted as an established fact that 'the number of agents of the German Secret Police at this moment working in our midst on behalf of the Intelligence Department in Berlin are believed to be over five thousand'.[230] The scale of their activities, he alleged, was being concealed by the War Office and the police 'for fear of creating undue panic'.[231] The Government's business managers knew that it was only a matter of time before the press so magnified the threat of Germany that it would be wholly unable to oppose the loss of civil liberties required to protect Britain. That moment arrived with the Agadir

[224] *Hansard*, 5th ser., XXIX, 18 Aug. 1911, col. 2252.

[225] *Hansard*, 4th Ser., CLXXVIII, 11 May 1908, col. 674.

[226] *Morning Post* (21 Mar. 1908).

[227] A. Palmer, 'The History of the D Notice Committee', in C. Andrew and D. Dilks, *The Missing Dimension: Governments and Intelligence Communities in the Twentieth Century* (London, 1984), 227–8.

[228] PRO, ADM1/8030.

[229] D. French, 'Spy Fever in Britain, 1900–1915', *Historical Journal*, 21: 2 (1978), 356–62.

[230] W. Le Queux, *Spies of the Kaiser* (London, 1909), p. x.

[231] Ibid. 112–13.

crisis of 1911, and the newspapers' articulate insubordination of three years earlier was duly replaced by a deferential silence.[232] At the same time, the government decided to adopt an earlier suggestion of the Director of Naval Intelligence, that it should try a more indirect solution to the problem of controlling the newspapers:

a simple method, worthy of trial, is to put the press to their honour in the schoolboy sense of the term, prior to any experiments which the board may wish to keep secret, by issuing a communiqué to the press association stating what is going to be carried out and asking them to co-operate in the publication of information likely to be of value to foreign countries.[233]

Once the appropriate mode of discourse had been identified, it proved possible to institute the D Notice Committee in 1912 without even informing Parliament, let alone seeking legislative sanction.[234]

More generally, the failure of the dogs to bark was a consequence of their assumption that they would continue to be fed. The issue of official secrecy in Victorian and Edwardian Britain was about the control rather than the volume of public communication.[235] From the 1873 Treasury Minute onwards, the state's principal concern was not with what was disclosed, but with who disclosed it. Whilst a prolonged campaign was conducted against attempts by journalists to suborn junior civil servants, senior officials were permitted to maintain a steady stream of information on and off the record.[236] Over the years, as governments became more defensive and newspapers more enterprising, there was a breakdown of trust that the rules would be voluntarily observed, but little questioning of the game itself. Editors and their now frequently honoured proprietors[237] were open to persuasion that the blanket clauses of the two Official Secrecy Acts would not destroy the gentlemanly relations they enjoyed with upper reaches of the establishment.

The final reason why the state was able to pass an Act which left their powers to prohibit the communication of official information so ill-defined lay in the unwritten character of the constitution which the legislation was supposed to defend. The French Revolution had taught Burke and his successors that the absence of a formal statement of rights and powers constituted a bulwark against sudden change. What once the hand of men had put down on paper

---

[232] The most trenchant account of the Government's manoeuvring between 1908 and 1911 is to be found in the *Report of the Departmental Committee on Section 2 of the Official Secrets Act of 1911*, i. 23–5.

[233] Cited by Palmer, 'History of the D Notice Committee', 232.

[234] D. G. T. Williams, 'Official Secrecy in England', *Federal Law Review*, 3: 1 (June 1968), 23; Palmer, 'History of the D Notice Committee', 234–5; Hooper, *Official Secrets*, 223; Thurlow, *Secret State*, 43. The official name of the body was the 'Admiralty, War Office and Press Committee'.

[235] Birkinshaw, *Freedom of Information*, 70.

[236] Z. Steiner, 'The Last Years of the Old Foreign Office, 1898–1905', *Historical Journal*, 6: 1 (1963), 66; J. D. Gregory, *On the Edge of Diplomacy* (London, 1929), 265; Koss, *The Rise and Fall of the Political Press in Britain*, i. 219–22, 412.

[237] J. Walker, *The Queen has been Pleased* (London, 1986), 95–6.

could be torn up and rewritten at will. However, in 1904, as various drafts of the Second Official Secrecy Act were in preparation, the French sociologist Émile Boutmy published a stimulating study of the characteristics of the English, in which he dared to draw the opposite conclusion. In times of relative tranquillity, he argued, the imprecision of the constitution and the associated vagueness of political theory did indeed encourage the slow and painless advance of freedom. He cited as an example the abolition of press controls earlier in the nineteenth century. But in times of crisis the reverse was the case: 'The State intervenes with less hesitation and in a more absolute form than in France, because what it has to face are contingent facts, not imperative principles.'[238] The evidence of history was that the past alone was an inadequate safeguard of individual liberties. When a government convinced itself and its supporters that the nation was in peril, he wrote, 'its intervention was of necessity less scrupulous, more decided and more radical, than is elsewhere the case, because it came into collision, not with an idea of absolute and distinctly imperative right, but with historical precedent'.[239] Boutmy's gaze was fixed on the rise of socialism, to which he thought the British constitution uniquely vulnerable. He did not consider the prospect of a Liberal Government, set about by external and internal enemies, intervening with so few scruples and so much dispatch.

The Importance of Being Secret

The first event of Oscar Wilde's *annus mirabilis et horribilis* of 1895 was the opening of *The Ideal Husband* on 3 January. In the audience were the Prince of Wales, A. J. Balfour, Joseph Chamberlain, and many members of the Government.[240] They were presented with a drama whose plot was nothing if not topical. A rising young politician, Sir Robert Chiltern, is being blackmailed by an adventuress, Mrs Cheveley, who wants him to withdraw an impending critical report on the 'Argentinean Canal' in which she has invested. Her weapon is a letter she has acquired which reveals a secret crime Chiltern had committed at the very beginning of his career. In an early exchange Chiltern attempts to dismiss the matter: 'You have lived so long abroad, Mrs. Cheveley, that you seem to be unable to realise that you are talking to an English gentleman'—to be met with the tart reply that, 'I realise that I am talking to a man who laid the foundations of his fortune by selling to a Stock Exchange speculator a Cabinet secret'.[241] It transpires that Chiltern, who had 'the double misfortune of being well-born and poor',[242] had once yielded to temptation and sold to Baron Arnheim inside in-

---

[238] É. Boutmy, *The English People* (London, 1904), 286.
[239] Ibid. 273.
[240] R. Ellmann, *Oscar Wilde* (London, 1987), 404.
[241] O. Wilde, *An Ideal Husband*, in *Plays* (Harmondsworth, 1954), 169.
[242] Ibid. 181.

formation on the Government's impending purchase of the Suez Canal shares. At the end of the play Chiltern finally escapes from her clutches when she is in turn blackmailed by the cynical Lord Goring over the theft of some jewellery. A chastened Chilton re-establishes his reputation with a brilliant Commons speech, but declines a proffered Cabinet seat to spend more time with his wife who had displayed a simple, humbling trust in the integrity of her ideal husband. The play attracted packed houses, and was followed six weeks later by the yet more successful opening of *The Importance of Being Earnest*. In mid-April, however, both plays were suddenly taken off as the secret of Wilde's affair with Lord Alfred Douglas was exposed. Following the highly publicized failure of his libel action against the Marquess of Queensberry, Wilde was prosecuted for homosexuality, and ended the year in Reading Gaol.[243]

The tragedy of Wilde's fall was prefigured by his comedy. Chiltern's secret crime which eventually found him out was committed eighteen years earlier when he was 22, at the same time and at the same age, as Richard Ellmann points out, that Wilde had contracted syphilis at Oxford.[244] He presents a set of characters whose lives are intimately linked by public and private secrets. Their relationships turn on the fine but critical distinction between honourable and dishonourable secrecy, which is parodied by Lord Goring in a famous disquisition on domestic confidences:

Secrets from other people's wives are a necessary luxury in modern life. So, at least, I am always told at the club by people who are bald enough to know better. But no man should have a secret from his own wife. She invariably finds it out. Women have a wonderful instinct about things. They can discover everything except the obvious.[245]

There is a sense throughout of impending disaster—'You know you are standing on the edge of a precipice,'[246] Mrs Cheveley warns Chiltern—and a far-sighted apprehension of the destructive role of the press in a new era of official rectitude: 'Nowadays', she continues,

with our modern mania for morality, everyone has to pose as a paragon of purity, incorruptibility, and all the other seven deadly virtues—and what is the result? You all go over like ninepins—one after the other. Not a year passes in England without somebody disappearing. Scandals used to lend charm, or at least interest, to a man—now they crush him. And yours is a very nasty scandal . . . Suppose that when I leave this house I drive down to some newspaper office, and give them this scandal and the proofs of it! Think of the loathsome joy, of the delight they would have in dragging you down, of the mud and mire they would plunge you in.[247]

High politics connected fiction and fact. Queensberry's vindictive fury against his younger son's lover was ignited by the suicide in the summer of

---

[243] C. Craft, *Another Kind of Love* (Berkeley, 1994), 136–9.
[244] Ellmann, *Oscar Wilde*, 387.
[245] Wilde, *An Ideal Husband*, 180.   [246] Ibid. 169.   [247] Ibid. 170.

1894 of his heir, Lord Drumlarig, who apparently feared the revelation of an affair with Lord Rosebery, the Liberal Prime Minister at the time of Wilde's arrest.[248] But as in the play, the real issue at the trials was not affairs of state, but the more general matter of formal and informal controls of the boundaries between public and private conduct. For much of the century that was now drawing to a close, improper sexual relations had shared with the improper communication of official information the character of double secrecy. Just as there was an unwritten conspiracy not to acknowledge practices of controlling information which were widely known to exist, so open recognition was denied to the problem of sodomy.[249] The function of this response, as Alan Sinfield has written, was 'not to conceal knowledge, so much as to conceal the knowledge of the knowledge'.[250] Local police-forces dealt enthusiastically with this transgression of the increasingly firm conventions of male sexuality, but for much of the nineteenth century it remained a vice whose name politicians were reluctant to utter. Labouchère's amendment to the 1885 Criminal Amendment Act under which Wilde was prosecuted was, like the first Official Secrets Act four years later, passed into law with a minimum of debate inside or outside Parliament.[251]

Wilde's trial demonstrated what could happen when the issue was finally given the oxygen of national publicity. The personal disaster accompanied a decisive shift in the meaning of the behaviour. This was partly an accident of timing. A trial even six months earlier might have had a different result for the history of both the theatre and the unspeakable vice. It was also a consequence of the tensions which had built up in the culture of honourable reserve. The code of the Victorian gentleman had been developed as a means of encasing the disruptive potential of liberalism in a structure of self-discipline. Increasingly its inculcation was the responsibility of a reformed education system, but the lessons in masculinity that this was delivering were decidedly ambiguous. More was learnt at Eton and Harrow than the virtues of loyalty, team spirit, and public service.[252] However provisional Gathorne-Hardy's calculation that 25 per cent of public-school boys of this era 'had sexual relations with each other on a regular basis',[253] there can be little doubt that in a court full of well-educated legal officers, Wilde will not have been alone in his knowledge of other men. His difference lay in the social status of his partners. The most damming evidence at the second trial was not the relationship with Douglas, which was long since physically dormant, but the details provided by one of the

---

[248] Ellmann, *Oscar Wilde*, 402.

[249] For further discussion of this issue, see the important forthcoming Ph.D thesis of Harry Cocks: 'Abominable Crimes: Sodomy, Law and Society, 1830–1885' (Manchester University).

[250] A. Sinfield, *The Wilde Century* (London, 1994), 8.

[251] J. Weeks, *Coming Out: Homosexual Politics in Britain from the Nineteenth Century to the Present* (rev. edn., London, 1990), 14–15.

[252] On sexual scandals in public schools in the 1870s and 1880s, see ibid. 17.

[253] J. Gathorne-Hardy, *The Public School Phenomenon, 597–1977* (London, 1977), 164.

new race of private detectives of his purchase of the services of working-class boys.[254]

The offence was compounded by the absence of contrition. When he was finally driven out of the world of subterfuge and blackmail in which he had lived for so long, Wilde made his stand on the right of the artist to define his own standards of conduct. As he had done since his days at Oxford, he represented liberalism as the negation of self-restraint, of Hellenism untrammelled by Hebraism.[255] The culture of the schooled gentleman was opposed by the anarchy of his educated *alter ego*. It was the sheer fragility of the boundary that forced a more emphatic labelling of deviance. The sodomite became the homosexual, not a man with a weakness, but a weakness which undermined all that manhood stood for. By this means, the activity was forced further into the private realm, but the condition emerged into the glare of public debate. In ways which were to be repeated in other contexts, the application of the law defined the secret but undermined the possibility of maintaining its secrecy.

---

[254] The ground for the trial was prepared by the Cleveland Street scandal five years earlier, which also involved the purchase by the high-born of the services of the low-born. Weeks, *Coming Out*, 19.

[255] L. Dowling, *Hellenism and Homosexuality in Victorian Oxford* (Ithaca, 1994), 117–24.

| # PUBLIC KNOWLEDGE, 1911–1945

Perfect Trust

Three years after he had supervised the passage of the Official Secrets Act, the Prime Minister wrote a long love letter to a close friend and contemporary of his daughter:

Can we ever forget those divine hours on Saturday & Sunday? They are part of us both, beyond the reach of chance or change—an ineffaceable memory—the little sheltered slope with the long grass, and the dogs in attendance, and the delicious alternations of silence & speech; and later on, the twilight on the wooden bench in the garden, with the moon & the evening star & the Great Bear, and—but it is too cruel to recreate what, until the lapse of many weary days & nights, we cannot renew. The price of absence & separation is heavy indeed, but not too heavy if (as I firmly believe) there is even more for us in the future than there has been in the past . . .

He then turned to another aspect of his affairs:

Now I will tell you a great *secret*. French intends,—if he can get Joffre's assent, and if Joffre can spare enough men to fill the gap—to 'disengage' as they call it i.e. to unlock his troops from their present position, and to make with his whole force a great outflanking march via Amiens, Arras, Douai, Tournay, to the line across Belgium from Brussels to Cologne. He thinks he could do it in a week or 9 days, and the long march would be good for his troops. It would relieve Antwerp (wh. is going to be sorely pressed) take in the Germans in their flank & rear, break up their communications, & if successful put an end to the invasion of France. It is a great scheme (heartily approved by Kitchener) and I hope Joffre won't thro' timidity or over caution put spokes in the wheel . . .[1]

Asquith's correspondence with Venetia Stanley began a few months after the legislation in 1911. From the outset, the personal endearments and private gossip were interspersed with news of public affairs and discussion of political developments. Rather than disciplining his pen, the advent of the First World

---

[1] H. H. Asquith, *H. H. Asquith, Letters to Venetia Stanley*, selected and ed. M. and E. Brock (Oxford, 1982), 256.

War destroyed all pretence of self-censorship. Until May 1915 he wrote unceasingly, giving full details of virtually every Cabinet meeting during the critical early months of the war, as well as the most vital military and diplomatic information.

The affair and the correspondence through which mainly it was conducted were kept hidden at the time, but are now matters of historical record. Asquith's later biographers have made extensive use of the material contained in the letters, which were carefully edited for publication by Michael and Eleanor Brock in 1982.[2] There remains, however, much to be learned from the Prime Minister's epistolary dalliance. His unbuttoned transgression of the 1911 Act raises a set of issues about the relationship between regulation, trust, and privacy in the era of mass communication and total war.

At one level the liaison represented the high tide of correspondence as a mode of expression. Asquith was one of the last of the prime ministers who wrote by hand not only as a duty but also as a pleasure.[3] The fluent, lengthy letters were composed after, between, and sometimes even during Cabinet meetings. As with so many of his class and generation, he found it easier to give voice to his deepest feelings when distance had silenced direct utterance. His younger and lower-born successor Lloyd George preferred to conduct his public business by talk rather than by pen, and his love life in bed rather than on paper.[4] Moreover, this was letter-writing in the most ordinary sense of the term. Asquith rarely made use of the private messengers at his disposal. Each envelope, regardless of the sensitivity of its contents, was merely stamped and dropped into the nearest letter-box. On the last day of 1914, for instance, a detailed discussion written from Walmer Castle about the future command of the armed forces was curtailed not by its confidentiality but by the local collection times:

I told you *very secretly* about Sir A. Murray: the French are very keen to get rid of him as Chief of our staff: they don't seem to have any very specific charge against him except that he speaks poor French & is not *sympathique*. Both K & I think that Robertson is the right man to succeed him. Winston is for Haig, but it would be almost impossible to replace him where he is. This is *most private*. Darling I could go on talking to you for a long time, but I must get this off by the 2 p.m post, which will give it a chance of reaching you to-morrow morning.[5]

The correspondence represented the ultimate vindication of the long campaign waged by the Post Office since the 1840s to establish an unquestionable reputation for efficiency and integrity. Asquith was utterly confident that the

---

[2] See R. Jenkins, *Asquith* (London, 1964); S. Koss, *Asquith* (London, 1976); G. H. Cassar, *Asquith as War Leader* (London 1994); Asquith, *Letters to Venetia Stanley*.

[3] Jenkins, *Asquith*, 257, 346.

[4] On Lloyd George's aversion to writing letters, see S. Roskill, *Hankey, Man of Secrets*, Vol. 1, 1877–1918 (London, 1970), 340. On Neville Chamberlain, see below, p. 176.

[5] Asquith, *Letters to Venetia Stanley*, 349.

letters would not be delayed, mis-delivered, or lost, and that they would not be opened and read by anyone other than his inamorata. At one stage he contemplated using the telegraph to speed the interchange, but decided it would be too dangerous unless the lovers went to the trouble of devising their own code.[6] The postal service alone guaranteed privacy. It was a totally secure repository of the innermost secrets of his heart and his country.

As elsewhere in this episode, however, Asquith represented an unresolved tension between the old and the new. At exactly the moment when he was committing his political life to the hands of the postman, he was reluctantly sanctioning an irreparable breach in the sanctity of the mails. As we have seen, postal espionage had quietly recommenced in the early 1880s, and the scope of the secret warrants had been widened as domestic and overseas pressures grew in the closing years of the Edwardian era.[7] Nonetheless, the Home Office maintained its traditional distaste of large-scale censorship right up to the outbreak of hostilities. Initially the security services responded to this difficulty by the equally time-honoured device of extending covert activity without seeking official, let alone public, sanction. But when, in November 1914, a censorship form was inadvertently left in an MP's envelope, the Government was forced to adopt an organized policy.[8] Asquith was persuaded to establish the War Trade Intelligence Department to place the work on a legal footing. Between the first and last shots of the First World War, the number of postal and cable censors grew from one to nearly 5,000,[9] and although their work was scaled down with the Armistice, there was no possiblity of a return to the far more restricted pre-war system.

The genie could not be put back into the bottle because the relationship between communication and national security had been decisively altered by the experience of international conflict.[10] In the late nineteenth century the spy-catchers were preoccupied with the almost medieval problem of observations being made of fixed fortifications. The subsequent transmission of the information to the hostile country was a secondary consideration. However, as defence information became more technical, led by the naval arms race, and the spy networks became more organized, the focus of concern shifted to less physical processes. More and more the object of spies was paper-based technical knowledge, and the essence of their practice became communication over distance with other spies in their network and with their controllers at home. The rounding-up of the German spy ring at the outbreak of hostilities was made possible by the fact that, as the first historians of the naval secret service

[6] Asquith, *Letters to Venetia Stanley*, 191.
[7] See above, pp. 116–18.
[8] Andrew, *Secret Service*, 176–7.
[9] H. T. Fitch, *Traitors Within* (London, 1933), 127; N. Hiley, 'Counter-Espionage and Security in Great Britain During the First World War', *English Historical Review*, 101 (July 1986), 640.
[10] T. Richards, *The Imperial Archive: Knowledge and the Fantasy of Empire* (London, 1993), 113, 123–5.

put it: 'Intelligence men in all countries used the post with the utmost freedom, trusting to luck, presumably, that no suspicion attached to them.'[11] In this sense, the spies had much in common with Asquith, but their confidence was now fatally misplaced. The letters of the German agents were intercepted in the months before their arrest, and their postman, the London barber Karl Ernst, was the only one brought to trial.[12] Detection by breaking into the flow of cables and correspondence became and remained the basic task of counter-espionage.[13] Just as the spies exploited the perception that all knowledge was connected, so their foes depended on the fact that no spy was an island. Thus the attempt was made to intercept every letter or telegram leaving or entering Britain. 'After a time', recalled J. C. Silber, one of those employed in the work, 'the entire correspondence of the world was thus caught up in the fine-meshed net of the British censorship.'[14] So also, of course, was much private communication written to and from respectable British citizens. To avoid possible embarrassment, the Government took care to ensure that their secrets were read only by those raised in the culture of honourable discretion: 'the correspondence', noted Silber, 'was generally examined by ladies, who came mostly from the upper classes.'[15] Their status made them trustworthy, and their gender, according to the Special Branch officer Herbert Fitch, made them 'more methodological and painstaking'.[16]

For all his confidence, Asquith retained some sense of the enormity of the risk he was taking. A striking feature of the correspondence was his intermittent labelling of parts of the text as '*very private*', or '*most secret*', or 'for your private eye'. On the face of it, these occasional injunctions were somewhat superfluous, given that every second paragraph of every letter contained highly confidential material. Their insertion partly reflected a vestigial awareness by Asquith that some revelations were even more critical than others. Accounts of Cabinet debates would cause embarrassment if they found their way into the public domain, details of impending military manoeuvres, up to and including the planning of the Dardanelles campaign, could cost tens of thousands of lives and conceivably the entire war.[17] More specifically, the explicit appeals to Venetia's discretion served to emphasize the real function of the discourse. The secret relationship was bound together by a sharing of secrets.

---

[11] H. C. Bywater and H. C. Ferraby, *Strange Intelligence: Memoirs of Naval Secret Service* (London, 1931), 220.

[12] Andrew, *Secret Service*, 70–1.

[13] For a detailed, if at times highly coloured account of the use made of postal espionage in the campaign against German spies, see Fitch, *Traitors Within*, 100–91.

[14] J. C. Silber, *The Invisible Weapons* (London, 1932), 106.

[15] Ibid. 109. Three-quarters of the censors employed at the end of the war were women.

[16] Fitch, *Traitors Within*, 127.

[17] The scale of the threat to national security is briefly assessed in Cassar, *Asquith as War Leader*, 35.

It was scarcely a union of equals. Venetia apparently replied to the torrent of letters,[18] and as an intelligent, politically literate woman was capable of giving her opinion on the events of the day. But there was no possibility of reciprocal indiscretion. At every juncture she was hopelessly outgunned by the Prime Minister's arsenal of inside information. Asquith was not above exploiting his power in order to titillate. On 27 October 1914, for instance, he put on a display of self-censorship: 'Winston came here before lunch in a rather sombre mood. Strictly between you & me, he has suffered to-day a terrible calamity on the sea, which I *dare* not describe, lest by chance my letter should go wrong: it is known only to him & me, and for a long time will & must be kept secret.'[19] A mere twenty-four hours later, Venetia's aroused curiosity was satisfied:

The disaster of wh. I wrote to you in veiled language yesterday was the sinking of the *Audacious*—one of the best & newest of the super Dreadnoughts, with a crew of about 1,000 and 10 3.5 inch guns, off the North Coast of Ireland . . . It is by far the worst calamity the Navy has so far sustained, as she cost at least 2 1/2 millions.[20]

As Edward Shils observed, the 'secret with an aura of fatefulness' is the most seductive form of concealed knowledge.[21] In this case, secrecy was not only sexy, but a substitute for sex in what was an intense but most probably unconsummated relationship.[22]

Asquith himself had no doubts about the true meaning of his indiscretion. A few days after naming the sunken dreadnought, whose fate the Government was still trying to keep out of the newspapers, he stepped back from the flow of news to survey the course of the correspondence:

I have written to you with more confidence & fullness & intimacy (a thousand times) than I ever have to any other human being, and the 'huge & growing pile', which already takes up so much room in your box, covers some of the most soul-stirring events that have happened or are likely to happen in our time . . . I believe hardly any one (indeed, no-one) knows so much of its real inner history as you do. Perfect love coupled with *perfect trust* is the best boon that life can give . . .[23]

There was no hyperbole here. Venetia had indeed been granted a ringside seat at the greatest armed conflict for a century. She had been in receipt of history as it was made, an epistolary witness to a conflict more dependent on transmissible knowledge than any before. The couple were bound together by the

---

[18] Her letters have not survived, but there is a strong sense in Asquith's correspondence of a continuing exchange, and of Venetia commenting upon the news she was receiving, sometimes at Asquith's direct request.

[19] Asquith, *Letters to Venetia Stanley*, 287.

[20] Ibid. 290.

[21] E. A. Shils, *The Torment of Secrecy* (London, 1956), 27.

[22] The balance of opinion is that the heated nature of the endearments reflected the conventions of Edwardian letter writing rather than a physical relationship. In any event, they spent a good deal of their time at a distance from each other, linked only by their correspondence. See Jenkins, *Asquith*, 365; Koss, *Asquith*, 140–1; Cassar, *Asquith as War Leader*, 34.

[23] Asquith, *Letters to Venetia Stanley*, 299–300.

deaths that would come to so many men if the secrets escaped the correspondence. Trust was at once a prior condition and a necessary consequence of the revelations. The prospect of their exposure lay at the heart of the relationship. As Georg Simmel wrote just a few years before the war: 'secrecy is surrounded by the possibility and temptation of betrayal; and the external danger of being discovered is interwoven with the internal danger, which is like the fascination of an abyss.'[24]

In the event it was not the Prime Minister but the man whose trust was betrayed. As far as is known, the letters remained in Venetia's box. Neither the military nor the Cabinet secrets leaked out, although given the extent to which Venetia moved in official circles, it is difficult to be certain that she kept entirely to herself the political gossip to which she was privy. It was otherwise, however, with her affections. In the early months of 1915, with the war poised on a knife-edge, two members of the Government were secretly writing love letters to the same woman during Cabinet meetings.[25] Venetia eventually accepted the suit of the younger and unmarried man, Asquith's friend and protégé Edwin Montagu,[26] the Chancellor of the Duchy of Lancaster, and for several agonizing weeks allowed Asquith to continue pouring out the confidences of his heart and his government. 'I think this week has taught us to know one another better than ever before—if that were possible . . .'[27] he wrote just four days before Venetia finally revealed to him her own great secret.

The pitiful and pitiable outcome of Asquith's infatuation seems not to have unduly affected the fate of his ailing Ministry.[28] Just five days after replying to Venetia—'As you know well, *this* breaks my heart',[29]—he successfully negotiated the end of the last Liberal Government and the creation of the first War Coalition. If his correspondence collapsed the division between the realms of the public and the private, his outward conduct observed a rigid distinction. He had a detached gift for convincing women, consecutively and concurrently, that they were the sole repository of his confidences. In spite of the liaison, Margot Asquith still believed that he told her 'every secret, things he tells no one in the world'.[30] There were successors to Venetia, though never again the

---

[24] Wolff, *The Sociology of Georg Simmel*, 333. Simmel's analysis of secrecy was mainly written in 1908.

[25] See, for instance, Asquith to Venetia, 25 Feb. 1915, and Montagu to Venetia, 19 Apr. 1915. Asquith, *Letters to Venetia Stanley*, 287, 447–8, 554–5.

[26] He had been Asquith's Private Secretary between 1906 and 1910.

[27] Asquith, *Letters to Venetia Stanley*, 587: 7 May 1915.

[28] There remains some debate as to whether Asquith's political life was at all influenced by this event. Koss thinks not, and whilst Cassar believes that the calamity did have a major effect on him, he does not argue that the course of the political crisis was measurably altered by Venetia's announcement. The more significant personal betrayal was by Lloyd George. Cassar, *Asquith as a War Leader*, 99–100; Koss, *Asquith*, 186–7.

[29] Asquith, *Letters to Venetia Stanley*, 546–7.

[30] From a letter to Edwin Montagu. She was aware of Asquith's relationship by this time and admitted to jealousy of it. Asquith had told her that it should not interfere with their marriage, and had managed to convince her, as Margot wrote, that 'he shows me all his letters & all Venetia's'. Asquith, *Letters to Venetia Stanley*, 546–7; 6 Apr. 1915.

haemorrhage of official information, if only because he had none to tell after 1916. The significance of the affair lay less in its relevance to the conduct of the war and more in its exposure of the tensions in the growing structure of public secrecy. As well as supplying the definitive case history of the eroticism of apocalyptic secrets, Asquith was representative of the more mundane but critical inconsistencies in the legal and constitutional traditions Britain was fighting to preserve.

Cabinet secrecy was an obvious problem. Asquith's conduct was an exaggerated form of a now-established tradition of simultaneously deploring and practising the leakage of information. He rounded on those of his colleagues he suspected of loose talk,[31] but in spite of the rigours of war, his Cabinet was notoriously porous, to the despair of the rigid Kitchener, who famously declined to share military secrets with his colleagues until they agreed first to divorce their wives. A year after the end of the affair, Asquith's Coalition added a new regulation (27A) to the Defence of the Realm Act, which extended its coverage to Cabinet proceedings, and made journalists liable to prosecution for printing confidential documents. In the Commons, the Home Secretary, Sir Herbert Samuel, piously intoned the 'ancient rule' that 'the secrecy of the Cabinet is as essential and necessary a part of the working of our democratic Constitution as the publication of the proceedings of the House of Commons'.[32] Some subversive voices in the debate argued that 'the wonderful secrecy of Cabinet proceedings . . . is a custom observed rather in the breach than in the practice',[33] that the definition of a 'confidential document' was too vague, and that by extending the law to cover the receivers of deliberately leaked information the Cabinet was punishing innocent and honourable parties for its own transgressions, but the regulation was passed and after the War formed the basis of the extension of the Official Secrets Act in 1920.

Asquith ended his prime-ministerial career at a moment of transition in the conduct of Cabinet business. Until he finally left office in December 1916, no formal record was made of its proceedings. Alongside his daily summary to Venetia, he had to write a less spicy letter to the King, usually every other day. At the heart of the modernization of Cabinet procedure carried through by Lloyd George was the institution of a formal system of agendas, prepared memoranda, and systematic minutes under the supervision of the obsessively secret Maurice Hankey (whose secrets Asquith had nonetheless conveyed to Venetia).[34] This overdue transition from speech to paper as the basic working medium of the Cabinet created a new layer of inconsistency and conflict in the maintenance of secrecy. Once the war was safely won, ex-minister after ex-minister, beginning with Lloyd George himself, flouted the regulations they

---

[31] Koss, *Asquith*, 152.
[32] *Hansard*, 8 May 1916, col. 415.
[33] Ibid., col. 406.
[34] Asquith, *Letters to Venetia Stanley*, 387–8: 15 June 1915.

had themselves created by raiding the Cabinet documents in order to subsidize their retirement and establish their own place in the historical record.[35]

In his old age Asquith was anxious both to repair his finances and challenge the account of his unforgiven successor, but lacked the materials with which to do this. He had not kept a diary, and had discouraged his colleagues from doing so on the grounds that Cabinet discussions would be freer in their absence.[36] His solution was to ask Venetia for the return of his letters, which contained almost as full a record of Cabinet proceedings as Hankey would later write. The second volume of *Memories and Reflections* commenced with the outbreak of war in 1914. It was prefaced with a brief discussion of the ethics of writing contemporary history:

There seems to me no occasion why, after a decent interval, such a journal should not, with all possible verification of details, be published with the same freedom and fullness as the correspondence of the dead. There is no more ground for a permanent embargo of secrecy in the one case than in the other.[37]

However, he was not free to give a full and free explanation of the source of the account that followed. The narrative up to May 1915 took the form of what appeared to be contemporary notes but which were in fact unacknowledged extracts from the letters, with the endearments and occasional injunctions to secrecy carefully excised.[38] There was no mention of Venetia at all, nor of the correspondence, save a vague reference to 'letters to a few intimate friends, which they have been good enough to place at my disposal'.[39] Thus the confidential journey of public affairs to the private domain was reversed, as the amatory discourse was translated into official history. Venetia became a ghost in her own story, invisible to all save herself and her quondam lover.

Asquith's amoral manipulation of the rules of secrecy placed him squarely in the tradition of the contemporary constitutional order. In essence, keeping public secrets was a transitive rather than a reflexive procedure. Those at the head of the political and bureaucratic hierarchies imposed absolute obligations on their subordinates but felt themselves free to exercise such discretion as was consonant with their flexible sense of honour. It is doubtful whether Asquith could in fact have been successfully prosecuted under the Official Secrets Act in the event of a letter falling into the wrong hands. The legislation merely prohibited the unauthorized disclosure of official information; as head of the Government he might have mounted a defence of self-authorization.

---

[35] Naylor, *A Man and an Institution*, 42–126, 266–318. K. Middlemas, 'Cabinet Secrecy and the Crossman Diaries', *Political Quarterly*, 47: 1 (1976), 40–4.

[36] B. Thomson, *The Scene Changes* (London, 1939), 236. Three members of the Cabinet were nonetheless keeping diaries (Churchill, Harcourt, and Crewe).

[37] H. H. Asquith, *Memories and Reflections, 1852–1927* (London, 1928), ii. 1.

[38] Ibid. 3–75.

[39] Ibid. 2.

He was without question in breach of his Privy Councillor's Oath, from which only the monarch could release him, but the penalties here were less clear.

During his period as wartime leader Asquith set in motion an irreversible extension of the confidential state. He was himself fascinated by the new-found capacity of the government to block communication. As the British Expeditionary Force was assembled in the early days of the war, he observed to Venetia that: 'There has never been anything more wonderful than the persistent & impenetrable secrecy in which everything both on sea & land continues to be enveloped . . . It enables one to realise how easily & how soon any part of the world might be isolated from the rest.'[40] Through the clouds of war, the Government and its agencies glimpsed unprecedented possibilities of controlling the flow of information within and across the nation's boundaries. Alongside the postal censorship and the Defence of the Realm Act, the military and civilian counter-espionage services underwent a rapid expansion from their very narrow base in 1914. During the course of the hostilities their combined numbers grew from 127 officers and men of all ranks to 1,500, with their total budget increasing from £25,000 to £200,000.[41] 'Intelligence' became a necessary condition of operation not just for the professional spycatchers but for a host of Government departments. The nineteenth-century bureaucratic passion for statistics was replaced with a thirst for systematic knowledge about attitude and behaviour. By the middle of the war the battle against subversive employees of enemy states was all but won, and attention was turned to the potential malcontents and traitors working for the much-enlarged British war machine.[42] The momentum of covert surveillance was now unstoppable; targets were invented to provide work and justify budgets, or to give effect to hitherto suppressed animosities against dissenting ideologies and organizations.

There were tensions and doubts in the higher reaches of Government. Asquith himself had a patrician distaste for the periodic bouts of spy mania. But the problem of accommodating the wholesale erosion of pre-war safeguards was resolved not just by the unprecedented national crisis, but also by two key elements of continuity from the Edwardian culture of secrecy. First, it was always supposed that the problem lay outside the ruling order (except in the case of those with German ancestry or surnames). Spying on pacifists, harassing malingerers in munitions factories, or infiltrating left-wing organizations need not reflect upon or alter the behaviour of those in command of the state. The new generation of professional secret-keepers, such as Basil Thomson of Special Branch and Maurice Hankey of the Committee of Imperial Defence

[40] Asquith, *Letters to Venetia Stanley*, 165: 11 Aug. 1914.

[41] N. Hiley, 'British Internal Security in Wartime: The Rise and Fall of P.M.S.2, 1915–1917, '*Intelligence and National Security*, 1 (1986), 396.

[42] Hiley, 'Counter-Espionage and Security', 653–60. The transition from German spies back to anarchists and other domestic subversives is well described by Fitch, *Traitors Within*, 76.

and the Cabinet Office, were seen less as all-pervading controllers and more as official nannies whose fussing advice was by turns tolerated, evaded, and ignored. Secondly, many of the key developments occurred out of the sight not only of the general public and their Parliamentary representatives, but often of the Cabinet as well. The decision not to establish the security services on a statutory basis had been taken in 1909, confirming an established policy of maximizing flexibility and minimizing controversy, and the exigencies of war enabled the convention of secrecy about secrecy to flourish. Although the regulatory framework of the Defence of the Realm Act had to be debated, no such sanction was requested or given for the growth of the security services or, crucially, for the shift in the focus of their work from foreign agents to domestic subversives.[43] Both operational and strategic policy was mostly left to the heads of the agencies involved. Ministers either did not know what each other were doing, or collectively had no consistent lines of report and command in the field of secret surveillance. Their consciences were clear because they were largely empty.

The central characteristic of this period was that of an exponential rise in publicly significant knowledge contained within a nineteenth-century tradition of public confidentiality. In any context, the amount of secrecy is a function of the volume of sensitive information. Asquith's amatory correspondence was conditioned by the fact that he knew far more secrets than any preceding Prime Minister, but shared much the same attitude to their control. So it was more generally. The legislation of 1911 represented both a major turning-point in the state's acquisition of knowledge about its population, and the consolidation of the Victorian approach to the policing of official information. Prior to the National Insurance Acts, no long-term record was made of any British citizen beyond the snapshot entries in the parish register and decennial census, and the annual demand for income tax from those wealthy enough to pay it. With varying degrees of consistency, larger episodes were recorded for social and economic casualties by the prisons, workhouses, and visiting charities, and for those in employment by the occupational bureaucracies of the uniformed public service, especially the Post Office, and a handful of private employers, such as the railway companies.[44] Now the welfare system, which was radically enlarged by the wartime Separation Allowances and the Unemployment Insurance Act of 1920, generated a mass of sensitive, extended material about virtually every working-class family in the kingdom. A record office at Kew soon contained details of the employment histories of almost 12 million citizens.[45] The middle classes were largely spared this intrusion for another generation, except insofar as they had to render an annual account to the Inland Revenue.

---

[43] Hiley, 'Counter-Espionage and Security', 660.
[44] See Jayaweera *et al.*, *Pathways and Prospects*.
[45] H. C. Emmerson and E. C. P. Lascelles, *Guide to the Unemployment Insurance Acts* (London, 1928), 4.

If the nineteenth century was the epoch of the ledger, and the late-twentieth that of the computer, this was the era of the card index. It was first introduced in 1876,[46] developed by pioneering voluntary and commercial organizations in the succeeding decades, and decisively embraced by the state just before and during the First World War. The tens of thousands of personal cards created by the security services and not erased by the Armistice were only one aspect of a wholesale and continuing expansion of public data collection. Everywhere private details, usually in the form of abbreviated, abstracted, or invented life histories, were being stored away, with the subjects unable to influence their form, content, or further exploitation. The practice raised in a new and complex form the issue of trust in relations between the state and its newly enfranchised citizens. Outside the overheated prime-ministerial love letters, there could be no perfection of reciprocal confidence, but rather an unstable mixture of reluctant trust and incipient paranoia. The state sought information covertly because it feared illegitimate protest, and overtly because it accepted the legitimacy of at least some of the needs of the working-class family economy. The balance between what the public had a right to keep secret from the state and vice versa had to be renegotiated. The subjects of the growing domestic archive, who increasingly encountered their lives as objectified knowledge, were prepared to confide in a state which displayed a new respect for their personal dignity, but were inclined to mistrust both the methods and the ends of the inspection. The only controls lay in the *ad hoc* administrative regulations which were introduced in accordance with the bureaucratic cast of mind which underpinned and was in turn confirmed by the Official Secrets Act.[47] As peace returned, the inconsistencies between modern forms of acquiring sensitive information and traditional means of preventing access to it remained unresolved.

The Confidential Community

The one feature which above all linked the wartime Cabinets and the peacetime domestic population was a love of gossip. As for the politicians, so for the inhabitants of the tightly knit working-class neighbourhoods, the informal exchange of news and opinion was more than merely recreational. Here the notions of private and public spheres had always had little to do with the entities deployed by political theorists. They referred rather to the social spaces in-

---

[46] For a survey of its limited early use in business, see A. Lofft, *Understanding Accounting in its Social and Historical Context* (New York, 1988), 96–114.

[47] For a ferocious attack on the scope of 'delegated legislation', whose growth was seen to have been greatly accelerated by the war, see C. Allen, *Bureaucracy Triumphant* (Oxford, 1931), esp. 7–8, 10, 54, 79.

side and outside the home. There was a constant movement between these arenas, especially for the women left behind when their husbands went out to work. The exchange of news and opinions, the endless process of review and judgement, of comfort and censure, were the means by which the tensions between the interior and exterior worlds were negotiated.[48]

From its formation onwards, the seclusion of the household was a fundamental objective of all its members. Couples embarked on matrimony to escape the surveillance of their parents at home and their peers in the streets where most of their courtship took place. A physically distinct housing unit was held to be a necessary condition of marriage, to be secured before the wedding if possible, or if not, as soon thereafter as could be arranged. Separation was far more important than comfort. The young miner Bert Coombes recalled his relief when he and his new bride finally graduated from a rented room to their own home: 'Despite its many drawbacks, it was a house to ourselves, where we could talk without being overheard.'[49] Achievement was measured in terms of the capacity to erect barriers to communication. Majorie Spring Rice observed in her *Working Class Wives* of 1939, that

In England, side by side with the passionate wish to preserve the integrity of the family, there is found the determination to keep it as a whole as separate as possible from other families and from any outside intrusion. There was for a long time in this country an inherent dislike of flats amongst rich and poor alike, because to share a staircase or lift with another family, to have another family living overhead or underneath, was considered a violation of that privacy which is the family's inalienable right.[50]

The more outsiders looked in on the communities of the poor, the more comfort they took from their discovery of an aspiration which transcended class and confirmed national identity. As a speaker in a Commons debate on housing policy proclaimed: 'With regard to the question of popularity, there can be no doubt that a house with a garden is the Englishman's castle, it is the pride of the Englishman and the envy of the Continent.'[51]

However, except for the minority able to take advantage of the new council estates, neither a garden nor a fully self-contained domestic life was a possibility.[52] The castle of most working men and women was still so bare and

---

[48] On the scope and function of gossip in this period, see M. Tebbutt, 'Women's Talk? Gossip and "Women's Words" in Working-Class Communities, 1880–1939', in A. Davies and S. Fielding (eds.), *Workers' Worlds: Cultures and Communities in Manchester and Salford, 1880–1939* (Manchester, 1992), 49–68. Also Moore, *Privacy*, 268.

[49] B. L. Coombes, *These Poor Hands* (London, 1939), 131. Also J. Walsh, *Not Like This* (London, 1953), 81.

[50] M. Spring Rice, *Working-Class Wives* (London, 1939; 1981), 15.

[51] *Hansard*, 5th Series, 332, 3 Mar. 1938, col. 1321. The Glasgow tenements needed a different narrative.

[52] On the growth of the ideology of 'self-containedness' and seclusion, see Muthesius, *The English Terraced House*, 249.

overcrowded that the occupants were constantly forced out of doors in search of release and relaxation.[53] If husbands were in employment, they had a journey to make in the morning, and afterwards money to spend in public houses. Their wives were left with the neighbours, on but rarely over the threshold.[54] Here social contact was founded on the trading of information. A shared fascination in what the Durham miner's daughter Mary Craddock called the 'intricacies of human relationships' determined the substance of the conversation.[55] The strategy of each participant was to exchange the smallest number of her own secrets for the largest volume of her neighbours'. Emotional and material solace was only possible if the veil over private troubles was lifted a few inches, but if it was torn aside altogether, all sense of self-respect was lost, and with it the right to share in the network of mutual aid. Shared deprivation drew the women together, but the struggle for respectability required the preservation of a discreet reserve.[56] 'We did not need telling', recalled Richard Hoggart of inter-war Hunslet, 'that "good fences make good neighbours" even if the fences were only in the mind and the physical division only a thinnish party wall.'[57] The capacity to control the release of information about the household's circumstances was a mark of relative prosperity. Total transparency was a condition of absolute poverty. The battle was lost when it was no longer possible to conceal the consequences of malnutrition or the shaming devices adopted to ward off destitution.[58]

The dependency of character on concealment was most evident in the ritual at the pawnbrokers. This means of borrowing reached its peak around the time of the 1911 Official Secrets Act, and declined only very slowly in the following two decades.[59] 'People tried to be proud by not admitting they used the services of these shops,' wrote the 'Manchester Lad', C. W. Whiteley, 'but most people reluctantly used them.'[60] They did so because such expensive forms of credit were the most rational means of ironing out the peaks and troughs in a hard-pressed family economy. The search for both cash and anonymity gave the premises a unique atmosphere, as the future playwright Ted Willis recalled:

They were dark, discreet, secret places, which had to be entered by a side door and where conversation was carried on in low whispers from small cubicles. The counter and the dividing partitions were high enough to preserve some degree of

[53] J. Blake, *Memories of Old Poplar* (London, 1977), 12.

[54] On the 'taboo' on entering other houses except in emergencies, see D. Gittins, *Fair Sex: Family Size and Structure, 1900–1939* (London, 1982), 139–40.

[55] M. Craddock, *A North Country Maid* (London, 1960), 51. Also R. Hoggart, *The Uses of Literacy* (Harmondsworth, 1958), 120–31; J. Seabrook, *The Everlasting Feast* (London, 1974), 157.

[56] Bell, *At the Works*, 318; J. Bourke, *Working-Class Cultures in Britain, 1890–1960* (London, 1994), 142–3.

[57] R. Hoggart, *A Local Habitation: Life and Times, 1: 1918–1940* (London, 1968), 76.

[58] Vincent, *Poor Citizens*, 3.

[59] M. Tebbutt, *Making Ends Meet: Pawnbroking and Working-Class Credit* (London, 1983), 137 and *passim*.

[60] C. W. Whiteley, 'A Manchester Lad/Salford Man', TS (Keele), 11. Also W. Greenwood, *How the Other Man Lives* (London, 1939), 230–9; D. Bailey, *Children of the Green: A True Story of Childhood in Bethnal Green, 1922–1937* (London, 1981), 40.

privacy, and it was not always possible to know what the person in the next cubicle was putting up for pawn, or redeeming.[61]

The really poor presented their goods in person; the less poor paid a penny to a child or to an old woman who specialized in such work to deputize for them; the respectable housewife watched through her curtains the shame of her neighbours.

Those whom one contemporary study of slum life termed 'The Secret People'[62] were secret in a double sense. In the face of outsiders, the community was bound together by its sense of exclusive knowledge.[63] Strangers were as far as possible kept in ignorance, especially where the sanctioned behaviour of the neighbourhood transgressed official values or regulations. 'If there was the odd secret deal', recalled Elsie Goodhead of the back streets of Derby, 'no one told the police.'[64] The wall of confidentiality could be so thick as to deaden the sound of the outside world altogether. 'Sometimes', she wrote, 'it seemed that the West End was enclosed—that the rest of Derby did not exist. Everybody knew everybody. Strangers hardly ever ventured there and if they did it was usually on business of some kind which was conducted as hastily as possible.'[65] Newcomers were accepted only when they had proved their fitness to enter the collective oral archive. Within the community, however, the strategies of communication were much more complex. From the perspective of the detached and semi-detached suburban villas, which were becoming the template of middle-class civilization,[66] street gossip appeared an undiscriminating flow of public discourse. In practice it was a constantly shifting pattern of exposure and suppression, as the participants sought both to repair and defend the limitations of their private lives.[67] The direction of history in this period was towards a lowering of the barriers between the neighbourhoods and a raising of those between individual households. What Jerry White has termed the 'fetishisation of home-based privacy'[68] began to infect working-class households whose earnings had remained at least stable during a period of long-term deflation. For some it was a matter of a gradual retreat as marginal increases in prosperity created more comfort in the home and less need to run the gauntlet of the casual inquisition which began once the front door was opened. For others it was a sudden translation to a municipal estate with its unimaginable

[61] E. H. Willis, *Whatever Happened to Tom Mix? The Story of One of My Lives* (London, 1970), 69. Also D. Scannell, *Mother Knew Best: An East End Childhood* (London, 1974), 42.

[62] H. Marshall and A. Trevelyan, *Slum* (London, 1933). Title of opening chapter (pp. 1–36).

[63] P. Ayers, *The Liverpool Docklands* (Liverpool, 1988), 67; J. White, *The Worst Street in North London* (London, 1986), 72–80.

[64] E. E. Goodhead, *The West End Story, Derby During the Depression: A Social and Personal History* (Matlock, 1983), 25.

[65] Ibid. 28.

[66] On privacy and the suburban semi, see P. Oliver, I. Davis, and I. Bentley, *Dunroamin: The Suburban Semi and its Enemies* (London, 1981), 91.

[67] Tebbutt, 'Women's Talk?', 63; Hoggart, *A Local Habitation*, 75, 127.

[68] White, *Worst Street in North London*, 134.

delights of private sanitation and enclosed gardens, and its unknown problems of absent relatives and silent neighbours.[69]

The process of opening up to the outside world was also uneven and ambiguous. At the noisiest but most unobtrusive level, there was a continual increase in street traders bringing to the doorstep an ever-widening range of goods and services. The callers were a means of connecting their customers to a national consumer network, and brought with them scraps of news and opinion from beyond the horizon of the locality. They were outsiders in name only, at best of only marginally superior status, and in times of mass unemployment often only one step ahead of destitution. The more difficult issue was the response given to those representing non-indigenous bodies of knowledge and expertise who were also an increasing presence in the neighbourhood. These visitors were more professional than their pre-war counterparts, and in most cases more powerful. They demanded new forms of trust, and threatened new assaults on privacy.

The trajectory of change can be glimpsed in the fate of the Anglican clergy, who had spearheaded the drive back into outcast communities during the closing decades of the nineteenth century. Although they had in large part discarded their dreams of a comprehensive home-visiting campaign which would reach every part of every fallen household in the parish, they were still encouraged to venture out and meet their flock in its natural habitat. To many in the church hierarchy, there was a real danger that the new generation of clergy was giving up the task in the face of the indifference or hostility of those upon whom they called. The Bishop of Winchester feared that, 'through the abandonment of visiting the Church is losing hold on parish after parish'.[70] According to the Bishop of Durham's *Ad Clerum*, the most influential manual for ordinands of the period, 'one of the main sources of pastoral inefficiency in the English clergy today is their ignorance of their own people . . .'[71] This was especially true of the large town parishes, where a powerful cultural identity was developing about which most of their priests knew little and understood less.

The solution appeared to be an intensification of the pre-war moves towards better training and more sophisticated methods of organization. The new incumbent needed first of all a plan, without which, advised the author of *The Parson and his Problems*, 'many clergy attempt this house-to-house visiting, waste their energy and vitality on what is often a complete failure, and becoming embittered or lazy according to temperament, give up visiting

---

[69] For a sensitive study of the gains and losses of moving to a new estate, see A. Hughes and K. Hunt, 'A Culture Transformed? Women's Lives in Wythenshawe in 1930', in Davies and Fielding, *Workers' Worlds*, 74–96. For a vivid account of moving from Poplar to a two-bedroomed council house in Dagenham, and then fleeing back to the warmth of kin and neighbours, see Blake, *Memories of Old Poplar*, 46.

[70] Cited in R. C. Joynt, *The Church's Real Work* (London, 1934), 53.

[71] H. H. Henson, *Ad Clerum* (London, 1937), 148.

altogether'.[72] The contemporary priest, like every other modern professional, needed to be a master of the card index. This was to be used to divide up the urban parish into manageable units, and to constitute a transferable record of the personal histories of every household which permitted a spiritual intrusion.[73] The information on these cards was to be obtained only from the subjects themselves, although it might be necessary to adopt an oblique approach to the more sensitive areas of past conduct. It was important that the clerical visitor keep aloof from the street information network: 'Do not let people gossip about their neighbours', urged the author of *The Parish Priest in his Parish.* 'It is very dangerous, though there are a few saints whom you can trust, and get information from, when you need to.'[74]

This self-imposed exclusion from the collective archive of personal habits, aspirations, and values, highlighted the essential problem of the parish visitor. He had to construct an autonomous channel of communication bounded by an absolute trust that the transmitted private secrets would not be misused or misapplied. It is evident from the advice manuals that confidentiality remained a serious problem within the profession. At the heart of the matter was the seal of the confessional, which as the standard guide of the period put it, 'is the obligation imposed upon the priest to keep secret everything made known to him by natural, divine, and ecclesiastical law, and admits of no exception'.[75] But even at this most formal level, the 'mental safe' in which the information was to be locked, was all too easily left ajar. 'This may be done', explained *The Parish Priest at Work,*

in speaking in a loud voice at confession; in speaking in sermons of sins heard in confession in a way likely to lead to identification, especially when it is done by a priest who has heard few confessions, or who has few penitents; by change of conduct towards a penitent; by injudiciously warning parents about their children; by speaking to penitents about their confessions unless invited to do so.[76]

If this was the fate of secrets gained in the confessional, so much greater was the danger where the material was not governed by the 113th canon of the Canons of 1603.[77]

[72] J. B. Goodliffe, *The Parson and his Problems* (London, 1933), 79.

[73] See e.g. Joynt, *Church's Real Work*, 54; C. R. Forder, *The Parish Priest at Work* (London, 1947), 266–70. Less technocratic manuals remained committed to the ruled notebook for family histories. See J. T. Inskip, *The Parish Idea* (London, 1905), 239.

[74] A. L. Preston, *The Parish Priest in his Parish* (London, 1933), 14. Also H. E. Savage, *Pastoral Visitation* (London, 1903), 47.

[75] F. G. Belton, *A Manual for Confessors* (London, 1916), 89.

[76] Forder, *Parish Priest at Work*, 325.

[77] 'If any man confess his secret and hidden sins to the Minister . . . we do straightly charge and admonish him, that he do not at any time reveal and make known to any person whatsoever any crime or offence so committed to his trust and secrecy (except they be such crimes as by the laws of this realm his own life may be called into question for concealing the same), under pain of irregularity' (cited by Belton, *Manual for Confessors*, 90–1).

In the end, the only security that could be offered the parishioner lay in the conscious self-discipline of the visitor. No amount of regulation could stand in for character. Henry Savage's *Pastoral Visitation* summarized what was needed:

it is required always that he shall be a gentleman in the truest Christian sense of the name; a man of unfailing courtesy and sympathy, of truth and fairness in word and deed; one who holds control of himself and knows how to keep his own counsel, and theirs. Englishmen assume that they can implicitly trust their clergyman, and woe to the influence of him who through self-conceit, or selfishness, or rudeness, or by an unbridled tongue, once betrays this loyal trust.[78]

In the Established Church the concept of honourable secrecy remained at the core of the approach to gaining public confidence. The properly raised, properly trained clergyman always knew what he should not say and where. The mutually reinforcing qualities of good breeding and instinctive discretion would smooth a path to the hearth and the heart of the doubting parishioner. As *The Church's Real Work* explained: 'A man's home is his castle, and is to be approached with the gracious courtesy which is the mark of a gentleman. The poorer the home the more call there is for this. Official or patronising airs are to be abjured, and as the visitor goes on his genial way he will have need of tact.'[79]

However, mental constructs which still functioned within the formal apparatus of the state were increasingly redundant at the level of domestic visitation. In the era of mass democracy, the gap between the corridors of Whitehall and the back streets of Whitechapel was widening. The point had been made with unanswerable logic in an unusually clear-sighted guide to parish work written by C. F. Rogers back in 1905: 'The *visit* is not a social call such as would be paid in the houses of the rich.'[80] A gentleman would never arrive uninvited on the doorstep of another gentleman, still less would he contemplate visiting a respectable married woman in the absence of her husband. What above all was missing was any sense of reciprocity. The clergyman was expected to make, not receive calls. Having taken tea with a working-man's wife, he did not look to see her in his own parlour the next afternoon. The greater the stress on gentlemanly reserve, the more indefensible became the entire ritual:

The very fact that such a visit is made is a gross impertinence, and sets up a false relation at once, which effectually prevents the caller from ever getting really to know the people on whom he calls. It is not necessary, therefore, to dwell on the complete failure of house-to-house visitation, to point out how it is resented by the poor, to speak of the bad reacting effect on the character of the man whom it puts continually in a false position, or to enlarge on the natural repugnance universally felt to the task.[81]

---

[78] Savage, *Pastoral Visitation*, 8.
[79] Joynt, *Church's Real Work*, 55. Also J. Watts-Ditchfield, *The Church in Action* (London, 1913), 61.
[80] C. F. Rogers, *Principles of Parish Work* (London, 1905), 188.
[81] Ibid. 188–9.

No matter how hard the clergyman tried, patronizing airs were inescapable. Advising the vicar to share a smoke with the man of the household (unless it was really unspeakable shag),[82] was never going to be enough to establish the exchange on anything like an equal footing. The Church was caught in a dilemma. It was too worried about its parochial ignorance to withdraw from the practice or to return to the mid-nineteenth-century tactic of making contact through tracts and leaflets,[83] but too wedded to its social status to abandon the whole edifice of honourable secrecy. Thus, in this period it was forced to condemn cohort after cohort of new curates to learn over again the lesson spelled out by Rogers, that condescension and communication were no longer as compatible as once they had been.

It was left to the emerging profession of social work to attempt a more creative response to this problem. As it pursued its journey from the spiritual to the secular sphere, it was forced to face up to much the same difficulty. In 1920 the public-school-educated Mayor of Stepney condensed his experience of missionary labours in the East End into a book entitled *The Social Worker*. 'The first qualification', wrote Clement Attlee,

for any one who wishes to engage in social work is sympathy. The social worker is coming, as a rule, from a class that has many advantages of wealth, leisure and education, and is endeavouring to share these advantages with others who are less well circumstanced and whose surroundings and opportunities are wholly different.[84]

Social distance had to be recognized as an obstacle rather than an advantage in gaining the trust of those who needed assistance. This entailed a systematic enlargement of the bureaucratic initiatives of the Charity Organisation Society in order to counteract its legacy of intrusive paternalism.

By the early post-war years, the occasional lecture courses established in the 1890s had developed into a full-scale programme of accredited institutional education.[85] Half-a-dozen universities had created departments of social service and administration which were awarding their own certificates and diplomas.[86] Each course had a practical element in which students undertook a supervised placement in an approved charity or local-authority scheme, where they were encouraged to reflect on the problems of conflicting backgrounds and values. Disciplined self-awareness was seen, if not as the solution then at least as the point of departure for the long journey towards creating a relationship based on mutual respect. As part of this endeavour, greater effort was

---

[82] See the discussion on this matter in P. Green, *The Town Parson* (London, 1929), 53.

[83] Mass tract distribution was no longer commended, although there were those urging the use of more ambitious parish newsletters and magazines. See L. S. Hunter, *A Parson's Job* (London, 1931).

[84] C. R. Attlee, *The Social Worker* (London, 1920), 126.

[85] M. Sewell, 'The Beginnings of Social Training, 1890–1903', in E. Macadam, *The Equipment of Social Workers* (London, 1925), 25–32.

[86] Attlee, *Social Worker*, 145.

made to widen the social base of recruitment to the courses, and to encourage those from privileged backgrounds to spend at least a token period in manual employment. As the leading theoretician of social work in the period put it, 'there can be no doubt that simple natural contact with fellow workers on equal terms which such an experience would afford would do much to break down barriers and to obliterate that objectionable social worker touch of un-conscious condescension which is so difficult to avoid'.[87] The role of volunteers was redefined. Where once they had been valued because of their indepen-dence of the constraint of earning a living, now they were seen as potential part-time representatives of the toiling masses themselves. To this end, tenta-tive efforts were made to build bridges with trade unions and the various pres-sure groups which were springing up in the field of family welfare.

The trainee social workers were also indoctrinated in the overriding impor-tance of keeping formal, transferable records of their home visits. In part it was a matter of integrating the nascent social-work movement with the growing structure of official welfare. As an increasing range of bodies organized their work around case papers and card indexes, the systematic summary of indi-vidual or family history became the essential unit of professional exchange.[88] More generally, it was a means of imposing greater rigour on the process of interrogation. Here again, the innovation of the COS was deployed against its ideology. With proper training in completing the case papers it would be pos-sible to diminish the perceived assault on domestic secrecy. There is, explained Attlee,

the general dislike that every one has to having his most private affairs made public. The art of collecting information requires not only thoroughness but im-mense tact in order to avoid wounding the self-respect of those who apply for relief: this tact is not always forthcoming, with the result that the applicant to the C.O.S. feels that he has to abandon all privacy and all self-respect.[89]

There was no overnight revolution. Progress was slow both in transforming the outlook of the social worker and in recognizing the complex problems of secrecy inherent in the increasing dependency on transmissible records. Whilst trained visitors were to be more sensitive to the issue of domestic re-serve, they were encouraged to share the resulting information indiscrimi-nately across the professional networks. The disjunction between vertical and lateral confidentiality, which had been a feature of the developments in the later nineteenth century, remained largely intact. However, there was a clear direction of change, and more than anything else it was this which condi-

---

[87] E. Macadam, *The Social Servant in the Making* (London, 1945), 61.
[88] For a full account of the statutory and professional encouragement of systematic record keep-ing in the various branches of relief and welfare, see E. Macadam, *The New Philanthropy* (London, 1934), 94–7. Also E. Eve (ed.), *Manual for Health Visitors and Infant Welfare Workers* (London, 1921), 85–6, 119–21.
[89] Attlee, *Social Worker*, 66.

tioned the response to the emergence between the wars of a wholly new form of domestic visitation. As was stressed in the previous chapter, the Insurance Acts of 1911, together with the Old Age Pensions Act of 1908, represented a critical decision to divorce the granting of relief from the destruction of privacy. Although the concession of trust to the family economies of the labouring poor was reluctant and incomplete, it did appear to constitute a sea-change of attitude and administrative practice, at once a consequence of the growth of the franchise and a precondition of the move towards full political citizenship in 1918. However, the dramatic fivefold increase in the cost of public welfare in the immediate aftermath of peace, coupled with a sudden downturn in the economy, exposed the latent lack of confidence in the financial morality of the dependent poor.[90]

In February 1922 a fresh species of visitor came knocking on the door of distressed households. As the Insurance Fund plunged into deficit, investigating officers were appointed to check the statements of every claimant, and a limited means test was introduced for those whose benefits were no longer covered by their insurance contributions.[91] Apart from a brief period between 1924 and 1925, means-testing and the accompanying inspections were a fact of life for the casualties of the economy throughout the remainder of the inter-war period. Alongside the domestic intrusions, unemployed workers faced regular questioning at the labour exchanges, particularly during the period of the Genuinely Seeking Work Test under which 3 million claims were disallowed between 1921 and 1930.[92] The proliferating forms of interrogation were a consequence of a double breakdown of trust. Under pressure of mounting costs, increasing unemployment, and growing left-wing militancy, the state lost confidence in the capacity of those in distress to behave honestly in applying for benefits, or legally if the benefits were withdrawn. The only solution was to maintain the welfare system, albeit in an endlessly modified form, and to institute new patterns of surveillance over both the collective bodies of the unemployed and the individual family economies. Thus, the National Unemployed Workers' Movement had undercover Special Branch members sitting on its National Administrative Committee and tapping its phones,[93] and, especially

[90] B. B. Gilbert, *Social Policy, 1914–1939* (London, 1970), 25–32; P. Abrams, 'The Failure of Social Reform, 1918–20', *Past and Present*, 24 (1963), 44; R. Lowe, 'The Erosion of State Intervention in Britain, 1917–24', *Economic History Review*, 31 (May 1978), 270.

[91] A. Deacon, *In Search of the Scrounger* (London, 1976), 26–8.

[92] Ibid. 9.

[93] J. Halstead, R. Harrison, and J. Stevenson, 'The Reminiscences of Sid Elias', *Bulletin of the Society for the Study of Labour History*, 38 (Spring 1979), 45; R. Hayburn, 'The Police and the Hunger Marchers', *International Review of Social History*, 17: 3 (1972), 627–32; W. Hannington, *Never on Our Knees* (London, 1967), 142–3, 146–7; R. Croucher, *We Refuse to Starve in Silence* (London, 1987), 203–21; J. Morgan, *Conflict and Order* (Oxford, 1987), 248–9; T. Bunyan, *The Political Police in Britain* (London, 1976), 120–1. The phones of the Communist Party were tapped continuously from the later 1920s. P. Fitzgerald and M. Leopold, *Strangers on the Line: The Secret History of Phone Tapping* (London, 1987), 38; Thurlow, *The Secret State*, 158–69.

after the institution of the full household means test in 1931, every claiming family had an inspector periodically sitting at its kitchen table counting its possessions.

The outcome of the decline in trust was an increase in secrecy. Behaviour central to the struggle for existence now had to been hidden from view. There was a widespread conflict between the new devices of the state and the traditional strategies of the poor. The rules of the labour exchanges and the means tests penalized the two basic responses to poverty, seeking casual employment and sharing resources within the family.[94] 'It led', recalled Ted Willis, 'to a shameful game of hide-and-seek between investigators and the unemployed.'[95] There was no compunction about engaging in this level of deceit, but neither was there any pride. The minor victories were bought at a cost to self-respect. As she struggled to manage her growing family in an Oldham slum, Jane Walsh found that minor household tasks were taking on a new, degrading significance: 'What did worry me was that I did not feel strictly honest any more ... I felt mean, washing and sewing in the dead of night to earn a few extra pence. I dared not hang the washing outside in case the Means Test man caught me. Every shilling I earned would have been deducted from Charlie's dole.'[96] This discomfort was reinforced by the regulations which, in both their substance and their application, assumed that claimants were guilty of deception unless they could prove otherwise.

The endless round of public interrogation made every aspect of private life a potential secret. Deprivation had always promoted concealment. Wives struggling to make ends meet attempted to hide their compromises from their husbands, couples combined to screen their family's defeats from all outside gaze. As the casual labourer Archie Hill wrote: 'The secrets of poverty, in an era of poverty, had to be kept from open knowledge. Otherwise all my strength could be gone and the world would kick me in the teeth with mockery and contempt.'[97] Now the defence of domestic information had a new focus, uniting the often fissiparous households against a common enemy. In Walter Brierley's vivid fictionalized account of the means test, the embittered wife was reunited with her husband in their time of trial: 'She blamed him for the poverty of the home, yet she blamed the Means Test investigators for the violation of it; she stood shoulder to shoulder with him when the man came poking into their secrets.'[98] The whole experience was a grotesque parody of the official celebration of domestic privacy:

[94] Vincent, *Poor Citizens*, 70–9.
[95] Willis, *Tom Mix*, 110. Also J. Dash, *Good Morning Brothers* (London, 1969), 10; W. Oxley, 'Are You Working?', in J. Common (ed.), *Semen Shifts* (London, 1938), 126.
[96] J. Walsh, *Not Like This* (London, 1953), 82.
[97] A. Hill, *A Cage of Shadows* (London, 1977), 33.
[98] W. Brierley, *Means-Test Man* (Nottingham 1983; 1st pub. 1935), 204.

The master and mistress of a household—the two heads of a home—husband and wife in their castle—English—And this man sat where those friends had sat, he was like a lord and they stood trembling before him. It was something else besides a means test, it tested one's soul, one's being, and the soul and the being were poorer every time.[99]

It may be argued against the more melodramatic representations of the means test that the protestors lacked a knowledge of history. The original workhouse test had in many respects represented a far more comprehensive assault on the dignity of the dispossessed. Unlike the hated Boards of Guardians in their Victorian heyday, the new bureaucracy had more limited powers, more precise regulations, and a formal appeal system.[100] At the summit of their ambition, the philanthropic ladies had demanded the exposure of a much wider range of personal secrets than the most energetic National Insurance inspector would ever wish to know. However, the force of the reaction was derived precisely from the sense that the new species of home visitor represented a reversal of the historical momentum. The process of the inspection negated every principle of the theory of domestic interviewing being developed by the nascent social-work profession. In the new training manuals it was, for instance, axiomatic that the outsider observed all the formalities of polite society in calling upon a household, no matter how destitute it might be. Now the front door was only a token obstacle to invasion. Ernie Benson, an unemployed engineer living in the tight-knit community of Hunslet celebrated in Hoggart's *Uses of Literacy*, recalled the visits of the inspectors:

They would very often enter the house after giving a peremptory knock without waiting to be asked in, and sometimes they didn't even bother to knock. Usually they would demand to look into the food cupboards or the cellars to see if there was food stored away. They would closely question the householder about the furniture and other household effects.[101]

There was a common hostility amongst the unemployed towards these procedures and the individuals who carried them out. Yet just as gossip was a means of both resolving and generating conflict amongst hard-pressed families, so the new welfare system both consolidated and fractured the unity of the poor locality. Whilst households struggled to conceal their secrets, their neighbours secretly attempted to expose them. Ernie Benson recounted a particular interrogation about his spare-time activities:

---

[99] Ibid. 263.

[100] On the operation of the courts of referees, see M. Cohen, *I Was One of the Unemployed* (London, 1945), 149–51; Elias, 'Reminiscences', 8–10; J. Connolly, *An Easy Guide to the New Unemployment Act* (London, *c*.1935), 13.

[101] E. Benson, *To Struggle is to Live: A Working Class Autobiography*, Vol. 2 (Newcastle-upon-Tyne, 1980), 30.

'Well I have a letter here which says you do quite a fair amount of boot repairing for other people,' and he held up an envelope with a letter inside. 'That's interesting. Can I have a look at it?.' 'No, you can't.' 'Who is the writer?' 'I won't tell you that.' 'Is it an anonymous letter?' 'Yes' he admitted. 'Well, in that case chuck it in there' I said, indicating the waste paper basket. 'I can't do that, I must place it before the committee.'[102]

The unsigned letter to those in authority, which a century earlier had been a device for collectively threatening the well-being of the privileged,[103] was now a means of individually endangering the last resources of the deprived. In essence, the National Insurance system was a means of redistributing resources within the working class. Those in work made an enforced and rising contribution to those out of work, placing an inevitable strain on structures of mutual sympathy and trust. The common currency of gossip—who had found what new job, who was sharing whose bed, who had purchased which new commodity—suddenly became charged with an official significance. Too indignant to let an unjustified advantage pass, but too ashamed to make an open report, someone along the street wrote anonymously to the inspectors.[104] As George Orwell discovered in his journey through the Depression-hit northern towns, amidst the warmth and solidarity 'there is much spying and tale-bearing'.[105]

There was little new in this procedure. In 1867 Edwin Waugh's celebration of the strengths of the Lancashire factory community in the face of the cotton famine was forced to concede that 'the poor are not always kind to the poor . . . it is not uncommon for the committees to receive anonymous letters, saying that so and so is unworthy of relief, on some ground or other. These complaints were generally found to be either wholly false, or founded upon some mistake.'[106] We have seen how so slight an issue as dog licences was stimulating a flow of denunciations to the Inland Revenue a decade later.[107] Wherever there was an outside agency with the authority to affect the well-being of a community and the bureaucracy to acquire and mobilize knowledge, there was the temptation of neighbourly betrayal. Linda Pollock reports a lively trade in malicious reporting to the sixteenth-century church courts.[108] All that was specific

---

[102] E. Benson, *To Struggle is to Live: A Working Class Autobiography*, 38–9. The encounter degenerated into a shouting match, and Benson's relief was suspended for five weeks, including the Christmas period.

[103] Thompson, 'The Crime of Anonymity'; E. J. Hobsbawm and G. Rudé, *Captain Swing* (Harmondsworth, 1973), 73, 88, 93–4, 103–4, 111, 113, 116, 132, 166, 171–5; Vincent, 'Communication, Community and the State', 170–3.

[104] F. W. Bakke, *The Unemployed Man: A Social Study* (London, 1933), 94; H. L. Beales and R. S. Lambert (eds.), *Memoirs of the Unemployed* (London, 1967), 153; Deacon, *In Search of the Scrounger*, 59.

[105] G. Orwell, *The Road to Wigan Pier* (Penguin edn., Harmondsworth, 1989), 72.

[106] E. Waugh, *Home-Life of the Lancashire Factory Folk During the Cotton Famine* (London, 1867), 51. The committees in question were those charged with giving relief to the families plunged into destitution by the crisis in the market.

[107] See above, Ch. 3, p. 78.

[108] Pollock, 'Living on the Stage of the World: The Concept of Privacy among the Elite of Early Modern England', 82–3.

to the inter-war period was the scale of the external institution and the presence of alternative organizations. For those engaged in building unions of the unemployed in the teeth of government intimidation and espionage, this subversion from below was the last straw. Thus, for instance, Harry Goldthorpe commented on his difficulties in organizing a branch of the NUWM in Bradford: ' "Informing" was the sort of thing that struck at the very roots of our attempts to organise ourselves against those who inflicted poverty upon us. Our handicaps were big enough without the burden of rats in our midst.'[109]

Even from the viewpoint of the authorities, the flow of defamatory information was something of a mixed blessing. To begin with, the newly recruited investigating officers were actively encouraged to tap into the local information network. According to a survey of methods of 'Investigating Claims for Benefit' conducted in 1929, they were advised to begin next door to the claimant, calling 'ostensibly in error' and allowing 'the line of enquiry to develop in accordance with the reception given by the neighbour'.[110] Other suitable sources of knowledge were insurance agents, small shopkeepers, Poor Law Relieving Officers, and the police. This approach had long been the practice of the Charity Organisation Society, which only in 1929 formally adopted a policy of asking the permission of the applicants before making enquiries of employers and relatives. It was still debating the morality of asking neighbours and shopkeepers as the new decade began.[111]

At the same time, the callow, barely trained inspectors quickly discovered that it was virtually impossible to separate truth from falsehood as they ventured into the quagmire of neighbourhood feuds and alliances. Suspicions were often raised by anonymous letters, but when these were pursued it was stated that nothing was known about a given applicant, or that he was spending every waking hour looking for employment, or that he was not interested in work and never got out of bed until dinner-time. 'With regard to the first two replies', observed the official in charge of the distressed north-west region,

notwithstanding an assurance that the information is confidential, it is felt that the persons interviewed are actuated by the desire not to be involved in any unpleasant consequences, whilst the last reply is frequently traced to jealousy or antagonism against the applicant's neighbour, for example, his own benefit having been disallowed.[112]

The head of the Scottish Division reported that direct interrogations were often difficult because the claimant 'may feel a certain amount of resentment that a claim to benefit has resulted in invasion of his domestic privacy', and indirect questioning was largely useless because,

[109] H. Goldthorpe, *Room at the Bottom* (London, 1959), 24.
[110] *Investigation of Claims for Benefit* (1929), App. 1, PRO, PIN7/160.
[111] Roof, *A Hundred Years of Family Welfare*, 159.
[112] PRO, PIN7/160.

strife between neighbours and particularly those residing in tenements, is not uncommon and . . . accordingly, a neighbour may present to an Investigating Officer an account of a claimant's movements etc., which is not in accordance with the facts. It is also possible that neighbours may be close friends and may therefore present a favourable position which is not in accordance with the facts.[113]

As Leo Besani has written, 'paranoia is a necessary product of all information systems'.[114] The warfare between the poor neighbourhoods and the scarcely well-paid inspectors was a product of the collision between two hitherto discrete information systems, one informal, the other newly bureaucratized, and both under almost unbearable pressure as the Depression deepened. The serpentine manoeuvres of oblique enquiries and shaded responses, of openly hiding true secrets and secretly transmitting false ones, resulted only in maladministration and embittered relationships. Trust was everywhere a victim, as real money was wasted by a state convinced it was on the edge of bankruptcy, and real hunger was experienced by households certain they now had a genuine right to subsistence.

There was no resolution in sight, merely a gradual institutionalization of mistrust as the rules for the new game were refined and the penalties for failure were reduced by the recovery of the economy in the later 1930s. Some attempt was made to improve the transparency of the system. The first official guides were published,[115] and applicants were allowed to sign a written summary of the officially defined facts in their case. Nonetheless, much remained hidden. In 1929 it was revealed that investigating officers were instructed to attach a further secret page to their reports, on which they were to record their general views of the applicant as a confidential briefing for the inspector in any appeal before the Court of Referees.[116] In traditional fashion, the Opposition denounced the practice as 'something entirely un-British' and the Government deplored the exposure of departmental regulations which it was not at liberty to publish.[117] A decade later there was a Parliamentary challenge to the behaviour of the investigating officers of the new Unemployment Assistance Board in seeking information not just about the material circumstances of applicants but about their 'private lives, and the views held by them on political and other subjects',[118] and on this occasion the Ministry of Labour agreed to issue new instructions limiting the range of questions.

Gradually, ground-rules were developed to meet at least some of the fears of

---

[113] PRO, PIN7/160.

[114] Cited in Richards, *Imperial Archive*, 114.

[115] See Emmerson and Lascelles, *Guide to the Unemployment Insurance Acts*. The guide was first published in 1926. It was clear and well organized, although its 244 pages must have been intended for those who would advise the unemployed, rather than the mass of claimants. On the attempts to publicize the regulations, see Lowe, 'Bureaucracy Triumphant or Denied?', 301–2.

[116] *Hansard*, 225, 27 Feb. 1929, cols. 2122–3.

[117] Ibid., cols. 2122, 2131.

[118] Ibid., 5th Series, 336, 26 May 1938, col. 1357.

applicants that their responses would find their way to third parties. It became an established policy, later confirmed by the code for investigating officers under the sweeping new post-war welfare system, that personal details were to be withheld from commercial interests or lawyers seeking evidence in divorce hearings.[119] However, inspectors were encouraged to collaborate closely with parallel bodies within the official apparatus, such as labour exchanges and rating authorities. An attempt was also made to curtail, or at least focus, the use made of the local information network. In the words of the new code of 1948:

Enquiries of neighbours and local tradesmen in cases of benefit irregularities should be made only very exceptionally where the investigating officer is satisfied that an offence has been committed and all that is required is confirmation of evidence already held. Where such enquiries are made, they should be conducted with the utmost discretion.[120]

The inter-war period witnessed both the heyday of the confidential community and the beginning of its decline. Never before had the urban working-class neighbourhood been so settled and so confident of its identity, and never again was it to be so cohesive and so powerful. The use and abuse of gossip encapsulated much of the trajectory of change. The casual conversations on the doorsteps, over the washing-lines, and in the corner shops, defined the limits of domestic secrecy and patrolled the boundaries of the collective realm of knowledge. The combination of a slow overall rise in living standards and a widespread exposure to unemployment began to make this form of discourse both less desirable and more dangerous. It became possible for larger numbers of families to retreat further into their households, restricting to a minimum the involuntary exposure of their affairs to the prying tongues of their neighbours. At the same time, the dense networks of information exposed the separate families to external surveillance in just the same way that the complex modern communication systems were proving vulnerable to foreign espionage. The process of change fragmented not only the communities themselves, but also the external agencies which sought to break into the secrets of their inhabitants.

Gérard Vincent writes of France in the 1920s: 'three authorities continued to preside over private life: the confessor in the spiritual realm; the notary in the material realm . . . and the doctor in the realm of the physical.'[121] In Britain this was true, if at all, only within a narrow social band. The lawyers were scarcely relevant to the two-thirds of the population who owned less than £100;[122] the

---

[119] *Draft Code for Investigation of Benefit Irregularities, National Insurance and Family Allowances* (Jan. 1948), PRO, PIN7/284. Also PRO, PIN7/227.

[120] PRO, PIN7/284.

[121] Vincent, 'A History of Secrets?', 147.

[122] John Hilton calculated that in 1938 one-third of the population had no identifiable resources, and a further third owned less than £100. J. Hilton, *Rich Man, Poor Man* (London, 1938), 25–31.

medical profession's engagement with family secrets was radically incomplete, as we shall see in the following section; and whereas once the Established Church had aspired to a central role in extracting and exchanging private information, now it was increasingly pushed to the margin as its traditions of honourable secrecy were rendered obsolete. The major initiatives in this period were being taken by employees of the state and local authorities. The nascent social-work profession was attempting to develop a discipline based on a respect for the privacy of the working-class home, whilst the new welfare bureaucracy appeared to be doing exactly the opposite. Much of the heat generated by the inquisition of the means test inspectors arose from precisely this collision between the two official approaches, the one reflecting the new dignity of the enfranchised poor citizens, the other the new threat of their raised expectations. The problem of establishing coherent relations of trust between the increasingly private home and the ever-more intrusive state had barely been recognized by the time civil society was once more subordinated to war.

The Facts of Life

An abiding difficulty of the topic of secrecy is establishing a scale of significance. Much of the current and historical commentary on official confidentiality appears to be dealing with matters of acute national importance, yet is open to the charge of irrelevance to the deeper concerns of the contemporary population. Asquith's amatory correspondence was a case in point. It courted military catastrophe and political destruction, but in the final account merely broke the heart of a man whose emotions were more readily repaired than the lines of troops on the Somme. Equally it may be argued that, of the reforms of 1911, the attack on domestic secrecy engendered by the later implementation of the new welfare system caused more tangible psychological and material suffering than any of the new controls imposed over official secrecy. The most extreme example of the private importance of blocked communication in this period lies in an area in which the state was most reluctant to intervene at all. In 1929 Marie Stopes, the self-dramatizing figurehead of the birth-control movement, published an anthology of letters under the resonant title of *Mother England*. It comprised, she claimed, 'the self-written record of the dumb class of working mothers of whose lives history has taken no cognisance'.[123] They had contacted her seeking information denied them by every other formal or informal agency they had tried to

---

[123] M. C. Stopes, *Mother England* (London, 1929), p. v. See also Ruth Hall's anthology of letters sent to Marie Stopes from 1918 onwards: *Dear Dr Stopes: Sex in the 1920s* (London, 1978). The collection includes seventeen letters from *Mother England* (pp. 37–45).

consult.[124] Taken together they conveyed more desperate mental and physical pain, and more raw anger at the concealment of knowledge, than any other text produced during the period of this study.

In one sense, the correspondents were merely filling out the blank spaces in Stopes's script. Their aspirations to fulfilled motherhood and their assault on medical conservatism dramatized the message of her many writings.[125] But the letters were not written for publication, and the frequent clumsiness of the prose style amplified rather than concealed their message. 'So Dear Doctor', concluded an appeal from a nursing mother worried about a further pregnancy,

I am writing to you for a little help not that I mind being a mother because I love babies but I suffer depression so bad when carrying and my troubles have been so heavy of late that I am only asking to have a few years between them as these are so young and times so hard to keep them as we ought to do so I shall await your advice patiently.[126]

They wrote of fears which dominated every waking moment of their existence. 'Can you write me and advise me how to prevent having any more children', appealed another mother, 'to be as ill as I am its fairly a dread all the time and it takes such a lot of your life.'[127] At the very least they conveyed a constant apprehension of further gynaecological and material difficulties; at their most intense they portrayed women on the verge of total collapse. 'So you see', wrote a mother about to undergo childbirth for the tenth time, 'it is terrible to me to keep having these children. The confinement itself is also a terror to me as I have such hard times.'[128] With maternal mortality actually rising after the war,[129] the issue in some of the correspondence was quite literally one of life or death. On occasions the letter itself was written by a worried husband: 'again I have made a slip', confessed one who found it impossible to practice abstinence, 'and I love my wife very dearly and I am worried out of my life because I really think another baby would kill her.'[130]

Neither the pain nor the fear was new to the twentieth century. What had changed, and what caused the letters to be written, was the sense that they were no longer necessary or inevitable. Marie Stopes's abiding achievement was to bring the topic of birth control into the domain of public and polite

---

[124] The book in fact consisted of all the letters written by correspondents with surnames from A to H in a file from 1926. Despite the title, a number were in fact written by the husbands of troubled wives.

[125] A. McLaren, *A History of Contraception: From Antiquity to the Present Day* (Oxford, 1992), 221.

[126] Stopes, *Mother England*, 55.

[127] Ibid. 26–7.

[128] Ibid. 6.

[129] A. Leathard, *The Fight for Family Planning* (London, 1980), 37. The rate increased from 3.91 per thousand in 1921 to 4.12 in 1926.

[130] Stopes, *Mother England*, 42.

discourse. Her first major work, *Married Love*, owed much to the pioneering writing of Havelock Ellis,[131] but whilst his books initially were banned, her celebration of connubial sexual fulfilment became an instant best-seller on its publication in 1918.[132] The success of her career between the wars was founded on an unrivalled grasp of two fundamental characteristics of the new century: the right to personal fulfilment and the power of mass communication. She argued, in clear, unambiguous language, that women had the same capacity and need for sexual pleasure as men, and that within marriage they were not required to sacrifice their health and well-being to the dictates of their reproductive systems and the dicta of churchmen and doctors: engaged or married couples were supplied for the first time with a vocabulary for communication about sexual matters. In promoting her case, Stopes seized upon the possibilities of the new media with immense skill and energy. The initial publication was followed by sundry tracts, guides, and anthologies, by poetry, plays, and journalism, by well-publicized legal actions, by mass meetings and organizations, and even by films. Only the newly founded British Broadcasting Corporation, in all its Reithian rectitude, proved resistant to her message, and was to remain so until almost the end of her life.[133] Whilst her ideas were nowhere near as original as she claimed, she had managed to create by the mid-1920s so much sheer noise about the possibilities of medically and morally respectable contraception that even the poorest and least educated of new mothers knew that there was now choice in their lives.

The problem was how to obtain the information which had at last been released from the realm of furtive secrecy. The thirst for knowledge conveyed by the letters which poured in to Marie Stopes partly derived from a growing sense of the inadequacy of informal systems of instruction. Although she romanticized the distant past, Marie Stopes was a well-informed observer of her own era: 'In this country, in modern times, the old traditions, the profound primitive knowledge of the needs of both sexes, have been lost, and nothing but a muffled confusion of individual gossip disturbs a silence, shamefaced or foul.'[134] Daughters looking to their mothers for advice were faced by a discreet reserve, which extended to every other experienced relative or neighbour.[135] As one correspondent told Stopes, 'I married knowing practically nothing of what married life would be—no one ever talked to me and told me

---

[131] For a lively account of the debt owed by Stopes to Ellis, see the memoir of her great American rival: Margaret Sanger, *My Fight for Birth Control* (New York, 1931), 101. Stopes always denied Sanger's claim that she was entirely ignorant of all birth-control methods until Sanger told her whilst she was writing *Married Love*.

[132] A. Maude, *Marie Stopes: Her Work and Play* (London, 1933), 137. The book eventually sold three-quarter of a million copies in England.

[133] R. Hall, *Marie Stopes* (London, 1977), 321.

[134] Stopes, *Married Love*, 18.

[135] D. G. Gittins, 'Married Life and Birth Control Between the Wars', *Oral History*, 3: 2, (1975), 54–6; R. Porter and L. Hall, *The Facts of life: The Creation of Sexual Knowledge in Britain, 1650–1950* (New Haven, 1995), 251–4.

things I ought to have known—and I had a rude awakening.'[136] The only prospect of free conversation lay in the exchange of myths and half-truths between adolescent girls as they studied and worked together. This pooling of mutual ignorance could not constitute an adequate preparation for the crises which lay ahead.[137] In moments of most acute need, the overstressed mother received contradictory and incomplete advice from those about her. 'Mrs. A.—— B.——' wrote describing a life of 'one constant worry' about further conceptions: 'Some say I should "learn a wrinkle", others that it is "disgusting", and others that is my fault as I have three boys and no girls, and yet no one tells me what to do.'[138]

The authority of indigenous sources of knowledge was being further undermined and fragmented by the increasing exposure of working-class mothers to professional medical intervention. The Maternity and Child Welfare Act of 1918 had consolidated the pre-war innovations by requiring all local authorities to set up maternity and child-welfare committees which could finance free neighbourhood clinics. Here mothers received detailed information on every aspect of childbirth, save how to avoid it. The clinics were forbidden by the 1924 Circular 517 on *Maternal Mortality* to give contraceptive advice,[139] and although there was some variation of attitude amongst both leaders of the profession and general practitioners (some of whom were now women), most refused to engage in a form of preventive medicine for which they had received no training.[140] Through their growing contact with doctors and with trained midwives and health workers, this generation of mothers was far more certain about the consequences of pregnancy than any of its predecessors, but no wiser about what to do.[141] The more vociferous the propaganda of Marie Stopes and her movement, the less acceptable became the yawning gap between diagnosis and remedy. Stopes herself, whose doctorate was in palaeobotany (the first ever awarded to a woman), not medicine, was from the outset bitterly critical of the refusal of doctors to transmit their knowledge to those who most needed it. The main protagonists of her first theatrical presentation of her views, *Our Ostriches*, which was produced at the Royal Court in 1923, were Evadne Carrillon, a superficial young woman, 'but with serious eyes and a well-balanced rather intellectual face, suggesting the possibility that once she is stirred there may be depths in her not yet represented', and Doctor Verro Hodges, a youthful, intelligent, but initially conventional member of his profession. Act 1 ends with a

---

[136] Stopes, *Mother England*, 9.

[137] F. Greene, *Time to Spare: What Unemployment Means* (London, 1935), 29–30.

[138] Stopes, *Mother England*, 84–5.

[139] Leathard, *Fight for Family Planning*, 33.

[140] J. Peel, 'Contraception and the Medical Profession', *Population Studies*, 18 (1964), 137–40, surveys the debate within the profession in the 1920s. Marie Stopes did receive some letters from doctors in poor areas seeking information on birth-control techniques which they themselves lacked. Hall, *Dear Dr Stopes*, 103.

[141] J. Bourke, *Working-Class Cultures in Britain, 1890–1960* (London, 1994), 55–6; Gittins, *Fair Sex*, 42.

medical grounds. In other words, the right to information was to be defined by the health professionals, not the mothers. The post-war birth-control movement had been strongly motivated by a desire to break up the structures of secret knowledge which surrounded the extensive use of abortion, and to diminish the appeal of secret devices and abortifacients widely advertised in the press. It had been increasingly concerned that the conservatism of the church and the doctors was driving the search for information underground as wives sought to bridge the growing gap between their desires and their fears. At one level, the concessions of 1930 represented an attempt to unify the forces of official wisdom and to reinforce their power and status in the lives of women less and less fatalistic about their future.

Downward communication was still strictly policed, and upward communication largely non-existent. Marie Stopes's engagement with the reproductive practices of working-class families was at once egalitarian and patronizing, sympathetic and contemptuous.[155] There was a real concern for the sexual rights of uneducated women, and an unfeigned anger at their treatment by their better-qualified superiors. On the other hand, in common with much of the birth-control movement, she was dismissive of all their existing knowledge and practices,[156] and argued vociferously that their continuing ignorance was threatening 'race suicide' as 'low-grade stocks' overwhelmed the 'high-grade'.[157] In some respects the refusal to take seriously what couples already knew was of greater long-term significance than what now seems the profoundly offensive eugenics. Stopes was hostile not only to abortion but to condoms and coitus interruptus, thus discounting most of the means other than abstinence (to which she was also opposed) and delayed marriage (to which she was not) by which conceptions had in the past been limited.[158] In their missionary enthusiasm, the campaigners made little attempt to subject their preferred devices to proper clinical trials, and even less to ask couples what worked for them.[159] Women were told they knew nothing, and sent to the nurse for instruction in the fitting of a 'Dutch cap' and the use of a douche. However, as an unusually sensitive and dispassionate study of an experimental clinic in Cambridge pointed out, the employment of this method presented acute practical difficulties:

[155] See e.g. her *A Letter to Working Mothers* (1919).

[156] McLaren, *History of Contraception*, 225–7.

[157] M. C. Stopes, *Contraception: Theory, History and Practice* (London, 1923), 7–12, 394–5. For more comprehensive treatments of the eugenicist case, see G. Pitt Rivers, *Weeds in the Garden of Marriage* (London, 1931); G. Whitehead, *Birth Control: Why and How* (London, 1929), 122–37. For a balanced summary of the variety of motives behind the birth-control campaigns, see E. Lindsay and A. D. Lindsay, *Birth Control and Human Dignity* (London, 1929), 33–4.

[158] She believed that nothing should be done to prevent contact at ejaculation, as the semen was absorbed through the vagina and invigorated the female partner.

[159] One of the very few large-scale surveys of the period found that coitus interruptus and the sheath were still the most widely used methods. E. Charles, *The Practice of Birth Control* (London, 1932), 173.

The vast majority of our patients have no bathroom or any suitable sanitary facilities for douching. In many cases they share a single out-door lavatory with lodgers or another family. They live in tiny, overcrowded houses, and more often than not share their bedroom with several children. The woman has no place in the house where she can go in privacy and be alone, much less where she can prepare and administer a douche.[160]

In practice, there was a complex structure of material and emotional factors impeding the free flow of information between those anxious to limit their families and those who were now legally free to help them. Effective advice required a proper understanding of the obstacles to change in the lives of poor mothers. 'Ignorance and fear,' observed the Cambridge study, 'more often than not reinforced by poverty and overwork, must be reckoned with before the woman is condemned as feckless and unworthy of further sympathy.'[161] It was far from easy for any individual, however desperate or enlightened, to step aside from entrenched family and neighbourhood conventions. In Cambridge it was found that: 'A great many patients come to the Clinic quite secretly, determined to conceal their visit from their mother-in-law or their grandmother, who disapproves of birth control, or from their neighbour, who would be likely to broadcast the news.'[162] It was for this reason that many campaigners preferred to integrate contraceptive services with the less sensitive maternity clinics, rather than set up a separate system. Even so, there remained a deep-seated reluctance to expose the body to intimate examination, particularly by a male doctor, or to reveal the details of its past to however sympathetic a listener. As with other forms of well-meaning intervention in the problems of the poor, it soon became evident that effective assistance required a reconstruction of a broad strand of the individual's life history. In this context, the problems of discourse were particularly acute. Few women of any social class or educational background had any experience of talking freely about their sexual practices,[163] a matter which Marie Stopes had striven to address through her frank naming of parts in her publications. They lacked a vocabulary or a readily available narrative, and where something might be said, embarrassment or guilt drove them to evasion or silence.[164] The Cambridge clinic found that the first stories which were extracted were usually incomplete or wrong. In the confused responses, births were muddled or omitted, 'and very often miscarriages and deliberate abortions, which were at first concealed, came to light later'.[165]

[160] L. S. Florence, *Birth Control on Trial* (London, 1930), 65.

[161] Ibid. 70.

[162] Ibid. 48.

[163] Middle-class women did write to Marie Stopes in large numbers, seeking information not about birth control but about many other aspects of sexual relations which they had never previously been able to discuss. Hall, *Dear Dr Stopes*, 153–91.

[164] McLaren, *History of Contraception*, 225.

[165] Florence, *Birth Control on Trial*, 24.

Secrecy was a natural condition of reproduction. In her writings, Marie Stopes had advocated a new axis between privacy and publicity. The free flow of contraceptive information would make possible a new level of domestic comfort into which the compact family could retreat from the bustle of the world. It was a message daily reinforced by the promotion through mass advertising of the family as a unit of consumption presided over by the caring housewife.[166] Conversely, increasing domestic prosperity would purchase the separate space in the house within which women could apply the knowledge they had gained from the open discourse about birth-control methods. In practice, both cultural and material pressures made it extremely difficult for working-class women to set up this virtuous circle. The absence of privacy in the home, and the enforced exposure to the eyes and tongues of the neighbours, discouraged the search for new means of limiting conceptions. Middle-class woman took much more readily to contraceptive appliances in this period.[167] In many respects the confidential letter was the most natural form of communication of sexual matters. It was a measure of progress that, whereas this was once only written in reply to advertisements for secret devices, cures, or abortifacients, now it was also being sent to supposed medical authorities such as Stopes. Ambition and confidence were slowly growing, and as they did, the birth-rate was continuing to fall throughout the lower reaches of society. But in the absence of dramatic improvements in physical conditions, and in the face of the failure of professional experts at first to talk to and then to listen to the new generation of working-class mothers, most of their thoughts and fears remained shrouded in fear and darkness.

The Nice and Jealous Honour

In his *Memories and Reflections* of 1928 Asquith gave what was becoming the standard encomium on the officials who had supported him during his long ministerial career:

The English Civil Service is unique in the world. Performing as it does, in a country where party divisions often cut deep, and where the House of Commons is jealously on the watch to guard against the encroachments of 'bureaucracy', the most confidential and responsible functions, essential to the efficiency and continuity of successive Governments, it has never incurred the suspicions of corruption or bias, and is carried on with rare disinterestedness by men who are debarred from publicity or self-advertisement, and many of whom have deliberately forgone the rewards of successful ambition which would have been almost certainly theirs in other walks of life.[168]

The combination of self-denial and self-censorship, of corporate neutrality and individual effacement, not only served the country but in an important sense

---

[166] Gittins, *Fair Sex*, 42. [167] McLaren, *History of Contraception*, 234.
[168] Asquith, *Memories and Reflections*, ii. 251.

defined its superiority over the upstart states of the modern times. Elsewhere, bureaucrats lacked the capacity or the will to police themselves. They were either entrammeled by formal regulation or enmeshed in bribery or both. As Britain struggled to maintain its status in an increasingly competitive international environment, it could with confidence proclaim the virtues of those who were forbidden by their ethos to sing in praise of themselves. We are now governed, wrote Lord Hewart in a famous attack on its enlarged powers a year later, by 'what it is a commonplace to describe as the best civil service in the world'.[169]

The consolidation of national pride in so incorruptible and uncommunicative a body was achieved in spite of the rapid growth in its size and cost. Between the outbreaks of the two World Wars, the number of non-industrial civil servants increased from 280,900 to 387,400,[170] and the expenditure on central government rose from a fifteenth to a quarter of Gross National Product.[171] As a consequence of the expansion of the welfare and education systems, the machinery of government was now a presence in the lives of citizens as never before, particularly in the case of the households and communities of the working class. The development of the infrastructural power of the state both required and made possible levels of information-gathering hitherto practised only on the new native populations of the Empire.[172] Whereas most of the significant knowledge about an individual had been held by the family and neighbourhood and by the workplace and its organizations, now a mounting proportion was generated and stored by outside officials. Despite the tensions traced earlier in this Chapter, the level of public trust in the civil service appeared to keep pace with its multiplying card indexes. There was a broad confidence that the state bureaucracy (which was rarely addressed as such) was fit not only to hold but to determine when to release the sensitive detail in its possession.

The maintenance of this deference in an era of political change and crisis was not left to chance. High on the agenda of the first designated head of the Civil Service was the promotion of a corporate image for the disparate departments he was trying to weld into a single body.[173] Warren Fisher, who was described by an eyewitness of the time as possessing 'a charming, youthful face', but 'bad, weak, obstinate hands',[174] responded to the arrival of mass democracy by relentlessly cultivating the public reputation of Whitehall. His strategy was most clearly exposed in the 'Francs Case' of 1928, where three diplomatic officials

---

[169] Lord Hewart, *The New Despotism* (London, 1929), 13.

[170] T. Balogh, *The Apotheosis of the Dilettante* (London, 1959), 89.

[171] R. Lowe, 'Bureaucracy Triumphant or Denied? The Expansion of the British Civil Service, 1919–1939', *Public Administration*, 62: 3 (1984), 291.

[172] On the growth of the infrastructural state, see M. Mann, 'The Autonomous Power of the State: Its Origins, Mechanisms and Results', in J. Hall (ed.), *States in History* (London, 1986), 111–14; G. Poggi, *The State: Its Nature, Development and Prospects* (Cambridge, 1990), 31–2.

[173] Chapman and Greenaway, *The Dynamics of Administrative Reform*, 191.

[174] A. Bridge, *Permission to Resign* (London, 1971), 56.

were arraigned on a charge of insider dealing in the currency markets. In the event they were acquitted of the specific charge of misusing confidential information in what had been a misguided and unsuccessful speculation, but the three-man Board of Enquiry headed by Fisher severely criticized them for transgressing the 'honour and traditions' of their calling. 'The Civil Service,' explained the Board, 'like every other profession, has its unwritten code of ethics and conduct for which the most effective sanction lies in the public opinion of the Service itself, and it is upon the maintenance of a sound and healthy public opinion within the Service that its value and efficiency chiefly depend.'[175] The Report then went on to give a classic definition of the substance of the code which both engineered and was patrolled by popular confidence:

Practical rules for the guidance of social conduct depend also as much upon the instinct and perception of the individual as upon cast-iron formulas: and the surest guide will, we hope, always be found in the nice and jealous honour of the Civil Servants themselves. The public expects from them a standard of integrity and conduct not only inflexible but fastidious, and has not been disappointed in the past.[176]

This statement constituted the bridge between the mid-nineteenth and late twentieth-century civil service. Its somewhat archaic formulation of 'nice and jealous honour' echoed the terminology of Cornewall Lewis's promulgation of the doctrine of 'honourable secrecy' in 1855,[177] yet it was regarded as so relevant to the modern official that it was regularly cited to new recruits throughout the remainder of the period covered by this book.[178] The timeless quality of the pronouncement reflected two key characteristics of the increasingly Treasury-dominated organization. First, the British administrative system still resisted the continental tradition of public law, by which the attributes, capacities, and authority of the state bureaucracy were enshrined in statute and monitored through the courts.[179] Yet it retained the same need to establish its credentials as a professional body with an accepted moral right to exercise a control over an increasing volume of sensitive information. With the almost complete absence of the external regulation which had been given to the professions themselves, the definition and maintenance of a corporate ethos became

---

[175] *Report of the Board of Enquiry Appointed by the Prime Minister to Investigate Certain Statements Affecting Civil Servants*, PP 1928, VII (1928), 20.

[176] *Report of the Board of Enquiry to Investigate Certain Statements* (1928), 36.

[177] See above, Ch. 2, p. 34.

[178] For an early embodiment in a standard summary of civil service ethics, see N. E. Mustoe, *The Law and Organisation of the British Civil Service* (London, 1932), 55. On its application in the early 1950s, see T. A. Critchley, *The Civil Service Today* (London, 1951), 58; in the 1960s and early 1970s, First Division Association, 'Performance Standards in the Public Service: A Report by a Sub-Committee of the First Division Association', *Public Administration*, 50 (Summer 1972), 118–20; in the 1980s, D. Johnstone, 'Facelessness: Anonymity in the Civil Service', *Parliamentary Affairs*, 39: 4 (1986), 413.

[179] For an early argument that it was time that Britain began to investigate the merits of a system of administrative law, see Allen, *Bureaucracy Triumphant*, 22.

more critical with every passing year and with the passage of every new piece of legislation extending the responsibilities of government. The 'inflexible and fastidious' standards were not merely the outer clothing of the organization but its very skeleton. In their perceived absence, the structure would collapse.

Secondly, the reworking of the gentlemanly ideal which had been undertaken during the middle decades of the previous century was still held to be valid. In a polity struggling to keep its distance from the spread of totalitarian regimes elsewhere in Europe, the principle of intense, constant self-restraint remained at the centre of civilized behaviour.[180] The more complex the relations between citizens, and the greater the temptation to resolve conflict by individual or collective violence, the more relevant was the particular notion of honour which Warren Fisher was seeking to entrench and refurbish. Through their long process of acculturation in the public schools and Oxbridge colleges, which more than ever determined entry to the upper ranks, the civil servants gained the right to demand the confidence of society at large.[181] Whilst to some contemporary and many later critics, Whitehall as a whole and the Treasury in particular were in this period of crisis turning away from the modern world, the leaders of the civil service were convinced that their combination of selfless efficiency and inner-disciplined integrity placed them on its leading edge.

Between the wars, self-confidence and self-denial went hand-in-hand down the corridors of Whitehall. From the more troubled years of the 1960s and beyond, this seemed a golden era in both internal morale and external reputation.[182] Such an achievement rested on a double closure. In his ambition to promote a single, powerful *esprit de corps* under the aegis of the Treasury, Fisher found it necessary to curtail the presence of freewheeling outsiders who had not been through the appropriate processes of institutional socialization. The recruitment of able specialists from industry or the universities which had been a feature of the Edwardian social reforms and the wartime emergency was brought firmly to an end.[183] Almost half the permanent secretaries between

---

[180] For a general discussion of the relationship between the state and self-restraint, see N. Elias, *The Civilising Process*, Vol. 2, *State Formation and Civilisation* (Oxford, 1982), 229–328.

[181] On the growing dominance of Oxford and Cambridge, which supplied 63% of Permanent Secretaries between 1900 and 1919, and 69% between 1920 and 1944, see Theakston and Fry, 'Britain's Administrative Élite: Permanent Secretaries, 1900–1986', 132; J. S. Harris and T. V. Garcia, 'The Permanent Secretaries: Britain's Top Administrators', *Public Administration Review*, 26: 1 (Mar. 1966), 31–5; H. J. Laski, *Parliamentary Government in England* (London, 1938), 321. Their hold on recruitment had been strengthened by the post-war introduction of an oral examination. C. Hetzner, 'Social Democracy and Bureaucracy: The Labour Party and Higher Civil Service Recruitment', *Administration and Society*, 17: 1 (May 1985), 102.

[182] See e.g. the comments in Lord Fulton, *The Civil Service: Report of the Committee 1966–68*, Vol. 1, pt. 2 (London, 1968), 1092. Also M. Beloff, 'The Whitehall Factor: The Rise of the Higher Civil Service 1919–1939', in G. Peele and C. Cook (eds.), *The Politics of Reappraisal, 1918–39* (London, 1975), 210.

[183] Hennessy, *Whitehall*, 59; J. R. Greenaway, 'Warren Fisher and the Transformation of the British Treasury, 1919–1939', *Journal of British Studies*, 23 (1983), 128.

1900 and 1919 had entered the civil service from some other occupation, compared with 15 per cent between 1920 and 1944.[184] Once inside Whitehall, the officials were beleaguered by an increasingly strident press, a far more representative Parliament, and an electorate sensitized as never before to the significance of the state and its actions.[185] The pressures reinforced the need to enhance the distinctiveness of the corporate ethos, and to emphasize that in an era of unprincipled mass communication, the civil servants alone were capable of keeping their silence. They were virgins in the whorehouse; their virtue resided in their difference and in their abstinence.

The problem was whether and by what means control over the disclosure of information could be imposed across the full range of government business. There was in this period a sharp divergence in the success with which discipline was exercised over the masters and the subordinates of the Whitehall officials. At the superior level, the leading members of the civil service were from the outset engaged in little more than a damage-limitation exercise. The creation of the Cabinet Secretariat in 1916 enabled its secretary, Maurice Hankey, to assume the responsibility of keeper of state secrets, but he rapidly discovered that his authority could not be taken for granted. In theory, the systematic committal of Cabinet business to paper offered the possiblity of a much more effective policing of the storage and transmission of sensitive material, and a much sharper definition of the offence of improper communication. In practice, the multiplication of paper fed an exponential growth in the public appetite for accounts of critical issues of the current moment and recent past. On the one hand, there was Hankey trying to insist that the Privy Councillor's Oath covered all the records his office was now manufacturing in such abundance; on the other there was the seemingly limitless capital, both financial and political, that could be made from transferring the material to books and newspapers. An attempt to insist on the return of all official documents in the private possession of members of the War Cabinet was largely abandoned in 1919, and thereafter the Secretariat was unable to prevent almost all the major players of the First World War, military and civilian, recycling the paper into self-justifying histories and memoirs.[186]

As the individuals involved were too powerful to be defeated by a frontal attack, their would-be censors had to adopt two less heroic and more oblique tactics. The first was to deploy the Official Secrets Act against the lesser figures in order to intimidate the larger. In 1932 Compton Mackenzie, the novelist and current Lord Rector of Glasgow University, wrote an account of his war experiences, motivated, as almost all the other martial autobiographers claimed to be, by a desire to correct errors in a competing version, in this case one written

---

[184] Theakston and Fry, 'Britain's Administrative Élite: Permanent Secretaries, 1900–1986', 135.

[185] J. Kingsley, *Representative Bureaucracy* (London, 1944), 221–4.

[186] Middlemas, 'Cabinet Secrecy and the Crossman Diaries', 40–3; K. Middlemas, *Politics in Industrial Society* (London, 1979), 362–5; Young, *The Crossman Affair*, 132–42.

by none other than Sir Basil Thomson, the former head of Special Branch.[187] The contested ground was wartime Greece, where Mackenzie, or 'Z' as he had christened himself, had served with theatrical vigour as head of counter-intelligence.[188] He was prosecuted on a charge of revealing the procedures he had developed, the names of some of his colleagues, and, most scandalously, the identity of his controller, the fabled 'C', Mansfield Cumming.[189] To take such Draconian action over so minor an aspect of the hostilities so long after so much else had been published was at first sight puzzling. However, Mackenzie maintained that he was given the real explanation by a friendly official: 'I understand the Government intend to make an example of you if they can, in order to warn Lloyd George and Winston Churchill that they can go too far in using information they could only have acquired in office.'[190] The point was re-inforced by the judge at the trial, which, in order to dramatize the enormity of the offence, was held entirely *in camera*. He was satisfied that the defendant was 'an honourable man', who was right to plead guilty to the charge: 'It must be obvious to everybody that when confidential documents get into the hands of public servants—servants of the Crown—however long they might keep them in secret, it was not for such servants to decide when such documents were to be published.'[191] The issue, as it almost always had been since the first Official Secrets Act of 1889, was the maintenance not of security but of authority.

Two years later the exercise was repeated. The new victim was Edgar Lans-bury, the son of the Leader of the Opposition, who was prosecuted under the Act for including material from Cabinet papers in a biography of his father.[192] On this occasion the real target was not just the wartime figures, but George Lansbury himself, who had been one of the few to vote against the 1911 Official Secrets Act, and more recently was thought to be responsible for the publica-tion in the *Daily Herald* of the details of the Cabinet debate which had preceded the downfall of the Labour Government in 1931.[193] However, there was little evidence that either the insubordinate Lansbury or the invulnerable Lloyd George and Churchill were at all moved by these token executions, and later in

[187] Mackenzie claimed that Thomson, whose career had been ruined by the Hyde Park affair (see above, p. 17), had been paid by the exiled Greek royal family to write his book (*The Allied Secret Service in Greece*, London, 1931). Mackenzie had already published two memoirs of the period, *Gallipoli Memories* (London, 1929) and *Athenian Memories* (London, 1932). The third, which was to concentrate more specifically on his war work, was to be entitled *Greek Memories*. This was eventually published, in an expurgated form, in 1939. For a full account of Mackenzie's side of events, see C. Mackenzie, *My Life and Times: Octave Seven, 1931–1938* (London, 1968), 83–106, App. C, 305–11.

[188] Linklater, *Compton Mackenzie*, 151 ff.

[189] For accounts of the episode, see R. Kidd, *British Liberty in Danger* (London, 1940), 93–5; Linklater, *Compton Mackenzie*, 243–50.

[190] Mackenzie, *My Life and Times: Octave Seven*, 84. His biographer endorses this view: Linklater, *Compton Mackenzie*, 248–9.

[191] *The Times* (13 Jan. 1933), 9. Mackenzie did not share this estimation of his crime, but had reluc-tantly pleaded guilty, not daring to incur the cost of a long trial, and was fined £100 with £100 costs.

[192] E. Lansbury, *Lansbury, My Father* (London, 1934).

[193] Hooper, *Official Secrets*, 54–6.

the year the Government adopted a different tactic of trying to draw a line under what it hopefully termed the 'dying class of War Memoir',[194] and tightening the procedures to prevent the emergence of a new genre of political life histories. In a paper marked 'SECRET, Publication of Cabinet Documents', it deplored the fact that: 'In a large number of cases since the War, extracts, particularly from War Cabinet and other similar Secret Papers, have been published in War Memoirs and kindred works without any application for sanction having been made.'[195] Whereas in the past, 'the number of these cases of unauthorised publication greatly exceeds the number of cases where application for sanction to publish has been made and obtained',[196] henceforth access to Cabinet papers for the purpose of writing history was to be strictly controlled, and Privy Councillors were to be reminded that the Crown was the 'trustee of the confidence of a Minister, past or present, who has given his oath'.[197] With splendid irony, the first major victim of the new regime was Hankey himself, who in 1943 was refused permission to publish his own memoirs by his immediate successor as Cabinet Secretary on the grounds that his revelations would destroy the 'trusted relationship' between civil servants and their Ministers. Hankey spent most of his retirement trying to get the ban lifted as a new generation of war memoirs began to appear, before finally publishing an expurgated version in 1961, two years before his death.[198]

This combination of consistent intention and uncertain application was visible in the broader history of the Official Secrecy Acts in this period. In 1920 a Bill was introduced to incorporate elements of the Defence of the Realm Regulations into the 1911 Act. These covered minor issues relating to postal and telegraph espionage, but also consolidated the offence of receiving unauthorized material under both Sections 1 and 2.[199] There was a strong element of familiarity about the Government's tactics in the debate. It tried to slip the Bill first through the Lords, as one speaker put it, 'sub silentio',[200] surrounding the proceedings with what an MP described as an 'atmosphere [of] barricades in Downing Street, secret police scattered about this very building, the galleries cleared, everyone apparently in a panic—the fear of the people'.[201] However, unlike 1889 and 1911, the Parliamentary managers were unable to prevent a substantial debate breaking out in both Houses, which produced the first modern argument over the relationship between secrecy, the state, and the liberty of the individual.

---

[194] 'Publication of Cabinet Documents', 31 Jan. 1935, p. 5. PRO, PREM1/171.

[195] Ibid. 2–3.

[196] Ibid.

[197] Ibid. Also Middlemas, 'Cabinet Secrecy', 43; Young, *The Crossman Affair*, 132.

[198] Naylor, *A Man and an Institution*, 271–5, 287–9.

[199] For useful summaries, see Baxter, *State Security, Privacy and Information*, 34–5; Thurlow, *Secret State*, 119; Kidd, *British Liberty in Danger*, 87–8. The text is to be found in Franks, *Departmental Committee on Section 2 of the Official Secrets Act 1991*, i. 112–14.

[200] *Hansard*, 5th Series, 135, 2 Dec. 1920, col. 1541. Also col. 1550.

[201] Ibid., col. 1566.

From the Government's perspective, the series of crises which had led to the 1911 Act and then the wartime regulations marked a permanent watershed. The choice was not whether to dismantle all the controls, but how far to consolidate them. In terms of the threat from abroad, Ministers were seized with the fear that the continuing growth of complex information systems was playing into the hands of the secret agents. 'Unfortunately', observed the Attorney-General, Lord Hewart, 'one of the things which increase and develop in an imperfect world is the ingenuity of spies, and another is the elaboration of the systems and methods of spying.'[202] At home, unemployment was rising past a million, the unions were planning concerted action, and the Russian Revolution was exercising a dangerous appeal. Basil Thomson, now 'Director of Intelligence', instituted a long-term programme of surveillance of protest movements, particularly those of the unemployed, and was sending the Home Office a stream of alarmist reports.[203] The Bill's supporters claimed in the debates that, in the words of Captain Thorpe, 'the State is in great danger and no power which would tend to protect it should be withheld from the Government'.[204] Its critics protested that the Government was wilfully confusing internal and external threats, and refusing to abandon powers it had only been granted at a time of genuine national emergency. 'It is another attempt', claimed Sir Donald McClean,

to clamp the powers of war on to the liberties of the citizen in peace, and unless this House turns away this strangle-hold of bureaucracy, before another twelve months are over, we shall find that this Government has, with the aid of the Members of this House, curtailed in a manner which is most inimical to the true interests of social order those liberties of the British subject, upon which the progress of this country at home and abroad has so long rested.[205]

Having sacrificed so much to defeat Germany, the Government was developing a concept of the state, argued another speaker, that owed more to Treitschke and the Prussians than to any indigenous tradition of liberty.[206]

In accordance with a practice which went all the way back to 1844, the Bill's sponsors defended themselves by making precise appeals to the past and giving vague undertakings about the future. There could be no disagreement with the term 'prejudicial to the interests of the state' because that was already in the

---

[202] Ibid., col. 1537. Curiously, one of the chief spycatchers of the era, Herbert Fitch, came to hold the opinion that the war had marked not the beginning but the end of the great era of spies, who had been driven permanently from the field by the superior technical powers of their opponents. Fitch, *Traitors Within*, 191.

[203] Morgan. *Conflict and Order*, 93–4, 111. A similar programme of surveillance was undertaken in Canada at this time. Thanks to the use of Access to Information requests, historians have been able to form a much more detailed knowledge of its extent. See G. S. Kealey and R. Whittaker (eds.), *R.C.M.P. Security Bulletins: The Early Years, 1919–1929* (St Johns, Newfoundland, 1994).

[204] *Hansard*, 5th Series, 135, 2 Dec. 1920, col. 1562.

[205] Ibid., col. 1546.

[206] Ibid.

1911 Act, to which no serious objections had been raised. And there should be no fear that journalists would now be prosecuted for printing material which Cabinet Ministers were leaking with impunity, because, said Lord Hewart, it was inconceivable that any gentleman of the press would ever wish 'to retain for some purpose prejudicial to the safety or interests of the State an official document which he has no right to obtain'.[207] In a later intervention Hewart unwisely went further and denied that the Bill was breaking any new ground at all. Section 6, which covered the receipt of unauthorized material, did not, he advised, relate to Cabinet papers or the general run of official documents, but merely to 'passports, passes, permits, and certificates and the like'.[208]

The lack of detail about future application was partly a deliberate evasion, amounting in the case of the final assurance to a straightforward falsehood, and partly a conscious strategy of retaining flexibility in an increasingly uncertain world. When in 1923 some MPs raised suspicions of an unannounced growth in letter-opening, they were met with the standard refusal to confirm or deny: 'It would not be in the public interest to give particulars concerning the warrants in force at any one time.'[209] The Government had no intention of tying its hands by opening its practices to any more Parliamentary inquiry than was absolutely necessary. However, in exposing the press to prosecution when it was still unable to discipline its own Ministers, it had given a hostage to fortune. Unnecessary harm was done to Government–newspaper relations in 1930, when the Labour Attorney-General Sir William Jowitt sanctioned under Section 6 the vigorous interrogation of a journalist suspected of improperly receiving an advance warning of the impending prosecution of Gandhi.[210] Resentment was finally translated into a campaign against the amended Act by the decision in 1937 of Lord Hewart himself, now raised to Lord Chief Justice, to reject the appeal of an obscure Manchester journalist obscurely prosecuted under the Act for not disclosing the source of leaked police information. To the charge of hypocrisy was now added that of dishonesty.

Matters came to a head the following year when the press and the Conservative anti-appeasers engineered a major public controversy over a clumsy attempt by the Attorney-General to threaten Churchill's son-in-law, Duncan Sandys, with the Act for deploying unauthorized official information in a Parliamentary question critical of the state of London's air defences.[211] The cry was raised of Parliamentary sovereignty. The charge that the Executive was undermining the pillars of democracy through its obsession with secrecy caused the establishment of a rare Select Committee to investigate the operation of the

---

[207] *Hansard*, 5th Series, 135, 2 Dec. 1920, col. 1539.

[208] Ibid., col. 1578.

[209] Ibid. 163, 10 May 1923, col. 2554.

[210] The details of the event are to be found in the Commons debate on the issue: ibid. 238, 12 May 1930, cols. 1446–53.

[211] For a full account, see *First Report from the Select Committee on the Official Secrets Acts* (1938), PP 1937–8, VII, pp. vii–xxiv. Also Parry, 'Legislatures and Secrecy', 773–81.

Official Secrets Acts. This rehearsed the possibility of further legislation to guarantee the immunity of MPs from the Act, but rejected it in a classic restatement of the virtue of unwritten conventions: 'The privileges of parliament, like many other institutions of the British constitution, are indefinite in their nature and stated in general and sometimes vague terms. The elasticity thus secured has made it possible to apply existing privileges in new circumstances from time to time.'[212] Tradition was the best preparation for modernity: 'Any attempt to translate them into precise rules must deprive them of the very quality which renders them adaptable to new and varying conditions, and new or unusual combinations of circumstances.'[213] However, tradition was also clearly vulnerable to ill-formulated legislation, and before the Select Committee made its final report, Chamberlain's Government brought in a Bill to reform the more contentious aspects of the 1920 Act. In the event this failed because of inadequate drafting and then lack of time, and Britain went back to war equipped with a partially discredited set of secrecy laws.

Compared with the prosecutions which flowed from the secret letters sent to National Insurance inspectors, the actual use of Section 2 of the Official Secrets Acts between the wars was slight. But from the moment in 1919 when the full force of the law was brought to bear on a hapless War Office clerk who had transmitted details of uniform contracts to a tailoring firm, it was apparent that inequality was to be the hallmark of its application.[214] The only consistency in the actions sanctioned by a series of Attorney-Generals was that they were directed at those either in the lower ranks of the state apparatus or outside its reach altogether. The single occasion when the Act was brought indirectly to bear on a member of the ruling party, albeit a dissenting backbencher, provoked precisely the kind of public debate governments strove to avoid. In the meantime the flow of unattributed information from the senior ranks of Ministers increased both in its volume and its sophistication. In his *Parliamentary Government in England* of 1938, Harold Laski observed that 'there are few Cabinet meetings in which the modern Press is not a semi-participant. Ministers, sometimes the Prime Minister, give to its organs inspired communications intended to promote opinion towards the direction which they desire.'[215] This applied particularly to moments of crisis in the Cabinet, beginning in 1921 with the resignation as Secretary of State for India of Asquith's successful rival in love, Edwin Montagu, and culminating in the high drama of the summer of 1931, but also to the general run of business. Gradually, attempts were made to formalize the channels of communication. Lloyd George, who made more out of selling his Cabinet secrets than any other politician of the

---

[212] *Report from the Select Committee on the Official Secrets Acts* (1939), PP 1938–9, VIII, p. xiv.
[213] *Select Committee on the Official Secrets Acts*, p. xiv.
[214] Drewry, 'The Official Secrets Acts', 90.
[215] Laski, *Parliamentary Government in England*, 254.

period,[216] was the first to employ an official spokesman, the reassuringly named Sir Geoffrey Shakespeare, and Neville Chamberlain, who, in the tradition of Asquith, regularly committed summaries of Cabinet business to the post—although in his case to his sister not his lover[217]—was the first to appoint a press officer to Number 10, a career civil servant from the Forestry Commission.[218] The Foreign Office also established a 'News Department' with its own salaried staff.[219] In Laski's view, what purported to be a move towards greater transparency was precisely the reverse: 'My own feeling is strong that it is the wrong kind of development. It has led to efforts to hinder criticism, to the retailing of inspired gossip, to the conversion of what is in fact propaganda into what appears to be genuine news, for which there is nothing to be said.'[220]

The outcome of these varying means of controlling the release of official information was an ambivalent endorsement of national identity. In one sense the sheer messy confusion of the apparatus and its half-hidden operation seemed quintessentially British. In an era when the open and systematic destruction of civil liberties was the fate of an increasing proportion of the European population, it remained possible to celebrate the ramshackle mixture of hypocrisy, inequality, and conflict which had characterized the interwar domestic polity. Orwell captured precisely the right tone of cynical pride in his essay *The Lion and the Unicorn*, written at a moment when virtually every European country was in the grip of totalitarian regimes: 'The whole conception of the militarised continental state, with its secret police, its censored literature and its conscript labour, is utterly different from that of the loose maritime democracy, with its slums and unemployment, its strikes and party politics.'[221] However, unlike the complacent Victorian contrast between indigenous liberty and foreign tyranny, there were now disturbing areas of overlap. Unemployment and strikes had institutionalized the role of secret policemen in Britain, and the threat of political violence had led to a curtailment of some traditional rights of association and protest, particularly through the Incitement to Disaffection Act of 1934 and Public Order Act of 1936. As J. D. Kingsley in his *Representative Bureaucracy* of 1944 observed: 'During these years when the unity of the middle class state was first clearly impaired by a militant proletariat, the area of civil rights everywhere contracted in England.'[222]

This contraction was real, but not always visible, and still less was it possible

---

[216] He reputedly was paid £90,000 by the *Daily Telegraph* for the rights to his memoirs.

[217] He wrote extensively to his younger sister Hilda throughout his inter-war ministerial career, conveying a good deal of technically secret political gossip. H. M. Hyde, *Neville Chamberlain* (London, 1976), 34–7, 61–2, 68, 72, 76, 80, 85–6; Young, *The Crossman Affair*, 137.

[218] J. Margach, *The Abuse of Power* (London, 1978), 21–53.

[219] Palmer, 'History of the D Notice Committee', 237–8.

[220] Laski, *Parliamentary Government*, 343.

[221] G. Orwell, *The Lion and Unicorn* (London, 1941), 121–2.

[222] Kingsley, *Representative Bureaucracy*, 222.

to view it as a coherent pattern. The key to the prevailing tone of uneasy celebration was the obscurity of the growth in controls. Although the state had been forced to legislate on official secrecy, and at the beginning and end of the inter-war period had been compelled to allow some Parliamentary discussion of the subject, the application of the Acts was so limited and inconsistent that it was difficult either to appreciate their benefits or to focus opposition to them. The operations of Special Branch and MI5 were occasionally objected to by their victims, but were never the subject of formal sanction or debate. Whilst the growing power of the state bureaucracy was causing occasional concern, not least to Lord Hewart,[223] reservations about its ethos of honourable secrecy were contained by its projected reputation for integrity and competence. Parliament was free, and, as Harold Laski assured the Americans in 1936, 'there is no British institution of which all citizens are, on the whole, more proud or more justly proud than the civil service'.[224] Yet the difficulties over Cabinet confidentiality and the spasmodic application of almost limitless Secrecy Acts raised ill-defined suspicions that all was not as well as once it was. Always there was pride, but increasingly there were doubts. J. B. Priestley, travelling through England the year after Hitler's accession to power, found himself looking over his shoulder as he hymned his nation's praises:

All over the world the shutters are being closed, the blue pencils are being sharpened, the gags and seals and chains and warrants for summary arrest are being brought out. There is some liberty yet in England. Milton could be living at this hour . . . I know that things happen in England, chiefly behind the scenes. No doubt letters are opened, persons are followed, pressure is brought to bear here and there. I am not fool enough to think that a travelling novelist has seen it all. It is a pity that we spoil a fine record by allowing a few contemptible moves of this kind to be made. We are told—sometimes when one of these dirty little bits of business is being put through—that at all costs we must keep our England, but the England to keep is the England worth keeping, the country of the free and generous temper.[225]

The nearest there was to an integrated critique of official secrecy in this period is to be found in the work of the Union of Democratic Control before, during, and after the First World War. What began as an attack led by Arthur Ponsonby, a left-wing Liberal MP and former diplomat, on the concealed manoeuverings surrounding the Moroccan crisis of 1911,[226] developed into a full-

---

[223] See his sweeping attack in *The New Despotism* of 1929. Also the similar onslaught in Allen, *Bureaucracy Triumphant*, and in R. Muir, *How Britain is Governed* (London, 1930), 58–64.

[224] H. J. Laski, 'The British Civil Service', *Yale Review*, 26: 2 (Dec. 1936), 350.

[225] J. B. Priestley, *English Journey* (London, 1934), 412. Cf. the protests made by E. M. Forster about 'the blows which are being struck against freedom in my country secretly and quietly.' E. M. Forster, 'Liberty in England', *Abinger Harvest* (Harmondsworth, 1967), 79.

[226] On the use of secret diplomacy in the decade before the outbreak of war, see Temperley, 'British Secret Diplomacy from Canning to Grey', 21–30.

scale campaign as the descent into catastrophic armed conflict confirmed all his warnings.[227] The Union, whose membership stretched across to the Independent Labour Party and sections of the Labour Party including Ramsay MacDonald,[228] set out a wide-ranging political and social diagnosis of the conduct of British foreign policy. The seat of the illness was the Cabinet, which was increasingly resistant to control by Parliament, and wilfully reluctant to expose its decisions to public scrutiny. The Foreign Office was the most obvious symptom of the malaise, as it formed policy and negotiated treaties out of sight of the expanding electorate. There were always enough leaks, whether authorized or otherwise, to raise suspicions, but never enough communication to inform a public debate. 'This semi-secrecy', wrote Ponsonby, 'combined with official silence is the surest way of creating scares. Diplomacy has been the pastime of a small privileged class, and for centuries that class has been the governing class.'[229] Sections of the Government machine, it was argued, had insulated themselves from the nineteenth-century triumph of liberalism. 'In this age of what is supposed to be democracy', claimed an article on 'The Foreign Office Autocracy',

the nation is rather less the master in its own house than it was in the periods of aristocratic and oligarchic rule. Our most vital transactions are managed for us behind closed doors by that secret committee called the Cabinet, which is supposed to be, but in a great many essential matters is not, responsible to the nation through the House of Commons.[230]

The proposed reforms ranged from establishing a Parliamentary Select Committee to review the conduct of foreign affairs to the first of Woodrow Wilson's Fourteen Points which demanded the end of secret diplomacy in the post-war world. At the centre of the Union's critique of the system which, it claimed, had plunged Europe into Armageddon, were a set of the purest liberal convictions. A progressive society and an orderly international system demanded the maximum intercourse between citizens and between nations. Secrecy promoted mistrust and instability, argued Ponsonby: 'A freer and franker communication of policy and information by the Governments to the peoples, not only here but in all countries, would in itself be a safeguard against sudden alarms and mischievous rumours.'[231] The open exchange of opinion was in turn both a condition and a product of the free expression of talent. The old landed elites

---

[227] On the early history of the movement, see M. Swartz, *The Union of Democratic Control in British Politics during the First World War* (Oxford, 1971). On the alleged secret agreements associated with the Moroccan crisis, see E. D. Morel, *Ten Years of Secret Diplomacy: An Unheeded Warning* (4th edn., Manchester, 1916).

[228] For Macdonald's views, see his Foreword to Morel's *Ten Years*. There were nine Union members in the 1924 Labour Cabinet. Harrison, *The Transformation of British Politics, 1860–1995*, 62.

[229] A. Ponsonby, *Democracy and the Conduct of Foreign Affairs* (London, 1912), 11.

[230] S. Low, 'The Foreign Office Autocracy', *Fortnightly Review*, NS 541 (Jan. 1912), 1.

[231] Ponsonby, *Democracy and Control of Foreign Affairs*, 18–19.

founded their power on mystery, and defended it by denying access to their knowledge. The Foreign Office in particular represented a last redoubt of the declining order, its civil servants drawn from a narrow social base, its political superiors able to deploy the excuse of national security to prevent all external scrutiny of its actions. As in the market-place, so in competition between nations, rational men, fully informed of the costs and benefits of alternative goods, would always choose those which promised the most secure and comfortable existence. James Bryce addressed the issue of diplomatic secrecy in his classic *Modern Democracies* of 1921. He accepted that there had to be some confidentiality in this field, but urged that ways should be found of diminishing its dangers: 'The risk that secrecy and discretion will be abused will be gradually lessened the more public opinion becomes better instructed on foreign affairs, and the more that legislatures learn to give unremitting attention to foreign policy.'[232]

The attack on official secrecy mounted by the Union of Democratic Control and its sympathizers could hardly have been more wide-ranging. The causes of the problem were located in the structure of both government and society, and its consequences in the preventible slaughter of millions of men. Yet the impact of the campaign on the practice of domestic government remained marginal. It deeply influenced the objectives of Labour's distinctive foreign policy between the wars, but at the level of international strategy rather than Parliamentary control of the Foreign Office, whose behaviour was little altered by either the Union's campaign or by the arrival and departure of the two minority Labour administrations.[233] The failure of the campaign to constitute a focal point for all those concerned with the growing restrictions on the flow of official information arose from a double misreading of history. First, there was a tendency to assume that the diplomats represented an anomalous element in the development of an open, meritocratic public bureaucracy. The Foreign Office was contrasted with what was projected as a far more progressive home civil service.[234] For this reason the Union turned away from a broader engagement with the politics of the 1920s, its secretary E. D. Morel refusing to join forces with the ILP for fear of diluting his attack on the conduct of international relations.[235] Secondly, it was supposed that official secrecy itself was an abnormality in the modern world. There was little recognition that it represented a defining characteristic of a contemporary bureaucracy, or that its particular British form could be projected as the rational and flexible means of

[232] J. Bryce, *Modern Democracies* (London, 1921), ii. 419. Also B. Crick, *The Reform of Parliament* (London, 1964), 7.

[233] On the rapid re-establishment of secret diplomacy after the war, notwithstanding the Covenant of the League of Nations, see C. Parry, 'Legislatures and Secrecy', *Harvard Law Review*, 67: 5 (Mar. 1954), 739.

[234] See e.g. Ponsonby in *Democracy and Diplomacy* (London, 1915), 18.

[235] Swartz, *Union of Democratic Control*, 102.

responding to the demands of the future. In reality, the honourable and secret civil servant, whatever his Department, was the outcome, not the negation, of the liberal reforms of the preceding century.

The inheritance by the Labour Party in the 1920s of the mantle of Opposition did little to encourage the emergence of a systematic critical analysis of the rapidly expanding civil service. It lacked any coherent view of the state on first entering office in 1915 as a junior member of Asquith's Coalition, and whilst it had acquired a socialist constitution by the time of the first minority Government in 1924, its attitude towards the machinery of government remained piecemeal and incoherent.[236] Of the leadership, only Arthur Henderson, who had seen the civil service at first hand during the war, was prepared to mount an attack on an institution 'swathed in red tape, hampered by tradition, conservative by instinct, saturated with class prejudice . . . a more effective check upon the reforming impulse than even a Parliament dominated by aristocratic and capitalist influences'.[237] However, he was anxious to confirm that democratic control over the machine could be achieved 'without a violent break with the past'.[238] The Party as a whole had confidence both in the capacity of the reformed franchise to deal with remaining pockets of undemocratic behaviour in the administrative system, and in the willingness of the civil service, whatever its background and private views, to work constructively with a reforming government.[239] As was to be the case after 1945, the ability of the bureaucracy to meet the challenge of the new welfare legislation did much to win the trust of the inexperienced Ministers. They were much more concerned about the successful implementation of the 1911 Insurance Acts than about the implications of the contemporary Official Secrets Act.

It seemed possible to accept the Fabian view that the civil service had no inevitable class interest of its own and was a necessary instrument for the realization of the Party's goals. The Fabian leaders Sidney and Beatrice Webb themselves were not blind to the defects of the machine, but shared the standard view of ex-prime ministers that it was an institution *sans pareil* in the modern world. Their *Constitution for the Socialist Commonwealth of Great Britain* of 1921 was a prospective rather than retrospective work, but nonetheless rehearsed the familiar theme: 'It has been the supreme good fortune of Great Britain that she has, during the past century, developed a Civil Service of exceptional capacity and integrity'.[240] There were problems with its attitude to communica-

---

[236] B. Jones and M. Keating, *Labour and the British State* (Oxford, 1985), 2–21; K. Theakston, *The Labour Party and Whitehall* (London, 1992), 25–53.

[237] A. Henderson, *The Aims of Labour* (London, 1918), 62.

[238] Henderson, *The Aims of Labour*, 62.

[239] W. B. Gwynn, 'The Labour Party and the Threat of Bureaucracy', *Political Quarterly*, 19: 4 (1971), 388.

[240] S. and B. Webb, *A Constitution for the Socialist Commonwealth of Great Britain* (London, 1920; 1975), 67.

tion, but these had to be set in the context of both the positive aspects of its code of honour, and the external checks on its behaviour: 'The great mass of government to-day is the work of an able and honest but secretive bureaucracy, tempered by the ever-present apprehension of the revolt of powerful sectional interests, and mitigated by the spasmodic interventions of imperfectly comprehending Ministers.'[241] Moreover, in a point rarely made by other critics, they argued that the limitations of the state bureaucracy paled into insignificance when set against the 'jealous secrecy in which the 1400 separate colliery companies at present enshroud their operations . . . and the bureaucratic concealment which to-day marks alike the Post Office and the railways'.[242] It was indeed the case that across the commercial sector, little progress had been made towards greater openness. Adverse trading conditions in the 1920s actually increased the tendency to withhold sensitive information from shareholders and the general public. Following Companies Acts in 1928 and 1929, an annual profit-and-loss account had to be published, but there was no control over its content, and nothing was done to prevent its manipulation by the widespread use of secret reserves.[243]

Strains of left-wing thinking, particularly the Guild Socialism Movement, which were much more seriously concerned about concentrations of bureaucratic power, remained marginal influences in the 1920s. More typical of the mainstream was J. H. Thomas's *When Labour Rules* of 1920, which said not a word about the machinery of government.[244] Ramsay MacDonald, whose two-volume *Socialism and Government* was equally silent on the subject,[245] combined an undue reverence for the dignified elements of the constitution with a mistrust of the press made all the more comprehensible after its treatment of his first administration. Whether or not the Zinoviev Letter caused or merely confirmed Labour's loss of the 1924 General Election, it had a permanent effect on the outlook of the leadership.[246] The Cabinet stumbled into the Gandhi incident in 1930 partly to prove its credentials as a responsible administration after an embarrassing series of leaks, and partly to intimidate the newspapers.[247] There was a shift in emphasis after the disaster of 1931, and a number of writers, particularly Laski and Stafford Cripps, began to address the need to

---

[241] Ibid. 69.

[242] Ibid. 195.

[243] J. R. Edwards, 'The Accounting Profession and Disclosure in Published Reports, 1925–1935', *Accounting and Business Research* (Autumn 1976), 289–303; Edwards, *History of Financial Accounting*, 126–42; Lee 'Company Financial Statements', 36.

[244] J. H. Thomas, *When Labour Rules* (London, 1920).

[245] J. R. MacDonald, *Socialism and Government*, 2 vols. (London, 1909). There was one brief reference to the possibility of decentralizing administration to the municipalities (ii. 121).

[246] Three days before the election in October 1924, the *Daily Mail* published a letter purportedly written by the President of the Comintern, urging both the Communist Party and sympathetic Labour Party members to promote a revolution. Serving and former members of the security services were involved in the forgery. Porter, *Plots and Paranoia*, 166–7.

[247] Margach, *Abuse of Power*, 44.

reform the institutions of the state as a precondition of an effective future Labour Government.[248] But amidst the talk of abolishing the Treasury and suspending the constitution, there remained a deep respect for the traditions of the service. Cripps held back from a wholesale replacement of officials 'by persons of known Socialist views',[249] and although Laski was becoming increasingly critical of the role of the gentleman,[250] he was still prepared to endorse the received image of the administrative machine: 'I have no reason to suppose that the civil servants of this country, even though they may not be socialists, would do no other, in general, than serve socialist ministers with the same loyalty and devotion they give to other parties. Their sense of professional honour is too high and too deep-rooted for it to be otherwise.'[251] Even on its radical fringe, Labour recognized Warren Fisher's characterization of the ideal bureaucrat.

Water on the Brain

A year after his conviction under the Official Secrets Act, Compton Mackenzie exacted his revenge. Forbidden to publish an uncensored history of espionage, he wrote instead a farce, which contained as much truth about its subject as any work of non-fiction. *Water on the Brain* narrated the exploits of Major Blenkinsop, recruited by the Director of Extraordinary Intelligence to replace an officer who had published a novel

which might have smashed up the whole of the Secret Service . . . he wrote what he honestly thought was a completely misleading picture of the Secret Service as it really is. The consequence is that any foreign agent who read's Chancellor's novel knows perfectly well what the British Secret Service is not, and to know what it is not is half-way to knowing what it is.[252]

The essence of the elaborate, paranoid bureaucracy which he inhabited was that its identity was unknown. Secrecy was every bit as important as the service itself, explains the Director: 'it stands to reason that if the Secret Service was no longer secret it would cease to be the secret service. After all, we're not cabinet ministers. We can't afford to talk.'[253] In anticipation of Le Carré, its operators

---

[248] J. E. Cronin, *The Politics of State Expansion* (London, 1991), 122–6.

[249] S. Cripps, 'Can Socialism Come by Constitutional Methods?', in C. Addison *et al.*, *Problems of a Socialist Government* (London, 1933), 64.

[250] See e.g. his fierce attack on their activities in all kinds of institutional power in, *The Danger of Being a Gentleman* (London, 1940), 13–29.

[251] H. J. Laski, *Democracy in Crisis* (London, 1933), 104. Also, Hetzner, 'Social Democracy and Bureaucracy', 113–15.

[252] Mackenzie, *Water on the Brain*, 38.

[253] Ibid. 16.

were known as 'plumbers', and Blenkinsop's immediate superior, 'N', employed the ingenious field-name of 'Captain W. S. Churchill'. The organization was expanding rapidly. As the Director observes: 'We're finding it a little easier to get money nowadays. There's so much of this bloody communism about. The people at the top are frightened. They think that we're the only thing that stands between them and the first lamp-post.'[254] It had doubled the 'Secret Vote' and was continually spawning new sections with impenetrable initials whose sole purpose was to protect the secrecy of the existing departments. Blenkinsop's own office needed the cover of another: 'That's where the Safety of the Realm Division comes in. Old P. who is the D.S.R.D. has a special set of sleuths who devote the whole of their time to preventing people from finding out what M.Q.99(E) means.'[255] As in the best of farces, it was a universe which seemed utterly logical to those within it, and completely absurd to those outside. At the end of the book, fearing that the location of their headquarters has been exposed in another novel, the Service secretly converts the building into an asylum 'for civil servants whose minds have given way under the strain of their responsibilities', hoping that foreign spies will believe that the mad officials are real British agents.[256]

The sobering aspect of Mackenzie's extended joke was how long it was to last. His explanation, for instance, of the anonymity of the Director was to hold good for the next half-century: 'One of the important things about it is not to let any foreign agent guess who is the head of the Secret Service. After all, war may break out any moment, and if the head of the Secret Service is known, what chance do we stand against the enemy?'[257] The persistence of the nonsense, as Mackenzie realized, was a function of the interdependence of the forms of pretence. Like the cry of the small boy in the tale of the Emperor's New Clothes, to which the book made explicit reference, it would require only one shaft of truth to bring the entire edifice tumbling to the ground. In the more immediate context, Mackenzie was insisting that the inverted logic of the secrecy legislation and the espionage bodies which both applied and were protected by it, was destroying all sense of perspective in matters of national security. As he commented at the time of his trial,

This phrase official secrets has become a bogy for the whole country and is used with extreme skill always to suggest in the mind of the general public that an act approaching espionage has been committed, an act against the safety of the realm. Any man accused of violating the Official Secrets Act in whatever ridiculous way runs the risk of creating in the public mind a prejudice against himself, so much has the sinister aspect been forced upon people.[258]

---

[254] Ibid. 15.
[255] Ibid. 39.
[256] Ibid. 307–8.
[257] Ibid. 40.
[258] Quoted in Kidd, *British Liberty in Danger*, 93.

The conflation of internal and external threats, and the obsessive secrecy about the operation of the secrecy system, made it impossible for the modern citizen either to understand the purpose of the new laws or to defend himself against their application.

In one sense, the suitability of the genre of farce to describe the British secret services was a measure of their relative harmlessness. It would have been a less appropriate form of commentary on the clandestine agencies of contemporary totalitarian regimes. The Gestapo, for instance, replicated aspects of the British welfare bureaucracy, setting up its card indexes and exploiting the eagerness of neighbour to denounce neighbour. Like the National Insurance inspectors, its officers were plagued by the volume of false accusations, in peace and in war. 'Malicious gossip' was at once a reportable offence and the form of reporting.[259] Yet there remained a difference between the notification of benefit reduction and the postcard by which the Gestapo politely invited suspects for interrogation at headquarters. For all his irritation and inconvenience, Mackenzie, who was a highly paid writer, was merely fined,[260] not sent to a concentration camp or shot. This Chapter has argued that measurable physical suffering, death, and the fear of death, were the province of structures of state and professional secrecy which lay largely outside the Official Secrets Acts and the espionage services. Only in areas such as the infiltration of the National Unemployed Workers' Movement was there a clear line of consequence between the expansion of official secrecy and the material well-being of sections of the population.

Aside from its reflection of a broader unease about the use and abuse of the concept of national security, the resonance of *Water on the Brain* was to be found principally in its depiction of the growth of publicly significant knowledge leading not to the widening of channels of communication but to the creation or reinforcement of closed systems of information. The reticence of the gentleman could increasingly be seen not only as a guarantee of his honour but also as a symbol of a wider failure to enlarge social communication in a nominally democratic nation. As D. W. Brogan observed in *The English People* of 1943: 'The difficulties of intercourse between various layers of English society are not merely matters of accent. They are matters of posture, or emphasis, of ease or diffidence in speech.'[261] The private world of M.Q.99(E) had its counterparts in the increasingly cohesive and introspective Whitehall culture, and in the still-defensive communities of the urban poor. The growth of the mass media and the role of government had instigated some opening up of contacts between the rulers and the ruled, but for differing reasons these had failed to fulfil their

---

[259] R. Gellately, *The Gestapo and German Society* (Oxford, 1990), 64, 129–59.

[260] Although the fine and imposed costs amounted to only £200, the further attendant legal costs and loss of royalties, did, nonetheless, precipitate a serious crisis in his financial affairs. Mackenzie, *My Life and Times: Octave Seven*, 115–16.

[261] D. W. Brogan, *The English People* (London, 1943), 98.

potential. They had resulted in a highly manipulative and inconsistent relationship between senior politicians and the press, or had been compromised by the hostile intrusion of those charged with policing the growth in state expenditure on the underprivileged. Those with power had insufficient confidence in the institutions of popular democracy; those without had too little trust in the institutions of the democratic state.

| # CITIZENSHIP AND SECRECY, 1945–1972

The King of the Underworld

Billy Hill was the first modern product of the public fascination with the hidden world of the professional criminal. The scion of an Irish family of thieves in the Dickensian slum of Seven Dials, he completed his education in Borstal and by his early twenties was running his own gang of housebreakers, 'the best screwing team in London'.[1] He pioneered motorized smash-and-grab raids, and through a combination of careful organization and the discreet use of his knife to scar the faces of potential rivals, built up a criminal empire in London during the 1930s. As with so many entrepreneurs, he had a good war, selling for large profits what previously he had been forced to steal, and as a result of a post-war territorial settlement could claim to be the 'top man of Britain's underworld' by the late 1940s.[2] A smartly dressed teetotaller, he lived in a modest flat in Barnes and entertained celebrities and journalists in his own West End night club. His vanity was fed by the newspaper men who enjoyed his hospitality and in return promoted him to the rank of monarch. Each side had an interest in dramatizing his authority over the criminal fraternity. The austere new society was eager to read about the secret life of a colourful but respectable rogue, a lawbreaker capable of ordering the disorderly.[3] In 1955 his notoriety was confirmed by the publication of an autobiography which attempted to combine an adventure story with an amateur ethnography of the subculture in which he had lived.

A leading theme of his account was the arcane vocabulary of his calling, which reflected its elaborate behavioural code, and at the same time protected it from exposure to outsiders. This was especially useful, he argued, as a defence against the increasingly sophisticated attempts by the police to penetrate his organization. He was well aware that his phone was routinely tapped, but was unconcerned: 'I would like to see the faces of some Post Office officials when

---

[1] Billy Hill, *Boss of Britain's Underworld* (London, 1955), 27.

[2] Ibid. 15.

[3] For a more broadly focused response to the same market, see J. Phelan, *The Underworld* (London, 1953). On Hill's career and its background, see D. Campbell, *The Underworld* (London, 1996), 37–41, 44–8.

they listen to conversations. Our language of the underworld was not evolved for Post Office clerks.'[4] The police themselves were not convinced by his literary claim to respectability, and renewed their surveillance in 1956 as the King of the Underworld became embroiled in a violent struggle with a group of usurpers led by Jack 'Spot' Comer. They tapped Hill's phone in his flat, recording his conversations not just with his gang but with his barrister, Patrick Marrinan, who was also from an impecunious Irish background. When Marrinan made a rash attempt to interfere physically in the arrest of two of Hill's henchmen at the Bridewell in Dublin, the Attorney-General, with the consent of the Home Secretary, permitted the transcripts to be handed to the Bar Council for a disciplinary hearing.

Marrinan was arraigned before the Benchers of the Honourable Society of Lincoln's Inn in June 1957, charged with soliciting work from clients and accepting instruction directly from them, and with the more diffuse and much more serious offence of 'association on terms of personal friendship and familiarity with Billy Hill and Albert Dimes and other persons in a manner unbecoming to a gentleman and a barrister'.[5] He was accused of betraying the honour of his profession by immersing himself too completely in the private realm of the underworld king. The clinching evidence came from the transcripts. It was not so much the substance of the conversations as their medium. Billy Hill's language was fit to be read by respectable people, but not to be spoken by them. Marrinan's familiarity with the criminal argot, his capacity to use phrases such as 'easy as kiss your hand',[6] were fatal to his defence, which was conducted by the future Conservative Attorney-General Michael Havers. At one level, the hapless barrister was guilty of little more than excessive enthusiasm caused by a combination of indigence and naivety. He was already an outsider in a profession for which he had been too poor to afford a pupillage, and in retrospect it was not wise to have asked Hill to solve his young family's housing problems by finding them a flat in the same building. There were, nonetheless, profound ethical considerations at issue. The Bar Council, citing a century-old directive of Cockburn, saw itself acting

for the protection of the profession that it might not be disgraced by having among its members those who disregarded its honour, and for the protection of the public that their confidence that the rank of barrister was a sufficient test of the trustworthiness and honour of individual members of the Bar might not be misled or abused.[7]

The contest between the complete integrity of the senior professional body and the personal livelihood of one its least-regarded juniors could only have

---

[4] Hill, *Boss of Britain's Underworld*, 2.
[5] *The Times* (28 June 1957), 10.
[6] Ibid. (1 July 1957), 4.
[7] Ibid. (29 June 1957), 4.

one outcome. Marrinan was duly disbarred, in spite of his pitiful plea to be allowed to go abroad and practice where there was no possibility of causing further embarrassment to his peers. However, basing such high-flown proceedings on evidence gained by secret surveillance whose very existence was concealed from the defendant when he was first questioned about his offences, was fraught with danger. A heated debate broke out within the Bar Council about the propriety of the hearings, with the Chairman, the former Labour Attorney-General Hartley Shawcross, further accused of trying to gag discussion of the matter. At the same time, the issue was raised in Parliament, where Rab Butler sought with some difficulty to defend the decision of his recent predecessor, Gwilym Lloyd George, to release the transcripts. He attempted to fall back behind the traditional right not to answer any questions on the exercise of the Home Secretary's prerogative, and found himself accused by, amongst others, the young Barbara Castle, of introducing precisely those tactics of state repression which the country had fought a world war against.[8]

In this context, the sword of honour was double-edged. Just as in the first controversy over the interception of communication in 1844, *The Times* was up in arms, its fury undimmed and its rhetoric unchanged by the passage of years. It was, proclaimed its leader page, 'An Odious Practice': even if telephone tapping was undertaken in the national interest, 'it is so repugnant to every idea of what constitutes freedom within a society; it has attached to it so much the aura of the police state, that the question has to be asked whether even in this highest cause it should be allowed'.[9] As before, it was not inclined to repose confidence in the secretly exercised discretion of the Home Secretary, the more so as the concurrent persecution of nuclear protestors revealed a want of self-control and sense of proportion amongst those in authority:

The strangest things can happen, as we are seeing just now, when it is possible for loyal but anxious citizens to be smeared with a Communist taint because they sincerely believe that the dropping of hydrogen bombs, even for testing purposes, is an evil thing. Yet everything to-day is calm and no one would suggest such people's telephones would at present be tapped. But governments are as capable of hysteria as individuals.[10]

To clinch its argument it raised the ghost of the great bogeyman of the early Victorian liberals:

It is worth remembering that METTERNICH had the highest motives for his postal spying system. Yet not one person in ten thousand would condone it now. There are many other legitimate resources, which do not threaten the ordinary citizen, open to the State to fight conspiracy. It is worth considering whether we are in enough

---

[8] *Hansard*, 5th Series, 571, 6 June 1957, cols. 1461–2, 1480–2, 1494; 7 June 1957, cols. 1565–6; 573, 11 July 1957, cols. 541–2; 574, 24 July 1957, cols. 402–3; 31 July 1957, cols. 1247–8.

[9] *The Times* (8 June 1957), 7.

[10] Ibid.

danger or whether the number of people caught by this particularly hateful device is worth all the unease and suspicion it must cause.[11]

Faced with mounting criticism, the Bar Council announced a rare open inquiry, to 'allay public misgivings regarding a case tainted by the odious practice of phone tapping',[12] whilst the Government adopted the less transparent mechanism of a committee of three Privy Councillors to undertake what would be the first and to date only major inquiry into the interception of communications since the Secret Select Committee Report of 1844. Both the chairman, the judge, and distinguished criminal lawyer Sir Norman Birkett, and the Conservative representative, Walter Monckton, had gained extensive experience of security systems and the control of information during the Second World War.[13] Their report, to which the third member, the Labour foreign affairs spokesman Patrick Gordon Walker appended a minor note of dissent, was published in October. In almost every respect it was founded upon the inquiry into the opening of Mazzini's correspondence a century earlier. It repeated not just sections of the earlier text, but the basic strategy of deploying history to defuse a crisis in the use of modern communication technology. The past stood as both the authority for present practice and the justification for its continuation.

As in 1844, the initial difficulty was that of establishing a legal basis for the interception of telephone calls. The report revealed that as late as 1937, more than half a century after the introduction of the service, the police and the security agencies were tapping lines without any form of official sanction at all.[14] Belatedly it had then been decided, without any public debate or announcement, to bring the practice within the system of Home Office warrants which existed for opening correspondence. That merely transferred the issue of legitimation back a stage. In 1937, as in 1957, there was still no direct statutory authority for any public surveillance of private letters. 'The origin of the power to intercept communications', confessed Birkett, 'can only be surmised.'[15] The usual sources for legal definition were largely silent: 'It is a singular circumstance that the source of the power has never been the subject of judicial pronouncement, and the text-book writers have not discussed it in any fullness.'[16] All that was left was history, and especially the 1844 report which stood both as the fullest compendium of what could be gleaned about the more distant past and, *de facto*, as a source of legal argument in its own right. 'It is significant',

[11] Ibid.

[12] Ibid. (4 July 1957), 12.

[13] Birkett had been chairman of the appeals committee against internment orders, and Monckton successively Director-General of the Censorship Bureau and of the Ministry of Information. H. M. Hyde, *Norman Birkett* (London, 1964), 470–2.

[14] *Report of the Committee of Privy Councillors Appointed to Inquire into the Interception of Communications* [Birkett], Cmnd. 283 (1957), 13–14. See also Fitzgerald and Leopold, *Stranger on the line*, 114.

[15] *Report . . . into the Interception of Communications*, 5.

[16] Ibid. 7.

concluded the Privy Councillors, 'that both Committees avoided any discussion of the source of the authority upon which the Secretary of State exercised his power, and were content to recognise the existence of the power to intercept communications, and to rely upon the various statutes which refer to the existence of the power.'[17]

It was impossible to draw the authority out of the shadows. The law could never be viewed directly, but only obliquely through the lesser regulations defining the powers of Post Office employees.[18] The vexed question of whether the statutes previously lost in the mists of time could be deployed to cover the unforseen technology of electronic communication was resolved by means of a complex analogy involving aeroplanes and Richard I. However, if this opaque legal reasoning satisfied the Privy Councillors, it was less clear that it convinced the public at large. There was a major contradiction at the heart of the report, which its findings did nothing to resolve. On the one hand, it was evident from the initial controversy that little had changed in popular sensitivities over the years since Sir James Graham had been pilloried. 'The feeling still persists', admitted the Councillors, 'that such interceptions offend against the usual and proper standards of behaviour as being an invasion of privacy and an interference with the liberty of the individual in his right to be "let alone when lawfully engaged upon his own affairs".'[19] Patrick Gordon Walker was of the view that in the age of modern citizenship, 'public repugnance to the interception of communication' had actually increased.[20] As had been the case in 1844, it was partly that letters, and by extension, telephone calls, lay so close to the expression of private identity, and partly that the peculiarly British mode of surveillance was so associated with the tradition of official secrecy. Natural suspicion was compounded by the concealment of both means and ends: 'The powers of interception are in the hands of State officials. They are exercised in secret, and the extent of the exercise and the purposes for which the powers are exercised are not publicly known.'[21]

On the other hand, the Privy Councillors were too immersed in the early Victorian tradition to break free of the structure of informality and concealment. It set out its position on openness on the very first page: 'Following the example of the Secret Committee of both Houses of Parliament appointed in 1844 to consider the same problem that has been referred to us, we decided not to publish the evidence and so informed those who gave evidence before us.'[22] Although the bare statistics of warrants issued between 1937 and 1956 were given in an Appendix, the report recommended that this practice should not be repeated, as it 'would greatly aid the operation of agencies hostile to the

---

[17] *Report . . . into the Interception of Communications*, 5.
[18] For a critical discussion of this mode of legal reasoning, see Baxter, *State Security, Privacy and Information*, 160–4.
[19] *Report . . . into the Interception of Communications*, 29.
[20] Ibid. 38.   [21] Ibid. 30.   [22] Ibid. 5.

State if they were able to estimate even approximately the extent of the inter-ceptions of communications for security purposes'.[23] All that was conceded was that, henceforth, proper secret records should be kept of the warrants. In 1947, as the Cold War intensified, the Security Service had caused the destruc-tion of the card index held by the Home Office, in case it fell into the wrong hands. Now at least the state was to be trusted with its own memory, even if it was to be denied to the general population.

The summary of warrants listed at the end of the report revealed a significant shift of balance in the form of interception. In the period since phone-tapping was made subject to Home Office control, the number of war-rants had multiplied fourteen times, outstripping those for written communi-cation for the first time in 1955. The statistics seriously understated the amount of wartime surveillance, when all internal telephone trunk lines had been tapped without any formal sanction,[24] and paid no attention to the growing work of GCHQ,[25] but taken on their own terms, they confirmed that the rapid growth in the use of electronic technology was adding a new dimen-sion to the 'odious, invidious and obnoxious' activities which had first aroused public disquiet a century earlier. In spite of this, the report recommended that there should be no alteration to the machinery of surveillance or to Parlia-ment's control over it. It contented itself instead with a series of lesser reforms, including the discontinuation of general or undated warrants, and the prohi-bition of the secondary use of transcripts such as had taken place with Billy Hill's conversations.[26] Having lifted a corner of the blanket covering the inter-ception of communications, the report concluded that it should once more be laid down and disturbed no further.

Birkett's failure to resolve the tension between the mentality of the Penny-Post era and the implications of the electronic age stemmed from the pe-culiar combination of continuity and crisis which characterized the post-war society. By refusing to open up what a *Times* leader on the publication of the re-port described as a practice 'popularly associated with the worst excesses of the police state',[27] the inquiry had made transparent a set of problems which were ingrained in the relationship between the new forms of citizenship and the ex-panding channels of information. The first of these, which will be the concern of the next section of this chapter, was how far the obsession with secrecy pro-voked by the general rise of the Cold War and the specific issue of nuclear tech-nology, would influence the development of democratic institutions. The unpublished evidence heard by the inquiry 'overwhelmingly established' that

---

[23] Ibid.

[24] N. Stammers, *Civil Liberties in Britain During the 2nd World War* (London, 1983), 133–7.

[25] Fitzgerald and Leopold, *Stranger on the Line*, 120–1.

[26] On the limited nature of the Report's findings, see R. Wacks, *The Protection of Privacy* (London, 1980), 36–7; S. McCabe, 'National Security and Freedom of Information' in L. Gostin (ed.), *Civil Liberties in Conflict* (London, 1988), 192; Madgwick and Smythe, *The Invasion of Privacy*, 100–4.

[27] *The Times* (1 Nov. 1957), 11.

there were 'continuous organised and dangerous efforts to spy out secrets of the State' and to 'spread subversion and to penetrate the apparatus of the Government and work of high security'.[28] The submissions reinforced a truth which had been apparent since the emergence of modern espionage systems just before the First World War, that the key targets of the security services were not individual spies but the communication networks which linked them together. New technology was at once the objective and the Achilles heel of the nation's enemies. So far from requiring a dismantling of the structures of surveillance, it justified a continuing expansion. The critics of phone-tapping might argue that the application of scientific discovery rendered obsolete traditional forms of secrecy, but those charged with defending the nation's security argued the reverse.

The willingness of the three Privy Councillors to endorse both the necessity and the effectiveness of the work of the security services, and the acceptance by both Parliament and the press of the unsubstantiated claims of the Report, raised a second set of questions about the persistence of institutional deference in the modern welfare state. There might be little surprise that *The Times* should replicate exactly its behaviour in 1844, beginning by demanding the total abolition of heinous practices whose existence it had never suspected, and ending by welcoming an almost complete whitewashing of Government procedures by an inquiry held *in camera*. Men of great probity had looked at the matter, and such reservations as the paper may have had were assuaged by the leaked information that the Privy Councillors had at least resisted pressures from the security services to censor their final report.[29] There was a daunting circularity about the acceptance of authority. The press behaved as it had done a century earlier, and the verdict it condoned was justified by reference to the reports on the Mazzini affair. It was enough for the Privy Councillors that all the Home Secretaries since the war were satisfied with the safeguards on the exercise of their powers: 'just as the Secret Committee of the House of Lords in 1844 were impressed by the witnesses who had held high office, we too in our turn, were impressed by this unanimity of opinion.'[30] So complete was the resemblance that they were impelled to fall back on the original wording:

'it is the concurrent Opinion of Witnesses who have held high Office, and who may be most competent to form a sound Judgment, that they would reluctantly see this Power abolished ...' We repeat this sentence as representing the view of the Secretaries of State who have been good enough to give evidence before us.[31]

More striking was the rapid evaporation of the wrath of the Labour Party and the unions. The initial exposure of the tapping of Billy Hill's phone led not only

---

[28] *Report ... on the Interception of Communications*, 26.
[29] *The Times* (1 Nov. 1957), 11.
[30] *Report ... into the Interception of Communications*, 31–2.
[31] Ibid. 32.

to vigorous questioning in the House but to an emergency motion carried unanimously by the annual conference of the Post Office Engineering Union which was in session in Blackpool. This spoke of the opening of the 'floodgates of police states' and condemned the Home Secretary for depriving the country of freedoms which its citizens had lately laid down their lives to defend.[32] By contrast, the publication of Birkett's report five months later[33] was greeted with silence inside and outside Westminster. In the end the TUC did not see the issue as fundamental to the rights of its members, and the Labour leadership was content to keep whatever comments it wished to make behind the closed doors of the Privy Council. No backbencher broke ranks, and it was left to the Liberal leader Jo Grimond to register a token dissent. The rhetoric of protest had looked back to the Victorian concerns for individual liberty rather than forward to the issues raised by the post-war expansion in government over which Labour had presided. There was no sense that the creation of the welfare state was provoking a more general crisis in public control over the acquisition and use of information about the affairs of private citizens. By one means or another, officials were collecting and storing an unprecedented volume of highly sensitive personal details, but a decade after Labour's historic election victory, the constitutional implications of the growth of such archives had yet to be addressed. Except where the security services got hold of them, more activity merely meant more card indexes. The powerful message delivered by the Birkett Report, and accepted by the Parliamentary left, was that there was little need to disturb traditions of official secrecy which had been established when Whitehall was in possession of infinitely less knowledge about the habits and circumstances of the population.

Deference was a function of trust, which in turn was sustained by notions of honourable conduct. The third set of questions raised by the incident was whether the structures and frontiers of ethical behaviour needed to be redrawn in the face of the increased volume of communication between the state and its citizens. The controversy had been generated by a double breach of traditional boundaries. The policing of national security had apparently merged with the Bar Council's control of professional honour, just as Marrinan's twin desire for justice and a livelihood had drawn him too far into the hidden world of Billy Hill. The immediate outcome of the legal and Parliamentary inquiries was a restoration of the status quo. Marrinan was sacrificed in the name of gentlemanly conduct, and the Government agreed to prohibit any overt overlap between official and private surveillance practices. There should be no future confusion between the way professions and the state kept their respective secrets. In the longer term, however, more difficult questions

[32] *The Times* (8 June 1957), 4.
[33] The report was published six weeks later than its date of 18 September, while arguments took place with the security services about censorship of its contents. For an account of its publication, see Fitzgerald and Leopold, *Stranger on the Line*, 119.

remained to be faced about whether sectors of the population hitherto excluded from the tight, privileged universe of the older professions either needed or could mobilize similar levels of control over their essential knowledge. Modern citizenship implied, amongst much else, the right to determine what to communicate and by what means. Rab Butler, who presided over the controversy, had come to national prominence as promoter of a major extension of national education. But whether citizens as individuals could effectively implement their new skills, or whether they needed to come together in organizations before they could either gain control over essential information or be trusted with it, remained to be established. Only in the realm of the King of the Underworld were the rules still clear. 'He nearly died', wrote Billy Hill of one victim of gang warfare: 'In accordance with our code he did not talk, and for being a good boy he was paid a monkey for his trouble.'[34]

The Nuclear Age

In March 1948, as the final stones in the arch of the welfare state were being put in place, the Prime Minister came to the House to announce that the Government had lost confidence in the integrity of the civil service. The Official Secrets Acts of 1889 and 1911 had marked the first defeat for the culture of honourable secrecy whereby the conduct of public servants was to be guaranteed. The legal sanctions signified a recognition that informal means of policing conduct were an insufficient safeguard in the face of the growth in the size of the machinery and in the scale of the threat from the nation's enemies, but their principal function was to reinforce rather than replace the traditional processes of ensuring conformity to the ethic of public service. Now it seemed that neither the elaborate internal systems of recruitment, induction, and supervision, nor the Draconian clauses of the Official Secrets Acts were strong enough to resist a new set of dangers:

there are certain duties of such secrecy that the State is not justified in employing in connection with them anyone whose reliability is in doubt. Experience, both in this country and elsewhere, has shown that membership of, and other forms of continuing association with, the Communist Party may involve acceptance by the individual of a loyalty, which in certain circumstances can be inimical to the State.[35]

The international conspiracy of communism was so powerful yet so intangible that normal methods of detecting or preventing the propensity for betrayal

---

[34] Hill, *Boss of Britain's Underworld*, 9.

[35] *Hansard*, 5th Series, 448, 15 Mar. 1948, col. 1703. On the background to the statement, see B. Cathcart, *Test of Greatness: Britain's Struggle for the Atom Bomb* (London, 1994), 87–9.

were ineffective. There were undoubtedly members of the Party who were perfectly loyal to their country, Attlee admitted, 'but there is no way of distinguishing such people from those, who, if opportunity offered, would be prepared to endanger the security of the State in the interests of another Power'.[36]

This sense that, in this most critical area, the state could be excluded from the mentality of even its most senior employees, was profoundly disturbing. Trust had been contaminated by the explosion of the atomic bombs over Japan. Immediately the war was over, the Cabinet Defence Committee began a search for a new policy to control the disclosure to foreign countries of the technical information which clearly was now central to the defence capability of any great power.[37] By 1947 the Chiefs of Staff had become so alarmed by the situation caused by the simultaneous relaxation of wartime Defence Regulations and intensification of Russian espionage that they were privately urging the Cabinet that 'known members of the Communist Party should be excluded from secret work'.[38] Behind the scenes, the Security Service had already begun quietly to encourage the transfer of suspect civil servants to less sensitive work, and it was concern that the growing volume of its activity might attract unwelcome publicity that led to Attlee's statement in the Commons.[39]

This was the traditional method of extending secrecy. First of all action was taken without notification, then Parliament was given a brief announcement to which objection was made only by those on the wilder shores of the left, most notably the Communist Willie Gallacher, who accused the Government of 'grovelling to the Tories and the big dollar boys of America'.[40] The Labour movement in general raised few objections to the principle of employing the secret policemen who before the war had paid such close attention to its own activities. Trade union leaders were enjoying their unprecedented and largely unpublicized access to the corridors of power, and were not averse to the stigmatizing of the Communist sympathies which were shared by disruptive elements within their own organizations.[41] The mechanism which the Treasury introduced later in the year was in its way equally British.[42] The right of liberty of conscience was to be maintained. Party membership would not lead to dismissal, only to transfer. The Permanent Secretaries were to retain their autonomy in staffing matters, being advised rather than controlled by the Security

---

[36] *Hansard*, 5th Series, 448, 15 Mar. 1948, col. 1704.

[37] PRO, CAB21/2554.

[38] Ibid.

[39] P. Hennessy and G. Broomfield, 'Britain's Cold War Security Purge: The Origins of Positive Vetting', *Historical Journal*, 25: 4 (1982), 967. P. Weiler, *British Labour and the Cold War* (Stanford, 1988), 220; Lustgarten and Leigh, *In From the Cold*, 130–2.

[40] *Hansard*, 5th Series, 448, 15 Mar. 1948, col. 1704.

[41] Weiler, *British Labour and the Cold War*, 226, 273–5.

[42] The attempt to maintain a balance between secrecy and freedom is discussed in Thurlow, *Secret State*, 287–96.

Service and free of any direct interference by Parliament.[43] Trade union concern was placated by the appointment of the retired General Secretary of the Union of Post Office Workers as one of the three-member tribunal set up to hear appeals. Everything was to be done as quietly as possible. The mechanism was to be embodied in administrative regulation rather than legal process, on the traditional grounds of flexibility and avoidance of unnecessary public controversy.[44] Although there was covert manipulation of the media, which gave extensive coverage to right-wing propaganda,[45] there were no systematic campaigns against individuals, no public hearings on either the procedures or on specific cases. Attlee resisted a call to set up a Select Committee on un-British activities but instead established a Cabinet Committee on 'Subversive Activities', whose very existence, like all such bodies, was an official secret.[46] In order that no light be shed on the operation of the vetting system, civil servants appealing against judgments were denied representation or the right of cross-examination. As Attlee explained to the anxious Vincent Tewson, General Secretary of the TUC: 'Given the need to safeguard secret sources of information, we cannot have these cases investigated by a judicial tribunal under the normal forensic process, including the questioning of the evidence by the civil servant's own advocate.'[47]

The sense of continuity of approach in dealing with the freedom of expression of public employees was reinforced by the publication the following year of the Committee of Enquiry on the Political Activities of Civil Servants. This sought to reconcile the fact that, 'the life of every citizen is being directly and acutely affected by all grades of the hierarchy',[48] with the growing expectations of political citizenship on the part of what were now more than a million industrial and non-industrial government workers, double the number in the mid-1930s. In the view of the Committee it remained axiomatic that, 'the political neutrality of the Civil Service is a fundamental feature of British democratic government and is essential for its efficient operation'.[49] It confirmed that all those above most of the minor, manipulative and industrial grades should still be forbidden to write letters to the press, or publish books, articles, or leaflets setting out their views on party political matters. However, the broadening of the public sphere which had taken place since 1945 did offer the possibility of less sensitive forms of participation, which could be policed by the

[43] M. R. Joelson, 'The Dismissal of Civil Servants in the Interests of National Security', *Public Law* (1963), 51–5.

[44] D. C. Jackson, 'Individual Rights and National Security', *Modern Law Review*, 20 (1957), 365–6.

[45] Weiler, *British Labour and the Cold War*, 229.

[46] Hennessy and Broomfield, 'Britain's Cold War Security Purge', 966–7.

[47] PRO, PREM8 948. Letter, 21 Dec. 1948. The implications of this 'cardinal fault' in the British procedures are examined from an American perspective in Jackson, 'Individual Rights and National Security', 376.

[48] *Report of the Committee on the Political Activities of Civil Servants* (1949), Cmnd. 7718, p. 15.

[49] Ibid. 15.

established traditions of behaviour. 'In the sphere of public affairs which are not matters of party controversy,' the Committee concluded, 'civil servants should be given more latitude to play their part in the normal activities of citizenship, so long as they do so in an unofficial capacity and observe the code of reserve.'[50]

At this level the culture of honourable secrecy was still alive and well and capable of further flexible adjustments to cope with a changing world. Set against the proliferating forms of paranoia and persecution in the United States, the British approach to loyalty in public life seemed notably restrained and civilized.[51] Past errors were left in the past. One of the most influential fellow-travellers of the 1930s, John Strachey, eventually became Secretary of State for War in the final year of the Attlee Governments.[52] Yet, as had been the case in the Edwardian era, the code of reserve in British politics was capable of harbouring profound breaches of established conventions of thought and behaviour. Limited though it was in its original form, the new vetting procedure, which let the Security Service into Whitehall in search not just of members of the Communist Party but of those maintaining some association with them, represented a critical, and in the view of contemporary scholars of public administration, unnecessary loss of confidence in the existing combination of internal and external controls.[53] At the heart of the developments, concealed and protected by the code of discretion, was what *The Times* had correctly diagnosed in its attack on phone-tapping as a form of government hysteria. This was true not only of the transfer of civil servants from secret work, but of the entire management of the nuclear programme, both military and civilian. The combination of unprecedented international threats and continuing internal restrictions on communication and debate caused those at the head of government progressively to lose all sense of proportion. As one detailed study of nuclear decision-making concluded: 'in Britain one feels that secrecy having begun as a necessity continued as a convenience and eventually became an obsession.'[54] If the British response was in every sense quieter than the American, it was in its own way just as irrational.

In a rare House of Commons discussion of nuclear policy in 1952, Churchill claimed to have been 'rather astonished' to discover on return to office that since 1945 well over £100 million had been spent on atomic energy without Parliament's knowledge.[55] His surprise was doubly misleading. In the first place, the efforts made by Attlee to deny discussion of the programme not only

---

[50] Ibid. 31.

[51] The best study of the American experience remains Shils, *Torment of Secrecy*.

[52] D. Caute, *The Fellow-Travellers* (London, 1977), 341.

[53] E. N. Gladden, *Civil Service or Bureaucracy?* (London, 1956), 152; T. A. Critchley, *The Civil Service Today* (London, 1951), 60.

[54] R. Williams, *The Nuclear Power Decisions* (London, 1980), 324.

[55] Cited in M. Gowing, *Independence and Deterrence: Britain and Atomic Energy, 1945–1952*, Vol. 2, *Policy Execution* (London, 1974), 46.

to MPs but also to the majority of his Cabinet replicated the behaviour of Churchill during the war, and were largely maintained when the Conservatives returned to power in 1951.[56] Secondly, part of the explanation for Attlee's success in maintaining secrecy was due to the willing collaboration of the Opposition, which abstained from any criticism either of the policy itself or of the means by which it was being hidden from public scrutiny. Nonetheless, the scale of the deception and concealment was remarkable. The costs of the exercise were buried in the general sub-headings of the Ministry of Supply vote; the formulation of policy was confined to a handful of ministers and advisors, of whom the most prominent, Sir John Anderson, was a leading member of the Opposition front bench; the decision to build a bomb was taken in January 1947 but not announced until May 1948; and no debate on the substance of nuclear policy took place in Parliament throughout either of Attlee's administrations.[57] Under advice from the Chiefs of Staff, Attlee agreed in 1947 that 'special arrangements should be put in place to make sure that the programme remained secret',[58] and these were to prove effective. Compared with the controversy on defence expenditure immediately before the war, when Churchill himself was continually embarrassing the Government with information leaked from inside the defence establishment,[59] the achievement of silence, no less than the intention, demands explanation.

In this matter, as elsewhere in this study, whilst the desire to maintain secrets reflected a lack of trust, so the capacity to do so demanded an investment of trust on the part of those excluded from communication. The loss of confidence had both an international and a domestic dimension. Under the secret clauses of the Quebec Agreement of 1943, later given more public form in the Washington Declaration of November 1945, Britain and the United States were to pool information on the development of a weapon which could have so significant an impact on the conduct of war and peace. The breaking of this agreement by the McMahon Act of August 1946, together with the equally abrupt cessation of lend-lease and the collapse of a joint policy on Palestine, severely jolted confidence in the reliability and goodwill of the American government.[60] At the same time, the deterioration of relations with Russia de-

[56] The active decision-making was confined to a defence subcommittee of the Cabinet, although its minutes were subsequently circulated to the whole Cabinet. Churchill did permit a full Cabinet discussion of the decision to build the hydrogen bomb in 1954. Harrison, *Transformation of British Politics*, 295.

[57] The fullest account of the secrecy surrounding the issue is to be found in M. Gowing, *Independence and Deterrence. Britain and Atomic Energy, 1945–1952*, Vol. 1, *Policy Making* (London, 1974), 5, 6, 21–8, 33–7, 49–56, 204, 281, 302–3; *Policy Execution*, 116–53. See also J. Baylis, *Ambiguity and Deterrence: British Nuclear Strategy, 1945–1964* (Oxford, 1995), 36–58; K. Harris, *Attlee* (London, 1982), 282–90.

[58] Baylis, *Ambiguity and Deterrence*, 54.

[59] R. Pyper, 'Sarah Tisdall, Ian Willmore, and the Civil Servant's "Right to Leak" ', *Political Quarterly*, 56: 1 (Jan.–Mar. 1985), 78.

[60] Cathcart, *Test of Greatness*, 16–21; A. Danchev, 'In the Back Room: Anglo-American Defence Cooperation, 1945–51', in R. J. Aldrich (ed.), *British Intelligence, Strategy and the Cold War, 1945–51* (London, 1992), 228.

stroyed the frail hopes amongst the Labour leadership that a new structure of co-operation could be constructed around the mutual problems of nuclear destruction and the sharing of atomic secrets.[61] The newly created United Nations established a short-lived Atomic Energy Commission, but the British Government rapidly lost enthusiasm for international collaboration, especially with nominally socialist regimes in the East. Whatever idealism about the world-wide brotherhood of man Ernest Bevin brought to the Foreign Office soon evaporated, nowhere more completely than in the field of atomic energy, which he came to see purely as a great power issue.[62] His lifelong hatred of Communism fed and was in turn strengthened by the intensification of the Cold War, just as his combative relations with the left wing of his own party was confirmed by his sojourn amongst the most elite group of mandarins in Whitehall.[63] On this most critical area of defence policy, he and Attlee had little more faith in the judgement and loyalty of Labour backbenchers than did the Conservatives, and as they faced the difficult task of filling the shoes of the war hero Churchill, were all the more anxious to establish their credentials as responsible upholders of the security of what was still the third-greatest power in the world.

Conversely, the absence of protest about the prolonged subterfuge and silence was a tribute to the strength of the deference with which the communication of official information was still surrounded. It was of course the case that on particular issues, at critical moments, key individuals and groups did not know what they were missing. Sir Henry Tizard, for instance, was kept in the dark by Churchill during the war, then as head of the Defence Research Policy Committee of the Ministry of Defence was not told of the decision to manufacture the atomic bomb until six months after it had been taken.[64] Yet after Hiroshima, no Member of Parliament, no defence expert, no journalist, no politically conscious member of the public, could be wholly unaware that steps were being taken which would have profound implications for the nation's survival. This much was made clear little more than a year after the bomb was dropped, when the second reading debate took place on the Atomic Energy Bill, which established state control over the whole field of nuclear research. The blocking of communication was both a consequence and a cause of the legislation. As with the loyalty of civil servants, in this critical sphere of national security the Government had little faith in codes of conduct or the Official Secrets Acts. Clause 11 of the Bill forbade any unauthorized disclosure of information about either fundamental research or its application, and

[61] Baylis, *Ambiguity and Deterrence*, 36.

[62] A. Bullock, *Ernest Bevin: Foreign Secretary* (Oxford, 1985), 185–92, 352–3; J. Saville, *The Politics of Continuity: British Foreign Policy and the Labour Government, 1945–46* (London, 1993), 92–7.

[63] R. Jenkins, *Nine Men of Power* (London, 1974), 77; M. A. Fitzsimons, *The Foreign Policy of the British Labour Government, 1945–1951* (Notre Dame, Ind., 1953), 27–9; Weiler, *British Labour and the Cold War*, 228.

[64] Baylis, *Ambiguity and Deterrence*, 56–8.

Clause 12 permitted the withholding of the details of nuclear patents.[65] Although Attlee continued to pay lip service to the 'hope that international arrangements will make state secrecy unnecessary',[66] the new restrictions graphically signalled his determination to go it alone. The McMahon Act two months earlier had marked the end of any realistic prospects of sharing knowledge with the only existing nuclear power, and, as a number of backbench critics pointed out, the secrecy clauses in the Bill confirmed that Britain was now turning its back on the rest of the world. By refusing to give further information on the programme, the Government left little doubt about its existence or significance.

To an extent, the system of controls was itself responsible for the subsequent absence of discussion. It was noted during the debate on the Bill that, 'scientists would be precluded, under Clause 11, from giving information to a Member upon which he could come to this House and ask the Minister to give an account of his actions. Parliamentary control, in this matter of atomic energy is almost unreal.'[67] Journalists found themselves thrust back into the pre-1914 world of security paranoia. As with the German threat, so with the red menace, there was a price to be paid for the dramatization of an external enemy. The 'D' Notice system, which had fallen into abeyance after the First World War, was retained after the defeat of Hitler.[68] The gentleman's agreement was deployed in 1947 and 1948 to forbid stories on the location or progress of work on the bomb.[69] Yet the press regulations were voluntary, and neither the scientific community nor Parliament registered more than a token protest when Attlee clothed the entire project in secrecy. He sought to reconcile the inevitable tension between freedom of intellectual enquiry and the danger to national security by the time-honoured device of leaving the restrictions as general as possible and endowing Ministers with the power to release information at their discretion. The assurance that the powers would be used sensibly and in moderation was not borne out by practice, which became increasingly rigid as the research progressed, but other than an occasional unanswered question in the House of Commons, no one broke ranks. The docility of the media, the electorate, and virtually the whole of Parliament, including the majority of the Cabinet, contrasted sharply with the more vociferous debate and more open administration in America. Attlee inherited and obsessively exploited a tradition of passive trust in the capacity of Government to determine the rules of

---

[65] On the breach in the patent rules for communication, see T. H. O'Dell, *Inventions and Official Secrecy: A History of Secret Patents in the United Kingdom* (Oxford 1994), 115–21; B. C. Reid, *Confidentiality and the Law* (London, 1986), 16.

[66] *Hansard*, 5th Series, 427, 8 Oct. 1946, col. 47.

[67] Ibid., col. 83.

[68] It had been revived during the war, and was continued. Palmer, 'The History of the D Notice Committee', 240.

[69] Gowing, *Independence and Deterrence*, ii. 134–7; 452–3.

communication in cases of national interest.[70] His unchallenged (and in practical terms quite unnecessary)[71] subversion of the basic decision-making structure in Cabinet, his total repression of information about such basic facts as the very existence of the Aldermaston station, reflected the licence which the British culture of secrecy vested in the highest level of Government. What drove him on, and what silenced criticism of his methods, was not, in the end, the measurable concern to prevent the Russians gaining an illicit advantage or the Americans losing yet more respect for our competence, but rather the immeasurable scale of the bomb itself. Attlee was bound to his audience in a pact of non-communication by what Shils has identified as 'a secret with an aura of fatefulness, a secret in which the apocalypse dwells'.[72] This was the most fascinating and most persuasive secret of all, and there was nothing in the British conventions of controlling information which could prevent its full flowering.

The consequences could be assessed in practical terms. Margaret Gowing, in her definitive study of the nuclear programme, has identified confused direction, organizational inefficiency, problems of recruitment, low staff morale, trivialization of public perception, and difficulties in negotiating effectively with the Americans.[73] In the broader context of the creation of a new era of popular democracy, the effects were more diffuse but no less important. The blanket of secrecy created a barrier between the two great sources of potential progress in the post-war world. On the one hand, the multiform welfare state promised to integrate political ideology, popular consent, and intellectual endeavour, nowhere more powerfully than in the National Health Service which received Parliamentary approval in 1948, just as Attlee announced the decision to build the bomb and revealed the purge procedure for civil servants. On the other hand, the walling-up of both the military and civilian nuclear programmes made it increasingly difficult to establish a coherent relationship between the creative capacity of this unprecedented source of energy and any aspect of the expanding public sphere.[74] Whereas the newly accessible doctors and the newly built hospitals represented the dedication of scientific expertise to the service of democracy, the silent work of the nuclear laboratories signified dark suspicion, unclear purpose, and unverifiable achievement. The contrast was drawn by a Labour backbencher in the debate on the Atomic Energy Bill:

---

[70] On Attlee's 'obsessive and ill-tempered' concern for secrecy, see Cathcart, *Test of Greatness*, 85.

[71] It is improbable that the full Cabinet would have objected if it had been allowed a proper debate on the subject, rather than merely being informed once the decision had been taken. Hennessy, *Whitehall*, 710.

[72] Shils, *Torment of Secrecy*, 27. Also, Bok, *Secrets*, 191–200.

[73] Gowing, *Independence and Deterrence*, i. 280–1; ii. 116.

[74] Williams, *Nuclear Power Decisions*, 329.

We have seen the benefits of this citizenship of the world in the sphere of science. It should be an example to the rest of us in every other department of man's activity. If, now, we are to clamp the narrow confines of an Official Secrets Act upon the work of many scientists in this country ... it will obstruct their efficiency, and the attainment of the greatest possible benefit in this country of the use of atomic energy.[75]

Although they occasionally chafed at the restrictions, the scientists allowed their ingrained fascination for hidden knowledge, their continuing need for funds, and their professional requirement to assert priority over their discoveries, to gain precedence over their powerful need for free communication within their national and international community and between themselves and the public on whose behalf and with whose taxes they were employed.[76] The money continued to flow, with little Parliamentary knowledge and less critical evaluation. The work of the Atomic Energy Authority was not subject to any rigorous assessment until the first investigation of the Select Committee on Science and Technology in 1967.[77] Ten years earlier a potentially disastrous fire at Windscale had been covered up by Macmillan, whose instinctive horror of openness in any area of nuclear energy placed him squarely in the tradition of his predecessors in Downing Street.[78] The scientists themselves paid a price for the failure to expose crucial issues of national security, state expenditure, and public health to democratic scrutiny. When the first British bomb was successfully detonated at Monte Bello in October 1952 there was a limited acknowledgement of the outstanding achievement of those who had led the programme, but their research rapidly retreated into the shadows. By this time the arrest in February 1950 of Klaus Fuchs, the head of theoretical physics at Harwell, and the subsequent flight to Russia of another senior Harwell physicist, Bruno Pontecorvo, had begun to increase popular suspicions of a group of men whose agenda was at best concealed from the public and at worst treasonably opposed to its interests. The conviction grew that those who consented to work in secret had secrets of their own to hide. The glad confidence in the value of science to the citizens of the welfare state was replaced by a less trusting and respectful attitude to those charged with discovering the hidden mysteries of nature.

The Harwell spy cases, followed by the defection of the diplomats Burgess and Maclean in 1951, reinforced the twofold crisis in confidence upon which the British independent programme had been founded. The serious breaches of security caused the Americans to halt the slow moves towards a reopening of the channels of international communication, and increased doubts about the

---

[75] *Hansard*, 5th Series, 427, 8 Oct. 1946, col. 71.

[76] For a useful survey on the debate over the tension between openness and secrecy in this sphere, see Himrod, 'Secrecy in Modern Science', 103–36.

[77] Williams, *Nuclear Power Decisions*, 31.

[78] R. Rhodes James, *Official Secrecy: An Historian's View* (London, 1990), 15.

established mechanisms for reading the minds of public servants, especially those possessed of a university education, which was no longer seen as a sufficient guarantor of ethical conduct.[79] The outcome was the addition of positive vetting to the purge procedure which had been in operation since 1948. The new scheme, approved just before the second Labour Government fell and implemented by the Conservatives in 1952, introduced an active assessment of the subject's character to the more objective test of political affiliation. The vetting covered not just those actually undertaking secret work, but those who might come in contact with information about it, and candidates for promotion to the post of Under Secretary and above, irrespective of their field of operation.[80]

The new system was reviewed four years later by a Conference of Privy Councillors, which confirmed that the main danger to national security was no longer professional foreign spies but professional domestic bureaucrats vulnerable to communist pressure. For this reason, the procedures should remain in place, in spite of the erosion of trust which they represented. The Conference was in no doubt that, as the White Paper on its confidential report put it, 'some of the measures which the State is driven to take to protect its security are in some respects alien to our traditional practices'.[81] The gentlemanly code of honour was compromised by the requirement that departments 'inform themselves of serious failings such as drunkenness, addiction to drugs, homosexuality or any loose living that may seriously affect a man's reliability'.[82] The conventions of discreet reserve were threatened by the inevitable incitement to 'tale-bearing and gossip'.[83] Established judicial procedures jarred with an appeal system, which denied victims representation or access to the information held against them, and excluded altogether those penalized for moral defects alone. And two centuries of progress in civil liberties were compromised by the need to give precedence to the national interest rather than the private citizen in this murky world of innuendo and suspicion: 'the Conference is of the opinion that in deciding these difficult and often borderline cases, it is right to continue the practice of tilting the balance in favour of offering greater protection to the security of the State rather than in the direction of safeguarding the rights of the individual.'[84]

It may be argued, however, that it was precisely tradition which enabled the scheme to survive, in spite of trade union complaints about the detail of the

---

[79] A. Sinclair, *The Red and the Blue: Intelligence, Treason and the Universities* (London, 1986), 4–8, 157–60.

[80] The best summary of the evolution of the purge process and positive vetting is to be found in *Security Procedures in the Public Service* [Radcliffe] (1962), Cmnd. 1681, 14–16. Also, Joelson, 'Dismissal of Civil Servants', 52–6; M. Hollingsworth and R. Norton-Taylor, *Blacklist: The Inside Story of Political Vetting* (London, 1988), 22–6.

[81] The text of the White Paper is given in 'Security Precautions in the British Civil Service', *Public Administration*, 35 (Autumn 1957), 299.

[82] Ibid. 298.

[83] Ibid.   [84] Ibid. 299.

procedures and the broader if equally ineffectual protests of the newly formed Campaign for the Limitation of Secret Police Powers.[85] Above all, there was no noise. As had been the case since 1889, the official Opposition refrained from open protest. When the White Paper was discussed in the Commons, the Labour leadership was conspicuously silent, and even the young firebrand Anthony Wedgwood Benn expressed his gratitude 'that security in this country has never become a matter of party dispute'.[86] There was no public vilification or even naming of civil servants with suspect loyalty, and those who suffered the roughest justice were too low in the hierarchy to be noticed.[87] The much-publicized excesses of McCarthyism, which reached its zenith as positive vetting was being consolidated, enabled the state to renew a comfortable practice of contrasting British constraint with foreign excitability. On numbers alone, there was a case to be made. In the first decade of positive vetting only 163 out of more than a million civil servants were the subject of action. Less than a third of these lost their jobs, and one in five were actually reinstated following investigation and appeal.[88] The American security purges, by comparison, resulted in the dismissal or resignation of 24,500 named federal civil servants.[89]

Even on its own terms, the determination to avoid unnecessary publicity could be counter-productive. The 1962 Radcliffe Inquiry on Security Procedures in the Public Services, called after the discovery of the Portland Spy Ring and a controversy over 'D' Notices, concluded that 'the biggest single risk to security at the present time is probably a general lack of conviction that any substantial threat exists'.[90] There were, however, less visible dangers, which had serious long-term consequences. The central question was how far the departures from traditional practices represented a genuine attempt to adapt the past to meet the demands of the future. In the event, the customary secrecy about secrecy concealed a broader failure to devise effective machinery for dealing with modern problems. If it was the case that the enhanced significance of official secrets and the declining confidence in the established legal and cultural processes of ensuring loyalty demanded new forms of surveillance, there was little evidence that asking awkward questions about drink and sex actually achieved more than further embarrassment. A major reason why there were so few actions was that the conception of character weakness remained at the level of a public school headmaster. On the one hand, the categories were so broad as to implicate half the service; on the other, the linkage between moral turpitude and national betrayal was so weakly articulated as to

---

[85] See below, pp. 246–7.

[86] *Hansard*, 5th Series, 550, 21 Mar. 1956, col. 1296.

[87] See the comments of Sir Kenneth Younger in ibid., col. 1257.

[88] Joelson, 'The Dismissal of Civil Servants', 57.

[89] Hennessy and Brownfeld, 'Britain's Cold War Security Purge', 970; Hollingsworth and Norton-Taylor, *Blacklist*, 26.

[90] *Security Procedures in the Public Services*, 33.

prevent intervention in any but the most extreme instances. As Radcliffe admitted, the vices which the investigators were looking for 'do not present themselves as necessarily the most dangerous traits from a security point of view and they do not in practice make a very firm base for action against a person as a security risk'.[91]

The investigations themselves were supervised by Section C of the Security Service (still popularly known as MI5), whose role was significantly enhanced in this period. It was a matter partly of new tasks, and partly of new technology. In the 1950s spying entered the electronic age with a vengeance. To the existing techniques of intercepting communication was added an ever-widening array of eavesdropping devices. The precise extent of the bugging of embassies, Communist Party buildings, and other self-selected targets is obscured by the dubious reliability of the chief published witness of the work,[92] and by the more general failure to adjust the machinery of democratic control in the light of the new powers and responsibilities. The formal restatement of the duties and accountability of the Security Service, issued secretly by the Home Secretary Sir David Maxwell Fyfe in 1952, represented no advance on the former position. Where previously the Service had been under the direct authority of either the Minister of Defence or the Prime Minister, now the Home Secretary was to exercise only the most distant control over an entity which was not itself part of the Home Office. Under the new directive, he was to be 'furnished with such information only as may be necessary for the determination of any issue on which guidance is sought'.[93] Necessity was to be defined not by the politician but the spies, whose terms of reference were so loosely drawn as to leave them free to decide who comprised a danger to the defence of the realm and what constituted subversion. The addition by Lord Denning in 1963 of the phrase of 'by unlawful means' did little to clarify the matter.[94]

The staff in whom such unquestioning trust was reposed were, as before, drawn from a restricted social group and possessed of an even narrower range of right-wing opinions.[95] Not only were they unrepresentative of post-war society in general, they were far more confined in their views and background than the civil service whose loyalty they were now charged with policing. Nowhere were the inadequacies of vetting more apparent than in the process by which the vetters themselves were appointed and managed. Such limitations became more significant as the definition of subversion imperceptibly widened. Whilst Britain escaped the wholesale collapse of barriers between private opinion and national security which occurred at the height of the American witch-hunts, there was a slow enlargement of the realm of legitimate intervention by the

---

[91] Ibid. 18–19.
[92] Peter Wright. See *Spycatcher: The Candid Autobiography of a Senior Intelligence Officer* (Richmond, Victoria, 1987). See, for instance, 54–71.
[93] Baxter, *State Security, Privacy and Information*, 97–8.
[94] Porter, *Plots and Paranoia*, 196.   [95] Ibid. 186–7.

state. The transition was uneven. In the case, for instance, of the BBC it was a matter of expanding a secret procedure for vetting staff which had been set up in 1937. Attempts by some local authorities to conduct mini-McCarthyite purges from the late 1940s onwards enjoyed only limited success.[96] But in industry the Economic League, which had been set up in 1919 to supply employers with information on potentially subversive workers, found demand for its services growing so rapidly that it was able to set up a separate vetting section in 1950. There had always been intricate but informal personnel and policy links between MI5 and the League, whose founder had previously served as Head of Naval Intelligence in the First World War.[97] Now the state itself began to turn its attention more systematically to subversion in organized labour. Signs of this shift were visible in 1962, when Radcliffe drew attention to communist penetration of the civil service unions.[98] As the direct threat from the Communist Party itself weakened, the stage was set for the development of a much broader programme of surveillance of those whose interference in the economic progress of the country was seen as increasingly dangerous.[99]

Britain strode into the nuclear age protected by patched clothing designed for a time when dreadnoughts constituted the leading edge of defence technology, and waiters with German accents represented the chief threat to national security. In a sense, the structures of official secrecy which reached their final form in the Edwardian era were intended precisely to allow this quiet adaptation to unforeseeable challenges. The ability of the post-1945 state to enlarge the controls over communication with a minimum of legislation or public debate can be seen as the true measure of their strength and flexibility. There remained, nonetheless, a growing discrepancy between the significance of new forms of knowledge to the citizens of the welfare state, and their capacity to gain an effective oversight over whether, why, and by what means it was being concealed from them. With the dropping of the first atomic bomb, the critical issue for every democracy became how to draw the line between the beneficial and destructive capacities of scientific discovery. In Britain a clear view of the debate was obscured by the undifferentiated blocking of communication about every aspect of the nuclear programme and by the concealment of the work of the Security Service, which was itself embracing new technology in its struggle against subversion by Russia.

In the midst of the post-war boom, the strains between modern requirements for information and traditional controls over its transmission were contained without too much difficulty. Only occasionally was it possible to gain an insight into their extent. In many respects, the 'D' Notice system represented the height of the state's achievement in this field. The continuing acceptance

---

[96] Hollingsworth and Norton-Taylor, *Blacklist*, 9–11.
[97] Ibid. 146–50.
[98] *Security Procedures in the Public Service*, 9.
[99] C. Aubrey, *Who's Watching You* (Harmondsworth, 1981), 41–3.

by newspaper editors of the hidden but voluntary system of censorship enabled the Government to maintain restrictions over coverage of nuclear issues and the security agencies whilst persisting in its public commitment to a free press. When Radcliffe reviewed the arrangements in 1962, he found that the procedures introduced on the eve of the First World War were perfectly adapted to the conduct of the Cold War. In February 1967, however, there was a sudden hiccup in the machinery when the *Daily Express* published a story by Chapman Pincher under the headline 'Cable Vetting Sensation'. His revelation that private cables and telegrams to overseas destinations were routinely made available to the Security Service appeared to be in direct contravention of a 'D' Notice of October 1961 which forbade any mention of 'the various methods used in the interception of foreign communications for secret intelligence purposes.'[100] Radcliffe was duly requested to conduct a second inquiry, which exposed the dangers of conducting the defence of national security by means of informal contacts in the restaurants and clubs of London. The breakdown of the system had begun when the Secretary of the 'D' Notice Committee, Sammy Lohan, met Chapman Pincher over lunch and failed clearly to explain the Government's objection to the story.[101] It had concluded when the Foreign Secretary George Brown, a man not renowned for his late-night sobriety, had made a 2 a.m. call to the paper's proprietor, who was summoned to the phone in the porter's lodge of the Garrick Club, where he was dining. As Radcliffe's report drily remarked,

the situation was one well calculated to produce misunderstandings on both sides. The Foreign Secretary was speaking on an open line and for reasons of security was unable to make any detailed reference at all to the secret activities which he understood to form the basis of the story. He was under the impression that Sir Max knew about the story which was going to appear in his paper and about its contents. In fact Sir Max did not at that time know anything about it at all and had no idea to what the Foreign Secretary was referring.[102]

In the event, this classic of non-comprehension resulted in little more than a temporary embarrassment for the Government. George Wigg, Labour's security co-ordinator and the staunchest friend of the Security Service in any administration of the period, had been worried that the publication of Radcliffe's inquiry might provoke disquiet about relations between the press and the Security Service: 'to judge by the postbag of No. 10, however, it put the public to sleep. The Prime Minister received twelve letters on the subject, I received one.'[103] If this was blocked communication as high comedy, the 'D' Notice system was also at the centre of the greatest national tragedy of the period. In the

[100] *Report of the Committee of Privy Councillors Appointed to Inquire into 'D' Notice Matters* (1967), Cmnd. 3309, p. 7; Williams, 'Official Secrecy in England', 24–5.

[101] Palmer, 'The History of the D Notice Committee', 244–5.

[102] *Report . . . into 'D' Notice Matters*, 13.

[103] Lord Wigg, *George Wigg* (London, 1972), 348.

late summer of 1956 the Downing Street Press Officer, William Clark, caused a Notice to be issued forbidding the press to run stories on the gathering and dispatch of troops for the Middle East.[104] This unenforceable instruction was the most formal element of a mounting campaign of pressure and intimidation conducted by an increasingly unstable Prime Minister. Eden's desperate attempt to rescue by one bold action his waning personal authority and Britain's declining imperial role was founded on a multiple deception of the public and Parliament. A weak leader, whose vile temper, according to Clark, was the 'one of the best-kept secrets' in Whitehall,[105] was reacting to growing press criticism, particularly from normally loyal newspapers such as the *Daily Telegraph*, by embarking on a military adventure which would justify a return to levels of manipulation and control enjoyed by his great predecessor during the struggle against Germany. Just as Nasser had become Hitler, and Suez the Rhineland, so journalists were once more to be loyal propagandists for an embattled state.[106]

The confusion between personal and strategic objectives characterized both the enterprise itself and the means by which it was conducted. Eden was endlessly on the phone to editors, his resentment of criticism for failing to exercise the smack of firm government merging with his need to keep from the papers any reference to the secret collaboration with France and Israel over the intended invasion of Egypt. As an exasperated Clark noted in his diary, 'ministers want the press to be quiet about our military preparations because they are politically embarrassing; but fool themselves into thinking they are only asking for military censorship in the national interest'.[107] This blurred distinction facilitated the critical transition from bending to breaking the truth. It enabled men who considered themselves honourable persistently and blatantly to lie not only to the electorate and the Opposition but to most of their colleagues in government.

The abiding mystery of Suez is not so much why Eden shrouded the enterprise in secrecy, as why he thought he could get away with doing so. His actions were not only a crime but clearly a blunder. The Americans rapidly discovered what had happened, and it was only a matter of time before the general outline of the conspiracy would become known at home. The immediate reason lay in the power which an overexcited Prime Minister now enjoyed to exclude vital information even from other senior members of the Government. The intelligence services, whose conspiratorial role in this affair is still largely concealed by the unavailability of the relevant files, were operating out of sight of both

---

[104] W. Clark, *From Three Worlds* (London, 1986), 169–70.
[105] Ibid. 160. For an equally unflattering portrait of Eden's temperament, see E. Shuckburgh, *Descent to Suez: Diaries, 1951–56* (London, 1986), 345; S. Lucas, *Britain and Suez: The Lion's Last Roar* (Manchester, 1996), 32–3. On the rapid erosion of Eden's personal authority in the early months of his premiership, see K. Kyle, *Suez* (London, 1991), 89; A. Nutting, *No End of a Lesson* (London, 1967), 25.
[106] Margach, *The Abuse of Power*, 113.
[107] Clark, *From Three Worlds*, 173.

the Cabinet and the Foreign Office.[108] The Prime Minister may have known of their plans to assassinate Nasser by poisoning his coffee, but he shared little with his colleagues. It is a matter of nice calculation whether more Cabinet members were kept in the dark by Attlee on the bomb or by Eden on Suez. Both post-war premiers were exploiting a tradition of restricting the flow of information in Cabinet which had been in place at least since the time of Salisbury.[109] Any dissent could be contained by the culture of discreet reserve whose masochistic strength was never more effectively displayed. Many civil servants involved in the exercise were opposed to it, as were some members of the Government. However, the critics observed the convention of suffering in silence. The only public servant to leave office specifically in protest at the lies was the Government Press Officer himself, who had nonetheless continued to promulgate them until the fighting was finished. He left with a minimum of publicity, having spent his last hours in office concocting a press release on the only resignation of a politician directly involved in the scandal, that of the Foreign Office Minister Anthony Nutting, which successfully obscured the reason why. Nutting, for his part, wrote but then tore up a resignation speech, having convinced himself that he ought not to spill the beans on his colleagues for as long as they were still running the country.[110] He only put pen to paper when Labour was safely in office, but even then had to fight a battle with the Cabinet Office to publish his account.[111]

The anticipated docility of the press was a function partly of its formal and informal intimidation during the crisis, and partly of its more general relationship with the Government. Since 1945 Ministers had become increasingly professional in their dealings with journalists, exploiting with growing skill their freedom to authorize their own breaches of official secrecy. Devoid of any absolute right to information about defence and diplomacy, specialists in these fields were alternatively fed and starved until they accepted the rules of the game. In a thoughtful essay on Cabinet secrecy and foreign policy, Clark presented an authoritative analysis of the mechanism and its consequence:

By its control of the sources of information, however, and by the implied threat that criticism of policies would lead to a less full flow to that correspondent; by co-opting all of its diplomatic correspondents into a cosy club of those in the know, I fear that the Government (under both parties) did manage the news of our foreign policy, so that the public got a smug and insular view of the world and our place in it. For Britain this meant a failure to realise how comparatively weak we were and

---

[108] Scott Lucas has recently pieced together some of the activities of MI6, partly on the basis of CIA material which is becoming available. *Britain and Suez: The Lion's Last Roar*, 35–7.

[109] See above, Ch. 3, p. 80.

[110] Nutting, *No End of a Lesson*, 159–62.

[111] The details of the dispute are given in P. Hennessy, 'No End of an Argument: How Whitehall Tried and Failed to Suppress Sir Anthony Nutting's Suez Memoir', *Contemporary Record* 1: 1 (Spring 1987).

how fragile the Empire/Commonwealth was, how far Europe was prepared to go without us, and how little our 'Special Relationship' meant to America.[112]

The final reason for Eden's naive confidence in his almost schoolboyish dishonesty was his calculation that achievement of the ends would obliterate doubts about the means. In the short term, the strength of the conventions of reserve and deference in Whitehall and the press was sufficient to carry the Government through the humiliation of defeat, although Eden himself was finished. In the longer term, a disaster which owed everything to the lack of national self-awareness raised for the first time serious questions about the systems of internal communication which had prevented Britain from understanding her changing position in the world.

Welfare and Honour

The centenary of the Northcote–Trevelyan Report fell in 1954. It provoked a series of public reassessments of the reforms in the light of the changing role of the civil service in the post-war world. A number of these were delivered by Sir Edward Bridges himself, who had been head of the service since the advent of the Attlee's Government in 1945. In June he addressed a celebratory dinner at the Mansion House in London. His central theme was the value of continuity in his profession. Having supervised the transformations wrought by Labour and the subsequent return of the Conservatives, he was proud of the record of his staff: 'I know this body of men and women believe intensely in the tradition which has been established of serving the State fairly and devotedly without bias or prejudice.'[113] It was an achievement which, he recognized, had been bought at the cost of public recognition and respect: 'The anonymity of Civil Servants has, indeed, led to a fable that they are rather different from other people, lacking perhaps in the full range of human sympathies and understanding.'[114] This was a misleading but perhaps inevitable outcome of the contrast between the adamantine reserve of the administrators and the high passions and heroic deeds of the era.

In an effort to instruct a wider audience in the character of the hundred-year-old institution, the BBC commissioned a series of programmes, which included contributions by Bridges and by Sir Ernest Gowers, whose career in Whitehall had begun half a century earlier. The emphasis of his retrospective was altogether different. What struck him most was not continuity in spite of change, but adaptation in response to it. The major development had been in the field

---

[112] W. Clark, 'Cabinet Secrecy, Collective Responsibility, and the British Public's Right to Know about and Participate in Foreign Policy Making', in T. M. Franck and E. Weisband (eds.), *Secrecy and Foreign Policy* (New York, 1974), 207.

[113] Text of speech delivered by Bridges on 21 June 1954. PRO, T273/222.

[114] Ibid.

of communication: 'Fifty years ago, there was no great difficulty in observing both in substance and in form this principle of a silent service with Ministers as its only spokesman.'[115] The transformation in the size of government, which he had helped to set in motion as Principal Private Secretary to Lloyd George in 1911, and then as the first Chief Inspector of the National Health Insurance Commission, had created a immense gulf between the present in the past. In his youth, only the politician had a voice:

But the upheavals of two wars and the coming of the Welfare State have changed all that. Government no longer holds aloof from our daily lives: on the one hand it re-stricts the freedom of the individual in countless ways for the benefit of the com-munity; on the other hand it has undertaken the duty of helping us through the changes and chances of life before the cradle until after the grave. All this falls on the civil service, and demands constant contact with the public at many levels. Under the pressure of events the curtain that used to veil the service has burst at the seams.[116]

There was some common ground between Bridges and Gowers. Both had been struck by the problem of official correspondence. The qualitative change in the role of government was producing a quantitative shift in the volume of letters written by civil servants. A significant proportion of these were ad-dressed to citizens who had little or no experience of communicating with bu-reaucrats. The abstruse language and arcane syntax which had once bound together officials and a more select audience now constituted a serious barrier to the fulfilment of the post-war reforms. In 1948 Bridges commissioned Gowers to write what was intended as a manual for officials but which became a best-selling guide to the use of English in a wide range of public and private contexts. *Plain Words*, and its successor, *The ABC of Plain Words* in 1951, explained in appropriately transparent prose how civil servants should write clear, acces-sible letters to every kind of reader.[117] Nonetheless, Gowers and Bridges were ap-proaching the opening up of government from quite different directions. Whereas for the former, greater clarity was both a symbol and an agent of the transformation of Trevelyan's legacy, for the latter, it represented the removal of certain inefficiencies in an otherwise perfectly preserved machine. Bridges, for instance, regarded the post-war growth in government information officers as an evil made necessary by the embarrassment increasingly experienced by officials in their dealings with journalists.[118] As he explained in his *Portrait of a*

---

[115] E. Gowers, 'The Civil Service and the Public', BBC talk, 1954. PRO, T273/222, p. 2.

[116] Gowers, 'The Civil Service and the Public', 2.

[117] HMSO published the two works in a single volume, *The Complete Plain Words* in 1954, and this later became a much-reprinted Pelican paperback. For an account of the impact of Gowers's work on the 'language of bureaucracy', see J. Delafons, 'Working in Whitehall: Changes in Public Administration, 1952–1982', *Public Administration*, 60: 3 (Autumn, 1982), 255–6.

[118] On the spread of government information officers, who first made their appearance in 1936, see J. P. W. Mallalieu, *'Passed to You Please'* (London, 1942), 83–9; May and Rowan, *Inside Information* (London, 1982), 186–8; Margach, *The Abuse of Power*, 86–99.

Profession in 1950, the essential convention of anonymity 'makes the average civil servant uncomfortable and infelicitous in his relations with the Press'. This awkwardness encouraged in staff a tendency to 'hedge or confine themselves to what has been said. The disease is so endemic that we have had to call in gentlemen from Fleet Street to help us out of our difficulties.'[119]

An indication of whether the conservative or revolutionary approach was to prevail can be found in another contribution to the centenary. Attlee wrote an article for a commemorative edition of the *Political Quarterly* which distilled his experience of government since first entering Churchill's wartime coalition. His celebration of continuity outdid even Bridges. 'The civil service in the higher ranks', he proclaimed, 'has not only a long personal experience but also has that mysterious tradition of the office wherein is somehow embalmed the wisdom of past generations.'[120] At the heart of that tradition was the act of denial, the acceptance of anonymity and the consequent abdication of the right of self-defence: 'the civil servant soon learns that sufferance is the badge of all their tribe.'[121] In composing what amounted to a love-letter to Whitehall, Attlee was returning thanks to the officials whose unsung work had made possible the creation of the welfare state. He was also mounting another in a series of public vindications of the state bureaucracy whose growing powers were coming under increasing attack from the right. As early as 1947 he had been on his feet in the Commons, adding himself to the long list of prime ministers who regarded the civil service as 'the best in the world . . . whose devotion to the public interest is unsurpassed'.[122]

Attlee's sugary compliments contained a hard core. His protection of the essential conventions of the civil service was more than just rhetorical. A mere fortnight after taking office, he issued a set of notes headed 'Precaution Against Unauthorised Disclosures of Information'. These insisted that, 'all servants of the Crown, whether Ministers, members of the Fighting Services or Civil Servants, must be most careful to observe due discretion in regard to all matters of State'.[123] The document made it crystal clear that the increase in public debate about government actions demanded an equal and opposite reaction by all those with information about them. After working under Churchill during the war, Attlee had no illusions about relations with the media:

Experience has shown that leakages of information have often occurred as a result of the skilful piecing together by representatives of the Press of isolated scraps of information each in itself is apparently of little importance, gathered from several

---

[119] E. Bridges, *Portrait of a Profession: The Civil Service Tradition* (Cambridge, 1950), 29.

[120] C. R. Attlee, 'Civil Servants, Ministers, Parliament and the Public', *Political Quarterly*, 25: 4 (Oct.–Dec. 1954), 309. For a discussion of Attlee's reverence for the senior civil service, see Theakston, *The Labour Party and Whitehall*, 34, 105–7.

[121] Attlee, 'Civil Servants, Ministers, Parliament and the Public', 314.

[122] *Hansard*, 5th Series, 439, 24 June 1947, col. 198.

[123] PRO, CAB129/4/282, p. 3. On the issuing of this document, see P. Hennessy, 'The Attlee Governments, 1945–51', in P. Hennessy and A. Seldon (eds.), *Ruling Performance* (Oxford, 1989), 52.

sources. The only safe rule is, therefore, never to mention such matters even in the form of guarded allusions, except for those who must be informed of them for reasons of State, until the time has come when disclosure, in whole or in part, is authorised.[124]

The new dawn of socialism was being greeted with a full-scale restatement of the approach to secrecy enshrined in the legislation of 1889 and 1911. Just as the Acts were principally employed to educate rather than punish, so Attlee's central concern was to inculcate a special mentality. In the heady atmosphere of victory such restraint was difficult to impose, and three months later Attlee was forced to return to the topic, issuing a 'Top Secret' memorandum on the 'Secrecy of Cabinet Proceedings' and re-circulating his first note. A series of leaks, he complained, had damaged both the efficiency and reputation of the administration: 'No Government', he reminded his colleagues, 'can be success- ful which cannot keep its secrets.'[125] Ministers were responsible both for their own behaviour and for the example they set their civil servants. It was their task not just to impose discipline but to cultivate and embody a culture of self- restraint:

the problem of secrecy cannot be solved solely by rules, however carefully drawn, re- stricting the circulation of papers. The essential point is the observance of a high standard of discretion by all who acquire knowledge of such information in the course of their duties—an attitude of mind which puts first the interests of the Government as a whole and subordinates everything to that end.[126]

As many commentators have noted, Attlee was by temperament the least loquacious of prime ministers, and by experience already deep in the embrace of the senior officials with whom he had worked so well during the war.[127] Yet the vigour with which he sought to emphasize the continuity of approach to official communication was a reaction as much to the future as to the past. The apparent disjuncture between institutional conservatism and legislative radi- calism concealed a powerful element of congruity, which deepened as the new welfare state took form. At the heart of the relationship was a particular con- struction of professionalism. In part it was a matter of establishing the con- ditions for implementing the manifesto. Although service in the wartime coalition had greatly enhanced Labour's reputation as a party of government, it had yet to prove itself as an autonomous administration.[128] A leaky Cabinet reflected amateurism rather than socialism. It was not the first step on the road to the new Jerusalem, but a dissipation of effort which might prevent the des- tination ever being reached. There were good practical reasons for keeping

[124] PRO, CAB129/4/282, p. 3.
[125] *Secrecy of Cabinet Proceedings, Note by the Prime Minister*, 9 Nov. 1945. PRO, CAB129/4/282, p. 1.
[126] Ibid. 2.
[127] See, most recently, K. Theakston, *The Civil Service since 1945* (Oxford, 1995), 4.
[128] On Labour's continuing need to be seen to be fit to govern, see E. P. Thompson, 'The Secret State', in *Writing by Candlelight* (London, 1980), 165.

journalists at arm's length. The veteran Parliamentary correspondent James Margach wrote of this period that he had 'never known the Press so consistently and irresponsibly, political, slanted and prejudiced'.[129] On every side there were traps for the unwary, as Dalton was to discover when he inadvertently disclosed details of the Budget to the *Evening Standard* in 1947. Just as gossip could terminate an individual career, so collective indiscipline would undermine the entire enterprise of reform.

This calculation rested in turn on a more progressive engagement with the management of Whitehall. Although Labour had devoted insufficient attention to the machinery of government as it prepared itself for power in the 1930s, the topic could scarcely be ignored as the welfare programme and nationalization multiplied the functions of the administrative machinery.[130] During the war G. D. H. Cole had argued that the cosy gentlemen's world of senior administrators had to be opened up. A reconstructed state could not be run by officials who 'belong, with relatively few exceptions, to one or another of a very small group of clubs in or near Pall Mall, where they meet regularly and transact many of their inter-departmental affairs in a pleasant, unofficial way'.[131] In 1947 the Fabians published a critique of the civil service which set the agenda of debate for the next quarter of a century. It attacked the seeming remoteness of the staff, but saw this as a matter of internal efficiency rather than external relations with politicians and the public: 'Extra-departmental training, later recruitment and more circulation between the Civil Service and other employment will do a good deal to break down the Brahminical aloofness, and the general training of young recruits must hammer home the need for officials to behave like human beings.'[132] The Fabians were much more concerned about the movement of personnel than the flow of information. There was a need for more exchanges with professional managers and scientists in other sectors of the economy, and for an increased flow of recruits to the higher from the executive grades. The only recommendation in the field of communication was that forms should be better designed, and moves to professionalize the public relations work of departments should be accelerated. The emphasis throughout was on expertise at the senior level. The report, and most of the subsequent analysis, was confined to the administrative grades which in 1947 still numbered only 4,200 out of two-thirds of a million non-industrial civil servants. The

[129] Margach, *Abuse of Power*, 86.

[130] For an exploration of the need to address the nature of the civil service in consequence of the likely post-war expansion of the role of the state, see G. D. H. Cole, 'Reconstruction in the Civil and Municipal Services', *Public Administration*, 20 (1942), 3–8.

[131] Ibid. 4. In fact, the proportion of Permanent Secretaries who belonged to one or more such clubs reached an all-time high of 80% between 1945 and 1964. Theakston and Fry, 'Britain's Administrative Élite: Permanent Secretaries, 1900–1986', 145.

[132] Fabian Society, *The Reform of the Higher Civil Service* (London, 1947), 57. Many of these points were also addressed in the contemporary study by H. R. Greaves, *The Civil Service in the Changing State* (London, 1947), esp. 51–79.

front-line staff whose letters to the public Gowers was trying to make plainer received scant attention.

Amidst the calls for greater training and wider application of expert knowledge, the curtain veiling the machinery of government remained largely intact.[133] During the making of the welfare state, a destructive dialectic was established between censure and secrecy. As early as 1947, before most of the reforms had taken effect, the Fabians found that 'at the moment the Civil Service probably comes in for more criticism than any other institution in the country'.[134] Attlee and his colleagues responded to these attacks by seeking to control yet more tightly the lines of communication with the public and pursuing forms of modernization which had negligible impact on the popular perception or experience of the ever-more intrusive and overworked administrators. As the Labour Government drew to a close, a study of the new middle class discovered that a key achievement of Trevelyan's reforms, to which Bridges had attached particular importance, was fading fast: 'In theory, the British people have always detested the idea of bureaucracy, but realising that their civil servants were not bureaucrats in the strict, opprobrious sense of the word, they regarded these officials before with respect, perhaps slightly tinged with amusement. This attitude is changing rapidly.'[135] The officials were still anonymous, but no longer invisible. A stereotype was taking form which belied the celebration of a century's progress. According to Critchley's *The Civil Service Today* of 1951, 'civil servants are all too often regarded as a particularly odious breed of State spies with sealed lips and the proud motto, "Stealth, Secrecy, Snooping".'[136]

For the time being, the tensions were held in check by the immense institutional and moral authority of Bridges and his colleagues.[137] They rose to the challenge of creating new machinery with enthusiasm, their self-respect enhanced by their evident capacity to work with those stigmatized for so long as unfit to govern, and by their acknowledged ability to increase their responsibilities without compromising their integrity.[138] As G. D. H. Cole wrote 1950,

It is a great thing which we take nowadays so much for granted as often to forget how great it is, that this established Civil Service of ours is, for all practical

[133] Theakston, *The Civil Service since 1945*, 64–73.

[134] Fabian Society, *The Reform of the Higher Civil Service*, 5.

[135] R. Lewis and A. Maude, *The English Middle Class* (London, 1950), 116. On Bridges's pride in a service which was not a bureaucracy, see Gladden, *Civil Service or Bureaucracy?*, 26, 134.

[136] Critchley, *The Civil Service Today*, 13. Also Gladden, *Civil Service or Bureaucracy?*, 17, 136; Greaves, *The Civil Service in the Changing State*, 51.

[137] On Bridges's personal integrity, and his 'almost monastic regard for his personal interests', see R. A. Chapman, *Ethics in the British Civil Service* (London, 1988), 308–11; Theakston, *The Civil Service since 1945*, 46–7.

[138] See e.g. the account of honesty as an ingrained habit of senior civil servants in C. K. Munro, *The Fountains in Trafalgar Square* (London, 1952), 59.

purposes, incorruptible. Not merely do its members not take bribes; they are for the most part continuously on their guard against much more subtle and insidious forms of corruption.[139]

As had been the case since the mid-nineteenth century, if there was secrecy, there was also honour. Amidst the centenary celebrations in 1954, this axis was threatened by the Crichel Down affair, which involved malpractice by officials dealing with the auction of Crown-held farmland. The resignation of the Minister concerned, Sir Thomas Dugdale, vindicated (for the last time) the doctrine of ministerial responsibility, but still left the civil service facing awkward questions about its conduct. The subsequent inquiry found that a principal cause of the maladministration had been 'the passionate love of secrecy inherent in so many minor officials'.[140]

In the aftermath of the report Bridges gathered the Permanent Secretaries together in the Treasury to formulate a response. It had to be accepted that 'an impression was abroad that there was a general tendency for Civil Servants to suppress facts in their submission to Ministers and so mislead them'.[141] But the Permanent Secretaries concentrated their attention not on the central issue of relations between politicians and civil servants, but rather on how to avoid the 'humiliation' of having their confidential, and in some cases 'semi-formal' correspondence exposed to public scrutiny by such an event.[142] To this there were three responses. First, the enforced circulation given to this material had 'produced no change in the legal position under the Official Secrets Act, and comment of the type which had been regarded as privileged would remain so'.[143] Secondly, whilst the campaign to eradicate 'the stiffness, sometimes verging on pomposity, of the official letter' had been beneficial, 'the meeting took the view that, in general, informality in correspondence had gone too far'.[144] It was dangerous to dress in vulgar underwear in case you were knocked down in the street. Thirdly, for those in closer contact with an increasingly mistrustful public, there was a need for more 'training in the techniques of public relations'.[145] By reinforcing the rules, censoring colloquialisms, and improving personnel management, confidence would be restored. In the meantime, Bridges wrote to all civil servants, reminding them of Warren Fisher's injunction after the

[139] G. D. H. Cole, 'Reform in the Civil Service', in *Essays in Social Theory* (London, 1950), 225. For a rather more sceptical account of public morals, which ascribed the absence of scandal in part to a desire not to notice them, see Brogan, *The English People*, 50.

[140] *Public Inquiry ordered by the Minister of Agriculture into the Disposal of Land at Crichel Down*, Cmd. 9176 (June 1954), 27.

[141] *Note of a Meeting Held in Sir Edward Bridges' Room at the Treasury on Friday, 30 July, 1954*, PRO, T222/661.

[142] On the concern felt by senior civil servants at the failure of the Official Secrets Act to prevent the actions of named civil servants entering the public domain, see Delafons, 'Working in Whitehall: Changes in Public Administration 1952–1982', 256–7.

[143] PRO, T222/661.

[144] Ibid.   [145] Ibid.

Francs Case, that they should be 'inflexible but fastidious' in the execution of their duties.[146]

This tendency to regard openness as an issue of efficiency and the avoidance of embarrassment rather than democracy and the interests of citizens persisted throughout the consolidation of the post-war reforms. During this period the major challenge to this approach came not from left-wing theorists but from the more impersonal force of the expansion of government machinery which Labour had set in motion. By coincidence, 1954 also saw the publication of the Grigg Report on departmental records, whose recommendations were embodied in the 1958 Public Records Act, which established for the first time a specific legal power of access to official material.[147] The driving force behind the reform was the growth in material being generated by departments. Grigg discovered that 'the greatly extended part played by the Government in the economic and industrial life of the country, together with the advent of the welfare state, have increased enormously the amount of papers created in the course of Government administration'.[148] The newly created Ministry of Supply, for example, was producing twelve miles of documents every year,[149] but there was no systematic policy governing the release of papers to the Public Record Office by departments, or from it to the general public. Bureaucratic convenience rather than political philosophy lay behind the legislation, which left the state with the latitude to refuse access to material more than fifty years old (reduced to thirty years in 1967), if it was deemed to breach undertakings to confidentiality, if it was thought likely to cause distress to private individuals, or if it merely seemed against the public interest to do so.[150] There was no appeal against decisions on these issues, and there was a blanket prohibition on anything to do with nuclear, intelligence, or civil defence matters. But however limited in intention, and however compromised by the tradition of vaguely specified and secretly exercised discretion, the outcome was as near as Britain was to get to a Freedom of Information Act in the post-war era.

A second, and in some ways more significant, breach in the Whitehall approach was made by the 1957 Franks Committee on Administrative Tribunals and Enquiries. Here again, the central problem was the increasing role of government in the lives of citizens. Since the 1930s, the work of appeal tribunals in the planning and welfare fields in particular had grown dramatically, placing mounting pressure on the procedures by which the final decisions were taken. In the course of the report, Franks met the Whitehall defence of secrecy head on. He accepted that there was an argument that in planning inquiries

---

[146] Chapman, *Ethics in the British Civil Service*, 312. Also see above, Ch. 4, pp. 167–8.

[147] M. Roper, 'Access to Public Records', in R. A. Chapman and M. Hunt (eds.), *Open Government* (London, 1989), 83–6.

[148] *Report of the Committee on Departmental Records* [Grigg] (1954), Cmnd. 9163, p. 18.

[149] *Report of the Committee on Departmental Records*, 27.

[150] D. G. T. Williams, 'Official Secrecy in England', *Federal Law Review*, 3: 1 (June 1968), 47.

'the Minister ought not to be exposed to the difficulty and embarrassment which would arise from the disclosure of differences between his decision and the recommendations of the inspector',[151] and that greater transparency might cause inspectors to be less frank with ministers. But these requirements had to be balanced against the need to give citizens the information they required to defend themselves from governments whose programmes presented an ever-greater threat to the enjoyment of their property. Publishing inspectors' reports would enable the public to understand how the appeal system worked, and would prevent Ministers from withholding from inquiries information which they could deploy at 'the later and secret stage'.[152] What finally tilted the argument in favour of openness was the issue of Ministerial responsibility, which hitherto had been kept off limits by senior civil servants. With planning appeals now running at 6,000 a year, the pretence of transferring accountability from civil servants to politicians could no longer be sustained. 'We are impressed', concluded Franks, 'by the need for some further control beyond that which Parliament, in theory, though not always in practice, can exercise. There is no doubt that publicity is in itself an effective check against arbitrary action.'[153]

A powerful rearguard action by Whitehall frustrated legislation in this field,[154] and in the end the release of reports on planning inquiries was achieved by an administrative decision in 1962.[155] Nevertheless, deploying the convention of ministerial responsibility as an argument against rather than for official secrecy marked a turning-point in the debate.[156] A similar, though less visible transition was taking place in the review of the operation of the nationalized industries. As elsewhere, government intervention had generated an outpouring of professionally produced information. Set against the practices of the previous owners, and of firms elsewhere in the private sector, the annual reports of the Boards were open and informative.[157] In spite of the Companies Act of 1947 and 1948, which extended disclosure requirements, the level of detail in reports to shareholders was still very much at the discretion of the directors.[158] The consumer councils of the nationalized industries, by contrast, gave customers unprecedented statutory rights to ask for information and

---

[151] *Report of the Committee on Administrative Tribunals and Enquiries* [Franks] (1957), Cmnd. 218, p. 72.

[152] Ibid. 71.

[153] Ibid. 73.

[154] The hostility of Whitehall is described in Delafons, 'Working in Whitehall: Changes in Public Administration 1952–1982', 257–8.

[155] R. Wraith, *Open Government: The British Interpretation* (London, 1977), 18; Williams, 'Official Secrecy in England', 42.

[156] S. de Smith, 'Official Secrecy and External Relations in Britain: The Law and its Context', in T. M. Franck and E. Weisbrand, *Secrecy and Foreign Policy* (New York, 1974), 314.

[157] W. A. Robson, *Nationalised Industry and Public Ownership* (London, 1960), 276.

[158] C. W. Nobes and R. H. Parker, 'The Development of Company Financial Reporting in Great Britain, 1844–1977', in T. A. Lee and R. H. Parker, *The Evolution of Corporate Financial Accounting* (New York and London, 1984), 200; Edwards, *A History of Financial Accounting*, 209–13.

make representations about the service they received.[159] However, the work of the councils was hampered by their shortage of staff, their narrow democratic base, and by their dependence for technical knowledge on the managers whose performance they were supposed to monitor.[160] Furthermore, the value of the public reports was severely qualified by the defensiveness of the directors. The average board, concluded the first academic study of their publications,

has no intention whatever of revealing its failures or inefficiencies; on the contrary, it is desperately anxious to cover them up. Things that have gone wrong are not mentioned, concealed behind vague, bromidic generalisations, or ascribed to the impact of forces over which the industry concerned has no control.[161]

More seriously, there was a growing sense that the central decision-making process was being hidden from view altogether. Rather than developing a new model of control and accountability as the state engaged more closely with industry, the implementation of nationalization was reinforcing time-honoured practices. At the highest level, procedures conformed to what a 1960 study of the sector described as 'the widespread habit of English life of preferring an informal understanding or gentlemanly "persuasion" to a formal instruction or legal document'.[162] Lacking a clear sense of how to reconcile the national interest with commercial forces, Labour, and more particularly the Conservatives after 1951, sought to fudge the issue behind closed doors. Exposed to criticism that they were doing too little or too much, they instinctively clothed the scale and substance of their intervention in an old, familiar coat. As the 1952 study noted, 'in spite of the clear theoretical distinction that exists between a nationalised industry and a government department, it seems that a convention is being established whereby the relationship between Minister and Board is as confidential as that between Minister and Permanent Secretary'.[163] But unlike other aspects of government, this traditional form of secrecy conflicted with specific legal commitments to openness. In the context of the requirement to communicate to employees, customers, and the electorate in general, there was a particular force in the charge made in the *Political Quarterly* in 1955 that Ministers 'have exercised their responsibility in private and not answered for it in public'.[164] The battleground of nationalization, which was to be traversed by twenty-five major select committee inquiries between 1956 and 1976, became a further arena of debate about the reality of ministerial accountability.

[159] Wraith, *Open Government*, 36–8.
[160] P. S. Florence and H. Maddick, 'Consumers' Councils in the Nationalised Industries', *Political Quarterly*, 25: 3 (July–Sept. 1953), 266–7; W. Ashworth, *The State in Business, 1945 to the mid-1980s* (London, 1991), 166.
[161] A. H. Hanson, 'Report on the Reports', *Public Administration*, 30 (Summer 1952), 113.
[162] Robson, *Nationalised Industry and Public Ownership*, 161–2.
[163] Hanson, 'Report on the Reports', 122.
[164] E. Davies, 'Government Policy and the Public Corporation', *Political Quarterly*, 26: 2 (Apr.–June 1955), 116.

By the mid-1960s Bridges's confident vision of continuity appeared increasingly at odds with the enlarged responsibilities and raised expectations of the government machine. The Fabians returned to the civil service in 1964, drawing attention to 'the tendency to be too closed and secretive in the formation of policy'.[165] It was becoming clear that the upper reaches of the civil service were so locked into their ways as to be incapable of generating reform from within. Since the war, a subtle but critical shift had taken place in the foundations of secrecy. In the Preface to his *Reform of Parliament* of 1964, Bernard Crick observed that,

Of all the governments in the free world the British administration is certainly the most restrictive in giving access to information about its operations to either scholars or journalists: this I take to be not just the old arrogance of an administrative and political elite, which is used to minding its own business, but a new uncertainty about the efficacy of the system.[166]

The suspicion that secrecy was now a function more of weakness than strength had been raised by the Suez debacle, and strengthened by the tawdry drama of the Profumo affair. Within Whitehall, the element of masochism which had always been associated with the burden of anonymity was a further obstacle to the formulation of a constructive response to the deepening unpopularity. The official who had served as secretary of the Fulton Committee later observed that,

if you think back to the first half of the sixties, it is undeniable that the civil service had grown a poor image—and that this had communicated itself quite widely throughout society . . . The belief that civil service organisation was a gently ossified muddle staffed by intelligent, urbane but managerially innocent mandarins became the accepted wisdom of the day. And to some extent, at least, we let this happen. We fell to that insidious spiritual temptation—the thing that really does mark the mandarin—the feeling that to be misunderstood by the ignorant is inevitable, and that to be traduced as a result is our peculiar badge of honour.[167]

To the critics of what appeared an increasingly remote elite, the badge was losing its shine. Self-sacrifice was becoming indistinguishable from self-interest. The equation between honour and secrecy was beginning to generate more negative than positive results.

On the left there had long been voices, notably that of Harold Laski, urging a second Northcote–Trevelyan Report.[168] As the centenary passed, doubts were raised, particularly by Tommy Balogh, about whether the addition of

---

[165] Fabian Society, *The Administrators: Reform in the Civil Service* (London, 1964), 17. For a discussion of the Fabian approach to the post-war reform of government, see Hetzner, 'Social Democracy and Bureaucracy', 115–16.

[166] Crick, *The Reform of Parliament*, p. xii.

[167] Richard Wilding, cited in A. Sampson, *The New Anatomy of Britain* (London, 1971), 237–8.

[168] Theakston, *Labour Party and Whitehall*, 73.

supposedly scientific methods of personality assessment to the conventional examinations had not shifted the emphasis back to the system of class self-recruitment which had characterized the unreformed civil service.[169] Richard Crossman and G. D. H. Cole sought to respond to the concern of middle-class floating voters by drawing their party's attention to the increasing unpopularity of the state bureaucracy.[170] During the 1950s such appeals were largely ignored. The Labour leadership was still basking in the glow of its post-war achievements, and the unions were disinclined to criticize the civil servants who were struggling to embody the objectives of the welfare state. Herbert Morrison's *Government and Parliament*, which praised the long-established relationship between politicians and Whitehall, and resolutely defended official secrecy, was probably the most representative text of the era.[171] A decade after the centenary, however, the momentum of criticism accelerated sharply. Concerns about inefficiency, class bias, remoteness, and unaccountability coalesced around the notion of closure. The civil service maintained barriers against outsiders, against new ideas, and against public interrogation.[172] There is a general tendency, claimed the Fabians, 'to be too closed and secretive in the formation of policy'.[173] The return to office of a Labour Government committed to modernizing outdated institutions increased the pressure for a second fundamental review of the machinery of government.[174] In 1966 the Fulton Committee was duly established, charged with casting fresh light on a body which no longer seemed capable of renewing itself.[175]

In a much-cited passage, the final report, which was published in 1968, delivered the first authoritative condemnation of the structure of official communication: 'We think that the administrative process is surrounded by too much secrecy. The public interest would be better served if there were a greater amount of openness.'[176] What was most significant about this judgement, however, was its context. Fulton chose to locate his discussion of secrecy in a chapter on 'The Civil Service and the Community'. The issue was seen first of all, as it had been by Bridges, in terms of efficiency. What the community required above all was 'greater professionalism among both specialists and administrators'.[177] This goal would be furthered if there was a more extensive flow of information from the periphery to the centre, and if those on whose behalf the

---

[169] Balogh, *The Apotheosis of the Dilettante*, 91.

[170] Cole, 'Reform in the Civil Service', 244; Gwynn, 'The Labour Party and the Threat of Bureaucracy', 390–8.

[171] H. Morrison, *Government and Parliament* (3rd edn., London, 1964), 26–7, 320–38. The book was first published in 1954.

[172] The criticisms are marshalled in W. A. Robson, *The Governors and the Governed* (London, 1964), 18.

[173] Fabian Society, *The Administrators*, 17.

[174] Jones and Keating, *Labour and the British State*, 140–6.

[175] Theakston, *The Civil Service since 1945*, 86–108.

[176] Lord Fulton, *The Civil Service*, Vol. 1, *Report of the Committee, 1966–68* (London, 1968), Cmnd. 3638, p. 91.

[177] Ibid. 91.

officials were acting were told more about what was being done for them. The Benthamite argument that democracy required the free exchange of opinion was dressed up in the modern language of community politics. A pale imitation of a basic principle was embodied in a commitment to a cautious, incremental growth in contacts with the public: 'In our view, therefore, the convention of anonymity should be modified and civil servants, as professional administrators, should be able to go further than now in explaining what their departments are doing, at any rate so far as concerns managing existing policies and implementing legislation.'[178] Administrators and politicians were urged to display greater confidence in the value of communication, and criticized for giving 'great and sometimes excessive weight to the difficulties and problems which would undoubtedly arise from a more open process of administration and policy making'.[179]

It was a lost chance.[180] As the Treasury official William Ryrie pointed out in the most substantial submission to the Committee, the issue of anonymity involved much more than civil servants multiplying their press releases and talking to a wider range of outside experts. The steeply declining morale of what once had been 'a rather self-satisfied elite',[181] was a consequence of the nineteenth-century system of government, which demanded a constant flow of decision-making up to the top of the department in order that the political head could exercise formal accountability to Parliament. This not only deprived officials of public recognition, but prevented them from exercising the kind of personal responsibility for their tasks which was essential both for job satisfaction and for the development of professional levels of efficiency. With the consolidation of the welfare state, major structural reform had gained a particular urgency. It was not only that the Victorian model no longer supplied a realistic description of the level of supervision which any Minister or Permanent Secretary exercised over the vastly increased business of departments. It was also that the agreement about the role of government which the post-war reforms had engineered offered a once-in-a-century window of opportunity for overhauling the administrative structure. Northcote–Trevelyan had exploited such a moment, now was the time to repeat the achievement: 'To reform the machinery of government radically while the role of government was in doubt was difficult; the new consensus should make it easier to find a generally acceptable basis of ideas for remodelling the machinery of government, and the Civil Service as part of it.'[182]

---

[178] Lord Fulton, *The Civil Service*, 93.

[179] Ibid. 92.

[180] On the limitations of Fulton, see Hennessy, *Whitehall*, 190–5; Sampson, *New Anatomy of Britain*, 237–40.

[181] Lord Fulton, *The Civil Service*, Vol. 5, *Proposals and Opinions* (London, 1968), Cmnd. 3638, pt. 2, p. 1092.

[182] Ibid. 1086.

Instead Fulton ring-fenced the doctrine of ministerial responsibility, and transferred consideration of a fundamental change in the law on official secrecy to a further report.[183] This appeared a year later in the form of a White Paper entitled *Information and Public Interest*, which demonstrated just how deeply embedded was Bridges's restricted conception of bureaucratic professionalism. Rather than seeing the commitment to more open relations with the community as a stepping-stone to a major transfer of rights to information, the White Paper used it as an argument against any legislative change at all. The multiplication of channels of communication, the continuing growth in the volume of government publications on every aspect of society's well-being, made it less rather than more feasible to tamper with the blanket prohibition on improper communication. 'There would', it concluded, 'be the greatest difficulty in defining satisfactorily what categories of information should qualify for this special protection and what should not, because the range of information which may need this protection is so varied.'[184] There was no need for public concern about the Official Secrets Acts, 'they do not inhibit the authorised release of information in any way; they affect only disclosures of official information made without authority'.[185] That there might be a fundamental problem with the structure of authority within the government machine, and between the state and its citizens, was not considered. Openness in the pursuit of efficiency did not conflict with secrecy in the defence of the national interest.

The Record of Welfare

The Younger Report of July 1972 was and remains the only large-scale official study of privacy ever carried out in this country. The genesis of the report was the attempt in 1969 by the Labour backbencher Brian Walden to introduce a general law on the subject. A committee of inquiry was the price for defeating the Bill, but, as the report pointed out, the significance of the issue extended well beyond short-term Parliamentary tactics: 'The demand that more systematic attention should now be paid to this problem has been growing since the end of the Second World War. The starting point was the experience of totalitarian regimes, both Nazi and Communist, which claimed the right to more or less unlimited interference by the public authorities with the private lives of their citizens.'[186] Declarations of a right to privacy by the United Nations and the Council of Europe had been integral to the post-war reconstruction of democratic institutions. The principle conformed to the long-standing British

---

[183] Ibid., i. 92.
[184] *Information and Public Interest*, Cmnd. 4089 (June, 1969), 11.
[185] Ibid. 11.
[186] *Report of the Committee on Privacy* [Younger], Cmnd. 5012 (1972), p. 5.

tradition of measuring liberty by the absence of public intervention in the domestic sphere. Hitler and Stalin were descendants of the pre-twentieth-century
tyrants whose exercise of secret power denied the private individual the right
to keep his own secrets. However, the practice of embodying an abstract right
in statute law conflicted with the equally well-preserved British tradition of
confining such matters to the realm of civil remedy or social sanction.[187] A quarter of a century after the end of the war, some way had to be found of reconciling the expectations of free citizens with the conventions of the legal system
which ostensibly guaranteed their liberties.

The initial strategy adopted by Younger was to stress that both the causes of
the increasing disquiet about privacy, and many of the more powerful remedies, were located in forces well outside the political arena. 'From a wider point
of view', wrote the report, 'concern for the protection of privacy has been
stimulated by the growing pressures exerted by modern industrial society
upon the home and daily life.'[188] It echoed the complaint of Warren and Brandeis in 1890, that the dynamics of mass living, and in particular of mass communication, were generating unacceptable threats to the inner world of the
modern family. At the same time countervailing tendencies could be detected
in the new urban civilization. Whilst the decline of gossip raised worries about
the weakening of the bonds which held society together, it did relieve householders of the constant surveillance of their neighbours.[189] And in the press of
people, a new kind of space was emerging:

The commuter on the rush-hour train may have lost room to move or even breathe,
but the privacy which he enjoys may not be less than that of his ancestors travelling
on the open road because he is anonymous to those who press about him. This
anonymity of our overcrowded urban and suburban society protects privacy at least
as effectively as the scope for greater physical separation which prevailed in the
past.[190]

Half a century earlier, the great German critic of modernization and
tyranny, Walter Benjamin, had also noted how the transport systems which
had made possible the conurbations were creating new forms of social
contact:

Interpersonal relationships of people in big cities are characterised by a markedly
greater emphasis on the use of the eyes than on that of the ears. This can be attributed chiefly to the institution of public conveyances. Before buses, railroads and
trams became fully established during the nineteenth century, people were never
put in the position of having to stare at one another for minutes or even hours on
end without exchanging a word.[191]

---

[187] Such provision as the common law did provide for the protection of privacy is explored by
J. Jacob and R. Jacob, 'Protection of Privacy', *New Law Journal*, 119: 5377 (13 Feb. 1969), 157–9.

[188] *Report of the Committee on Privacy*, 6.

[189] Ibid. 23.   [190] Ibid. 23.

[191] W. Benjamin, *Illuminations* (London, 1973), 193.

The metropolis was an arena in which the divorce between the inner and outer world was becoming ever-more marked. In the streets, people observed but did not listen; at home they communicated but were no longer observed. For Younger, as for earlier commentators, the more prosperous sections of society were in the vanguard of change:

As a result of these developments the modern middle-class family of two parents and their children, relatively soundproofed in their semi-detached house, relatively unseen behind their privet hedge and rose trellis, travelling with determined reserve on public transport or insulated in the family car, shopping in the supermarket and entertained by television, are probably more private in the sense of being unnoticed in all their everyday doings than any sizeable section of the population in any other time or place.[192]

At the beginning of the century, Georg Simmel had observed of his native Berlin that 'the modern style of life . . . has produced an entirely new measure of reserve and discretion, especially in the large cities'.[193] Now, as the leafy interwar suburbs began to mature, and the nuclear family reached its apogee of stability and security, the capacity to control what was known of your personal affairs and feelings, to maintain a 'determined reserve' in an overcrowded world, had never been greater.

There was growing evidence, furthermore, that the welfare state was beginning to universalize this condition. In the aftermath of the reforms, the urban working-class community came under scrutiny from a new generation of sociologists. Their interest was stimulated by the recognition that a way of life which had taken form in the late-nineteenth and early-twentieth centuries was becoming obsolete. It was still possible to discover and write about such neighbourhoods, but increasingly they were seen as relics of a past age. Areas of towns and cities which once had been viewed as destructive of all established customs and values were now regarded as exemplars of a fast-disappearing 'traditional' community.[194] In Bethnal Green and elsewhere, investigators were able to find social entities bound together by a network of street conversations. Peter Townsend, for instance, identified the role of the 'good neighbour' in the East End of London, who not only 'could supply a drop of vinegar or a pinch of salt if you ran short', but also 'provided street-corner news and gossip about the neighbourhood, about other families and about the community. She was the go-between, passing news from one family to another, one household to another.'[195] As had always been the case, there were well-policed limits to these structures of communication. The conversations were a source of censure as

---

[192] *Report of the Committee on Privacy*, 24.

[193] Wolff, *Sociology of Georg Simmel*, 336. Also Vincent, 'Secrecy and the City', 341–4.

[194] The best survey of this body of research is to be found in R. Frankenberg, *Communities in Britain: Social Life in Town and Country* (revised edn., Harmondsworth, 1969). See also Bourke, *Working-Class Cultures*, 156.

[195] P. Townsend, *The Family Life of Old People* (London, 1957), 121.

well as support, and where possible were confined to neutral territory out of doors. Townsend found that 'nearly two-thirds of the old people claimed they did not go regularly into the home of a neighbour and a neighbour did not visit them. Such marked reserve was, perhaps, largely a means of preserving marital and family relationships but also a means of avoiding personal antagonisms.'[196] Households under the greatest pressure, such as the sample of unusually large families studied by Hilary Land, found it particularly difficult to engage in relationships in which they were unable to reciprocate gifts and favours.[197] Deprivation was at once consoled and confirmed by gossip. The absence of material resources enforced a reliance on public exchanges of news and services which were vital for maintaining some semblance of a functioning private household.[198]

The fragile balance between participation and withdrawal in these traditional neighbourhoods demanded constant vigilance.[199] It was a comforting but at the same time fraught pattern of communication.[200] There can be little surprise, therefore, that when the investigators turned to the municipal housing estates which were accommodating an ever-larger proportion of the urban working class, they found that the chains of gossip were significantly shorter. Young and Willmott followed the movement of families from Bethnal Green to a new estate where relationships between neighbours were conducted on a 'window-to-window, not face-to-face' basis.[201] The world of strangers began not at the edge of the community but at the boundary of domestic space. The official handbook to the great Dagenham council estate reminded tenants that their front door is 'the gateway to your particular castle. You can close it like a fortress against the outside world.'[202] Surrounding this rented castle was the carefully tended moat of the garden, with its front gate which tenants were abjured to shut quietly: 'banging is bad for the latch and annoying to the neighbours.'[203] The home was seen as a place of absolute rather than relative privacy. The most rigorous comparative study of the period was conducted by J. M. Mogey on an old and a new settlement in Oxford. Here he discovered that the transition caused a dramatic curtailment of the network of conversation:

For most families the surrounding neighbourhood, apart from the two or three families met face-to-face, was considered an unfriendly place, even a place where people hostile to some of the things you cherished might be living. In the face of

---

[196] P. Townsend, *The Family Life of Old People*, 122.

[197] H. Land, *Large Families in London* (London, 1969), 81–4.

[198] E. Roberts, *Women and Families: An Oral History, 1940–1970* (Oxford, 1995), 207–11.

[199] For a detailed account of such problems in a surviving traditional community, see K. Coates and R. Silburn, *Poverty: The Forgotten Englishmen* (Harmondsworth, 1970), 93–9, 106–9.

[200] Bourke, *Working-Class Cultures*, 157–9.

[201] M. Young and P. Willmott, *Family and Kinship in East London* (Harmondsworth, 1962), 163. Also J. Tucker, *Honourable Estates* (London, 1966), 83–5.

[202] Dagenham Municipal Housing Estates, *Tenants' Handbook* (Gloucester, 1949), 19.

[203] Ibid. 13.

such an attitude a strengthening of relations within the family and a cautious exchange of gossip between immediate neighbours might be expected to take place.[204]

The physical territory of the estate was no longer coextensive with the sphere of informal communication. At best, oral contact was maintained with those in contiguous houses rather than adjacent streets.

There was a sense of nostalgia for the warmth and openness of the information networks of the old communities, and an apprehension that the residents of the council estates would be imprisoned inside their newly equipped houses, with no corner-shops or pubs in which to reconstitute social relations.[205] However, it was evident that there were powerful gains amidst the losses. Not only did the new arrangements enhance the defence of domestic space which had always been the ambition of the most impoverished slum dweller, but they also permitted new levels of intimacy within the family and a more active and deliberate strategy of making contacts outside it. Foreign observers had frequently identified a national tradition of restricted communication within as well as between families. In 1945 Pierre Maillaud published *The English Way*, a friendly if bemused portrait of the nation with whose aid his country had finally defeated the totalitarian regimes. 'There are', he wrote, 'fewer walls in England than in France or in Italy. There is no secrecy, even less privacy than elsewhere, in the household itself.'[206] Yet the physical openness coexisted with an emotional closure: 'Within the household itself, within that open household unguarded from without, there seems between its members to be a high degree of individual reserve and discretion, of individual self-defence against excessive intimacy.'[207] Nowhere were these barriers higher and more impermeable than in the classic slum, where a rigid division of labour between husband and wife left them struggling on separate battlefields, the occasional opportunities for emotional contact undermined by constant physical and emotional weariness.[208] Mogey found that in the traditional community, there was more conversation between women in the street than between couples inside the home:

Adults put little emphasis on the ability to talk and the verbal expression of emotion is neither wished nor possible. In marriage both partners keep fairly rigidly to their household roles. Serious friction is handled by avoiding contact and by emphasising getting along together rather than any more positive harmony in the marriage relationship; a minor everyday friction is rarely allowed to rise to the level of conscious expression.[209]

---

[204] J. M. Mogey, *Family and Neighbourhood: Two Studies in Oxford* (Oxford, 1956), 153.
[205] Young and Willmott, *Family and Kinship*, 147, 154.
[206] P. Maillaud, *The English Way* (London, 1945), 48.
[207] Ibid. 49. Also J. Bailhache, *The Secret of the English* (London, 1948), 78.
[208] Vincent, *Poor Citizens*, 20.
[209] Mogey, *Family and Neighbourhood*, 154–5.

So entrenched a tradition of reserve could not be overturned by a single change of residence, but it was possible to detect in the home-centred new estates more relaxed and open patterns of discourse. More leisure time was spent inside more comfortable domestic spaces, and the rehoused families displayed 'a heightened ability to communicate desires and wishes'.[210]

Outside the home the families were able to exercise much greater discretion in the personal contacts they made and maintained. In the traditional community the social network was given; in the new estates choices could be made about which neighbours to get to know, and on what terms. With improvements in physical communication, including the possession for the first time by more prosperous sections of the working class of a motor car and then a telephone, friendships could relax the tight bonds of space. The destruction of the giant of 'squalor' was one of the five objectives of Beveridge's welfare state. Once the council-house building programme escaped the material shortages of the immediate post-war years, the new estates increasingly became the standard environment of the manual worker and his family. Between 1945 and 1971 the privately rented sector declined from just over a half to under a fifth of the housing stock, whilst council housing grew from an eighth to nearly a third.[211] If there was still a significant gap in terms of both status and facilities between the municipal and owner-occupied developments, there was, at this most basic level of social interaction, a genuine convergence of class experience. On the one hand, as sociologists widened their focus to include the middle-class households it was discovered that they too exchanged gossip with their neighbours.[212] On the other, the council tenants were beginning to negotiate the boundaries of communication with the kind of freedom which once had been the privilege of their social superiors.[213]

The opportunities for determining the level of reserve in the conduct of relationships within and beyond the household increased as the era of depression and austerity was left behind. In part this was a straightforward function of material prosperity, as rising standards of living brought enhanced domestic comfort and greater possibilities of secluded transport and communication to larger sections of the population. The narrow band of respectable working-class families who could afford to keep themselves to themselves was steadily widened.[214] And in part it was a consequence of government intervention, not only at the level of macroeconomic management but also in the form of direct involvement in the most basic areas of human activity. The capacity to exercise greater control over personal communication was bought at the expense of an

---

[210] Mogey, *Family and Neighbourhood*, 156.

[211] R. Lowe, *The Welfare State in Britain since 1945* (London, 1993), 251.

[212] C. Bell, *Middle Class Families* (London, 1968), 139–46.

[213] On friendship patterns in contemporary middle-class estates, see P. Willmott and M. Young, *Family and Class in a London Suburb* (London, 1960), 99–110. On the cross-class ambition for domestic privacy, see E. Hahn, *England to Me* (London, 1950), 63.

[214] Roberts, *Women and Families*, 212.

enlarged national and local public sector whose implications went largely unnoticed in the first quarter-century of the welfare state. Nowhere was this more clearly the case than in the field of housing itself. In place of the intrusive and at times exploitative private landlord, there developed a large bureaucracy possessed of immense powers over the lives of the modern citizen. Eligibility for council accommodation, transfer up waiting-lists, allocation to particular estates and subsequent movement between them, and behaviour inside the dwellings and their gardens were subject to decisions of officials under the nominal control of elected councillors and the notional supervision of central government.

In theory, the structure of local democracy and formal regulation represented a major advance on the arbitrary and unaccountable powers of the myriad of small landlords. In practice, the shift of control to the tenants was severely compromised by the way in which the housing bureaucracies interpreted their responsibilities. The paternalist culture established by Octavia Hill in the pioneering schemes of the later nineteenth century was kept alive by the new generation of officials.[215] Before 1980 the tenants possessed no right to participate in the management of their estates, and only the most limited ability to challenge the rules by which their engagements with the local authorities were conducted. With a growing volume and variety of stock, administrators exercised increasing discretion in determining and applying the criteria by which households were given and permitted to occupy accommodation. Their approach was conditioned by a general sense that the tenants were answerable to officials for their conduct and not vice versa. The interpretation of the rules allowed them wide areas of discretion, and occasional interventions by councillors served only to increase the sense of a system at once rigid in its construction and unpredictable in its impact on the lives of individual families.

The inequality of the relationship between those given employment by this branch of the welfare state and those given homes was particularly apparent in the realm of knowledge. At the strategic level the planning of new estates and of the built environment in general was so shrouded in secrecy that in 1968 the authorities were obliged by law to demonstrate that they had consulted local opinion in formulating plans. Existing or prospective tenants found it extremely difficult to grasp the detail and significance of the ever-more complex regulations which were so critical to their domestic well-being. A major theme of the influential television film *Cathy Come Home*, which was one of the first documents to raise serious questions about the benevolence of local government, was the inability of the homeless couple to negotiate the labyrinthine system of forms and waiting-lists and reach the promised land of a house in newly constructed estate. Once a family approached the local authority, it be-

---

[215] S. Merrett, *State Housing in Britain* (London, 1979), 200–9.

came the subject of a confidential file which would come to contain a range of personal information only distantly related to a tenancy.[216] The collection of such material, which was derived from a variety of sources, including reports from housing inspectors and other welfare agencies, newspaper cuttings, and information culled from neighbours, was justified in terms of the housing authority's responsibility to fit the family to the appropriate accommodation. Standards of domestic morality and cleanliness were observed and filed as part of a strategy of maintaining the quality of entire neighbourhoods. Street gossip had been replaced by formal record as a means of policing conduct, with far greater consequences for transgression, and much less opportunity for discovering or influencing fact and judgement.

Elsewhere, the supportive role of the neighbourhood information networks began to be assumed by employees of the rapidly expanding personal social services. As a 1971 discussion paper on confidentiality from the newly formed British Association of Social Workers explained, 'a great deal of their work is concerned with the type of communication which in more favourable circumstances or in less complex societies is dealt with on the level of kinsfolk and friends'.[217] The task of the professional visitor was to enter into a relationship with a family in order to 'acquire knowledge, pertinent to the situation but painful to the teller, which in different circumstances would already be known to a trusted friend and would have to be talked about and certainly not recorded'.[218] As we have seen in earlier chapters, the issue of creating and controlling such records had been central to the slow, incomplete professionalization of welfare work since the late nineteenth century. With the establishment of the welfare state, the translation of informal conversation to formal archive highlighted the confused but critical relationship between new forms of public bureaucracy and new kinds of private citizenship.

At the outset there was little evidence that the Beveridge revolution had achieved a matching transformation in the outlook of the employees in the reshaped social services, most of whom had been trained between the wars in methods developed by the Charity Organisation Society. The first guide to the new structure, Cherry Morris's *Social Case-Work in Britain* of 1949, did recognize that 'co-operation in the social services of the local authority raises the whole question of confidentiality',[219] but neither she nor subsequent commentators in the 1950s had many new answers. For most of the first two decades of the welfare state, the multiplication of numbers and categories of home visitors caused organizational confusion and impeded any coherent reconsideration of their duties towards those families whose histories they sought to dis-

---

[216] S. Weir, 'Housing', in R. Delbridge and M. Smith (eds.), *Consuming Secrets* (London, 1982), 63–4.
[217] British Association of Social Workers, *Discussion Paper no. 1. Confidentiality in Social Work* (London, 1971), 3.
[218] Ibid. 3.
[219] C. Morris (ed.), *Social Case-Work in Great Britain* (London, 1954 edn.), 161.

cover.[220] At best, new recruits were reminded of their ethical responsibilities as professionals and cautioned not to make too copious notes in front of the householder. The tendency was for the scale of recording interviews to increase rather than diminish.[221] Problems concerning the management of the subsequent documents were to be resolved by an essentially paternalist judgement on the interests of the client. Margaret McEwan's 1956 textbook for health-visitor students suggested that the question of how much information should be passed to other social workers rested 'on whether the result will be to the ultimate good of the family or individual'.[222] In practice, as the Younghusband working party on social workers discovered in 1959, the information stored in local authority offices was treated with culpable carelessness:

During one of our visits we passed through a general office also used by the public for inquiries. We saw papers relating to an unmarried mother (whose name and status was clearly visible in the heading) lying in a correspondence tray close to the public inquiry desk. In another instance we found case records were kept in unlocked filing cabinets in the general office.[223]

Not until the mid-1960s did the personal social services really begin to respond to the challenge laid down by the vision of an integrated welfare system based on a new valuation of citizen's rights. A period of expansion and debate culminated in the Seebohm Report of 1968 and the subsequent 1970 Local Authority Social Services Act. The establishment of unitary social services departments was designed to bring to an end the damaging rivalries between the different categories of welfare workers, thereby enhancing public confidence in social work and broadening the service delivered to those increasingly seen as clients rather than supplicants. In his highly influential report, Seebohm isolated the fundamental cause of the conflicts and inefficiencies which had undermined the ambitions of this critical area of welfare provision:

the tradition which leads to the present difficulties is understandable but it derives from views of professional practice that are increasingly anachronistic. In many fields today, problems of any seriousness are rarely dealt with by individuals, but by teams; a large number of professional persons, medical and others, may be involved in dealing, for instance, with a single hospital admission. Confidential information is exchanged freely; otherwise the work could not be done properly.[224]

He had no patience with those clinging to outmoded conceptions of professionalism. It was time to abandon the nineteenth-century model which

---

[220] E. Younghusband, *Social Work in Britain: 1950–1975* (London, 1978), i. 31–5; Lowe, *Welfare State in Britain*, 261–71.

[221] The Family Welfare Association, *The Family, Patients or Clients?* (London, 1961), 37.

[222] M. McEwan, *Health Visiting* (2nd edn., London, 1957), 105.

[223] *Report of the Working Party on Social Workers* [Younghusband] (London, 1959), 170.

[224] *Report of the Committee on Local Authority and Allied Personal Social Services* [Seebohm] Cmnd. 3703 (1968), 199.

stressed the discrete individual working within a corporate body whose jealously guarded identity was derived from its unique practices and objectives. A new era of collective endeavour in society had to be matched by a fresh spirit of co-operation amongst those charged with resolving its problems. The growth of bureaucratized welfare, reinforced by developments in information technology which were creating limitless possibilities of storing and linking records, 'necessitates', he argued, 'reconsideration of traditional attitudes to confidentiality'.[225] Effective deployment of knowledge derived from clients was still not taking place: 'the obstacles arise from real or assumed differences in professional status. These will not disappear until social workers, doctors, teachers, nurses, administrators and others realise that they are all members of a team and accept the team approach to family problems.'[226]

Guides to every branch of the personal social services stressed that confidentiality was a necessary condition of communication between the welfare worker and the client. Felix Biestek's *The Casework Relationship* of 1961, the standard text of its time, made clear the attitude of the individual from whom such sensitive knowledge was sought:

He communicates this secret information upon the condition, at least implicitly made, that it is necessary for the help he is seeking. He assumes that the information will not go beyond the persons engaged in helping him . . . Therefore the caseworker's preservation of secret information is an essential quality of the relationship. If a client ever became aware of an individual caseworker's violation of confidentiality, the relationship would be destroyed.[227]

Yet increasingly the caseworker was required to take part in regular conferences, which were conducted by means of sharing this secret information with representatives of other agencies.[228] The transformation of the personal social services urged by Seebohm was founded on the replacement of a casual by a formal exchange of private details. In the past, co-ordination of endeavour had been conducted through a kind of professional gossip. Now all was to be structured, with the transmission of records itself to be recorded.

The difficulty of reconciling the personal relationship between welfare worker and client with the bureaucratic relationship between one professional and another was compounded by the concurrent attack on the paternalistic attitudes inherited from the pre-war era. It was no longer acceptable for the visitor alone to determine what was communicated inside the home and beyond it. Much greater respect had to be paid to the dignity and discretion of the householder. As Evelyn Davison's 1965 textbook pointed out, 'there is a

---

[225] *Report of the Committee on Local Authority and Allied Personal Social Services*, 199.
[226] Ibid. 199.
[227] F. P. Biestek, *The Casework Relationship* (London, 1961), 121–2. Also J. Clegg (ed.), *Dictionary of Social Services* (London, 1971), 19.
[228] On the growth of case conferences, see M. Saunders, *Health Visiting Practice* (London, 1968), 98; H. Cunningham (ed.), *The Principles of Health Visiting* (London, 1967), 242–5.

subtle danger of a caseworker thinking that, because a client seeks her help, she has a right to know everything. A client has a right to his own secrets, a right to decide how much of his intimate affairs he wishes to reveal. This right must be respected.'[229] It was partly a matter of extending the status of full citizenship to the poorest and most marginal of the population, and partly of recognizing at last that maintaining control over private knowledge was crucial to the recovery process. Seeking the permission of the client for subsequent communication of personal secrets should be an integral element of the therapy. 'The consent of the client', argued Davison, 'to consultation with another person or agency about his affairs is important not only for the preservation of confidence but also because it is a way in which self-responsibility can be exercised.'[230]

It was far from clear how welfare workers were to resolve the latent conflict between the newly discovered rights of their clients and the newly established authority of the integrated social work departments. The most that Seebohm could offer was an appeal to their professional judgement to guide them through the maze. There were, however, unresolved pressures within the new structures which made the balanced exercise of such judgement almost impossible. The drive towards co-ordination which was central to the transformation of the personal social services involved forging close relations not just between the branches of welfare work which had grown up during the recent decades, but also, and critically, between the comparatively new occupations and the much older and more powerful medical bodies. It became evident that the most valuable currency which the less respected and secure groups possessed was the recorded information about their clients. This was particularly the case with the health visitors and district nurses, who since 1948 saw themselves occupying a key position between social workers and doctors. As the Ministry of Health noted of the health visitor in 1956, 'her main value to others will often be the detailed knowledge she has of a wide range of families in need'.[231] The 13 million calls a year that were now being made were generating information on the social and physical background of the family which could greatly aid the process of medical care. The problem was how to form an effective working relationship with general practitioners who during the first half of the century had paid little regard to their activities. According to *The Principles and Practices of Health Visiting*, 'this is best attained if the health visitor calls on the doctor at the most convenient times, and is prepared to share her knowledge of the family background when necessary'.[232]

Gradually, more formal connections were established. Health visitors were

[229] E. H. Davison, *Social Casework* (London, 1965), 28.

[230] Ibid., *Social Casework*, p. 29.

[231] Ministry of Health, *Health Visiting: Report of a Working Party on the Field of Work, Training and Recruitment of Health Visitors* [Jameson] (1956), 116.

[232] R. Hale, M. K. Loveland, and G. M. Owen, *The Principles and Practices of Health Visiting* (Oxford, 1968), 41.

attached to pioneering group practices, district nurses were directly linked to surgeries in 1968, and following the recommendations of Seebohm, experimental projects were launched to co-ordinate the activities of medical social workers and doctors.[233] The auxiliaries expected the trade in records to be two-way. As they assisted the doctor to devise a more informed programme of treatment, so they would gain access to knowledge which would facilitate their home visits. 'I find it a great help', wrote a health visitor in 1967, 'working in the surgery, to have access to the whole family's medical records, usually including those of grandparents . . . it is a great help in providing that so essential family background when we meet families in difficulties.'[234] It could not be assumed, however, that the medical profession was prepared for this wholesale invasion of the confidential relationship between doctor and patient. The bureaucratization of general practice had been successfully resisted in the negotiations which led to the creation of the National Health Service in 1948. In the same year, the newly formed World Medical Association had issued the Declaration of Geneva, which required the doctor to promise to uphold 'the honour and noble traditions of the medical profession' and to 'respect the secrets which are confided in me, *even after the patient has died*'.[235] The Hippocratic Oath was alive and well in the welfare state. The British Medical Association saw no need to alter its position in the light of the new structure. As a doctor explained in 1953, 'in recent years the policy of the Association has been that of complete secrecy under all circumstances, with a sole exception that a doctor might warn others against possible infection of venereal disease in an affected patient'.[236] With the exception of long-standing legislation on notifiable diseases, the model of the individual doctor engaged in an enclosed private relationship with an individual patient remained intact. A decade after the NHS was founded the assistant secretary of the BMA was still able to assure his colleagues that 'the general interest and the common welfare require that the patient shall be able to rely with full confidence upon the secrecy of all communication made to the doctor'.[237]

By the time the Younger Committee reported, however, the medical establishment was beginning to modify its stance. Pressure came from the experimental introduction of team practices in primary medicine, and the much more dramatic growth in the size and significance of the hospital sector, where

[233] L. Hockley, *Feeling the Pulse* (London, 1966), 73–4; M. F. Antrobus, *District Nursing* (London, 1985), 1; Younghusband, *Social Work in Britain*, i. 157–8.

[234] G. Flack, 'The Health Visitor's Work in a Group Practice—A Personal Account of the Early Days', in P. J. Cunningham (ed.), *The Principles of Health Visiting* (London 1967), 44. Also, M. K. Chisholm, *An Insight into Health Visiting* (London, 1970), 92–3.

[235] Cited in C. Hawkins, *Mishap or Malpractice?* (Oxford, 1985), 306. Emphasis in original. The declaration was reissued in 1968 and 1983. See M. Phillips and J. Dawson, *Doctor's Dilemmas: Medical Ethics and Contemporary Science* (London, 1985), 121; Campbell, *Moral Dilemmas in Medicine*, 195.

[236] Cited in Phillips and Dawson, *Doctors' Dilemmas*, 120.

[237] S. J. Hadfield, *Law and Ethics for Doctors* (London, 1958), 55. Hadfield was the Assistant Secretary of the BMA.

lateral collaboration between doctors and vertical association between medical and lay staff was inescapable. In a memorandum to the Committee the BMA acknowledged that, 'it is no longer practicable to look upon the single physician as the patient's sole confidant in any serious illness, and it is assumed by public and profession alike that any contact with the complex medical machinery of today implies acquiescence in some degree of extended confidence'.[238] Nonetheless, it was still very uncertain about how to define or police the outer reaches of this enlarged realm. Sharing personal records amongst doctors was one thing; embracing other workers in the circle of confidentiality was quite another. The BMA could only offer the patronizing hope that the outsiders would be influenced by its moral example:

We think the public has confidence in the ethical standards of the medical profession, but may not realise that at present the confidentiality of written medical records depends upon adherence to a strict code of conduct, not only by doctors who give a responsible lead but also by a large number of lay people who may have access to such records in the course of their daily work.[239]

There was little evidence that the medical profession would easily trust the ancillary workers, and no obvious mechanism for ensuring compliance with their own standards. In the end, Younger merely concurred with the doctors that 'there are dangers to privacy presented by the growing tendency for people outside the strictly medical field—social workers, researchers, demographers, administrators and others in, for example, hospitals and group practices—to acquire medical information about individuals'.[240]

At the heart of the tensions between the ancillary workers and both their clients and their medical collaborators was the unresolved issue of official bureaucracy. The hierarchical teams through which the services of the new welfare state increasingly were delivered threatened structures of confidentiality built upon relations of trust between individuals, whether home visitor and householder or doctor and patient. By the early 1970s the outline of the problem was becoming clearer, but not the solution. The tendency on the part of both the ancillary workers and the doctors was to fall back on professional ethics, which the former were still anxious to claim, and the latter to defend. But this paternalist appeal to a privileged moral code raised disputes within the ranks of the caring professions, and did not sit easily with the new language of citizen rights. The alternative approach, which was to respond to the impact of the state by generating new forms of legislative protection, was confined at this stage to the fringes of the debate.

The one area in which individual privacy was intended directly to be enhanced by the extension of state welfare was that of income transfer. The

---

[238] Memorandum by British Medical Association to Younger Committee. *Report of the Committee on Privacy*, 109.
[239] Ibid.   [240] Ibid. 114.

central virtue of the insurance principle, which lay at the heart of Beveridge's programme, was that it reduced to a minimum the need to visit the homes of the poor to enquire into their circumstances. After the bitter experience of the inter-war household means test, the prospect of delivering relief without exposing domestic secrets was immensely attractive to claimants and officials alike. Even the National Assistance Board, responsible for the small and supposedly declining minority not fully covered by insurance, was determined to forge a new relationship with those still required to reveal their finances. Difficulties of communication were now seen as a consequence of natural reticence rather than deliberate evasion. Overcoming them required extra effort by the official rather than greater openness by the claimant: 'If the Board's officer is to discover and deal with the problems of the people he visits,' explained the 1954 NAB report, 'he must be observant, and sometimes he must be persistent (though still tactful) in his enquiries, for many people, especially old people, are reluctant to speak of their difficulties, particularly to an official.'[241] The Board set out to gain the confidence of those it was charged with assisting, and in turn offered its trust to those dependent on the state. As the 1961 Annual Report concluded, 'in the Board's experience the overwhelming majority of those who apply to them are honest, truthful people in need of real help'.[242] Where money alone was not the solution, it saw itself operating, in the decades before unitary social service departments, a referral service to the proliferating municipal and voluntary agencies.[243]

Temptation could not be expelled entirely from this new Eden. Mechanisms for detecting fraud remained in place, but the state was determined to distance itself from the crude and degrading practices which had aroused such resentment before the war. The code for investigating benefit irregularities prepared for the introduction of the new system in 1948 required that,

enquiries of neighbours and local tradesmen in cases of benefit irregularities should be made only very exceptionally where the investigating officer is satisfied that an offence has been committed and all that is required is confirmation of evidence already held. Where such enquiries are made, they should be conducted with the utmost discretion.[244]

Eventually, the insurance system would displace means tests altogether; in this interim phase, neither the officials nor those amongst whom the claimants lived and worked felt able to relax their guard entirely. The culture of suspicion could not be eradicated overnight, but the attempt was made to reduce the damage it caused in relations between neighbours. 'It will be readily under-

[241] *Report of the National Assistance Board for the Year ended 31st December, 1954*, Cmnd. 9781 (London, 1955), 19.

[242] *Report of the National Assistance Board for the Year ended 31st December, 1961*, Cmnd. 1730 (London, 1962), 41.

[243] Vincent, *Poor Citizens*, 136–7.

[244] PRO PIN7/284, p. 105.

stood', explained a Board circular, 'that the notice which officers may feel bound to take of an anonymous submission in any particular case can be said to involve a special degree of responsibility for protecting the informant . . . In particular, letters from common informers should not be shown to the persons stigmatised.'[245] The officials were advised not to carry copies of the unsigned accusations with them on their visits, nor to quote directly from them. The mistrust was to be contained by secrecy. Replacing open by discreet suspicion would enhance the sense of common citizenship.

Although the number of claimants for means-tested relief was much higher than expected when the new system came into operation, and thereafter rose rather than fell, it remained possible to retain the illusion of a new culture of trust throughout most of the next two decades. This was largely because the majority of the 8 million or so visits a year made by the Board's inspectors in the 1950s were to the homes of pensioners, two-thirds of whom were women. Elderly widows were not generally suspected by either neighbours or officials of concealing undeclared jobs or lovers. In 1960 only 2,000 prosecutions for benefit fraud were made, and of these, just forty-five involved pensioners.[246] However, as traditional family structures began to decay and the long post-war boom came to an end, the figure of the able-bodied pauper once more began to stalk the imaginations of those who contributed to welfare benefits and those who administered them. By 1971 the number of claimants for means-tested relief, renamed supplementary benefit in 1966, had reached 3 million, triple the initial level, and a growing proportion of these were either lone mothers or unemployed males. In response to a vociferous campaign in sections of the press, the Conservative Government set up a committee of inquiry on the 'abuse of social security benefits' under Sir Henry Fisher. Its report in 1973 supplied the most detailed analysis of the state's policing of welfare ever undertaken. There was no doubt that the practice of covert accusation was both flourishing and valued. The report found that 'an appreciable proportion of the abuse which is detected comes to light through anonymous letters'.[247] This was especially the case with non-contributory benefits, where such correspondence constituted the single biggest category of evidence in 1971.[248] Two-thirds of the letters concerned earnings, and almost a quarter cohabitation or fictitious desertion.

With prosecutions rising, and what the report termed 'popular sympathy' falling,[249] it was necessary to define the official attitude to a practice which challenged long-standing traditions of civil liberty and more recent aspirations to common citizenship. As Fisher admitted, 'the historical precedents for

---

[245] PRO PIN7/361 Circ. G94/37.

[246] V. George, *Social Security: Beveridge and After* (London, 1968), 97.

[247] *Report of the Committee on Abuse of Social Security Benefits* [Fisher] Cmnd. 5228 (1973), 198.

[248] Ibid. 276. 'Table 2, Supplementary Benefit Fraud. How cases considered in December 1971 came to light.'

[249] Ibid. 140.

official encouragement of delation are unattractive. It would not conduce to good relations within the community if neighbours were encouraged to inform on neighbours.'[250] On the other hand, such denouncements, together with information gathered more directly from people in the area, could not be ignored. In the case of single mothers, for instance:

People gossip, and inquiries of this nature are likely to reveal to neighbours that the woman concerned is on supplementary benefit and is suspected of cohabitation. We share the distaste which has been widely expressed for this method of inquiry, and for the use of neighbours as witnesses, but we consider that investigation would be unduly hampered if it were to be forbidden.[251]

In the end, the report came to the 'clear conclusion that there should be no official encouragement of informing'.[252] The only solution to the state's embarrassment was to transfer the moral responsibility to the informers themselves. The state could deny that it was asking for such denouncements, and also that it was refusing to read them. By this heroic double negative its hands could be kept clean whilst the campaign against fraud was prosecuted with renewed vigour.

There remained the issue of the exchange of confidential information between the national and local authority welfare agencies. The various groups of home visitors whose labours the National Assistance Board had once tried to co-ordinate were now in unitary social work departments and increasingly aware of their distinct responsibilities towards the poor. As Fisher recognized, 'it is difficult for these social workers, who generally rely on the co-operation of clients and mutual confidence, to disclose to the appropriate Ministry details of circumstances of mis-use of funds or fraudulent application for benefits'.[253] Since the foundation of the Charity Organisation Society a century earlier, the lateral transfer of confidential knowledge had been a key device in the perpetual war against mendicancy. Now this exchange was drying up—less than 4 per cent of supplementary benefit fraud cases in 1971 stemmed from information from 'other Government Depts. and local authorities'[254]—and there was a danger that the increasingly self-confident welfare professionals would develop an adversarial role towards the state income support system. An obligation to maintain the trust of clients could easily merge with an ambition to advance their interests in encounters with an increasingly stressed means-test bureaucracy. All that Fisher could do was exhort local offices

to take steps to ensure that social workers understand the necessity for what the Departments do in order to prevent and detect abuse, and that it is in the interest of claimants themselves and of the community of which they form a part that

---

[250] *Report of the Committee on Abuse of Social Security Benefits* 198 ('delation' was a somewhat obscure term for informing against).
[251] Ibid. 142–3. [252] Ibid. 198.
[253] Ibid. 199. [254] Ibid. 276.

such measures should be taken, and to dispel any idea that in the matter of abuse the concern of social workers and others should be regarded as in some way different from or opposed to that of the Departments.[255]

The only leverage which the offices possessed was the shared respect of one professional for another. Just as the social workers were now obtaining degrees, so the benefit inspectors were being sent on university courses. Only by improving their ethical standards could they gain the confidence of those in possession of claimants' secrets: 'If the Departments are to secure the co-operation and sympathy which they require from social workers and other professional people, they must be scrupulous in the care with which they investigate any complaint by such people of improper or oppressive treatment of claimants.'[256]

For much of the early period of the welfare state, the performance of the economy obscured the growing conflict between privacy and bureaucracy. Directly or indirectly, the state was democratizing the capacity to maintain a 'determined reserve' amidst the pressures of urban living and mass communication. In daily relations with friends and neighbours and in occasional encounters with national or local government, it was becoming easier to patrol the boundaries of personal knowledge. All the while, however, the archive of personal information held by those paid out of the public purse was growing. For as long as unemployment and inflation were low, latent tensions could be absorbed by the culture of public trust which the Beveridge system had been designed to create. The Younger Report was commissioned just before the symptoms of malaise in the post-war economy turned into a full-scale illness. This partly explains why it failed so comprehensively to respond to the scale of the problem. Having begun by associating the anxiety about privacy with the legacy of totalitarian oppression, it concluded by endorsing the role of culture as a bulwark of individual liberty:

the law is only one of the factors determining the climate of a democratic society and it is often only a minor factor. Education, professional standards and the free interplay of ideas and discussion through the mass media and the organs of political democracy can do at least as much as the law to establish and maintain standards of behaviour.[257]

The inquiry endorsed a polarity between the public and the private realms which was no longer tenable. Having been forbidden by its terms of reference to address the behaviour of the police and security services, it too readily assumed that the state was not an issue in the remaining topics of investigation. The only area in which the report accepted that change required additional government intervention was that of new technology. Computers and electronic surveillance devices justified legislation, but other difficulties could be dealt with by more traditional safeguards. The press, whose alleged intru-

---

[255] *Report of the Committee on Privacy*, 199.
[256] Ibid. 199.   [257] Ibid. 206.

sion into the lives of the well connected had led to the inquiry, was seen more as a remedy than a problem. Otherwise there remained the great standby of 'professional standards'. However, as we have seen there were increasing conflicts between individual and bureaucratic models of professional behaviour, and between the paternalism inherent in the professional ideal and the rights asserted by the individual citizen of the welfare state. In many respects, the greatest beneficiaries of the Beveridge reforms had been the middle class, both as recipients of free benefits and services and as employees of the structures which supplied them. Their corporate values were now to resolve the threats their work posed to the discreet reserve of the less privileged citizens.

At issue—as in one form or another it had been for a century—was the permeable boundary between privacy and secrecy. The post-war welfare reforms embodied a reclassification of the personal archive of the poor as legitimate privacy rather than illegitimate secrecy. Prosperity plus bureaucratized welfare engendered the sense of public trust which the transition demanded. However, growing economic dislocation together with intensifying difficulties of official confidentiality threatened to reverse the process, with clients of the bureaucracies losing control of the transmission of their secrets and their neighbours communicating them more freely to inquiring inspectors. The appeal to culture which concluded the Younger Report could only obscure this dilemma. It mistook the aspiration for the remedy, preventing a clear analysis of the implications of the growing state archive, and thus, in a broader sense, inhibiting a broader understanding of the relationship between private and official secrecy.

Secrecy and the Maiden

On 5 February 1960, the newly elected Member of Parliament for Finchley, dressed in a coat frock of bronze and black brocade, buttoned down the front, with a black velvet collar, rose to give her maiden speech.[258] Margaret Thatcher had passed Napoleon's first test of success, the possession of luck. As soon as she won her seat in the 1959 General Election, she came second in the ballot for private members' Bills. She was too ambitious to waste the opportunity on an idiosyncratic venture, and in too much of a hurry to observe the convention of devoting her first words in the House to an uncontentious issue. Instead she consulted the Whips' Office on an appropriate topic, and launched her political career in a widely reported twenty-seven minute peroration, made virtually without notes, introducing the Public Bodies (Admission of the Press to Meetings) Bill.

[258] R. Lewis, *Margaret Thatcher* (London, 1985), 26. Also E. Money, *Margaret Thatcher, First Lady of the House* (London, 1975), 57–8.

The Bill, which became an Act later in the year,[259] was the first effective attempt to limit official secrecy since an earlier and widely evaded attempt to open up local government sponsored by the Labour MP Arthur Henderson in 1908.[260] Indeed, for the next three decades almost all the legislation to reduce closed government and protect the secrets of private citizens was the responsibility either of Margaret Thatcher personally, or of administrations which she led. Labour and Liberal backbenchers introduced more Bills, often of a more radical nature, but she actually changed the law. Her entry into the lists of open government warriors was the consequence of Conservative anger at the behaviour of a number of Labour-controlled local authorities during a newspaper dispute in 1958, when they had excluded strike-breaking journalists from council meetings.[261] The target was the unions rather than the rights of the press, but the rhetoric ran all the way back to Bentham: ' "Publicity is the greatest and most effective check against any arbitrary action" ', she proclaimed, 'That is one of the fundamental rights of the subject.'[262] Appeals to efficiency were dismissed in the name of a higher principle: 'the paramount function of this distinguished House is to safeguard civil liberties rather than to think that administrative convenience should take first place in law.'[263]

A number of left-wing Labour MPs were attracted to this eloquent defence of democracy and free speech, especially another forceful young woman, Barbara Castle, who made common cause with the Member for Finchley throughout the passage of the Bill. Ranged against them were the spokesmen for local government, who made a determined attempt to defeat the legislation both in the debates and in the accompanying procedural manoeuvres.[264] Although the county councils were known to be unhappy about the Bill, it was the municipal authorities which led the opposition. Barbara Castle tried to claim open government for her party, arguing that 'it is conservatism which needs secrecy to survive and not socialism',[265] but all the serious hostility came from her own side. Charles Pannell, for instance, ex-Mayor of Erith and Vice-President of the Association of Municipal Corporations, complimented Margaret Thatcher on 'rather a beautiful maiden speech', and then denounced her Bill on the grounds that it would destroy the 'camaraderie' between opposing councillors, who would henceforth be tempted to play to the gallery, and that it would fatally compromise the neutrality of the officials who served them. There was

[259] Under the slightly shortened title of the Public Bodies (Admission to Meetings) Act.

[260] For a summary of the legislation in this field, see T. Harrison, *Access to Information in Local Government* (London, 1988), 1–12. On the long-term tradition of secrecy in local government, see Williams, 'Official Secrecy in England', 42–3.

[261] H. Young, *One of Us* (London, 1990), 44–5.

[262] *Hansard*, 5th Series, 616, 5 Feb. 1960, col. 1351. The quote was from Lord Franks.

[263] Ibid., cols. 1357–8.

[264] On the complex negotiations behind the scenes during the passage of the bill, see, Money, *Margaret Thatcher*, 57–9.

[265] *Hansard*, 5th Series, 616, 5 Feb. 1960, col. 1391.

altogether too much exposure of government in the modern age. 'I reject the Bill', he concluded, 'out of my experience and a deep conviction that reticence is a fine and decent quality, far more desirable that the garish desire for publicity which seems to oppress our civilisation today.'[266] Granting access to the press in the name of freedom of information cut little ice with these practical socialists. Arthur Skeffington, who held the resonant title of Joint President of the British Section of the Council of European Municipalities and Council of Commonwealth Municipalities, regarded newspapers as just another form of capitalism. There were no holy principles involved in the issue, and no case for giving 'a special privilege to representatives of a commercial organisation, for, after all, the Press exists to sell newspapers'.[267]

In place of statutory rights, the Labour local government representatives argued for custom and informality. What was needed, asserted the former Mayor of Acton, was 'material trust, confidence and respect between the local public body and the Press. This can only be achieved by understanding and by working together over long period of years and not by any Act of Parliament.'[268] It was an insult to minority parties to suppose them incapable of exposing wrongdoing by controlling groups on councils, and a misunderstanding of the nature of local democracy to insist on legal safeguards. If there had been occasional abuses in the past, these could be dealt with by a code of practice. Instead of insensitive intervention by the courts, it would be sufficient to 'leave it to the good sense of locally elected bodies to decide the actual detailed course of action they will take'.[269] The appeal to culture rather than law, to anonymity rather than publicity, to efficiency rather than communication, replicated to the point of parody the arguments put forward in defence of Whitehall secrecy. What central and local government shared were tightly knit groups of individuals secure in their power and expecting the trust of those on whose behalf they exercised it. Party ideology was of significance only in that it permitted the Labour councillors to be overtly dismissive of the rights of the press. What separated the two layers of the political process was the persuasive tradition of honourable discretion in the administrative grades of the civil service, and the much weaker sense of professional identity in the town halls. The councils of Erith and Acton lacked friends and influence and thus were doomed to be pioneers of open government.

In practice, the councils soon developed new techniques for evading the spirit of the Act, and further legislation was required in 1972 and 1980.[270] The conflict did nothing to enhance their standing in the Conservative Party; what-

---

[266] *Hansard*, col. 1420.
[267] Ibid., col. 1380.
[268] Ibid., col. 1376.
[269] Ibid., cols. 1372–3.
[270] Harrison, *Access to Information in Local Government*, 9–12. For early warnings on the extent of non-compliance, see *The Times* (31 Dec. 1962), 11. Also Delbridge and Smith, *Consuming Secrets*, 15–19; Williams, 'Official Secrecy in England', 43; Wraith, *Open Government*, 39–40.

ever doubts Margaret Thatcher may have had about local authorities before she made her maiden speech can only have been confirmed by the attitudes it exposed. This entrenched indifference to rights of information in the municipalities was important on its own terms, given the greatly enhanced role of locally administered welfare, housing, and educational services in the lives of the mass of the population. Corruption scandals in the early 1970s revealed how abuse of trust could flourish amidst the continuing secrecy of many local authority committees.[271] The issue also reflected a more general dilemma for the democratic left. Tony Benn argued in a 1970 Fabian tract that 'the theme of publicity versus secrecy should be a natural one for a future Labour Government',[272] but there was little in the record of the preceding quarter of a century to support this expectation. In office, under both Attlee and Wilson, the Labour Party had showed an instinctive deference to the culture of official secrecy and a willingness to evoke the cry of national security when faced with both overseas and domestic problems. Wilson willingly deployed MI5 against the seamen's strike in 1966,[273] and famously declined to describe the machinery of secrecy in his otherwise exhaustive account of the process of government.[274] He cited with approval Macmillan's reassertion of the tradition of clothing secrecy in secrecy, gave two brief paragraphs on the structure of control, and concluded: 'The prime minister is occasionally questioned on matters arising out of his responsibility. His answers may be regarded as uniformly uninformative. There is no further information that can usefully or properly be added before bringing this Chapter to an end.'[275]

Even in opposition, the Labour Party's practices mirrored those of the state. 'It is difficult to convey to modern readers,' writes the veteran journalist John Cole, 'or even to younger journalists, the secrecy which enshrouded such bodies as Labour's National Executive Committee in the fifties and early sixties.'[276] Both the main political parties, together with the trade unions who were bound ever-more tightly into the corporate state, regarded 'all their meetings as gatherings of a Masonic Lodge'.[277] For socialists detached from the traditional structures of the Labour movement, there was a seamless quality about the behaviour of government and opposition, regardless of which side happened to be holding power. In 1972 Richard Crossman reviewed his recent experience in and out of office:

One problem we face is the English addiction to secrecy. The Shadow Cabinet meets (officially) in secret. So do the Cabinet and the N.E.C. We have to have all our battles,

---

[271] P. Fennell, 'Local Government Corruption in England and Wales', in M. Clarke (ed.), *Corruption: Causes, Consequences and Control* (London, 1983), 18–19.

[272] *The New Politics: A Socialist Renaissance*, cited in T. Benn, *Office Without Power: Diaries, 1968–72* (London, 1989), App. V, p. 515.

[273] Aubrey, *Who's Watching You*, 43; E. P. Thompson, *Writing by Candlelight* (London, 1980), 159–62.

[274] See Ch. 9 of Wilson, *The Governance of Britain* (London, 1977 edn.), 204–5.

[275] Ibid. 205.

[276] J. Cole, *As It Seemed to Me* (rev. edn., London, 1996), 27.   [277] Ibid. 27.

not on the floor of the House of Commons with the Tories present, but in our own party enclaves where only the comrades are present, and where the issue can really be discussed . . . and it is this which makes our addiction to secrecy so damaging—because democracy only functions if the democratic process takes place in public.[278]

Growing concern about the extent of public secrecy became the subject of a series of reports by established or newly created pressure groups from the mid-1960s onwards. In one of these, State Research's *Review of Security and the State, 1978*, E. P. Thompson mounted a fierce attack on the record of the left since 1945, accusing it of 'dulling the nerve of outrage' by implementing or failing effectively to oppose a major extension of confidential government. Beginning with Attlee's willing embrace of the machinery of the Cold War, the Party had pursued the wrong kind of national consensus:

The bureaucratic statism towards which Labour politicians increasingly drifted carried with it a rhetoric in which the State, in *all* its aspects, was seen as a public good, a defence of working people, or of the little man, against private vested interests. The dividing line between the Welfare State and the Police State became obscure, and bureaucracy, in every form, waxed fat in this obscurity.[279]

In one sense, this was a gross exaggeration. The welfare state had in many respects enhanced the capacity of the traditional constituents of the Labour Party to determine the limits of what was known of their lives, and whilst control of the expanding public archive of personal information was causing increasing difficulties, there were no grounds for associating the social services or the Supplementary Benefit Commission with, for instance, the East German STASI which had been called into being in the name of socialism during these years. Yet Thompson was right to identify an incomprehension of the problems inherent in the enlargement of the post-war bureaucracy as the connecting link between the realms of social and national security. The issue of obscurity had a double charge. On the one hand, the conventions of official reserve had been extended rather than challenged by the increased responsibilities of central and local government. On the other hand, the traditional refusal to make public the extent of blocked communication had prevented an effective assessment of the damage that was being caused. Secrecy concealed the failings of the post-war British state, and the failure to understand the machinery of state made it impossible to grasp the problem of secrecy.

By the time Wilson led the Labour Party back to power the cracks were beginning to show in the structures created by his predecessor. Declining international authority combined with growing economic problems at home

---

[278] R. Crossman, *Inside View* (London, 1972), 99.

[279] E. P. Thompson, 'Introduction', in State Research, *Review of Security and the State, 1978* (London, 1978). The essay was reprinted as 'The Secret State' in Thompson's *Writing by Candlelight*, 149–80.

were eroding the passive trust in government which Attlee had inherited and exploited. As Bernard Crick's *The Reform of Parliament* observed in 1964:

It is no accident that a rash of demands has suddenly sprung up for legal safeguards against all sorts of actions hitherto trusted to the discretion of public authorities; phone-tapping, immigration procedures, press access to council meetings, employment policy regarding race, the 'right' of assembly etc.[280]

The concept of 'civil liberties' began to gain currency in the debate about the relation between the state and society.[281] Margaret Thatcher's initiative prefaced a series of unofficial Bills on privacy,[282] and a growing discussion of the practice of government and the rights of citizens. Four months after her maiden speech, she was one of a minority of Conservatives to vote in favour of a motion urging the government to implement the Wolfenden Committee's recommendations on the legalization of private homosexual acts.[283] In this context, the tradition of concealing knowledge (of the knowledge) of such practices was breaking down under pressure of a series of highly publicized prosecutions and the association of homosexuality with national security following the defection of Burgess and MacLean.[284] As the journalist and Conservative MP Bill Deedes explained,

there had been little or no public discussion or report on this subject. Until lately, the English have cherished a reluctance—which is widely recognised—to talk freely on subjects such as this. Perhaps this national characteristic and this lack of discussion is why we now find ourselves in this difficulty.[285]

The solution, which was delayed until the indifference of Labour traditionalists such as Callaghan and Wilson could be overcome,[286] was to reverse the path taken by official secrecy. Under the 1967 Sexual Offences Act, the force of the law was to be replaced for consenting adults by the discipline of what Wolfenden had described as 'strong social forces'.[287]

Elsewhere, little changed. The absence of effective reform of the state was

---

[280] Crick, *The Reform of Parliament*, 8; Christoph, 'A Comparative View', 28.

[281] Harrison, *The Transformation of British Politics*, 146.

[282] See the Bills introduced by Lord Mancroft (14 Feb. 1961), Alexander Lyon (8 Feb. 1967), and Brian Walden (26 Nov. 1969). Mancroft's Bill was specifically concerned with intrusion by the media, but Lyon's and especially Walden's, which was based on a draft by *Justice*, attempted a much broader defence of privacy.

[283] The motion was introduced by another ballot winner, the Labour MP Kenneth Robinson. It was defeated by 213 votes to 99.

[284] P. Higgins, *Heterosexual Dictatorship: Male Homosexuality in Postwar Britain* (London, 1996), 15–140. S. Jeffrey-Poulter, *Peers, Queers and Commons* (London, 1991), 13–72.

[285] *Hansard*, 5th Series, 625, 29 June 1960, col. 1462. J. Weeks, *Coming Out: Homosexual Politics in Britain from the Nineteenth Century to the Present* (rev. edn., London, 1990), 162.

[286] See Richard Crossman's account of the debate in Cabinet when Roy Jenkins finally persuaded them to give official support to Abse's backbench Bill. R. Crossman, entry for 27 Oct. 1966, *The Diaries of a Cabinet Minister* (London, 1975), ii. 97.

[287] Jeffrey-Poulter, *Peers, Queers and Commons*, 30.

associated with a particular construction of professionalism which characterized this era. It was not just that the Labour Party was still in the throes of its long love affair with the expert which it had inherited from its Fabian ancestors; nor that the Conservatives once back in office had become similarly enamoured. It was rather that the perceived malfunctions of the national and local bureaucracies appeared not to question but rather to endorse a further extension of the professional ideal. The recourse to the strengths of those who were members of the chartered professions or who claimed professional status within public service, was made in the name of modernization. In an era in which official bureaucracy was at long last beginning to attract obloquy for its self-perpetuating conservatism, the professional ideal offered a combination of meritocratic recruitment, scientific practice, and dedication to the common good. It could prevent public service from turning in on itself, and through the tradition of self-policed conduct could supply a guarantee of ethical behaviour in the increasingly complex dealings with private citizens. If it did not guarantee open government, it did at least proffer open minds within the existing structures, and a self-policing defence against the abuse of bureaucratic power. Those on the right could ease their fears of the expanding state without recourse to further legislation; those on the left could advocate progressive reforms without sacrificing their faith in the role of government.

There were, however, two particular difficulties with this solution. The first was that the latent tension between the autonomous individual and the corporate institution was becoming increasingly exposed as professional practice itself became bureaucratized. It was more difficult to sustain the myth of disinterested public service, and less possible to contrast the personal discourse of professional to client with the hierarchical processes of central and local government. This was as true of the nuclear scientists as it was of the personal social workers. The second was that the professional ideal reinforced rather than undermined the subordinate relationship between the citizen and the state. The ideal was in essence an exclusive construction, to be professed only by the minority capable of undergoing the technical and ethical initiation procedures. Its promotion conflicted with the increasingly vocal assertion of individual rights on the part of the least significant of the members of the new welfare society. The appeal to the culture of professionalism evaded this challenge, but at the same time confined the momentum for reform. The protests were mounted by experts in the name of experts.

In 1956 the forerunner of all the modern pressure groups for open government issued its manifesto. The Campaign for the Limitation of Secret Police Powers was called into being to protest about the abuses of positive vetting. It attracted a galaxy of the alternative great and good, including Henry Moore, J. B. Priestley, Kenneth Tynan, Peter Ustinov, Bertrand Russell, Christopher Fry, and the Wegdwood Benns *père et fils*. According to its pamphlet, *The Secret Police and You*, the organization was the product of a 'spontaneous concern' about the undermining of civil liberties through the use of 'denunciations by unidentified informers and allegations by the secret police.'[288] There was a public meeting in Caxton Hall, but little more. The problem, as the Campaign recognized, was that 'there has not yet been a "public outburst"; and nothing less is needed to reverse the machine which authority has set in motion'.[289] Such an outburst never came on this or any other issue in the period. The connections between the interests of individual citizens in enhancing their command over their lives and what was known about them, and the instincts of government to control and conceal, were never properly articulated. By the time the more radical demands began to surface in the early 1970s, the consensus about the role of the state which would have sustained fundamental reform, was dissolving in the face of accelerating national decline.

[288] Campaign for the Limitation of Secret Police Powers, *The Secret Police and You* (London, 1956), 1. The particular case which provoked the launching of the Campaign was the attempt to dismiss a scientist from Imperial Chemicals. The Campaign also took up the case of Ronald Frankenberg, a young anthropologist refused entry to St Vincent for alleged Communist sympathies. He was forced to abandon field-work in the West Indies, and instead conducted research into British community life—see n. 194 above.

[289] Ibid. 15.

| # Secrecy and Reform, 1972–1989

Implicit Authorization

At the beginning of the fourth volume of his 1972 report, Lord Franks recorded a moment of enlightenment. His committee on Section 2 of the Official Secrets Act had spent a fortnight interrogating the leading members of the civil service, and finally he understood the relation between law and practice: 'The doctrine to which we have been listening is that every civil servant may be authorised, either by the consent of his superior or by his duty in carrying out the job which he is doing, to communicate to the outside world.'[1] At the head of government departments, 'Ministers are certainly more or less self-authorising', and below them, a senior civil servant would in most cases 'authorise himself in terms of the job he was doing'.[2] The 'doctrine of implicit authorisation' might appear to conflict with the terms of both the 1911 Act and the declarations which were signed on entering and leaving government employment. However, explained Lord Franks,

if you look at the language of the Act itself, which only talks about what is unauthorised and not what is authorised, you can get this doctrine of authorisation, explicit and implicit authorisation, self-authorisation, out of it; it is consistent with the Act. Therefore the practice has built up in the Civil Service over time which from their point of view explains to them what they are doing.[3]

Lord Franks's penetration of the mystery of official secrecy marked not the invention of the doctrine but rather its arrival in the public arena. Little notice had been taken of a fleeting exposition in the pre-war Select Committee on the Official Secrets Acts.[4] Now, full weight was given to the account which had been extracted from the Permanent Secretaries. Amidst the obfuscation normally surrounding the topic, the doctrine of implicit authorization possessed the sig-

---

[1] *Departmental Committee on Section 2 of the Official Secrets Act 1911* [Franks] (London, 1972), iv. 9.
[2] Ibid. On the doctrine, see also de Smith, 'Official Secrecy and External Relations in Britain: the Law and its Context', 327.
[3] *Departmental Committee on Section 2 of the Official Secrets Act 1911*, iv. 9.
[4] *Report from the Select Committee on The Official Secrets Acts* (1939), 16–17. Evidence of the Attorney-General, Sir Donald Somervell.

nal virtue of describing the real world. In particular, it accounted for the disparity between the exponential increase in official communication since 1911 and the continuing infrequency of prosecutions under Section 2.[5] The still unnameable Director-General of the Security Service insisted in his evidence that 'it is an official secret if it is in an official file',[6] yet he was failing to prevent the network of formal and informal contacts between government and the press becoming daily more elaborate. The Franks Committee had been established partly in response to the concerns about civil service secrecy raised by the 1968 Fulton Report, and partly as a consequence of trenchant criticisms of the Act made in February 1971 by the judge in the trial of Jonathan Aitken and three others for publishing in the *Sunday Telegraph* confidential information about the conduct of the Nigerian Civil War.[7] The strength of the doctrine was that it allayed fears about the closure of government and refuted claims that the law was inoperable.

Lord Franks himself combined a legendary personal reticence with a wide experience of the official machine and a firm belief in open government.[8] He was attuned to the outlook of those he was interrogating, and alert to the significance of his discovery. 'The whole doctrine of implicit authorisation', he suggested to Sir William Armstrong, the head of the home civil service, 'has been constructed as a way of living on the basis of what the Act says.'[9] It represented an unobtrusive accommodation of the law to the pressures of modern democracy. Just as the state was first driven to legislate in 1889 by mistrust of the lower reaches of the civil service, so the doctrine was modulated by seniority. Sir James Dunnett, the Permanent Secretary of the department responsible for the Admiralty clerks and artisans who had caused such concern nearly a century earlier, explained the double standard:

To be quite honest my experience is that below deputy secretary civil servants have jolly little direct contact with journalists—they may occasionally meet them at some cocktail party laid on by the Ministry, but in the average Government Department the contacts between journalists and civil servants, except for top levels, are pretty few and far between.[10]

Those who had survived the entry procedures to the administrative sector and had spent two or three decades gaining promotion could safely be trusted to authorize themselves under the Act. 'If you cannot rely upon them to have a reasonable measure of discretion as to how they deal with journalists,' argued

---

[5] Between 1945 and 1971 there were twenty-three prosecutions under Section 2 of the Act, involving a total of thirty-four defendants, of whom two-thirds were civil servants. Wraith, *Open Government*, 16–17.

[6] *Departmental Committee on Section 2 of the Official Secrets Act 1911*, iii. 249.

[7] D. G. T. Williams, 'Official Secrecy and the Courts', in P. R. Glazebrook (ed.), *Reshaping the Criminal Law* (London, 1978), 162; Aitken, *Officially Secret*, p. 198; Thomas, *Espionage and Secrecy*, 208–9.

[8] A. Danchev, *Oliver Franks: Founding Father* (Oxford, 1993), 162–3, 196–7.

[9] *Departmental Committee on Section 2 of the Official Secrets Act 1911*, iii. 107.

[10] Ibid. 90.

Dunnett, 'I think there is something lacking in them as under secretaries or deputy secretaries.'[11] The great majority of government employees would never be exposed to the temptation of cocktail parties, and would be silenced by the law or internal regulation if subjected to some other pressure to communicate with the world outside.

There was nothing unique in this double standard. The contemporary French civil service allowed its senior officials far more latitude than their subordinates. But across the Channel the licence was public knowledge, not least because the upper ranks still enjoyed the right abandoned by British civil servants a century earlier of writing in the press under their own names.[12] At home, all contact with journalists was unattributable, and Franks's belated identification of the practice did not of itself resolve the problems associated with it. There were grounds for arguing that the doctrine was revealed at just the moment when it could no longer paper over the cracks in the edifice of official secrecy. In practice, it reinforced rather than qualified the power of the state to set the rules of communication. Where the Act gave officials the right to determine what the public should know, so the unwritten rules governing implicit authorization were their private possession. The existence of the doctrine was not admitted until questions were asked, and its actual operation remained shrouded in darkness.[13] This redoubling of official reserve intensified long-standing difficulties. Most obviously, Dunnett's model of relations with the press was increasingly inapplicable to the broad swathe of government service which now had intricate contacts with the public beyond the confines of Whitehall and its tightly organized lobby system. Hundreds of thousands of civil servants were creating archives and taking decisions which were of keen interest to innumerable local newspapers and specialist magazines. Junior officials could gain little guidance from an unwritten convention, and in the absence of any confidence in their right to authorize themselves, sought safety in silence. For their part, correspondents were frustrated by the absence of reliable maps of the terrain upon which they worked. The line between authorized and illegal communication was invisible until it was crossed. 'The net result', complained the Press Council, 'is that both journalists and Civil Servants spend their lives walking through an ancient minefield. Most of the mines are now dud, but one may at any moment blow up in their faces.'[14]

The insecurity of the press was matched by growing uncertainty amongst those who sought to control the flow of information. Self-authorization was being eaten away by self-doubt. Dunnett himself became ensnared in double negatives as he attempted to justify the status quo: 'a good deal of thought has

[11] *Departmental Committee on Section 2 of the Official Secrets Act 1911*, iii. 90.

[12] D. Clark, 'Open Government: The French Experience', *Political Quarterly*, 57, 3 (July–Sept. 1986), 280–1.

[13] Williams, 'Official Secrecy and the Courts', 162; R. M. Thomas, 'The Secrecy and Freedom of Information Debates in Britain', *Government and Opposition*, 17 (1982), 303.

[14] *Departmental Committee on Section 2 of the Official Secrets Act 1911*, ii. 316.

been given in Whitehall over certainly the last five or six years to this whole issue, and I think I would be wrong not to say that the corporate judgment of my colleagues is that a substantial amount would be lost if one did not have broadly the present scope of the Act.'[15] The confident defence of honourable secrecy mounted in earlier decades by Warren Fisher and Edward Bridges was being replayed in a much more minor key. Self-censorship had always been presented as a form of self-denial, but now the element of personal suffering was invading the principle itself. A succession of Permanent Secretaries confessed to anxiety about the role of the law in official communication. When Sir William Armstrong was asked whether an unused Act was a bad thing, he replied that it was 'a conclusion to which I found myself coming from time to time, and I have personally tried to wrestle with this'.[16] These long nights of the soul had rarely afflicted his predecessors. No serving official was prepared to abandon the system, but none were capable of delivering a ringing endorsement.

The difficulty facing Armstrong and his colleagues was that the growing argument for reducing secrecy about secrecy was matched by an intensification of the pressures which had led to the creation of the original structure. Whilst the civil service was gradually losing the confidence of the electorate, the mandarins were less inclined to invest trust in their staff than ever they had been. The Cold War remained a corrosive influence, with the head of the Security Service informing the Franks Committee that 'there is virtually no information about this country or indeed about any country in the west which the Russian Intelligence Service is not anxious to obtain'.[17] The fears which had been given flesh in the late 1940s and early 1950s still stalked the corridors of Whitehall. At any level there was the risk that, as Sir Douglas Allen of the Treasury put it, 'the code of the service may not be all that strong against a man who has another code of his own'.[18] The dangers multiplied in proportion to the distance from the centre. It was the modern-day equivalent of the temporary writers who caused the greatest anxiety—the junior clerks who arrived without a history, the 'girls who get married, go off to have babies and then come back',[19] the tens of thousands of employees who viewed the civil service as not a vocation but a perch in a varied or truncated career. So little was known about the past or future of the typists that those employed on sensitive work were having to be re-vetted every year.[20] Such troublesome but indispensable staff were beyond the reach of convention or regulation. Explicit trust, let alone implicit authorization, had no abode at the penumbra of the system.

Under pressure, the mandarins seemed unable to specify anything. They could neither let go of the Official Secrets Act nor give a clear account of why and how it operated. All Armstrong could say when pressed on the limits of his

---

[15] Ibid. iii. 102. [16] Ibid. 121. [17] Ibid. 259.
[18] Ibid 158. [19] Ibid. 36. [20] Ibid. 73.

self-authorization was that, 'I do find it very difficult to define that line, but I have never found it difficult in practice to know when I was approaching it'.[21] If he could not describe the rules to himself, there seemed little prospect of the outside world reaching an understanding of the procedures which controlled their access to official information. The only guide was the unwritten tradition of the service which policed the boundaries of acceptable conduct. The notion of culture, which once had served as a guarantor of the honour of secrecy, now served only to deepen the obscurity with which it was surrounded. Sir Burke Trend, who as Secretary of the Cabinet shared with Armstrong the responsibility of setting the standards of official secrecy, defended the continuing existence of the Act on the grounds that 'I think in some rather indefinable way the climate changes if there is not a fairly absolute sanction at the end of the road'.[22] Not only the implementation but the very purpose of the legislation was and could only be implicit.

The year 1972 marked a turning-point in the relationship between the law and the communication of information. The Franks Report, which recommended the replacement of the catch-all Section 2 by a specific definition of the categories of official documents requiring legal protection, was published in September, just two months after the Younger Report on privacy. In the General Election of October 1974 Labour's manifesto was the first to include a commitment to open government,[23] and during the succeeding decade and a half all the major parties, together with an increasingly strident body of pressure groups, took up the cause of legislative reform in a variety of contexts. Scarcely a year passed without a Bill being presented to Parliament by the Government or a backbencher, and a series of important Acts found their way on to the Statute Book, culminating in 1989 in the first serious revision of the law on official secrecy since 1911. On the face of it, a sea change was taking place in attitudes to access to information. Deference to the right of the state to determine what it allowed into the public domain was in sharp decline, as was confidence in the ability of a range of government, professional, and commercial bodies to make responsible use of new technologies of storage and transmission. Before 1972 vocal concern had been confined to misuse of the Official Secrets Acts by the state and the invasion of privacy by the press. Thereafter the campaigns widened to incorporate the interests of consumers denied information about goods, householders unable to identify environmental dangers, and clients fearful that personal details were being abused by those who provided them with services.[24]

Each protest had its own motives and objectives, but there did appear a com-

---

[21] *Departmental Committee on Section 2 of the Official Secrets Act 1911*, iii.

[22] Ibid. 337.

[23] In 1970 the Conservative Manifesto had included a less specific commitment to eliminate unnecessary secrecy and review the Official Secrets Acts.

[24] For a summary of the broadening of the campaigns after 1972, see Michael, *The Politics of Secrecy*, 195.

mon theme. The culture of informal trust exemplified by the doctrine of implicit authorization was to be replaced by a far more explicit contract between modern citizens and every agency in possession of information derived from or relevant to them. The apprehensions and aspirations were summarized in calls for a broad Freedom of Information Act, a general protection of privacy, and a wholesale reform of the constitutional conventions which had hitherto denied the possibility of either. Bills were drawn up based on legislative forms which were becoming increasingly common in other liberal democracies, such as the Freedom of Information Acts which Australia, Canada, and New Zealand all passed in 1982.[25] The Campaign for Freedom of Information and Charter 88 demanded nothing less than a total transformation of the ways in which the rights of citizens were embodied in law. They sought to exploit an atmosphere of dissent and distrust to mount an epochal attack on the culture of unwritten powers and practices.

Franks himself had prefigured the scale of the agitation in his observation cited in the opening chapter of this book, that secrecy involved not just the law, but 'constitutional arrangements, political tradition, and national character, habit and ways of thought'.[26] There was a sense of a general crisis in the control of information, of a widespread breakdown of confidence in those with the power to block its communication. Both the malaise and the remedies were conceived in the widest terms. At the same time, it was far from obvious that the sequence of prospective or actual reforms did reflect a systematic analysis of the past or a coherent vision of the future. Neither Younger nor Franks endorsed the more general prescriptions put before them. The former denied the possibility of a general right of privacy, and the latter resisted the case for an all-embracing Freedom of Information Act. In both instances, the appeal to culture was a justification for limiting rather than expanding the legislative programme. From one perspective, the pair of reports, which were much the most substantial official inquiries into the control of information ever undertaken in this country, made a powerful case for breaking with constitutional convention; from another, they performed the time-honoured function of evoking unwritten tradition as a bulwark against radical change.

The difficulty of establishing a consistent perspective on the magnitude of the need for reform was compounded by three particular characteristics of the debate. At the outset, the position of the state was less straightforward than it might appear. In general terms, the issue was easily stated. As the editor of the *Evening Standard* told the Franks Committee, 'there is a growing alienation between the Government and the people. There is in our view a growing distance

---

[25] Australia enacted its Freedom of Information Action in March, Canada its Access to Information Act in June, and New Zealand its Official Information Act in December 1982. For compact surveys of this legislation, see R. Thomas, 'The Experience of Other Countries', in R. A. Chapman and M. Hunt (eds.), *Open Government* (London, 1989); R. Hozell, 'Freedom of Information in Australia, Canada, and New Zealand', *Public Administration*, 67 (Summer 1989), 189–210.

[26] See above, Ch. 1, p. 12.

between the governed and the governors.'[27] Support for this opinion was wide-spread and growing. Since at least the time of Suez, critics of the political process had argued that official secrecy and the attitudes which it embodied both symbolized and concealed the declining efficacy of government. Administrators and their political masters were out of touch with broader currents of change, and protected from exposure to modernizing forces by their ability to keep searching criticism at bay. Electors in turn were less and less willing to believe that they were engaged in a genuine dialogue with those who exercised power on their behalf. The solution was termed open government, which would replace the closed state, or freedom of information, which would compel the state to justify rather than assume secrecy. However, the boundaries of such objectives resisted definition. The events of 1972 marked a historic missed opportunity to articulate the relationship between the right of citizens to control what was known of their own affairs and their right to determine what they knew of the state's activities. Younger was forbidden to examine the invasion of privacy by public agencies, and subsequent attempts by Shirley Williams and others to engage in an integrated debate about both reports were frustrated.[28]

Furthermore, the state itself was becoming a contested category. Official secrecy was predicated on a single entity over which the writ of an all-embracing law could run. Together with making pension contributions, 'signing the Act' was one of the few ways of recognizing formally the existence of the civil service. The problems which had always been encountered at the frontiers of this realm, particularly in respect of private defence contractors, were becoming more complex as the state multiplied its engagement with industry and the professions, and its own forms became more diverse. The public encountered national and local bureaucrats in an ever-more varied range of contexts, each of which posed its own problems of communication. It was by no means obvious that the need to know about the content of meat inspectors' reports was of the same order and required the same legal or normative framework as the need to know about social workers' files, or that either had much in common with the right to learn the number and cost of nuclear warheads under construction. The challenge to the structure of official secrecy was in part a critique of a monolithic, exclusive conception of government which had been devised in the heyday of Victorian liberalism and no longer accorded with the aspirations of the late-twentieth-century citizen.[29] The argument advanced from both ends of the political spectrum, that blocked communication was a device to protect the private interest of an enclosed bureaucracy, could be met by dissolving the boundaries between professional and civilian administrators, or be-

---

[27] *Departmental Committee on Section 2 of the Official Secrets Act 1911*, iv. 45.
[28] Thomas, 'Freedom of Information in Britain', 297.
[29] Poggi, *The State*, 10.

tween public service and commercial enterprise. In either circumstance, the task of defining a consistent set of regulations to control the flow of public information became less rather than more straightforward.

As the state apparatus threatened to break up, so also did the community it was required to serve. A second apparently homogeneous factor in the reform campaign was the sense that the revolution in electronic communication was provoking a systemic failure in constructions designed for an age in which writing and filing letters were the characteristic forms of transmission and storage.[30] By their nature, telecommunications and computers connected people and linked information. Yet their impact was far from unifying. The private household became still more private as the home could supply access to knowledge and entertainment which previously required participation in a wider neighbourhood. In turn, the enclosed family encountered difficulties in controlling access to information in a more complex set of circumstances. Where once such issues as personal files and secret surveillance were confined to a limited number of public or qualified bodies, now they embraced an ever-broadening range of official, professional, and commercial agencies, each with their own methods and objectives. As this happened, the categories of citizen, client, and consumer began to appear much less stable than once they had been. Younger and Franks recognized the significance of technological changes which in 1972 were still in their infancy, but both based their inquiries and recommendations on divisions between the private and the public which were increasingly under threat. If general reform were to be possible, it could only be at the expense of generalized identities which previously had informed the approach to control.

A final problem lay with the reformers themselves. The great strength of the mounting campaign for greater freedom of information was the close match between form and content. The 1960s witnessed the emergence of a new force in the political process. Pressure groups were not a fresh invention. They had grown up alongside the modern liberal state and helped to create its key institutions[31]—as we have seen, the civil service itself had been deeply influenced in its formative phase by the agitation of the Administrative Reform Association a century earlier[32]—but during the first two Wilson administrations single-issue protest organizations began to move into the centre of the political stage. They were staffed for the most part by a fresh generation of university-educated activists who deployed their skills of analysis and advocacy in the press and the burgeoning electronic media. Their lifeblood was infor-

---

[30] For early warnings of the implications of computers for the control of personal information, see G. B. F. Niblett, 'Computers and Privacy', in B. C. Rowe (ed.) *Privacy, Computers and You* (Manchester, 1972), 17–23; P. Sieghart, *Privacy and Computers* (London, 1976), 58–76.

[31] On their role in the making of the post-Reform Act state, see Harrison, *The Transformation of British Politics*, 157–64.

[32] See above, Ch. 2, pp. 35–6.

mation, gathered from or communicated to the decision-makers.[33] Whereas the more conventional interest groups were content to exchange technical knowledge with civil servants behind closed doors,[34] the new protest organizations had a natural interest in open government, and frequently found themselves objecting to secrecy or exploiting leaks from politicians and civil servants.[35] In this sense, bodies such as the Outer Circle Policy Unit or the Campaign for Freedom of Information were at the heart of the new pressure-group movement. The success of parallel organizations in prising open the system assisted their work, and in turn, their agitation enhanced the powers of every other campaign.

Yet the pressure groups themselves reflected the fragmentation of the democratic process. Traditional party organizations with their all-embracing programmes were seen as less and less able to convey the interests of an increasingly diverse constituency.[36] The single-issue campaign was a symptom of the impoverishment of the political structure and raised acute questions about coherence and representation. If it was claimed that open government or major constitutional change would cure the crisis of legitimacy, it could also be argued that the objectives of the pressure groups were without focus and the methods were devoid of authority. James Callaghan, who was to exercise a profound influence over the Labour Party's remaining opportunities to implement reform before 1989, was one of the few non-governmental witnesses in the Franks inquiry broadly to advocate the retention of Section 2.[37] Central to his position was a view that the Popes of open government had no divisions. The noise in sections of the press was merely the chatter of well-connected journalists and professional activists who stoked up self-referential campaigns with no roots in the real world occupied by working people worried about jobs and prices. There was little substance in the protests and less votes in acceding to them. Once Labour regained power, the case for change would have to do battle with both the embrace of the civil service and the profound scepticism of politicians raised in the traditional democratic structures which were now under attack. If the declining confidence in the implicit systems of the established order offered the prospect of fundamental reform, those who sought to achieve it faced a serious problem in marshalling their forces during the remainder of the period.

[33] On the growing mutual dependence of pressure groups and government, with both sides increasingly dependent on the information the other could give, see Drewry and Butcher, *The Civil Service Today*, 184–6.

[34] G. Alderman, *Pressure Groups and Government in Great Britain* (London, 1984), 101.

[35] The growing engagement of pressure groups with the control of information is discussed in J. Cornford, 'The Right to Know Secrets', *Listener*, 100 (31 Aug. 1978), repr. in A. May and K. Rowan (eds.), *Inside Information* (London, 1982), 38. Also I. Galnoor, 'Government Secrecy: Exchanges, Intermediaries and Middlemen', *Public Administrative Review*, 35 (Jan.–Feb. 1975), 35–42; J. Jacob, 'Some Reflections on Governmental Secrecy', *Public Law* (1974), 26.

[36] Alderman, *Pressure Groups and Government in Great Britain*, 17.

[37] For his evidence, see *Departmental Committee on Section 2 of the Official Secrets Act 1911*, iv. 179–93.

Dickering and Dispute

Four days before Christmas 1988, the Home Secretary opened the Second Reading of a Bill which, he claimed, was 'bolder and more open than anything attempted by any Government since the war . . . The present law is both too wide and too weak. After 16 years of dickering and dispute since the Franks report, I believe the time has come to settle on a successor to section 2 of the Official Secrets Act of 1911.'[38] At the publication of the report, such a history was not anticipated. Despite doubts that it recommended too little or too much, there was broad agreement that legislation was inescapable. Edward Heath had entered office full of plans for civil service reform, and committed by his manifesto to 'eliminate unnecessary secrecy'.[39] He commissioned and formally welcomed the Franks Report, and could claim that only the fall of his Government prevented its implementation. His successor, Wilson, picked up the torch, and in October 1975 established a Cabinet Committee to plan the fulfilment of his manifesto pledge to open government.[40] The parties seemed divided only by the matter of urgency. Five years after the initial discussion of the report, the Opposition used a Supply Day to launch a fierce attack on Government inaction. No less a firebrand than Leon Brittan denounced Labour's arguments for caution as 'intellectually disreputable and politically cowardly', and argued that 'the very existence of the law as it stands faces the Press with an ever-present implied threat and helps to perpetuate the all-pervading atmosphere of secrecy that has for far too long pervaded British government'.[41]

If the professed objectives were shared, so also was the obvious obstacle to fundamental change. The most significant event following the Franks Report took place not at home but in the Middle East. The impact on the shaky British economy of the Gulf War and the attendant rise in oil prices stalled what remained of Heath's programme of reform,[42] and condemned the subsequent Wilson and Callaghan administrations to a life of short-term crisis management. Too much attention had to be paid to the outcome of government to

[38] *Hansard*, 6th Series, 144, 21 Dec. 1988, col. 460. For readers defeated by the Home Secretary's vocabulary, to 'dicker' is to engage in petty bargaining.

[39] Hennessy, *Whitehall*, 220–42; K. Theakston, 'The Heath Government, Whitehall and the Civil Service', in S. Ball and A. Seldon (eds.), *The Heath Government* (London, 1996), 100.

[40] The Committee, MISC 89, divided itself into two, one dealing with the Home Office's responsibility for the criminal aspects of the issue, the other with the Civil Service Department's responsibility for enhancing the quality of official communication. B. Donoughue, *Prime Minister* (London, 1987), 121–2; Kellner and Crowther Hunt, *The Civil Servants*, 266–7.

[41] *Hansard*, 5th Series, 951, 15 June 1978, col. 1270–1.

[42] The record suggests that Heath's enthusiasm for reforming the process (as distinct from the structure) of the civil service, and for attacking the traditions of secrecy, evaporated soon after taking office. See Theakston, 'The Heath Government, Whitehall and the Civil Service', 75–105.

permit the investment of time and energy in the issue of process.[43] Until 1979 the mandarins were allowed by the politicians to set the agenda in the case of both secrecy and the organizational changes recommended by Fulton.[44] They were able to turn to their advantage the view that progress was as much a matter of culture as of law. During and after the major inquiries, significant changes were taking place without high-profile Parliamentary intervention. In 1973, for instance, civil servants were for the first time shown on television at work discussing a new Bill with politicians and interest-groups. The veil covering the budgeting process was lifted in the early 1970s with the publication of an annual White Paper outlining the Government's expenditure strategy. Elsewhere, greater consultation at the early stages of legislation was being encouraged by the device of Green Papers, which were introduced in 1967 and used widely by the Heath administration.[45] More advice was sought from outside Whitehall, openings for professional experts were created in key areas, and ministers expanded the practice of appointing their own advisors to their private offices.[46] Within the civil service, the written code of conduct, ESTACODE, now placed a positive emphasis on communication with the outside world. The section on 'Official Information' began: 'The need for greater openness in the work of Government is widely accepted.'[47] Civil servants were enjoined to make the 'fullest possible exposition' of government policies to Parliament and the electorate, and to create a 'better public understanding' about the process of decision-making.

This solution to the problem of change was unobtrusive but also unstable. There remained deep uncertainty about the relation between attitudes and beliefs and current or future law. On the one hand, critics of Franks argued that decisive legal reform was essential if the culture was to be shaken out of its complacency.[48] On the other, Whitehall urged that the potential for internal advance was sufficient to render unnecessary further legislation. In either case, the long-term role of the Official Secrets Act was increasingly unclear. The continuing capacity of Section 2 to inflame its opponents and embarrass the government was demonstrated within weeks of the appearance of the Franks Report when detectives raided the offices of the *Railway Gazette* in search of the source of a leaked review of railway closures which had been published by the *Sunday Times*, whose editor was then interviewed and cautioned under

---

[43] P. Hennessy, 'Oiling the Machine', in B. Pimlott, A. Wright, and T. Flower (eds.), *The Alternative* (London, 1990), 180.

[44] On the Administrative Class determining what of Fulton was to be implemented, see Kellner and Crowther-Hunt, *The Civil Servants*, 98; Theakston, *The Civil Service since 1945*, 96.

[45] H. Street, 'Secrecy and the Citizen's Right to Know: A British Civil Libertarian Perspective', in T. M. Franck and E. Weisbrand (eds.), *Secrecy and Foreign Policy* (New York, 1974), 340.

[46] C. Seymour-Ure, 'Great Britain', in I. Gilnoor (ed.), *Government Secrecy in Democracies* (New York, 1977), 158–69. For a more general account of the direction of change, see R. Clarke, *New Trends in Government* (London, 1971), 104–7.

[47] Cited in Wraith, *Open Government*, 33.

[48] See e.g. Street, 'Secrecy and the Citizen's Right to Know', 350.

the Act.[49] This heavy-handed use of legal machinery to deal with what was little more than a passing political irritation merely endorsed the widespread view that the Act was becoming unworkable in its present form. Labour's response to this dilemma on its resumption of office in 1974 was to adopt a policy of determined inaction. With the prospect of a new Bill receding over the horizon, it quietly decided to exploit the discretionary powers of the Attorney-General not to sanction any further use of Section 2 except in the most grave circumstances.[50] After a century of extending official secrecy with a minimum of debate, its central feature was being abolished without formal announcement.

Whilst the law was falling further into disrepute, public respect for the civil service continued to decline.[51] The worsening economy both postponed reform and undermined resistance to it. The Treasury's slow moves towards openness stalled as economic indicators became identified with national survival.[52] Labour's enthusiasm for a Freedom of Information Act rapidly cooled when Roy Jenkins, as Home Secretary, paid a fact-finding visit to the United States in January 1975, and convinced himself that it would impose unacceptable costs on an already overstretched budget.[53] At the same time the machinery of state, which outwardly appeared little altered by the series of inquiries, was an easy scapegoat for national failure.[54] In 1970 William Armstrong conceded in a survey of his service that increasingly it was perceived as remote and staffed by mandarins,[55] and events during the following decade did nothing to soften this image. As one disenchanted former official wrote in 1978, 'in the last four or five years . . . heavy taxation, cuts in services to the public and the recession in the private sector have given a bitter edge to jokes about overstaffing and waste in the public service'.[56] In his view, the protection which the Official Secrets Act was held to afford incompetent or self-serving bureaucrats was central to the growing hostility.[57] When a Home Office Minister tried to explain the operation of implicit authorization to the Commons, he was laughed at by Opposition MPs.[58] Rather than compensating for the shortcomings of the Act, confidence in the informal practices of the civil service was being damaged by it.

[49] A. Sampson, 'Secrecy, News Management, and the British Press', in T. M. Franck and E. Weisbrand (eds.), *Secrecy and Foreign Policy* (New York, 1974), 219; Street, 'Secrecy and the Citizen's Right to Know', 340; Jacob, 'Some Reflections on Governmental Secrecy', 39; Hooper, *Official Secrets*, 11–12.

[50] M. C. Hunt, *Open Government in the 1980s* (Sheffield, 1980), 2.

[51] Theakston, *The Civil Service Since 1945*, 114.

[52] Lord Croham, *Would Greater Openness Improve or Weaken Government?* (Salford, 1984), 5.

[53] D. Wilson, 'The Struggle to Overcome Secrecy in Britain', in D. Wilson (ed.), *The Secrets File* (London, 1984), 127; Kellner and Crowther Hunt, *The Civil Servants* (1980), 265.

[54] Hennessy, *Whitehall*, 260.

[55] W. Armstrong, *The Role and Character of the Civil Service* (London, 1970), 5.

[56] L. Chapman, *Your Disobedient Servant* (London, 1978), 94. See also the criticisms in the contemporary pamphlet, Justice, *The Citizen and the Public Agencies* (1976).

[57] Chapman, *Your Disobedient Servant*, 124.

[58] *Hansard*, 5th Series, 951, 15 June 1978, col. 1264.

As demands for major reform became more vociferous in Parliament and outside,[59] Whitehall made one last attempt to seize the initiative. In July 1977 Sir Douglas Allen (later Lord Croham), who had succeeded Armstrong as head of the Home Civil Service and was himself about to retire, issued the only comprehensive directive on openness ever made in this period.[60] A letter of guidance was issued to Permanent Secretaries requiring them to publish as a matter of course all background material relating to policy studies and reports, unless specifically forbidden to do so by their Ministers.[61] At the same time it was announced that greater use was to be made of Green Papers, and that departments were to make more effort to respond 'positively and sympathetically' to specific requests of information from MPs, the public, journalists, and scholars.[62] In transferring the burden of proof from those who wished to communicate to those who did not, and in drawing a line between the facts and analysis supplied by civil servants and the confidential advice they gave, Allen sought to create a radical yet practical and inexpensive departure from the time-honoured practice of secrecy.[63] As he later claimed, it was 'a more important step than is often given credit for'.[64]

It was also an almost complete failure. Between May and October 1978, twenty-eight departments produced just over 200 items, but the flow soon diminished to a trickle. Peter Hennessy, then writing for *The Times*, was refused access in July 1978 to background papers on the White Paper on the Official Secrets Act which had just been published.[65] In response to his request, officials produced the perfectly circular argument that the Croham directive, which stemmed from Franks's recommendations on open government, was inapplicable because all the relevant facts in the new White Paper were to be found in the Franks Report itself. 'Those with a taste for irony', observed *The Times*, 'can only exult.'[66] Croham's successor as civil service head, Sir Ian Bancroft, was less

---

[59] For a critical account of the origins of the Directive, see T. Barnes, *Open Up! Britain and Freedom of Information in the 1980s* (Fabian Tract, 1980), 3. Barnes claimed that the Government was trying to take some of the heat out of demands for reform, which had been on display in the brief Parliamentary debate held in Nov. 1976. See *Hansard* 5th Series, 919, 22 Nov. 1976, cols. 1878–87.

[60] The significance of the report was discussed in detail in a Radio 4 programme, *On Secrecy*, made by Peter Hennessy and broadcast on 25 June 1992. On retiring later in the year, Allen became Lord Croham, and his guidance is usually known as the 'Croham Directive'. The spirit and some of the substance of the Directive was recently embodied in the Open Government Code promulgated in 1994.

[61] D. Wass, *Government and the Governed* (London, 1983), 88; Baxter, *State Security, Privacy and Information*, 56; Harden and Lewis, *The Noble Lie: The British Constitution and the Rule of Law*, 145; Hennessy, *Whitehall*, 368; Kellner and Crowther-Hunt, *The Civil Servants*, 267–71.

[62] See the account based on an official press notice in *The Times* (8 Aug. 1977) 1, and the Leader on the same day, 13.

[63] On the preoccupation with keeping down costs, see Wilson, 'The Struggle to Overcome Secrecy in Britain', 127; *The Times* (5 Aug. 1977), 1.

[64] Lord Croham, 'Is Nothing Secret?', *Listener* (7 Sept. 1978), 298.

[65] Kellner and Crowther-Hunt, *The Civil Servants*, 269.

[66] *The Times* (20 July 1978), 17.

committed to the issue, and the directive was effectively dead by the time Margaret Thatcher buried it on taking power.[67]

The true significance of Allen's initiative was the demonstration it gave of the limits of internal reform. Permanent secretaries still enjoyed qualified autonomy, and implementation of the directive was left to their discretion. In spite of Allen's efforts, it proved all too easy to plead expense in declining to publish, and the Civil Service Department made little attempt to police observance.[68] One directive could not transform a tradition, and in the absence of external scrutiny there was, as ever, no means of knowing what was being withheld or on what basis. As Sir Douglas Wass, joint head between 1981 and 1983, observed in a Reith Lecture, 'critics have rightly noted that the control of information remains firmly in Whitehall's hands and that there is no provision for checking up on, or auditing the observance of the directive. The citizen has to depend on the unsupervised conscientiousness of officials and ministers.'[69] Croham himself reflected publicly on his experience, and by 1984 had become a reluctant convert to the cause of a Freedom of Information Act. He was still enough of a civil servant to be sceptical of the larger claims made for such an innovation and to remain concerned about its potential cost. But he no longer had confidence in the capacity of the bureaucracy to generate its own momentum for change, and was increasingly worried about the damage being caused to both its external reputation and internal discipline by continuing legislative inaction. Reform would have its drawbacks, he argued,

but it is also possible to hope that greater openness would help to restore trust and confidence. It is indeed on these grounds that, having always believed in greater openness than we have had, I have come to the view that we should have a right to freedom of information, provided that adequate protection is retained for vital secrets and for privacy, and that there is no suggestion that deliberate breaches of confidence by public employees should go unpunished.[70]

Lord Croham had begun his career as the profession entered its Indian Summer of approbation after the Second World War.[71] He was reluctantly abandoning Edward Bridges's commitment to official secrecy in order to return the service to the levels of self-discipline and self-respect that Bridges had promulgated and personified. It was unclear, however, that after the failure of reform in the 1970s there was any road back to this land of lost content. Croham's successor viewed his inheritance with little optimism: 'The British civil service—like most of the public services—has entered the 80s with its stock in

---

[67] H. Young, 'The Thatcher Style of Government', in May and Rowan, *Inside Information*, 274.

[68] Barnes, *Open Up!*, 3.

[69] Wass, *Government and the Governed*, 89.

[70] Croham, 'Would Greater Openness Improve or Weaken Government?', 15.

[71] He had briefly entered the Board of Trade in 1939, but his career did not really begin until after the war, when he joined the Cabinet Office in 1947.

the public's eye particularly low and with its morale badly dented.'[72] Soon after she took office, Margaret Thatcher invited Ian Bancroft and his fellow Permanent Secretaries to a dinner, which, according to *The Downing Street Years*, 'was one of the most dismal occasions of my entire time in government'.[73] The meal was an epochal disaster, confirming all the new Prime Minister's prejudices which had taken form when she was patronized and bullied by her staff as a junior Pensions Minister in 1961. There were no more dinners, and none of the encomiums for the best civil service in the world that had littered the memoirs of her predecessors, irrespective of their politics. Henceforth, the most that civil servants could expect from their masters was, as Bancroft observed, 'words of praise forced out through clenched teeth'.[74] The Prime Minister felt no affection for Whitehall officials other than her personal staff, and a disdain bordering on contempt for their culture.[75] Her attack on their faltering attempts at modernization took two forms, neither of which enhanced the trust and confidence that those at the head of the service were seeking to rebuild.

In the first instance, the strategy of easing the flow of information by internal directive and the *de facto* suspension of the law was halted in its tracks. The Tories had little interest in open government as a goal in its own right, and no patience with an undisciplined flow of information. After an attempt to introduce a more focused Official Secrets Act was frustrated by the coincident exposure of the Keeper of the Queen's Pictures as a former Russian spy,[76] the corpse of the old Act was resurrected. In the first seven decades of its existence, Section 2 was deployed about once every two years. In the first five years of Thatcher's regime it was used once every eighteen weeks. Eleven civil servants were prosecuted, compared with none under the 1974–9 Labour Governments, and five under the preceding Heath and Wilson administrations.[77] Contemporary assessments of the role of the Act still stressed its capacity to reinforce the ethos of secrecy,[78] but there were indications that this sudden resort to what was now

---

[72] I. Bancroft, 'The Civil Service in the 1980s', *Public Administration*, 59 (Summer 1981), 139. Also Delafons, 'Working in Whitehall: Changes in Public Administration 1952–1982', 270.

[73] M. Thatcher, *The Downing Street Years* (London, 1993), 48.

[74] Cited in D. Wass, 'The Civil Service at the Crossroads', *Political Quarterly*, 56: 3 (July–Sept. 1985), 232. See also Bancroft's bitter protest at the 'unwonted criticism' to which he and his colleagues were now exposed, in Bancroft, 'The Civil Service in the 1980s', 144.

[75] Hennessy, *Whitehall*, 592.

[76] In Nov. 1979, following the revelations in Anthony Boyle's *Climate of Treason*, the Government publicly admitted that Anthony Blunt had been given immunity from prosecution back in 1964. Porter, *Plots and Paranoia*, 208–9; Baxter, *State Security*, 36.

[77] Regan, 'Anonymity in the British Civil Service: Facelessness Diminished', *Parliamentary Affairs* 39: 4 (1986), 424. Also Drewry and Butcher, *The Civil Service Today*, 173; Lustgarten and Leigh, *In From the Cold*, 223. In 1991 Joe Haines, Wilson's Press Officer, claimed that Margaret Thatcher had used the Act more than all the governments between 1911 and 1979 put together. J. Haines, 'The Ventriloquist's Dummy Who Made it to Stardom', *The Times* (15 May 1991).

[78] See e.g. Jonathan Aitken in *Hansard*, 5th Series, 960, 19 Jan. 1979, col. 2137; F. F. Ridley, 'Political Neutrality, the Duty of Silence and the Right to Publish in the Civil Service', *Parliamentary Affairs*, 39: 4 (1986), 445; P. Nairne, 'Policy-Making in Public', in R. A. Chapman and M. Hunt (eds.), *Open Government* (London, 1989), 42; Kellner, 'The Lobby, Official Secrets and Good Government', 280.

a thoroughly discredited device was having the reverse effect. A retired Under Secretary observed in 1986 that,

for a variety of reasons the present administration does seem to be particularly preoccupied with confidentiality in relation to its affairs and with problems of presentation and of public image . . . the danger which is inherent is that well-conceived presentation can slide over into excessive secrecy in all sorts of ways. And too much secrecy can produce—and seems to me to have produced—its own consequence in terms of a greater tendency for leaks to appear.[79]

Margaret Thatcher was by no means the first post-war Prime Minister to be plagued by unauthorized communication.[80] The growing sensitivity of governments was a function of the widening gap between the ambition of controlling their public presentation and the difficulty of doing so. As Whitehall press officers multiplied,[81] and expenditure on government publicity rose to reach £200 million a year by 1989,[82] so also did the range of agencies which sought to expose the hidden workings of the state. The two central devices for policing the flow of information, the 'D' Notice and lobby systems, remained in place,[83] and Thatcher's own press officer, the pugnacious Bernard Ingham, raised the art of media manipulation to a new level. In his hands, the doctrine of implied authorization was a potent weapon. 'I must tell you', he informed the Independent Broadcasting Authority on one occasion, 'that I—and I am sure my colleagues—have never regarded the Official Secrets Act as a constraint on my operations. Indeed I regard myself as licensed to break that law as and when I judge necessary.'[84] But however brutally the lobby was treated, and however supinely it responded, there existed beyond this privileged group a proliferating mass of specialized journals and interest-groups continually seeking to establish their own lines of communication with Ministers and civil servants. The methods of gathering and disseminating news were becoming daily more diverse, as were those of recording it. Developments in information technology caused further difficulties. The growing presence in government offices of the photocopier and then the FAX machine meant that illicit communication was no longer dependent on theft or memory as in the time of the prototype leaker, Charles Marvin.[85]

---

[79] Regan, 'Anonymity in the British Civil Service: Facelessness Diminished', 426.

[80] Edward Heath, for instance, had launched thirty official inquiries into unauthorized communication in his term of office. Margach, *The Abuse of Power*, 182. For a lively account of Harold Wilson's obsession with leaks, see Crossman, *The Diaries of a Cabinet Minister*, ii. 331, 334, 424.

[81] May and Rowan, *Inside Information*, 91.

[82] P. Birkinshaw, *Reforming the Secret State* (Buckingham, 1990), 53.

[83] G. Kaufman, *How to be a Minister* (London, 1980), 171; Kellner, 'The Lobby, Official Secrets and Good Government', 276–81; Kellner and Crowther-Hunt, *The Civil Servants*, 281; Ponting, *Secrecy in Britain*, 33.

[84] Cited in C. Hitchens, 'What is this Bernard', *London Review of Books*, 13: 1 (10 Jan. 1991).

[85] See above, Ch. 2, pp. 78–82. For a discussion of the impact of photocopying on leaking, see *Hansard*, 5th Series, 960, 19 Jan. 1979, col. 2206.

These structural pressures interacted with a more human drama of confidence and betrayal. The prosecutions, the endless and usually fruitless internal searches for the sources of leaks, created a worsening climate of mutual suspicion. Civil servants felt themselves both demeaned and manipulated by their political masters. The Prime Minister made no secret of her intention of intervening in the cycle of promotion, particularly at the highest levels, nor of her view that a talented public official was a modern oxymoron. The professed desire to destroy the post-war conventions of consensus politics implicitly threatened the neutrality of senior advisors, particularly as interpreted by ambitious or ideologically driven Ministers. It is possible to refute the charge of crude politicization.[86] Permanent Secretaries were chosen more for qualities of personality than party conviction, and, as Peter Hennessy has pointed out, those appointed to head the service in this era could have held the position under any government since Northcote–Trevelyan.[87] Few serious changes were made to roles and duties, and there was no great influx of outsiders. Nonetheless, there was a widespread belief that Thatcher's Governments neither understood nor respected the culture of the service, and that they were blurring the interests of party and state in a way that compromised the integrity of permanent officials.

Leaking information became self-fulfilling protest. The more excessive the Government's response, the more justified it seemed.[88] Like Charles Marvin a century earlier, Sarah Tisdall was a junior clerk in the Foreign Office. But her decision in 1983 to transmit to the *Guardian* details of the planned deployment of cruise missiles was motivated not by personal gain but a principled opposition both to nuclear weapons and what she considered to be the manipulation of Parliament by her political head Michael Heseltine.[89] The law was now well prepared for this 'cheap and untrustworthy class of people',[90] and she received a six-month jail sentence under Section 2 the following year. Unauthorized disclosure reflected the worst each side thought of the other. Civil servants no longer trusted Ministers to make responsible use of the vast powers of controlling information vested in them by the Official Secrets Act; politicians no longer trusted their advisers to observe their traditions of discreet reserve.

In this context, Clive Ponting's leaking of a confidential internal inquiry into the sinking of the *General Belgrano* during the Falklands War was a representative drama. Whilst working as an assistant secretary in the Ministry of Defence in 1984, he became convinced that the Government was requiring its officials

---

[86] P. Barberis, 'Whitehall since the Fulton Report', in id. (ed.), *The Whitehall Reader: The UK's Administrative Machine in Action* (Buckingham, 1996), 15–16.

[87] Hennessy, *Whitehall*, 674.

[88] On the 'politically neurotic' pursuit of opponents of her defence policies, see A. Marr, *Ruling Britannia: The Failure and Future of British Democracy*, (rev. edn., London, 1996), 177–8.

[89] R. Pyper, 'Sarah Tisdall, Ian Willmore, and the Civil Servant's "Right to Leak",' *Political Quarterly*, 56: 1 (Jan.–Mar. 1985), 73–6.

[90] See above, Ch. 3, p. 81.

to assist in a campaign to mislead Parliament, and in protest sent details of the report he had helped prepare to the Labour MP Tam Dalyell.[91] It was not that most senior civil servants approved of the action, nor that they would have done the same themselves if placed in a similar position. Rather, Ponting was giving dramatic expression to a set of pressures which in one form or another were being experienced by all his colleagues. He believed that his superiors, in particular his Secretary of State, Michael Heseltine, were breaching the code of honourable conduct which bound official to Minister in the exercise of their duties. His action, and his highly publicized trial under Section 2, made him the most notorious public servant since Marvin. Although he escaped prison thanks to one of the rare but highly symbolic acts of defiance by juries which have played so large a part in the history of English civil liberties,[92] Ponting lost his job, and was condemned to join the ranks of those who eke out a living writing about secrecy. The Government survived, as did his Minister until the Westland affair in 1986, which again raised serious doubts about the ethical conduct of senior politicians. The sequence of improper communications of official information changed nothing except the need for change. By the mid-1980s, those committed to the traditional balance of law and culture were becoming increasingly beleaguered.

Earlier crises of behaviour in the civil service, notably the Francs and Crichel Down affairs,[93] had been the occasions of a restatement of standards and duties which had lit the path of a succeeding generation of officials. Sir Robert Armstrong, joint head of the service from 1981 and sole head from 1983, did his best to uphold this practice. After a series of leaks during the 1983 election campaign, he wrote a letter to Permanent Secretaries reminding them that whilst the formal requirements of the Official Secrets Act were important, the real issue for the civil service was the maintenance of 'the trust which Ministers, and those who may at some future date be Ministers, have traditionally placed in it', and 'the confidence of Parliament and the public as being a non-political service of Government'. This could only be achieved by reasserting 'the values and the sense of professional obligation and loyalty which will make such leaks unacceptable and unthinkable at any time'.[94] The exhortation had little discernible effect, and following a further series of unauthorized disclosures culminating in the Ponting case, he circulated a 'Note of Guidance on the Duties and Responsibilities of Civil Servants in Relation to Ministers', in which he

---

[91] The most detailed accounts of the leaking and the subsequent trial are to be found in R. Norton-Taylor, *The Ponting Affair* (London, 1985); T. Dalyell, *Misrule: How Mrs. Thatcher has Misled Parliament from the Sinking of the 'Belgrano' to the Wright Affair* (London, 1987); R. Thomas, 'The British Official Secrets Acts 1911–1939 and the Ponting Case', in Chapman and Hunt (eds.), *Open Government*, 95–112. See also Ponting, *Secrecy in Britain*, 64–5; Baxter, *State Security*, 45; Burkinshaw, *Freedom of Information*, 79–81; Robertson, *Freedom, the Individual and the Law*, 134–6.

[92] This was, however, the first such act of defiance by a jury which had previously been vetted.

[93] See above, Ch. 4, pp. 167–8, and Ch. 5, pp. 216–17.

[94] Cited in Hennessy, *Whitehall*, 664–5.

stressed that the official's principal loyalty was to 'first and foremost the Minister of the Crown', not some private construction of the public good'.[95]

If the first encyclical was ignored, the second was positively counterproductive. In seeking to reawaken the tradition of his great predecessors, Armstrong served only to demonstrate its obsolescence. In the words of a contemporary commentator, it was seen by many inside and outside the service as 'an unhelpful restatement of outdated constitutional platitudes, inappropriate to circumstances in which the civil service has become increasingly demoralised and alienated from its traditionally accepted role'.[96] Armstrong made no pretence of going beyond Fisher and Bridges. 'I am not conscious that I altered the doctrine in what I said,' he told the Commons Treasury and Civil Service Committee, 'though I did not use exactly the same words'.[97] The Committee subsequently issued a critical report which wondered whether 'the principles of the 1930s . . . are adequate for the 1980s', and confirmed that Section 2 of the Official Secrets Act was 'now unenforceable'.[98] A number of witnesses to the Committee, including Sir Douglas Wass who had shared the headship with Armstrong, doubted whether an internal system of appeal for officials concerned about ethical issues would resolve the crisis of trust between civil servants and Ministers.[99] Complaining to the Head of Home Civil Service would not alter the conduct of their political superior, and, as the 'Note of Guidance' made clear, even if the official made the final protest of resignation, 'he or she will still be bound to keep the confidences to which he or she has become privy as a civil servant'.[100]

Wass himself deplored breaches of confidentiality. 'The leak', he had written in 1983, 'is a blatant breach of the rules under which we play the games of government . . . the proper route to openness is by changing the rules, not by breaking them.'[101] But whilst Armstrong hoped that his Note would 'steady nerves',[102] and that by example and exhortation the old order could be restored, Wass, together with a growing number of retired senior officials and their increasingly vocal professional body, no longer believed this to be possible.[103] Honour and secrecy, for so long the twin sentinels of the civil service tradition,

[95] For a copy of the text, House of Commons Treasury and Civil Service Committee Sub-Committee 1985–86, *Civil Servants and Ministers: Duties and Responsibilities, Minutes of Evidence*, 27 Nov. 1985, Annex A. A slightly revised version was incorporated in the Civil Service Management Code, and is reprinted in Barberis, *Whitehall Reader*, 113–17.

[96] G. Drewry, 'Ministers and Civil Servants', *Public Law* (Winter 1986), 515.

[97] Treasury and Civil Service Committee, *Duties and Responsibilities*, 17.

[98] Cited in Drewry, 'Ministers and Civil Servants', 517.

[99] Ibid. 519.

[100] Treasury and Civil Service Committee, *Duties and Responsibilities*, 9.

[101] Wass, *Government and the Governed*, 99. He returned to the point two years later, placing particular emphasis on the 'breaches of trust' caused by leaks by Ministers. Wass, 'The Civil Service at the Crossroads', 232.

[102] Treasury and Civil Service Committee, *Duties and Responsibilities*, 31.

[103] W. Plowden, *Ministers and Mandarins* (London, 1994), 112–15.

were now at war with each other. Whereas the exercise of discreet reserve had embodied a high level of trust between officials and politicians, and between the state and the electorate at large, now its frequent breakdown reflected a steep decline in mutual confidence. The First Division Association argued that both sides of the equation needed to be addressed. The legal framework had to be overhauled,[104] and the convention of unwritten behavioural standards had to be challenged. Since 1972 it had become increasingly concerned about the absence of a public discussion of this issue. As it pointed out, the massive Fulton Report of 1968 had examined everything 'except the question of ethical standards which determine how civil servants perform their work in relation to the loyalties they observe and the conflicts they perceive, merely observing that the integrity of the British civil service was unquestioned'.[105] Such silence was no longer acceptable. In reaction to Armstrong's Note, the Association began work on drafting a formal code of ethics which would embrace both officials and their Ministers.[106] The era of implicit regulation was drawing to a close.

Margaret Thatcher's second line of attack on the dismal state bureaucracy eventually resulted in the most far-reaching reform since the modern civil service was consolidated under Warren Fisher between the wars. It took nearly a decade and three election victories before the reconstruction began in earnest. At the outset it seemed easier to change people rather than structures.[107] On gaining office, she discovered that the weakness of the formal constraints on her authority over both her Ministers and her officials was well suited to the combination of ideological radicalism and constitutional conservatism that characterized her regime. She put to death the few achievements of Fulton and Franks which might have formed the basis for internally generated change—the Civil Service Department, the Central Policy Review Staff, the Croham Directive—and instead brought in an outsider, Sir Derek Rayner from *Marks and Spencer*, to shake up the metabolism and reduce the costs of public service.[108] A series of 'efficiency scrutinies' were undertaken and a vigorous attempt was made to reduce the reliance on paper records which had expanded unchecked since well before Northcote–Trevelyan. Rayner's labours were embodied in the 1982 White Paper, *Efficiency and Effectiveness in the Civil Service*, and the subsequent

[104] For early signs of interest in some form of freedom of information legislation on the part of the FDA and other civil service unions, see S. H. Dresner, 'How Would a British Freedom of Information Act Work in Practice?', in *Secrecy, or the Right to Know* (London, 1980), 16; Wilson, 'The Struggle to Overcome Secrecy in Britain', 137.

[105] First Division Association, 'Performance Standards in the Public Service', 168.

[106] A prototype code was produced in 1986, and in 1994 a full draft code was drawn up in conjunction with the Treasury and Civil Service Committee. *Ethics in the British Civil Service*, 305; Plowden, *Ministers and Mandarins*, 116. The text of the 1994 Code is reprinted in Barberis, *Whitehall Reader*, 130–1.

[107] Margaret Thatcher summarized the evolution of her approach in *The Downing Street Years*, 48–9.

[108] Hennessy, *Whitehall*, 592–610; Drewry and Butcher, *The Civil Service Today*, 201–3; Theakston, *The Civil Service Since 1945*, 128–31.

Financial Management Initiative (FMI).[109] The aim was to produce a new generation of civil service managers capable of deploying the techniques of setting targets and measuring performance which had been developed in the better-run sectors of industry.

In its way, this management revolution was as concerned about information as Franks and the subsequent campaigners for the reform of secrecy. The emphasis, however, was not on what the public and the Government knew about each other, but rather on what the Government knew about itself. Officials were encouraged to communicate with outsiders so that they might learn the implications of what they themselves were doing. The only deliberate concession to openness in this period was the overhaul of the Select Committee system established by Crossman in the late 1960s. Fourteen new committees were established, which were to maintain a permanent working relationship with specific Government departments. The reform, claimed Norman St John-Stevas, as he introduced it to the Commons in 1979, 'will be an important contribution to greater openness in government, a kind that is in accord with our parliamentary arrangements and our constitutional tradition'.[110] MPs were given direct access to civil servants who could be called before them to explain the actions of their departments. It represented a deliberate qualification of the creaking doctrine of ministerial accountability, and a marked reduction in the anonymity of officials. Substantial numbers of named civil servants were now required to make the journey from Whitehall to the Palace of Westminster, and their interrogation resulted in a significant increase in the volume of information conveyed to Parliament and available for consultation by journalists and the public.[111]

The overall impact, however, fell some distance short of the kind of revolution which the efficiency drive was trying to achieve elsewhere.[112] A determined effort was made by Whitehall to relocate the new system within the conventional structures of secrecy. A set of rules issued in 1980 insisted that an official called before a committee 'would remain subject to Ministerial instructions as to how he should answer questions', and would not discuss advice given to ministers, or any issues 'in the field of political controversy'.[113] As controversy was Margaret Thatcher's preferred mode of discourse, the latter restriction was of particular importance. The tendency to treat every aspect of

---

[109] For an insider's summary of the efficiency campaign, see R. Butler, 'The Evolution of the Civil Service—A Progress Report', *Public Administration*, 71: 3 (Autumn 1993), 398–400.

[110] Cited in P. Baines, 'History and Rationale of the 1979 Reforms', in G. Drewry (ed.), *The New Select Committees* (Oxford, 1989), 15.

[111] M. Hunt, 'Parliament and Official Secrecy', in Chapman and Hunt, *Open Government*, 76; G. Drewry, 'The 1979 Reforms—New Labels on Old Bottles', in id. (ed.), *The New Select Committees* (Oxford, 1989), 389; Chapman, *Ethics in the British Civil Service* 296.

[112] Harden and Lewis, *The Noble Lie*, 99–100; Marr, *Ruling Britannia*, 156.

[113] Passages from the *Memorandum of Guidance for Officials Appearing before Select Committees* (known as the 'Osmotherly Rules' after the assistant secretary who drafted them), cited in Hennessy, *Whitehall*, 362. A revised version of the rules is reprinted in Barberis, *Whitehall Reader*, 223–9.

policy as a party issue limited the ability of both civil servants and MPs to engage in an open, objective pursuit of knowledge.[114] Tensions grew between politicians and officials and amongst the groupings within the committees. The consequence was a marked increase in leaks to the press of their private deliberations. In 1985 these became the subject of a critical inquiry by the Commons Committee of Privileges, which found that a number of newspapers, particularly *The Times*, were in breach of a Parliamentary resolution of 1837.[115] Journalists were unimpressed by this use of elderly precedent to halt the erosion of confidential government. 'What I think you are looking at', the *Guardian's* editor told the Committee of Privileges, 'is a situation where something has broken down which either has to be shored up by more bricks and mortar or looked at pragmatically and, frankly, dismantled.'[116]

At the centre of the breakdown was the doctrine of ministerial accountability. Although its death had been announced by political scientists for decades,[117] it had survived as the crumbling keystone of the arch of bureaucratic secrecy. By the mid-1980s it was under attack from every quarter. At one level, Ministers themselves were often unaware of the formulation of policy as the Prime Minister increasingly used Cabinet committees to bypass discussion in the full Cabinet. Although the traditional refusal to identify the existence of these bodies was relaxed slightly in 1983, they remained a secret within a secret of government, obscuring the dynamic of the decision-making process.[118] The literal truth of Ministers maintaining a direct oversight of all that was done in their name had been untenable since at least the Liberal welfare reforms which accompanied the 1911 Official Secrets Act, but now it was ceasing to function even as an acceptable myth. This was a consequence partly of the further expansion of government, partly of the growing sense that the convention was being deliberately exploited by Ministers to claim improper credit and evade proper blame,[119] and partly of a declining enthusiasm on the part of civil servants for their role in the charade. As one retired senior official observed in 1986, 'the thrill of non-recognition' was being experienced less and less often by those brought up to accept anonymity as the badge of their calling.[120]

In an administration in which greater efficiency was a far more important objective than increased communication, it was to be expected that the long-overdue reform of the doctrine should be undertaken in the name of better management rather than open government. The *FMI* had exposed the difficulty of operating a late-twentieth-century bureaucracy on the basis of a

---

[114] Hunt, 'Parliament and Official Secrecy', 71.

[115] The issues are summarized in Committee of Privileges, 1984–85, *Second Report, Premature Disclosure of Proceedings of Select Committees* (1985), pp. iii–v.

[116] Ibid. 59–60.

[117] See e.g. Crick, *The Reform of Parliament*, 189–90.

[118] R. Brazier, *Constitutional Practice* (Oxford, 1988), 109–10; Baxter, *State Security*, 112.

[119] Chapman, *Ethics in the British Civil Service*, 297.

[120] Regan, 'Anonymity in the British Civil Service: Facelessness Diminished', 424.

mid-nineteenth-century model of accountability.[121] It was impossible for heads of sections to assume responsibility for performance if decision-making was funnelled through an orderly hierarchy to a single administrative and thence political head, and if non-specialist officials were constantly moved from post to post. As a consequence, the most important structural reform since North-cote–Trevelyan was set in motion in the aftermath of the Conservatives' third election victory.[122] What became known as 'Next Steps Agencies' were to be created wherever it was possible to separate the delivery of a service from the strategic direction of the department. Within a decade they were to contain three-quarters of the existing civil service, which had declined from 732,300 to 579,600 since 1979.[123] Each agency would have a chief executive, recruited by open advertisement on a fixed-term contract, and directly responsible to the Minister for meeting targets set out in a framework document.[124] Success was to be measured in terms less of public service and more of customer satisfaction.[125] The agencies were to develop their own methods of selection and employment, with the Civil Service Commission reduced to a quality-assurance function.[126]

In 1993, with two-thirds of the old establishment now in the agencies, Sir Robin Butler, who had assumed control of the home civil service just as the 'Next Steps' initiative was launched, reviewed the tasks ahead:

I see the greatest challenge facing the civil service in the last years of the century as the need to combine the greater efficiency, flexibility and standards of service resulting from the management changes of the last twenty years, with the maintenance of the integrity, probity and cohesion which I have just described.[127]

'Integrity' was the key term. The dictionary gives two definitions, 'material wholeness' and 'soundness of moral principle'.[128] In the Northcote–Trevelyan tradition, the meanings acted upon each other. A single service, with a single mode of entry and a single set of working conditions, employing, especially at the senior levels, staff with a single social and educational background and a single career ahead of them, provided the structural context for the development, transmission, and policing of a single code of ethical behaviour. It had taken half a century for the service to become more than a sum of its departmental parts, but since at least the time of Warren Fisher, wholeness

---

[121] Harrison, *Transformation of British Politics*, 377–9.

[122] The initiative was in fact ready for publication before the election, but was kept secret to avoid unnecessary controversy.

[123] Drewry and Butcher, *The Civil Service Today*, 200.

[124] For an early warning of the problems of defining the separate spheres of accountability, see R. A. Chapman, ' "The Next Steps": A Review', *Public Policy and Administration*, 3: 3 (1988), 4–6.

[125] A. Davies and J. Willman, *What Next? Agencies, Departments and the Civil Service* (London, 1991), 70.

[126] On the early history of 'Next Steps', see Hennessy, *Whitehall*, 618–22; Drewry and Butcher, *The Civil Service Today*, 222–8.

[127] Butler, 'The Evolution of the Civil Service—A Progress Report', 405–6.

[128] See the *Shorter Oxford English Dictionary* (1983 edn.).

of body and soundness of principle had existed in a state of mutual dependence.[129] The question now was whether the cultivation of a distinctive occupational ethos in each agency would be a sufficient response to what Andrew Marr described as the 'curdling of the culture of public service with that of the narrower culture of the market'.[130]

There were and remain doubts about whether such an outcome was possible, the more so as the reform was preceded by a decade of disparagement of public service. Such uncertainty was inescapable, given that 'Next Steps' was variously proclaimed as the relaunching of the civil service for the next millennium and the necessary preparation for its complete dismemberment.[131] But we may conclude with the optimistic view, represented by a study conducted by the Institute for Public Policy Research whilst Butler was defining his agenda for the rest of the 1990s. *Ministers and Mandarins* identified a new consonance between structure and ethos.[132] Just as 'Next Steps' involved the disaggregation and refocusing of the bureaucracy to meet the demands of the citizen as active customer, so it would be possible to unbundle and reconstitute its behavioural standards to meet the requirements of the customer as active citizen. Lowering the barriers between the state and the market would expose areas of shared moral behaviour, and promote trust between them. Rethinking issues such as the kind of person who should exercise executive responsibility, and the criteria that should be established for measuring performance, provided a long-overdue opportunity for interrogating what now appeared a confused and contradictory pattern of values and attitudes. Whilst some aspects of the traditional code, such as 'honesty, personal disinterestedness, a respect for intelligence, an enormous capacity for hard and often rapid work, loyalty to colleagues' needed to be retained, others should now be pensioned off, including, 'conservatism, caution, scepticism, elitism, a touch of arrogance and, too often, a deeply-held belief that the business of government can be fully understood only by government professionals'.[133] Above all, the 'core element of the "executive mentality"', that 'governments may conceal the truth from citizens *in the citizen's own best interests*', might now be addressed: 'Accustomed to operating largely in secret, officials and ministers understandably come to believe that secrecy—or, at least, openness only at the government's discretion—is essential . . . One way to modify this ethic is to challenge it from within, by sufficient movement between Whitehall and the world.'[134] The new public management,

---

[129] R. A. Chapman, 'The End of the Civil Service?', *Teaching Public Administration*, 7: 2 (1992), repr. in Barberis, *Whitehall Reader*, 188–9.

[130] Marr, *Ruling Britannia*, 230.

[131] Davies and Willman, *What Next?*, 65–6; Theakston, *Whitehall Since 1945*, 141.

[132] Plowden, *Ministers and Mandarins*, esp. 70–4.

[133] Ibid. 74.

[134] Ibid. The possibilities for promoting greater openness through the Next Step Agencies are also assessed in an earlier IPPR study: Davis and Willman, *What Next?*, 70–5.

in other words, could provide the lever for finally prising apart honour and secrecy.

Citizens, Clients, and Consumers

The Younger Report of 1972 tried and failed to establish a comprehensive definition of privacy which would satisfy a judge or a Parliamentary draughtsman. However, it was in no doubt where the heart of the matter lay in the eyes of the general public: 'The evidence we have received indicates that the main concern about what is termed invasion of privacy involves the treatment of personal information.'[135] Some of the problems arose from external assaults on the domestic archive by the press or various surveillance agencies, but the bulk of the fears stemmed from failures to maintain the secrecy of personal details entrusted to individuals and organizations in return for assistance or services. Confidentiality required a contract between two parties which set limits to the disclosure of private information to a third.[136] The scope and complexity of these agreements, traditionally assumed rather than codified, imposed rather than negotiated, had widened continuously since the beginning of the period covered by this study. The Younger Report marked not the culmination but merely a staging-post in the growth of the pressures surrounding the contracts. Developments which were already apparent, particularly the spread of electronic means of storing and transmitting data, and the bureaucratization of professional activities, continued apace throughout the 1970s whilst a variety of legislation remained in draft form. The only achievement of the decade was the 1974 Consumer Credit Act which gave potential borrowers the right to interrogate a file held on them by a credit reference agency.[137] By the time Margaret Thatcher took office, the era of informal, unwritten safeguards was drawing to a close. However, the road to reform was by no means clear. The development of enforceable models of confidentiality raised questions of power and trust to which there were no easy answers.

Since their first manifestation as the late-nineteenth-century home-visiting movement, the personal social services had been acutely exposed to the major cross-currents in the confidential relationship. Following the reorganization of social work departments in 1970, the rapidly expanding profession began to pay systematic attention to the dilemmas with which it had long wrestled.

---

[135] *Report of the Committee on Privacy* [Younger], Cmnd. 5012 (1972), 10.

[136] For useful working definitions of confidentiality, see J. Clegg (ed.), *Dictionary of Social Services* (London, 1971), 19; P. Parsloe, 'Social Services: Confidentiality, Privacy and Data Protection', in P. Pearce *et al.*, *Personal Data Protection in Health and Social Services* (London, 1978), 84; F. Gurry, *Breach of Confidence* (Oxford, 1984), 3; M. H. Kottow, 'Medical Confidentiality: An Intransigent and Absolute Obligation, *Journal of Medical Ethics*, 12 (1986), 117.

[137] Hewitt, *Privacy*, 4–5.

Discussion Paper No. 1 of the newly formed British Association of Social Workers in 1971 was on the subject of *Confidentiality in Social Work*. It concluded that strict discipline in the use of knowledge 'pertinent to the situation but painful to the teller' was critical to the establishment of 'that essential trust without which all relationships between person and person and between individuals and groups become useless distortions of truth and justice'.[138] There was a real danger that this requirement would be overwhelmed by the sheer scale of the responsibilities placed upon the profession by the relentless expansion of the welfare state. As a BASW member observed,

One of the prices we pay for increased occupational, social and welfare benefits of all kinds is the necessary requirement to share and entrust personal and private information to an ever widening range of organisations and persons . . . we run the risk that we may lose control of that information and have no knowledge of how it may be subsequently used.[139]

There was growing concern about the absence of any detailed guidance on this most sensitive issue,[140] and four years later a formal code of ethics was promulgated as part of the strategy of asserting the identity and authority of the profession.[141] According to its 'principles of practice', the social worker 'recognises that information clearly entrusted for one purpose should not be used for another purpose without sanction. He respects the privacy of clients and confidential information about clients gained in his relationship with them or others.'[142] At this stage the profession was doing little more than distilling accumulated wisdom and practice. However, significant developments were taking place in the theory of social work, and by the end of the decade these began to impact on the concept of confidentiality in a way which made the 'social work model' the benchmark for all organizations struggling to reform their controls.[143]

Signs of change could be detected in the 1980 BASW report entitled *Clients are Fellow Citizens*. Particular emphasis was placed on sharing not only the generation of knowledge but also the determination of its use.[144] An active citizen had the right to self-direction, and effective social work required that clients should be enabled to make their own decisions about key aspects of their lives,

[138] British Association of Social Workers, *Discussion Paper No. 1, Confidentiality in Social Work* (London, 1971), 3–4.

[139] M. Murch, 'Privacy—No Concern of Social Workers?', *Social Work Today*, 2: 5 (3 June 1971), 7.

[140] See, for instance, the complaint about the absence of such guidance in R. Bessell, *Interviewing and Counselling* (London, 1971), 195.

[141] For a discussion of the role of codes in the politics of professionalization, see D. Watson (ed.), *A Code of Ethics for Social Work* (London, 1985), 9–10.

[142] Ibid. 3.

[143] For a contemporary discussion of the emergence of this model, see Thompson, 'The Nature of Confidentiality', *Journal of Medical Ethics*, 62.

[144] The report is discussed in D. Shemmings, *Client Access to Records: Participation in Social Work* (Aldershot, 1991), 71.

including the maintenance of their privacy.[145] The issue of control was moved from the protection of the professional relationship to the centre of the treatment itself.[146] According to a contemporary study of social work ethics, the key question was 'whether confidentiality will help to empower, or undermine empowerment of the individual'.[147] A proper response demanded an informed awareness of the dilemmas inherent in the deployment of personal information on the part of both the social worker and the client. It was now accepted that this dimension of secrecy could never be an absolute. Both the givers and receivers of confidences faced a complex set of decisions to which there were few given answers.[148] This in turn required that the contract between them be made fully explicit. As Phyllida Parsloe wrote in 1988, 'the confidence which the worker needs to be frank with the client is more likely to exist where the agency has a clear policy about the form and content of records and has developed guidelines about who may have access to them and with whom they may be shared'.[149] Openness was a reciprocal process. Professionals could gain more effective access to the hidden recesses of clients' lives if clients fully understood the rules governing the further transmission of their secret stories. The listeners had to publicize the criteria by which their professional judgement was exercised, and could no longer merely assume the consent of the speakers to subsequent breaches of the confidential relationship. The convention of implied authorization, which in its way had been as central to social work as to the civil service, was to be abandoned.

The debate within the profession was shortly translated into a linked series of administrative and legislative reforms. In 1983 a Department of Health and Social Security circular established the policy of giving clients access to their own records, subject to specified safeguards.[150] The increasing proportion of social work records stored on computer were covered by the passage of the Data Protection Act the following year, which belatedly embodied one of the main recommendations of the Younger Report. Any personal information held in a machine-readable form was not to be used for any but the original purpose for which it was collected, and the subjects of the data were given the right of inspection and where necessary correction or erasure.[151] In the case of social work, exceptions were subsequently permitted where access would cause serious mental or physical harm to the subject or lead to the identification of a

---

[145] C. L. Clark with S. Asquith, *Social Work and Social Philosophy* (London, 1985), 31–2; M. Horne, *Values in Social Work* (Aldershot, 1987), 9.

[146] M. Frankel, 'Files on Ourselves: Fact or Fiction?', in Wilson, *The Secrets File*, 98.

[147] M. L. Rhodes, *Ethical Dilemmas in Social Work Practice* (1986), 80.

[148] For a detailed recent examination of the complexity of the issues involved in confidentiality, see T. Bond, *Standards and Ethics for Counselling in Action* (London, 1993), 121–42.

[149] Parsloe, 'Social Services: Confidentiality, Privacy and Data Protection', 41.

[150] Circular LAC83(14). Harrison, *Access to Information in Local Government*, 60–1; Shemmings, *Client Access to Records*, 3

[151] For a full summary of the Act, see P. Birkinshaw, *Government and Information: The Law relating to Access, Disclosure and Regulation* (London, 1990), 180–209.

third party.[152] The provisions of the legislation were extended to non-electronic records in social work and council housing by the Access to Personal Files Act of 1987.[153] Meanwhile, the Local Government (Access to Information) Act of 1985, which furthered the work begun by Margaret Thatcher a quarter of a century earlier, made the activities of social work departments more open to public scrutiny.[154] The road which began with home visitors developing record-keeping systems in the closing decade of the nineteenth century ended on 1 April 1989. With the publication of a further circular the users of social service departments became fully able to employ the right of access to their files.[155]

Social work was neither the sole cause nor the only beneficiary of the new structure of statutory regulation. But of all the bodies affected by the reforms of the 1980s, it displayed the closest match between internally generated codes and externally imposed controls. There was a genuine consonance between professional ethics and formal rules. Clients had been accepted as citizens with basic rights of privacy, citizens had been recognized as participants in a complex structural process which rendered confidentiality a relative rather than an absolute concept. The endlessly difficult question of reconciling the individual practitioner–client relationship with the bureaucratic forms of vertical command and horizontal collaboration had been addressed by an insistence on open discussion based on mutual respect. By these means, a real attempt had been made to integrate rather than oppose the control of information with the conduct of professional practice.

There were limits, nonetheless, to the scale and relevance of this achievement. At the outset, it was far from clear that the 'social work model' fully applied even to those who described themselves as social workers. Not only were there the gaps between theory and practice which might be found in any organization adapting to new codes and regulations, but also the boundaries of social work were still very ragged. There were many employed by local government and subject to its legal framework who were not trained or qualified members of professional bodies or covered by their codes of ethics.[156] Even for those secure in their occupational identity, the rules and laws offered only a distant and provisional guide to the resolution of the most acute issues of suffering and privacy. This was particularly the case with the physical and sexual

---

[152] The exceptions were embodied in a subject access modification order made in 1987.

[153] Harrison, *Access to Information in Local Government*, 83–4; Shemmings, *Client Access to Records*, 4–8.

[154] Parsloe, 'Social Services: Confidentiality, Privacy and Data Collection', 34; Birkinshaw, *Government and Information*, 154–170. For a positive assessment of the outcome of the Act across the whole field of local government, see J. Steele, *Public Access to Information: An evaluation of the Local Government (Access to Information) Act 1985* (London, 1995), 61–4.

[155] Circular LAC(89)2. Shemmings, *Client Access to Records*, p. ix.

[156] The Lindop Committee had noted that in the late 1970s, 'around 60% of social workers have not been professionally trained'. *Report of the Committee on Data Protection* [Lindop], Cmnd. 7341 (1978), 224; Watson, *Code of Ethics for Social Work*, 22.

abuse of children. Here the many achievements of social workers were unsung and the occasional errors broadcast to the nation in a way which made White-hall's hairshirt of anonymity seem a positive luxury. No code could guarantee the uncovering of every domestic secret or the proper communication of every scrap of knowledge which was collected.[157] A series of scandals culminating in the Cleveland sexual abuse inquiry of 1987 forced difficult reassessments of the methods of domestic inquiry and the strategies of transmitting the resulting information within social work departments and beyond them to cognate agencies such as the police and the health services.

The outlines of the model were also threatened by continuing developments in the methodology of social work. Concerns were expressed that over the years bureaucracy and professionalism had devalued rich traditions of helping those in need. It was argued that instead of sitting in a central office admiring their qualifications, social workers should be based in a locality where it would be possible to enrich rather than bypass informal networks of assistance. They would immerse themselves in a community or 'patch', absorbing knowledge about pressures and resources in the neighbourhood, stimulating mutual sup-port systems, and thereby dissolving problems before they became the 'cases' around which the profession had organized its disciplines for more than a cen-tury. In this approach, social workers became less the authoritative outside ex-perts and more an internal information exchange, seeking out and mobilizing details of domestic misfortune, making particular use of local intermediaries such as publicans and shopkeepers. These were, of course, precisely the figures upon whom successive generations of benefit inspectors had sought to base their surveillance work.[158] As a number of critics pointed out, the new tech-nique threatened to reverse all that had been achieved in the field of confiden-tiality. 'At a time', wrote Robert Pinker in 1982, 'when profound disquiet is being expressed about the indiscriminate and often *unreported* collection of in-formation about ordinary citizens by public and private bodies, we are now in-vited to endorse the creation of a proliferation of local data banks based largely on hearsay, gossip and well-meaning but uninvited prying.'[159] Licensing un-qualified if benevolent residents to 'enquire into the personal circumstances of citizens who may neither have asked for help nor committed any offence' would reawaken all the difficulties with privacy which the home visitors once had encountered. Proponents of the new method responded by evoking the 'sensitivity and professionalism' of social workers as a guarantee of confiden-tiality, which returned the issue to its point of departure.[160]

[157] For a discussion of the inherent dilemmas of working in this field, see B. Campbell, *Unofficial Secrets* (London, 1989), 4–9.

[158] See above, pp. 237–9.

[159] R. Pinker, 'An Alternative View', in National Institute for Social Work, *Social Workers, their Role and Tasks* (1982), App. B, 254–5.

[160] See M. Bayley, 'Values in Locally Based Work', in S. Shardlow (ed.), *The Values of Change in Social Work* (London, 1989), 56–7.

If there could be no final resolution of the tensions within the 'social work model', there were still greater difficulties in applying it to other categories of confidential behaviour. This was immediately apparent as attempts were made to establish common standards of practice with the various agencies with which, as the child abuse enquiries regularly reported, it was vital that the social workers shared their information.[161] The reforms of the 1980s resulted in only a partial convergence of attitude and behaviour. The most striking disparity was between the two professions directly engaged in the welfare of society. The doctors were reluctant to abandon their entrenched mistrust of the record-keeping practices of most forms of social work. As late as 1988, an authoritative review of the field observed that, 'at the time of writing, the management of confidential information between these two services is the matter causing greatest concern. Social service departments are worried that doctors may refuse to give them information, or at least refuse, unless there are very stringent safeguards.'[162]

At the heart of the difficulty was the issue of authority. It has been persuasively argued that the reason why social work set the pace of change was its continuing professional insecurity.[163] With its status and responsibilities still in dispute, there was much to be gained from developing formal codes of practice and negotiating explicit contracts with clients. Furthermore, its structural weakness made it easier for the state to impose regulation upon it. A case in point was the Access to Personal Files Act, which began life as a backbench Bill introduced by the Liberal MP Archie Kirkwood and supported by the Campaign for Freedom of Information. It was intended to apply to manual records held by a broad range of statutory and commercial bodies, including the health services, but in exchange for permitting its legislative passage, Ministers narrowed the scope of the Bill to two aspects of local government, which since 1960 had been compelled to march in the vanguard of openness.[164]

The doctors initially wished to engage in the debate over confidentiality on their own terms. The limitations of the Hippocratic Oath as a guide to the control of information in the modern health service had been apparent well before 1970, but it was not until a decade later that a serious attempt was made to develop a set of guidelines which had some bearing on the real complexities of the practitioner–patient relationship. The underlying tensions caused by the need to collaborate with other qualified and lay workers within and beyond the realm of medicine, and by the need to uphold public health as well as private

---

[161] For surveys of the range of bodies with whom modern social workers needed to share their records, see R. Lacey, 'Social Workers and their Records', in P. Hewitt (ed.), *Computers, Records and the Right to Privacy* (Purley, 1979), 77; *Report of the Committee on Data Protection*, 225.

[162] Parsloe, 'Social Services: Confidentiality, Privacy and Data Protection', 89.

[163] Thompson, 'The Nature of Confidentiality', 62.

[164] Birkinshaw, *Government and Information*, 173; Harrison, *Access to Information in Local Government*, 85–7.

well-being, had been latent ever since the profession began to remake itself in the early nineteenth century.[165] The National Health Service had not invented hospitals, nor the need for communication with other caring and disciplinary services.[166] What turned half-acknowledged difficulties into a widely recognized crisis was the rapid growth in the role of information technology.[167] Although the computerization of records was in prospect at the time of the Younger Report, the Committee on Data Protection six years later found that the bulk of personal files were still held in manual form, including the biggest single personal numbering system in the country, the index of 51 million patients and their doctors held in Stockport.[168] Thereafter, computers steadily replaced paper, and then began to displace people. Machines were developed to read other machines, and by the end of the 1980s the new technology was moving from storing to creating knowledge about therapeutic intervention as telemedicine enabled doctors to manage the needs of patients at a distance.[169] Diagnostic material derived by electronic means could now be transmitted in space or time by telephone, fax, video, microwave, and broad-band links. The figure of the lone doctor entering the answers to oral questions on a battered card disappeared into history, accompanied by such confidence as still existed in the established conventions for policing the transmission of personal information.

At the same time, the BMA belatedly began to shed its appearance of 'a London gentleman's club concerned only that its members behave like gentlemen and that "bounders" should be evicted'.[170] Having resisted all requests for a written code of ethics until 1949, it responded to the creation of the National Health Service by publishing a short pamphlet which, like Percival's *Medical Ethics* of 1803, was largely confined to the proprieties of conduct between doctors and with other professions.[171] Another three decades passed before the task of adjusting the traditional mindset to the radically altered content and context of medicine was addressed. Following the creation of a new BMA committee on medical ethics in 1979, a *Handbook* was compiled for the use of

---

[165] M. Stacey, *The British General Medical Council and Medical Ethics* (Philadelphia, 1991), 166.

[166] For nineteenth-century difficulties, see above, pp. 52–6. On the increase in the complexity of hospital organization and the consequences for confidentiality, see Hawkins, *Mishap or Malpractice?*, 217.

[167] The limited acknowledgement of growing problems made by the BMA to the Younger Committee is discussed in Wacks, *The Protection of Privacy*, 126–7. On the growing sense of crisis caused by computers in the late 1970s, see J. Dawson, 'State of Medical Records', in P. Hewitt (ed.), *Computers, Records and the Right to Privacy* (Purley, 1979), 80; F. H. Pheby, 'Changing Practice on Confidentiality: A Cause for Concern', *Journal of Medical Ethics*, 8 (1982), 12.

[168] *Report of the Committee on Data Protection*, 65–6.

[169] British Medical Association, *Medical Ethics Today: its Practice and Philosophy* (London, 1993), 38–9.

[170] Stacey, *The British General Medical Council and Medical Ethics*, 175.

[171] British Medical Association, *Ethics and Members of the Medical Profession* (London, 1949). For a discussion of the evolution of the BMA's approach to guidance on medical ethics since its formation, see BMA, *Medical Ethics Today*, pp. xxv–xxvi.

practitioners.[172] This flatly restated the Hippocratic principle that 'a doctor must preserve secrecy on all he knows', but acknowledged a number of general exceptions, including patient consent and 'the doctor's overriding duty to society'.[173] The relatively simple prescriptions of the *Handbook* exposed the distance the profession had yet to travel. The debate about the rights of patients and the challenge of information technology was only beginning. As a review of the implications of computing for medical records noted in 1979, 'absolute personal privacy is incompatible with a multi-disciplinary approach to medical care and this dilemma is unresolved at present'.[174] The turning-point was the establishment of the Inter-Professional Working Group on Access to Personal Health Information, which in 1984 produced a lengthy code of guidance on the lateral transmission of medical records.[175] This still tended to leave resolution of difficult issues to the discretion of the individual doctor,[176] but it marked a decisive retreat from the language of absolute secrecy which had informed the approach of the profession since the Hippocratic Oath had been revived in the late eighteenth century.

The belated recognition that records had always been communicated to other professionals raised questions about why they were traditionally withheld from their subjects. As the BMA later observed, 'in the past, the concept of confidentiality meant that health records were kept secret from patients themselves'.[177] Gradually the notion of right of access, already entrenched in other caring professions, began to percolate through the medical hierarchy. It was propelled in this direction by the general concern about information technology. Computerized medical records were embraced by the 1984 Data Protection Act, although an exemption was later granted where subject access might, in the doctor's judgement, cause serious harm to the patient or reveal the identity of a third party.[178] There was also a new emphasis on the role of openness in the therapeutic process. Trust began to be distinguished from deference. In place of the passive acceptance of the integrity of the professional, a more active process of consent was advocated.[179] Patients would be more likely to reveal the

---

[172] The full title of the new body was the Committee on Standards of Professional Conduct and on Medical Ethics. The *Handbook* was first published in 1980, and regularly revised.

[173] British Medical Association, *The Handbook of Medical Ethics* (London, 1984 edn.), 12.

[174] Dawson, 'State of Medical Records', 80.

[175] Phillips and Dawson, *Doctors' Dilemmas*, 128. The prevailing practice of passing records with the 'patients implied consent' between doctors and nurses outside the surgery is discussed in M. Illing and B. Donovan, *District Nursing* (London, 1981), 141.

[176] Frankel, 'Files on Ourselves', 88.

[177] BMA, *Medical Ethics Today*, 45.

[178] i.e. The Data Protection (Subject Access Modification) (Health) Order 1987.

[179] H. Francis and A. Mascara, 'The Keeper and the Bailey: Privacy and Confidentiality in Medicine', in P. Pearce (ed.), *Personal Data Protection in Health and Social Services* (London, 1988), 93–5; Kottow, 'Medical Confidentiality', 120. For a parallel advocacy of the negotiation of an 'informal participative contract' between health visitors and their clients in the matter of confidentiality, see S. Twinn and S. Cowley (eds.), *The Principles of Health Visiting: A Re-examination* (London, 1992), 30. Also C. Robertson, *Health Visiting in Practice* (Edinburgh, 1988), 142.

most sensitive details of their physical or mental condition if they could check for themselves that their disclosures were being recorded accurately and objectively.[180] Further, they should no longer be expected to rely on the discretion of the doctor to exercise the right of inspection. Although medicine was deleted from the 1987 Personal Files Act, patients were guaranteed the right to see summaries of their health supplied to employers and insurance companies by the Medical Reports Act of 1988, and finally were allowed full inspection of their secrets by the Access to Health Records Act of 1990.[181]

From the early 1980s onwards, doctors were engaged in both codifying and restricting the role of professional discretion in the control of personal information. They gained greater guidance and less freedom in their relations with their patients, whom they were encouraged to view as autonomous and reasoning beings rather than passive sufferers incapable of understanding the knowledge generated about their condition. In the textbooks, the all-embracing concept of professional conduct was qualified by more specific notions of clinical and ethical behaviour, with systematic training in the latter provided on a wider, if still inadequate, scale. More changed in a decade than in the previous two centuries, but the transformation was both troubled and incomplete. It was symptomatic that the basic question of who owned the medical records remained a matter of dispute. The Lindop Committee was assured they belonged to the state, but this was never accepted by the doctors who had compiled them.[182] The notion that possession might be transferred to the patients themselves, who could then read them at leisure and, if they chose, show them to their family or friends, was received with little enthusiasm when it was first broached.[183] Whilst the social workers had made a real attempt to merge the categories of client and citizen, the doctors still regarded the patient as a distinct entity, albeit with more rights and dignity than had once been the case. They continued to approach the issue of confidentiality along twin tracks, on the one hand anxious to develop a more open relationship with those they treated, on the other, concerned to exercise their obligations to the ever-more fraught notion of the public interest. Their belated recognition of the complexities involved in the management of personal information, and their requirement to observe new laws as well as their own constantly expanding codes of conduct, undermined the old certainties without replacing them with a coherent programme of action. Having ceded some of their authority to the

---

[180] P. Ley, 'Giving Information to Patients', in J. R. Eiser (ed.), *Social Psychology and Behavioral Medicine* (Chichester, 1982), 357.

[181] The 1990 Act gave patients access to health records made after 1 Nov. 1991, and to information recorded earlier if needed to understand what was written later. BMA, *Medical Ethics Today*, 45; Birkinshaw, *Government and Information*, 176–7, 178–9.

[182] *Report of the Committee on Data Protection*, 69; Pheby, 'Changing Practice on Confidentiality', 16; BMA, *Medical Ethics Today*, 41.

[183] M. L. M. Gilhooly and S. M. McGhee, 'Medical Records: Practicalities and Principles of Patient Possession', *Journal of Medical Ethics*, 17 (1991), 141–3.

state, and a little of their discretion to their patients, they found the bound-aries of their own responsibilities increasingly difficult to recognize, and the old, simple invocation to secrecy less and less easy to apply. As Phillips and Daw-son remarked in their *Doctors' Dilemmas* in 1985, 'it is hardly surprising that doctors themselves appear confused when the principle is applied with so little consistency'.[184]

At issue was the authority of the profession. It was no longer clear where the rights of the patients should end, nor where the responsibilities of the less qualified members of the health bureaucracies should begin. The suspicion amongst the social workers that the doctors still had reservations about their status was well founded. In its major statement of medical ethics published in 1993, the BMA cautioned that

a great risk to confidentiality arises out of the multiplicity of repositories of health information where it is controlled by a number of different health professionals, administrators and social workers—all of whose records are subject to different criteria for disclosure, to a range of possible others from trainees to town councillors.[185]

Whilst limited progress had been made in relations with fellow professionals, the problem of lay participation was about to get worse. Alongside the partial break-up of the civil service into Next Steps Agencies, the Conservative Govern-ment set about creating an internal market within the National Health Service. Doctors and other medical professionals had their contracts transferred to Hos-pital Trusts which were controlled by unelected lay boards and charged with promoting competition amongst providers. As in the commercial sector from which many of the board members were drawn, information about the work of the hospitals became a market-sensitive commodity. In addition to their oblig-ations to their patients, their profession, and society at large, the doctors, together with nurses and others involved in the process of treatment, were now required to observe a duty of confidentiality to their Trusts.

The politically inspired encroachment of the public and professional sectors by the commercial realm highlighted the distinctiveness of the control of com-munication in fields where profit was the nominal goal. Full privatization and the halfway house of internal markets were both justified by their impact on closed information systems. The need to measure performance in terms of bal-ance sheets would disclose true costs, expose hidden inefficiencies, and place in the hands of the patients and consumers the knowledge required to exercise free and informed choice. The market would exploit to the full the potential of electronic information systems, with the state confined to its proper role of establishing the regulatory framework necessary for maintaining a climate of

---

[184] Phillips and Dawson, *Doctors' Dilemmas*, 137.
[185] BMA, *Medical Ethics Today*, 38. Also 66. For a similar discussion of the more specific problems in dealing with lay people in child-abuse cases, see 293.

trust. Both the benefits and the dangers of the late-twentieth-century revolution in communications challenged the conventional boundaries of public and private performance. Inquiries such as the Younger and Lindop Reports, and reforms such as the Data Protection Act and the 1990 Computer Misuse Act, responded to the anxieties of clients, customers, and citizens alike. The authority of government and the expertise of lawyers and technicians were mobilized to create structures of confidence which would permit a full-scale attack on the encrusted paternalism of bureaucrats and professionals. With the potential for abuse under control, the road was open for the private individual to challenge the traditional monopolies of knowledge.

The question was how far the market was capable of fulfilling the expectations which had been placed upon it. Its own traditions offered little comfort. As we have seen in earlier chapters, the world's first industrial economy resisted the imposition of the formal disclosure regulations which developed amongst its rivals. Throughout the nineteenth century and most of the first half of the twentieth, the patterns of discipline had much in common with the public sector. Gentlemanly capitalists placed the same reliance on the discretionary release of information as gentlemanly administrators. As with taxpayers, shareholders were told no more than those who managed their affairs wished them to know. The difference was that in commerce, the cultural controls on honourable conduct were weaker, and the incidence of every kind of fraudulent behaviour correspondingly greater. After the Second World War, however, signs of change became visible. In common with the service sector, reform was driven by a combination of internal professional debate and external political pressure, most powerfully from Europe. The 1948 Companies Act represented a move towards more formal regulation,[186] although the interpretation of its disclosure requirements was still left to the judgement of the accountancy profession. As in social work and medicine, a further two decades elapsed between the first recognition of a problem and the commencement of significant action. In 1970 the profession began to codify its responsibilities in this field, and in the succeeding years showed an increasing interest in the precision and efficacy of its ethical rules.[187] Following the report of the Dearing Committee in 1988, the Accountancy Standards Board was established in 1990, which produced a Statement of Aims the following year. At the same time, the state started to expand its role. The Labour Government passed the Employment Protection Act of 1975 which imposed an obligation to reveal knowledge necessary for collective bargaining. After 1979 the Conservative administrations successfully opposed the imposition of further Common Market regulations on communication with the workforce,[188] but they did move towards the harmonization of laws on disclosure to shareholders. The Companies Acts of

[186] See above, pp. 218–19.
[187] D. Alexander and A. Britton, *Financial Reporting* (3rd edn., London, 1993), 211–12, 253–4.
[188] Barnes, *Open Up!*, 7.

1981 and 1985 marked a decisive break with the conventional British emphasis on informality.[189]

Underpinning these changes was a need to exchange power for trust. As consumers and shareholders became more informed, and pressure groups and fund managers more professional, it was necessary to cede an element of control over the process of disclosure in order to preserve confidence in specific transactions and in the market as a whole. The move towards greater transparency was, however, far from straightforward. There were powerful and still largely unexplored forces at work within bureaucratized companies which created and re-created internal and external boundaries of communication. Survival and success within large organizations required the careful deployment of knowledge about the substance and performance of the segmented role which the individual employee performed. It was advantageous to claim possession of information or skills denied to competitors within the hierarchy, to manipulate the presentation of achievement, and to conceal evidence of error or failure. Once intellectual property had been established, tactical alliances with other key players could be formed on the basis of its discreet exchange.[190] Secrecy was both a function of power and means of compensating for its absence.[191]

Business provided as rich an example as any other organization of Simmel's perception of the powerful bonds of trust created by the sharing of secret information.[192] In turn, the enterprise as a whole strengthened the commitment of its employees by the sense of collective possession of privileged knowledge denied to rivals and the public at large. Discipline was reinforced by personal contracts which forbade the disclosure of information gained during the course of employment.[193] Whatever the theories of perfect competition prescribed, the instinct of a firm was to keep to a minimum the volume of data about its activities which might come into the possession of any agency which might curtail its operations, which included not only customers and competitors but the state and its own shareholders. A major study of American firms observed that, 'just as there seems to be a powerful human need for a certain degree of privacy manifested by people of every culture, the attitude of corporations toward the disclosure of information about their workings is so strong

---

[189] Alexander and Britton, *Financial Reporting*, 213–24, Edwards, *History of Financial Accounting*, 213–14.

[190] See the very useful discussion of these points in R. Jackell, *Moral Mazes: The World of Corporate Managers* (New York, 1988), 3–11, 118, 122, 133.

[191] D. Golding, 'Management Rituals: Maintaining Simplicity in the Chain of Command', in S. Linstead, R. G. Small, and P. Jeffcutt (eds.), *Understanding Management* (London, 1996), 83–4; S. P. Feldman, 'Management in Context: Culture and Organizational Change', in ibid. 125–7.

[192] See above, p. 14. M. N. Wexler, 'Conjectures on the Dynamics of Secrecy and the Secrets Business', *Journal of Business Ethics*, 6: 6 (1987), 473–7.

[193] On the incidence of confidentiality clauses in the contracts of employment of staff in large companies, see Y. Cripps, *The Legal Implications of Disclosure in the Public Interest* (2nd edn., London, 1994), 23.

as to appear almost a biological urge'.[194] The default position was silence. Where they wished to respond to the climate of greater openness, managers retained discretion as to which of the various stakeholders were given priority in the release of market-sensitive information.[195] The attitude towards the control of communication was inherently adversarial. In this sense, commerce was closer to the secret services than to Whitehall. The desire to increase trust did constant battle with the fear that any disclosed fragment might be the piece which enabled a competitor to complete the jigsaw.

The exchange of power for confidence was further complicated by the intervention of the courts. The last occasion when the legal control of information in manufacture became a matter of national debate was the patent-reform controversy of the mid-nineteenth century, which was discussed in Chapter 3.[196] The system which resulted was subject to further modifications, culminating in the 1977 Patents Act, which sought to align the domestic and EEC regulations.[197] Over the years, however, its significance steadily declined. The bureaucratization of production diminished the role of the lone inventor and his patentable discovery and stimulated use of civil actions to protect trade secrets. This application of the legal doctrine of confidentiality expanded out of sight of Parliament and the general public, until by the closing decades of the twentieth century it had become much the most common recourse for those wishing to restrict access to commercially sensitive intellectual property.[198] Action under this judge-made device was far more flexible and wide-ranging than under the cumbersome procedures of statutory patent law. Intervention by the courts required merely that any information of competitive value within a firm, including both its manufacturing processes and its business practices in general, was not public knowledge, that it had been transmitted to an employee under an obligation of confidentiality, that efforts had been made to keep it secret, and that an unauthorized disclosure had taken place.[199] In this context, industrial espionage by means of electronic surveillance or communication was of secondary if growing concern. The central problem was the disaffection and mobility of employees, as it had been ever since eighteenth-century artisans travelled to France with the earliest industrial inventions in their heads.[200] Recourse to the law both required and reinforced the establish-

---

[194] Stevenson, *Corporations and Information*, 51–2.

[195] C. Carnaghan, M. Gibbins, and S. Ikäheimo, 'Managed Financial Disclosures: The Interplay Between Accountability Pressures', in R. Munro and J. Mouritsen (eds.), *Accountability: Power, Ethos and the Technologies of Managing* (London, 1996), 166–79.

[196] See above, pp. 107–11.

[197] D. I. Bainbridge, *Intellectual Property* (London, 1992), 245; T. A. Blanco White, R. Jacob, and J. D. Davies, *Patents, Trade Marks, Copyright and Industrial Designs* (2nd edn., London, 1978), 16–17.

[198] A. Coleman, *The Legal Protection of Trade Secrets* (London, 1992), 2–18; J. Pooley, *Trade Secrets* (Berkeley, 1982), 13–55; R. B. Stevenson, *Corporations and Information* (Baltimore, 1980), 5–50.

[199] Coleman, *Legal Protection of Trade Secrets*, 4; Gurry, *Breach of Confidence*, 3–6, 90–7.

[200] M. Saunders, *Protecting your Business Secrets* (Aldershot, 1985), 38; Coleman, *Legal Protection of Trade Secrets*, 93.

ment of a culture of secrecy within the company. Unless the judge was convinced that such a culture existed, the action would fail, and if it succeeded, the award of punitive damages would impact on the workforce as a whole. Loyalty to the enterprise, during and beyond the period of employment, was the basic objective.

Since the mid-nineteenth century, the potential conflict between this branch of civil law and the criminal law in general had been recognized by the development of a public interest defence. Companies could not block communication if the purpose was to conceal illegal behaviour.[201] However, in the absence of a formal definition of this concept, it has proved very difficult for the lone whistle-blower to gain the confidence to resist the application of actions for breach of confidence by powerful corporations. Only where formal legal protection has been given to the principled leaker, as in the US Whistleblower Protection Act of 1989 (which applies to both the private and public sectors), has there been a redress of the balance of power. In Britain, action has yet to be taken on a recommendation from the Law Commission as long ago as 1981 that the device of confidentiality be transferred from common to statutory law.[202] The territory remains a playground for company lawyers and a minefield for dissenting employees.

The use of breach of confidence to supplement statutory controls of information or frustrate legal obligations to openness is nowhere better illustrated than in what was for the consumer the most critical interface between industry and the state. Britain had invented the device of official inspection of productive processes liable to damage public health. Beginning with the establishment of the Alkali Inspectorate in 1804, a range of agencies had grown up armed with duties of inquiry and report. Following the post-war programme of nationalization, their work, as we have seen, had been supplemented by a parallel structure of consumer councils charged with monitoring the performance of public utilities. In practice, the proliferating volumes of information which were laid before Parliament all too rarely revealed the extent or precise causes of threats to consumer safety.[203] The bulk of the legislation defining their responsibilities of investigation and communication contained powerful exclusion clauses designed to protect the organization's presumed trade secrets, whatever the form of its ownership. In 1972 the Franks Report on Secrecy listed sixty-one Acts embodying restrictions on the flow of information from public agencies in addition to the catch-all Official Secrets Act, and a Parliamentary answer in 1987 suggested that in the intervening period these

---

[201] Cripps, *Legal Implications of Disclosure*, 25–9.

[202] As this book is in press, a government-backed Private Member's Bill (The Public Interest Disclosure Bill) is going through Parliament.

[203] M. Frankel, 'How Secrecy Protects the Polluters', in D. Wilson (ed.), *The Secrets File* (London, 1984), 22–46; M. Frankel, 'The Environment', in D. Delbridge and M. Smith (eds.), *Consuming Secrets* (London, 1982), 95–121; Barnes, *Open Up!*, 6.

had more than doubled.[204] The existence of these prohibitions, and the reluctance fully to exploit the remaining possibilities of communication, reflected a deference to the market and a heightened sensitivity to the role of secrecy in any kind of manufacturing or service industry. It was argued that resistance to inspection would be unmanageable unless full consideration was given to the need for confidentiality, and that the model of organization as a domain of private knowledge applied as much to the public as the commercial sector. In the pharmaceutical industry, for instance, where the threat to public health was at its most acute, the Government readily accepted its responsibility to adjust publication to avoid damage to trade secrets.[205] The Alkali Inspectorate itself surrounded its activities with a 'cloak of secrecy' which kept the public at arm's length from its dealings with companies guilty of pollution.[206] The conflicts between the needs of producer and consumer were real, but a rational, open resolution was impeded by the long tradition of assuming rather than demonstrating the commercial value of confidentiality.[207]

Rather than the consumer as active citizen deploying the power of the state to erode the restrictions of the law of equity, there was a growing prospect of the reverse process taking place. As the Official Secrets Acts became increasingly inoperable, governments began to explore the possibility of imposing controls on communication by means of breach of confidence actions. Rulings were obtained, first in relation to the publication of the Crossman *Diaries* and later during the *Spycatcher* saga, which indicated that the creaking device of 'signing the Act' could be supplemented by enforceable obligations of personal trust which all civil servants were deemed to have assumed in accepting employment.[208] It is of some interest to trace the stepping-stones over which Lord Widgery carried the action from the private to the public domain in his landmark 1967 judgement:

I cannot see that the courts should be powerless to restrain the publication of public secrets, while enjoying the *Argyll* powers in regard to domestic secrets. Indeed, as already pointed out, the court must have power to deal with publication which threatens national security, and the difference between such a case and the present

[204] *Departmental Committee on Section 2 of the Official Secrets Act 1991*, i. App. V, pp. 132–3; *Hansard*, 6th series, 108, 21 Jan. 1887, written answers cols. 560–1. The Hansard list contained 131 laws.

[205] C. Rayner, *The Right to Know: A Spoonful of Secrets* (London, 1993), 2.

[206] The phrase is from G. Richardson, with A. Ogus and P. Burrows, *Policing Pollution: A Study of Regulation and Enforcement* (Oxford, 1982), 46.

[207] The Royal Commission on Environmental Protection, for instance, concluded that 'the refusal to release information on grounds of confidentiality tends to become a reflex action, without specific reference to the question of whether commercial interests are truly at risk'. Cited in Frankel, 'How Secrecy Protects the Polluter', 26.

[208] Young, *The Crossman Affair*, esp. 196–200; D. G. T. Williams, 'The Spycatcher Saga', *Dalhousie Law Journal*, 12: 2 (Nov. 1989), 210, 223–4; C. Munro, 'Confidence in Government', in L. Clarke (ed.), *Confidentiality and the Law* (London, 1990), 7–11; D. Goldberg, 'Executive Secrecy, National Security, and Freedom of Information in the Untied Kingdom', *Government Information Quarterly*, 4: 1 (1987), S1–6; Thomas, *Espionage and Secrecy*, 77–84, 123–41; Baxter, *State Security, Privacy and Information*, 75–9; Naylor, *A Man and his Institution*, 307–8.

case is one of degree rather than kind. I conclude, therefore, that when a Cabinet Minister receives information in confidence the improper publication of such information can be restrained by the court, and his obligation is not merely to observe a gentleman's agreement to refrain from publication.[209]

The basis upon which the law was brought in to reinforce honourable secrecy was, ironically, one of the most distasteful episodes in the long fall from grace of the aristocracy. The Duchess of Argyll had succeeded in preventing publication of details of her colourful private life on the grounds that marital confidence took precedence over marital chastity.[210]

From the state's point of view, this use of the courts had the advantage of comparative speed, reliability, and lack of drama. Injunctions could be obtained at any hour of the day or night to prevent rather than merely punish publication; the matter was in the hands of judges rather than unpredictable juries; and the penalty of fines rather than imprisonment reduced the danger of creating martyrs.[211] The difficulty was that the notion of 'public interest' was easier to deploy in favour of openness. It could be argued that where the ostensible purpose of the organization was service to the public rather than to shareholders, the burden lay with the plaintiff to prove that society would benefit from concealment rather than with the defendant to prove that it would be harmed.[212] Equity also was more sympathetic to discretionary assessments of time and harm, unlike Official Secrets Act prosecutions, where, until the Ponting jury defied the judge's direction, the issue was solely the breach of authorization. For this reason the state's success in extending the scope of a branch of law developed largely in the context of private business was qualified by defeats in the Crossman and *Spycatcher* cases over questions of public damage and prior publication.[213]

The inconsistent pattern of reform in the commercial sector illustrated the impossibility of dissociating confidential relationships from relations of authority. Progress was not a zero-sum game in which the former naturally grew as the latter diminished. The rules controlling the dissemination of secrets held between two parties always tended towards asymmetry. In commerce, the fiction of structures being composed of a series of implied contracts between autonomous private individuals concealed complex strategies of

---

[209] Cited in Cripps, *Legal Implications of Disclosure*, 165.

[210] It was argued by the defendants that her action should be disallowed because she 'did not come to equity with clean hands'. Gurry, *Breach of Confidence*, 100; Reid, *Confidentiality and the Law*, 150–1.

[211] Lustgarten and Leigh, *In from the Cold*, 279–82.

[212] Munro, 'Confidence in Government', 9–10.

[213] In the Crossman case, the defence argued that the public interest in maintaining the confidentiality of Cabinet proceedings would not be seriously harmed by the publication of material relating to meetings ten years earlier, and in the *Spycatcher* case, the prosecution faced persistent difficulties with the argument that the book and its contents had become too widely available to meet the condition that the material was not already in the public domain.

control. In the professions, the trust between the social worker and the client, the doctor and the patient, was traditionally founded on an engineered deference. Radical change took place in this period only when the act of consent was aligned with the purpose for which the confidences were obtained. If active participation in a welfare or healing process was held to enhance the prospect of success, so also the use of the relevant personal information required a conscious exercise of choice. As any liberal theorist knew, choice depended on information; the process of keeping secrets had to be as transparent as possible. The virtue of the social work model which emerged at the end of this period was that clients were in possession of written safeguards, and were to be supplied with as much detail as possible about the journeys their private secrets were likely to take. The more the relativity of confidentiality was acknowledged, the more important it was that the source of the personal archive was fully informed of the inevitable complexity of the decisions which would have to be taken about it.

Problems arose when the transfer of authority was resisted, as was long the case in the medical profession, or where the rules of the game remained partially obscure, as in the case of commercial confidentiality. In contrast to many informal safeguards, the civil action of breach of trust was legally enforceable, and in contrast to much statutory protection, it possessed valuable elements of flexibility and proportionality. But it failed the tests of transparency and transfer of power. The dynamics of authority were unclear and at worst heavily tilted towards the hierarchies of command in commercial and, latterly, public and quasi-public organizations. The widening use of the device constituted a quiet counter-current to the noisy debate about statutory reform. The deployment of the obligation of confidentiality became a device for asserting the private interests of a bureaucracy against the needs of those it was intended to serve.[214] The strategy of merging customer, client, and citizen was all too often frustrated by precisely the claim to control private secrets which had first given rise to it.

Protest

Midway through the second period of Conservative office, the Home Secretary stood up in the House of Commons to proclaim a revolution. Almost a century and a half after the first demand for explicit legal controls over the interception of communications, the government was at last proposing to act. Leon Brittan dwelt upon the significance of the moment:

It is clear that we are providing, for the first time, a clear and comprehensive statutory framework for the interception of communications. Even more important, we

---

[214] C. Medewar, *Social Audit Consumer Handbook* (London, 1978), 4.

are creating, for the first time, a new criminal offence of unauthorised interception. Most important of all we are providing, for the first time, a means of redress, and an effective one, for those wishing to complain that interception has been improperly authorised.[215]

There was no novelty in the basis of public concern. As Brittan himself put it, 'interception of communications is always highly distasteful; it is a major intrusion of privacy'.[216] From Mazzini to Marrinan, the same arguments had been put forward, to be met by a blanket refusal even to discuss Home Office practice, let alone place it on a statutory footing. Now, at last, the ice appeared to be breaking up. Between 1985 and 1989 more legislation was passed relating to the secret behaviour of the state than at any time since the frenetic period just before the First World War. After James Callaghan's government had successfully resisted demands for intervention in spite its evaporating majority, Margaret Thatcher's administrations, secure in their purpose and their power, seemed to be yielding to protest on every front.

The immediate cause of reform was the final decline of Britain's moral ascendancy in Europe and its Empire.[217] In the heyday of Victorian liberalism, it had been axiomatic that any imitation of practice on the continent or in the newly annexed territories could only mark a step backwards in the progress of the nation's political freedoms.[218] Signs of diminishing confidence could be detected well before the end of the nineteenth century, but it was not until the commencement of democratic reconstruction after 1945 that the scale of change became fully visible. The rebuilding of the Western European states ravaged by totalitarianism and war, the quickening of decolonization and the maturing of former imperial possessions such as Canada and Australia, together with the associated declarations of human rights, provided domestic critics of the British political culture with an increasing range of instruments and examples with which to further their campaigns. The 1985 Interception of Communications Act was precipitated by a judgement of the European Court of Human Rights in August 1984 that Britain was in breach of Article 8 of the European Convention on Human Rights, which guaranteed the protection of privacy for individuals, their families, and their correspondence.[219] The case in question concerned an antiques dealer named Malone, who in 1978 had been tried for receiving stolen property after his telephone had been tapped by the police.[220] Almost exactly a century after the arrival of the telephone in Britain,

---

[215] *Hansard*, 6th Series, 75, 12 Mar. 1985, col. 151.

[216] Ibid.

[217] See the argument put forward, *inter alia*, by Neal Ascherson, in 'Mocking of Monarchy Tilts the Power Axis', The *Independent on Sunday* (17 Jan. 1993), 23.

[218] See above, pp. 5–6.

[219] Lustgarten and Leigh, *In from the Cold*, 53.

[220] Aubrey, *Who's Watching You*, 70; Fitzgerald and Leopold, *Stranger on the Line*, 133–6; Baxter, *State Security, Privacy and Information*, Wacks, *Protection of Privacy*, 167–72, 40–4; L. J. Lloyd, 'The Interception of Communications Act 1985', *Modern Law Review*, 49 (Jan. 1986), 86–8.

he made the first legal challenge to this form of interception, citing, amongst other authorities, Warren and Brandeis on the right to personal privacy.[221] Having failed to gain redress in the national courts, he turned to Europe and eventually secured a ruling that English law in this area failed to provide clear and transparent safeguards against arbitrary action. As a signatory to the Convention, the Government came under pressure to introduce a reform which would for the first time identify the scope of the state's authority in this field.

Leon Brittan was departing from the tradition of Sir James Graham more out of necessity than conviction. As his Labour counterpart observed in the debate: 'He boasted that it is the first statutory limitation on interception. That is true. But the Government never wanted to do it. They have been dragged kicking and screaming all the way.'[222] As recently as 1980 it had defeated an attempt by the backbencher Bob Cryer to introduce a Control of Interception Bill, and the following year had overturned a Labour-sponsored amendment to the Telecommunications Bill passed by the House of Lords.[223] The decision to respond so swiftly to the defeat in Europe reflected the intersection of several additional pressures, as was argued in a letter to *The Times* on the day of the Second Reading debate by a former President of the European Commission:

I believe that the present position has become untenable and that the previous practice cannot continue. This is partly because we have become a more inquisitive and iconoclastic society, and partly because this Government has deliberately damaged the nexus of consent. Actions may be taken with the tacit support of 90 per cent of the House of Commons which should not be done with the support of 60 per cent, particularly if even that lower figure is generally inflated by the vagaries of the electoral system . . . A rolling back of the frontiers of State surveillance is necessary.[224]

The changed society which Roy Jenkins discovered on his return from Brussels was as much a consequence of the increased deployment of information technology as a cause of the growing unease about its misuse. In the early 1840s the intense political concern about postal espionage arose from changing patterns of private and public communication which heightened sensitivity to the altered behaviour of the state. By the same measure, the growing intensity of the debate over phone tapping stemmed from accelerating developments in the electronic transmission of information. In 1957, when the Home Office buried the last outburst of protest, telephones and televisions were installed in only a minority of households, and the broadcasting services were still encased in a deferential relationship to government.[225] A quarter of a century later, two-

---

[221] D. G. T. Williams, 'Telephone Tapping', *Cambridge Law Journal*, 38 (Nov. 1979), 226.

[222] *Hansard*, 6th Series, 75, 12 Mar. 1985, col. 170.

[223] On the attempt to modify the 1981 Telecommunications Act, see P. Goodrich, 'Freedom of the Phone', *Liverpool Law Review*, 11: 2 (1981), 44.

[224] *The Times* (12 Mar. 1985), 15.

[225] On the spread of televisions, which were installed in 47.2% of households in 1957, see S. Bowden and A. Offer, 'Household Appliances and the Use of Time: The United States and Britain Since the 1920s', *Economic History Review*, 47: 4 (1994), 746.

thirds of homes were connected to the phone network, and 97 per cent were receiving BBC and ITV programmes, which were beginning to assume the role of informed critic of the political process previously the monopoly of the printed word.[226]

There was an increasing demand for information about the communication of information, and a growing body of experts able to make use of the opportunities offered by the new media to supply it. Like the writers of the unstamped press at the very beginning of the period covered by this book, these technically literate journalists were at once the subjects and the objects of their protests. The two best-informed commentators on the machinery of state secrecy at this time, Crispin Aubrey and Duncan Campbell, were prosecuted under the Official Secrets Act in 1977, together with an army corporal named John Berry, for publishing classified material about signals intelligence.[227] Having received only light sentences, they were free to exploit their notoriety and knowledge in a range of further reports and books. It was Campbell's exposé of the organization of the modernized phone-tapping system in the *New Statesman* in 1980 which supplied the bulk of the data upon which later campaigners based their technical arguments.[228] As in the early 1830s, the Government was in a double bind. The more it attempted to enforce its regulations, the more it dramatized the message of its opponents. The most striking combination of ineffective repression and specialist reporting came on the eve of the second reading of the Interception of Communications Bill in 1985. The Independent Broadcasting Authority was persuaded to mount an unsuccessful attempt to ban a Channel 4 programme entitled *MI5's Official Secrets* on the grounds that it might be in breach of Section 2 of the Official Secrets Act. The only consequence of the intervention was the enlargement of the audience for a series of revelations by Cathy Massiter and another unnamed MI5 officer about the widespread monitoring by the security services of domestic organizations, and the subsequent exploitation of the material in the Commons debate just six days later.[229]

What was so alarming about the new detail was its imprecision. At the time of Birkett it was possible to chart the changing balance between epistolary and telephonic interceptions on an almost like-for-like basis. Although there was always the prospect of a single warrant sweeping up many letters or conversations, there did appear to be some boundaries to the possibilities of surveillance. The conduct of postal espionage continued much as before, but with the creation of a new national telephone-tapping centre in London linked to com-

---

[226] On the growth during the 1970s of broadcast journalism and the resulting 'plethora of programmes focusing on political issues', see Barnes, *Open Up!*, 2.

[227] The initials of the defendants endowed the event with the title of the 'ABC trial'. For a full if partial account of the drama, see Aubrey, *Who's Watching You?*, 11–13.

[228] A collected and updated edition of the reports was published as D. Campbell, *Phonetappers and the Security State* (London, 1981).

[229] They were referred to at length in the main Opposition speech by Gerald Kaufman. *Hansard*, 6th Series, 75, 12 Mar. 1985, cols. 167–8.

puters capable of triggering recordings and transmitting their contents directly to other branches of the security services, and with an unknown volume of interceptions taking place through the satellite-based technology at GCHQ, the scope of electronic intervention now seemed limitless.[230] The introduction in 1980 of the next generation of telephone exchanges, cosily entitled 'System X', which avoided the need to instal cumbersome physical taps on lines, further increased anxiety. In these circumstances, the fact that the official number of warrants had more than tripled between 1958 and 1979 was almost beside the point.[231] The more journalists wrote about the organization of the system, the less acceptable became the state's silence about the rules for its use. Parliamentary questioners were referred back to the Birkett Report, which in turn referred back to 1844 and thence to time immemorial. Little comfort was given by the publication of an eight-page White Paper in 1980 and the subsequent concession of an annual review by a distinguished judge.[232] Information on the Government's terms was no longer enough.

The Labour Party was towed along in the wake of the journalists and pressure groups. Systematic interest in secret surveillance only commenced at the close of its period of office in 1979, when a Home Affairs Group on the intelligence services was established.[233] Although it maintained informal links with the investigative reporters, and facilitated the publication of their findings, it did not produce its own research until 1984.[234] After the publication of the Younger Report the issue had been kept alive only by the exertions of a handful of libertarian MPs such as Alex Lyon, who in 1973 launched a vain pursuit of the Home Secretary following claims that the phone of the editor of the *Railway Gazette* had been bugged.[235] Even when the Party became formally committed to a complete overhaul of the system, enthusiasm amongst its hierarchy was patchy at best, to the mounting frustration of a few vocal left-wingers such as Peter Hain and Ken Livingstone. In the debate on the Interception of Communications Bill, James Callaghan, a former Home Secretary as well as the preceding Prime Minister, could only bring himself to say that the legislation represented a 'slight advantage' over the procedures he once had policed.[236] Any attempt to codify the powers of the Home Office in the field of the secret services was likely, in his view, to raise as many problems as it resolved.

---

[230] See Campbell's contemporary account in *Phonetappers and the Security State*, Ch. 2. Also R. Norton-Taylor, *In Defence of the Realm?* (London, 1990), 77–8; Fitzgerald and Leopold, *Stranger on the Line*, 50–82; Wacks, *The Protection of Privacy*, 37.

[231] 'Phone Tapping', *Labour Research*, 73: 4 (Apr. 1984), 90.

[232] See *The Interception of Communications in Great Britain*, Cmnd. 7873 (1980). The first review was conducted in 1981 by Lord Diplock, who had been a member of the Security Commission since 1971. He found the system to be in perfect health.

[233] Campbell, *Phonetappers and the Security State*, 40.

[234] See, 'Phone Tapping', *Labour Research*.

[235] Fitzgerald and Leopold, *Stranger on the Line*, 72–3; Madgwick and Smythe, *The Invasion of Privacy*, 106; Sampson, 'Secrecy, News Management and the British Press', 219.

[236] *Hansard*, 6th Series, 75, 12 Mar. 1985, col. 193.

A central difficulty, as it had been since the mid-1960s, was the shared history. Cathy Massiter's revelations about the widespread bugging of organizations capable of challenging government policy in the industrial and security fields applied to both Labour and Conservative periods of office. If the last great miners' strike, which ended just as the Interception of Communications Bill was going through the Commons, represented the most intense use of telephonic surveillance against trade unions ever seen, there were plenty of other examples from years when the labour movement's political wing held power, including the bitterly fought Grunwick Strike of 1978.[237] Exactly what Labour Home Office Ministers were told of the activities of the secret services for which they were nominally responsible was never clear. Merlyn Rees, who held the post at the time of Grunwick, supported the 1985 Bill on the grounds that 'it is impossible for a Home Secretary, dealing with all the various aspects of a wide Department, even to pretend that he knows all that is going on in MI5'.[238] Nonetheless, as Barbara Castle pointed out in her diaries, the Cabinet must have suspected the source of the confidential reports it received so regularly on the conduct of industrial disputes.[239] From the mid-1960s onwards the Labour Party was as much the cause as the vehicle of the growing sense of unease about the interception of communications, and had as much to lose from the release of Secret Service documents into the public domain. The volume of complaints from trade unions and pressure groups about interference with their calls and correspondence increased sharply during the 1974–9 Labour Government, and formed the basis of the campaign against the Conservative administrations in the first half of the 1980s.

Roy Jenkins's second argument for structural change in the management of the secret services was that the legitimacy of informal controls was conditional on the maintenance of a particular political culture. The problem in 1985 was not so much the intrinsic weakness of the current arrangements as the erosion of the constitutional conventions in which they were encased. By deliberately setting out to destroy the post-war consensus, Margaret Thatcher had undermined the trust which the exercise of unwritten powers required. In the absence of consensus over the aims of Government policy, there could be no confidence in the hidden exercise of the means. Jenkins's analysis was based on a somewhat foreshortened view of history. The lineaments of the peculiarly British form of the secret state had been established a century before the emergence of 'Butskellism', and had weathered many a political storm in the meantime. However, as election victory followed election victory after 1979, the dangers of an 'elective dictatorship', first outlined by Lord Hailsham in 1976, seemed ever more

---

[237] Campbell, *Phonetappers and the Security State*, 22; R. Norton-Taylor, 'The Slick Spymaster', *Guardian* (20 June 1994).

[238] *Hansard*, 6th Series, 75, 12 Mar. 1985, col. 182.

[239] Fitzgerald and Leopold, *Stranger on the Line*, 40.

real.[240] In this sense, the concessions made by the Conservatives during the 1980s in the control of the secret state were a consequence as much of their strengths as their weaknesses. A partial departure from the tradition of unwritten powers of surveillance was an acceptable price to pay for the immense authority they remained able to exercise under the unwritten constitution.

Whilst the 1984 European Court ruling precipitated legislation, the form it took reflected the Conservatives' successful resistance of a continental right of privacy. Younger had recommended a case-by-case approach to the issue, with the emphasis on safeguards against modern electronic forms of surveillance, and in this sense the Interception of Communications Act was a companion piece to the Data Protection Act of the previous year. The initial strategy had been to exclude the security services from the public debate over the implications of new information technology. But restricting the terms of reference of both the Younger and Lindop inquiries could not prevent the connections being made by increasingly well-informed critics. Pressure was intensified by the ruling in the Malone affair that the civil right to confidentiality could not be applied to telephone conversations.[241] The Vice-Chancellor hearing the case was moved to make a public protest about the legal vacuum in which the interception of calls existed. In response, the Government was able to adopt the tactic, later applied to other aspects of the secret state, of introducing rules of engagement which embodied a minimum of precision and accountability. The law was framed so as to offer the least concession to the broader arguments for civil liberties, and the smallest opportunity to MPs and electors wishing to monitor the work of the secret services.

Henceforth warrants could be issued on one of three grounds: protection of national security, prevention of serious crime, and protection of the economic well-being of the country.[242] With the exception of the notion of serious crime, none of the categories was otherwise defined. The third issue, which again was to reappear later, was a further instance of the state turning weakness into strength. The relative under-performance of the post-war economy had been a long-term factor in undermining public confidence in the entire edifice of official secrecy. Opacity seemed increasingly unable to guarantee either honour or efficiency. The response of successive governments from the 1960s onwards—Labour just as much as Conservative—was to bring sensitive areas of economic performance under the black umbrella of national security. In the absence of any specific assurances to the contrary, almost any action by a player in the market, including in particular a trade union, could be held to be caus-

---

[240] Lord Hailsham, 'Elective Dictatorship', Richard Dimbleby Lecture, 1976.

[241] Coleman, *Legal Protection of Trade Secrets*, 84–5.

[242] For a compact summary of the Act, see Birkinshaw, *Government and Information*, 34–5; Lloyd, 'The Interception of Communications Act 1985', 89–92; Lustgarten and Leigh, *In From the Cold*, 53–64.

ing it potential damage. Secrecy was once more presented as a sentinel of public progress. The only safeguard against the abuse of these loosely described powers was an annual report by a commissioner and the right of appeal to a newly constituted tribunal, whose role was confined to determining whether the Home Secretary had been acting in good faith in applying the Act.[243] It was possible to complain, but not to know anything about how the appeal was considered, nor to appeal against the outcome. In other countries, especially in Germany, subjects of phone taps had the right to a full account of what had been done to them, and why.[244] This was not the British way. Leon Brittan patiently explained how, as ever, secrecy needed to be encased in secrecy: 'It would clearly, however, be ridiculous for somebody to be able to discover whether an interception had been directed against him simply by applying to the tribunal. That is why the tribunal cannot operate in public. But it will have full access to all the facts and arguments.'[245]

The extent to which the concession of statutory regulation implied no necessary alteration of the traditional mindset was confirmed at the end of the debate on the Interception of Communications Bill, when the junior Home Office Minister David Waddington announced the appointment of a new Head of MI5 but refused to name him. He further declined to answer any questions about individual cases of phone tapping, citing a statement by James Callaghan in 1978 in support of his position.[246] Having allowed the Parliamentary draughtsmen into the world of espionage, it could only be a matter of time before their attentions were turned to the Secret Service itself, but the Government now had a working model which it could safely apply. Thus, three years later Douglas Hurd, Brittan's successor as Home Secretary, rose in the Commons to proclaim another fundamental break with the past:

The Bill gives Parliament for the first time this century, the opportunity to establish a framework for the Security Service and to weld it into legislation. A month ago no one suspected that we were about to launch a substantial reform of this kind. Now, so fast does the political kaleidoscope shift, those who in their hearts were amazed at the boldness of what we proposed take it for granted and press for more.[247]

As with phone tapping, the shift in the kaleidoscope had been precipitated by difficulties with the European Court of Human Rights. In 1988 the Government seemed likely to lose a case brought against it by members of Liberty over the absence of adequate definition and oversight of the powers of the Security

---

[243] Baxter, *State Security, Privacy and Information*, 174–94, provides a lengthy discussion of the powers of the tribunal and the difficulties of giving precise interpretations of the grounds for issuing warrants.

[244] On the practice in Germany, see Goodrich, 'Freedom of the Phone', 95–6; Lloyd, 'The Interception of Communications Act 1985', 93.

[245] *Hansard*, 6th Series, 75, 12 Mar. 1985, col. 163.

[246] Ibid., cols. 252–4.

[247] Ibid., 143, 15 Dec. 1988, col. 1104.

Service.[248] It responded by introducing a White Paper and then the Security Service Bill which was explicitly modelled on the 1985 Act. The legislation, which received the Royal Assent in April 1989, specifically related to the domestic espionage structure created by Royal Prerogative in 1909, although as with the interception of communications, it was merely giving statutory recognition to practices which had enjoyed an unacknowledged existence in one form or another since at least the seventeenth century. The legal definition of the powers of the Service was only marginally more precise than the internal statement drawn up by Maxwell Fyfe in 1952 and endorsed by Lord Harris in 1975.[249] It was to protect national security from the agents of foreign powers, and 'from actions intended to overthrow or undermine parliamentary democracy by political, industrial or violent means; and to safeguard the economic well-being of the United Kingdom against threats posed by the actions of persons outside the British Islands'. The only protection given to the nation against the Security Service itself was a specific prohibition of actions furthering the interest of any political party, and the creation of a Commissioner to review the issuing of intercept warrants and other activities, together with a tribunal to hear complaints from aggrieved citizens. The Home Office maintained reserve powers to censor the annual reports of the Commissioner to Parliament and to clothe the work of the tribunal in secrecy.[250] In common with the similar appeals procedure under the 1985 Act, a subject of Security Service action could not learn of even the existence, let alone the detail, of a warrant if it was found to have been legally granted, and there was no avenue of further appeal to an outside judicial body.[251]

Beyond the immediate problem of Europe, the concession of formal regulation could be seen as the product of principle or expediency. As Jonathan Aitken observed in the Second Reading debate, the latter appeared more persuasive: 'the big issue in the Bill, which is the first in the history of the Security Service, is probably not civil liberties, but the confidence, effectiveness, efficiency and judgment of the security services.'[252] All four qualities of the domestic espionage operation had been in manifest decline during the 1980s. There were landmark events, such as the unmasking of Geoffrey Prime in 1982 and Michael Bettaney in 1985, both of whom had been recruited

---

[248] G. Robertson, *Freedom, the Individual and the Law* (London, 1989), 155; Birkinshaw, *Reforming the Secret State*, 6–8.

[249] I. Leigh and L. Lustgarten, 'The Security Service Act 1989', *Modern Law Review*, 52 (Nov. 1989), 804–5; Birkinshaw, *Reforming the Secret State*, 36. The text of the Maxwell-Fyfe Directive is reprinted in Lustgarten and Leigh, *In From the Cold*, App. 1, p. 517.

[250] On the secrecy surrounding the system of report and appeal, see Birkinshaw, *Government and Information*, 34–40; Baxter, *State Security, Privacy and Information*, 117–19; Norton-Taylor, *In Defence of the Realm?*, 40–1; Robertson, *Freedom, the Individual and the Law*, 156.

[251] Leigh and Lustgarten, 'The Security Service Act 1989', 825–30.

[252] *Hansard*, 6th Series, 143, 15 Dec. 1988, col. 1130.

and retained despite spectacular personality defects.[253] The long-drawn-out *Spycatcher* affair made nonsense of the Government's attempts to pretend that the Security Service did not really exist,[254] and left it with the choice of admitting that the organization had virtually run out of control, or that one of its most experienced men was a compulsive fantasist.[255] Wright's revelations about the so-called 'Wilson Plot' of 1974 to 1976 suggested that there was merit in both allegations.[256] The precise nature of the encounter between inherently paranoid security officers and an increasingly paranoid Prime Minister remains impossible to determine.[257] At the very least there was a total collapse of trust, with the event brought to an end only by Wilson's early resignation. The central argument of the Service's critics was that secrecy not only permitted but caused the shortcomings of personnel and procedure. As the Labour Home Affairs spokesman Roy Hattersley put it, 'MI5's errors are the errors of inbreeding. Its mistakes are the mistakes of a closed society that does not have to account for the legality and efficiency of its operations.'[258] With the Government seemingly unable to stem the flow of damaging stories, the need to regain the trust necessary to maintain secrecy seemed increasingly urgent.

The utter absurdity of the traditional refusal to acknowledge the work of the organization or name its head, and the sheer scale of the Service's shortcomings in the recent past, deflected attention from the failure of the campaign for more general reform. The Opposition was able to give a grudging welcome to an Act which, as in 1985, made only a token concession to civil liberties, because it did represent a formal response to a range of outstanding abuses. Commentators might point out that both the definition of powers and the system of Parliamentary oversight fell far short of the arrangements now in force in sister democracies,[259] but the Act could be presented as at least a step towards a more rational and orderly structure of control and operation. It could also be seen, however, as a licence for the Service to advance into the next decade with renewed self-confidence, with the token restrictions more than compensated for by the opportunities for self-aggrandisement which were permitted to open, legally recognized organizations. Its Head could emerge from the shadows to give carefully managed presentations of the value of the Service,

---

[253] Prime was employed at GCHQ. Bettaney was the first MI5 agent to be convicted for spying. The former was a paedophile, the latter a drunk.

[254] D. G. T. Williams, 'The Spycatcher Saga', *Dalhousie Law Journal*, 12: 2 (Nov. 1989), 214.

[255] On the impact of the affair on the subsequent legislation, see Norton-Taylor, *In Defence of the Realm*, 10–11.

[256] Wright, *Spycatcher*, 369–72. According to Wright the original plot was modelled on the Zinoviev Letter forgery of 1924 (see above, Ch. 4. n. 246).

[257] For a lively and sane attempt, see Porter, *Plots and Paranoia*, 210–13.

[258] *Hansard*, 6th Series, 143, 15 Dec. 1988, col. 1116.

[259] Ewing and Gearty, *Freedom under Thatcher*, 176.

and as a new mission was sought following the ending of the Cold War, it could bid to enlarge its spheres of action at the expense of other public agencies such as the police.[260]

In 1980 a Fabian tract reviewed the rapid escalation of protests against secrecy in the previous few years, and looked forward with eager anticipation to the coming struggle: 'The 1980s will be the decisive decades for Britain for freedom of information. For the first time there is a highly motivated coalition of interests determined not only to reform the Official Secrets Act but also to introduce a statutory "right to know".'[261] At the end of the decade attention was finally given to the 1911 Act, but the outcome was as ambiguous as the other reforms to the secrecy system, and the Freedom of Information Bill, which was first presented to Parliament in March 1984,[262] remained a distant aspiration. From the perspective of the highly motivated coalition, the 1980s turned out to be eventful but in the end largely indecisive.

The most obvious reason for the lack of clear-cut progress was the simple reality of Conservative electoral hegemony. For eleven years the country was led by a Prime Minister whose maiden enthusiasm for open government had been replaced by a set of attitudes ranging from indifference to outright hostility.[263] As her opponents were to discover, this form of Conservatism was more than capable of adapting to its purpose the modern techniques of mass communication. When faced with challenges to official secrecy, it was not content merely to decline to answer questions and wait for the fuss to go away. Indicative of its approach was Michael Heseltine's special unit inside the Ministry of Defence, later supplemented by a Ministerial Committee on 'Nuclear Weapons and Public Opinion', which broke new ground by integrating secret surveillance with open campaigning in an onslaught on the burgeoning disarmament movement.[264] The Government had authority and in specific instances was prepared to enforce its will over every kind of coalition of interests. This was notably the case at the Government Communications Headquarters (GCHQ), whose purpose and activities were never fully revealed.[265] The decision in 1984 to ban trade union membership because of an alleged threat to na-

---

[260] On MI5's increasing mastery of public relations, especially after the appointment of Stella Rimmington as its Head in 1991, see Norton-Taylor, 'The Slick Spymaster', *Guardian* (20 June 1994).

[261] Barnes, *Open Up!*, 1.

[262] The Bill was introduced by the Liberal leader David Steel, assisted by the Campaign for Freedom of Information, formed in January. Wilson, 'The Struggle to Overcome Secrecy in Britain', 134; Thomas, 'The British Official Secrets Acts 1911–1939 and the Ponting Case', 111–12.

[263] Young, 'The Thatcher Style of Government', 273.

[264] Ewing and Gearty, *Freedom under Thatcher*, 61–5; *Secret Society: Cabinet*, Broadcast on Channel 4, April, 1991.

[265] The scale of its interceptions of telephone conversations passing in and out of Britain was not exposed by the Birkett Report, and not effectively covered by the 1985 Interception of Communications Act. Its very existence was not acknowledged until May 1983. See Fitzgerald and Leopold, *Stranger on the Line*, 50–1, 120; Baxter, *State Security, Privacy and Information*, 184–94.

tional security was maintained in the face of widespread and prolonged domestic and international protest.[266]

The often brute fact of Conservative power is not, however, a sufficient explanation of the complex mixture of concession, evasion, and resistance which characterized the response to the protest movements of the 1980s. Attention also needs to be paid to the resources and tactics of their opponents. At the very end of the period covered by this book, an authoritative analysis of the campaigns for reform was delivered by Merlyn Rees, who had been a signatory of the epochal Franks Report in 1972 and then served as Home Secretary from 1976 and 1979 as the attempts to secure legislation began to gather momentum. 'So my key words are these', he concluded, '—and I apologise if I've been unnecessarily gloomy—the battle has been won these past ten or fifteen years, but it is no good winning the intellectual battle if there are insufficient troops on the ground to actually translate it into legislative victory at the end of the day.'[267] Rees was a politician; by troops he meant the voters who won elections rather than the leader-writers who merely commented upon them: '*The Guardian* can go on for however long it likes about open government and reform of the Official Secrets Act, but I can tell you that in my own constituency of 75,000 electors I would be hard pressed to find many who would be interested in what I am talking about.'[268] This was not just the wisdom of hindsight. Whilst in office he had argued that the volume of column inches which campaigners were securing in the liberal press was not replicated by the weight of mail in his postbag,[269] nor did it reflect the attitudes of those outside the metropolitan middle class.[270]

This analysis rested on a number of constructions. In the first place it assumed a gap between attitude and agitation. Opinion polls conducted throughout this period gave no support to the view that freedom of information was the private passion of the chattering classes.[271] The growing majority in favour of the principle showed little variation by class or residence. Only the elderly displayed slightly less enthusiasm, but even here it was a matter of

---

[266] H. Lanning and R. Norton-Taylor, *A Conflict of Loyalties—GCHQ 1984–1991* (Cheltenham, 1991), 43–209.

[267] M. Rees, 'The Parameters of Politics', in Chapman and Hunt, *Open Government*, 37.

[268] Ibid. 32. His constituency was Leeds South.

[269] For a discussion of his use of this argument at the time of the publication of the White Paper on Official Secrecy in 1978, see Thompson, 'The Secret State', 150; Michael, *Politics of Secrecy*, 207; G. Drewry, 'Openness and Secrecy in British Government', in T. N. Chaturvedi (ed.), *Secrecy in Government* (New Delhi, 1980). On the quality of public interest in civil liberties in general, see J. Griffiths, 'The Democratic Process', in P. Wallington (ed.), *Civil Liberties 1984* (Oxford, 1984), 86.

[270] Rees argued this in Cabinet. See T. Benn, *Conflicts of Interest: Diaries, 1977–80* (London, 1990), 314 (entry for 22 June 1978). On the significance of this perception to Callaghan, see P. Whitehead, 'The Labour Governments, 1974–1979', in P. Hennessy and A. Seldon (eds.), *Ruling Performance* (Oxford, 1989), 260.

[271] Goldberg, 'Executive Secrecy . . .', 41–4; Michael, *The Politics of Secrecy*, 216. *Labour Research* reported in 1984 the findings of 'a MORI poll' that 84% of respondents did not think the police should have the power to tap phones. See, 'Phone Tapping', 90.

indifference rather than outright hostility.[272] It was evident that votes would not be lost by including the issue in an election manifesto. What was less clear was how far the party would suffer from failing to implement such a promise. For the Labour Prime Ministers of the era, if not for Rees himself, the polarization between stolid voters and excitable campaigners was an easy device for dismissing a cause for which there was little natural sympathy. Whilst the party had been formally committed to some kind of legislation since 1974, Wilson was too weary and still too much in love with Whitehall to press for reform, and his successor too deferential to the constitution and too preoccupied with economic crisis.[273] Callaghan's reluctant conversion to the reform of Section 2 of the 1911 Act was a matter more of tactics than principle. He was extremely annoyed by his inability to prevent or punish the leaking to *New Society* in 1976 of Cabinet discussions about implementation of the new Child Benefit Act.[274] The Child Poverty Action Group, one of the most effective of the new generation of pressure groups, was able to use the secret documents to prevent the Government abandoning its commitment to the scheme (in the name of commonsense trade unionists).[275] It added insult to injury by using the opportunity to deliver a homily on the progress of open government:

Britain is a secretive society. All kinds of government decisions are wrapped in clouds of unknowing. For years there has been a growing amount of talk about greater devolution to the level of the individual, and about greater open-ness in decision-making. But how much of this has come about? About as much as could be balanced on the back of one of the fast-vanishing sixpences.[276]

The Cabinet was embarrassed, but as Section 2 of the Official Secrets Act was no longer thought to be usable, nothing could be done. In response, Callaghan informed the Commons in July 1976 of his intention to reform the Act, 'in a way which will make its coverage both more limited and more effective'.[277] Thus was born the 'armalite rifle versus blunderbuss' strategy, to which Labour was

---

[272] See e.g. the 1986 survey which found that 16% of those aged over 55 registered a 'don't know' answer, double the proportion of younger respondents. A majority of this age group (59%) were nonetheless in favour. Campaign for Freedom of Information, *Public Attitudes Towards Freedom of Information* (London, 1986), 2. Similar but smaller variations were recorded in a 1991 survey: Market and Opinion Research International (MORI), *State of the Nation, 1991* (London, 1991).

[273] On Wilson, see above, pp. 243–4. Also C. Ponting, *Breach of Promise: Labour in Power, 1964–1970* (London, 1989), 175. Callaghan's affection for the traditional aspects of government is well conveyed in his autobiography, *Time and Chance* (London, 1987), esp. 395–7, 406–8, 461. Tony Benn, a member of Callaghan's Cabinet, claimed in 1988 that 'Jim Callaghan was bitterly opposed to open government. Everybody knew that. Everybody knew it at the time.' *Hansard*, 6th Series, 143, 15 Dec. 1988, col. 507.

[274] Kellner and Crowther Hunt, *The Civil Servants*, 267.

[275] For a retrospective account of the event, and the general problems of pressure-group action in this area, see F. Field, *Poverty and Politics* (London, 1982), esp. 43–5.

[276] [F. Field], 'Killing a Commitment: The Cabinet and the Children', *New Society* (24 June 1976).

[277] *Hansard*, 5th Series, 913, 1 July 1976, col. 653. At the same time an inquiry was mounted into Cabinet secrecy, which recommended a tightening of the existing procedures. *Report of the Committee of Privy Councillors on Cabinet Document Security* [Houghton], Cmnd. 6677 (London, 1976), 2–7.

committed until 1979 and the Conservative governments thereafter.[278] The antique device of the catch-all Section 2 was to be replaced by a more focused and therefore more operational definition of the areas of official information which were protected by the law. In the event, Callaghan shied away from exposing the issue to open debate in the Commons, where he no longer had a secure majority, and in the early years of Thatcher's regime the blunderbuss was pressed back into action.[279] However, a further series of misfires, culminating in the Ponting acquittal, reminded the Conservatives of the unreliability of the weapon, and the Act of 1989 may be seen as a belated fulfilment of Labour's undertaking.

Labour had persistent difficulty in viewing reform of the secrecy laws as an integral rather than optional element of its programme. The historic failure to think seriously about the machinery of state had been partly remedied since the war by an engagement with the efficiency of Whitehall, and there was renewed interest in the confining traditions of the bureaucracy following the electoral defeat in 1979.[280] But the larger issue of constitutional change was never anchored in the party's strategy.[281] 'There is something about a proposal for reforming the constitution that releases the inhibitions in a Member of Parliament . . .', observed James Callaghan. 'In debate the subject lays itself open to inventive minds to spin the most fanciful theories and arguments into wild arabesques that can only be brought to earth by the use of the Parliamentary guillotine.'[282] The field was seen as the playground of a motley band of parliamentary outsiders who belonged neither to the heartland of the labour movement nor to the corridors of power. 'The individuals who supported open government or reform of the Official Secrets Act', wrote Merlyn Rees, 'were their own worst enemies. They all had brilliant ideas on what they wanted to do, but could not agree what was the lowest common denominator of what they wanted to get through.'[283] This view was entrenched in the early years of defeat, when the few leading members with a genuine intellectual interest in the issue defected to form the Social Democratic Party,[284] and the remainder of the party showed itself vastly more interested in its own constitution than that of the country at large. As Callaghan's generation was gradually replaced by

---

[278] The terms were actually used by the Conservative MP Sir Hugh Fraser in a debate on reform of the Official Secrets Act later in the year. *Hansard*, 5th Series, 919, 22 Nov. 1976, col. 1887. On its contemporary use by Merlyn Rees, see Theakston, *The Labour Party and Whitehall*, 183.

[279] Ewing and Gearty, *Freedom under Thatcher*, 139.

[280] Jones and Keating, *Labour and the British State*, 151; Theakston, *Labour Party and Whitehall*, 191.

[281] For a jaundiced view of the depth of Labour's interest, see J. A. G. Griffith, *Public Rights and Private Interests* (Tivandrum, 1981), 85–6.

[282] Callaghan, *Time and Chance*, 502.

[283] Rees, 'The Parameters of Politics', 32. Also Wraith, *Open Government*, 6.

[284] On the loss of momentum on the issue of open government with the departure of Jenkins for Brussels in 1976, see Donoughue, *Prime Minister*, 121. On the views on open government of two of the leading defectors, see S. Williams, *Politics is for People* (Harmondsworth, 1981), 185; D. Owen, *Face the Future* (London, 1981), 303–10.

the modernizers, greater sympathy was shown both to specific items of reform and to the general system of government which had allowed a party which never won more than 43.9 per cent of the votes to impose its will on the majority of the population with such uncompromising vigour.[285] Once Neil Kinnock became leader in 1983, there was a consistent commitment to the principle of freedom of information, yet the party went into the 1990s still bereft of a coherent programme of Whitehall reform.[286]

There was an additional difficulty in identifying what Rees termed the 'common denominator' of reform. Refocusing the Official Secrets Act was not interchangeable with 'open government', which might be achieved simply by hiring more press officers and improving the clarity of public documents, and neither were necessarily the same as 'freedom of information', which implied a statutory reversal of the convention that all official material was secret unless otherwise specified, and could be extended to include a range of non-governmental bodies and the protection of privacy.[287] Given the clear structural affinities between the unwritten constitution and the informal rules for controlling official communication, there was a further debate about whether serious reform could be achieved in isolation, or whether, as Charter 88 argued after its launch during the tercentenary of the Glorious Revolution, 'freedom of information and open government' needed to be embedded in a complete overhaul of the constitutional apparatus and the passage of a Bill of Rights.[288] At the level of the public concern which campaigners sought to raise and politicians to counter, there were at best two unifying factors. In practical terms, the most urgent interest was not in information produced by the government and withheld from the electorate, but in material generated by individuals and their families and misused by the agency which held it. Legislation was more likely at the interface between privacy and secrecy rather than secrecy and government, and for this reason it was no accident that the first major reform of the decade was the 1984 Data Protection Act, which was centred on the use rather than the ownership of information technology.

If confidentiality was the first general issue, the second was confidence. More than any other form of conduct, secrecy requires trust, and the growing crisis in the 1980s in relation to every form of blocked communication was above all a product of a widespread decline of faith in the bodies which controlled the flow of information. As the government challenged the overarching claims of

---

[285] On the move of the Labour Party back to the 'libertarian centre' later in the 1980s, see Harrison, *The Transformation of British Politics*, 147.

[286] Theakston, *The Labour Party and Whitehall*, 203.

[287] The development of the different concepts is examined in Goren, *Secrecy and the Right to Know*, 27–34.

[288] See the text of Charter 88, which received its first signatures on 30 Nov. 1988. The movement's arguments for reform in this field, which was one of twelve linked demands, are summarized in its leaflet, *Freedom of Information* (London, 1992). For a survey of the growing campaign for a Bill of Rights, see H. Fenwick, *Civil Liberties* (London, 1994), 77–112.

the professions, so the electorate turned away from the grand narratives of the state. In this context, the ever-increasing ambition of the campaigners both reflected and challenged the public mood. A consistent erosion of trust did not necessarily create support for an integrated programme of reform. At one level, the Campaign for Freedom of Information and Charter 88 were throwbacks to the Benthamite optimism about the transforming power of knowledge and rational reform which had informed the debate at the beginning of the period covered by this book. From its creation in 1984, the former body argued passionately for the impact on citizens, clients, and consumers of the free flow of information,[289] and as the 1980s came to an end signatures were sought for a Charter which demanded the most radical change in the constitution since at least 1688, if not well before. But neither within the decade nor for at least the first two-thirds of the next, did either movement achieve its larger ends, despite the intellectual and organizational energy invested in them. Reformers as much as their opponents were victims of the fragmentation of confidence. The pressure groups for open communication were both strengthened and weakened by an erosion of support for the players in the old corporate state. They recruited disillusioned activists, but lacked the physical and ideological resources that the defeated labour movement once had. As election after election was lost, they were faced with the reality that the only effective reforms were general, and the only feasible ones were partial.[290]

For these reasons, campaigners in the 1980s were never fully in control of the process of reform. They could not even claim full credit for such progress as was made. It may be argued that genuine revolutions are a consequence as much of war within as of war without. If there was any substance in the claims of Brittan and Hurd that they were engineering major change, it was in some part because of division and conflict within the ruling order. The most significant voices in the decade may not have been the tireless advocates for openness, such as Maurice Frankel and Des Wilson, but rather the retired Permanent Secretaries who cautiously embraced the cause,[291] or the increasingly vocal ethical committees of the professions who sought a new relationship between expert and client, and between informal and statutory regulation. Equally the growing dissonance between British practice and the conventions and innovations of other European countries and former members of the empire may have done as much to accelerate legislation as the organized protests at home. The scale of the dissension marked the era off from its predecessors, and created a climate of constantly heightened expectation. But at the end of the day those in

---

[289] See Wilson, *The Secrets File*, for an early collection of arguments on behalf of the Campaign. On the first phase of its work, see Goldberg, 'Executive Secrecy . . .', 44–7.

[290] Hunt, *Open Government in the 1980s*, 7–8.

[291] The civil service unions also began to move in the direction of legislative reform. For early support, see Dresner, 'How would a British Freedom of Information Act Work in Practice?', in *Secrecy, or the Right to Know*, 16.

authority maintained sufficient command of their retreat to ensure that there was no fundamental change of power or principle in the control of communication.

Keeping the Secret

The state's role in the shifting world of secrecy and privacy was marked in 1989 by two centenary enactments. Legislation which had set the framework for the development of twentieth-century systems of intervention and regulation was the subject of major reforms designed to determine the pattern of control until well into the next millennium. The most complex of these built upon the foundations of the first 'Children's Charter', the Prevention of Cruelty to Children Act of 1889, which had established a long-term balance between the powers of government and the rights of families. The privacy of the domestic sphere, which hitherto had been sacrosanct for all but the poorest in the community, was qualified by the creation of new offences of cruelty and neglect, and new devices of discovery and punishment.[292] The informal inquisition of the charity visitors was complemented by statutory mechanisms of inquiry and exposure. In the interests of their children, parents lost their absolute possession of the secrets of the home. The field was intermittently revisited by Parliament, particularly in 1908 and 1948, and during the 1980s pressure grew for a complete overhaul of the duties and responsibilities of all those now involved in the welfare of the most vulnerable members of society. The outcome was a Bill which, according to the Solicitor-General, represented 'the first attempt to establish a unified and consistent code of law covering the care and upbringing of children in both the public and private spheres'.[293]

The case for reform emerged from a wide-ranging debate about public and private responsibilities, but its urgency stemmed from a series of highly publicized child-abuse cases, commencing with the death of Maria Colwell in 1972 and culminating in the Cleveland affair of 1987 and the subsequent inquiry conducted by Lord Justice Butler-Sloss. Just as the physical and sexual assaults on children appeared to highlight a more general malaise of authority and morality, so the individual reports revealed fundamental difficulties in the relationships between professionals and those for whom they were responsible. At the heart of the matter was what Butler-Sloss described in the Introduction to her report as the 'pressure to keep the secret'.[294] This pressure came from outside the child, 'from the family, mother, siblings and the extended family as

---

[292] H. Hendrick, *Child Welfare: England, 1872–1989* (London, 1994), 53–4. The Poor Law Guardians already possessed powers of intervention, although these were not widely used.

[293] *Hansard*, 6th Series, 151, 27 Apr. 1989, col. 1183. The Children's Bill had started its legislative journey in the Lords at the end of the previous year.

[294] *Report of the Inquiry into Child Abuse in Cleveland 1987* [Butler-Sloss], Cm. 412 (London, 1988), 6.

well as the abuser',[295] and from within. Victims set up barriers to communication out of a sense of shame or complicity, or of a misplaced desire to protect those by whom they should be protected: 'Children may elect not to talk because of genuine affection for the perpetrator and an awareness of the consequences to the perpetrator, to the partner, to the family unit, or for an older child an understanding of the economic considerations in the break-up of the family and the loss of the wage earner.'[296] Protection and punishment depended on the extraction and effective deployment of this secret knowledge.[297] The accumulated evidence pointed to shortcomings at every level. Either the professionals failed to penetrate the closed world of the abusive relationship, or, as in the Cleveland case, they invested too much confidence in physical indicators of assault. Where knowledge was obtained, there were critical obstacles to its transmission amongst what could be as many as seventy-two different professional bodies which might become involved in a case of suspected abuse.[298] The inquiry into the first of the sequence of tragedies concluded that, of the relevant factors, 'the greatest and most obvious must be that of the lack of, or ineffectiveness of, communication and liaison',[299] and this remained the most common finding in more than thirty subsequent reports in the period covered by this chapter.[300]

New legislation demanded a full-scale reconsideration of the spheres of authority of professions, the state, and private society. The search was driven partly by a revived emphasis on the integrity of the family, and partly by the breadth of concern about the performance of the welfare organizations. The right blamed them for undermining the authority of parents, the left for bullying working-class families whose problems stemmed from larger failings in society and the economy.[301] Social workers in particular were in a double bind. They frequently lacked the resources to generate sufficiently detailed bodies of knowledge about potentially troubled families, yet the more their ignorance was exposed, the more threatened was their funding. Many of the problems of inter-agency communication were attributable, as they always had been, to inequalities of status and power, yet the more tragedies which hit the headlines, the less secure they became in their dealings with clients and professionals alike. The outcome was a series of reforms to both the procedures and concepts

[295] Ibid. 7.

[296] Ibid.

[297] For a discussion of these problems, see B. Campbell, *Unofficial Secrets* (London, 1989), 4–9.

[298] P. Reder, S. Duncan, and M. Gray, *Beyond Blame: Child Abuse Tragedies Revisited* (London, 1993), 65.

[299] Department of Health and Social Security, *Report of the Committee of Inquiry into the Care and Supervision Provided in Relation to Maria Colwell* (London, 1974), 86.

[300] Reder, Duncan, and Gray, *Beyond Blame*, 60. See the similar findings of two official surveys of the reports: Department of Health, *Child Abuse: A Study of Inquiry Reports, 1980–1989* (London, 1991), 99; Department of Health and Social Security, *Child Abuse: A Study of Inquiry Reports, 1973–1981* (London, 1982), 48.

[301] For a particularly fierce attack on the presumptions of professionals, see S. Bell, *When Salem Came to the Boro: The True Story of the Cleveland Child Abuse Crisis* (London, 1988).

of child-care which attempted to strike a new balance between public and private responsibilities. In the words of the Home Office Minister introducing the Bill: 'local authorities and other agencies should be ready to help where this reduces the risk of family breakdown . . . such services should be provided in voluntary partnership with parents and in a way that promotes family relationships as fully as possible.'[302] Private and public family law was merged, and the interest of the child was formally given priority in resolving conflict. The removal of the child from the home was made the subject of a new structure of court orders. Parental rights would be conditional on the performance of their duties, professional intervention was to be discreet, supportive, and subject to the authority of the courts. Wherever possible, the search for knowledge was to be collaborative rather than inquisitorial. Efforts were made to reduce the paternalism of the professional approach, and to endorse the principle of informing witnesses of the use that would be made of their confidences. The trust of society in the system would reflect the trust families could invest in those charged with helping their children.

The 1989 Children's Act was not the final chapter. The legislation embodied assumptions about the value and strength of the nuclear family which were and will remain issues of intense debate. In the particular instance of abuse, the dilemmas posed by the child's keeping of secrets could not be resolved at a blow. How the boundaries of privacy were negotiated within and beyond the family would remain a difficulty. As Butler-Sloss had written,

there is no easy solution to this problem with the responsibilities for protection of children suspected of having been abused, the element of secrecy inherent in family sexual abuse, the likelihood that if true an offence has been committed, the wishes of the child and the duty of confidentiality between doctor and patient.[303]

Nonetheless, the Act did represent a genuine search for consensus and clarity. In contrast to the prevailing Government style, the legislation was preceded by full consultation with the interested parties, and guided through Parliament with a minimum of conflict.[304] It was in several senses a liberal compromise which embodied statutory definitions of the rights and responsibilities not only of the state but also of the professions and the most vulnerable of its citizens. It recognized the essential relativity of controls over private and public knowledge, and established agreed and transparent mechanisms for at least attempting to resolve the dilemmas which would always arise.

---

[302] *Hansard*, 6th Series, 151, 27 Apr. 1989, col. 1111. The minister was David Mellor, who was later to encounter his own difficulties with the press and family breakdown.

[303] *Report of the Inquiry into Child Abuse in Cleveland 1987*, 212.

[304] There were arguments about detail, but the Opposition broadly supported the Bill throughout its passage. N. Parton, *Governing the Family: Child Care, Child Protection and the State* (London, 1991), 147–50.

Few of these virtues could be claimed for the second centenary enactment. Six days after the second reading of the Security Service Bill, the Home Secretary was back on his feet in the House of Commons introducing yet another supposed break with the past. The Official Secrets Bill addressed the shortcomings of the previous Acts of 1889 and 1911. Section 1, covering espionage, was left untouched, but the all-embracing Section 2 was replaced by a set of provisions designed to 'remove the protection of the law from the great bulk of sensitive and important information'.[305] Henceforth, criminal sanctions could be applied to improper disclosure in just six areas: security and intelligence, defence, international relations, crime, material obtained by special investigative powers, and material entrusted in confidence to other countries.[306] 'They are radical reforms,' concluded Douglas Hurd, 'because they open windows that have remained closed and cobwebbed, because they define clearly what has been confused for a long time, and because they strike in 1988 a balance that is designed for today.'[307] Whilst it was no longer possible to rush such legislation through Parliament in silence, extensive use was made of the guillotine and the three-line whip, and the Act which received the Royal Assent on 11 May 1989, and came into operation the following March, closely conformed to the Government's original intentions.

There is a tempting symmetry about the chronology of reform in the field of official secrecy. The 1911 Act stands precisely sixty-seven years from the first modern controversy over official secrecy, and from the introduction of its replacement, which was intended by its proponents to last as long again.[308] It is difficult, however, to sustain a long-wave explanation of change. Everything about the Act suggested that it was an error of timing, and that it was unlikely to survive for long a defeat of the Conservatives at the polls. In practice, the legislation opened more windows on the past than on the future. It removed from legal protection information which had already ceased to attract criminal penalties, and enshrined a set of attitudes and procedures which were and could only remain matters of intense controversy. The central issue was not so much the scope of the law as the exercise of authority. The Government resisted all attempts to modify or replace the pattern of its control over official information.[309] The Attorney-General's discretion to prosecute was untouched, the possiblity of an appeal to a judge or jury for an alternative conception of the

---

[305] *Hansard*, 6th Series, 144, 21 Dec. 1988, col. 462.

[306] For detailed commentaries on the Act, see Birkinshaw, *Reforming the Secret State*, 15–30; J. A. Griffith, 'The Official Secrets Act 1989', *Journal of Law and Society*, 16 (1989), 279–89; Baxter, *State Security, Privacy and Information*, 58–70.

[307] *Hansard*, 6th Series, 144, 21 Dec. 1988, col. 468.

[308] See e.g. the claim by Nicholas Budgen in one of the debates: 'We are legislating for a generation: we are not legislating for the next five years.' Cited in Birkinshaw, *Government and Information*, 27.

[309] The fate of a series of attempted amendments is examined in Griffths, 'The Official Secrets Act 1989', 279–85.

public interest was denied, the distinction within the six protected areas between licit and illicit communication rested as before on implied authorization derived from the duties of the post, and the blanket coverage of every other category of information was sustained by the Civil Service Pay and Conditions Code,[310] which was modified in the light of the Act to endorse the general obligation of confidentiality to the Crown, and by the recourse to the civil law of confidentiality whose relevance to government business had lately been confirmed in the courts. The only concession to the principle of proportionality in the exercise of controls was the obligation to prove that the disclosure of information would cause 'damage' to the protected categories.[311] As was readily admitted, the legislation resisted the full-scale transfer of rights which a full Freedom of Information Act would entail. There was no guarantee that it would increase the volume of communication between the Government and the electorate, and less expectation that it would have a material impact on the paternalism of Ministers or civil servants. It advanced Britain little further from the past, and no closer to the current arrangements in comparable states. The Act meant, argued Roy Hattersley for the Opposition, that 'the cocoon of unnecessary and debilitating secrecy by which Whitehall is surrounded will continue to deny the British people information about the actions of Government which is freely available in other countries'.[312]

Had such legislation been enacted at the beginning rather than the end of the period covered by this chapter, it is just possible that it might have fulfilled the expectations of those who drafted it. Although some specific recommendations of Franks were dropped, such as the exclusion from the law of all trivial information irrespective of the area, there was a general affinity with the report which in the mid-1970s was broadly supported by both major parties. But the years of dickering and dispute had taken their toll. The national context had become more fragmented and less deferential, and in the world outside both our friends and our enemies had moved on. Whereas Britain had contemplated major change but backed away from it, most of the liberal democracies with which we associated ourselves had embarked on a series of significant reforms. Australia, New Zealand, and Canada, for instance, placed their security services under proper democratic control.[313] The USA, France, and Germany adopted the Swedish model of laws which made access to information a right and placed the onus of proof on the state for withholding it.[314] The growing chorus of claims that, in the words of one recent constitutional study,

---

[310] On the operation of the Code in the field of disclosure in the 1980s, see Pyper, 'Sarah Tisdall, Ian Willmore, and the Civil Servant's "Right to Leak" ', 76.

[311] Lustgarten and Leigh, *In from the Cold*, 230–1, 237–40, 246.

[312] *Hansard*, 6th Series, 144, 21 Dec. 1988, col. 471.

[313] See the Australian Security Intelligence Organisation Act, 1979; the Canadian Security Intelligence Service Act 1984. Leigh and Lustgarten, 'The Security Service Act 1989', 806–13.

[314] France passed the Data Processing and Freedom Act in 1978. Clark, 'Open Government: The French Experience', 281.

'British governmental practice is among the most secretive in the western world',[315] was a product less of domestic decline and more of international advance. There was an air of instant obsolescence about the linked legislation on the security services and official secrecy,[316] most obviously in relation to the clauses dealing with national defence. In 1989 the Government placed the coping-stone on a new regime of statutory surveillance systems just as the Cold War was ending. The Official Secrets Act gave blanket protection to the practices defined by the 1985 Interception of Communications Act, and by the concurrent Secret Service Act, but the Berlin Wall was dismantled before it came into operation. Britain entered the last decade of the century with its defences against subversion newly entrenched, but with the external enemy in a state of advanced dissolution.

The Conservatives themselves were part-authors of the new uncertainties. The Official Secrets Act embodied a conception of a monolithic civil service which the Government was elsewhere bent on destroying. The attempt to rethink the historic divisions between the public, professional, and private sectors raised important questions about the common responsibilities of large-scale organizations to those they were committed to serving. The institutional iconoclasm of the Thatcher era had created opportunities for revisiting the ethical conduct of all kinds of bureaucratic structures. Long-standing dilemmas, which had been exacerbated by the spread of information technology, could now be addressed in a more fluid context. A new basis could be sought for entrusting individuals with control over significant information generated by organizations, and organizations with possession of sensitive information generated by individuals. Some progress was made towards enhancing the rights of citizens, customers, and clients, and embodying them in more formal regulations. Least advance was made by the state, whose token concessions to external regulation were accompanied by a continuing growth in the volume of secret information held on its inhabitants. In 1989 over half-a-million citizens were the subject of enquiries to the National Identification Bureau 'for the protection of national security'.[317] The limitations of reform were exemplified by the Official Secrets Act, which prevented any transfer of rights over crucial areas of public activity, resisted a genuine clarification of the criteria for withholding information, and sought to use the device of confidential obligation to generalize the more limited legal restrictions.

The difficulties were inherent in the Thatcher experiment. From the outset the market was used to interrogate the restrictive practices of the traditional bureaucracies, but its attitude towards the control and dissemination of information was at best inconsistent and at worst barely distinguishable from the structures of secrecy in the public sector. The doctrine of customer satisfaction

---

315 Harden and Lewis, *The Noble Lie*, 267.
316 Leigh and Lustgarten, 'The Security Service Act 1989', 802.
317 Lustgarten and Leigh, *In From the Cold*, 134–5.

suggested ways in which open communication might spread from commerce to government, but the fiction of confidential obligation indicated the possibility of a mutual reinforcement of devices for closure. The market did not fully trust its customers, and in the end the Government did not trust the market. The Act of 1989 was a measure of the Conservatives' entrenched reluctance to weaken the authority of the state. Faced with well-articulated demands for a Freedom of Information Act, they clung to a modified version of what they knew best. However impatient they might be with the culture of Whitehall, they had no intention of compromising its right to determine when and on what terms it shared its confidential knowledge with the people. The secrecy of keeping secrets remained in place.

CHAPTER SEVEN

THE BRITISH WAY

In 1989 Alan Bennett wrote a preface for his double bill *Single Spies* which had brought together his plays about two of the most celebrated traitors of modern times, Guy Burgess and Anthony Blunt.[1] His attitude towards the actions of his characters was conditioned by the changing perspectives of the era. After ten years of Margaret Thatcher, he was no longer certain of the significance of his topic:

It suits governments to make treachery the crime of crimes, but the world is smaller than it was and to conceal information can be as culpable as to betray it. As I write, evidence is emerging of a nuclear accident at Windscale in 1957, the full extent of which was hidden from the public.[2] Were the politicians and civil servants responsible for this less culpable than our Cambridge villains? Because for the spies it can at least be said that they were risking their own skins, whereas the politicians were risking someone else's.[3]

The inherent absurdity of international espionage had been celebrated in Compton Mackenzie's *Water on the Brain* half a century earlier. The contemporary aspect of Bennett's doubt was the sense that domestic secrecy was both more real and more destructive. It might make less entertaining drama (although Hollywood had dealt with the cover-up of nuclear accidents as early as 1978 in *The China Syndrome*), but it raised more acute issues of guilt and harm. Further, as the historical significance of spying was questioned, so was the identity of the nation which suffered betrayal. For Bennett, the act was far from straightforward. In *An Englishman Abroad*, he explained,

it is suggested that Burgess was a spy because he wanted a place where he was alone, and that having a secret supplies this. I believe this to be psychologically true, but there is a sense too that an ironic attitude towards that country and a scepticism about one's heritage are part of that heritage. And so, by extension, is the decision to betray it. It is irony activated.[4]

---

[1] *An Englishman Abroad*, on Burgess, was broadcast in 1983, and *A Question of Attribution*, on Blunt, in 1988.

[2] See above, Ch. 5, p. 202.

[3] Reprinted in A. Bennett, *Writing Home* (London, 1994), 214.

[4] Ibid. 211.

Bennett's voice was of its time. In 1951 the defection of Burgess and Maclean was viewed in more forthright terms. But he was right to detect a tradition which always stood at a distance from itself. The essentially oblique conception of national identity was a product of both the strengths and the weaknesses of the gentlemanly liberal state which took form in the early decades of the nineteenth century. It reflected a rationality of rule which was founded on an assertion of political self-restraint. What distinguished the liberal enterprise from the despotic regimes which flourished at its birth and from the totalitarian challengers of the following century was a positive abnegation of authority. It recognized the proper division between the state and civil society. Social and economic structures possessed their own logic and laws which could be appreciated but not appropriated by the political realm. The responsibility of politicians was to delineate the separate spheres and to create the conditions in which each could flourish in the presence of the other.[5] Regulation was justified only when it promoted self-regulation. Those with power faced the endless task of policing their own boundaries. Liberalism, in the words of a recent study, was 'not about governing less but about the continual injunction that politicians and rulers should govern cautiously, delicately, economically, modestly'.[6]

The capacity of the liberal state to fulfil its obligations was greatly facilitated by the revolution in communications which accompanied its birth. The Reform Act of 1832 was swiftly followed by the construction of the first sections of the railway network and by the associated introduction of the Penny Post which exploited and subsidized the new transport system.[7] Distance was further disconnected from time by the subsequent invention of the telegraph and the telephone. The rapid acceleration in the transmission of information displayed the scope and limits of government. Without the unitary state and its developing infrastructure, none of the new devices would have been possible. The railway companies and their capital market required a legislative framework, the Penny Post needed a public monopoly and a heavy if hidden subsidy, the telegraph network was nationalized once its potential was established. Everywhere the state was present in creating the conditions for a precipitous increase in the density of private interactions. Social and economic structures were enriched and at the same time the overt presence of government was reduced. As knowledge could be communicated to the centre and troops dispatched from it with so much greater ease, it became possible to maintain authority throughout the realm without large permanent garrisons or obtrusive physical surveillance. Further, as a virtuous circle was established between

---

[5] Crouch, 'Sharing Public Space: States and Organized Interests in Western Europe', 180.

[6] A. Barry, T. Osborne, and N. Rose, 'Introduction', in *Foucault and Political Reason: Liberalism, Neo-Liberalism and Rationalities of Government* (London, 1996), 8.

[7] On the interdependence of the Penny Post and the fledgling railway companies, see Vincent, *Literacy and Popular Culture*, 46–9.

the use of literacy and the demand for education, so the capacity of the private citizen to act as a rational, informed critic of the powers of government was enhanced.

Mass communication was a quintessential but contingent liberal achievement. Within a few decades of the first steam train carrying the first mailbag, every state with a pretence to modernity possessed some kind of national network. The founding of the Universal Postal Union in 1875 symbolized the progress of the century.[8] It proved possible to establish a uniform service across continents and oceans, irrespective of language, culture, and form of government. Correspondence, and the associated means of transmitting people and information, was adaptable to political traditions of all kinds. If in one context it strengthened the private sector against the public, in another it equipped the state with unprecedented weapons of intrusion and discipline. The defining issue was not the presence but the control of the new mechanisms. What distinguished the liberal from the illiberal regime was how communication was blocked. Britain established its identity against much of the rest of the world by its claim that its public discourse was open to inspection and its private was closed. The individual was free to write to a Member of Parliament or a Minister with the expectation of a reply, and to exchange letters with other individuals with the assurance that the mail would not be intercepted. Thus, employees in the rapidly expanding official bureaucracy spent most of their time reading, filing, and responding to correspondence, and the beneficiaries of the growing economy devoted increasing proportions of their work and recreation to epistolary intercourse.

Between the ideal and the execution stood the matter of confidence. The Whig governments which presided over the coming of the railways and the Penny Post emerged out of the most dangerous constitutional crisis since the Glorious Revolution. The boundaries of the political nation and the limits of legitimate state action were the subject of the most vigorous challenges as the new systems were introduced. At the same time, a growing pile of Blue Books was revealing in convincing detail the alarming otherness of the proliferating communities of the urban poor. It was critical that the new ministries allayed suspicion by distancing themselves from the repressive mechanisms of the old order and by declining to exploit the despotic potential of the infrastructure they were creating. Yet they also needed to retain reserve powers of defence on behalf of both the government and the propertied classes who now possessed the franchise. The real threats in the present cast long shadows into the future. The solution to this dilemma was a double negative. As Henry Taylor wrote in *The Statesman* of 1836: 'A secret may be sometimes best kept by keeping the secret of its being secret.'[9] By this means the ambitions of the liberal state could

---

[8] Robinson, *Britain's Post Office* (London, 1953).
[9] Taylor, *The Statesman*, 89.

be reconciled with its fears. Less self-confidence would have rendered the policing of communication more blatant, more would have rendered it unnecessary. Declining to communicate the control of communication preserved the state's moral authority without sacrificing its physical safeguards.

The achievement of this peculiar combination of assertion and denial rested on an appeal to history which partially obscured the historical identity of the British liberal enterprise. In 1844 and in every subsequent public debate through to the 1980s, a timeless past was evoked to justify silence about secrecy. Precedent which had no specific origin and little discernible form was deployed to evade disclosure. The means by which the post Reform Act state sought to strike the characteristic liberal balance between the public and the private realm remained half-hidden from view. Secrecy became the virtue that dared not speak its name. In the long quiet, the attribution of vice could never convincingly be countered. The task for historians is as much to interrogate popular accusations as to question official denials. Everywhere their gaze is deflected from the concrete to the abstract. Statutory powers and written safeguards are in most cases replaced by such assurances as custom and duty can supply. The mounting body of criticism against, in particular, the Official Secrets Act of 1911 often masks the fact that from 1889 to 1989 any decision to deploy Parliamentary draughtsmen in this field was seen as a defeat by the government of the day. Had the strategy which took its modern form amidst the challenge of Chartism survived unscathed, there would have been no laws, no debates, no public inquiries, nothing except a succession of Home Secretaries rising in the House to evoke the behaviour of their predecessors in defence of their silence.

It was not so much that British political culture was inherently secretive, but rather that in the British version of a liberal state, secrecy was inherently a cultural form. This was true of its negative aspect, where attacks were smothered by tradition, and also of its creative dimension. The attempt to keep secrecy secret redoubled the requirement of trust which any blocked communication imposes. In the absence of a clear legal definition of the right to withhold official information or interrupt its flow, the ethical basis of government and in particular of its professional servants was thrust into the foreground. Attitudes and values, and the means by which they were inculcated and displayed, became not merely the cladding but the very framework of the edifice which was constructed after 1832. Everything depended on voluntary restraint, which in turn required the transmission and development of broader forms of cultural capital. Self-discipline could never be guaranteed by the self alone. It had to be taught and policed by a multiplicity of informal and formal structures, beginning with the family and ending with the ministry rule-book. In the aftermath of the Reform Bill crisis, with the cries of old corruption still resounding through the radical discourse and the possibilities for the abuse of communication systems increasing exponentially, the achievement of a new tradition of public trust seemed far from inevitable. Yet out of the turmoil emerged a structure of values and behaviour of notable power and resilience.

The marriage of honour and secrecy was made in a liberal heaven. Just as the Reform Act state represented not the defeat of the landowning elite but rather its accommodation to the rising middle class, so the new spirit of public service integrated the self-restraint of the gentlemanly ideal with the self-discipline of the professional ethos. Just as the modern rationality of rule implied a modesty of government, so the control of official communication displayed a negation of personal interest. The union was at once buried in history and consciously on the leading edge of change, looking back to an era when privilege was justified by the risk of death in combat and forward to a century in which selfless efficiency and cultivated integrity stood out against the amoral bureaucracies of mass destruction. It was both the badge of a particular social elite and an epitome of the national character. The British reserve was celebrated with proud deprecation at home and with admiring satire abroad. Above all, it delivered its promise. If the proclamation of the world's best civil service was becoming an increasingly empty ritual during the post-war decades, there was throughout much of the period a legitimate contrast to be drawn with the want of competence and morality in the public offices of earlier centuries and of contemporary states. In view of the recent characterization of secrecy as the British disease, it needs to be stressed that for the most part this study has not been an exercise in pathology.

The code of honourable secrecy was a product in equal measure of confidence and insecurity. Much of its strength was derived from the association of abstract values with the material advantages of birth and education brought together in the middle decades of the nineteenth century by the reformed public schools and the colleges of Oxford and Cambridge. At the same time the pervasive sense of closure inherent in the code reflected the constant and growing threat from below. As formal marks of rank and privilege faded and the lower orders were admitted to the outer reaches of the political nation and the lower rungs of the meritocratic ladder, so the need to sustain artificial barriers increased. The more open the competition for authority and status, the more resolute was the attempt to police the boundaries of character and knowledge. Hence the frequent appearance in these pages of embarrassment as a determinant of blocked communication. This feature of the civilizing process, argues Elias, 'arises characteristically on the occasions when a person who fears lapsing into inferiority can avert this danger neither by direct physical means nor by any other form of attack'.[10] The more subtle and differentiated the prohibitions in society, the greater the opportunities of shame. Secrecy was the natural guardian of embarrassment. Time after time, the cry of

---

[10] Elias, *The Civilising Process: 2. State Formation and Civilisation*, 292.

national security dissolved on further investigation into the avoidance of moral discomfort.

In this gentlemanly liberal state, trust was a reciprocal requirement. Government Ministers had to obtain the confidence of the people in their fitness to exercise hidden powers, and in turn had to be convinced of the right of all sectors of society to conduct their lives behind closed doors. As he introduced one of the more substantial of a series of failed private members' Bills on the control of information during the last quarter of this century, Clement Freud proclaimed that, 'a democracy maintains an equilibrium between publicity, privacy and secrecy'.[11] In practice, the democratic system inaugurated in 1832 found it extremely hard to strike a stable and lasting balance between the separate categories of blocked communication. There was a persistent tendency for the key terms to dissolve into each other. In 1868, for instance, with the political nation being widened for the second time and an intense debate taking place over the publicity which should be attached to the act of casting a vote, G. J. Holyoake attempted to resolve the prevailing ambiguity:

There are two descriptions of secrecy—an infamous secrecy and an honourable secrecy. The base kind of secrecy is that employed in mean, furtive or criminal acts, as when a man lies, conceals the truth in giving evidence, or clandestinely filches from another. But there is a second description of secrecy which is manly, as when I lock my doors against intrusive or impertinent people—or when I exclude others from meddling with my affairs without my consent—or when I provide for the protection of my own interest in my business or my family. This is necessary and justifiable secrecy. In these cases I merely exercise the right of personal privacy in what concerns me primarily, vitally, and concerns me alone.[12]

But even the appropriation from the public sector of the concept of honourable secrecy failed to achieve a permanent set of distinctions. Without the authority of a social and educational elite behind it, honour was difficult to define and defend. The difference between infamous and manly secrecy could become merely a matter of perspective. The British tradition of reserve was by turns a virtue or a vice according to the stresses within the liberal enterprise. To simplify a long and complex history, blocked communication was labelled privacy when a section of society was trusted to conduct its own affairs, and secrecy when it was not. Equally, households upheld their privacy when they trusted the state and other external agencies, and consciously kept secrets when they felt unable so to do.

Perhaps the most obvious and powerful of the forces controlling change throughout this study was the basic factor of success. The longevity of the tradition of official secrecy was in the first instance a consequence of the gentlemanly liberal state's ability to supply growth with integrity, security

---

[11] *Hansard*, 5th Series, 960, 19 Jan. 1979, col. 2144.
[12] Holyoake, *A New Defence of the Ballot*, 3–4.

with efficiency. The serious challenge to the concordat which took form in the second third of the nineteenth century only began to gain strength once doubts spread about the capacity of the official machine to sustain Britain's economic and strategic position in the world. If Suez was not the cause of the disillusion, it was the defining moment. The clear interdependence of government deception and international humiliation in 1956 created for the first time an audience for those who had been arguing that the structures of closure were disabling the management of our overseas and domestic affairs. In the midst of the long post-war boom, it was still possible to strike a positive balance sheet, but never again would the association between honour and secrecy be taken for granted. By the same measure, the willingness of the state to extend to the least of its citizens the fundamental right not to communicate was conditioned by the performance of the national economy. Rising standards of living made it easier for the poor to achieve the same levels of privacy as their social superiors, and more feasible for the growing ranks of officials to refrain from intrusive inquiring. Conversely, the outbreaks of mass unemployment between the wars and again from the mid-1970s exposed the persisting reluctance to permit those dependent on the state to maintain control of their own narratives. Trust was in the end a function of both private and public prosperity, and secrecy a reflection of both domestic and corporate indigence.

Growth was itself a mixed blessing. It relaxed tensions and promoted confidence, but brought in its trail a series of problems which at the outset were barely visible. An expansion of the state was not itself a negation of liberalism, providing that it served to enhance rather than erode the vitality of the burgeoning civil society. Two related features of the culture of secrecy which emerged in the Victorian era made it particularly difficult to accommodate subsequent developments. The first was that welfare reforms designed to promote active citizenship were implemented by administrative structures founded on a passive consumption of information. Lord Croham, who knew whereof he spoke, summarized the dilemma in the year that the Campaign for Freedom of Information was founded:

The increases in the powers and in the resulting accumulation of new kinds of information in the possession of the British Government tended to reinforce the propensity to secrecy which is inherent in all Government and had been substantially reinforced by war. Most of the highly difficult tasks assumed by Government would have been made much more difficult by advance knowledge of the Government's intentions or of the detailed instructions given to its negotiators and controllers. At the same time many of those tasks required public understanding of the issues because acceptance of the policies was necessary for their success. Plenty of information was published but only when the Government chose to do so.[13]

---

[13] Croham, *Would Greater Openness Improve or Weaken Government?*, 3.

Croham was referring specifically to the period of his own career as a senior civil servant, but his analysis applied to the whole era of modern welfare provision which began in the epochal year of 1911, when both the National Insurance and Official Secrets Acts were passed. Amidst the excitement of Liberal social reform and the drama of approaching war, the implicit contradiction between these two pieces of legislation was not apparent. In the lives of the poor, material advancement and command of personal information had always been mutually reinforcing goals. More broadly, the health of the liberal enterprise had been conditional on a simultaneous expansion of engagement with the political sphere and knowledge of its activities. It was at the point when the whole of the population was embraced by the state that the twin aspects of emancipation were formally set against each other.

The second difficulty arose from the vast growth in the size and complexity of what are known in the international sphere as non-governmental organizations. In a model liberal world, there was a bare minimum of bureaucratic structures standing between individual citizens and the political entities called into being to enhance and protect their freedom. At the time of the 1832 Reform Act it was indeed the case that the manufacturing processes of the world's first industrializing economy operated with a tiny complement of clerks, that the few recognized professions, apart possibly from the church, were loose associations of private practitioners, and that voluntary bodies were either benign charities dedicated to achieving their own redundancy, or malign combinations doomed by the laws of political economy. The problem of the bureaucratic deployment of information was confined to a small group of public servants who in the nineteenth century successfully resisted the label of bureaucrats. As the decades passed, the increasing complexity of social and economic relations generated ever-more permanent and intricate organizations. The masthead of the *Poor Man's Guardian*, which was the principal unstamped journal of the radical campaign throughout the Reform Bill crisis, famously proclaimed that 'Knowledge is Power'. In post-Reform Act Britain, the phrase was as true in reverse. Control of the information necessary to sustain or gain advantage was everywhere perceived to be dependent on structured action. Even in the home there was a necessary correlation between the size of domestic institution and the capacity to manage significant knowledge. Individuals by themselves could never adequately police their own secrets.

The vulnerability of the isolated citizen was a consequence of the particular British construct of gentlemanly liberalism. The absence from the beginning to the end of the period covered by this study of a statutory definition of privacy or of a general right to official information threw critical emphasis on the constraints of cultural tradition. In the case of state officials, all that prevented an abuse of the proliferating information in their possession was a set of values and instincts, reinforced until 1889 by nothing more than hidden departmental regulations. The subsequent Official Secrets Acts were designed not to defend the public from government, but government from the growing number of its employees who were beyond the influence of the code of gentlemanly restraint. Outside the public sector, similar battles to assert authority by means of establishing control over secret information were fought by an increasing range of interest groups. Over time, a compromise was struck between the state, traditionally suspicious of secret organizations, and various collectivities increasingly in need of legal sanction in order to function. In exchange for an open description of their purposes and a visible commitment to ethical behaviour, institutions ranging from trade unions to middle-class professions were permitted to police their own universes of knowledge. Granting a licence to what Harriet Martineau had lately denounced as the 'secret organisation of trades' marked the coming of age of the liberal enterprise. The state now felt able to trust independent bodies of working men who were explicitly committed to defending their bargaining powers by maintaining the greatest possible control over the transmission of workplace skills and knowledge.[14] In the same way, it was because the state found itself looking at an adapted version of its own ideal of disinterested public service that it felt able to bestow charters on more and more professional groups whose strategies were founded on the restriction of access to their trade secrets.

A pluralist society made up of a host of enclosed organizations protected and supervised at a long distance by the state was an acceptable modification of liberalism to meet the needs of a complex world. There was, however, a contradiction at the heart of this settlement, which became more apparent as the various categories of private-sector bureaucracy grew in size and significance during the twentieth century. Each organization represented an assertion of power over those less able to organize. This was true not only of professions in relation to non-certificated experts and to clients or patients, but of trade unions in relation to the 'dishonourable' labourers, and of the increasingly bureaucratized manufacturers in relation to their customers. In the face of the multiple monopolies of knowledge, private individuals found it more and more difficult to generate the command over information which, according to the liberal model, they required to function effectively as citizens, or as players in the market-place for goods and services. Just as their only protection from the abuse of official secrecy was the code of civil servants reinforced by the increasingly threadbare myth of ministerial responsibility, so their only defence against the misuse of professional or commercial information was the concept of public service reinforced by the increasingly strained notion of free competition. Informal structures of private knowledge which had once offered some sense of security, such as the gossip networks of the urban working-class communities, were at the same time being eroded by slum clearance and new forms of mass entertainment. The consequence was a growing sense of crisis about

---

[14] For the struggle over the prevention of the formal codification of working practices in the nineteenth century, see Vincent, *Literacy and Popular Culture*, 104–19.

the restrictive practices of every kind of bureaucracy, inside and outside the public sector. There was a general erosion of the trust which in one way or another all such bodies required of those dependent on the knowledge they possessed.

Throughout the 1970s and 1980s the response of government was a confused attempt to realign the rhetoric of individual liberty with the conventions of the unwritten constitution. A series of legislative devices was introduced as a substitute rather than a preparation for a general transfer of rights to information. In this context, the record of the organized left, with some notable individual exceptions, has hitherto been largely indistinguishable from that of the right. Throughout this history, the Labour Party has been the epitome of the non-barking dog. The Liberals have sometimes pushed the issues forward, but in the arena of blocked communication all parties have been held back by their subscription to the liberal tradition. Secrecy as a cultural form, as a set of essentially paternalist moral imperatives, doubly distorts the picture. Despite the efforts of an ever-more energetic band of campaigners, the blanket of hidden restrictions continues to obscure the scale of the information which is held back from those who lack either statutory rights or organizational capacities. And despite the series of official inquiries and public debates, the appeal to a diffuse set of normative practices still impedes a clear sense of the relations of power at the heart of the various systems of blocked communication.

There is, however, no road back to the arrangements and conventions which once made Britain so distinctive amongst modernizing countries. This is partly because of the growing significance of international law, which increasingly makes it impossible to measure national superiority by the distance from the legislative regimes in neighbouring states. But it is also because of the terminal decline of the social category which stood at the centre of the culture of secrecy and which to outsiders seemed to be so characteristic of the national identity at large. The matter was recently put with typical disrespect by the Italian newspaper *La Stampa* following the revelation of royal secrets by Princess Diana's quondam lover, the public-school educated former army officer James Hewitt: 'Was this once not the island of true gentlemen? The country which codified acceptable behaviour? Tact, reserve, respectability, correctness. Today, the tables have been turned and Britain is the country of boorishness, rudeness and coarseness.'[15] In this particular respect, as more generally, the ethical basis of authority in Britain stands in need of reform.

---

[15] *La Stampa* (4 Oct. 1994), translated and reprinted in the *Guardian* (5 Oct. 1994), 6.

Afterword

The book ends as Mrs Thatcher's career moved to its conclusion, and was written during the course of the fourth consecutive Tory Administration. It went to press, however, in the immediate aftermath of a political landslide. Tired Conservatism was replaced by New Labour, committed, amongst much else, to reforming the control of official information. Seven months later, the subject of this book was consigned to the past. A White Paper was published outlining what the Prime Minister described as a 'fundamental and vital change in the relationship between the government and the governed.' 'The traditional culture of secrecy', he wrote in the Preface, 'will only be broken down by giving people in the United Kingdom the legal right to know.'[1]

The scale of the proposed legislation came as a surprise to campaigners who had feared the worst when the manifesto pledge was omitted from the first Queen's Speech in order to undergo further consultation. It appeared as if the pressures and pleasures of power would once again frustrate an objective with which Labour had been associated for a quarter of a century. Instead, to widespread applause, a radical reform was outlined which had every prospect of becoming law before the end of the century. The proposed Freedom of Information Act would, in the words of the White Paper, 'provide the people of this country, for the first time, with a general statutory right of access to the information held by public authorities.'[2] The principle that communication was the privilege of the state rather than the citizen was at last to be reversed. Henceforth, it would be for officials to prove the harm caused by disclosure, and not for the enquirers to demonstrate the benefit. The default position, to be embodied in a public interest test, was 'a presumption of openness'.[3] In making a judgment on the release of information, public officials would have to ensure, 'That the decision is in line with the overall purpose of the Act, to encourage government to be more open and account-able.'[4] The consequence would be not only an informed electorate, but a trans-formed state. As the Chancellor of the Duchy of Lancaster stated at a conference on his White Paper, 'I personally believe that Freedom of Information is

---

[1] *Your Right to Know. Freedom of Information* (December 1997) Cm 3818, Preface.
[2] Ibid., para 1.3.
[3] Ibid., para 3.1.
[4] Ibid., para 3.20.

going to change the whole political culture in Britain. It will sweep away the obsession with secrecy.'[5]

The election victory which paved the way to reform was itself a product of the accelerating decline of respect for political morality. The closing flurry of accusations about covert payments to MPs for asking Parliamentary Questions was merely the final act of a long drawn-out drama of scandals, of which the most serious was the revelation about arms sales to Iraq. In the view of the then Leader of the Opposition, the subsequent Scott Report 'showed that the culture of secrecy permeates almost every single aspect of government activity.'[6] Fundamental reform was necessary in order to re-establish the trust which both politicians and the civil service required for the exercise of their authority. The White Paper accepted in its first paragraph that, 'the perception of excessive secrecy has become a corrosive influence in the decline of public confidence in government.'[7] The most striking evidence of the Administration's intent was the regulatory framework which was proposed for the right to know. It was not enough to declare a new principle and leave civil servants and their ministers to implement the procedures. Only by refusing to trust officials and politicians could a culture of trust in public life be re-established. A powerful Information Commissioner was to be appointed, independent of Whitehall and Parliament, with sweeping powers to order disclosure, gain access to records and deal with complaints about excessive delays and costs. In the case of deliberate obstruction by officials, a warrant could be obtained to enter and search premises, and a criminal offence would be established 'for the wilful or reckless destruction, alteration or withholding of records relevant to an investigation of the Information Commissioner'.[8] Gone were the days of confiding in the honour of public servants. The proposed machinery assumed the worst, and set about preventing it.

The approach contrasted strongly with the final attempt of the previous Administration to come to terms with the pressure for reform. As compensation for defeating a large-scale private member's bill sponsored by the Labour MP Mark Fisher, it introduced in 1994 a *Code of Practice on Access to Government Information*. This in effect revived and extended the Croham Directive of 1977. Officials were committed to publishing facts and analysis behind major policy proposals, explanatory material on a department's dealings with the public, and reasons for administrative decisions. The Code applied to those areas of the public sector subject to the Ombudsman, who would investigate allegations of non-compliance.[9] It was the last in a long series of attempts to reform in order

---

[5] Speech to Freedom of Information Conference, Church House, London, February 2, 1998.

[6] *Speech by the Rt. Hon. Tony Blair MP, Leader of the Labour Party at the Campaign for Freedom of Information's annual Awards ceremony, 25 March 1996.*

[7] *Your Right to Know*, para. 1.1.

[8] Ibid., para 5.14.

[9] A parallel Code was introduced for the National Health Service in 1995.

to prevent reform. The Code embodied no statutory rights, no precedence over existing controls, no access to documents as distinct from official summaries, and was subject to no less than fifteen categories of exemption. These occupied more than half the Code, ranging through harm caused to international relations or the management of the economy to 'information relating to confidential communications between Ministers and her Majesty the Queen or other Members of the Royal Household'.[10] The Code was given little publicity, and the Ombudsman received only forty-four complaints in 1996, taking an average of almost a year to deal with the half which merited investigation. Open government was still being conducted on the government's terms.

For the White Paper, cultural change was both a consequence and a condition of legislation. Nothing could be achieved without a shift from informal to formal regulation, but a Freedom of Information Act would only be effective if officials, politicians, and the Information Commissioner accepted the obligation to promote its objectives:

Overseas experience shows that statutory provisions need to be championed within government itself if openness is to become part of the official culture rather than an irksome imposition. We believe that this sort of culture change has taken place in some countries—the USA and New Zealand are examples. We see no reason why it should not also be possible in the UK, despite a more entrenched culture of secrecy extending back at least to the 19th century and the Official Secrets Acts from 1889 onwards.[11]

The tradition of being secret about secrecy was to be replaced by one of being open about openness.

The pervasive appeal to cultural transformation throughout the White Paper and the accompanying commentaries by politicians and civil servants were justified by the substance of the proposals. A genuine attempt was being made to re-think the interaction between formal regulation and informal tradition. Both the significance and the difficulty of achieving change in the mentality of public officials had been grasped, and there was in prospect the first major break with the past since the civil service tradition took shape in the middle decades of the nineteenth century. The proposals were conservative only in the sense that they embodied a desire to restore public confidence in the integrity of government. The White Paper was welcomed by the General Secretary of the Association of First Division Civil Servants, whose organization had been campaigning for such a reform for fifteen years. The unprecedented external regulation of his members would be justified by their reclamation of the high moral ground that once they occupied: 'if the public trusts government more, then it will trust and respect the civil service.'[12] The problems

---

[10] *Code of Practice on Access to Government Information* (London, 1997 edn.), Part II, section 3.
[11] *Your Right to Know*, para 7.2.
[12] Speech to Freedom of Information Conference, Church House, London, February 2, 1998.

posed by the White Paper were largely ones of ambition rather than its absence. If the notion of culture signalled the scale of the enterprise, it also raised a series of questions about the boundaries of change.

One feature which struck every commentator was the sheer breadth of the new system. It was intended to cover not only all government departments, including the Next Step agencies, but local government, quangos, privatized utilities, public service broadcasting, the National Health Service, and state education. The White Paper represented a dramatic reversal of the progressive narrowing of the concept of public service which had been under way since the early 1980s. However, the Labour Government shows few signs of wishing to rescind the structural changes which were implemented by the Conservatives, and it remains to be seen whether a single regulatory framework can be applied to what is now so heterogenous a collection of bodies.

A case in point is the crucial issue of harm tests. The distance between the White Paper and the preceding Code can be measured by the reduction of the fifteen exclusion categories to seven, with six of them (national security, defence and international relations; law enforcement; personal privacy; commercial confidentiality; safety of the individual, the public and the environment; and information supplied in confidence) subject to a 'substantial harm' test which would require officials to establish the scale of damage likely to be caused by a particular disclosure. This introduced an element of proportionality to the prohibition of communication. It would no longer be sufficient to deny access to information on grounds which amounted to nothing more than inconvenience or embarrassment. The quantity of misfortune would have to be demonstrated by the official, and set against the assumed public interest in openness.

The seventh exclusion category, 'the integrity of the decision-making and policy advice processes in government', was, however, to be subject to a test merely of simple harm. In a passage which bore all the hallmarks of a hand-to-hand struggle with Whitehall, it was explained that the maintenance of collective responsibility, the political impartiality of public officials, the requirement for 'free and frank' discussion between officials and ministers, and the need to prevent premature disclosure of decisions still under consideration, were of such transparent significance, that it would be superfluous to prove the extent of the potential misfortune. These were the issues which the mandarins had for decades advanced against the concept of freedom of information. It had always been argued that the neutrality and efficiency of the government's senior advisers would be fatally compromised by a wholesale reversal of their right to control the flow of information. The price for the abandonment of this principle was a formal differentiation between the quality of their concerns and those of every other sensitive area of public affairs.

As had been the case with all statutory intervention in the field of government communication since the first Official Secrets Act of 1889, there was a sense of reform being driven by the interests of an elite group of civil servants. The White Paper explained that, 'in framing our proposals on decision-making and policy advice, we see the factors determining the harm test here as likely to apply particularly to high-level government records (Cabinet and Cabinet Committee papers, Ministerial correspondence and policy advice intended for Ministers, whether from government departments or other public bodies).'[13] Yet every one of the multifarious group of agencies, utilities, quangos, health trusts, and even universities covered by the proposed legislation had its own command structure, each with its concerns for the confidentiality of collective decision-making. It is unclear whether the traditions of Whitehall are now to be entrenched in every management committee of every kind of public body, and what would be the justification for privileging this aspect of their work over those categories subject to the more rigorous test of substantial harm.

A further concession to the past was the refusal in the White Paper to coun-tenance the repeal of the 1989 Official Secrets Act. Although this reworking of the 1911 Act had excluded many areas of government activity, it preserved controls over a number of loosely defined categories,[14] and gave blanket pro-tection to the external and internal security services. Unlike the proposed Freedom of Information Act, there was no transfer of rights, only a simple test of damage and no external appeal to a concept of public interest. A particular virtue of the White Paper is its determination to address the whole complex of controls over information. The new Act would either have precedence over or require the further reform of the two hundred or so statutory prohibitions which have accreted around government communication. The Official Secrets Act, together with the 1985 and 1989 legislation on the Interception of Communications and on the Security Services with which it formed a whole, would alone remain untouched. It is possible that as in the time of the previous Labour Government, the Official Secrets Act will be abolished by neglect, but the White Paper makes a point of insulating its harm tests from the more rigorous hurdles in the proposed Act.[15]

There was a potential conflict in the provisions of the existing and proposed legislation, and a fundamental contradiction between the spirit of the last attempt to shore up the 'traditional culture of secrecy' and that of the new ambition to lay it to rest. An equally intractable problem lay at the frontier between public service and private enterprise. Spokesmen for business gave a welcome to the proposed regime of open communication, which held out the prospect of access to immense volumes of potentially valuable information. Al-though there is some debate about whether the suggested flat-rate fee of £10 per request should be adjusted upwards for applications-for-profit, the scale of demand is likely to be so large as to support a new industry of companies

---

[13] *Your Right to Know*, para 3.12. [14] See above, chapter 6, p. 307.
[15] *Your Right to Know*, p. 3.19.

obtaining and re-processing official information for private clients. Money will be made out of openness, and costs will be incurred by the public sector which it must be hoped the Treasury is prepared to countenance.

The real difficulty is not one of money but of competing approaches to confidentiality. From the private sector's perspective there are three dangers. First, the proposed Act is intended to be retrospective. Information given in the past to government agencies in the expectation that it would be covered by the conventions of official secrecy may now become accessible. Secondly, enterprises which thought they had been transferred to the commercial sphere will find themselves once more subject to the disciplines of public service. The privatized utilities in particular have been in the forefront of manipulating the law of commercial confidentiality to repel unwelcome inquiry, and may now be subject to disclosure requirements far more rigorous than those facing the private-sector firms with which they are competing or collaborating. Thirdly, the proposed legislation will require that contracts between private companies and public bodies be made available for inspection. The costs of commercially-supplied services should be exposed, and unsuccessful bidders should be informed of the reasons for their failure. 'Commercial confidentiality', proclaimed the White Paper, 'must not be used as a cloak to deny the public's right to know.'[16]

It not yet evident that business has woken up to these threats, but neither is it clear that the government has found a way of resolving the inevitable conflicts, particularly as it pursues a policy of increasing the scope of public/private collaborative projects. The law of commercial confidentiality has become so pervasive that it can be applied to almost any practice where profit is at risk. As the White Paper accepts, 'there will of course be information—like trade secrets, sensitive intellectual property or data which could affect share prices—where disclosure would substantially harm the commercial interests of suppliers and contractors.'[17] In theory, disputes should be resolved by an appeal to the public interest in openness. In practice, the field will be a playground for m'learned friends. The White Paper says hopefully that 'relations between public authorities and the private sector need to rest on two-way openness and trust.'[18] The latter, however, has its own traditions of closure, and the legal means of protecting them. It remains to be seen whether the former can by example and by statue establish a regime of access which applies with equal effect to both sides of the divide.

A different aspect of the boundaries of the public sphere lay in the long-contested distinction between secrecy and privacy. Unlike the early 1970s, when the Franks and Younger Reports occupied entirely distinct compartments of the official mind, the new enterprise gave full recognition to the necessary relationship between the two categories of controlling communication.

---

[16] *Your Right to Know*, para 3.11.   [17] Ibid., para 3.11.   [18] Ibid., para 3.11.

The proposed Freedom of Information Act was to form part of a complex of legislation designed to guarantee the rights of citizens to determine what they knew about the state, and what the state knew about them. Concurrent reforms, especially the incorporation of the European Convention on Human Rights into domestic law, and the extension of the Data Protection Act from electronic to many paper-based records, would ensure that individual privacy would not be compromised by the anticipated heavy demand for personal information held by public bodies. The inevitable tensions between the privacy and openness regimes were to be countered by co-ordinating the drafting of the new legal frameworks to make them as compatible as possible, and by requiring the regulatory agencies, in particular the Information Commissioner and the Data Protection Registrar, to co-operate 'closely and effectively'. The proposed requirement to demonstrate 'substantial harm' where privacy was appealed to against openness was a further attempt to strike a working balance. There were no permanent solutions. On the one hand, it was necessary to protect third parties from the inadvertent disclosure of their secrets by other inquirers. On the other, as a number of campaigners have argued, it was important not give such complete protection to personnel records that it would be impossible to expose discrimination and victimization.

Finally there is the problem of boundaries as frontiers. The true measure of the ambition of the proposed Freedom of Information Act is that it is likely to rekindle the nineteenth-century pride in constitutional progress. From being amongst the most secretive of modern democracies, Britain stands to gain a system which would be one of the most comprehensive and rigorous yet implemented. The White Paper benefited greatly from the careful study that had been made of overseas experience, and the operation of the resulting Act will in turn demand the attention of every country concerned with open politics. Britain could know itself once more by the quality and quantity of the communications between the governors and the governed. Nonetheless the proud independence of the Victorian age cannot be revisited. In many respects the complex of reforms advanced by the new Labour Government represents a belated acceptance of the need to adapt domestic laws and practices to the requirements and behaviour of the European Community. There is no accompanying sense, however, that Britain's participation in the Community's institutions should be covered by the new legislation in any specific fashion. The White Paper recognizes merely the traditional distinction between home and foreign governments. 'International relations' are treated as an undifferentiated whole. If domestic political institutions are yielding their secrets, they are also losing their monopoly of power. What is said, written, and recorded elsewhere in the Community may now be relevant to the British citizen. Nothing in the new proposals indicates that the frontiers of government no longer always end at Dover. And whilst the subjection of international relations to the substantial harm test might provide a mechanism for recognizing the special case of EC information, there remains in the background the Official Secrets Act, with its yet more obsolete conception of national interest.

As has always been the case, the dilemmas of secrecy resolve themselves into issues of trust. If government becomes not merely the subject but the agent of openness, if the Information Commissioner serves not only as the regulator but the prophet of reform, the public may well invest sufficient confidence in the new system to enable it to overcome the difficulties which it will face. Goodwill has been evoked by proposals which are so large in their conception and so practical in their planning. At the time of writing, campaigners, ministers, and civil servants are sitting at the same table, sharing the same hopes. The reforms are born of a new moment of political and economic optimism, and may in turn lead to a fundamental change in the perception and role of public service. 'At last', claims David Clark, the minister in charge, 'there is a government ready to trust the people with a legal right to information'.[19]

Yet just as the boundaries of cultural change are open to dispute, so the depth of trust is still to be tested. New Labour is still gripped by old fears. It is giving power to the citizen but retaining methods for controlling domestic surveillance which have disfigured the democratic process since universal suffrage was enacted. It is combining a fresh respect for individual privacy with a renewed attack on the personal archives of welfare claimants, who have always exposed the confusion between privacy and secrecy. It is demanding the disclosure of the private sector's business with the public sector but is reluctant to mount a direct challenge on commercial confidentiality. It is conforming to European practices but is hesitant about our European identity. Having committed itself to abolishing the 'traditional culture of secrecy', these problems will have to be faced. The best hope for a successful outcome will be a clear grasp of the dimensions of the culture and of the trajectory of its development. In David Clark's view, when the history of the Blair Government comes to be written, the Freedom of Information Act will be remembered where the traffic of daily politics has been forgotten. In the reform of the culture of secrecy, history can only be made if first it is understood.

FEBRUARY 1998.

---

[19] *The Right Know*, Foreword.

BIBLIOGRAPHY

1. UNPUBLISHED SOURCES

Public Record Office, London (PRO)
  Cabinet Papers
  Home Office Papers
  Tenterden Papers
  Treasury Papers
  War Office Papers

Elsewhere
  WHITELEY, C. W., 'A Manchester Lad/Salford Man' (typescript, Keele University Library)

2. OFFICIAL PAPERS

Hansard.

Report from the Select Committee on the Law Relative to Patents for Invention (1829), PP (Parliamentary Papers) 1829, III.

First Report from the Select Committee on Public Documents (1833), PP 1833, XII.

Second Report from the Select Committee on Public Documents (1833), PP 1833, XII.

Administration and Operation of the Laws for the Relief of the Poor (1834), PP 1834, XXVII (Harmondsworth, 1974 edn.).

Report from the Select Committee on Medical Education (1834), PP 1834, XIII.

Report from the Select Committee appointed to inquire into the Management and Affairs of the Record Commission, and present State of the Records of the United Kingdom (1836), PP 1836, XVI.

Report from the Select Committee on Postage (1843), PP 1843, VIII.

Report from the Select Committee on the Post Office (1844), PP 1844, XIV.

Report from the Select Committee on Medical Registration (1847), PP 1847, IX.

Report from the Select Committee on Official Salaries (1850), PP 1850, XV.

Report and Minutes of Evidence taken before the Select Committee of the House of Lords (in) Letters Patent for Inventions (1851), PP 1851, XVIII.

Report from the Select Committee of the House of Lords on the East India Company's Charter (1852), PP 1852–3, XXX.

Reports of Committees of Inquiry into Public Offices (1854), PP 1854, XXVII.

Northcote–Trevelyan Report (1854), republished in *Public Administration*, 32 (Spring 1954).

Papers on the Re-Organisation of the Civil Service (1855), PP 1854–5, XX.

Seventh Report of the Postmaster General on the Post Office (1862).

Report from the Select Committee on Education (Inspectors' Reports) (1864), PP 1864, IX.

Tenth Annual Report of the Postmaster General on the Post Office (1864).

Eleventh Annual Report of the Postmaster General on the Post Office (1865).

Report Presented to the Trades Unions Commissioners by the Examiners Appointed to Inquire into Acts of Intimidation, Outrage, or Wrong Alleged to have been Promoted, Encouraged, or Connived at by Trades Unions in the Town of Sheffield (1867), reprinted in S. POLLARD (ed.), *The Sheffield Outrages* (London, 1967).

Eleventh and Final Report of the Royal Commissioners Appointed to Inquire into the Organisation and Rules of Trade Unions and other Associations (1869), PP 1868–9, XXXI.

Report from the Select Committee on Civil Service Writers (1873), PP 1873, XI.

First Report of the Civil Service Inquiry Commission [Playfair] (1875), PP 1875, XXIII.

Twenty-Seventh Annual Report of the Postmaster General on the Post Office (1881).

Premature Publication of Official Documents. Treasury Minute (13 Mar. 1884), PP 1884, LXII.

Second Report of the Royal Commission Appointed to Inquire into the Civil Establishments of the Different Offices of State at Home and Abroad [Ridley] (1888), PP 1888, XXVII.

Report as the Practice of Medicine and Surgery by Unqualified Persons in the United Kingdom (1910), PP 1910, XLII.

Report from the Select Committee on Patent Medicines (1913), PP 1913, X.

Fourth Report of the Royal Commission on the Civil Service [MacDonnell] (1914), PP 1914, XVI.

Report of the Board of Enquiry Appointed by the Prime Minister to Investigate Certain Statements Affecting Civil Servants (1928) PP 1928, VII.

First Report from the Select Committee on the Official Secrets Acts (1938), PP 1937–8, VII.

Report from the Select Committee on the Official Secrets Acts (1939), PP 1938–9, VIII.

Report of the Committee on the Political Activities of Civil Servants, Cmnd. 7718 (1949).

Report of the Committee on Departmental Records [Grigg] (1954), PP 1953–4, XI.

Public Inquiry ordered by the Minister of Agriculture into the Disposal of Land at Crichel Down, Cmd. 9176 (June 1954).

Report of the National Assistance Board for the Year Ended 31st December, 1954, Cmnd. 9781 (London, 1955).

Ministry of Health, *Health Visiting. Report of a Working Party on the field of Work, Training and Recruitment of Health Visitors* [Jameson] (1956).

Report of the Committee of Privy Councillors Appointed to Inquire into the Interception of Communications [Birkett] Cmnd. 283 (1957).

Report of the Committee on Administrative Tribunals and Enquiries [Franks], Cmnd. 218 (1957).

Report of the Working Party on Social Workers [Younghusband] (London, 1959).

Security Procedures in the Public Service [Radcliffe], Cmnd. 1681 (1962).

Report of the National Assistance Board for the Year Ended 31st December, 1961, Cmnd. 1730 (London, 1962).

Report of the Committee of Privy Councillors Appointed to Inquire into 'D' Notice Matters, Cmnd. 3309 (1967).

The Civil Service, Report of the Committee 1966–68 [Fulton] (London, 1968).

Report of the Committee on Local Authority and Allied Personal Social Services [Seebohm], Cmnd. 3703 (1968).

Information and Public Interest, Cmnd. 4089 (June, 1969).

Departmental Committee on Section 2 of the Official Secrets Act, 1911 [Franks], Cmnd. 5104 (London, 1972).

Report of the Committee on Privacy [Younger], Cmnd. 5012 (London, 1972).

Report of the Committee on Abuse of Social Security Benefits [Fisher], Cmnd. 5228 (1973).

Department of Health and Social Security, *Report of the Committee of Inquiry into the Care and Supervision Provided in Relation to Maria Colwell* (London, 1974).

Report of the Committee of Privy Councillors on Cabinet Document Security [Houghton], Cmnd. 6677 (London, 1976).

Report of the Committee on Data Protection [Lindop], Cmnd. 7341 (1978).

The Interception of Communications in Great Britain, Cmnd. 7873 (1980).

Committee of Privileges, 1984–85, *Second Report, Premature Disclosure of Proceedings of Select Committees* (1985).

House of Commons Treasury and Civil Service Committee Sub-Committee 1985–86, *Civil Servants and Ministers: Duties and Responsibilities, Minutes of Evidence*, 27 November 1985.

Report of the Inquiry into Child Abuse in Cleveland 1987 [Butler-Sloss], Cm. 412 (London, 1988).

Your Right to Know, Freedom of Information (December 1997)

Code of Practice on Access to Government Information (London 1997 edn.).

3. Printed Primary Sources

The Administration of the Post Office from the Introduction of Mr. Rowland Hill's Plan of Penny Postage up to the Present Time (London, 1844).

Administrative Reform Association, *Address of the Committee to the People of England* (10 May 1855).

——*Speech of Charles Dickens, Esq., Delivered at the Meeting of the Administrative Reform Association at the Theatre Royal, Drury Lane* (27 June 1855).

——*Appointments for Merit Discussed in Official Answers to Official Objections to the Abolition of Patronage* (London, 1855).

'Advertisements', *Quarterly Review*, 97 (1855).

ALLEN, C., *Bureaucracy Triumphant* (Oxford, 1931).

ARMSTRONG, W., *The Role and Character of the Civil Service* (London, 1970).

ASHWORTH, H., *Recollections of Richard Cobden, M.P., and the Anti-Corn Law League* (2nd edn., London, 1878).

ASQUITH, H. H., *Memories and Reflections, 1852–1927* (London, 1928).

——*H. H. Asquith, Letters to Venetia Stanley*, selected and ed. M. and E. Brock (Oxford, 1982).

ATTLEE, C. R., *The Social Worker* (London, 1920).

——'Civil Servants, Ministers, Parliament and the Public', *Political Quarterly*, 25: 4 (Oct.–Dec. 1954).

'Au Fait', *Social Observances: A Series of Essays on Practical Etiquette* (London, 1896).

BAILEY, D., *Children of the Green: A True Story of Childhood in Bethnal Green, 1922–1937* (London, 1981).

BAILHACHE, J., *The Secret of the English* (London, 1948).

BALOGH, T., *The Apotheosis of the Dilettante* (London, 1959).

BANCROFT, I., 'The Civil Service in the 1980s', *Public Administration*, 59 (Summer, 1981).

BANKS, A., *Medical Etiquette* (London, 1839).

BARROW, J., *An Auto-Biographical Memoir* (London, 1847).

BEALES, H. L. and LAMBERT, R. S. (eds.), *Memoirs of the Unemployed* (London, 1967).

BEETON, I., *The Book of Household Management* (London, 1895).

BELL, LADY, *At the Works* (London, 1907).

BELTON, F. G., *A Manual for Confessors* (London, 1916).

BENN, T., *The Right to Know* (Nottingham, 1978).

—— *Office Without Power: Diaries, 1968–72* (London, 1989).

—— *Conflicts of Interest: Diaries, 1977–80* (London, 1990).

BENNETT, A., *Writing Home* (London, 1994).

BENSON, E., *To Struggle is to Live: A Working Class Autobiography*, Vol. 2 (Newcastle-upon-Tyne, 1980).

BENTHAM, J., 'Of Publicity', in J. BOWRING (ed.), *The Works of Jeremy Bentham* (London, 1843).

BLAKE, J., *Memories of Old Poplar* (London, 1977).

BOSANQUET, C., *A Handy Book for Visitors of the Poor in London* (London, 1874).

BOUTMY, É., *The English People* (London, 1904).

BOWMAKER, E., *The Housing of the Working Class* (London, 1895).

BRATHWAIT, R., *The English Gentleman* (London, 1860; 1st pub. 1630).

BREND, W. A., *Health and the State* (London, 1917).

BRIDGE, A. *Permission to Resign* (London, 1971).

BRIDGES, E., *Portrait of a Profession: The Civil Service Tradition* (Cambridge, 1950).

BRIERLEY, W., *Means-Test Man* (Nottingham 1983; 1st pub. 1935).

British Association of Social Workers, *Discussion Paper No. 1: Confidentiality in Social Work* (London, 1971).

The British Code of Duel (London, 1824).

British Medical Association, *Secret Remedies* (London, 1909).

—— *Ethics and Members of the Medical Profession* (London, 1949).

—— *The Handbook of Medical Ethics* (London, 1984 edn.).

—— *Medical Ethics Today: Its Practice and Philosophy* (London, 1993).

BROGAN, D. W., *The English People* (London, 1943).

[BROWNE, W. J.], 'The English Gentleman', *The National Review*, 7: 38 (Apr. 1886).

BRYCE, J., *Modern Democracies* (London, 1921).

BULWER LYTTON, E., *England and the English* (Paris, 1833 edn.).

BUTLER, J. E., *Government by Police* (London, 1888).

BUTLER, R., 'The Evolution of the Civil Service—A Progress Report', *Public Administration*, 71: 3 (Autumn 1993).

BYERS, Sir J., 'Quackery—With Special Reference to Female Complaints', *British Medical Journal* (27 May 1911).

BYWATER, H. C. and FERRABY, H. C., *Strange Intelligence: Memoirs of Naval Secret Service* (London, 1931).

CALLAGHAN, J., *Time and Chance* (London, 1987).

Campaign for Freedom of Information, *Public Attitudes Towards Freedom of Information* (London, 1986).

Campaign for the Limitation of Secret Police Powers, *The Secret Police and You* (London, 1956).

CAMPBELL, LADY COLIN, *Etiquette of Good Society* (London, 1895).

'The Causes of Quackery', *British Medical Journal* (27 May 1911).

CARPENTER, A., 'Medical Etiquette', in R. C. GLENN, *A Manual of the Laws Affecting Medical Men* (London, 1871).

[CECIL, LORD R.], 'Competitive Examinations', *Quarterly Review*, 18 (Oct. 1860).

CHARLES, E., *The Practice of Birth Control* (London, 1932).

Charter 88, 'Freedom of Information' (London, 1992).

CHAUCER, G., *The Wife of Bath's Tale*, in E. T. DONALDSON (selected and ed.), *Chaucer's Poetry* (New York, 1958).

CHEADLE, E., *Manners of Modern Society* (London, 1872).

CHISHOLM, M. K., *An Insight into Health Visiting* (London, 1970).

CHURCHILL, W. S., *The World Crisis, 1911–1914* (2nd edn., London, 1923).

CLARK, W., *From Three Worlds* (London, 1986).

COHEN, M., *I Was One of the Unemployed* (London, 1945).

COLE, G. D. H., 'Reconstruction in the Civil and Municipal Services' *Public Administration*, 20 (1942).

—— 'Reform in the Civil Service', in *Essays in Social Theory* (London, 1950).

COLE, J., *As It Seemed to Me* (rev. edn., London, 1996).

COLLAR, G. and CROOK, C. W., *School Management and Methods of Instruction* (London, 1900).

COLLIER, P., *England and the English from an American Point of View* (London, 1910).

CONNOLLY, J., *An Easy Guide to the New Unemployment Act* (London, c.1935).

COOMBES, B. L., *These Poor Hands* (London, 1939).

CORYTON, J., *A Treatise on the Law of Letters-Patent* (London, 1855).

CRADDOCK, M., *A North Country Maid* (London, 1960).

CRIPPS, S., 'Can Socialism Come by Constitutional Methods?', in C. ADDISON *et al.*, *Problems of a Socialist Government* (London, 1933).

CROHAM, LORD, 'Is Nothing Secret?', *Listener* (7 Sept. 1978).

—— *Would Greater Openness Improve or Weaken Government?* (Salford, 1984).

CROSSMAN, R., *Inside View* (London, 1972).

—— *The Diaries of a Cabinet Minister*, 3 vols. (London, 1975).

The Czar Unmasked. Being the Secret and Confidential Communication between the Emperor of Russia and the Government of England relative to the Ottoman Empire (2nd edn. 1854).

Dagenham Municipal Housing Estates, *Tenants' Handbook* (Gloucester, 1949).

DALE, W., *The State of the Medical Profession in Great Britain* (London, 1875).

DALYELL, T., *Misrule: How Mrs. Thatcher has Misled Parliament from the Sinking of the 'Belgrano' to the Wright Affair* (London, 1987).

DASH, J., *Good Morning Brothers* (London, 1969).

DEFOE, D., *The Compleat English Gentleman*, ed. K. D. BUELBRING (London, 1900).

DICEY, A. V., *Introduction to the Study of the Law of the Constitution* (1885; 10th edn. London, 1959).

DICKENS, C., *Dombey and Son* (London, 1847–8).

—— *Bleak House* (Everyman edn., London, 1907).

DISRAELI, B., *Collected Edition of the Novels and Tales by the Right Honourable B. Disraeli*, Vol. 1, *Lothair* (London, 1870).

District Visitors, Deaconesses (London, 1890).

The District Visitor's Note Book (London, 1866).

DOYLE, A. CONAN, 'The Naval Treaty', in *The Penguin Complete Sherlock Holmes* (Harmondsworth, 1981).

DUNCAN (Lecturer on Elocution), *The Gentleman's Book of Manners or Etiquette; Showing How to Become a Perfect Gentleman* (London, 1875).

EVE, E. (ed.), *Manual for Health Visitors and Infant Welfare Workers* (London, 1921).

EDMONSTONE, Sir A., *The Christian Gentleman's Daily Walk* (London, 1850).

EMERSON, R. W., *English Traits* (London, 1883).

—— *Society and Solitude* (London, 1895 edn.).

EMMERSON, H. C. and LASCELLES, E. C. P., *Guide to the Unemployment Insurance Acts* (London, 1928).

ESCOTT, T. H. S., *England: Its People, Polity, and Pursuits* (London, 1890).

Fabian Society, *The Reform of the Higher Civil Service* (London, 1947).

—— *The Administrators: Reform in the Civil Service* (London, 1964).

The Family Welfare Association, *The Family, Patients or Clients?* (London, 1961).

FIELD, F., 'Killing a Commitment: The Cabinet and the Children', *New Society* (24 June 1976).

—— *Poverty and Politics* (London, 1982).

FITCH, H. T., *Traitors Within* (London, 1933).

First Division Association, 'Performance Standards in the Public Service: A Report by a Sub-Committee of the First Division Association', *Public Administration*, 50 (Summer, 1972).

FLACK, G., 'The Health Visitor's Work in a Group Practice—A Personal Account of the Early Days', in P. J. CUNNINGHAM (ed.), *The Principles of Health Visiting* (London 1967).

FLORENCE, L. S., *Birth Control on Trial* (London, 1930).

FORDER, C. R., *The Parish Priest at Work* (London, 1947).

FORSTER, E. M., 'Liberty in England', in *Abinger Harvest* (Harmondswroth, 1967).

FREELING, A., *The Gentleman's Pocket-Book of Etiquette* (8th edn, Liverpool, 1838).

'Gentlemen', *Cornhill Magazine*, 5 (Jan.–June 1852).

GILCHRIST, J. P., *A Brief Display of the Origin and History of Ordeals* (London, 1821).

GISBORNE, T., *On the Duties of Physicians Resulting from their Profession* (Oxford, 1847).

GOLDTHORPE, H., *Room at the Bottom* (London, 1959).

GOODHEAD, E. E., *The West End Story, Derby During the Depression: A Social and Personal History* (Matlock, 1983).

GOODLIFFE, J. B., *The Parson and his Problems* (London, 1933).

GOWERS, E., *The Complete Plain Words* (London, 1954).

GREEN, P., *The Town Parson* (London, 1929).

GREENE, F., *Time to Spare; What Unemployment Means* (London, 1935).

GREENWOOD, W., *How the Other Man Lives* (London, 1939).

GREG, W. R., *The Way Out* (London, 1855).

GREGORY, J. D., *On the Edge of Diplomacy* (London, 1929).

GREY, Earl, *Parliamentary Government* (London, 1858).

The *Guardian*.

The Habits of Good Society. A Handful of Etiquette for Ladies and Gentlemen (London, 1855).

HADFIELD, S. J., *Law and Ethics for Doctors* (London, 1958).

HAHN, E., *England to Me* (London, 1950).

HAILSHAM, Lord, *Elective Dictatorship*, Richard Dimbleby Lecture, 1976.

HALL, R. (ed.), *Dear Dr Stopes: Sex in the 1920s* (London, 1978).

HALSTEAD, J., HARRISON, R., and STEVENSON, J., 'The Reminiscences of Sid Elias', *Bulletin of the Society for the Study of Labour History*, 38 (Spring 1979).

HANNINGTON, W., *Never on Our Knees* (London, 1967).

HAYBURN, R., 'The Police and the Hunger Marchers', *International Review of Social History*, 17: 3 (1972).

HAZLITT, W., 'On the Look of a Gentleman', *The Plain Speaker* (1826), reprinted in P. P. HOWE (ed.), *The Complete Works of William Hazlitt*, XII (London, 1931).

HEATH, E., 'A State of Secrecy', *New Statesman and Society* (10 Mar. 1989).

HENDERSON, A., *The Aims of Labour* (London, 1918).

HENSON, H. H., *Ad Clerum* (London, 1937).

HERSTLET, E., *Recollections of the Old Foreign Office* (London, 1901).

HEWART, Lord, *The New Despotism* (London, 1929).

'H.F.', *Hints to District Visitors* (London, 1858).

HILL, A., *A Cage of Shadows* (London, 1977).

HILL, B., *Boss of Britain's Underworld* (London, 1955).

HILL, O. *Homes of the London Poor* (2nd edn., 1883: repr. London, 1970).

HILL, R. and G. B., *The Life of Sir Rowland Hill and the History of the Penny Postage* (London, 1880).

HILTON, J., *Rich Man, Poor Man* (London, 1938).

HINDMARSH, W. *Observations on the Defects of the Patent Laws of this Country with Suggestions for the Reform of Them* (London, 1851).

HOBSON, J. A., 'The Restatement of Democracy', *Contemporary Review*, 81 (1902).

HOGGART, R., *A Local Habitation: Life and Times, 1: 1918–1940* (London, 1968).

HOLYOAKE, G. J., *A New Defence of the Ballot* (London, 1868).

HORDER, T., 'Introduction', in J. MARCHANT (ed.), *Medical Views on Birth Control* (London, 1926).

How To Behave, A Pocket Manual of Etiquette (Glasgow and London, 1865).

How to Behave, or, Etiquette of Society (London, [1879]).

HUGHES, T., 'Anonymous Journalism', *MacMillan's Magazine*, V (Dec., 1861).

HUNTER, L. S., *A Parson's Job* (London, 1931).

INSKIP, J. T., *The Parish Idea* (London, 1905).

JACOB, W., 'Observations and Suggestions Respecting the Collation, Concentration, and Diffusion of Statistical Knowledge Regarding the State of the United Kingdom', *Transactions of the Statistical Society of London*, 1: 1 (1837).

JAMESON, A., 'On the Relative Position of Mothers and Governesses', *Memoirs and Essays* (1846).

The Joseph Rowntree Memorial Trust/MORI, *State of the Nation Survey* (York, 1995).

JOYNT, R. C., *The Church's Real Work* (London, 1934).

KAUFMAN, G., *How to be a Minister* (London, 1980).

KEALEY G. S. and WHITTAKER, R. (eds.), *R.C.M.P. Security Bulletins: The Early Years, 1919–1929* (St Johns, Newfoundland, 1994).

KERR, R., *The Gentleman's House* (2nd edn., London, 1865).

KIDD, R., *British Liberty in Danger* (London, 1940).

KIDDIER, W., *The Old Trade Unions from the Unprinted Records of the Brushmakers* (London, 1930).

KINGSLEY, J., *Representative Bureaucracy* (London, 1944).

The Ladies' Companion for Visiting the Poor (London, 1813).

The Lancet.

E. LANSBURY, *Lansbury, My Father* (London, 1934).

LE QUEUX, W., *Spies of the Kaiser* (London, 1909).

LEWIS, G. C., *A Dialogue on the Best Form of Government* (London, 1863).

LIEBER, F., *The Character of the Gentleman* (Cincinnati, 1846).

LINDSAY, E. and A. D., *Birth Control and Human Dignity* (London, 1929).

LOANE, M., *From their Point of View* (London, 1908).

—— *Neighbours and Friends* (London, 1910).

LOCH, C. S., *How to Help Cases of Distress* (London, 1883).

—— *Charity and Social Life* (London, 1910).

LOW, S., *The Governance of England* (London, 1904).

[McCULLOCH, J. R.], 'State and Defects of British Statistics', *Edinburgh Review*, 61 (Apr. 1835).

MACDONALD, J. R., *Socialism and Government*, 2 vols. (London, 1909).

MACFIE, R. A., *The Patent Question* (London, 1863).

MACKENZIE, C., *Water on the Brain* (London, 1933; 2nd edn., London, 1954).

—— *My Life and Times: Octave Seven, 1931–1938* (London, 1968).

MAILLAUD, P., *The English Way* (London, 1945).

MALLALIEU, J. P. W., *'Passed to You Please'* (London, 1942).

The Manners of the Aristocracy. By One of Themselves (London, 1881).

Market and Opinion Research International (MORI), *State of the Nation, 1991* (London, 1991).

MARSHALL, H. and TREVELYAN, A., *Slum* (London, 1933).

[MARTINEAU, H.], 'Secret Organisation of Trades', *Edinburgh Review*, CX (1859).

MARVIN, C., *Our Public Offices* (2nd edn., London, 1880).

MARX, K. and ENGELS, F., *Collected Works*, vol. 39 (London, 1983).

MASTERMAN, C. F. G., 'Realities at Home', *The Heart of Empire* (London, 1902).

MAURICE, M., *Governess Life* (1849).

[MAZZINI, J.], 'Mazzini and the Ethics of Politicians', *Westminster Review*, LXXXII (Sept.–Dec. 1844).

—— *Life and Writings of Joseph Mazzini* (new edn., London, 1891).

MEARNS, A., *The Bitter Cry of Outcast London* (London, 1883, repr. London, 1970).

'Medical Ethics', *British and Foreign Medico-Chirurgical Review* (July, 1848).

MILL, J. S., *On Liberty* (1859; London, New Universal Library edn., n.d.).

—— 'Thoughts on Parliamentary Reform', in *Collected Works of John Stuart Mill* (Toronto, 1977), vol. 19.

MILLAR, J., *The Gentleman's Handbook of Etiquette* (Edinburgh 18-), republished as *How to be a Perfect Gentleman* (London, 1989).

MITCHELL, B. R., *Abstract of European Historical Statistics* (2nd edn., London, 1981).

—— and DEANE, P., *Abstract of British Historical Statistics* (Cambridge, 1971).

MITCHELL, J. ['Captain Orlando Sabertash'], *The Art of Conversation* (London, 1842).

MONTAGUE, F. C., *The Limits of Individual Liberty* (London, 1885).

MOREL, E. D., *Ten Years of Secret Diplomacy: An Unheeded Warning* (4th edn., Manchester, 1916).

MORLEY, J. *The Life of Gladstone* (London, 1908).

Morning Post.

MORRISON, H., *Government and Parliament* (3rd edn., London, 1964).

MUIR, R. *Peers and Bureaucrats: Two Problems of English Government* (London, 1910).

—— *How Britain is Governed* (London, 1930).

MUNRO, C. K., *The Fountains in Trafalgar Square* (London, 1952).

NAIRNE, P., 'Policy-Making in Public', in R. A. CHAPMAN and M. HUNT (eds.), *Open Government* (London, 1989).

NEIL, C., *The Christian Visitor's Handbook* (London, 1882).

NEWMAN, J. H., *The Idea of a University*, ed. I. T. KER (Oxford, 1976).

NUTTING, A., *No End of a Lesson* (London, 1967).

'On the Anonymous in Periodicals', *New Monthly Magazine* (1853).

Operative Society of Masons, *Fortnightly Returns.*

ORWELL, G., *The Road to Wigan Pier* (1937; Penguin edn., Harmondsworth, 1989).

—— *The Lion and Unicorn* (London, 1941).

OWEN, D., *Face the Future* (London, 1981).

OXLEY, W., 'Are You Working?', in J. COMMON (ed.), *Seven Shifts* (London, 1938).

Pall Mall Gazette

PANTON, J. E., *From Kitchen to Garrett. Hints to Young Householders* (London, 1890).

PATCHETT MARTIN, A., *Life and Letters of the Right Honourable Robert Lowe, Viscount Sherbrooke* (London, 1893).

PERCIVAL, T., *Medical Ethics; or, a code of Institutes and Precepts adapted to the Professional Conduct of Physicians and Surgeons* (Manchester, 1803).

PETERS, C., *England and the English* (London, 1904).

PHELAN, J., *The Underworld* (London, 1953).

PHILBY, K., *My Secret War* (London, 1968).

PINNOCK, W., *The Golden Treasury* (London, 1848).

PITT-RIVERS, G., *Weeds in the Garden of Marriage* (London, 1931).

PONSONBY, A., *The Decline of the Aristocracy* (London, 1912).

—— *Democracy and the Conduct of Foreign Affairs* (London, 1912).

—— *Democracy and Diplomacy* (London, 1915).

PORTER, W. O., *Medical Science and Ethicks* (Bristol, 1837).

PRESTON, A. L., *The Parish Priest in his Parish* (London, 1933).

PRIESTLEY, J. B., *English Journey* (London, 1934).

Punch.

REES, M., 'The Parameters of Politics', in R. A. Chapman and M. Hunt (eds.), *Open Government* (London, 1989).

REILLY, S. A., *I Walk with the King* (London, 1931).

RICHMOND, M. E., *Friendly Visiting Among the Poor* (London, 1899).

[RICKARDS, G. K.], 'Trades' Unions', *Edinburgh Review*, 126 (1867).

RIVINGTON, W., *Medical Education and Medical Organisation* (London, 1879).

ROSEBERY, LORD, *The Duty of Public Service* (Edinburgh, 1898).

—— *Sir Robert Peel* (London, 1899).

ROGERS, C. F., *Principles of Parish Work* (London, 1905).

SANGER, M., *My Fight for Birth Control* (New York, 1931).

SAUNDBY, R., *Medical Ethics: A Guide to Professional Conduct* (London, 1907).

SAVAGE, H. E., *Pastoral Visitation* (London, 1903).

SCANNELL, D., *Mother Knew Best: An East End Childhood* (London, 1974).

'Security Precautions in the British Civil Service', *Public Administration*, 35 (Autumn, 1957).

SEELY, J. E. B., *Adventure* (London, 1930).

SEWELL, E. M., *Principles of Education* (1856).

SHUCKBURGH, E., *Descent to Suez: Diaries, 1951–56* (London, 1986).

SILBER, J. C., *The Invisible Weapons* (London, 1932).

SIMS, G. R., *How the Poor Live* (London, 1883).

SINCLAIR, A., *The Red and the Blue: Intelligence, Treason and the Universities* (London, 1986).

SMYTHE-PALMER, A., *The Ideal of a Gentleman* (London, [1908]).

The Society for Organising Charitable Relief and Repressing Mendicity, *House-to-House Visitation* (London, 1871).

SPRING RICE, M., *Working-Class Wives* (London, 1939; 1981).

STACK, J. H., *Our Government Offices* (London, 1855).

STANLEY, H. M., *The Autobiography of Sir Henry Morton Stanley* (London, 1909).

STEEL, F., *Ditcher's Row* (London, 1939).

STEER, M. H., 'Rescue Work by Women among Women', in Baroness Burdett-Coutts, *Women's Mission to Women* (London, 1893).

STEPHEN, C. E., *The Rt. Hon. Sir James Stephen: Letters with Biographical Notes* (Gloucester, 1906).

STOPES, M., *A Letter to Working Mothers* (1919).

—— *Contraception: Theory, History and Practice* (London, 1923).

—— *Our Ostriches* (London, 1923).

—— *Mother England* (London, 1929).

SURRIDGE, H. A. D., *A Manual of Hints to Visiting Friends of the Poor* (London, 1871).

TAINE, H., *Notes on England* (3rd. edn., London, 1872).

TAYLOR, H., *The Statesman* (1836; New York, 1958).

—— *The Autobiography of Henry Taylor* (London, 1885).

THATCHER, M., *The Downing Street Years* (London, 1993).

THOMAS, J. H., *When Labour Rules* (London, 1920).

THOMSON, B., *The Scene Changes* (London, 1939).

THOMSON, H. B., *Choice of a Profession* (London, 1857).

The Times.

TORRENS, T. M., *The Life and Times of the Right Honourable Sir James R. G. Graham* (London, 1863).

TRAILL, H. D., 'The Anonymous Critic', *Saturday Review*, 10 (1860).

[TROLLOPE, A.], 'The Civil Service as a Profession', *Cornhill Magazine*, III (Jan.–June 1861).

TUFNELL, E. C., *Character, Object and Effects of Trade Unions* (London, 1834).

'Unqualified Practice through the Post', *British Medical Journal* (27 May 1911).

VAUGHAN, R., *The Age of Great Cities* (London, 1843).

WALSH, J., *Not Like This* (London, 1953).

WARREN S. D. and BRANDEIS, L. D., 'The Right to Privacy', *Harvard Law Review*, 4: 5 (15 Dec. 1890).

WASS, D., *Government and the Governed* (London, 1983).

—— 'The Civil Service at the Crossroads', *Political Quarterly*, 56: 3 (July–Sept. 1985).

WATTS-DITCHFIELD, J., *The Church in Action* (London, 1913).

WAUGH, E., *Home-Life of the Lancashire Factory Folk During the Cotton Famine* (London, 1867).

WEALE, J., *Catalogue of Books on Architecture and Engineering, Civil, Mechanical, Military, and Naval, New and Old* (London, 1854).

WEBB, B., *My Apprenticeship* (Harmondsworth, 1938).

WEBB, S. and B., *Industrial Democracy* (London, 1897).

——*A Constitution for the Socialist Commonwealth of Great Britain* (London, 1920; 1975).

WEBER, M., *The Theory of Social and Economic Organisation*, ed. T. Parsons (New York, 1947).

——*From Max Weber*, ed. H. H. Gerth and C. Wright Mills (London, 1948).

WHITEHEAD, G., *Birth Control: Why and How* (London, 1929).

WHITE, F. W., *Birth Control and its Opponents* (London, 1935).

WIGG, LORD, *George Wigg* (London, 1972).

WILDE, O., *An Ideal Husband*, in *Plays* (Harmondsworth, 1954).

WILLIAMS, S., *Politics is for People* (Harmondsworth, 1981).

WILLIS, E. S., *Whatever Happened to Tom Mix? The Story of One of My Lives* (London, 1970).

WILLS, F., 'What is a Gentleman?', in id. (ed.), *Lay Sermons for Practical People* (London, 1890).

WILSON, H., *The Governance of Britain* (London, 1977 edn.).

WOLFF K. H. (ed. and trans.), *The Sociology of Georg Simmel* (Toronto, 1950).

'Work and Murder', *Blackwood's Magazine*, 102 (1867).

WRIGHT, P., *Spycatcher: The Candid Autobiography of a Senior Intelligence Officer* (Richmond, Victoria, 1987).

WRIGHT, T., *The Great Unwashed* (London, 1868).

4. SECONDARY SOURCES

ABRAMS, P., 'The Failure of Social Reform 1918–20', *Past and Present*, 24 (1963).

AITKEN, J., *Officially Secret* (London, 1971).

ALDERMAN, G., *Pressure Groups and Government in Great Britain* (London, 1984).

ALEXANDER, D. and BRITTON, A., *Financial Reporting* (3rd edn., London, 1993).

ANDERSON, O., 'The Janus Face of Mid-Nineteenth-Century English Radicalism: The Administrative Reform Association of 1855', *Victorian Studies*, 8 (Mar. 1965).

——'The Administrative Reform Association, 1855–1857', in Hollis, P. (ed.), *Pressure from Without* (London, 1974).

ANDREW, C., *Secret Service: The Making of the British Intelligence Community* (London, 1985).

ANDREW, D. T., 'The Code of Honour and its Critics: The Opposition to Duelling in England, 1700–1850', *Social History*, 5: 3 (Oct. 1980).

ANTROBUS, M. F., *District Nursing* (London, 1985).

ARANHYA, N., 'The Influence of Pressure Groups on Financial Reporting Statements in Britain', in T. A. Lee and R. H. Parker (eds.), *The Evolution of Corporate Financial Accounting* (New York and London, 1984).

ASCHERSON, N., 'Mocking of Monarchy Tilts the Power Axis', *Independent on Sunday* (17 Jan. 1993).

ASHWORTH, W., *The State in Business, 1945 to the mid-1980s* (London, 1991).

AUBREY, C., *Who's Watching You* (Harmondsworth, 1981).

AYERS, P., *The Liverpool Docklands* (Liverpool, 1988).

BAKKE, F. W., *The Unemployed Man, A Social Study* (London, 1933).

BAINBRIDGE, D. I., *Intellectual Property* (London, 1992).

BAINES, P., 'History and Rationale of the 1979 Reforms', in G. Drewry (ed.), *The New Select Committees* (Oxford, 1989).

BARBERIS, P., 'Whitehall since the Fulton Report', in P. Barberis (ed.), *The Whitehall Reader: The UK's Administrative Machine in Action* (Buckingham, 1996).

BARNES, T., *Open Up! Britain and Freedom of Information in the 1980s* (Fabian Tract, 1980).

BARRY, A., OSBORNE, T., and ROSE, N., 'Introduction', in *Foucault and Political Reason: Liberalism, Neo-Liberalism and Rationalities of Government* (London, 1996).

BAXTER, J. D., *State, Security, Privacy and Information* (London, 1990).

BAYLEY, M., 'Values in Locally Based Work', in S. Shardlow (ed.), *The Values of Change in Social Work* (London, 1989).

BAYLIS, J., *Ambiguity and Deterrence: British Nuclear Strategy, 1945–1964* (Oxford, 1995).

BECKETT, J. V., *The Aristocracy in England, 1660–1914* (Oxford, 1986).

BEHAGG, C., 'Secrecy, Ritual and Folk Violence: The Opacity of the Workplace in the First Half of the Nineteenth Century', in R. D. Storch (ed.), *Popular Culture and Custom in Nineteenth-Century England* (London, 1982).

BELL, C., *Middle Class Families* (London, 1968).

BELL, S., *When Salem came to the Boro: The True Story of the Cleveland Child Abuse Crisis* (London, 1988).

BELOFF, M., 'The Whitehall Factor: The Rise of the Higher Civil Service, 1919–1939', in G. Peele and C. Cook (eds.), *The Politics of Reappraisal, 1918–39* (London, 1975).

BENNETT, C. and HENNESSY, P., 'Introduction' to the Outer Circle Policy Unit, *A Consumer's Guide to Open Government* (London, 1980).

BENSMAN, J. and LILIENFELD, R., *Between Public and Private: The Lost Boundaries of the Self* (New York, 1979).

BESSELL, R., *Interviewing and Counselling* (London, 1971).

BIESTEK, F. P., *The Casework Relationship* (London, 1961).

BIRKINSHAW, B., *Freedom of Information: The Law, the Practice and the Ideal* (London, 1988).

—— *Government and Information: The Law relating to Access, Disclosure and Regulation* (London, 1990).

—— *Reforming the Secret State* (Buckingham, 1990).

BIRKS, M., *Gentlemen of the Law* (London, 1960).

BLAKELEY, B. L., *The Colonial Office, 1868–1892* (Durham, NC, 1972).

BLANCO WHITE, T. A., JACOB, R., and DAVIES, J. D., *Patents, Trade Marks, Copyright and Industrial Designs* (2nd edn., London, 1978).

BOEHM, K. *The British Patent System*, Vol. 1 (Cambridge, 1967).

BOK, S., *Secrets: On the Ethics of Concealment and Revelation* (Oxford, 1984).

BOND, T., *Standards and Ethics for Counselling in Action* (London, 1993).

BOURKE, J., *Working-Class Cultures in Britain, 1890–1960* (London, 1994).

BOURNE, J. M., *Patronage and Society in Nineteenth-Century England* (London, 1986).

BOWDEN, S. and OFFER, A., 'Household Appliances and the Use of Time: The United States and Britain Since the 1920s', *Economic History Review*, 47: 4 (1994).

BRASNETT, M. *Voluntary Social Action* (London, 1969).

BRAZIER, R., *Constitutional Practice* (Oxford, 1988).

BRIGGS, A., 'Robert Lowe and the Fear of Democracy', in *Victorian People* (Harmondsworth, 1965).

BROWN, L., *The Board of Trade and the Free Trade Movement, 1830–42* (Oxford, 1958).

—— *Victorian News and Newspapers* (Oxford, 1985).

BULLOCK, A., *Ernest Bevin: Foreign Secretary* (Oxford, 1985).

BUNYAN, T., *The Political Police in Britain* (London, 1976).

BURN, W. L., *The Age of Equipoise* (London, 1964).

BURNEY, I., 'Making Room at the Public Bar: Coroners' Inquests, Medical Knowledge and the Politics of the Constitution in Early-Nineteenth-Century England', in J. Vernon (ed.), *Re-reading the Constitution* (Oxford, 1996).

CAMPBELL, A. V., *Moral Dilemmas in Medicine* (Edinburgh, 1972).

CAMPBELL, B., *Unofficial Secrets* (London, 1989).

CAMPBELL, D., *Phonetappers and the Security State* (London, 1981).

CAMPBELL, D., *The Underworld* (London, 1996).

CARNAGHAN, C., GIBBINS, M., and IKÄHEIMO, S., 'Managed Financial Disclosures: The Interplay Between Accountability Pressures', in R. Munro and J. Mouritsen (eds.), *Accountability: Power, Ethos and the Technologies of Managing* (London, 1996).

CARTWRIGHT, T. J., *Royal Commissions and Departmental Committees in Britain* (London, 1975).

CASSAR, G. H., *Asquith as War Leader* (London 1994).

CATHCART, B., *Test of Greatness: Britain's Struggle for the Atom Bomb* (London, 1994).

CAUTE, D., *The Fellow-Travellers* (London, 1977).

CELL, J. W., *British Colonial Administration in the Mid-Nineteenth Century* (New Haven, 1970).

CHAPMAN, L., *Your Disobedient Servant* (London, 1978).

CHAPMAN, R. A., *The Higher Civil Service in Britain* (London, 1970).

—— *Ethics in the British Civil Service* (London, 1988).

—— ' "The Next Steps": A Review', *Public Policy and Administration*, 3: 3 (1988).

—— 'The End of the Civil Service?', *Teaching Public Administration*, 7: 2 (1992), reprinted in Barberis, *Whitehall Reader*.

—— and GREENAWAY, J. R., *The Dynamics of Administrative Reform* (London, 1980).

CHESTER, N., *The English Administrative System, 1780–1870* (Oxford, 1981).

CHRISTOPH, J. B., 'A Comparative View: Administrative Secrecy in Britain', *Public Administration Review*, 35 (Jan.–Feb. 1975), 28.

CLARK, A., 'Gender, Class and the Constitution: Franchise Reform in England, 1832–1928', in J. Vernon (ed.), *Re-reading the Constitution* (Cambridge, 1996).

CLARK, C. L. with ASQUITH, S., *Social Work and Social Philosophy* (London, 1985).

CLARK, D., 'Open Government: The French Experience', *Political Quarterly*, 57: 3 (July–Sept. 1986).

CLARK, W., 'Cabinet Secrecy, Collective Responsibility, and the British Public's Right to Know About and Participate in Foreign Policy Making', in T. M. Franck and E. Weisband (eds.), *Secrecy and Foreign Policy* (New York, 1974).

CLARKE, R., *New Trends in Government* (London, 1971).

CLEGG, J. (ed.), *Dictionary of Social Services* (London, 1971).

CLOKIE, H. M. and ROBINSON, J. W., *Royal Commissions of Inquiry* (Standford, 1937).

COLEMAN, A., *The Legal Protection of Trade Secrets* (London, 1992).

COLLINI, S. 'The Idea of "Character" in Victorian Political Thought', *Transactions of the Royal Historical Society*, 35 (1985).

COLLINS, R. 'Market Closure and the Conflict Theory of the Professions', in M. Burrage and H. Tortendahl (eds.), *Professions in Theory and History* (London, 1990).

CORFIELD, P. J., *Power and the Professions in Britain, 1700–1850* (London, 1995).

CORNFORD, J., 'The Right to Know Secrets', *Listener*, 100 (31 Aug. 1978), reprinted in May and Rowan, *Inside Information*.

—— 'Official Secrecy and Freedom of Information', in R. Holme and M. Elliott (eds), *1688–1988: Time for a New Constitution* (London, 1988).

COX, N., 'The Thirty-Year Rule and Freedom of Information: Access to Government Records', in G. H. Martin and P. Spufford (eds.), *The Records of the Nation* (Woodbridge, 1990).

CRAFT, C., *Another Kind of Love* (Berkeley, 1994).

CRAFT, N. F. R., 'Exogenous or Endogenous Growth? The Industrial Revolution Reconsidered', *Journal of Economic History*, 55: 4 (Dec. 1995).

CRICK, B., *The Reform of Parliament* (London, 1964).

CRIPPS, Y., *The Legal Implications of Disclosure in the Public Interest* (2nd edn., London, 1994).

CRITCHLEY, T. A., *The Civil Service Today* (London, 1951).

CRONIN, J. E., *The Politics of State Expansion* (London, 1991).

CROUCH, C., 'Sharing Public Space: States and Organized Interests in Western Europe', in J. Hall (ed.), *States in History* (Oxford, 1986).

CROUCHER, R., *We Refuse to Starve in Silence* (London, 1987).

CROWTHER, M. A., *The Workhouse System, 1834–1929* (London, 1983).

CULLEN, M. J., *The Statistical Movement in Early Victorian Britain* (Hassocks, 1975).

CUNNINGHAM, H. (ed.), *The Principles of Health Visiting* (London, 1967).

CURTIN, M., *Propriety and Position: A Study of Victorian Manners* (New York, 1987).

DANCHEV, A. 'In the Back Room: Anglo-American Defence Co-operation, 1945–51', in R. J. Aldrich (ed.), *British Intelligence, Strategy and the Cold War, 1945–51* (London, 1992).

—— *Oliver Franks: Founding Father* (Oxford, 1993).

DAVIES, A. and WILLMAN, J., *What Next? Agencies, Departments and the Civil Service* (London, 1991).

DAVIES, C., 'Professionals in Bureaucracies: The Conflict Thesis Revisited', in R. Dingwall and P. Lewis (eds.), *The Sociology of the Professions* (London, 1983).

DAVIES, E., 'Government Policy and the Public Corporation', *Political Quarterly*, 26: 2 (Apr.–June 1955).

DAVISON, E. H., *Social Casework* (London, 1965).

DAWSON, J., 'State of Medical Records', in P. Hewitt (ed.), *Computers, Records and the Right to Privacy* (Purley, 1979).

DEACON, A., *In Search of the Scrounger* (London, 1976).

DELAFONS, J., 'Working in Whitehall: Changes in Public Administration, 1952–1982', *Public Administration*, 60: 3 (Autumn 1982).

Department of Health, *Child Abuse: A Study of Inquiry Reports, 1980–1989* (London, 1991).

Department of Health and Social Security, *Child Abuse: A Study of Inquiry Reports, 1973–1981* (London, 1982).

DE SMITH, S., 'Official Secrecy and External Relations in Britain: The Law and its Context', in T. M. Franck and E. Weisbrand, *Secrecy and Foreign Policy* (New York, 1974).

DESMOND, A., *The Politics of Evolution: Morphology, Medicine and Reform in Radical London* (Chicago, 1989).

DIGBY, A. and SEARBY P., *Children, School and Society in Nineteenth-Century England* (London, 1981).

DONAJGRODZKI, A. P., 'New Roles for Old: The Northcote–Trevelyan Report and the Clerks of the Home Office, 1822–48', in G. Sutherland (ed.), *Studies in the Growth of Nineteenth-Century Government* (London, 1972).

—— 'Sir James Graham at the Home Office', *Historical Journal*, 20: 1, (1977).

DONOUGHUE, B., *Prime Minister* (London, 1987).

DOWLING, L., *Hellenism and Homosexuality in Victorian Oxford* (Ithaca, 1994).

DRESNER, S. H., 'How Would a British Freedom of Information Act Work in Practice?', in *Secrecy, or the Right to Know* (London, 1980).

DREWRY, G., 'The Official Secrets Acts', *Political Quarterly*, 44: 1 (1973).

—— 'Openness and Secrecy in British Government', in T. N. Chaturvedi (ed.), *Secrecy in Government* (New Delhi, 1980).

—— 'Ministers and Civil Servants', *Public Law* (Winter 1986).

—— 'The 1979 Reforms—New Labels on Old Bottles', in id. (ed.), *The New Select Committees* (Oxford, 1989).

—— and BUTCHER, T., *The Civil Service Today* (Oxford, 1988).

DUMAN, D., 'The Creation and Diffusion of a Professional Ideology in Nineteenth Century England', *Sociological Review*, 27 (1979).

DUNFORD, J. E., 'Robert Lowe and Inspectors' Reports', *British Journal of Educational Studies*, 25: 2, (June 1977).

DUTTON, H. I., *The Patent System and Inventive Activity During the Industrial Revolution, 1750–1852* (Manchester, 1984).

EDELSTEIN, L., 'The Hippocratic Oath: Text, Translation and Interpretation', *Bulletin of the History of Medicine*, Supplement 1 (1943).

EDWARDS, J. R., 'The Accounting Profession and Disclosure in Published Reports, 1925–1935', *Accounting and Business Research* (Autumn 1976).

—— *A History of Financial Accounting* (London, 1989).

ELIAS, N., *The Civilising Process*, Vol. 2, *State Formation and Civilisation* (Oxford, 1982).

ELLIS, A. *Educating Our Masters* (Aldershot, 1985).

ELLMANN, R., *Oscar Wilde* (London, 1987).

ERIKSON, A. B., *The Public Career of Sir James Graham* (Oxford, 1952).

ERNST, M. L. and Schwartz, A. U., *Privacy: The Right To Be Let Alone* (London, 1968).

EWING, K. D. and GEARTY, C. A., *Freedom Under Thatcher: Civil Liberties in Modern Britain* (Oxford, 1990).

FELDMAN, S. P., 'Management in Context: Culture and Organizational Change', in S. Linstead, R. G. Small, and P. Jeffcutt (eds.), *Understanding Management* (London, 1996).

FENNELL, P., 'Local Goverment Corruption in England and Wales', in M. Clarke (ed.), *Corruption: Causes, Consequences and Control* (London, 1983).

FENWICK, H., *Civil Liberties* (London, 1994).

FETTERLEY, D. D., 'Historical Perspectives on Criminal Laws Relating to Theft of Trade Secrets', *Business Law*, 25 (1970).

FIDO, J., 'The Charity Organisation Society and Social Casework in London 1869–1900', in A. P. Donajgrodzki (ed.), *Social Control in Nineteenth-Century Britain* (London, 1977).

FINER, S., 'Jeffersonian Bureaucracy and the Jeffersonian Tradition', *Public Administration*, 30 (1952).

FISSELL, M. E., *Patients, Power and the Poor in Eighteenth-Century Bristol* (Cambridge, 1991).

FITZGERALD, P. and LEOPOLD, M., *Strangers on the Line: The Secret History of Phone Tapping* (London, 1987).

FITZSIMONS, M. A., *The Foreign Policy of the British Labour Government, 1945–1951* (Notre Dame, Ind., 1953).

FLORENCE, P. S. and MADDICK, H., 'Consumers' Councils in the Nationalised Industries', *Political Quarterly*, 25: 3 (July–Sept. 1953).

FRANCIS, H. and MASCARA, A., 'The Keeper and the Bailey: Privacy and Confidentiality in Medicine', in P. Pearce (ed.), *Personal Data Protection in Health and Social Services* (London, 1988).

FRANKEL, M., 'The Environment', in D. Delbridge and M. Smith (eds.), *Consuming Secrets* (London, 1982).

—— 'Files on Ourselves: Fact or Fiction?' and 'How Secrecy Protects the Polluters', in D. Wilson (ed.), *The Secrets File* (London, 1984).

—— 'Addicted to Secrecy, Lies and Distortion', *Observer* (10 Apr. 1994).

FRENCH, D., 'Spy Fever in Britain, 1900–1915', *Historical Journal*, 21: 2 (1978).

FRIEDSON, E., *Professional Powers* (Chicago, 1986).

FREVERT, U., 'Honour and Middle-Class Culture: The History of the Duel in England and Germany', in J. Kocka and A. Mitchell (eds.), *Bourgeois Society in Nineteenth-Century Europe* (Oxford, 1993).

FRIEDRICH, C. J., 'Secrecy versus Privacy: The Democratic Dilemma', *Nomos* (New York, 1971).

GABIS, S. T., 'Political Secrecy and Cultural Conflict: A Plea for Formalism', *Administration and Society*, 10 (1978).

GALNOOR, I., 'Government Secrecy: Exchanges, Intermediaries and Middlemen', *Public Administrative Review*, 35 (Jan.–Feb. 1975).

GASH, N., *Sir Robert Peel* (London, 1972).

GATHORNE-HARDY, J., *The Public School Phenomenon, 597–1977* (London, 1977).

GELLATELY, R., *The Gestapo and German Society* (Oxford, 1990).

GEORGE, V., *Social Security: Beveridge and After* (London, 1968).

GILBERT, B. B., *The Evolution of National Insurance* (London, 1966).

—— *Social Policy 1914–1939* (London, 1970).

GILHOOLY, M. L. M. and McGHEE, S. M. 'Medical Records: Practicalities and Principles of Patient Possession', *Journal of Medical Ethics*, 17 (1991).

GIROUARD, M., *Life in the English Country House* (New Haven, 1978).

—— *The Return to Camelot* (New Haven, 1981).

GITTINS, D. 'Married Life and Birth Control between the Wars', *Oral History*, 3: 2, (1975).

——*Fair Sex: Family Size and Structure, 1900–1939* (London, 1982).

GLADDEN, E. N., *Civil Service or Bureaucracy?* (London, 1956).

GOLDBERG, D., 'Executive Secrecy, National Security, and Freedom of Information in the United Kingdom', *Government Information Quarterly*, 4: 1 (1987).

GOLDING, D., 'Management Rituals: Maintaining Simplicity in the Chain of Command', in S. Linstead, R. G. Small, and P. Jeffcutt (eds.), *Understanding Management* (London, 1996).

GOMME, A. A., *Patents of Invention: Origin and Growth of the Patent System in Britain* (London, 1946).

GOODRICH, P., 'Freedom of the Phone', *Liverpool Law Review*, 11: 2 (1981).

GORDON WALKER, P., 'Secrecy and Openness in Foreign Policy Decision-Making: A British Cabinet Perspective', in T. M. Franck and E. Weisbrand (eds.), *Secrecy and Foreign Policy* (New York, 1974).

GOREN, D., *Secrecy and the Right to Know* (Ramat Gan, 1979).

GOWING, M., *Independence and Deterrence: Britain and Atomic Energy, 1945–1952*, Vol. 1, *Policy Making*; Vol. 2, *Policy Execution* (London, 1974).

GREAVES, H. R., *The Civil Service in the Changing State* (London, 1947).

GREENAWAY, J. R., 'Warren Fisher and the Transformation of the British Treasury, 1919–1939', *Journal of British Studies*, 23, (1983).

GRIFFITHS, J., *Public Rights and Private Interests* (Tivandrum, 1981).

—— 'The Democratic Process', in P. Wallington (ed.), *Civil Liberties 1984* (Oxford, 1984).

—— 'The Official Secrets Act 1989', *Journal of Law and Society*, 16 (1989).

GURRY, F., *Breach of Confidence* (Oxford, 1984).

GWYNN, W. B., 'The Labour Party and the Threat of Bureaucracy', *Political Quarterly*, 19: 4 (1971),

HAKIM, C., 'Census Confidentiality in Britain', in M. Bulmer (ed.), *Census, Surveys and Privacy* (London, 1979).

HALE, R., LOVELAND, M. K., and OWEN, G. M., *The Principles and Practices of Health Visiting* (Oxford, 1968).

HALL, R., *Marie Stopes* (London, 1977).

HANSON, A. H., 'Report on the Reports', *Public Administration*, 30, (Summer, 1952).

HARDEN, I. and LEWIS, N., *The Noble Lie: The British Constitution and the Rule of Law* (London, 1986).

HARRIS, J. S. and GARCIA, T. V., 'The Permanent Secretaries: Britain's Top Administrators' *Public Administration Review*, 26: 1 (Mar. 1966).

HARRISON, B., *The Transformation of British Politics, 1860–1995* (Oxford, 1996).

HARRISON, T., *Access to Information in Local Government* (London, 1988).

HART, J., 'The Genesis of the Northcote–Trevelyan Report', in G. Sutherland (ed.), *Studies in the Growth of Nineteenth-Century Government* (London, 1972).

HAWKINS, C., *Mishap or Malpractice?* (Oxford, 1985).

HAGELL, R., 'Freedom of Information in Australia, Canada, and New Zealand', *Public Administration*, 67 (Summer 1989).

HENDRICK, H., *Child Welfare: England 1872–1989* (London, 1994).

HENNESSY, P., 'A Malign Legacy', *Index on Censorship*, 15: 6 (1986).

—— 'No End of an Argument: How Whitehall Tried and Failed to Suppress Sir Anthony Nutting's Suez Memoir', *Contemporary Record* 1: 1 (Spring 1987).

HENNESSY, P., 'Not by Teabags Alone', *Index on Censorship*, 17: 8 (1988).

—*Whitehall* (London, 1989).

—'The Attlee Governments, 1945–51', in P. Hennessy and A. Seldon (eds.), *Ruling Performance* (Oxford, 1989).

—'Oiling the Machine', in B. Pimlott, A. Wright, and T. Flower (eds.), *The Alternative* (London, 1990).

—'On Secrecy', Radio 4 broadcast, 25 June 1992.

—and BROOMFIELD, G., 'Britain's Cold War Security Purge: The Origins of Positive Vetting', *Historical Journal*, 25: 4 (1982).

HETHERINGTON, K., *The Badlands of Modernity* (London, 1997).

HETZNER, C., 'Social Democracy and Bureaucracy: The Labour Party and Higher Civil Service Recruitment', *Administration and Society*, 17: 1 (May 1985).

HEWITT, P., *Privacy* (London, 1977).

HIGGINS, P., *Heterosexual Dictatorship: Male Homosexuality in Postwar Britain* (London, 1996).

HILEY, N., 'The Failure of British Counter-Espionage against Germany, 1907–1914', *Historical Journal*, 28: 4 (1985).

—'British Internal Security in Wartime: The Rise and Fall of P.M.S.2, 1915–1917', *Intelligence and National Security*, 1 (1986).

—'Counter-Espionage and Security in Great Britain during the First World War', *English Historical Review*, 101 (July 1986).

HIMROD, D. K., 'Secrecy in Modern Science', in K. W. Bolle (ed.), *Secrecy in Religions* (Leiden, 1987).

HINGLEY, R., *The Russian Secret Service* (London, 1970).

HITCHENS, C., 'What is this Bernard', *London Review of Books* (13, 1, 10 Jan. 1991).

HOBSBAWM, E. J. and RUDÉ, G., *Captain Swing* (Harmondsworth, 1973).

—'Labour and Human Rights', in *Workers* (London, 1984).

HOCKLEY, L., *Feeling the Pulse* (London, 1966).

HOGGART, R., *The Uses of Literacy* (Harmondsworth, 1958).

HOLLINGSWORTH, M. and NORTON-TAYLOR, R., *Blacklist: The Inside Story of Political Vetting* (London, 1988).

HOLME, R., 'The Democratic Deficit', in B. Pimlott, A. Wright, and T. Flower (eds.), *The Alternative* (London, 1990).

HOOPER, D., *Official Secrets* (London, 1987).

HORN, P., 'Robert Lowe and HM Inspectorate, 1859–1864', *Oxford Review of Education*, 7: 2 (1981).

HORNBY, J. A., *An Introduction to Company Law* (London, 1957).

HORNE, M., *Values in Social Work* (Aldershot, 1987).

HOWITT, H., *The History of the Institute of Chartered Accountants in England and Wales, 1870–1965* (New York, 1984).

HUGHES, A. and HUNT, K., 'A Culture Transformed? Women's Lives in Wythenshawe in 1930', in A. Davies and S. Fielding (eds.), *Workers' Worlds: Cultures and Communities in Manchester and Salford, 1880–1939* (Manchester, 1992).

HUGHES, E., 'Sir James Stephen and the Anonymity of the Civil Servant', *Public Administration*, 36 (Spring 1958).

HUGHES, K., *The Victorian Governess* (London, 1993).

HULL, D., 'Openness and Secrecy in Science: Their Origins and Limitations', *Science, Technology and Human Values*, 51 (1985).

HUNT, M., 'Parliament and Official Secrecy', in R. A. Chapman and M. Hunt, *Open Government* (London, 1989).

HUMPHREYS, R., *Sin, Organized Charity and the Poor Law in Victorian England* (London, 1995).

HUMPHRIES, S., *A Secret World of Sex: Forbidden Fruit: The British Experience, 1900–1950* (London, 1994).

HUNT, M. C., *Open Government in the 1980s* (Sheffield 1988).

HURWITT, M. and THORNTON, P., *Civil Liberty* (4th edn., London, 1989).

HYDE, H. M., *Norman Birkett* (London, 1964).

——*Neville Chamberlain* (London, 1976).

ILLING, M. and DONOVAN, B., *District Nursing* (London, 1981).

JACKELL, R., *Moral Mazes: The World of Corporate Managers* (New York, 1988).

JACOB, J., 'Some Reflections on Governmental Secrecy', *Public Law* (1974).

JACOB, J. M., *Doctors and Rules* (London, 1988).

JACOB, M. C., *Living the Enlightenment: Freemasonry and Politics in Eighteenth-Century Europe* (Oxford, 1991).

JACKSON, D. C., 'Individual Rights and National Security', *Modern Law Review*, 20 (1957).

JAYAWEERA, H., MILES, A., SAVAGE, M., and VINCENT, D., *Pathways and Prospects: The Development of the Modern Bureaucratic Career, 1850–1950* (Cambridge, forthcoming).

JEFFREY-POULTER, S., *Peers, Queers and Commons* (London, 1991).

JENKINS, R., *Asquith* (London, 1964).

——*Nine Men of Power* (London, 1974).

JOELSON, M. R., 'The Dismissal of Civil Servants in the Interests of National Security', *Public Law* (1963).

JOHNSON, D. H., 'Criminal Secrecy: The Case of the Zande "Secret Societies"', *Past and Present*, 130 (1991).

JOHNSTONE, D., 'Facelessness: Anonymity in the Civil Service', *Parliamentary Affairs*, 39: 4 (1986).

JONES, B. and KEATING, M., *Labour and the British State* (Oxford, 1985).

JONES, M. (ed.), *Privacy* (Newton Abbot, 1974).

JONES, R., *The Nineteenth-Century Foreign Office* (London, 1971).

JONES, W. H. S., *The Doctor's Oath: An Essay in the History of Medicine* (Cambridge, 1924).

JUSTICE, *The Citizen and the Public Agencies* (1976).

KEATING, P., *Into Unknown England* (London, 1976).

KELLNER, P., 'The Lobby, Official Secrets and Good Government', *Parliamentary Affairs*, 36: 3 (1983).

——and CROWTHER-HUNT, Lord, *The Civil Servants: An Inquiry into Britain's Ruling Class* (London, 1980).

KENT, C., 'Higher Journalism and the Mid-Victorian Clerisy', *Victorian Studies*, 13 (1969).

KIERNAN, V., *The Duel in European History* (Oxford, 1988).

KIEVE, J., *The Electric Telegraph* (Newton Abbot, 1973).

KINZER, B. L., *The Ballot Question in Nineteenth-Century English Politics* (New York, 1982).

KITSON CLARK, G., ' "Statesmen in Disguise": Reflexions on the History of the Neutrality of the Civil Service', *Historical Journal*, 3 (1959).

KOSS, S., *Asquith* (London, 1976).

—— *The Rise and Fall of the Political Press in Britain*, Vol. 1, *The Nineteenth Century* (London, 1981).

KOTTOW, M. H., 'Medical Confidentiality: An Intransigent and Absolute Obligation', *Journal of Medical Ethics*, 12 (1986).

KYLE, K., *Suez* (London, 1991).

LACEY, R., 'Social Workers and their Records', in P. Hewitt (ed.), *Computers, Records and the Right to Privacy* (Purley, 1979).

LANNING, H. and NORTON-TAYLOR, R., *A Conflict of Loyalties—GCHQ 1984–1991* (Cheltenham, 1991).

LASKI, H. J., *Democracy in Crisis* (London, 1933).

—— 'The British Civil Service', *Yale Review*, 26: 2 (Dec. 1936).

—— *Parliamentary Government in England* (London, 1938).

—— *The Danger of Being a Gentleman* (London, 1940).

LEATHARD, A. *The Fight for Family Planning* (London, 1980).

LEE, T. A., 'A Brief History of Company Audits: 1840–1900' and 'Company Financial Statements: An Essay in Business History, 1930–1950', in T. A. Lee and R. H. Parker (eds.), *The Evolution of Corporate Financial Accounting* (New York and London, 1984).

LEES, A., 'The Metropolis and the Intellectual', in A. Sutcliffe (ed.), *Metropolis 1890–1940* (London, 1984).

LEES, A. J., *The Origins of the Popular Press in England, 1855–1914* (London, 1976).

LEIGH, D., *The Frontiers of Secrecy* (London, 1980).

LEIGH, I. and LUSTGARTEN, L., 'The Security Service Act 1989', *Modern Law Review*, 52 (Nov. 1989).

LETWIN, S. R., *The Gentleman in Trollope* (London, 1982).

LEWIS, J., *Women and Social Action in Victorian and Edwardian England* (Aldershot, 1991).

LEWIS, R. and MAUDE, A., *The English Middle Class* (London, 1950).

—— *Professional People* (London, 1952).

LEWIS, R., *Margaret Thatcher* (London, 1985).

LEY, P., 'Giving Information to Patients', in J. R. Eiser (ed.), *Social Psychology and Behavioral Medicine* (Chichester, 1982).

LINKLATER, A., *Compton Mackenzie: A Life* (London, 1987).

LLEWELLYN SMITH, H., *The Board of Trade* (London, 1928).

LLOYD, L. J., 'The Interception of Communications Act 1985', *Modern Law Review*, 49 (Jan. 1986).

LOFFT, A., *Understanding Accounting in its Social and Historical Context* (New York, 1988).

LONGFORD, E., *Wellington: Pillar of State* (London, 1972).

LOW, S., 'The Foreign Office Autocracy', *Fortnightly Review*, NS 541 (Jan. 1912).

LOWE, R., 'The Erosion of State Intervention in Britain, 1917–24', *Economic History Review*, 31 (May 1978).

—— 'Bureaucracy Triumphant or Denied? The Expansion of the British Civil Service, 1919–1939', *Public Administration*, 62: 3 (1984).

—— *The Welfare State in Britain since 1945* (London, 1993).

LUCAS, S., *Britain and Suez: The Lion's Last Roar* (Manchester, 1996).

LUSTGARTEN, L. and LEIGH, I., *In From the Cold: National Security and Parliamentary Democracy* (Oxford, 1994).

MACADAM, E., *The New Philanthropy* (London, 1934).

——*The Social Servant in the Making* (London, 1945).

MCCABE, S., 'National Security and Freedom of Information' in L. Gostin (ed.), *Civil Liberties in Conflict* (London, 1988).

MACDONAGH, O., *Early Victorian Government, 1830–1870* (London, 1977).

MCEWAN, M., *Health Visiting* (2nd edn., London, 1957).

MACHLUP, F. and PENROSE, E., 'The Patent Controversy in the Nineteenth Century', *Journal of Economic History*, 10 (1950).

MACKINNON, F., 'Notes on the History of English Copyright', in M. Drabble (ed.), *The Oxford Companion to English Literature* (Oxford, 1985).

MCLAREN, A., *A History of Contraception: From Antiquity to the Present Day* (Oxford, 1992).

MACLEOD, C., *Inventing the Industrial Revolution* (Cambridge, 1988).

——'Strategies for Innovation: The Diffusion of New Technology in Nineteeth-Century British Industry', *Economic History Review*, 45: 2 (1992).

MCLEOD, R. M. (ed.), *Government Expertise: Specialists, Administrators and Professionals, 1860–1919* (Cambridge, 1988).

MCILHINEY, D. B., *A Gentleman in Every Slum: Church of England Missions in East London, 1837–1914* (Allison Park, Penn., 1988).

MCMULLIN, E., 'Openness and Secrecy in Science: Some Notes on Early History', *Science, Technology and Human Values*, 51 (1985).

MACK SMITH, D., *Mazzini* (New Haven, 1994).

MADGWICK, D. and SMYTHE, T., *The Invasion of Privacy* (London, 1974).

MANN, M., 'The Autonomous Power of the State: Its Origins, Mechanisms and Results', in J. Hall (ed.), *States in History* (London, 1986).

MARCHAM, A. J., 'The Revised Code of Education 1862: Reinterpretation and Misinterpretations', *History of Education*, 10: 2 (1981).

MARGACH, J., *The Abuse of Power* (London, 1978).

MARIO, J. W., *The Birth of Modern Italy* (London, 1909).

MARR, A., *Ruling Britannia: The Failure and Future of British Democracy* (rev. edn., London, 1996).

MASON, P., *The English Gentleman: The Rise and Fall of an Ideal* (London, 1993).

MATHER, F. C., *Public Order in the Age of the Chartists* (London, 1959).

MAUDE, A., *Marie Stopes: Her Work and Play* (London, 1933).

MAURER, O., Jr, 'Anonymity vs. Signature in Victorian Reviewing', *Studies in English*, 27 (June 1948).

MAY, A. and ROWAN, K. (eds.), *Inside Information* (London, 1982).

MEDAWAR, C., *Social Audit Consumer Handbook*, (London, 1978).

MEDVEDEV, Z. A., *Secrecy of Correspondence Guaranteed by Law* (Nottingham, 1975).

MERRETT, S., *State Housing in Britain* (London, 1979).

MICHAEL, J., *The Politics of Secrecy* (Harmondsworth, 1982).

——'Privacy', in P. Wallington (ed.), *Civil Liberties 1984* (Oxford, 1984).

MIDDLEMAS, K., 'Cabinet Secrecy and the Crossman Diaries', *Political Quarterly*, 47: 1 (1976).

——*Politics in Industrial Society* (London, 1979).

MILLER, A. R., *The Assault on Privacy* (Ann Arbor, 1971).

MOGEY, J. M., *Family and Neighbourhood: Two Studies in Oxford* (Oxford, 1956).

MONEY, E., *Margaret Thatcher, First Lady of the House* (London, 1975).

MORGAN, G., *Organisations in Society* (London, 1990).

MORGAN, J., *Conflict and Order* (Oxford, 1987).

MOORE, B., *Privacy* (New York, 1984).

MORRIS, C. (ed.), *Social Case-Work in Great Britain* (London, 1954 edn.).

MULLEN, R., *Anthony Trollope* (London, 1990).

MUNRO, C., 'Confidence in Government', in L. Clarke (ed.), *Confidentiality and the Law* (London, 1990).

MURCH, M., 'Privacy—No Concern of Social Workers?', *Social Work Today*, 2: 5 (3 June 1971).

MUSTOE, N. E., *The Law and Organisation of the British Civil Service*, (London, 1932).

MUTHESIUS, S., *The English Terraced House* (New Haven, 1982).

NAYLOR, J. F., *A Man and an Institution: Sir Maurice Hankey, the Cabinet Secretariat and the Custody of Cabinet Secrecy* (Cambridge, 1984).

NIBLETT, G. B. F., 'Computers and Privacy', in B. C. Rowe (ed.), *Privacy, Computers and You* (Manchester, 1972).

NOBES, C. W. and PARKER, R. H., 'The Development of Company Financial Reporting in Great Britain, 1844–1977', in T. A. Lee and R. H. Parker (eds.), *The Evolution of Corporate Financial Accounting* (New York and London, 1984).

NORTON-TAYLOR, R., *The Ponting Affair* (London, 1985).

—— 'The Slick Spymaster', *Guardian* (20 June, 1994).

O'DELL, T. H., *Inventions and Official Secrecy: A History of Secret Patents in the United Kingdom* (Oxford, 1994).

OLIVER, P., DAVIS, I., and BENTLEY, I., *Dunroamin: The Suburban Semi and its Enemies* (London, 1981).

OLSEN, D. J., 'Victorian London: Specialization, Segregation and Privacy', *Victorian Studies* (March 1974).

OSBORNE, T., 'On Liberalism, Neo-Liberalism and the "Liberal Profession" of Medicine', *Economy and Society*, 22: 3 (Aug. 1993).

—— 'Bureaucracy as a Vocation: Governmentality and Administration in Nineteenth-Century Britain', *Journal of Historical Sociology*, 7: 3 (Sept. 1994).

PALMER, A., 'The History of the D Notice Committee', in C. Andrew and D. Dilks (eds.), *The Missing Dimension: Governments and Intelligence Communities in the Twentieth Century* (London, 1984).

PARRIS, H., *Constitutional Bureaucracy* (London, 1969).

PARSLOE, P., 'Social Services: Confidentiality, Privacy and Data Protection', in P. Pearce *et al.*, *Personal Data Protection in Health and Social Services* (London, 1978).

PARRY, C., 'Legislatures and Secrecy', *Harvard Law Review*, 67: 5 (Mar. 1954).

PARTON, N., *Governing the Family: Child Care, Child Protection and the State* (London, 1991).

PEEL, J., 'Contraception and the Medical Profession', *Population Studies*, 18 (1964).

PELLEW, J., *The Home Office, 1848–1914* (London, 1982).

PETERSON, M. J., *The Medical Profession in Mid-Victorian London* (Berkeley, 1978).

PHEBY, F. H., 'Changing Practice on Confidentiality: A Cause for Concern', *Journal of Medical Ethics*, 8 (1982).

PHILLIPS, M. and DAWSON, J., *Doctor's Dilemmas: Medical Ethics and Contemporary Science* (London, 1985).

PINKER, R., 'An Alternative View', in National Institute for Social Work, *Social Workers, Their Role and Tasks* (London, 1982).

PLOWDEN, W., 'Whitehall and the Civil Service', in R. Holme and M. Elliott (eds.), *1688–1988: Time for a New Constitution* (London, 1988).

—— *Ministers and Mandarins* (London, 1994).

POGGI, G., *The State: Its Nature, Development and Prospects* (Cambridge, 1990).

POLLOCK, L. A., 'Living on the Stage of the World: The Concept of Privacy Among the Elite of Early Modern England', in A. Wilson (ed.), *Rethinking Social History* (Manchester, 1993).

PONTING, C., *Breach of Promise: Labour in Power, 1964–1970* (London, 1989).

—— *Secrecy in Britain* (London, 1990).

POOLEY, J., *Trade Secrets* (Berkeley, 1982).

PORTER, B., *The Origins of the Vigilant State* (London, 1987).

—— *Plots and Paranoia* (London, 1989).

PORTER, R. and HALL, L., *The Facts of Life: The Creation of Sexual Knowledge in Britain, 1650–1950* (New Haven, 1995).

PROCHASKA, F. K., *Women and Philanthropy in Nineteenth-Century England* (Oxford, 1980).

PROUTY, R., *The Transformation of the Board of Trade, 1830–1855* (London, 1957).

PYPER, R., 'Sarah Tisdall, Ian Willmore, and the Civil Servant's "Right to Leak" ', *Political Quarterly*, 56: 1 (Jan.–Mar. 1985).

RAYNER, C., *The Right to Know: A Spoonful of Secrets* (London, 1993).

REDER, P., DUNCAN, S., and GRAY, M., *Beyond Blame: Child Abuse Tragedies Revisited* (London, 1993).

REGAN, C. M., 'Anonymity in the British Civil Service: Facelessness Diminished', *Parliamentary Affairs*, 39: 4 (1986).

REID, B. C., *Confidentiality and the Law* (London, 1986).

RHODES, G., *Inspectors in British Government* (London, 1981).

RHODES, M. L., *Ethical Dilemmas in Social Work Practice* (1986).

RHODES JAMES, R., *Official Secrecy: An Historian's View* (London, 1990).

RICH, P. J., *Elixir of Empire* (London, 1989).

—— *Chains of Empire* (London, 1991).

RICHARDSON, G., with OGUS, A. and BURROWS, P., *Policing Pollution: A Study of Regulation and Enforcement* (Oxford, 1982).

RIDLEY, F. F., 'Political Neutrality, the Duty of Silence and the Right to Publish in the Civil Service', *Parliamentary Affairs*, 39: 4 (1986).

RICHARDS, T., *The Imperial Archive: Knowledge and the Fantasy of Empire* (London, 1993).

ROBB, G., *White-Collar Crime in Modern England* (Cambridge, 1992).

ROBERTS, E., *Women and Families* (Oxford, 1995).

ROBERTS, J. M., *The Mythology of the Secret Societies* (London, 1972).

ROBERTSON, C., *Health Visiting in Practice* (Edinburgh, 1988).

ROBERTSON, G., *Freedom, the Individual and the Law* (London, 1989).

—— *Freedom of Information: The Cure for the British Disease* (London, 1993).

ROBERTSON, K. G., *Public Secrets* (London, 1982).

ROBINSON, H., *Britain's Post Office* (Cambridge, 1953).

ROBINSON, J. J., *Born in Blood: The Lost Secrets of Freemasonry* (London, 1989).

ROBSON, W. A., *Nationalised Industry and Public Ownership* (London, 1960).

——*The Governors and the Governed* (London, 1964).

ROGERS, A., *Secrecy and Power in the British State: A History of the Official Secrets Act* (London, 1997).

ROOF, M., *A Hundred Years of Family Welfare* (London, 1972).

ROPER, M., 'Access to Public Records', in R. A. Chapman and M. Hunt (eds.), *Open Government* (London, 1989).

ROSKILL, S., *Hankey, Man of Secrets*, Vol. 1, *1877–1918* (London, 1970).

ROSS, E., ' "Not the Sort that Would Sit on the Doorstep"; Respectability in Pre-World War London Neighbourhoods', *International Labor and Working Class History*, 27 (Spring 1985).

RUDMAN, H., *Italian Nationalism and English Letters* (London, 1940).

SAMPSON, A., *The New Anatomy of Britain* (London, 1971).

——'Secrecy, News Management, and the British Press', in T. M. Franck and E. Weisbrand (eds.), *Secrecy and Foreign Policy* (New York, 1974).

SAUNDERS, M., *Health Visiting Practice* (London, 1968).

SAUNDERS, M., *Protecting your Business Secrets* (Aldershot, 1985).

SAVAGE, M. and MILES, A., *The Remaking of the British Working Class, 1840–1940* (London, 1994).

SAVILLE, J., *1848* (Cambridge, 1987).

——*The Politics of Continuity: British Foreign Policy and the Labour Government, 1945–46* (London, 1993).

SEABROOK, J., *The Everlasting Feast* (London, 1974).

SEWELL, M., 'The Beginnings of Social Training, 1890–1903', in E. Macadam (ed.), *The Equipment of Social Workers* (London, 1925).

SEYMOUR-URE, C., 'Great Britain', in I. Gilnoor (ed.), *Government Secrecy in Democracies* (New York, 1977).

SHAPIN, S., *A Social History of Truth: Civility and Science in Seventeenth-Century England* (Chicago, 1994).

SHEMMINGS, D., *Client Access to Records: Participation in Social Work* (Aldershot, 1991).

SHILS, E. A., *The Torment of Secrecy* (London, 1956).

SHORT, M., *Inside the Brotherhood* (London, 1990).

SIEGHART, P., *Privacy and Computers* (London, 1976).

SINFIELD, A., *The Wilde Century* (London, 1994).

SMELSER, N. J., *Social Paralysis and Social Change: British Working Class Education in the Nineteenth Century* (Berkeley, 1991).

SMITH, F. B., 'British Post Office Espionage 1844', *Historical Studies*, 4 (1970).

——*The People's Health* (London, 1979).

——'Health', in J. Benson (ed.), *The Working Class in England, 1875–1914* (London, 1985).

SNELLING, R. C. and BROWN, T. J., 'The Colonial Office and its Permanent Officials, 1801–1914', G. Sutherland (ed.), *Studies in the Growth of Nineteenth-Century Government* (London, 1972).

SOLOWAY, R. A., *Birth Control and the Population Question in England, 1877–1930* (Chapel Hill, 1982).

STACEY, M., *The British General Medical Council and Medical Ethics* (Philadelphia, 1991).

STAFF, F., *The Picture Postcard and its Origins* (London, 1966).

STAMMERS, N., *Civil Liberties in Britain During the 2nd World War* (London, 1983).

STEDMAN JONES, G., *Outcast London* (Harmondsworth, 1976).

STEELE, J., *Public Access to Information: An Evaluation of the Local Government (Access to Information) Act 1985* (London, 1995).

STEINER, Z., 'The Last Years of the Old Foreign Office, 1898–1905', *Historical Journal*, 6: 1, (1963).

STEVENSON, R. B., *Corporations and Information* (Baltimore, 1980).

STREET, H., 'Secrecy and the Citizen's Right to Know: A British Civil Libertarian Perspective', in T. M. Franck and E. Weisbrand (eds.), *Secrecy and Foreign Policy* (New York, 1974).

STURT, M., *The Education of the People* (London, 1967).

SULLIVAN, R. J., 'England's "Age of Invention": The Acceleration of Patents and Patentable Invention during the Industrial Revolution', *Explorations in Economic History*, 26: 4 (1989).

SUMMERS, A., 'A Home from Home—Women's Philanthropic Work in the Nineteenth Century', in S. Burman (ed.), *Fit Work for Women* (London, 1979).

SUTHERLAND, D., *The English Gentleman* (London 1978).

SWARTZ, M., *The Union of Democratic Control in British Politics During the First World War* (Oxford, 1971).

TEBBUTT, M., *Making Ends Meet: Pawnbroking and Working-Class Credit* (London, 1983).

—— 'Women's Talk? Gossip and "Women's Words" in Working-Class Communities, 1880–1939', in A. Davies and S. Fielding (eds.), *Workers' Worlds: Cultures and Communities in Manchester and Salford, 1880–1939* (Manchester, 1992).

TEFFT, S. K. (ed.), *Secrecy: A Cross-Cultural Perspective* (New York, 1980).

TEMPERLEY, H., 'British Secret Diplomacy from Canning to Grey', *Cambridge Historical Journal*, 6: 1 (1938).

THEAKSTON, K., *The Labour Party and Whitehall* (London, 1992).

—— *The Civil Service Since 1945* (Oxford, 1995).

—— 'The Heath Government, Whitehall and the Civil Service', in S. Ball and A. Seldon (eds.), *The Heath Government* (London, 1996).

THEAKSTON, K. and FRY, G. K., 'Britain's Administrative Élite: Permanent Secretaries, 1900–1986', *Public Administration*, 67: 2 (Summer 1989).

THOMAS, R. M., 'The Secrecy and Freedom of Information Debates in Britain', *Government and Opposition*, 17 (1982).

—— 'The Experience of Other Countries', in R. A. Chapman and M. Hunt, *Open Government* (London, 1989).

—— 'The British Official Secrets Acts, 1911–1939 and the Ponting Case', in Chapman and Hunt, *Open Government*.

—— *Espionage and Secrecy: The Official Secrets Acts, 1911–1989 of the United Kingdom* (London, 1991).

THOMPSON, E. P., 'The Crime of Anonymity', in D. Hay *et al.* (eds.), *Albion's Fatal Tree* (Harmondsworth, 1977).

—— 'Introduction', in State Research, *Review of Security and the State 1978* (London, 1978).

—— *Writing by Candlelight* (London, 1980).

THOMPSON, I. E., 'The Nature of Confidentiality', *Journal of Medical Ethics*, 5 (1979).

THURLOW, R., *The Secret State: British Internal Security in the Twentieth Century* (Oxford, 1994).

TILLEY, J. A. C. and GASELEE, S., *The Foreign Office* (London, 1933).

TOWNSHEND, C., *Political Violence in Ireland* (Oxford, 1983).

TROUP, E., *The Home Office* (2nd edn., London, 1926).

TUCKER, J., *Honorable Estates* (London, 1966).

TURNER, E. S., *The Shocking History of Advertising* (London, 1952).

TWINN, S. and COWLEY, S. (eds.), *The Principles of Health Visiting: A Re-examination* (London, 1992).

VAILLÉ, E., *Le Cabinet noir* (Paris, 1950).

VELECKY, L. C., 'The Concept of Privacy' in J. B. Young (ed.), *Privacy* (London, 1978).

VERNON, J., *Politics and the People* (Cambridge, 1993).

—— 'Notes Towards an Introduction', in id. (ed.), *Re-reading the Constitution* (Cambridge, 1996).

VINCENT, C. E. H., *A Police Code and Manual of the Criminal Law* (London, 1881).

VINCENT, D., 'Communications, Community and the State', in C. Emsley and J. Walvin (eds.), *Artisans, Peasants and Proletarians, 1760–1860* (London, 1985).

—— *Literacy and Popular Culture* (Cambridge, 1989).

—— *Poor Citizens* (London, 1991).

—— 'Secrecy and the City, 1870–1939', *Urban History*, 22: 3 (Dec. 1995).

VINCENT, G., 'A History of Secrets?', in A. Prost and G. Vincent (eds.), *A History of Private Life*, Vol. V, *Riddles of Identity in Modern Times* (Cambridge, Mass., 1991).

WACKS, R., *The Protection of Privacy* (London, 1980).

WADDINGTON, I., *The Medical Profession in the Industrial Revolution* (Dublin, 1974).

—— 'The Development of Medical Ethics: A Sociological Analysis', *Medical History*, 19 (1975).

WALKER, J., *The Queen has been Pleased* (London, 1986).

WALSH, J., *Not Like This* (London, 1953).

WARD, J. T., *Sir James Graham* (London, 1967).

WATSON, D. (ed.), *A Code of Ethics for Social Work* (London, 1985).

WEEKS, J., *Sex, Politics and Society* (London, 1981).

—— *Coming Out: Homosexual Politics in Britain from the Nineteenth Century to the Present* (rev. edn., London, 1990).

WEILER, P., *British Labour and the Cold War* (Stanford, 1988).

WEIR, S., 'Housing', in R. Delbridge and M. Smith (eds.), *Consuming Secrets* (London, 1982).

WELSH, A., *The Hero of the Waverley Novels* (New Haven, 1963),

—— *George Eliot and Blackmail* (Cambridge, 1985).

WESTIN, A. F., *Privacy and Freedom* (New York, 1967).

WEXLER, M. N., 'Conjectures on the Dynamics of Secrecy and the Secrets Business', *Journal of Business Ethics*, 6: 6 (1987).

WHITE, J., *The Worst Street in North London* (London, 1986).

WHITEHEAD, P., 'The Labour Governments, 1974–1979', in P. Hennessy and A. Seldon (eds.), *Ruling Performance* (Oxford, 1989).

WILKINSON, R., *Gentlemanly Power* (London, 1964).

WILLIAMS, D., *Not in the Public Interest* (London, 1965).

WILLIAMS, D. G. T., 'Official Secrecy in England', *Federal Law Review*, 3: 1 (June, 1968).

—— 'Official Secrecy and the Courts', in P. R. Glazebrook (ed.), *Reshaping the Criminal Law* (London, 1978).

—— 'Telephone Tapping', *Cambridge Law Journal*, 38 (Nov. 1979).

—— 'The Spycatcher Saga', *Dalhousie Law Journal*, 12: 2 (Nov. 1989).

WILLIAMS, R., *The Nuclear Power Decisions* (London, 1980).

WILLMOTT, P. and YOUNG, M., *Family and Class in a London Suburb* (London, 1960).

WILSON, D., 'The Struggle to Overcome Secrecy in Britain', in id. (ed.), *The Secrets File* (London, 1984).

WILSON, H., *The Governance of Britain* (London, 1977 edn.).

WOHL, A. S., 'Sex and the Single Room: Incest among the Victorian Working Class', in id. (ed.), *The Victorian Family* (London, 1978).

WRAITH, R., *Open Government: The British Interpretation* (London, 1977).

WRIGHT, D. (rev. and ed.), *Guild's History of Freemasonry* (London, 1931).

YEO, E., 'Some Practices and Problems of Chartist Democracy', in J. Epstein and D. Thompson (eds.), *The Chartist Experience* (London, 1982).

YOUNG, A. F. and ASHTON, E. T., *British Social Work in the Nineteenth Century* (London, 1956).

YOUNG, D. M., *The Colonial Office in the Early Nineteenth Century* (London, 1961).

YOUNG, H., *The Crossman Affair* (London, 1976).

—— 'The Thatcher Style of Government', in A. May and K. Rowan (eds.), *Inside Information* (London, 1982).

—— *One of Us* (London, 1990).

YOUNG, M. and WILLMOTT, P., *Family and Kinship in East London* (Harmondsworth, 1962).

YOUNGHUSBAND, E., *Social Work in Britain: 1950–1975* (London, 1978).

YOUNGSON, A. J., *The Scientific Revolution in Victorian Medicine* (London, 1979).

5. UNPUBLISHED THESIS

KAMM, R. M., 'The Home Office, public order and civil liberties, 1870–1914', unpublished Ph.D thesis (Cambridge University, 1987).

INDEX